Expenditure

Income

1993

ECU 5,000,000

ECU 0

1980

ECU

ECU

ECU 1,200,000

ECU 1,000,000

ECU 800,000

ECU 600,000

ECU 400,000

ECU 200,000

ECU 0

The Netherlands

Other

Switzerland

Germany

Belgium

Japan

France

1993

ii

1980

MUSÉE DES BEAUX ARTS

EXPOSITION

AMSTERDAM ANVERS KARLSRUHE LA HAYE
LILLE MELUN SENART PARIS ZEEBRUGGE

v

Wages & salaries
39%

Services of third parties
25%

The Netherlands

Other

x

OMA Travel Behavior

550 nights

650,000 km

305 nights

360,000 km

1993

km traveled Rem Koolhaas

Nights in hotels Rem Koolhaas

Total km traveled

Total nights in hotels

S,M,

Small, Medium, La

Office for Metropo

Rem Koolhaas and

Edited by Jennifer

Photography by H

1995 The Monacel

rge, Extra-Large

litan Architecture

Bruce Mau

Sigler

ns Werlemann

Press

A

ABOLISH
To execute an intention amounts to abolishing a desire.

ABSENCE
The most beautiful is not to be present.

ACCEPTED
Okay, I was the kind of guy who had to be superior to everyone all the time, whenever I could. In some ways I was very vain, but everyone knew this about me, and it was an endearing part of me that my true friends were able to accept. Did this mean I wasn't really a saint?

ACCIDENT
Lorenz's discovery was an accident, one more in a line stretching back to Archimedes and his bathtub. Lorenz never was the type to shout *Eureka*. Serendipity merely led him to a place he had been all along.

ACCUMULATE
You git you a piece of land, by hook or crook, an' things start growin' on it, things accumulate on it, and the first thing you know it's completely out of hand, completely out of hand!

ACCURACY
Two men and a woman are standing in the field. One man has a tape measure in his hand. He is going to measure off the plot of land which he has received for a wedding present. His bride is there to make certain that not a millimetre of land is miscalculated.

AD INFINITUM
Causality depends on observed uniformity. This does not mean that a uniformity so far observed will always continue, but what cannot be altered is that the events so far have been uniform; that can't be the uncertain result of an empirical series which in its turn isn't something given but something dependent on another uncertain one and so on ad infinitum.

ADJUST
The resident workers, as contrasted with the field bees, are mostly younger adults. They too adjust their behavior on sunny days.

ADVANTAGE
No question about it: Papa's absence had its advantages. If he were home

First published in the United States of America in 1995 by The Monacelli Press, Inc.
10 East 92nd Street, New York, New York 10128.

Library of Congress Catalog Card Number: 94-76578
ISBN: 1-885254-01-6

Editor: Jennifer Sigler
Design: Bruce Mau Design, Inc., Bruce Mau with Kevin Sugden, and Nigel Smith, Greg van Alstyne, Alison Hahn, Chris Rowat
Design Management: Kevin Sugden
Monacelli Press Editor: Andrea E. Monfried
Monacelli Press Production: Steve Sears
Principal Photographer: Hans Werlemann
Image Research Coordinator: Kristina del Carmen
Dictionary: Jennifer Sigler
Fundraising: Donald van Dansik

Printed and bound in China

We gratefully acknowledge the generous support of the Netherlands Foundation for Fine Arts, Design, and Architecture, Amsterdam; Centre Canadien d'Architecture/Canadian Centre for Architecture, Montreal; Graham Foundation, Chicago; Sandra Simpson, Toronto; Netherlands Foundation for Architecture, Rotterdam; Netherlands Ministry of Education, Culture, and Science, Rijswijk; National Government Buildings Agency, The Hague; Prins Bernhard Fonds, Amsterdam; Euralille, Lille; Rotterdam Arts Council, Rotterdam; Juriaanse Foundation, Rotterdam; Getty Center for the History of Art and the Humanities, Los Angeles.

Introduction Architecture is a hazardous mixture of omnipotence and impotence. Ostensibly involved in "shaping" the world, for their thoughts to be mobilized architects depend on the provocations of others—clients, individual or institutional. Therefore, incoherence, or more precisely, randomness, is the underlying structure of all architects' careers: they are confronted with an arbitrary sequence of demands, with parameters they did not establish, in countries they hardly know, about issues they are only dimly aware of, expected to deal with problems that have proved intractable to brains vastly superior to their own. Architecture is by definition a *chaotic adventure*.

Coherence imposed on an architect's work is either cosmetic or the result of self-censorship. S,M,L,XL organizes architectural material according to size; there is no connective tissue. Writings are embedded between projects not as cement but as autonomous episodes. Contradictions are not avoided. The book can be read in any way.

To restore a kind of honesty and clarity to the relationship between architect and public, S,M,L,XL is an amalgam that makes disclosures about the conditions under which architecture is now produced. Its epic scale is both arrogant and hesitant. It tries to deflate and reflate architecture—to destroy and rebuild. On the basis of contemporary givens, it tries to find a new realism about what architecture is and what it can do. In other words, this is a painfully utopian enterprise.

The more architecture mutates, the more it confronts its immutable core. Yet S,M,L,XL is a search for "another" architecture, knowing that architecture is like a lead ball chained to a prisoner's leg: to escape, he has to get rid of its weight, but all he can do is scrape slivers off with a teaspoon.

the scrambled eggs for dinner would
have onions in them. If he were at
home they wouldn't have been permitted to gouge out the white of the
bread and eat only the crust. If he
were home they wouldn't have got
so much sugar.

ADVICE
Useless to ask a wandering man
Advice on the construction of a
house.
The work will never come to
completion.

AESTHETIC
Most aesthetic absolutes prove
relative under pressure.

AIR[1]
On the evening of Oct. 30, a team
working at the face at the French
section of the service tunnel 40m
below the bed of the Channel waited
for a thin steel probe, drilled through
from the British side of the tunnel,
to pierce the wall of chalk marl in
front of them. The 5cm-diameter
aperture created by the probe could
not be seen at first, but then the
British crew sent a blast of compressed air through the hole, blowing
out the last crumbs of marl. "From
that moment on," said one of the
workers, "we could feel the air from
the other side circulating."

AIR[2]
Air is 840 times lighter than water.

ALPHABETIZED
Rose had a kitchen that was so completely alphabetized, you'd find the
allspice next to the ant poison.

ALREADY
The tower-block was new, but
already decayed.

ALTERNATE
I understand how one can desert
a cause in order to experience the
sensation of serving another.
It would perhaps be pleasant to be
alternately victim and executioner.

ALWAYS[1]
I always wear tan pants.

ALWAYS[2]
What I'm trying to do in my buildings is always the same trick.

ALWAYS[3]
You always ask me the same
question.

AMSTERDAMS
52°21 N, 4°54 E: The Netherlands.
26°38 S, 30°40 E: South Africa.
30°44 N, 84°26 W: Georgia, U.S.
42°19 N, 114°35 W: Idaho, U.S.

42°56 N, 74°12 W: New York, U.S.
40°29 N, 80°56 W: Ohio, U.S.

ANAGRAM

Invent, invent wildly, paying no
attention to connections, till it
becomes impossible to summarize.
A simple relay race among symbols,
one says the name of the next, without rest. To dismantle the world into
a saraband of anagrams, endless.
And then believe in what cannot be
expressed. Is this not the true reading
of the Torah? Truth is the anagram of
an anagram.
Anagram = ars magna.

ANALOGY

Rule One: Concepts are connected
by analogy. There is no way to
decide at once whether an analogy
is good or bad, because to some
degree everything is connected to
everything else. For example, potato
crosses with apple, because both are
vegetable and round in shape. From
apple to snake, by Biblical association. From snake to doughnut, by
formal likeness. From doughnut to
life preserver, and from life preserver
to bathing suit, then bathing to sea,
sea to ship, ship to shit, shit to toilet
paper, toilet to cologne, cologne to
alcohol, alcohol to drugs, drugs to
syringe, syringe to hole, hole to
ground, ground to potato.

ANDROID

"We're not born; we don't grow up;
instead of dying from illness or old
age we wear out like ants. Ants
again; that's what we are. Not you;
I mean me. Chitinous reflex-
machines who aren't really alive."
She twisted her head to one side,
said loudly, "I'm not alive! You're
not going to bed with a woman.
Don't be disappointed; okay? Have
you ever made love to an android
before?"

ANGELIC

The baby, perfectly programmed,
opened his eyes and smiled.

ANIMALS

Foucault quotes Borges quoting a
certain Chinese encyclopedia in
which it is written that "animals are
divided into a) belonging to the
Emperor, b) embalmed, c) tame,
d) suckling pigs, e) sirens, f) fabu-
lous, g) stray dogs, h) included in
the present classification, i) frenzied,
j) innumerable, k) drawn with a very
fine camel hair brush, l) et cetera,

Medium

m) having just broken the water
pitcher, n) that from a long way
off look like flies."

ANONYMOUS
I would like to be anonymous, the
way the twelfth-century architects
and designers of Romanesque
churches were anonymous.

ANOTHER
Among those who are familiar with
the professional and academic
architectural scene, it may well be
thought that the last thing we need
is another work on architectural
theory.

APARTMENT
Now that I have grown old, I have
the feeling, when walking through
a cemetery, that I am apartment
hunting.

ARBITRARY
When I was in art school, the arbitrary was the biggest taboo. The
worst thing you could say about
someone's work was that it seemed
arbitrary — that it was just a
function of taste... People use the
word *arbitrary* when the set of decisions which brought the work into
being are too obscure. When people
cannot see those decisions, they feel
that the work is arbitrarily motivated.
I am interested in precisely that
state of mind. The point is that sometimes it is very hard to tell why something is the way it is. I am very
interested in situations in which I
thought I was doing one thing and
then realized that I was doing something very different.

ARCHITECTURE
What is the act of Architecture, what
are its elements, its conditions, its
materials, its motives?

ARITHMETIC
Can you point to something which
doesn't exist? Take books, for
example, that you gather together,
but abandon for a while, let's say
ten years. Then, you happen upon
them in the eleventh year only to
discover that you cannot put them
down. Where is the arithmetic in
that?

ARRIVAL
The elevator was finally there.

ARROGANT
Now you'll be classified as
arrogant if you don't want to sell
out. I think selling out is the basis
of humility as it's understood in

Large

our country. So look out.

ARTIFICIAL
Limca is artificially flavoured.
It contains no fruit juice or fruit
pulp.

ASSAULT
Pick up a magazine these days, and
you'll be assaulted by pages that
smell of a Rolls-Royce's leather
upholstery, or of lasagne, or even of
a new perfume. Invented at 3M
Corporation only a decade ago, the
strips contain microscopic balls full
of fragrance. When you scratch, or
tear back the flap, the balls rip open
and the scent rushes out. Giorgio
was the first company to advertise
their perfume with scent strips. Now
it's difficult to find a magazine that
doesn't smell.

ASSOCIATION
In daydreaming there is no attention
from the outset, and wherever this
is absent the course of association
must sink to the level of a dream-
state, to a slow progression according
to the laws of association and
tending mainly towards similarity,
contrast, coexistence, and verbal
associations.

ATRIUM
Usually situated just inside the
main entrance of the building, the
atrium is a large space, several
floors high. Furnished with ramps,
stairs, escalators, and elevators,
it gives the impression of kinetic
activity, of people coming in and
out of offices, going up and down
stairs, stopping in coffee lounges.
The aim of the atrium is to infuse
the employee with a sense of unity,
to promote a sense of belonging
to a whole, and therefore identify-
ing with it.

ATTRACTION
One Tokyo-based firm is planning
a 600-unit resort hotel on an 800-
square-mile cattle spread near the
old mining town of Tennant Creek
in Australia's Northern Territory.
The developers say the main attraction will be surroundings that most
Japanese never experience — wide
open spaces.

ATTRACTORS
Because these trajectories represent
the behavior of real physical systems,
the attractors and repellors in
a phase portrait represent the long-
term tendencies of a system. For

instance, a ball rolling downhill will
always "seek" the lowest point. If it is
pushed up a little, it will roll down
to its lowest point again. Its phase
portrait will contain a "point attractor": small fluctuations (the ball
being pushed up a little) will move
the trajectory (representing the ball)
away from the attractor, but then
the trajectory will naturally return
to it.

AU
Thus the researchers begin to stutter,
one by one, they tangle their tongue
on the word authenticity, in particular: *Au, au, au, au, au ...* and their
once eminent, scientific discussions
degenerate into banal quarrelling:
*Real! False! Real! False! Real!
False!* Coffee cups and potted plants
fly through the air in the office.
Dr. Witold Finkelstein observes them
with invisible, wicked glee.

AUDIENCE
Intellectuals need an audience, a
circle of people to whom they can
address themselves and who can
bestow recognition.

AUTHENTIC
The historical city is full of falsifica-
tions and manipulations that make
it impossible to talk about what is
authentic and what is not.

AUTHENTICITY
The authentic work is radically
bound to the moment of its emergence; precisely because it consumes
itself in actuality, it can bring the
steady flow of trivialities to a stand-
still, break through normality, and
satisfy for a moment the immortal
longing for beauty — a moment in
which the eternal comes into fleeting
contact with the actual.

AUTOMONUMENT
Beyond a certain critical mass each
structure becomes a monument,
or at least raises that expectation
through its size alone, even if the
sum or the nature of the individual
activities it accommodates does
not deserve a monumental expression. This category of monument
presents a radical, morally traumatic
break with the conventions of symbolism: its physical manifestation
does not represent an abstract ideal,
an institution of exceptional
importance, a three-dimensional,
readable articulation of a social
hierarchy, a memorial; it merely

Acknowledgments S,M,L,XL has a hybrid authorship. The book is a sequence of writings by **Rem Koolhaas** and projects by the Office for Metropolitan Architecture–**OMA**–given form by **Bruce Mau** and his office–**BMD**.

The Work: The Office for Metropolitan Architecture has been defined by a number of partnerships, formal and informal. OMA was founded in 1975 by **Rem Koolhaas, Elia Zenghelis, Zoe Zenghelis,** and **Madelon Vriesendorp,** who has remained an essential support. The Rotterdam office opened in 1981 with **Jan Voorberg, Kees Christiaanse, Ron Steiner,** and **Jo Schippers** as sequential partners. **Stefano de Martino, Alex Wall, Xaveer de Geyter, Jeroen Thomas, Willem-Jan Neutelings, Yves Brunier, Fuminori Hoshino, Floris Alkemade, Mark Schendel, Winy Maas, Alejandro Zaera,** and **Christophe Cornubert** have left their marks on individual works and contributed to the intelligence of the office as a whole. Euralille would have been unthinkable without **Donald van Dansik;** Congrexpo, without **François Delhay.** OMA's work has been deeply influenced by collaborations with **Cecil Balmond** from Ove Arup. **Petra Blaisse** has been crucial in the development of exhibitions, interiors, exteriors. **Hans Werlemann** has been an accomplice in the domain of visualization; **Vincent de Rijk, Frans Parthesius,** and **Herman Helle,** in the making of models that were also explorations. Individual clients—**Joop Linthorst, Lydie and Dominique Boudet, Carel Birnie, Jean-Paul Baietto, Ken-ichi Toh, Jan Geerlings, Marian Glaudi, Marc Hostettler, Jean-François and Hélène Lemoine**—have believed in OMA's work at critical moments. Support and criticism from **Peter Eisenman, Zaha Hadid, Charles Jencks, Philip Johnson, Jeff Kipnis, Andrew MacNair, Kayoko Ota,** and **Terence Riley** have been important.

The Book: Without **Jennifer Sigler** this book would not exist. She triggered its initial formula and sustained its momentum. **Andrea Monfried** provided valuable criticism of the text. **Kevin Sugden** managed its physical assemblage. **Gianfranco Monacelli** made possible its realization.

The book owes thanks to **Nigel Smith, Chris Rowat, Alison Hahn, Greg van Alstyne, Kathleen Oginski, Anita Matusevics, Vilip Mak, Robert Sorr,** and **Lewis Nicholson** of BMD; to **Steve Sears** of The Monacelli Press; to **Hans Oldewarris** and **Peter de Winter** of 010; to **Richard Hunt** of Archetype; to **Donald van Dansik, Jeroen de Rijk, Marja van der Burgh** of OMA and **Karla Huckvale** and **Lee Jacobson** of BMD for their administrative talents; to design assistants **Val Foster, Paul Backewich, Nathaniel Gray, Megan Oldfield, Tom Kyle, Jonathan Winton, Izumi Iizuka, Helmina Kim, Burton Hamfelt, Steve Snyder, Alaho Gehry,** and **Kevin Hope;** to **Daniel Castor** for his Singapore research; to **Kristina del Carmen** for her help collecting the visual material; to **Chidi Onwuka** and **Sarah Whiting** for their contributions to the Dictionary; to **Laura Bourland** for her editorial input; to **Christian Hubert** and **Sylvia Lavin** for their hospitality; to **Brian Boigon, Sanford Kwinter, Andrew MacNair, Donald McKay, David Morton, Mark Schendel,** and **Bisi Williams** for their assistance, advice, and critical involvement.

Finally, the authors would like to thank **Julia Bloomfield, Tom Reese,** and the **Getty Center for the History of Art and the Humanities** for supplying the runway from which the book took off in December 1992.

Exodus, or the Voluntary Prisoners of Architecture
City of the Captive Globe
House in Miami
Roosevelt Island Housing
Hotel Sphinx
The Story of the Pool
Welfare Palace Hotel
New Welfare Island
Extension of the Dutch Parliament
Residence for the Irish Prime Minister
Renovation of a Panopticon Prison
Housing Kochstrasse/Friedrichstrasse
Housing Lützowstrasse
Boompjes Tower Slab
Netherlands Dance Theater, Project I
Y-Plein Urban Planning
Oost III Housing and Shops, Y-Plein
School and Gymnasium, Y-Plein
Villas Antiparos
Hotel Therma
Police Station, Almere-Haven
Parc de la Villette
Exposition Universelle 1989
Netherlands Dance Theater, Project II
Checkpoint Charlie Housing
De Brink Apartments
Villa Dall'Ava
Churchillplein Office Tower
Byzantium
Bus Station, Rotterdam
House for Two Friends
Installation for the 1986 Milan Triennale
Morgan Bank
Parc Citroën Cevennes
Bay of Koutavous Reconstruction
Uithof 2000
Bijlmermeer Redevelopment
The Hague City Hall
Kunsthal
Ville Nouvelle Melun-Sénart

Rem Koolhaas
Elia Zenghelis
Madelon Vriesendorp
Zoe Zenghelis
Laurinda Spear
Ron Steiner
Livio Dimitriu
Richard Perlmutter
Derrick Snare
German Martinez
Elias Veneris
Katerina Galani
Andreas Kourkoulas
Zaha Hadid
Alan Forster
Stefano de Martino
Ricardo Simonini
Alex Wall
Batsheva Ronen
Norman Chang
Omri Eytan
Gerard Comello
Jan Voorberg
Paul de Vroom
Herman de Kovel
Kees Christiaanse
Brigitte Kochta
Luc Reuse
Georg Ritschl
Karin Rühle
Arjan Karssenberg
Willem-Jan Neutelings
Jeroen Thomas
Xaver de Geyter
Ruurd Roorda
Katerina Tsigaridas
Tony Adam
Dirk Hendriks
Matthias Sauerbruch
Dirk Alten
Götz Keller
Hans Werlemann
Thijs de Haan
Jaap van Heest
Frans Vogelaar
Mike Guyer
Georges Heintz
Jo Schippers
Eleni Gigantes
Stavros Aliferis
Klaas Kingma
George Tombros
Marty Kohn
Leo van Immerzeel
Vahe Kaloustdian
Frank Roodbeen
Yves Brunier
Garciela Torre
Art Zaaijer
Christian Rapp
Petra Blaisse
Wim Kloosterboer
Donald van Dansik
Christian Dellus
Maartje Lammers
Reni Keller
Barbara Burren
Gregor Mescherowsky
Fuminori Hoshino
Eric van Daele
Isaac Batenburg
Ramon Klein
Alexander Nowotny
Marc Peeters
Jennifer Sigler
Edith Winkler
Heike Lohmann
Mark Schendel
Alexa Hartig
Christophe Cornubert
Isabelle Menu

Exodus,

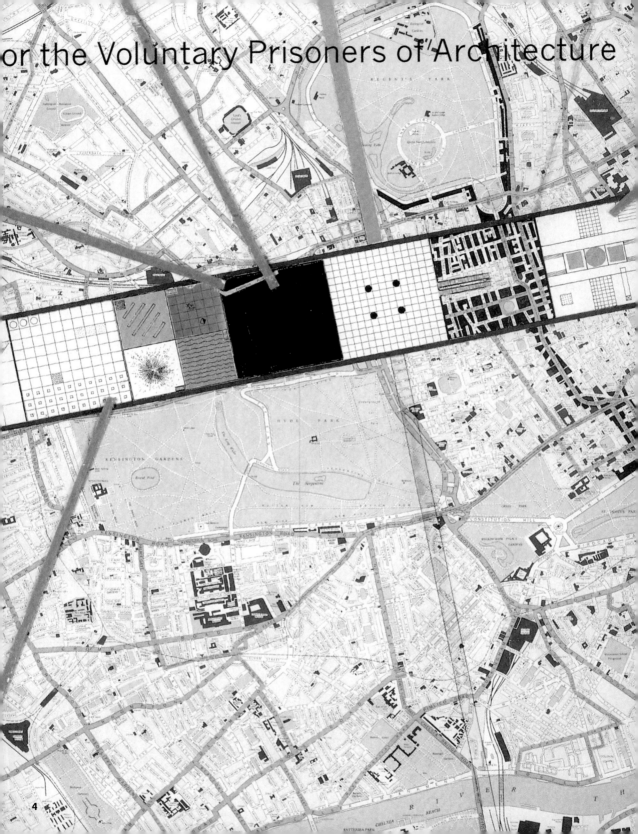

or the Voluntary Prisoners of Architecture

4

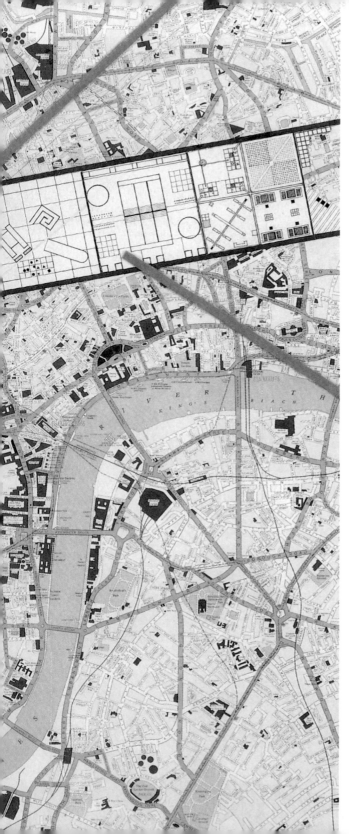

Prologue

Once, a city was divided in two parts.

One part became the Good Half, the other part the Bad Half.

The inhabitants of the Bad Half began to flock to the good part of the divided city, rapidly swelling into an urban exodus.

If this situation had been allowed to continue forever, the population of the Good Half would have doubled, while the Bad Half would have turned into a ghost town.

After all attempts to interrupt this undesirable migration had failed, the authorities of the bad part made desperate and savage use of architecture: they built a wall around the good part of the city, making it completely inaccessible to their subjects.

The Wall was a masterpiece.

Originally no more than some pathetic strings of barbed wire abruptly dropped on the imaginary line of the border, its psychological and symbolic effects were infinitely more powerful than its physical appearance.

The Good Half, now glimpsed only over the forbidding obstacle from an agonizing distance, became even more irresistible.

Those trapped, left behind in the gloomy Bad Half, became obsessed with vain plans for escape. Hopelessness reigned supreme on the wrong side of the Wall.

As so often before in this history of mankind, architecture was the guilty instrument of despair.

Architecture

It is possible to imagine a mirror image of this terrifying architecture, a force as intense and devastating but used instead in the service of positive intentions.

Division, isolation, inequality, aggression, destruction, all the negative aspects of the Wall, could be the ingredients of a new phenomenon: architectural warfare against undesirable conditions, in this case London. This would be an immodest architecture committed not to timid improvements but to the provision

Those strong enough to love it would become its Voluntary Prisoners...

of totally desirable alternatives.

The inhabitants of this architecture, those strong enough to love it, would become its Voluntary Prisoners, ecstatic in the freedom of their architectural confines.

Contrary to modern architecture and its desperate afterbirths, this new architecture is neither authoritarian nor hysterical: it is the hedonistic science of designing collective facilities that fully accommodate individual desires.

From the outside this architecture is a sequence of serene monuments; the life inside produces a continuous state of ornamental frenzy and decorative delirium, an overdose of symbols.

This will be an architecture that generates its own successors, miraculously curing architects of their masochism and self-hatred.

The Voluntary Prisoners

This study describes the steps that will have to be taken to establish an architectural oasis in the behavioral sink of London.

Suddenly, a strip of intense metropolitan desirability runs through the center of London. This Strip is like a runway, a landing strip for the new architecture of collective monuments. Two walls enclose and protect this zone to retain its integrity and to prevent any contamination of its surface by the cancerous organism that threatens to engulf it.

Soon, the first inmates beg for admission. Their number rapidly swells into an unstoppable flow.

We witness the Exodus of London.

The physical structure of the old town will not be able to stand the continuing competition of this new architectural presence. London as we know it will become a pack of ruins.

Reception Area

After crossing the Wall, exhausted fugitives are received by attentive wardens in a lobby between the Reception Area and the Wall. The consoling atmosphere of this waiting room is

7

Minimal training for new arrivals: overwhelming previously undernourished senses.

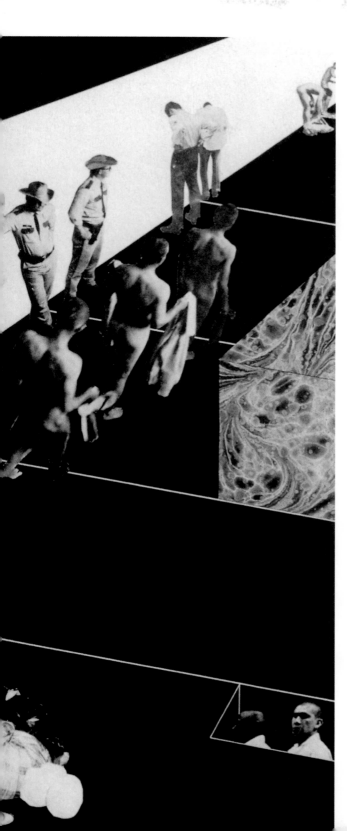

an architectural sigh of relief. The first step in the indoctrination program of the other side of the Wall is realized: the newcomers enter the Reception Area.

On arrival a spectacular welcome is given to all.

The activities inside the Reception Area require minimal training for new arrivals, which is only accomplished by overwhelming previously undernourished senses. The training is administered under the most hedonistic conditions: luxury and well-being.

The Reception Area is permanently crowded by amateurs who through their dealings exercise an inspired state of political inventiveness, which is echoed by the architecture. The senses are overwhelmed by thought.

The sole concerns of the participants are the present and the future of the Strip: they propose architectural refinements, extensions, strategies. Excited groups elaborate proposals in special rooms, while others continuously modify the model. The most contradictory programs fuse without compromise.

Central Area

The roof of the Reception Area, accessible from the inside, is a high-altitude plateau from which both the decay of the old town and the physical splendor of the Strip can be experienced.

From here, a gigantic escalator descends into a preserved fragment of the "old" London. These ancient buildings provide temporary accommodation for recent arrivals during their training period: the area is an environmental sluice.

Ceremonial Square

The other (west) side of the roof is completely empty, except for the tower of the Jamming Station, which will protect the inhabitants of the Strip from electronic exposure to the rest of the world. This black square will accommodate a mixture of physical and mental exercises, a conceptual Olympics.

Division, isolation, inequality, aggression, destruction: frontline of architectural warfare.

than 99% of men with baldness have male pattern baldness, which is a result of genetic and hormonal factors. Over two-thirds of the male population suffer from male pattern baldness, and most of them spend countless hours worrying about this curse which makes them look older than their years.

BALLS
At the AA, Rem said, "Sorry, I'm not gonna play with ping-pong balls." So he got a bad report! Almost thrown out!

BANG[1]
"BANG music, or Bad Ass New Groove, is a reaction against the commercialism of R&B and rap," explains frontman Bazerk. "Our recipe for success is our belief that every 15 or 30 seconds the beat should change — that way it never gets boring."

BANG[2]
The nail that sticks up will be banged down.

BATH
The Doctor, meanwhile, lay in a state of perfect contentment in a hot bath filled with blue crystals.

BAZAAR
The Blade Runner syndrome is the interfusion of crowds of people among a high-technological bazaar with its multitudinous nodal points — all of this sealed into an inside without an outside, which thereby intensifies the formerly urban to the point of becoming, or being analogous to, the unmappable system of late capitalism itself. The abstract system and its interrelations are now the outside, the former dome, the former city, beyond which no subject position is available so that it cannot be inspected as a thing in its own right, although it is a totality.

BEACH
Under the pavement, beach.

BEAT
He could hear it all; the sounds coming in through his ears and deep inside, in his heart and lungs, especially around the diaphragm, he felt the beat; the tap-tap-tap, as in frenetic intercourse, rhythm of the City's drum.

BEAUTIFUL
Our fine arts were developed, their types and uses were established, in times very different from the

audience. Overcharged by this spectacle, the Voluntary Prisoners descend to the ground floor looking for those willing and able to work out new elaborations.

Institute of Biological Transactions
The Institute sustains the Voluntary Prisoners through biological emergencies and physical and mental crises; it also demonstrates the harmless nature of mortality.

It is divided into four parts by a cruciform building. The first part, the hospital, contains the complete arsenal of modern healing, but is devoted to a radical deescalation of the medical process, to the abolition of the compulsive rage to heal. No forced heartbeats here, no chemical invasions, no sadistic extensions of life. This new strategy lowers the average life expectancy and with it, senility, physical decay, nausea, and exhaustion. In fact, patients here will be "healthy."

The hospital is a sequence of pavilions, each devoted to a particular disease. They are connected by a medical boulevard — a slow-moving belt that displays the sick in a continuous procession, with a group of dancing nurses in transparent uniforms, medical equipment disguised as totem poles, and rich perfumes that suppress the familiar stench of healing, in an almost festive atmosphere of operatic melodies.

Doctors select their patients from this belt, invite them to their individual pavilions, test their vitality, and almost playfully administer their (medical) knowledge. If they fail, the patient is returned to the conveyer; perhaps another doctor tries the patient, but it soon becomes apparent that the belt leads beyond the pavilions, through the cruciform building, and straight into the cemetery.

The mood here is continuously festive. The same smells, the same ethereal dance, are made still more human by the contrast between the ruthlessly formal layout of the plots and the unnaturalness of the dark green shrubbery.

In another part of the square, the Three Palaces of Birth, there is a statistical balance between births and deaths. The physical proximity of these events suggests the consolation of a causal relationship between the two, a gentle relay. The lowering of the average life expectancy creates an ambitious urgency; it does not allow the luxuries of underexploited brains, the artificial prolongation of childishness or wasted adolescence. The Three Palaces of Birth will also care for babies, educating them and turning them into small adults who — at the earliest possible date — can actively participate in life in the Strip.

In the fourth part, mental patients will be on display as in former days, not as themselves but as part of a well-produced exhibition of their delusions, sustained by the most advanced technical equipment: an infinite number of Napoleons, Florence Nightingales, Einsteins, Jesus Christs, and Joans of Arc, all in their custom-made uniforms.

Finally, the cruciform building, which separates the four compartments, contains the archives — records of all vital facts, developments, and life incidents of past and present Prisoners. Bureaucracy, so often criticized for its passion for control, contempt for privacy, and moral blindness, guarantees the Prisoners a new kind of immortality: this statistical treasure, linked to the most imaginative computers, produces not only instant biographies of the dead in seconds, but also premature biographies of the living — mixtures of facts and ruthless extrapolations — used here as essential instruments for plotting a course and planning the future.

Park of Aggression

In this recreational area, rudimentary structures were erected to correct and channel aggressive desires into creative confrontations. The unfolding ego/world dialectic generates the continuous emergence of conflicting ideologies. Their imposed coexistence invokes childish dreams and the desire to play.

The Park is a reservoir of sustained tension waiting to be released, a gigantic playground of flexible dimensions to accommodate the Strip's only sport: aggression.

Here, conflicts are reenacted: the staged battles dissolve the corrosive hysteria of good manners. On an individual level, the Park is a sanatorium where patients recover from remnants of Old World infections: hypocrisy and genocide. The diagnoses provide richer forms of intercourse.

The most prominent edifices are the two towers. One is infinite, a continuous spiral; the other, consisting of 42 platforms, has a familiar architectural style. Magnetic fields between these towers create a tension that mirrors the psychological motivations of their users.

Entry to the Park is free, and performances are continuous; visitors arrive alone, in pairs, or in small groups. The aggressive confidence of the players compensates for the electrifying uncertainty about the safety of the square tower. Inside the tower are shelves containing cells where visitors withdraw to vent suppressed hatred, freely abusing each other.

But these private antagonists are also spectators: the shelves serve as viewing galleries which overlook the larger platforms of the tower, provoking visitors to join groups involved in unknown physical transactions below. As remnants of shyness are overcome, visitors add their private energies to this incredibly demanding and mutant form of social behavior. In an agitated sleep, they ascend the tower; as they pierce each floor, their view of the activity below improves, and around the architecture of great height they experience an exhilarating new sensation of the unfolding spectacle.

As their tower leans forward, they push their antagonist into an abysmal fall through the relentless spiral of introspection. Its digestive movements consume excessive softness: it is the combustion chamber for the fat underneath the skin. The human

Nothing ever happens here...

missiles, helped by centrifugal acceleration, escape through a chosen opening in the walls of the spiral. They are objects of terrifying energy released into a trajectory of irresistible temptations.

The entire surface of the Park — the air above and the cavities below — becomes a full-scale battlefield. As the operations continue into the night they take on the appearance of hallucinatory celebrations against the backdrop of an abandoned world of calculated extermination and polite immobility.

As they return from their nocturnal adventure, the visitors celebrate their collective victories in a gigantic arena that crosses the Park diagonally.

The Allotments

To recover in privacy from the demands of intense collectivism, each Voluntary Prisoner has a small piece of land for private cultivation. The houses on these Allotments are built from the most lush and expensive materials (marble, chromium, steel); they are small palaces for the people. On a shamelessly subliminal level this simple architecture succeeds in its secret ambition to instill gratitude and contentment.

The Allotments are well supervised so that both external and internal disturbances can be avoided, or at least quickly suppressed. Media intake in this area is nil. Papers are banned, radios mysteriously out-of-order, the whole concept of "news" ridiculed by the patient devotion with which the plots are plowed; the surfaces are scrubbed, polished, and embellished.

Time has been suppressed.

Nothing ever happens here, yet the air is heavy with exhilaration.

The Avowal
To express their everlasting gratitude the
Voluntary Prisoners sing an ode to the
architecture that forever encloses them:

De ce terrible paysage,
Tel que jamais mortel n'en vit,
Ce matin encore l'image,
Vague et lointaine, me ravit.

Le sommeil est plein de miracles!
Par un caprice singulier,
J'avais banni de ces spectacles
Le végétal irrégulier,

Et, peintre fier de mon génie,
Je savourais dans mon tableau
L'enivrante monotonie
Du métal, du marbre et de l'eau.

Babel d'escaliers et d'arcades,
C'était un palais infini,
Plein de bassins et de cascades
Tombant dans l'or mat ou bruni;

Et des cataractes pesantes,
Comme des rideaux de cristal,
Se suspendaient, éblouissantes,
A des murailles de métal.

Non d'arbres, mais de colonnades
Les étangs dormants s'entouraient,
Où de gigantesques naïades,
Comme des femmes, se miraient.

Des nappes d'eau s'épanchaient, bleues,
Entre des quais roses et verts,
Pendant des millions de lieues,
Vers les confins de l'univers;

C'étaient des pierres inouïes
Et des flots magiques; c'étaient
D'immenses glaces éblouies
Par tout ce qu'elles reflétaient.

Insouciants et taciturnes,
Des Ganges, dans le firmament,
Versaient le trésor de leurs urnes
Dans des gouffres de diamant.

Architecte de mes féeries,
Je faisais, à ma volonté,
Sous un tunnel de pierreries
Passer un océan dompté;

Et tout, même la couleur noire,
Semblait fourbi, clair, irisé;
Le liquide enchâssait sa gloire
Dans le rayon cristallisé.

Nul astre d'ailleurs, nuls vestiges
De soleil, même au bas du ciel,
Pour illuminer ces prodiges,
Qui brillaient d'un feu personnel!

Et sur ces mouvantes merveilles
Planait (terrible nouveauté!
Tout pour l'oeil, rien pour les oreilles!)
Un silence d'éternité.

— Charles Baudelaire, *Les Fleurs du mal*

present, by men whose power of
action upon things was insignificant
in comparison with ours. But the
amazing growth of our techniques,
the adaptability and precision they
have attained, the ideas and habits
they are creating, make it a certainty
that profound changes are impending
in the ancient craft of the Beautiful.

BEAUTY[1]
Tuesday, May 13 1856
Take some copies to Michel.
Write to Moun,
to Urrie\s.
to Maria Clemm.
Send to Madame Dumay to know if
Mire\s …
That which is not slightly distorted
lacks sensible appeal; from which it
follows that irregularity — that is to
say, the unexpected, surprise and
astonishment — are an essential part
and characteristic of beauty.

BEAUTY[2]
And by beauty we mean simplicity,
largeness, and renewed severity of
discipline; we mean a return to
detachment and to form.

BED
I retire in bed, not just to sleep, but
to have lunch or dinner on a tray, to
sip a scotch and soda at the end of
the day, to make phone calls with my
push-button telephone. I hide there,
because that's where I find true
privacy. And I write in bed — every

The permanence

22

Rem Koolhaas

DELIRIOUS NEW YORK

of even the most frivolous item of architecture

DELIRIOUS NEW YORK
A Retroactive Manifesto for Manhattan

Rem Koolhaas

Manhattan is the arena of the terminal stage of Western Civilization:
Through the simultaneous explosion of human density and an invasion of new technologies, Manhattan became, from 1850, a mythical laboratory for the invention and testing of a revolutionary lifestyle: the *Culture of Congestion*.
Delirious New York is a polemical investigation of that Manhattan; it documents the symbiotic relationship between its mutant metropolitan culture and the unique architecture to which it gave rise. Though this book argues that it often appears that the architecture generated the culture.
Delirious New York exposes the consistency and coherence of the seemingly unrelated episodes of Manhattan's urbanism; it is an interpretation that establishes Manhattan as the product of an unformulated movement, *Manhattanism*, whose true program was so outrageous that in order for it to be realized, it could never be openly declared.
Delirious New York is the *retroactive manifesto* of Manhattan's architectural enterprise: it untangles the theories, tactics and dissimulations that allowed New York's architects to establish the desires of Manhattan's collective unconscious as realities in the Grid.

and the instability of the metropolis are incom

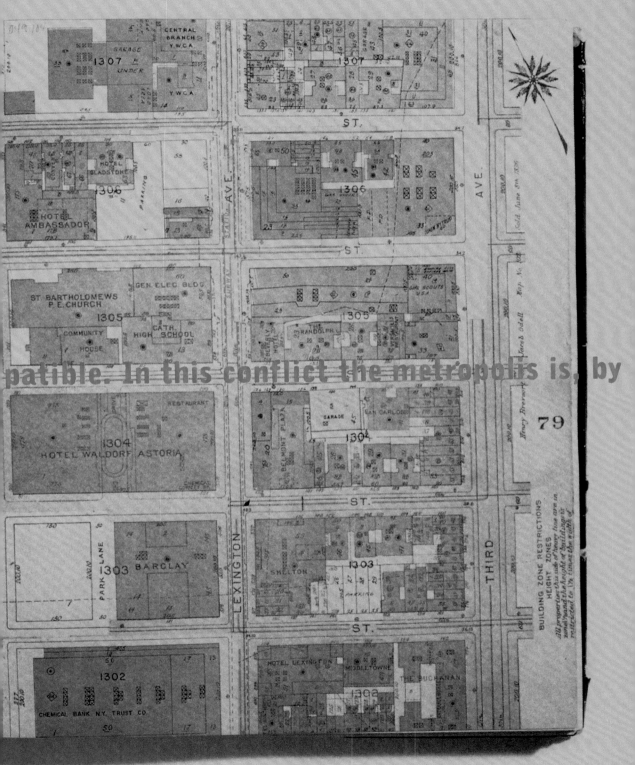

patible. In this conflict the metropolis is, by

Appendix: A Fictional Conclusion

The Metropolis strives to reach a mythical point where the world is completely fabricated by man, so that it absolutely coincides with his desires.

The Metropolis is an addictive machine, from which there is no escape, unless it offers that, too.

Through this pervasiveness, its existence has become like the Nature it has replaced: taken for granted, almost invisible, certainly indescribable.

This book was written to show that Manhattan had generated its own metropolitan Urbanism—a *Culture of Congestion*.

More obliquely, it contains a hidden, second argument: that the Metropolis needs/deserves its own specialized architecture, one that can vindicate the original promise of the metropolitan condition and develop the fresh traditions of the Culture of Congestion further.

Manhattan's architects performed their miracles luxuriating in a self-imposed unconsciousness; it is the arduous task of the final part of this century to deal with the extravagant and megalomaniac claims, ambitions and possibilities of the Metropolis *openly*.

After the chronicle in POSTMORTEM of the shriveling of Manhattanism—as if it had been too suddenly exposed to daylight—the Appendix should be regarded as a *fictional conclusion*, an interpretation of the same material, not through words, but in a series of architectural projects.

These proposals are the provi-

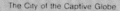

The City of the Captive Globe

sional product of Manhattanism as a conscious doctrine whose pertinence is no longer limited to the island of its invention.

The City of the Captive Globe

The City of the Captive Globe is devoted to the artificial conception and accelerated birth of theories, interpretations, mental constructions, proposals and their infliction on the World. It is the capital of Ego, where science, art, poetry and forms of madness compete under ideal conditions to invent, destroy and restore the world of phenomenal Reality.

Each Science or Mania has its own plot. On each plot stands an identical base, built from heavy polished stone. To facilitate and provoke speculative activity, these bases—ideological laboratories—are equipped to suspend unwelcome laws, undeniable truths, to create non-existent, physical conditions. From these solid blocks of granite, each philosophy has the right to expand indefinitely toward heaven. Some of these blocks present limbs of complete certainty and serenity; others display soft structures of tentative conjectures and hypnotic suggestions.

The changes in this ideological skyline will be rapid and continuous: a rich spectacle of ethical joy, moral fever or intellectual masturbation. The collapse of one of the towers can mean two things: 243

failure, giving up, or a visual Eureka, a speculative ejaculation:
A theory that works.
A mania that sticks.
A lie that has become a truth.
A dream from which there is no waking up.

At these moments the purpose of the Captive Globe, suspended at the center of the City, becomes apparent: all these Institutes together form an enormous incubator of the World itself, they are breeding on the Globe.

Through our feverish thinking in the Towers, the Globe gains weight. Its temperature rises slowly. In spite of the most humiliating setbacks, its ageless pregnancy survives.

The City of the Captive Globe (1972) was a first, intuitive exploration of Manhattan's architecture drawn before research would substantiate its conjectures.

ture is change—a state of perpetual animation—and the essence of the concept "city" is a legible sequence of various permanences—then only the 3 fundamental axioms on which the City of the Captive Globe is based—Grid, lobotomy and schism—can regain the terrain of the Metropolis for architecture.

The *Grid*—or any other subdivision of the metropolitan territory into maximum increments of control—describes an archipelago of "Cities within Cities." The more each "island" celebrates different values, the more the unity of the archipelago as system is reinforced. Because "change" is contained on the component "islands," such a system will never have to be revised.

In the metropolitan archipelago each Skyscraper—in the absence of real history—develops its own

244

instantaneous "folklore." Through the double disconnection of *lobotomy* and *schism*—by separating exterior and interior architecture, and developing the latter in small autonomous installments—such structures can devote their exteriors *only* to formalism and their interiors *only* to functionalism.

In this way, they not only resolve forever the conflict between form and function, but create a city where permanent monoliths celebrate metropolitan instability.

Alone in this century, the 3 axioms have allowed Manhattan's buildings to be both architecture *and* hyper-efficient machines, both modern and eternal.

The projects that follow are interpretations and modifications of these axioms.

Hotel Sphinx (1975-76)

Hotel Sphinx straddles two blocks at the intersection of Broadway and 7th Avenue, a site condition of Manhattan that (with few exceptions) has failed to generate its own typology of urban form.

It sits facing Times Square, its claws on the southern block, its twin tails to the north and its wings spreading across 48th Street, which dissects it.

The Sphinx is a luxury hotel as a model for mass housing.

The ground and mezzanine floors contain functions that are extensions and additions of the questionable facilities that give the Times Square area its character. They are designed to accommodate the luxuriant demand of sidewalk activities along Broadway and 7th Avenue.

The Hotel's main entrance lobby on 47th Street, facing Times Square

(and the Times Building) contains an international information center. This lobby also connects with the existing infrastructural facilities. A new subway station—complicated as a spider's web—will link all the subway stations that now serve the Times Square area.

The legs of the Sphinx contain escalators ascending to a large foyer serving theatres, auditoria, ballrooms, conference and banquet rooms. Over this zone, a restaurant forms the wings of the Sphinx. On one side it enjoys the view of a typical midtown street, on the other side of Nature, or at least New Jersey.

The roof of this restaurant is an outdoor playground and garden for the surrounding residential accommodation in the flanks of the structure.

This accommodation consists of a collection of any imaginable number of units: hotel bedrooms and other residential arrangements populate laterals with apartments and culminate in villas with private gardens on the terraced steps that descend in opposite directions to avoid the overshadowing that would result from the narrowness of the site, and to achieve better East-West views.

The twin towers that form the tail of the Sphinx contain north-facing double-height studio apartments, while the connecting middle section is an office block for the residents.

The neck of the Sphinx facing Times Square contains the residents' clubs and social facilities: this is the section over the Entrance Lobby and main auditorium, and below the circular head of the Sphinx. This section is divided by the number of clubs that occupy it. These are headquarters

Hotel Sphinx facing onto Times Square.

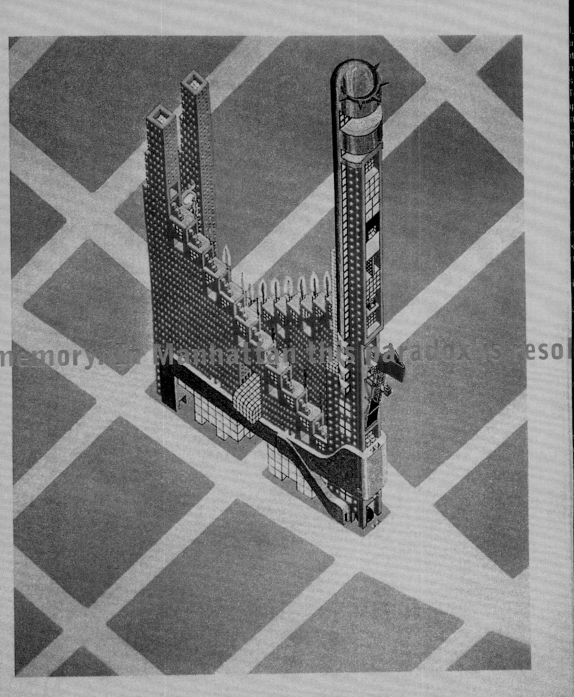

memory. In Manhattan this paradox is resolved

for the various trades and professions to which the residents belong, each displaying its identity and proclaiming its messages by means of the ideological billboard construction that clads the face of the tower, competing with the existing signs and symbols of Times Square.

The head of the Sphinx is dedicated to physical culture and relaxation. Its main feature is the swimming pool. A glazed screen divides the pool into two parts: indoor and outdoor. Swimmers can dive under the screen from one part to the other. The indoor section is surrounded by four stories of locker rooms and showers. A glass-brick wall separates these from the pool space. A spectacular view of the city can be enjoyed from the small open-air beach. Waves made in the outdoor part of the pool crash directly onto the pavement. The ceiling over the pool is a planetarium with suspended galleries for the audience and a semi-circular bar that forms the crown of the Sphinx; its patrons can influence the planetarium's programming, improvising new trajectories for the heavenly bodies.

Below the pool is a floor for games and gymnastics. A staircase and ladders connect the diving island in the pool to this floor and continue to the floor below, which contains steam-baths, saunas and massage parlor.

In the beauty parlor and hairdresser's (the lowest floor of the head of the Sphinx), residents relax. The chairs face the perimeter wall, which is clad in mirror glass. Below the part reflecting the face from a sitting position, a small porthole affords a view out towards the city below.

Finally a lounge, indoor/outdoor

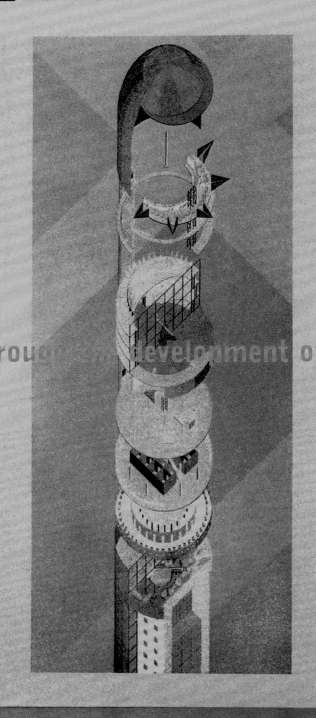

Hotel Sphinx : exploded axonometric of the
246 head of the sphinx.

restaurant and garden form the section that separates the head of the Sphinx from the clubs. This is the location of the jacking and twisting mechanisms of the head of Hotel Sphinx: in response to certain important events, the face of the Sphinx can be directed to "stare" at various points in the city. In response to the level of nervous energy in the Metropolis as a whole, the whole head can be jacked up or down.　　　　(E.Z.)

New Welfare Island
(1975-76)

Welfare (now Roosevelt) Island is a long (about 3 km), narrow (200 m on average) island in the East River, more or less parallel to Manhattan. Originally the island was the site of hospitals and asylum, generally a storehouse for undesirables."

Since 1965, it has been undergoing a half-hearted "urbanization." The question is: is it to be a true part of New York—with all the agonies that implies—or is it to be a civilized escape-zone, a kind of resort that offers, from a safe distance, the spectacle of Manhattan burning?

The island's planners have so far chosen the latter alternative—although no more than 150 m from Manhattan, it is now connected to the mother island merely by a cable-car (colored in a cheerful

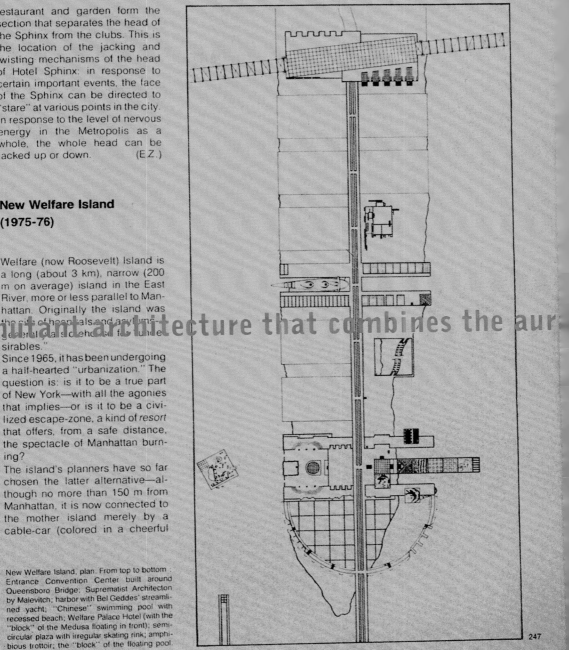

New Welfare Island, plan. From top to bottom : Entrance Convention Center built around Queensboro Bridge; Suprematist Architecton by Malevitch; harbor with Bel Geddes' streamlined yacht; "Chinese" swimming pool with recessed beach; Welfare Palace Hotel (with the "block" of the Medusa floating in front); semicircular plaza with irregular skating rink; amphibious trottoir; the "block" of the floating pool.

247

"holiday" purple) whose service could easily be suspended in case of urban emergencies.

For over a century, Welfare Island's dominant architectural incident had been the crossing of the monumental Queensboro Bridge that connects Manhattan to Queens (without an exit to the smaller island) and casually cuts Welfare Island into two parts. The area north of the bridge has now been developed by the Urban Development Corporation, a New York State agency, with a series of blocks that terrace down with equal enthusiasm to both Manhattan *and* Queens (why?), and which are arranged on both sides of a picturesquely kinked Main Street. "New Welfare Island," on the contrary, is a *metropolitan* settlement on the sector *south* of Queensboro Bridge, a stretch that coincides with the area between 50th and 59th Streets in Manhattan.

...architects, residing as a resuscitation of some of the features that made Manhattan's architecture unique: its ability to fuse the popular with the metaphysical, the commercial with the sublime, the refined with the primitive—which together explain Manhattan's former capacity to seduce a mass audience for itself. It also revives Manhattan's tradition of "testing" certain themes and intentions on smaller, experimental "laboratory" islands (such as Coney Island at the beginning of the century).

For this demonstration, the Manhattan Grid is extended across the East River to create 8 new blocks on the island. These sites will be used as a "parking lot" for formally, programmatically and ideologically competing architectures—which would confront each other from their identical parking spaces.

All the blocks are connected by 248 an elevated travelator (moving

pavement) that runs from the bridge southward down the center of the island: an accelerated architectural promenade. At the tip of the island it becomes amphibious, leaving the land to turn into a *trottoir* on the river, connecting floating attractions too emphemeral to establish themselves on land.

Those blocks that are not occupied are left vacant for future generations of builders.

From north to south, "New Welfare Island" so far accommodates the following structures:

1

Built around Queensboro Bridge without actually touching it is the Entrance Convention Center—a formal entrance porch to Manhattan that is, at the same time, a colossal "roadblock" separating the southern half of the island from the northern. An auditorium for mass meetings is slotted underneath the bridge; adjoining towers contain cellular office accommodation. Between them, above the bridge, they support a suspended glass object—whose steps reflect the curve of the bridge—that contains a stacked sports and entertainment center for the Conventioneers.

2

Buildings that were once proposed for New York, but for whatever reason aborted, will be built "retroactively" and parked on the blocks to complete the history of Manhattanism. One such building is a Suprematist "Architecton" stuck by Malevitch on a postcard of the Manhattan skyline—sometime in the early twenties in Moscow—but never received.

Due to an unspecified scientific process that would be able to suspend gravity, the involvement of Malevitch's Architectons with the surface of the earth was tenuous: they could assume, at any

moment, the status of artificial planets visiting the earth only occasionally—if at all. The Architectons had no program: "Built without purpose, [they] may be used by man for his own purposes. . . ." They were supposed to be "conquered" programmatically by a future civilization that deserved them. Without function, Architectons simply exist, built from "opaque glass, concrete, tarred felt, heated by electricity, a planet without pipes . . . the planet is as simple as a tiny speck, everywhere accessible to the man living inside it who, in fine weather, may sit on its surface. . . ."

3

In the middle of the "New Welfare Island" development is the harbor, carved out of the rock to receive floating structures such as boats—in this case Norman Bel Geddes' "special streamlined yacht" (1932).

4

South of the harbor is a park with a "Chinese" swimming pool in the form of a square, part of which is carved out of the island, while the complementary part is built out on the river. The original coastline has become three-dimensional—an aluminium Chinese bridge that follows in plan the line of the natural coastline. Two revolving doors at either end lead to locker rooms inside the two halves of the bridge

New Welfare Island, axonometric. Manhattan is on the left, Queens on the right, New Welfare Island in the middle. From top to bottom: Entrance Convention Center penetrated by Queensboro Bridge; Suprematist Architecton; harbor with streamlined yacht; "Chinese" swimming pool; Welfare Palace Hotel with raft; plaza; and river-trottoir. Opposite the UN Building on Manhattan Island is the Counter-UN standing on a small island. On Manhattan itself can be seen the "separation" of Hotel Sphinx and the RCA Building. In Queens is "desperation park" with its modern housing; the suburb; the Pepsi-Cola sign; and the Power Station. Approaching in the river is the floating pool.

(one for men, the other for women). Undressed, the sexes emerge from the middle of the bridge, from where they can swim to the recessed beach.

5

The tip of the island is occupied by Welfare Palace Hotel and a semi-circular plaza.

6

The travelator continues on the water to a point just south of 42nd Street. Along its way, it passes a small island opposite the United Nations Building, to which the Counter-UN has been attached: a slab that repeats the silhouette of the original, with an attached auditorium. The open space of this small island serves the recreational needs of the office workers of this Counter-UN·

The towers increase in height as they move away from Manhattan; the tops are so designed that they "stare" at Manhattan, especially at the RCA Building, which steps down toward the hotel.

The hotel has four facades, designed individually to respond to the specific formal and symbolic demands of their respective situations.

The southern facade, along the semi-circular plaza, is the dominant elevation. Three-dimensional fragments have dissociated themselves from the main slab to lead their own lives. The fragments have a double function: together, they form a decorative relief with an explicit figurative message—a city collapsing; separately, they provide differentiation of the hotel's accommodation—small palatial skyscrapers that can be reserved for private functions. The materials of the fragments are as diverse as possible—marble, steel, plastic, glass—providing the hotel with the history it would otherwise lack.

The ground floor of the Hotel is subdivided into a series of independent zones each with its own particular function.

The first zone—the sector closest

Welfare Palace Hotel: interior of restaurant/theater/nightclub: a merging of the twin themes of "Shipwreck" and "The Uninhabited Island." Dining spectators sit on terraces watching a floor show on the hull of the overturned ocean liner. Columns are disguised as lighthouses, piercing the dark with their erratic beams. Luxurious lifeboats move soundlessly through the gloomy space (painting by Madelon Vriesendorp).

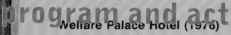

of program and activity that change constant

Welfare Palace Hotel (1976)

The Welfare Palace Hotel—a City within a City—occupies the block near the tip of the island. It accommodates 10,000 guests, and each day as many visitors again. It is a composition of seven towers and two slabs. The 10-story slabs are placed on the edges of the block to define the "field" of the Hotel. Since the island tapers toward the tip, the block of the hotel is incomplete, but the two slabs still run the full width of the island into the water so that the shore runs through the hotel as a geological fault. On the field between the slabs, six towers are arranged in a V formation, pointing at Manhattan. A seventh tower on the Queens side does not "fit" on the island; it has become a horizontal waterscraper with a roof-garden on its former facade.

Welfare Palace Hotel: Cutaway axonometric shows, consecutively on the ground floor: inundated theater/restaurant/night club (with uninhabited island, overturned ship, lighthouse columns, dining terraces, lifeboats), island-as-found-plaza with shopping; reception area of hotel; access to the horizontal water scraper (concealed between the rear 4 skyscrapers with park on top).

On each side of the Hotel's transverse axis is a long low slab—one overlooks the "Chinese" pool, the other the semi-circular plaza. The façade of this latter slab has been fragmented into a 3-dimensional mural which functions as luxury accommodation.

In "V" formation are 6 skyscrapers—each with its own club (whose respective theme is related to the mythology established on the ground floor of each tower).

Tower 1: locker rooms, square beach surrounded by circumferential pool; tower 2: ship's bridge as bar; tower 3: Expressionist club as climax of the mural; tower 4: vacant; tower 5: waterfall/restaurant; tower 6: Freud Unlimited Club.

The light blue in front of the hotel is an artificial skating rink; to the left of the hotel is a park with a "Chinese" swimming pool; in front of the Hotel is a gigantic 3-dimensional *Raft of the Medusa* executed in plastic (with a small area equipped for dancing).

250

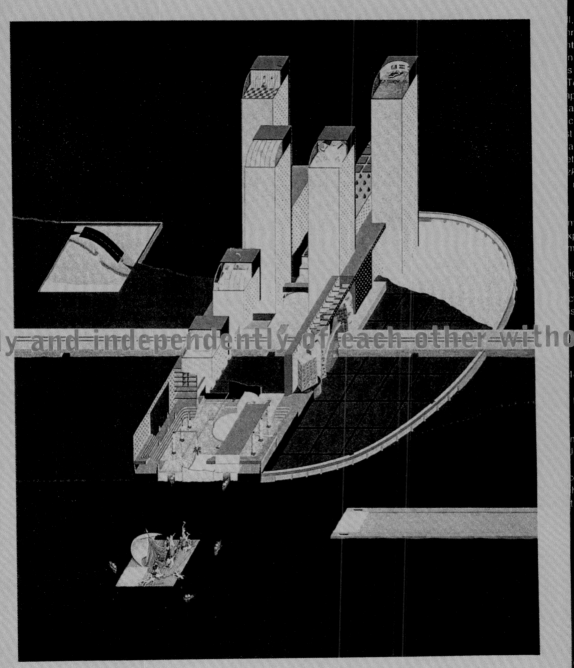

d, that
nning,
t and
n this
s an
Tech-
per a
an a
ctural
t and
attan.
ets in
zkrieg
mid-

pro-
ming'
xplicit
mong

iginal
pro-
ctural
stent
and

4 in

then
and
later
nhat-
Jrban

ce for
h is
t of a

ORK

After the shipwreck in the Mediterranean of the *Medusa*—a military vessel—the soldiers/castaways were left on their raft with only barrels of wine, guns and ammunition. In a premature and drunken panic they began to cannibalize each other on the second day of their journey. Saved on the 7th day of the shipwreck, they could easily have survived without eating anything at all.

This monumental expression of "loss of nerve" corresponds to the premature panic and loss of nerve about the Metropolis in the present moment of the 20th century.

to Manhattan—is a theater and nightclub-restaurant on the twin themes of *shipwreck* and *uninhabited island*. It holds 2,000 people—only a small percentage of the hotel's visitors. Its floor is inundated. A stage is carved out of the steel hull of an overturned, sinking ship. Columns masquerade as lighthouses, frantically piercing the darkness with their beams. Guests can sit, eat and watch performances on the terraces along the water or they may board the lifeboats—luxuriously equipped with velvet benches and marble table-tops—that emerge from a hole in the sinking ship to move slowly through the interior on submerged tracks. Opposite the sinking ship is a sandy island, symbolizing Manhattan in its virgin state. It can be used for dancing. Outside the Hotel, exactly between Manhattan and Welfare Island, floats a gigantic reproduction of Gericault's *Raft of the Medusa*; it is a symbol of Manhattan's metropolitan agonies—proving both the need and the impossibility of "escape." It is an equivalent of nineteenth-century public sculpture. When the weather permits it, the lifeboats leave the interior of 252 the Hotel to go out on the river.

They circle around the raft, compare the monumental suffering of its occupants to their own petty anxieties, watch the moonlit sky and even board the sculpture. A section is equipped as dance floor, relaying the music that is produced inside the Hotel through a cable telephone.

The second zone of the Hotel—open to the air—represents the island *as found*, and is lined with shops.

The third zone—where the course of the travelator is interrupted—is the reception area of the Hotel.

Beyond that is the fourth zone—the horizontal skyscraper with a park on top and conference facilities inside.

There is a different club at the top of each skyscraper. Their glass visors can retract to expose the club's activities to sunlight.

The themes of the clubs relate to the themes established directly below them on the ground floor, so that elevators shuttle between two interpretations of the same "story."

The first tower—above the uninhabited island on the ground floor—has a square beach and a circumferential swimming pool. A glass plate separates locker rooms for men and women.

The second tower—the only office building—is equipped with the "displaced" bridge of the sinking ship. Guests feel like captains here, drinking their cocktails in the euphoria of apparent control, oblivious to the disaster that occurs 30 floors below them.

The third tower is an expression istic environment, concluding the agitation of the south facade in a paroxysm of decorative arbitrariness.

The top of the fourth tower is vacant and awaits future, unspecified occupancies.

The top of the fifth tower, which stands in water, is a waterfall whose unpredictable reflections will be visible from the city.

The top of the sixth tower, the one furthest removed from Manhattan, is terminated by a three-dimensional allegorical interior that extrapolates and "predicts" the real destinies of the RCA, the Chrysler and the Empire State buildings, of whose tortured relationships the Hotel is the "postponed" offspring. That part of the semi-circular plaza in front of the Hotel which is not on the island, is turned into ice. North of the Hotel is the "Chinese" swimming pool

(R.K.)

The Story of the Pool (1977)

MOSCOW, 1923

At school one day, a student designed a floating swimming pool. Nobody remembered who it was. The idea had been in the air. Others were designing flying cities, spherical theaters, whole artificial planets. Someone *had* to invent the floating swimming pool. The floating pool—an enclave of purity in contaminated surroundings—seemed a first step, modest yet radical, in a gradual program of improving the world through architecture.

To prove the strength of the idea, the architecture students decided to build a prototype in their spare time. The pool was a long rectangle of metal sheets bolted onto a steel frame. Two seemingly endless linear locker rooms formed its long sides—one for men, the other for women. At either end was a glass lobby with two transparent walls: one wall exposed the healthy, sometimes exciting underwater activities in the pool, and the other fish agonizing in polluted water. It was thus a truly *dialectical* room, used for physical exercise, artificial sunbathing and socializing between the almost naked swimmers.

The prototype became the most popular structure in the history of Modern Architecture. Due to the chronic Soviet labor shortage, the architects/builders were also the lifeguards. One day they discovered that if they swam in unison—in regular synchronized laps from one end of the pool to the other—the pool would begin to move

slowly in the opposite direction. They were amazed at this involuntary locomotion; actually, it was explained by a simple law of physics: *action = reaction.*

In the early thirties, the political situation, which had once stimulated projects such as the pool, became rigid, even ominous. A few years later still (the pool was quite rusty now, but popular as ever), the ideology it represented became suspect. An idea such as the pool, its shiftiness, its almost invisible physical presence, the iceberg-like quality of its submerged social activity, all these became suddenly subversive.

In a secret meeting, the architects/lifeguards decided to use the pool as a vehicle for their escape to freedom. Through the by now well-rehearsed method of *auto-propulsion*, they could go anywhere in the world where there was water. It was only logical that they wanted to go to America, especially New York, so that the pool was a *Manhattan block* realized in Moscow, which would now reach its logical destination.

Early one morning in the Stalinist thirties, the architects directed the pool away from Moscow by swimming their relentless laps in the direction of the golden onions of the Kremlin.

NEW YORK, 1976

A rotating schedule gave each lifeguard/architect a turn at the command of the "ship" (an opportunity rejected by some hardcore anarchists, who preferred the anonymous integrity of continuous swimming to such responsibilities).

After four decades of crossing the Atlantic, their swimsuits (front and back panels were exactly the same, a standardization following a 1922 edict to simplify and ac-

celerate production) had almost disintegrated.

Over the years, they had converted some sectors of the locker room/corridor into "rooms" with improvised hammocks, etc. It was amazing how, after 40 years at sea, relationships between the men had not stabilized but continued to display a volatility familiar from Russian novels: just before arriving in the New World, there had been a flare-up of hysteria which the architects/swimmers had been unable to explain, except as a delayed reaction to their collective middle age.

They cooked on a primitive stove, living on supplies of preserved cabbage and tomatoes, and on the fish they found each daybreak washed into the pool by the Atlantic's waves (Although captive, these fish were hard to catch due to the pool's immensity).

When they finally arrived, they were aghast to find the Manhattan swim away from where they wanted to go, toward what they wanted to get away from.

It was strange how familiar Man-

First tentative landings of pool. Wall Street. A moving "block" joins the blocks of Manhattan's Grid.

253

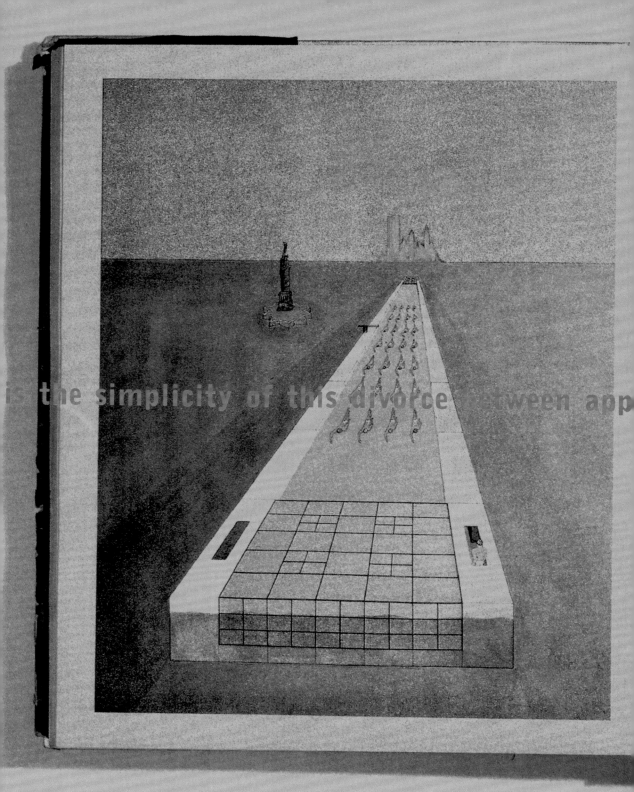

is the simplicity of this divorce between app

hattan was to them. They had always dreamt of stainless-steel Chryslers and flying Empire States. At school, they had even had much bolder visions, of which, ironically, the pool (almost invisible—practically submerged in the pollution of the East River) was proof: with the clouds reflected in its surface, it was more than a Skyscraper—it was a patch of heaven here on earth.

Only the Zeppelins they had seen crossing the Atlantic with infuriating velocity 40 years before were missing. They had expected them to hover over the Metropolis like a dense cloud drift of weightless whales.

When the pool docked near Wall Street, the architects/swimmers/lifeguards were shocked at the uniformity (dress, behavior) of the visitors, who swamped the craft in a brute rush through the lockers and showers, completely ignoring the facilities the architects had prepared for their clients.

Had Communism reached America while they were crossing the Atlantic? they wondered in horror. This was exactly what they had swum all this time to avoid, this crudeness, lack of individuality, which did not even disappear when all the businessmen stepped out of their Brooks Brothers suits. (Their unexpected circumcisions contributed to this impression in the eyes of the provincial Russians.)

They took off again in shock, directing the pool further upstream: a rusty salmon, ready—finally—to spawn?

3 MONTHS LATER

The architects of New York were uneasy about the sudden influx of Constructivists (some quite famous, others long thought to have been exiled to Siberia—if not executed—after Frank Lloyd Wright visited the USSR in 1937 and betrayed his Modern colleagues in the name of Architecture).

The New Yorkers did not hesitate to criticize the design of the pool. They were all against Modernism now; ignoring the spectacular decline of their profession, their own increasingly pathetic irrelevance, their desperate production of flac... suspense of their trite complexities, the dry taste of their fabricated poetry, the agonies of their irrelevant sophistication, they complained that the pool was so bland, so rectilinear, so unadventurous, so boring; there were no historical allusions; there was no decoration; there was no . . . shear, no tension, no *wit*—only straight lines, right angles, and the drab color of rust.

(In its ruthless simplicity, the pool threatened them—like a thermom-

eter that might be inserted in their projects to take the temperature of their decadence.)

Still, to have Constructivism over with, the New Yorkers decided to give their so-called colleagues a collective medal at a discreet waterside ceremony.

Against the background of the Skyline, the dapper spokesman of New York's architects gave a gracious speech. The medal had an old inscription from the thirties, he reminded the swimmers. It was by now irrelevant, he said, but none of Manhattan's present architects had been able to think of a new motto . . .

The Russians read it. It said THERE IS NO EASY WAY FROM THE EARTH TO THE STARS. Looking at the starry sky reflected in the narrow rectangle of their pool, one architect/lifeguard, still dripping wet from the last lap, answered for all of them: "We just went from Moscow to New York." Then they dove into the water to assume their familiar formation.

5 MINUTES LATER

In front of Welfare Palace Hotel, the raft of the Constructivists collides with the raft of the Medusa: optimism vs. pessimism.
The steel of the pool slices through the plastic of the sculpture like a knife through butter.

Arrival of the Floating Pool: after 40 years of crossing the Atlantic, the architects/lifeguards reach their destination. But they hardly notice it: due to the particular form of locomotion of the pool—its reaction to their own displacement in the water—they have to swim toward what they want to get away from and away from where they want to go.

Credits :

City of the Captive Globe: Rem Koolhaas, with Zoe Zenghelis.

Hotel Sphinx: Elia and Zoe Zenghelis.

New Welfare Island : Rem Koolhaas, with German Martinez, Richard Perlmutter; painting by Zoe Zenghelis.

Welfare Palace Hotel: Rem Koolhaas, with Derrick Snare, Richard Perlmutter; painting by Madelon Vriesendorp.

Between 1972 and 1976 much of the work on the Manhattan projects was produced at the Institute for Architecture and Urban Studies in New York, with the assistance of its interns and students.

255

Delirious New York proves above all, that Manhattan has been, from the beginning, devoted to the most rational, efficient and utilitarian pursuit of the irrational. In this vision Coney Island becomes an embryonic Manhattan, testbed of a Technology of the Fantastic, the Skyscraper a self-contained universe, Manhattan a man-made archipelago of architectural islands, Rockefeller Center the first and last fragment of a definitive Manhattan. The decline of this movement sets in with the European Modernist *Blitzkrieg* unleashed by Le Corbusier in the mid-thirties.

An appendix presents a series of projects that announce the 'second coming' of *Manhattanism*, this time as an explicit doctrine that can claim its place among contemporary urbanisms.

An impressive documentation of original materials and unpublished projects provides the evidence for this architectural manifesto, which reads, in its insistent tracing of subconscious clues and

heartedly to the needs of the metropolis. This

Rem Koolhaas was born in 1944 in Amsterdam.

He first was a film-script writer, then studied architecture in London, and moved to New York in 1972. A year later he became Visiting Fellow at Manhattan's Institute for Architecture and Urban Studies.

He is currently a partner in the Office for Metropolitan Architecture, which is devoted to the further development of a Culture of Congestion.

Cover by Madelon Vriesendorp

OXFORD UNIVERSITY PRESS, NEW YORK

41

architecture relates to the forces of the Gre

Copyright © 1978 Rem Koolhaas
Printed in France from type set in the United States

Library of Congress Cataloging-in-Publication Data

Koolhaas, Rem.
    Delirious New York.
        1. Architecture — New York (City). I. Title.
NA735.N5K66   720'.9747'1   77-17418
ISBN 0-19-520035-7

Originally published in English as *Delirious New York*
by Oxford University Press, New York, and Academy
Editions, London; in French as *New York Délire* by
Editions du Chêne, Paris.

stadt like a surfer to the waves.

New edition first published in the United States
of America (and in all countries not covered by
the co-publisher listed below) in 1994 by
The Monacelli Press, Inc., New York

New edition first published in the English language in
all countries of Europe, Japan, Korea, Taiwan, and the
U.K. and Commonwealth (except Canada) in 1994 by
010 Publishers, Rotterdam

Copyright © 1994 Rem Koolhaas
and The Monacelli Press, Inc.

Library of Congress Number: 94-076577
ISBN: 1-885254-00-8

book was written in longhand in the gorgeous comfort of my bedroom.

BEDS

This life is a hospital in which sick man is possessed by a desire to change beds. One would prefer to suffer by the stove. Another believes he would recover if he sat by the window. I think I would be happy in that place I happen not to be, and this question of moving house is the subject of a perpetual dialogue I have with my soul.

BEING THERE

Given the myriad of contending subprocesses in every cognitive act, how are we to understand the moment of negotiation and emergence when one of them takes the lead and constitutes a definite behavior? Or, in more evocative terms: How are we to understand the very moment of being there, when something concrete and specific appears?

BELLY

She had no navel. Gaze. Belly without blemish, bulging big, a buckler of taut vellum, no, whiteheaped corn, orient and immortal, standing from everlasting to everlasting. Womb of sin.

BERLIN

If you stand in the middle, where the circus was, you have completely different views coming out of four directions; really strange views of the past or of what still remains from the past, witnesses of everything that has happened. One can see something there that is uniquely Berlin and is rarely found in other cities — I mean the fully open, empty side and back walls of buildings, fire protection walls, that used to be covered by other buildings … If you like, these fire walls are historical documents. They tell of loss.

BEST

It gives the best massage I have ever received from a machine.

BETWEEN

I take another peek up and down the corridor. For a loony bin, it's awful quiet. Most rooms have double doors. The outside door only has a small glass window so you can look in at the crazies; the inside door has bars. I'm sittihg in the space between the two doors.

BEYOND

For anyone who, like Rem Koolhaas,

S

The pools were emptied.

Unlike the other temporary pavilions, which looked more like buildings, the German pavilion, which looked light, was too heavy to be moved easily. Since Germany was in a state of confusion, it was decided to leave the pavilion on loan to Spain until a decision could be made.

So it stood, a Gothic outpost in the land of the Moors. Meanwhile, the political situation in Spain became tense and the pavilion was forgotten as other problems became more pressing. Bombs exploded nearby.

For a few days it served as the headquarters for the Anarchists, but they quarreled about the use of the spaces. One of them made a plan so ridiculous, with such an absurd profusion of desks, cabinets, and chairs, that the result was catastrophic.

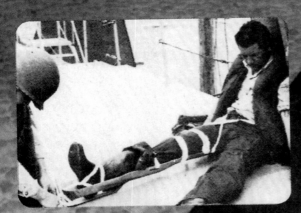

Because of this experience the Anarchists were the first to declare that modern architecture didn't work, and once again the pavilion was abandoned. Later it was badly damaged, becoming the first modern architectural ruin, but no

The new regime was determined to resolve the question of the pavilion. They disliked the fact that it had been the Anarchists' headquarters and so, being on good terms with the new government of its *Heimat*, they decided, as a friendly gesture

Since our "site" was curved, the pavilion had to be "bent."

The train journey was complicated. The railway tracks of each country were of different widths; many transfers were needed. After long delays the pavilion finally arrived in Berlin.

It was now an architectural orphan: its creator had just left for the USA.

The new government was against modernism and hardly even bothered to open the crates containing the pavilion. But its unacceptable modernity was a matter of context, and the marble slabs could serve other purposes.

First they were used on the set of a propaganda film aimed at homesick soldiers scattered around the world. With the precious stone as a pompous background, a voluptuous blonde sang a sentimental aria.

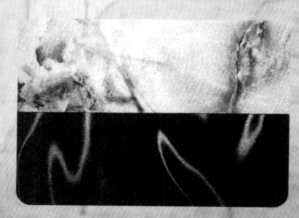

As decor (to soften the contours of the marble slabs and improve the acoustics), they were draped with purple satin, yellow silk, and red velvet.

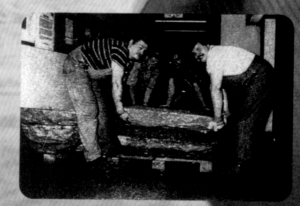

Next the marble was incorporated in the construction of a ministry, where it became the floor of the service entrance.

The war grew more intense. Berlin was bombed and the ministry was hit many times. A few days before the city was liberated the marble slabs cracked.

The ministry became an improvised hospital and camp.

57

In the euphoric time that followed the liberation, it was sometimes the scene of wild parties.

After the liberation, Europe had to be rebuilt. Each fragment, each particle of the pavilion was reused. The ministry was dismantled and the marble preserved. The other crates containing the pavilion were finally unpacked.

First the planners of the east side of the city suggested reassembling the entire pavilion as a gas station, for the time when each worker would own a car.

But the dimensions and the hidden module of the structure prevented that or any other use. Eventually it became the locker room for a gigantic sports complex planned for the 1952 Olympic Games.

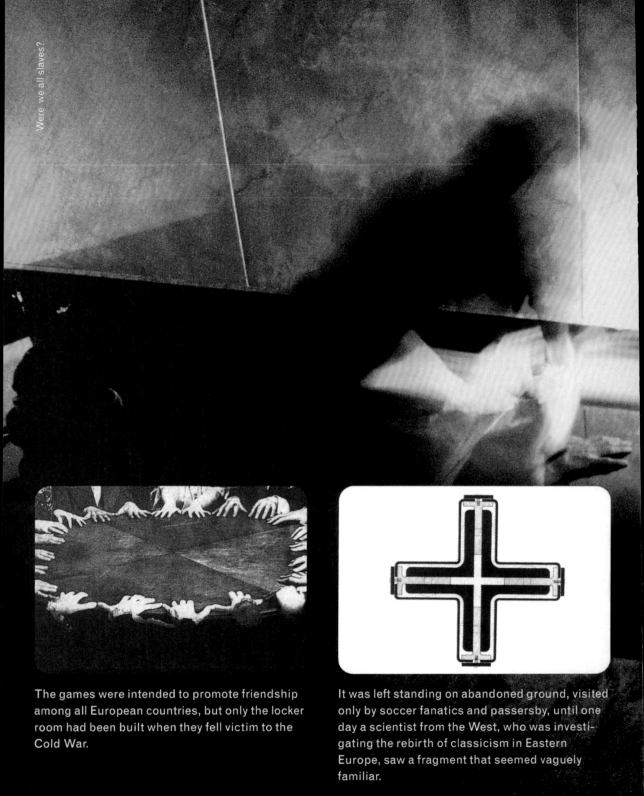

The games were intended to promote friendship among all European countries, but only the locker room had been built when they fell victim to the Cold War.

It was left standing on abandoned ground, visited only by soccer fanatics and passersby, until one day a scientist from the West, who was investigating the rebirth of classicism in Eastern Europe, saw a fragment that seemed vaguely familiar.

Dutch Section

divided the week up among different organs and members: Monday, hands; Wednesday, ears; Thursday, nose; Friday, hair; Saturday, eyes; and Sunday, skin ... Concentrating each night on just one area of his body allowed him to carry out the task of cleaning it and preserving it with greater thoroughness and attention to detail; and by so doing, to know and to love it more. With each individual organ and area the master of his labors for one day, perfect impartiality with regard to the care of the whole was assured; there were no favoritisms, no post-ponements, no odious hierarchies with respect to the overall treatment and detailed consideration of part and whole. He thought: My body is that impossibility; an egalitarian society.

BODY²

OMA's recent projects thus constitute *bodies* rather than *objects*. Body in the sense of material without *linguistic overcoding*; neither pure nor frag-mented forms, but *vague essences*: rounded, elongated, oblong ... No more constants, no more ideal forms, nor their fragments but instead their deformations.

BODY³

Just as we do not know what a spirit is, so we are ignorant of what a body is. We see certain properties, but what is this subject in which these properties reside? There are only bodies, said Democritus and Epicurus. There are no bodies, said the disciple of Zeno of Eden.

BODY⁴

Yet arguments based on the human body are fundamentally ahistorical and involve premises about some eternal "human nature" concealed with the seemingly "verifiable" and scientific data of physiological analysis. If the body is in reality a social body, if therefore there exists no pregiven human body as such, but rather the whole historical range of social experiences of the body, the whole variety of bodily norms projected by a series of distinct historical "modes of production" or social formations, then the return to some more "natural" vision of the body in space projected by phenom-enology comes to seem ideological, if not nostalgic.

A single glass element—the patio—is placed in the house to generate kitchen, dining, and living around it. Its glass floor lights a gym below. Two of the patio's walls are mobile; they can make it disappear entirely. A freestanding wall defines bedroom, study, and bathroom. Sliding panels extend it to create privacy.

In a parody of the archetypal Dutch section—
high water, dike, low land—this house
exploits its position on the embankment of an
unrealized highway; it consists of two layers—
a lower entrance floor at street level and a
"living" floor on the higher, water level.

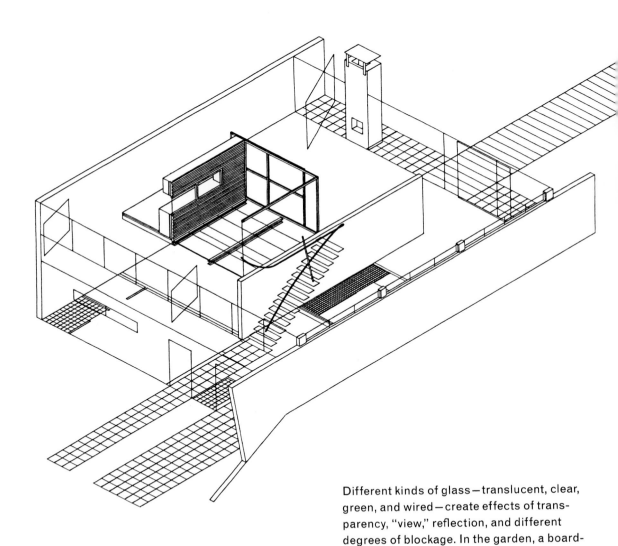

Different kinds of glass—translucent, clear,
green, and wired—create effects of transparency, "view," reflection, and different
degrees of blockage. In the garden, a boardwalk continues the passage through the house
with an exit toward the water.

0 | | | | | 5m

patio at night

BODY SNATCHER
(In former times) A person who dug
up dead bodies and sold them to
doctors for scientific study.

BOREDOM[1]
But the most exhausting thing of all
is boredom.

BOREDOM[2]
If my interest in the banal architecture of the 1950s and 1960s, the
derivatives of Ernesto Rogers and
Richard Neutra, seems a somewhat
boring source, I can only answer
that to die of boredom is not so bad.

BORING[1]
The thing that everybody finds out
about me once they really get to
know me is just how terrifically
boring I am, and how I aspire to
being boring. I'm sure eventually it
will turn everybody off of me
because my dream in life is to wear
sweats and go to a mall.

BORING[2]
I like boring things.

BORROWER
Bach was a great borrower. Not only
did he derive creative stimulus from
the works of such famous com-
posers as Vivaldi and Corelli, but
minor figures like Dieupart also provided him with useful ideas.

BOTH
Where something and nothing are
both qualities.

BOUCLIERS
Côté police, boucliers du Moyen
Age et grenades à faire pleurer.
Jamais encore on n'avait vu dans
Paris ces boucliers de tôle. Place
Maubert, les C.R.S. les inaugurent
pour se protéger contre une pluie de
projectiles divers: pierres, pavés et
même phares d'auto.

BOUDOIR
The boudoir is the fusion of body and
space. At the same time it is also
instrument and object and as such it
reveals desires, dreams, and thoughts.

BOUQUET
veux-tu venir Paulette oui ou non tu
nous emmerdes je veux dire à maman
que tu ne veux plus jouer et que tu
cherches à te rendre intéressante en
te développant de mille façons en
bouquet de fleurs japonaises.

BOXES
Who would have imagined we
would go this way. The pyramid ...
the cathedral ... and now, the skyscraper. We all live in little boxes ...

looking back

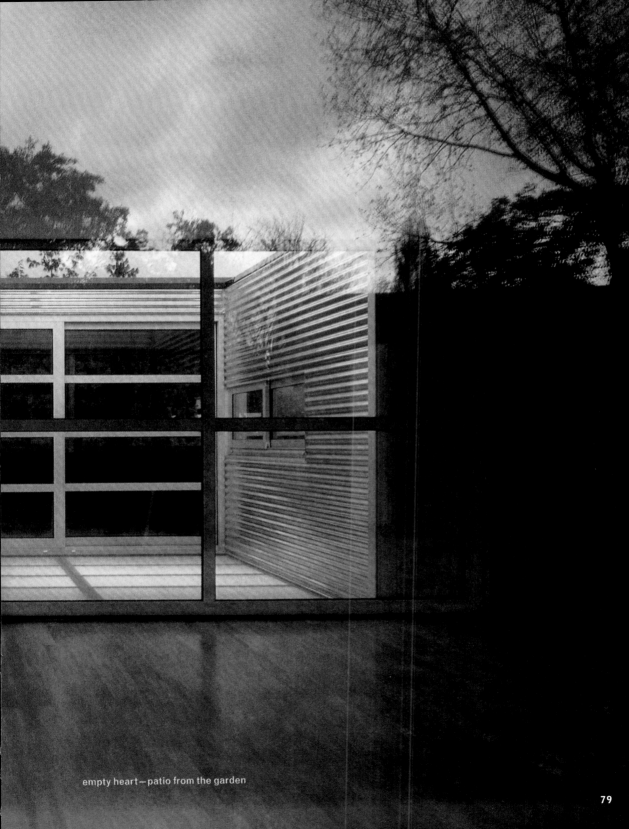

empty heart—patio from the garden

Dilemma of European architect building in Japan: Should the project be "as Western as possible"? Is it just another export like a van Gogh, a Mercedes, or a Vuitton bag? Or should it reflect the fact that it exists in Japan?

±13,000 Points

Nexus World Housing
Fukuoka, Japan
Completed 1991

Fukuoka context: sea, highway, site.

In Fukuoka, the character of the site reinforces this dilemma: the context is much more organized, less chaotic, than the typical Japanese city.

82

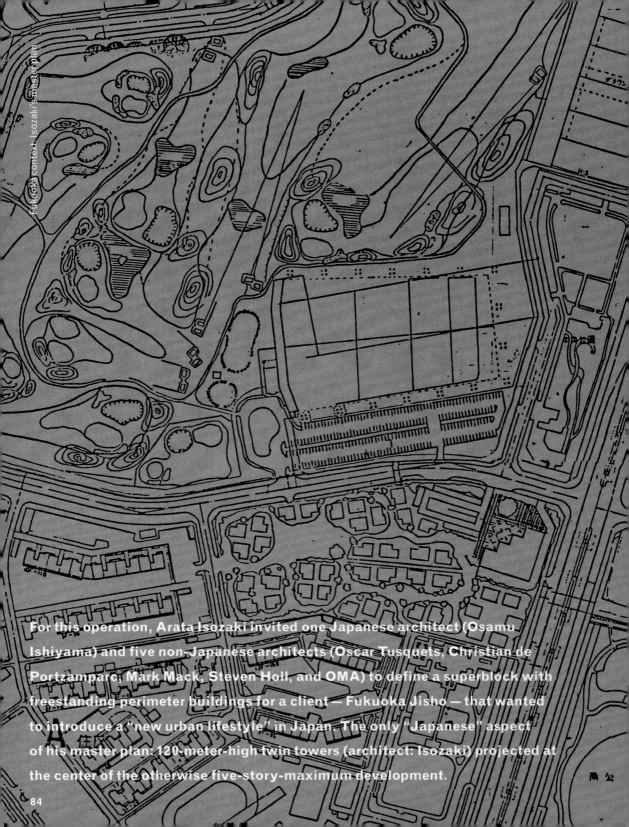

For this operation, Arata Isozaki invited one Japanese architect (Osamu Ishiyama) and five non-Japanese architects (Oscar Tusquets, Christian de Portzamparc, Mark Mack, Steven Holl, and OMA) to define a superblock with freestanding perimeter buildings for a client — Fukuoka Jisho — that wanted to introduce a "new urban lifestyle" in Japan. The only "Japanese" aspect of his master plan: 120-meter-high twin towers (architect: Isozaki) projected at the center of the otherwise five-story-maximum development.

九大留学生会館

亀公園

香椎郵便局

香椎中学校

B 住区

Oscar Tusquets
オスカー・トゥスケ
①

Arata Isozaki
磯崎 新
⑦

Christian de Portzamparc
クリスチャン・ド・ポルザンパルク
②

Osamu Ishiyama
石山 修武
③

Steven Holl
スティーブン・ホール
⑥

Rem Koolhaas
レム・クールハース
⑤

Mark Mack
マーク・マック
④

85

Like an earlier scheme in the shadow of the Berlin Wall, the project explores a fusion of the Roman city — sections of Pompeii, for instance, form continuous tapestries where houses never become objects — and similar experiments by Mies van der Rohe where individual courtyard houses are consolidated to form blocks. The centrifugal substance of modern architecture is condensed to generate urban form.

LEARNING JAPANESE

Rotterdam
Desperate phone call to Tokyo.
Our instructions for first
Japanese exhibition: display models freestanding
in space.
Their layout according to
incoming fax: all models
up against the wall.

Never-before-seen Japanese man steps
out of our elevator.
Hand him the phone; he saves
the day; immediate employment:
Fuminori Hoshino.

Tokyo
Japan, 7 days later.
First impression: the vastness
and shamelessness of its ugliness.

Being on intimate terms with the
utilitarian is major strength:
no frills, ever.

Europe, and even America, try
(with more or less success)
to create situations where
everything is as "good" as possible;
Japan lives (serenely?) with drastic
segregation between
the sublime, the ugly,
and the utterly without qualities.

Dominance of the last 2 categories
makes mere presence of the first
stunning:
when beauty "happens,"
it is absolutely surprising.

Schedule
Japanese schedule:
written prison that blocks freedom,
excludes improvisation, eliminates possibility,
voids time, plans non-event.

Living rooms emerging by night....

Instead of obligations embedded in generic
free time, free time in Japan
is exceptional condition excavated from
general condition of obligation.

Only free time that day — midnight:
run around Imperial Palace; darkness;
fall; deep wound. Trail of blood
back to hotel.
Ambulance crew entirely covered
in what seem man-sized
condoms, medical riot gear
(foreigner's blood considered dangerous).

Medical care: traditional.
First Tokyo visit:
untraditional; horizontal, immobile.
Think about it.

Blue
Fukuoka: young pink Chicago around
a blue bay.
(But all colors are blue in Japan.)

Eastern extremity of axis that runs
via Seoul and Moscow to Lille,
and eventually even to London,
maybe.

Like almost everywhere, the south
considered essence of attractiveness:
better climate, less history, more freedom.
Atlanta, Munich, Marseille:
people, activities, programs —
disconnected
from specifics of place —
gravitate toward zone of maximum *niceness*.
In Japan, that is Fukuoka.

Stacked highway, stainless steel "blinders,"
smell of oysters.

Site: flat; distant mountains; residential
area of almost East German neatness
near invisible sea;
could be anywhere.

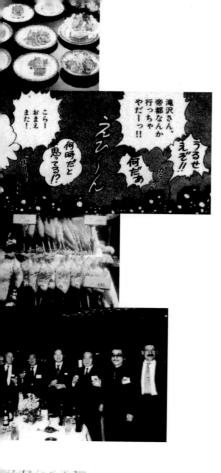

We

"We in Japan ...": obsessive refrain
over endless business dinners.

It announces:
1. probable failure of any project of
communication;
2. formal declaration of lack of
interest in "other side";
3. immutable "we" vs. unstable "they";
4. self-administered blanket-
amnesty for any future transgression;
5. beginning of strategic skirmish
assuring quick advantage over other side,
paralyzed by touristic eagerness;
6. first application of web of politeness
to immobilize enemy;
Japan equals England in surgical manners,
also in insular self-love.

"We" is the ghostwriter behind every Japanese "I."

Meal

Ground behind rectangular counter
for ±12 customers is,
in fact, basin. Chefs wearing rubber boots flick,
at imperceptible signal of patron,
specific fish — or at least water-based beings
(cold-blooded aquatic craniate vertebrates) —
through air toward rectangular window in tiled wall.
Behind window — facing customers — a cook
(is there a better name for a profession that is about
elegant killing? culinary henchman?)
follows, with a very sharp knife,
the last part of arc described by still
violently flapping sea creature,
dismembers and rearranges
it as festive, still-contracting
artwork before it lands
on plate,
center
of impeccable dish.

Sections of fish strung
together by dismembered arch of spine
transferred to table.

Levitating black concrete socle ...

Film of watery
blood drips
from window
back to basin,
which, as each meal proceeds,
turns slightly redder.

Breakfast
Uminonakamichi Beach Hotel,
end of peninsula prominently
protruding into ocean.
Nobody
swims in the sea;
it's always "out of season"
(even at 100°).

Breakfast: the impossible beauty
of its honeymooning couples,
more poignant still
in their lack
of visible intimacy.

It is always too cool to use the pool.

Ceremony
Opening of new Hyatt Hotel merged
(or is it spliced?)
with ceremony
for the 1992 Architectural Institute prize
for "best building in Japan":
lake-sized pool, laser show,
5,000 best friends (of the developers).

Tables of raw fish create Martian landscapes,
from pink to deep
red.

Suddenly on island in pool:
moving speech
by 3-man committee.
My interpretation: award grants access
to genetic material of Japanese architecture.
More modern version of "keys to the city":
"keys to the chromosomes."
From now on we can be
Japanese *Imagineers*.

Night roofline ...

Haiku
(for Mr. Toh)

Japanese client
gulp of melted snow
in Superdry desert

First steps into the vertical patio house...

Memo

Memo from Toyo Ito: Purely in terms of design, I find myself comparing you to a mechanical baseball pitching machine, the kind you see so often on Japanese batting practice ranges, where the ball is controlled perfectly without the emotional or spiritual agitation of a real pitcher. This leaves me with an impression of freshness that I have not often seen among architects in Europe, or anywhere else for that matter.

Soul

Toyo
Thank you
for comparing me
to a "mechanical baseball pitching machine."
Only from a Japanese
such a compliment
would not be an
insult.
Maybe there is
a certain efficiency in my character,
but in Europe
it is very dangerous
to admit
that you don't have a soul.

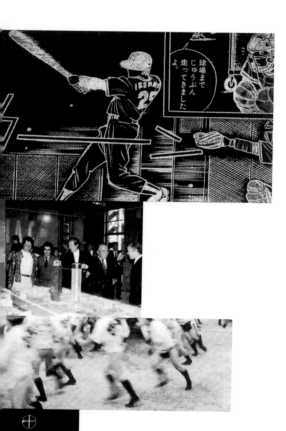

Party

Next party, club:
drink to new role—gene raider—
with glass full of living
fish (over 500);
no noticeable movement
beyond stomach.

Sudden intrusion of (naked under kimonos?)
barefoot singers roaring
Japanese a cappella—holy music.
For the Japanese, usually camouflaged
as neutral beings,
revealing virility is a decision
coming out of the blue.

Enters foot masseur/reader,
growling.
One foot quickly exposed;
inserts metal object in previously unsuspected
(nonexistent?) folds.
Calloused hands explore delicate surfaces.
"Excellent circulation,"

Down to Japanese room, up to green mountain . . .

Present-geisha: it is never clear
whose torture is worse, hers or yours.
She always seems the same age:
a theoretical 39.
White face cracked with anxiety,
hair a brittle helmet.
Please, no please, please, no please!

Yet, they may suddenly stand on their heads,
their hair voluptuous on the ground,
kimono dropping, real thighs, calves,
singing Western ballads
upside down:
extremes necessary to keep attention of
increasingly drunken *sans*?

Yielding, at the end of the meal, to Oedipal
pull of post-geisha:
some kind of witch — gray spiky hair
of a madwoman, almost no teeth; telling
hilarious stories, apparently
outrageous jokes — "*ach so, ach so*" —
crude elderly Ophelia
doubled over
with laughter, slapping her thighs ...
mother as one of the boys, finally.

Meeting
We had been 6 times to Japan,
each time for 7 days;
each day we had "meetings":
25 people together from 8 A.M. to 10 P.M.;
at each meeting: 200 – 400 points.
#1: please choose between 2 grays
for the bathroom;
#113: foundations don't work.
Mosaic tiles before the foundation:
Japanese inability
to define hierarchy?
Or deliberate scrambling
to keep foreigner on high alert?

More exciting hypothesis:
for Japanese
no point
ever unimportant.

Explains maddening attention to detail,
but also density of incredible quality.

As for the size of the meeting:
first thought: irrational, inefficient
to meet with entire organizations—
but after a meeting
everyone knows;
no distortions, deviations, destruction.

Now we have our own "Japanese meetings"
in Rotterdam:
endless table, schedule for everyone, no free time.
Nobody leaves the room before
all 300 decisions are made.

We all love it.   **1993**

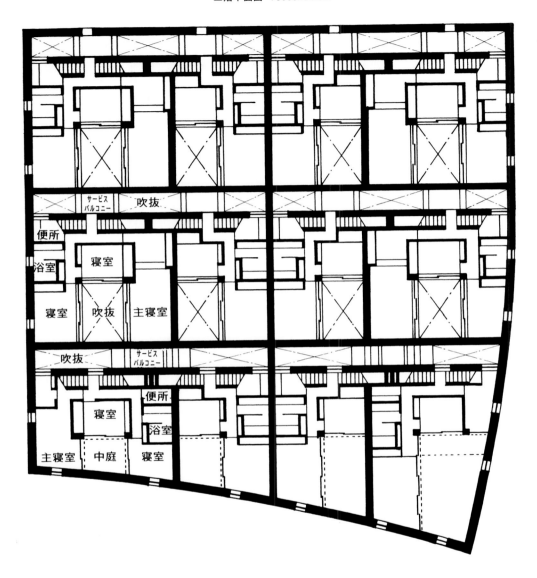

サービスバルコニー
吹抜

便所

浴室　寝室

寝室　吹抜　主寝室

吹抜　サービスバルコニー

便所

寝室

浴室

主寝室　中庭　寝室

主寝室 ：master bedroom

寝室 ：bedroom

便所 ：lavatory

浴室 ：bathroom

吹抜 ：void

中庭 ：patio

サービスバルコニー ：service balcony

0　　　　　　　　　　10m

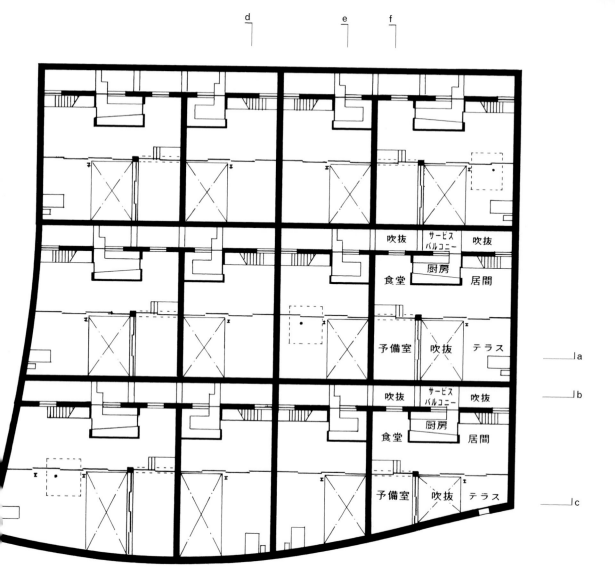

d　　　　e　f

吹抜　サービスバルコニー　吹抜
食堂　厨房　居間
予備室　吹抜　テラス

吹抜　サービスバルコニー　吹抜
食堂　厨房　居間
予備室　吹抜　テラス

a
b
c

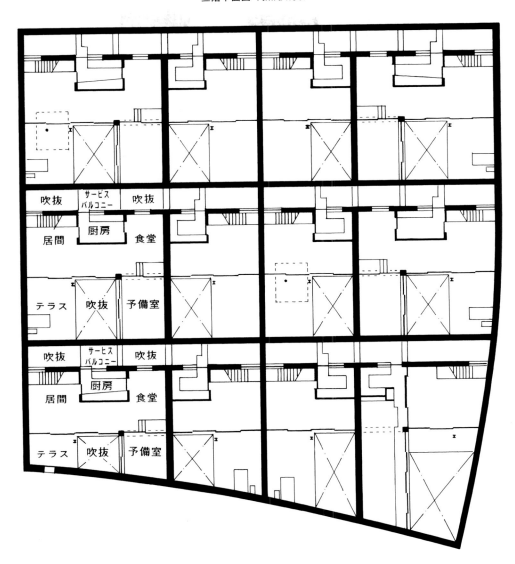

居間 : living room

テラス : terrace

食堂 : dining room

厨房 : kitchen

予備室 : extra room

吹抜 : void

サービスバルコニー : service balcony

0   10m

day of the shipwreck — they could easily have survived without eating anything at all. This monumental expression of "loss of nerve" corresponds to the premature panic and loss of nerve about the Metropolis in the present moment of the 20th century.

CAPITALISM
Capitalism is in the crossing of every kind of formation, always and by nature neocapitalism.

CAREFREE
They are waiting on the bench; that is, they are there before me and I hesitate under a tree, watching them smile and laugh, before advancing to make myself known. Then I ask them what they would like to do. They shrug their shoulders, look at one another, smile, laugh, and say they do not care.

CATHEDRAL[1]
The cathedral is inevitably the organizing element in any gothic city, and we therefore propose to start our visit there.

CATHEDRAL[2]
Well, I suppose these freeways made this town … and many others … possible. They're the cathedrals of our time. There are names for the various kinds of freeway drivers. The "slingshotter" … the "adventurer" … the "marshmallow" … the "nomad" … the "weaver." It's fancy driving … Things that never had names before now are easily described. It makes conversation easy.

CATHEDRAL[3]
The microchip is a cathedral.

CAUGHT
The apartment blocks looked like skyscrapers that, at the moment of being blown up and fracturing in two or three places, had been caught and laid flat on their sides.

CAUTION
This appliance was constructed to process normal household quantities.

CHANCE[1]
In a small town in Scotland they sell books with one blank page hidden someplace in the volume. If the reader opens to that page and it's three o'clock in the afternoon, he dies.

CHANCE[2]
If the universe is indeed spatially infinite, or if there are infinitely many universes, there would probably be some large regions

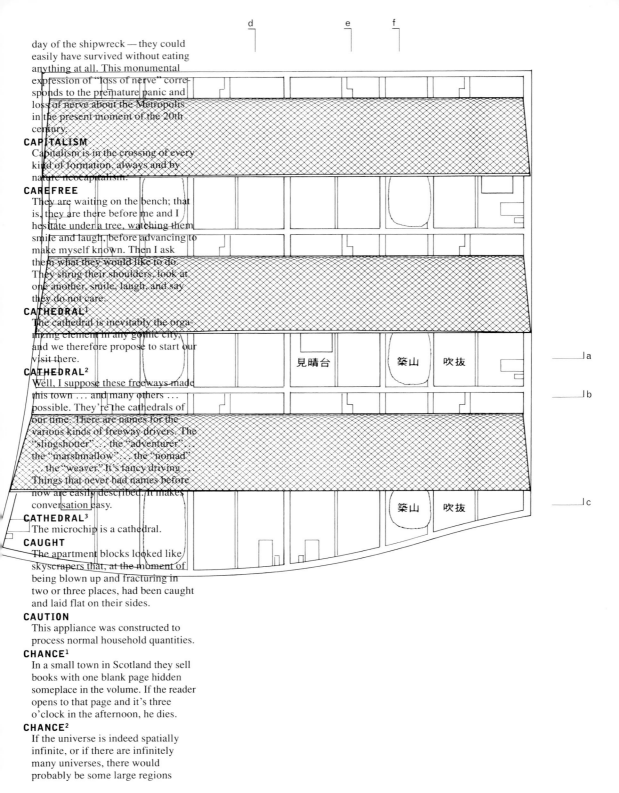

見晴台　築山　吹抜

築山　吹抜

屋根伏図 : roof

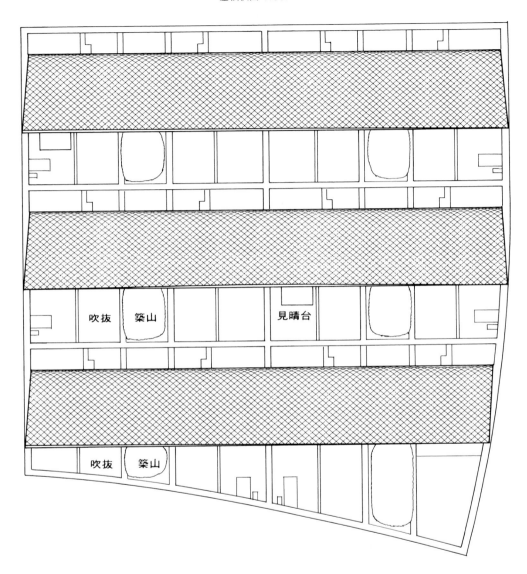

吹抜　築山　　　　　見晴台

吹抜　築山

見晴台 : balcony

築山 : green dome

吹抜 : void

0 | | | | | | | | 10m

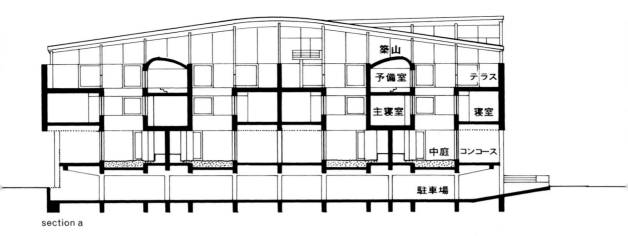

築山
予備室　テラス
主寝室　寝室
中庭　コンコース
駐車場

section a

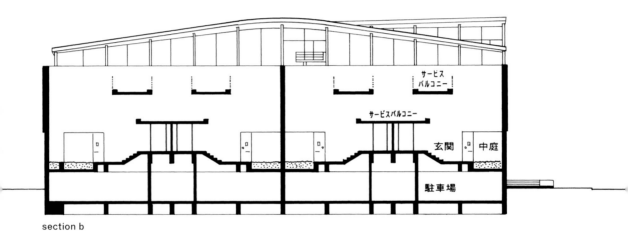

サービス
バルコニー
サービスバルコニー
玄関　中庭
駐車場

section b

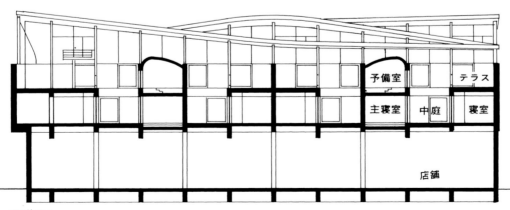

予備室　テラス
主寝室　中庭　寝室
店舗

section c

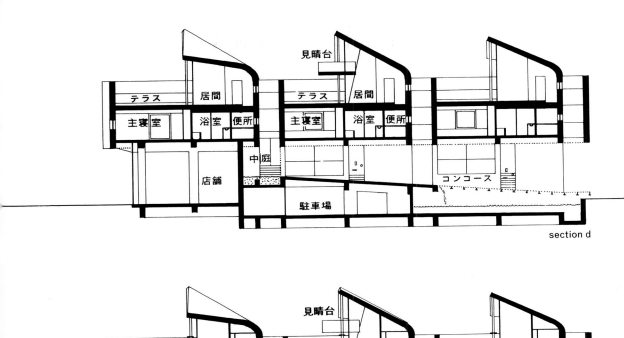

テラス　居間　　見晴台　テラス　居間

主寝室　浴室　便所　　主寝室　浴室　便所

中庭

店舗

駐車場　　　　コンコース

section d

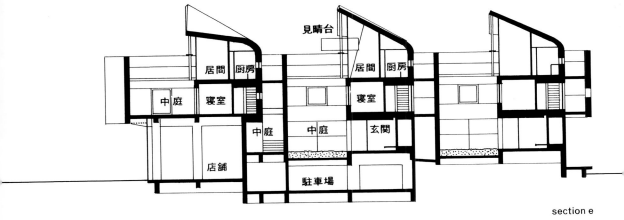

見晴台

居間　厨房　　　居間　厨房

中庭　寝室　　　　寝室

中庭　中庭　玄関

店舗

駐車場

section e

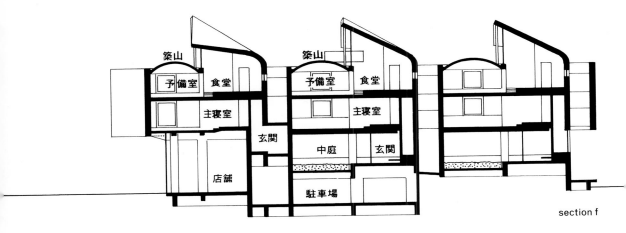

築山　　　　築山

予備室　食堂　　予備室　食堂

主寝室　　　主寝室

玄関

中庭　玄関

店舗

駐車場

section f

0　　　　　　　　　　　10m

somewhere that started out in a
smooth uniform manner. It is a bit
like the well-known horde of
monkeys hammering away on type-
writers — most of what they write
will be garbage, but very occasionally by pure chance they will type
out one of Shakespeare's sonnets.

CHANCE³
Chance, the phosphorescent word
that he will write on the black wall
when I turn out my light tonight.

CHANNEL
By changing the channel he could
change himself. He could go
through phases, as garden plants
went through phases, but he could
change as rapidly as he wished by
twisting the dial backward and forward. In some cases he could spread
out into the screen without stopping,
just as on TV people spread out into
the screen. By turning the dial,
Chance could bring others inside his
eyelids. Thus he came to believe that
it was he, Chance, and no one else,
who made himself be.

CHAOS¹
In the steeply curving corridor of the
centrifuge, the wind was howling
past, carrying with it loose articles
of clothing, pieces of paper, items
of food from the galley, plates and
cups — everything that had not been
securely fastened down. Bowman
had time for one glimpse of the
racing chaos when the main lights
flickered and died, and he was
surrounded by screaming darkness.

CHAOS²
You cannot aspire to it, you can only
be an instrument of it ... The only
relationship that architects can have
with chaos is to take their rightful
places in the army of those committed to prevent it, and fail. And it is
only in failure, by accident, that
chaos happens.

CHARACTERS
My Latin Quarter hat. God, we simply must dress the character. I want
puce gloves. You were a student,
weren't you? Of what in the other
devil's name? Paysayenn. P.C.N.,
you know: physiques, chimiques,
et naturelles. Aha. Eating your
groatsworth of mou en civet, flesh-
pots of Egypt, elbowed by belching
cabmen. Just say in the most
natural tone: when I was in Paris,
boul'Mich'.

Hotel Furka Blick dominates Furka Pass, an important connection between the Rhone and Rhine valleys. It is an agglomeration of two buildings: a ten-room chalet built in 1893 and a cube of 27 rooms built ten years later.

Neglect after the war left the hotel untouched: the dining room on the ground floor, the bedrooms without running water, the beds, the view.

The pass is open only during the summer months; the rest of the year the buildings are lost in mist and snow, as in a fairy tale.

Marc Hostetler owned a gallery in Neuchâtel. In 1978 he bought Hotel Furka Blick. He invited artists to spend part of the summer working, performing, intervening in the landscape, leaving traces in the buildings, confronting the other, "accidental" public: tourists, wanderers.

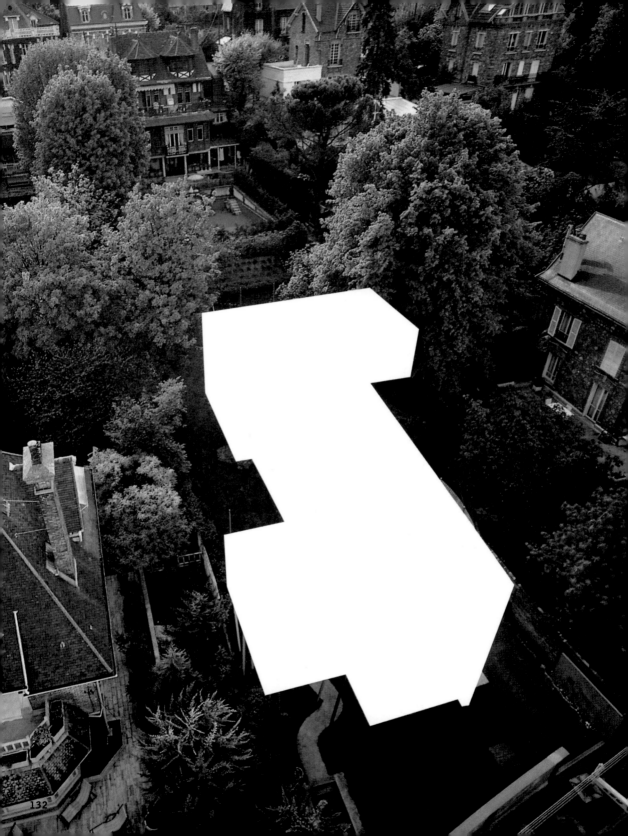

Obstacles

Villa Dall'Ava
St. Cloud, Paris, France
Completed 1991

Letter
It was handwritten in blue ink, obviously by someone who was very
passionate about architecture.

Reading it, you knew immediately that this was going to be a
mythological enterprise.

Desperation
It had a desperate tone: "Dear so-and-so, you are our last chance."
Something like that.

Competition
Later, we found out that they had already spent a long time searching
for the right architect. They had even held small competitions.

Scandal
We made an appointment. He would pick me up at Charles de Gaulle
Airport. When I came out, there was an enormous scandal: someone
was trying to kill a policeman.

It turned out to be him. The policeman had asked him to move,
but since he was waiting for his architect he had tried to run over the
policeman.

Introduction
That was our introduction.

Site
The site was beautiful — a Monet. It slopes toward the Seine.
Beyond it, the Bois de Boulogne, and beyond that a panoramic view
of the city; the Eiffel Tower is straight on axis. La Défense is
to the left.

Neighbors
It is surrounded by 19th-century houses, very picturesque;
diagonally across is a 1950s "Belgian" house with a tennis court.

the difference between his own class and the class of his character.

CLASSIC

"Classic" is henceforth the "flash" at the dawning of a new world — which will of course have no duration, for its collapse is already sealed with its appearance.

CLEFT

Then with a rapid sure movement he grasped the sides of the onlooker's head. With one hand he pulled violently to the left, with the other to the right. First the skull was cleft, and then the onlooker's body, with only the faintest brief moan, barely more than a sigh, parted down the middle. The two cleanly separated halves of the body toppled stiffly to the floor.

CLICHES¹

But you said that if we always talked logically and did not get into muddles, we could never say anything new. We could only say ready-made things. What did you call those things?

CLICHES²

Few men are innovators, and while it is vital not to inhibit those who are, it is equally vital to provide the others with a standard by which they can be guided; hence the need for a canon, for a contemporary vernacular, even for clichés.

CLIMATES

I went into the bathroom, started the shower and stepped in. I stood there long enough to get completely wet, then wrapped myself in a big, fluffy bath-towel and went out on to the balcony. Into thirty degrees below freezing.

CLIMAX

A well-planned life should have an effective climax.

CLOTHES¹

They seem to wear more clothes than other people. I mean the men wear shoes and socks when they go down to the lake and they have their cigarettes tucked into their socks. And the women wear earrings, hats, bracelets, watches, high heels. Sometimes you'll see someone with nothing on but a bandaid.

CLOTHES²

If the king is in effect naked, it is only insofar as he is under a certain number of clothes — fictitious, doubtless, but nonetheless essential

Intimidation I

Two of Le Corbusier's villas are nearby.

Intimidation II

The clients wanted a masterpiece.

Contradiction I

He wanted a glass house.
She wanted a swimming pool on the roof.

Urban/Suburban

Theoretically, it would be possible to see the Eiffel Tower while swimming.

Weight

It was a difficult issue to resolve: the weight of the pool resting on glass.

Columns

The engineer proposed columns to support the parents' apartment.

Butterfly

There are columns inside, but they are absorbed by the wall. The house floats like a concrete butterfly.

Contradiction II

The site was small.
The house was big.
It had to have the smallest possible footprint.

Pretzel

The zoning regulations described a kind of pyramidal pretzel that the house could not violate.

The site was surrounded by walls; it was already a kind of interior.

The small rectangle of the glass house represents the minimal footprint.

It is only a preliminary enclosure; the real house ends at the walls, where the "others" begin.

Building Permit

The permit process went very fast.
That was the last thing that went fast.

Fight

We got permission to build.
When the neighbors learned what was happening, they became very
unhappy. There had never been a house on the site.

Issue

The issue: does etched glass count as a wall?
It was debated all the way to the French Supreme Court.

Commuters

Anyway, we started.
The house was too expensive. Belgian contractors were cheaper.
It would be a house built by commuters.

Deserted

In the end, the lawyers deserted the clients.
They had to argue themselves.
They won.

Delay

Time passed. Time pressed.

Daughter

The daughter grew up. How would she inhabit the house that she
had destroyed — accidentally — as a model when she was seven?

Revision

The long wait was bad in some ways, but good in allowing endless
revision: it began as a beginner's house: strident, colorful, etc.; it
became a record of our own growing up.

Delay

Years passed.

Moved

We moved in to finish the house.
They moved in because it was still unfinished.
We became friends.

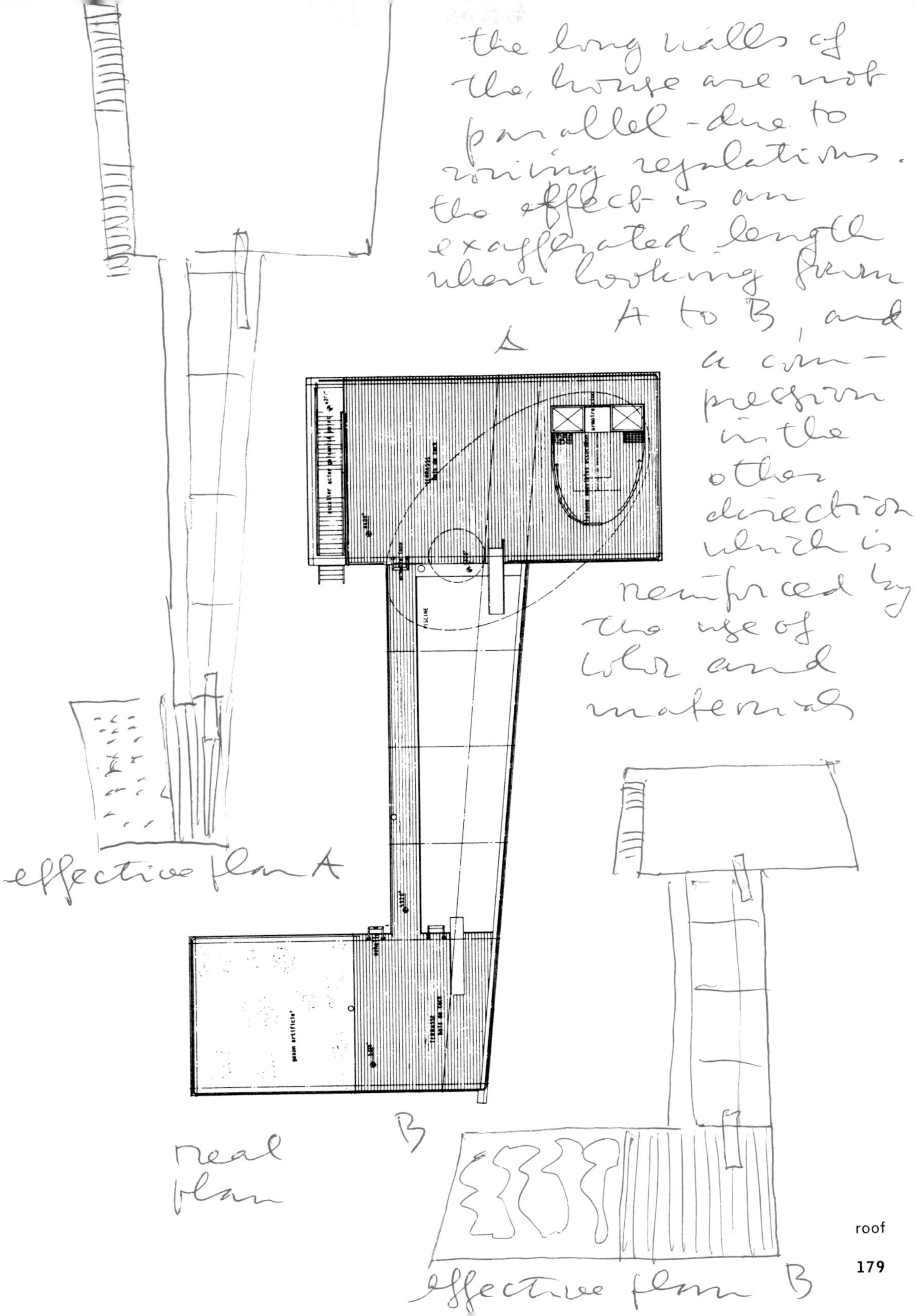

the long walls of
the house are not
parallel - due to
zoning regulations.
the effect is an
exaggerated length
when looking from
A to B, and
a com-
pression
in the
other
direction
which is
reinforced by
the use of
color and
materials

A

B

effective plan A

real
plan

effective plan B

roof

179

stripping railings:

i hate the ship metaphor. it
very hard to do without res
ocean liner from the 20-tie
case, the outlines also interl
the relation ships of the in
volumes

a cavity above
stairs used
for storage

échel

bois de teck
couverture bitumineux
isolant 800mm.
béton armé 200 mm.
peinture

5320*

membrane de pvc souple armée
isolant 80 mm.
béton armé 200 mm.
peinture

membrane de pvc souple armée
isolant 40 mm.
béton armé 200 mm.
plafonds de plaques de plâtre

parquet chêne
béton armé 200 mm.
plafond de tôle ondulée finition
aluminium

tôle ondulée finition aluminium
isolant 80 mm.
béton armé 200 mm.
peinture   2520*

2100*

armoires de contreplaqué

0000
revêtements en plaque ardoises
béton armé 200 mm.
isolant 80 mm.
stuc 10 mm.

caoutchouc
chauffage par le sol mm.
isolant 40 mm.
béton armé 200 mm.
2520

A   B   C   D   E   F

in the end the railing
became a minimal
ling not a
definitive container
version
tube bent
similar dimensions
to both side
original: i beam
resting on
tube.

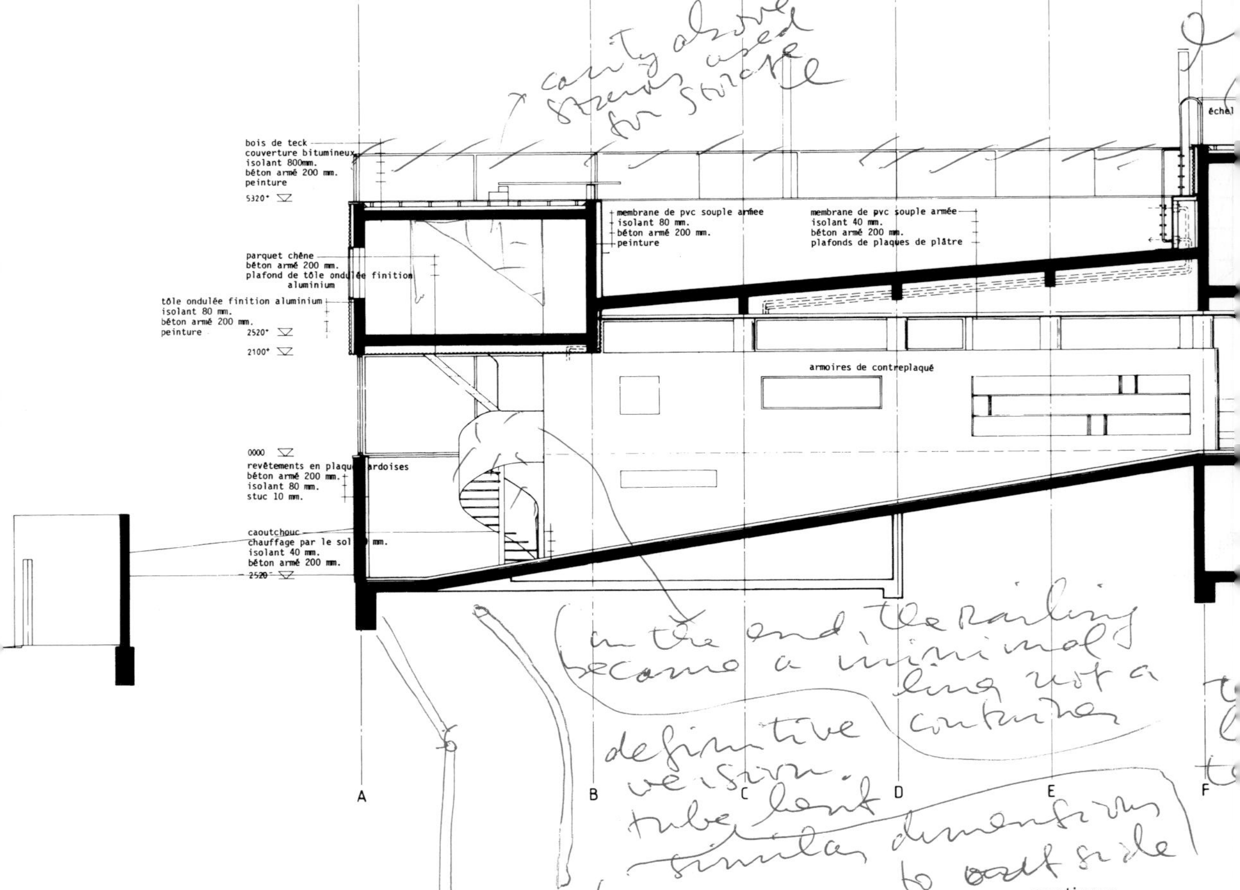

section a

ing one
...ting the
...tain
...with
duel

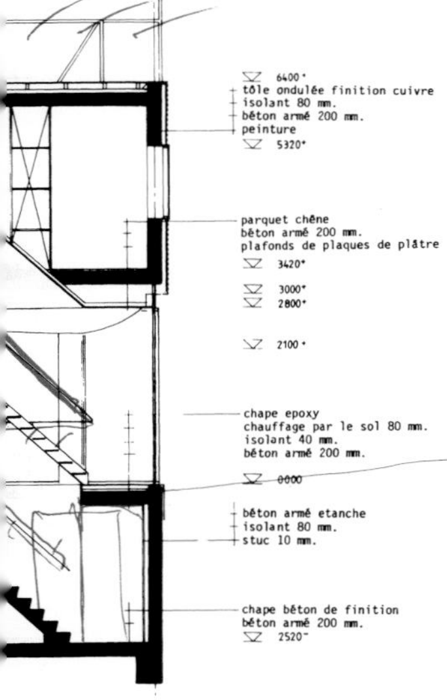

▽ 6400*
tôle ondulée finition cuivre
isolant 80 mm.
béton armé 200 mm.
peinture
▽ 5320*

parquet chêne
béton armé 200 mm.
plafonds de plaques de plâtre
▽ 3420*

▽ 3000*
▽ 2800*

▽ 2100*

chape epoxy
chauffage par le sol 80 mm.
isolant 40 mm.
béton armé 200 mm.
▽ 0000

béton armé etanche
isolant 80 mm.
stuc 10 mm.

chape béton de finition
béton armé 200 mm.
▽ 2520*

...rizntel lines
...d horrible in
...ning room
one 'stick' left

The house is actually
positioned in an
incredibly complex,
dense situation. It
is about its rela-
tionship with its
neighbours, its
context. The best
way to represent it
would be to take the
house as a frame
to describe its en-
vironment. It is not
an object!

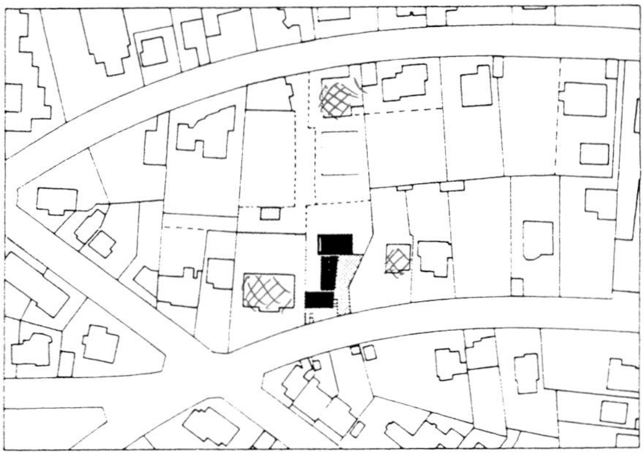

"those fellas ain't thinkin'. No sir, they just ain't usin' their heads."

COATING

Beauty is made up, on the one hand, of an element that is eternal and invariable ... and, on the other, of a relative, circumstantial element, which we may like to call ... contemporaneity, fashion, morality, passion. Without this second element, which is like the amusing, teasing, appetite-whetting coating of the divine cake, the first element would be indigestible, tasteless, unadapted, and inappropriate to human nature.

CODE

A man indicates his desire for a woman by winking. When a man winks, a woman is required to lower her eyes demurely. She is not allowed to look directly into the eyes of anyone she desires. However, if she is interested, she will not lower her eyes ... the man then twitches the corner of his mouth, indicating where he wants to meet her behind.

COINCIDENCE

There is always a moment when the image presses close to the sound. It is the moment of rhythmic coincidence between what is seen and what is heard. Three clashes of the cymbals — three flashes of light. Five chords played hell for leather — five images wedged together just as fast. To the devil with out-of-sync: the image is marching in step. And that is ultimately what it offers best. Otherwise, it strays, losing itself in diluted metaphor, repeating words superfluously. Thanks, but we had already got the message! Whilst there, crash, bang, wallop, blah, blah, blah, and the meaning is forgotten. Simply the call to order. The order of sensations. Rhythmic coincidence is the moment of truth. We see at last who gives the orders and who obeys. In case we had forgotten.

COLLAPSE

There is an enormous tension between the ostensible health of architecture and the actual erosion of its importance ... On the one hand, there is this triumphant atmosphere: an incredible amount of publications, incredible amount of programs, incredible amount of

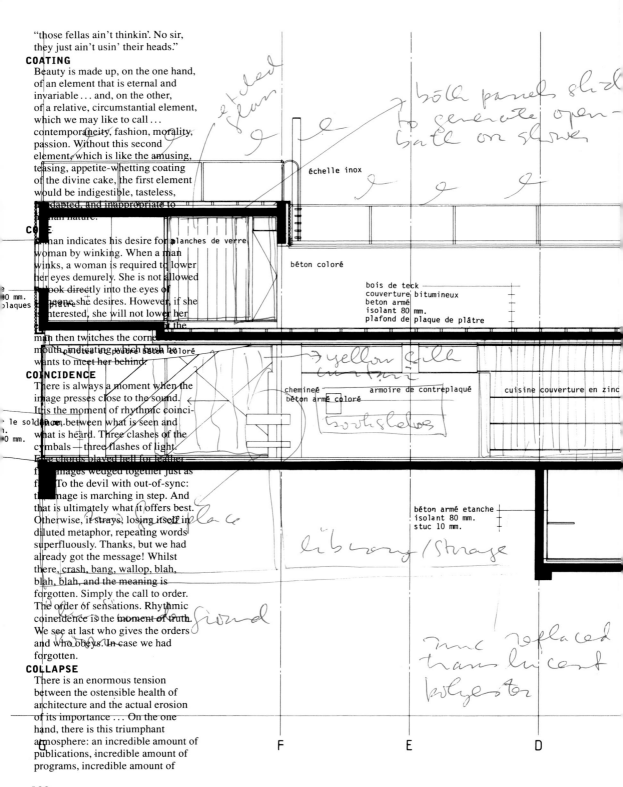

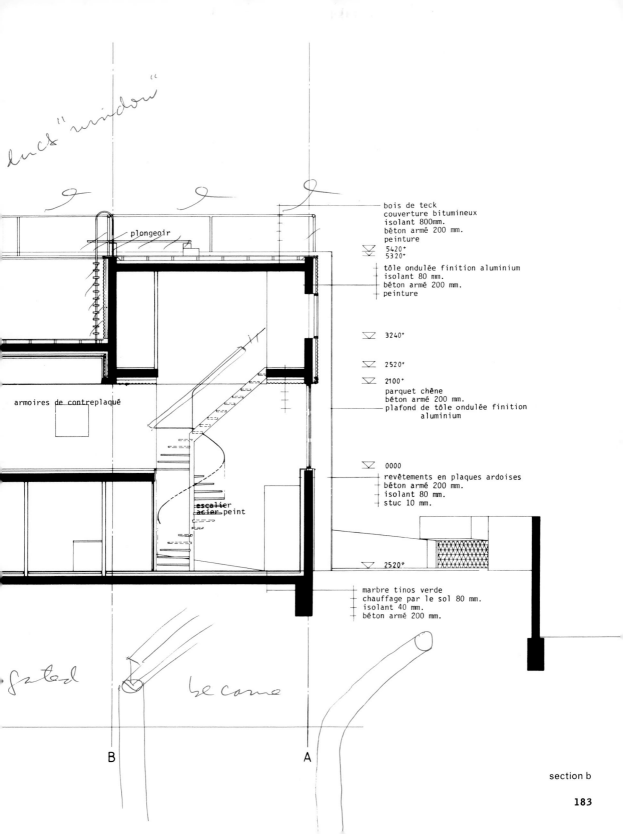

duct "window"

plongeoir

bois de teck
couverture bitumineux
isolant 800mm.
béton armé 200 mm.
peinture

▽ 5420⁺
5320⁺

tôle ondulée finition aluminium
isolant 80 mm.
béton armé 200 mm.
peinture

▽ 3240⁺

▽ 2520⁺

▽ 2100⁺

parquet chêne
béton armé 200 mm.
plafond de tôle ondulée finition
    aluminium

armoires de contreplaqué

▽ 0000

revêtements en plaques ardoises
béton armé 200 mm.
isolant 80 mm.
stuc 10 mm.

escalier
acier peint

▽ 2520⁺

marbre tinos verde
chauffage par le sol 80 mm.
isolant 40 mm.
béton armé 200 mm.

gated

become

B   A

section b

183

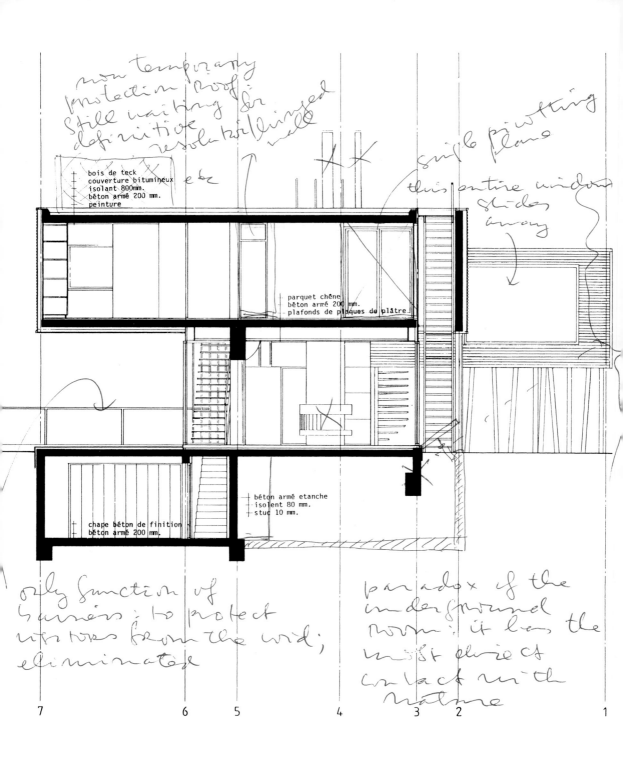

non temporary
protection roof.
still waiting for
definitive
resolution hinged wall

etc

bois de teck
couverture bitumineux
isolant 800mm.
bêton armé 200 mm.
peinture

single pivotting

this entire window
slides
away

parquet chêne
bêton armé 200 mm.
plafonds de plaques de plâtre

bêton armé etanche
isolent 80 mm.
stuc 10 mm.

chape bêton de finition
bêton armé 200 mm.

only function of
screens: to protect
windows from the wind;
eliminated

paradox of the
underground
room: it has the
most direct
contact with
nature

7   6   5   4   3   2   1

section f

Only 90°, Please

FUKUOKA JISHO
CO., LTD.

福岡地所株式会社／〒812 福岡市博多区博多駅東2-5-19
2-5-19 HAKATA-EKIHIGASHI HAKATA-KU FUKUOKA 812 JAPAN
PHONE:092-451-2787 TLX:723-219 FAX:092-473-6914

CHRISTIAN,
ABOUT THE ABRI'S :

1) MAKE SOMETHING VERY A-SYMETRICAL, SO THAT THE EFFECT OF 2 IDENTICAL OBJECT FACING EACH OTHER IS AT IS STRONGEST

2) I STILL THINK AN IMPOSSIBLY DIGNIFIED ABRI — LIKE MIES V.D. ROHE MEETS DECAUX — COULD BE INTERESTING. SO: NO FAKE MARBLE, REAL MARBLE.

GLASS PLATE ROOF
CHROMIUM PLATED COLUMN.
MABLE
RED VELVET CURTAIN "AGAINST THE ELEMENTS"

3) ONLY SIGN OF "VULGARITY". DIFFERENT VIDEO PROGRAMS, PROJECTED ON MARBLE WITH 3-D METAL LETTERS : ON OUTSIDE

ROBOTICS SWEETD ... etc: etc.

4) MAYBE IN EACH SLAB ; TV WITH VIDEO'S
DISCREET HOLES FOR VERY DISCREET SOUND.

5) IF YOU DO ALL OF THIS WELL, THE CONTRAST WITH THE BUS WILL BE O.K.

6) PLEASE : ONLY 90° ANGLES.
GOOD LU
Rem

SEE YOU!
PLEASE FAX FURTHER ACTIVITY

196

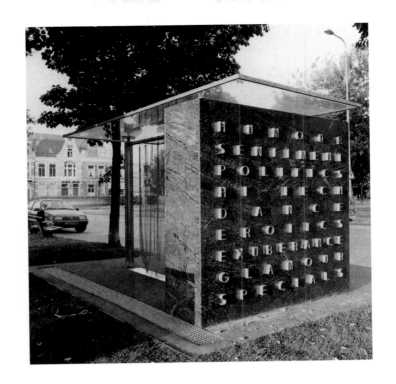

197

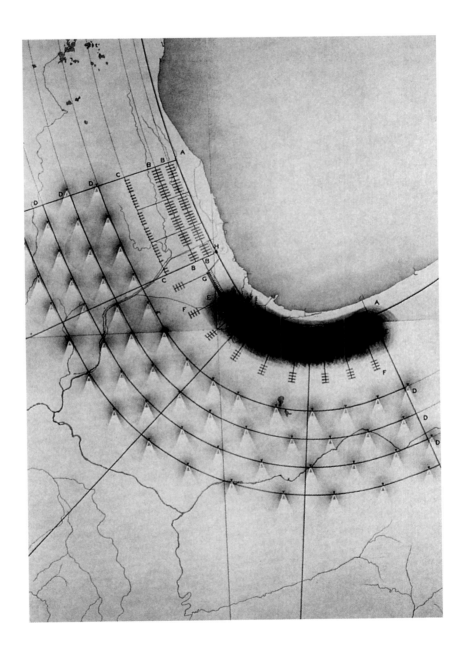

Construction of Cherbourg interchange. La Défense, early 1950s.

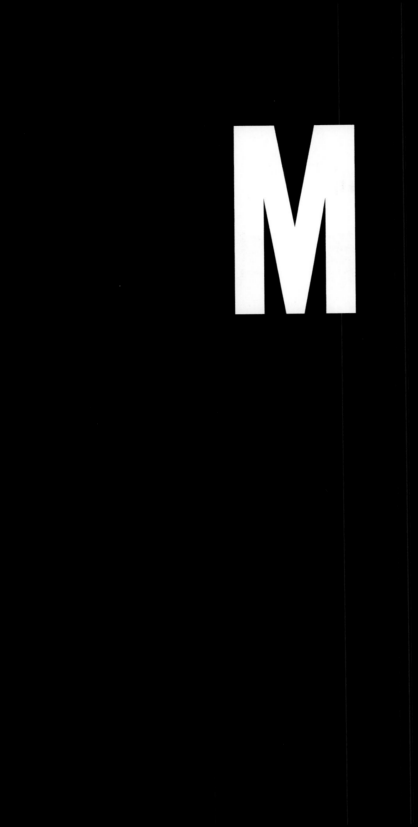

Field Trip

A(A) MEMOIR (First and Last...)

AA,[1] London, early seventies.

"Famous" students present megastructures made of sugar cubes to universal approval of grinning Archigramesque[2] teachers.

Peter Smithson[3] walks in—he wears a flowered shirt—winces, and turns back.

Cedric Price[4] pontificates on architectural modesty from interchangeable cards—early randomized discourse.

Jencks,[5] a dandy, is seen to assemble—according to amateur terrorist handbook—the first elements of the semiotic explosion.

A sulfurous Boyarsky[6] exposes Chicago's infrastructural underbelly.

School in upheaval about mystic takeover plot. Theory: there is only a limited amount of knowledge in the world which should *therefore* not be spread homogeneously or democratically—it would get too thin. Knowledge should be communicated to chosen few only.

Elia Zenghelis[7] perpetually threatens to walk away from it all...

A monstrously idealistic appearance by Louis Kahn.[8] Never again...

Tschumi,[9] frequently in periphery of my vision, already a perfectly formed typology — a teacher...

Superstudio[10] appearing on the horizon...

Incomparable mixture, in other words, of Celtic (or is it simply Anglo-Saxon?) barbarism and intellectual ferment. If there is a plot, in any school, it is the eternal one — simple Darwinian imperative maybe — of each generation trying to incapacitate the next under the guise of educational process. Here it is very noticeable and very expensive. (I was writing movie scripts to cover the costs.)

In this anarchic assembly, one of the rare remaining formal obligations for a diploma is so-called Summer Study: the documentation (measured drawings, photographs, analytical studies) of an existing architectural item, usually in a good climate — Palladian villas; Greek mountain villages of complicated, yet to be deciphered geometries; pyramids.

Intuition, unhappiness with the accumulated innocence of the late sixties, and simple journalistic interest drive me to Berlin (by plane, train, car, foot? In my memory, I'm suddenly there) to document *The Berlin Wall as Architecture.*

That year, the wall celebrates its tenth birthday. My first impression in the hot August weather: the city seems almost completely abandoned, as empty as I always imagined the other side to be. Other shock: it is not East Berlin that is imprisoned, but the West, the "open

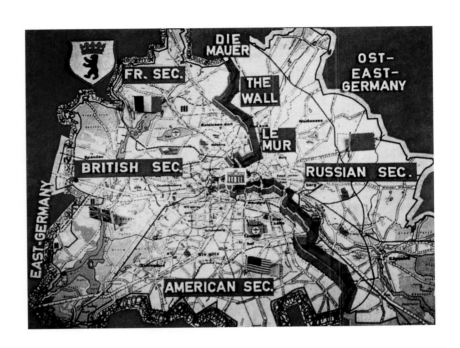

society." In my imagination, stupidly, the wall was a simple, majestic north-south divide; a clean, philosophical demarcation; a neat, modern Wailing Wall. I now realize that it *encircles* the city, paradoxically making it "free." It is 165 kilometers long and confronts all of Berlin's conditions, including lakes, forests, periphery; parts of it are intensely metropolitan, others suburban.

Also, the wall is not stable; and it is not a single entity, as I thought. It is more a *situation*, a permanent, slow-motion evolution, some of it abrupt and clearly planned, some of it improvised.

As if time is an accordion—a Disney[11] archaeology—all of its successive physical manifestations seem simultaneously present in this deserted city (holiday? exile? atomic threat?). In its "primitive" stage the wall is *decision*, applied with absolute architectural minimalism: concrete blocks, bricked-in windows and doors, sometimes with trees—implausibly green—still in front of them.

The scale of this phase is heroic, i.e., urban, up to 40 meters high.

In the next permutation, a second wall—this time of rough concrete slabs hurriedly piled on top of each other (by forced labor?)—is planned just behind the first. Only when this wall is finished is the first wall (the old houses) taken down. Sometimes, adding insult to injury, the street level—a portico, forever-empty shop windows, the striped poles of nonexistent barbers—is left as a kind of decorative pre-wall. This second wall is also unstable. It is continuously "perfected" through construction techniques—more and more prefabrication—

that finally give it ultimate form: the smooth, mechanical, *designed* wall taken down 20 years later. Topped by an endless row of hollow concrete cylinders, it is impossible to grip for those who might want to escape.

Directly behind the second wall: sand, treated like a Japanese garden. Below the sand: invisible mines. On the sand: antitank crosses — concrete intersections of the three-dimensional axial cross — an endless line of Sol LeWitt[12] structures. Beyond this zone: an asphalt path, barely wide enough for a jeep. (Do they avoid each other in the mined zone?) After that: a residual strip where German shepherds pace back and forth, patrolling the "park," baying at non-events. Beyond that, Gehry-like[13] chain-link fencing.

Those are the linear elements. Closely spaced together are natrium street lamps, their orange glow turned toward the West; then, wider apart: the architecture of the standardized doghouses. Still wider apart: guard towers emanating a visible military presence even when apparently unmanned; guns poking through narrow slits. Finally, inevitably at irregular intervals: the sections through the entire system represented by the border crossings.

This was the schematic profile. But in acts of obvious realism, it was not imposed on the city as consistent formula. The wall swelled to assume its maximum identity wherever possible, but along more than half its length, its regularity was compromised in a series of system-

people — mostly young men — had died in more or less disorganized attempts at escape: shot dead beyond the barbed wire, the sand, the mines; caught theatrically at the top of the wall.

A particular cruelty in the wall's permanent transformation from line to zone was that the distance that had to be crossed became longer and longer, exponentially increasing the risk, provoking ever more premature attempts at escape.

On a more premeditated level, there had been more fantastic attempts that relied either on hiding in vehicles that would cross the wall at the notorious checkpoints (eerily, it seemed that the most famous metropolitan crossings, such as Checkpoint Charlie, exercised the greatest attraction for those with the least interest in being discovered) or on circumnavigating the wall itself — either in the air or, in a more traditional vocabulary of prison escape, underground — using sewers, digging tunnels, starting from living rooms that seemed unchanged since the Third Reich.

(What architect — however Bataille-soaked[17] — could boast of its transgressive performance, of the sheer radicalism of its existence?) The wall was the transgression to end all transgressions.

Reverse Epiphanies

This was a field trip that spoiled the charms of the field; tourism that left a kind of scorched earth. It was as if I had come eye to eye with architecture's true nature.

1.

In the early seventies, it was impossible not to sense an enormous reservoir of resentment *against* architecture, with new evidence of its inadequacies — of its cruel and exhausted performance — accumulating daily; *looking at the wall as architecture, it was inevitable to transpose the despair, hatred, frustration it inspired to the field of architecture.* And it was inevitable to realize that all these expressions — the fanaticism of the tunnel diggers; the resignation of those left behind; the desperate attempts to celebrate conventional occasions, such as marriage, across the divide — were finally all too applicable to architecture itself. *The Berlin Wall was a very graphic demonstration of the power of architecture and some of its unpleasant consequences.*

Were not division, enclosure (i.e., imprisonment), and exclusion — which defined the wall's performance and explained its efficiency — the essential stratagems of *any* architecture?

In comparison, the sixties dream of architecture's liberating potential — in which I had been marinating for years as a student — seemed feeble rhetorical play. It evaporated on the spot.

2.

The wall suggested that architecture's beauty was directly proportional to its horror.

There was a dreadful "serial" beauty to the wall's systematic transformation from an invisible line on a map to a solid line of soldiers (that made it manifest), to barbed wire dropped on the line, to the first cementing of blocks: a fatality of "development" that perversely echoed, for instance, the sophistication of Schinkel's[18] thematic variations on architectural themes at Schloss Glienicke.

3.

On the same level of negative revelation, the wall also, in my eyes, made a total mockery of any of the emerging attempts to link form *to* meaning *in a regressive chain-and-ball relationship.*

It was clearly about communication, semantic maybe, but its meaning changed almost daily, sometimes by the hour. It was affected more by events and decisions thousands of miles away than by its physical manifestation. Its significance as a "wall" — as an object — was marginal; its impact was utterly independent of its appearance. Apparently, the lightest of objects could be randomly coupled with the heaviest of meanings through brute force, willpower.

There was no point in constructing the grammar of this new type of event. Yes, one could look at the first sections of the definitive wall, read into them a style or a language — a kind of Olivetti[19] aesthetics — connect them to modernism, declare them boring, imagine frantic layers of mimetic devices as compensation. *But on the eve of postmodernism, here was unforgettable (not to say final) proof of the "less is more" doctrine ...*

I would never again believe in form as the primary vessel of meaning.

4.

In my eyes, the wall also forever severed the connection between importance *and* mass.

As an object the wall was unimpressive, evolving toward a near dematerialization; but that left its power undiminished.

In fact, in narrowly architectural terms, the wall was not an object but an erasure, a freshly created absence. For me, it was a first demonstration of the capacity of the void—of nothingness—to "function" with more efficiency, subtlety, and flexibility than any object you could imagine in its place. It was a warning that—in architecture—absence would always win in a contest with presence.

5.

The wall had generated a catalog of possible mutations; sometimes the new object/zone slashed mercilessly through the most (formerly) impressive parts of the city; sometimes it yielded to apparently superior pressures that were not always identifiable.

Its range from the absolute, the regular, to the deformed was an unexpected manifestation of a formless "modern"—alternately strong and weak, imposition and residue, Cartesian and chaotic, all its seemingly different states merely phases of the same essential project.

I had not known what to expect on this journey. I had hoped to "do" the wall in a day and then to explore the rest of the cit(ies). It was so

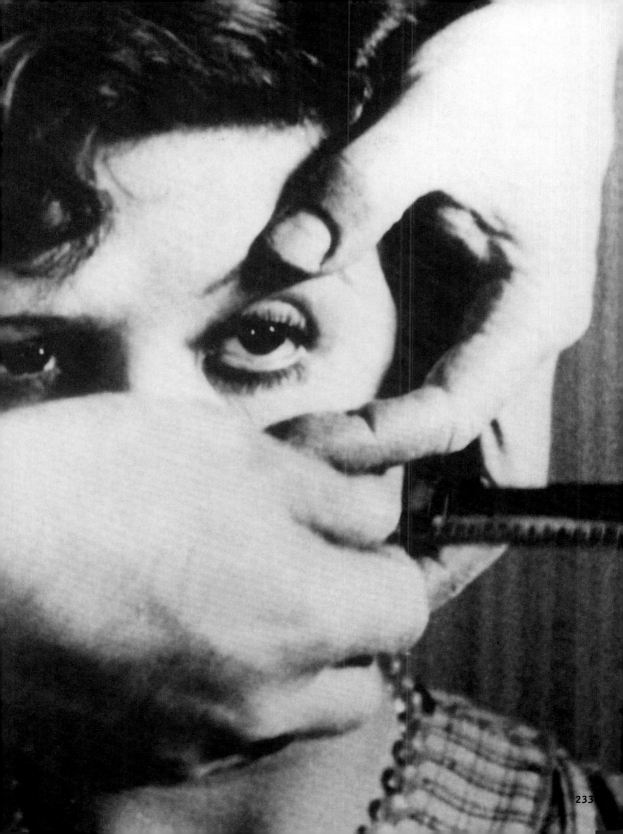

waved your arms at a record-player
do please realise that the machine is
conducting you.

CONFIDENCE[1]

At Weimar I have radically overturned everything ... I have talked to
the pupils every evening and I have
infused the poison of the new spirit
everywhere ... I have mountains of
strength and I know that our notions
will be victorious over everyone
and everything.

CONFIDENCE[2]

The net effect is a solid precise
response to the steering wheel that
gives confidence in the corners and
even eases the chore of steering
straight down the expressway.

CONFINED

They all preached in their black
gowns, as their fathers had done
before them; they wore ordinary
black cloth waistcoats; they had no
candles on their altars, either lighted
or unlighted; they made no private
genuflexions, and were contented
to confine themselves to such ceremonial observances as had been in
vogue for the last hundred years.

CONFUSED

I'm confused as to what's ugly and
what's pretty.

CONNECTED

Any point in a rhizome might be
connected to any other, and must be.

CONNECTIONS

Thanks to the Chunnel and TGV,
Lille will become the center of
gravity of a thirty-million-inhabitant
London-Brussels-Paris triangle,
which will ... create around the railway station the conditions for a
culture of congestion which up to
that moment belonged only to
Manhattan or Tokyo. The key word
is that of linking or connection:
"The programs will become abstract
inasmuch as by now they are no
longer tied to a specific place or city,
but fluctuate and gravitate opportunistically around the point offering
the highest number of connections."
This is indeed a reformulation of
the theory on dislocation of modern
capital, which actually moves toward
the most favorable places.

CONSTRUCTION[1]

Pieces are taken from Chrysler's
Plymouth and Imperial ads ... The
sex symbol is, as so often happens in
the ads, engaged in a display of

Revision

Study for the Renovation of a Panopticon Prison
Arnhem, Netherlands
1979 – 81

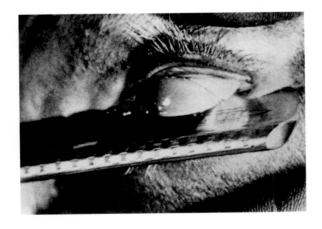

The aim of the Panopticon Principle was efficient production — of goods in the factory, health in the hospital, or reformed human beings in the prison.

Jeremy Bentham, diagram of a panopticon prison, 1791.

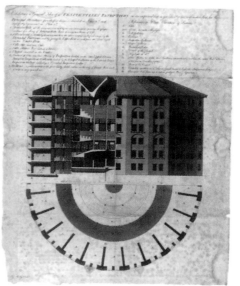

In 1979, as an informal consolation prize for not winning the Dutch Parliament competition, **OMA** was asked to study the possible renovation of the **Koepel** (dome) Prison in Arnhem to investigate whether the 100-year-old building could be made to function "for at least another 50 years" and to "embody present-day insights into the treatment of prisoners."
This text was written for the Ministry of Justice, where our positive answer created controversy; its defense of a clearly outdated architectural object seemed to ridicule 100 years of "progress."

The Arnhem Koepel Prison was built according to the so-called Panopticon Principle, invented in 1787 by the philosopher Jeremy Bentham. It is a universal principle of organization for situations in which a small group of supervisors monitors a much larger group of supervised: factory workers, hospital patients, lunatics, prisoners. The Arnhem Koepel represents the principle in its purest form: a single, all-seeing "eye" is placed dead center in a circle of the observed. The aim of the Panopticon Principle was efficient production — of goods in the factory, health in the hospital, or reformed human beings in the prison.

In 1882, when the Koepel was built, many considered its architecture too luxurious and feared that the compassion expressed in its accommodations might stimulate rather than deter crime. As one parliamentarian, a certain Wintgens, warned, "If they are constructing that prison in this grandiose manner, some — maybe even many — people may be tempted, after their daily work, to try to secure a place in that glorious resort at the expense of the State."

One hundred years later, the Panopticon Principle, with its mechanistic ideal — the naked power exercised by the authority in the center over the subjects in the ring — has become intolerable. In fact, without a single change in the architecture of the Koepel, its principle has been abolished. Guards have abandoned the center and now circulate randomly on the ground and the rings, among prisoners who are often released from their cells. In this transparent space, no action or inaction remains unnoticed. The central control post — the former "eye" of the panopticon — has become a canteen for the guards; they now sip coffee there, observed by the prisoners on the rings. Originally envisioned as empty, the entire interior is now often as busy as the Milan Galleria.

When the Koepel was built, solitary confinement was considered humane: it preserved the prisoner's anonymity. Those who had deviated from the right path could meditate, repent, better themselves, and — once reformed — start a new life. One hundred years later, solitary confinement has also become unacceptable; it is thought to make the prisoner unfit to return to society. This principle too has been abandoned. Communal facilities — for work, sports, visits — have been added to the institution. But while the Koepel itself survived the suspension of the

The central control post — the former "eye" of the panopticon — has become a canteen for the guards; they now sip coffee there, observed by the prisoners.

As the only visible manifestation of newness inside the Koepel, this intersection offers its residents a way out.

243

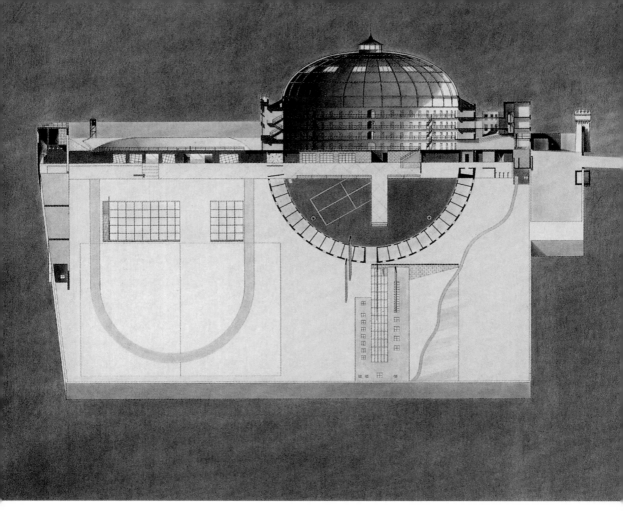

A "modern" prison architecture would consist of a *prospective archaeology*, constantly projecting new layers of "civilization" on old systems of supervision.

Two sunken streets extend across the prison grounds, constituting — in combination with the three cell rings and the Koepel floor — a limited public realm.

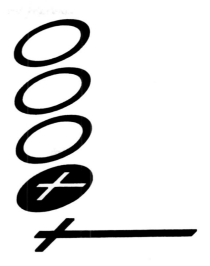

new street level the walls are invisible. The socle establishes a new datum: the former ground floor becomes the roof of the socle. Anticipating a drastic reduction of working hours and the need for other activities to fill the rest of the day, this organization allows for simultaneous use of the grounds in two shifts: one on the socle for sports, games, gardening; one in the socle. Halfway through the day the shifts trade places. Wherever possible and desirable, facades and activities are exposed to eliminate any sense of a basement.

The activities on the streets are grouped to give specific programmatic definition. "Central" facilities are projected at the intersection itself — shops, hairdresser, library, doctors, and meeting rooms for creative activities and discussion groups.

South Street leads to the visitors center; its facade is exposed by a sloping garden. From a waiting room, prisoners see visitors arriving from the main gate. The windows are tilted to avoid the suggestion of bars. North Street leads to a patio with kitchens, medical departments, and a separate pavilion for difficult prisoners. West Street leads to the most urban condition: four workshops, a sports center, and a hall for film, drama, religion.

Each workshop has a roof garden and a patio with a "park." The final section of the street is sunken further; filled with water, it becomes a swimming pool. A running track surrounds the socle.

The facades of the public domain are "luxurious" — glazed brick and marble; behind the facade, materials are spartan.

Koepel

In past decades, most emergency changes inside the Koepel have been made by using certain cells for other purposes, sometimes removing load-bearing walls to connect them. In this study, all of the facilities required for the Koepel to function as "home" — living quarters, dining rooms, bathrooms — are concentrated in two external satellites attached to the rings. The Koepel's interior is left intact while the extensions communicate the changes to the outside world.

With the satellites, each ring of 50 cells can be divided into two groups of ± 24 prisoners, without expressing these groupings in concrete. These 24 prisoners can be subdivided into smaller temporary entities by a further subdivision of the satellite. Communication between the rings, which are connected by

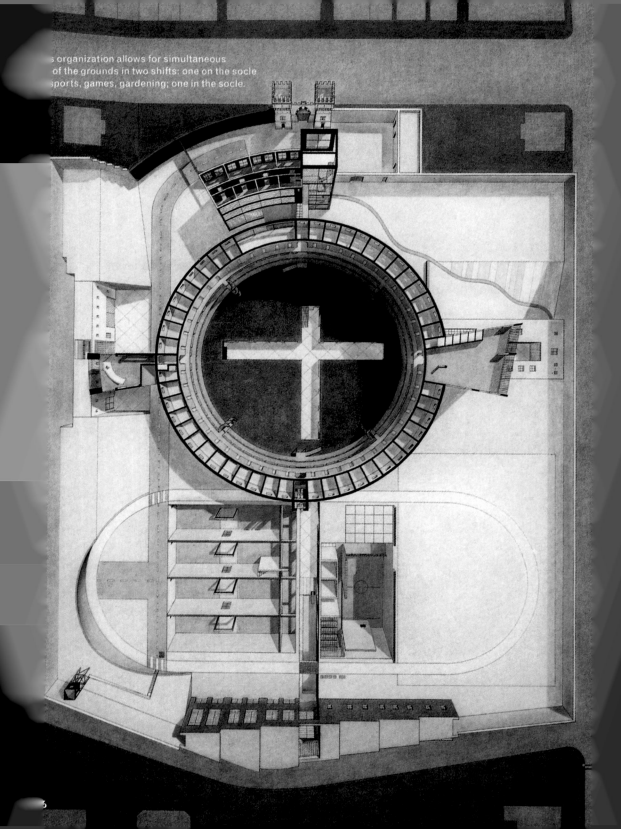

s organization allows for simultaneous
of the grounds in two shifts: one on the socle
sports, games, gardening; one in the socle.

small spiral staircases and two larger stairs, permits the formation of groups from different rings; prisoners can be part of several groupings.

With integration on the wane and the frank preference of some populations to stay together, the satellites offer a flexible regime: momentary constellations of prisoners subject to endless permutations. This possibility is especially important in a remand center where inmates are presumed innocent and where there is no guarantee of a stable statistical breakdown on which a group architecture could be based.

A third Koepel satellite is planned at the site of the present entrance building, opposite the main gate. It is generated through an outward projection of the panopticon center, creating a sector of an implied second ring, in this case offices. Four previously connected cells become rest areas for the guards. The outer wall of the Koepel is removed here so that the ring is invaded by a wedge of supervision.

For us, the prison embodied, in a way, 100 years of wisdom, or at least of experience. The new adds a layer of modernity without claiming to be definitive. It is neither more nor less safe than the old. The old maintains its iconographic deterrence, liberating the new from having either to ignore or to express the idea of incarceration. After the intervention, the Koepel represents the dismantled past, its former center crossed out, resting on a podium of modernity that is only concerned with improving the prisoners' conditions.   **1981**

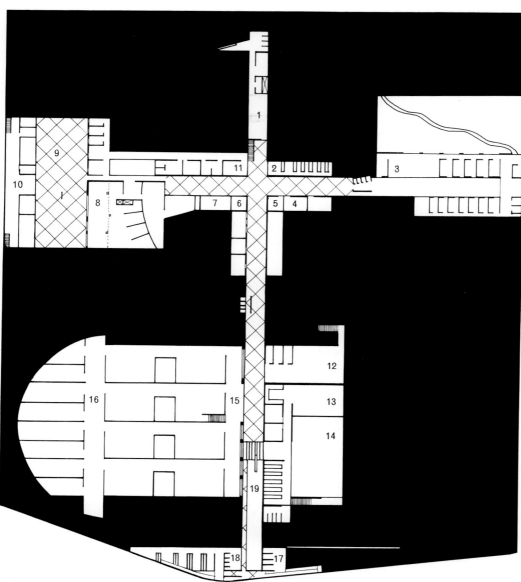

podium

1. service/reception area
2. library
3. visiting room and cells
4. free-expression room
5. barber
6. meeting room
7. shop
8. kitchen
9. patio
10. quarters for difficult prisoners
11. infirmary, dentist, doctor
12. multi-purpose room
13. judo
14. gymnasium
15. studios
16. storage
17. instruction room
18. guards' cloak room
19. pool

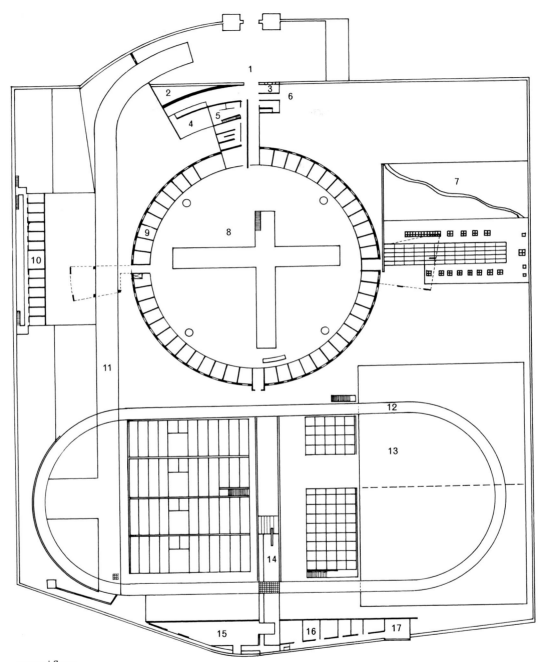

ground floor

1. entrance
2. lobby
3. porters' room
4. meeting room
5. reception
6. exit to visitors area
7. visitors garden

8. dome floor
9. cells
10. pavilion for difficult prisoners
11. storage
12. track
13. sports field
14. pool

15. guards' canteen
16. shops
17. instruction department

0   50m

The old maintains its iconographic deterrence,
liberating the new from having either to ignore
or to express the idea of incarceration.

The most complex aspect of the project was the extent to which programmatic, metaphoric, and formal intentions coincided with political issues. Within strict programmatic demands, the metaphor for a new beginning, the idea of culture as a system of continuously revised paradigms, and the crossing out of the center bond the utilitarian to the conceptual. What was surprising, finally, was the almost eager way in which an architectural solution was finally — after two years of heated discussion — embraced by the authorities as resolving the dilemma of other disciplines. The discredited claim for architecture's ability to intervene directly in the formation of culture and to resolve, through its crystallization, hopelessly contradictory demands — freedom and discipline — was seemingly vindicated.

But immediately after its acceptance, money ran out and the project was put on hold, indefinitely.

essence of the geodesic dome more conceptually than that distracting external figure ever could.

CONTRADICT

That's the idea, let's contradict each other.

CONTRIBUTIONS

Any account of knowledge has to take account both of the contribution of the world and the contribution of man. Every human endeavour, every activity, every art, every science is a product of a unique interaction between man and the world. Where man is most passive, he merely reflects and reports the world; this is pure discovery, if it ever exists. Where man is most active, the world's contribution lies merely in the provision of the raw materials; this is pure invention, if it ever exists.

CONTROL

What people make of my building is outside my control.

CONVERSATION

In Japan it is considered both uncomfortable to look at length into someone's eyes during a conversation and cold not to do so at all, so a precise balance has to be maintained. Most Japanese are unaware of this process and are shocked to find that in some countries conversation is carried on while looking into the eyes of the other person.

COPIED

You know something? If I'm copied well, I really don't mind. Unfortunately, most of the time I seem to be copied badly.

COPYRIGHT

Levine, that is, de-monstrates the grammatological writing appropriate to the age of mechanical reproduction in which "copyright" now means the right to copy anything, a mimicry or repetition which is originary, producing differences (just as in allegory anything may mean anything else).

CORE

In the city as centrifuge, this was the peaceful core, the eye of the hurricane. A great tranquility reigned in the square.

CORPORATE

The body is not one self but a fiction of a self built from a mass of interacting selves. A body's capacities are literally the result of what it

Programmatic, metaphoric, and formal intentions coincided with political issues.

Shipwrecked

**Housing Kochstrasse/Friedrichstrasse
Berlin, Germany
Competition, 1980**

The competition organized by **IBA (Internationale Bauausstellung)** asked each of 16 architects to develop an overall urban concept for the four blocks around the intersection of **Kochstrasse and Friedrichstrasse,** and then for a more specific architectural proposal for a single block, in this case for **Block 4,** which runs parallel to the wall and faces **Checkpoint Charlie.**

Modern architecture has been persistently criticized for its insistence on starting from scratch — its foundation on the tabula rasa. The area of Friedrichstrasse offers the advantage of already having been razed.
We interpreted the still profoundly damaged character of the site as a challenge to investigate the extent to which certain modern typologies and textures developed for Berlin — some first proposed for Friedrichstadt — can coexist with a classical street pattern and with the survivors of architectural ideologies of the recent and distant past, which are all now equally shipwrecked.
We looked at interventions in Friedrichstadt by Erich Mendelsohn, Mies van der Rohe, and Ludwig Hilberseimer, and at the courtyard schemes Mies developed for other locations in Berlin, to analyze the respective strengths and qualities of these textures and the new environments they might still generate.

1. Berlin Wall
2. Checkpoint Charlie
3. OMA's proposal for the four-block area
4. Erich Mendelsohn, Headquarters of the German
   Metallurgic Federation, 1929–30
5. Ludwig Hilberseimer, "City of Slabs," 1928
6. Mies van der Rohe, project for Friedrichstrasse, 192¹

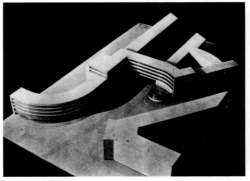

4

5

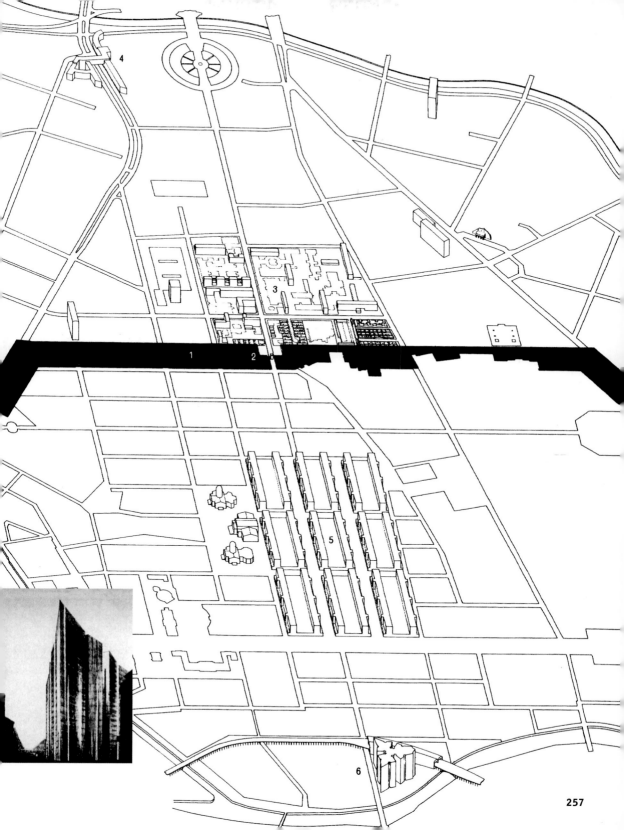

257

incorporates; the self is not only corporal but corporate.

COSTUME

I had to stretch the band to make the velvet ears fit. I pulled on the tights, which were elastic enough, and then the corset, which was snug across the chest. The green stilettos pinched less than I would have expected. I had never realized Barbara Ann had such big feet.

COUPLING

Another kind of coupling is found when two elements are more rigidly constrained into a constant relation-ship. This is often seen in machinery construction, when coupled parts are encompassed with a clamp or pierced with a bolt.

COURSE

Something is taking its course.

COVER-UP

Now as soon as the servant demon arrived in that country, he took on human form, and appeared to be as normal as any man. When the man saw that this change had taken place, he decided not to inform his family of the demon's true identity for fear that it might frighten them.

COWS

Dutch cows produce more milk than any other cows.

CRANES[1]

A sort of dredging machine. From the hidden cabin (small, closed, glassed-in) of a crane, I manipulate some levers and (I saw this done at Saintes-Maries-de-la-Mer at Easter), from afar, I plunge a mouth of steel into the water. And I scrape the bottom, grab some stones and algae that I bring back up to the surface in order to set them down on the ground while the water quickly falls out of the mouth.
And I begin again to scrape, to scratch, to dredge the bottom of the sea.
I barely hear the noise of the water from the little room...
Some alga, some stones...
Detached.

CRANES[2]

After Jerene xeroxed the article, she left the library. There was a brisk wind outdoors; she turned her collar up. Some construction was going on nearby — cranes working, lifting beams to the hardhatted men who swarmed the precarious frame of a

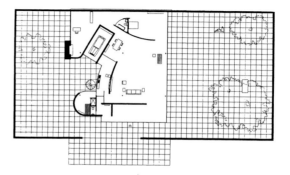

Mies van der Rohe, Hofhaus with garage, 1934.

The context of the four-block competition site is determined by the 18th-century grid, the remaining prewar structures generated by the grid, and the postwar reconstruction, which is usually at odds with the grid. The old buildings define and are defined by the street; the new buildings diffuse and dissolve it.

Since the recent rediscovery of the street as the core element of all urbanism, the simplest solution to this complex and ambiguous condition is to undo the "mistakes" of the fifties and sixties and to build once again along the plot lines of the street as a sign of a regained historical consciousness. This approach restores the grid, respectfully connects new buildings with the old, and attempts to hide most of the postwar buildings in an effort to render harmless the mistaken ideologies of the past four decades.

But it is important to resist that temptation, to avoid becoming part of a mindless pendulum movement where the acceptance of one particular architectural doctrine leads — as surely as day follows night — to the adoption of its exact opposite a few years later: a negative sequence in which every generation ridicules the previous one only to be annulled by the next. The effect of such a yes-no-yes sequence is antihistorical in that it condemns the discourse of architecture to become an incomprehensible chain of disconnected sentences.

A project for Kochstrasse/Friedrichstrasse should impose a conceptual framework, beyond the literalness of the street plan, that relates the existing buildings — whether or not they conform to the grid — and creates anchors for new insertions. Without this framework — a retroactive concept that makes sense out of the existing randomness — both the old architecture with its pathos of decay and the postwar architecture with its aura of forgotten optimism will remain in limbo.

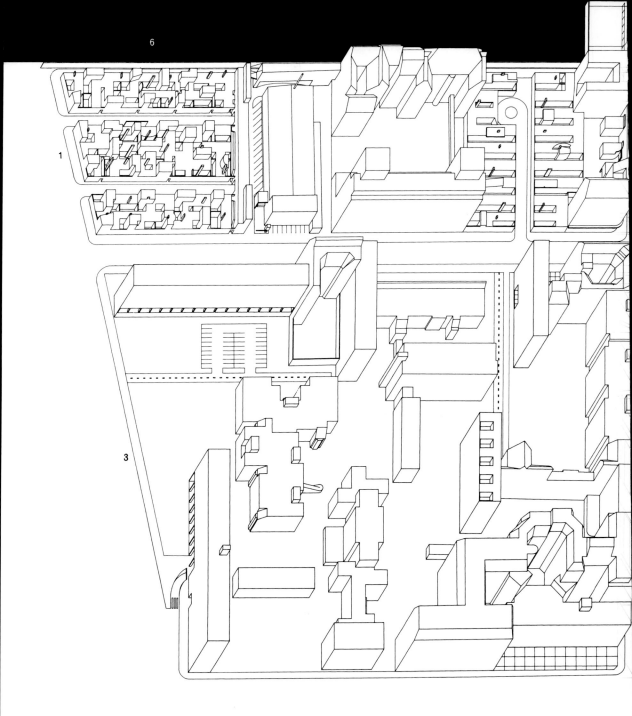

6

1

3

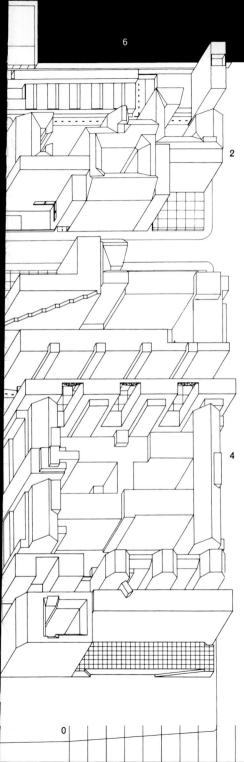

On Block 4, the critical issue was to design housing in the shadow of the Berlin Wall and the border control facilities of Checkpoint Charlie. In this peculiar context, the courtyard house — as reinvented in the 1920s by Mies, Hilberseimer, and Hugo Häring — is convincing because:

1. it creates a self-contained intimacy and serenity that is independent of circumstances; it creates a context while dissociating itself from context;

2. it responds to Berlin's decreasing population: it can maintain architectural intensity and urbanity with minimal material display and few inhabitants;

3. it invests imagination in the endless rearrangement of a small quantity of components.

The same strategy is applied to the smaller Block 5 and along the wall. On Block 6, almost a square, the area of the block is suggested — but never exactly defined — by additional slabs that absorb existing freestanding objects and street-wall fragments into a "pier-and-ocean" composition.

Hilberseimer's parallel slabs are projected on the narrow Block 7 and simply "deducted" when they collide with existing structures.

The four-block area along the wall.

1. Block 4
2. Block 5
3. Block 6
4. Block 7
5. Checkpoint Charlie
6. Berlin Wall

From west to east, Block 4 is divided into independent operations:
1. a housing section of 56 units accessible through two new streets, 1st Street and 2nd Street; all plots are identical — the larger types have a first-floor extrusion;
2. a row of workshops arranged between Kochstrasse and Zimmerstrasse to terminate the first housing section;

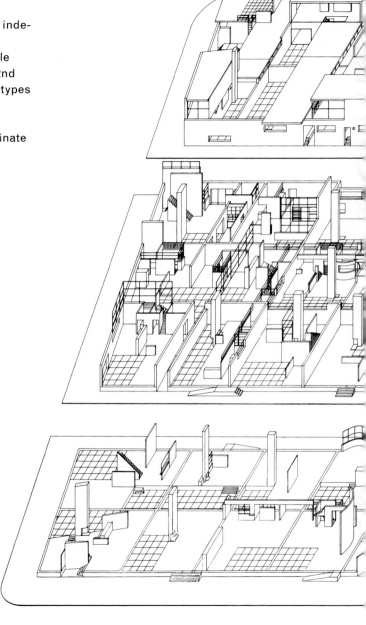

ALLIES

POLICE

CUSTOMS

3rd STREET

HERUNGEN

0   50m

second floor

ADMINISTRATION & DISPATCH REWAMAT

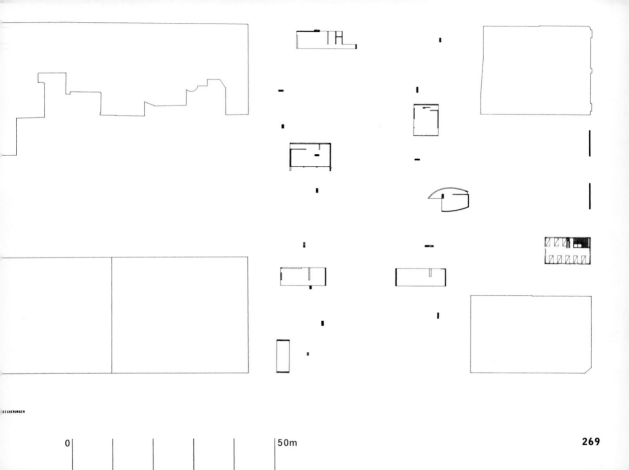

SICHERUNGEN

0   50m   **269**

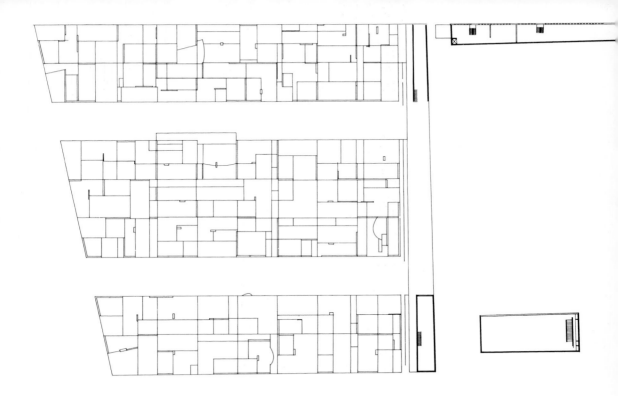

roof

272

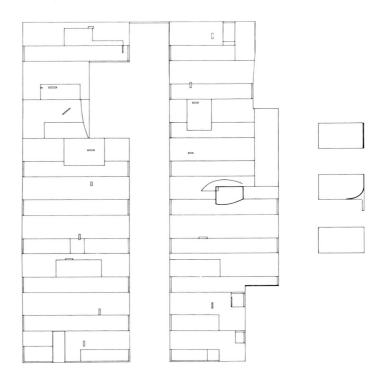

0   50m

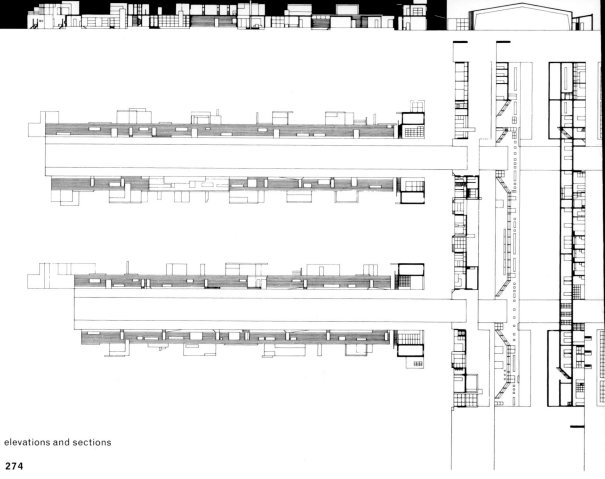

elevations and sections

Extension of the Dutch Parliament
The Hague, Netherlands
Competition, 1978

impulse, just the opposite of foresight, doing the most unexpected and wildest sort of thing. And at that moment precisely it could be said that there was a sort of saturation of reality, don't you think? Reality comes on fast, it shows itself with all its strength, and precisely at that moment the only way of facing it is to renounce dialectics, it's the moment for shooting somebody, jumping overboard, swallowing a bottle of gardenal like Guy, unleashing the dog, a free hand to do anything. Reason is only good to mummify reality in moments of calm or analyze its future storms, never to resolve a crisis of the moment. But these crises are like metaphysical outbursts, like a state that perhaps, if we hadn't chosen the path of reason, would be the natural and current state of *Pithecanthropus erectus*.

CROWDS
See **NUMBER**.

CUSHICLE
The Cushicle is an invention that enables a man to carry a complete environment on his back. It inflates out when needed. It is a complete nomadic unit — and it is fully serviced. It enables an explorer, wanderer or other itinerant to have a high standard of comfort with a minimum effort.

CYBER-SOMETHING
I don't know if the future is necessarily going to be cyberpunk or cyberprep, but it's going to be cyber-something. And as soon as they announce that skull implants are available, I'm gonna line up for mine... I'd like to add a few languages, be able to go without sleep, and obviously, I'd like to get a direct neural interface with my computer. That would be great.

CYBERSPACE[1]
A consensual hallucination experienced daily by billions of legitimate operators, in every nation...
A graphic representation of data abstracted from the banks of every computer in the human system. Unthinkable complexity. Lines of light ranged in the nonspace of the mind, clusters and constellations of data. Like city lights, receding...

CYBERSPACE[2]
Cyberspace, for those who haven't

Site plan indicating the zone within which the renovations could occur.

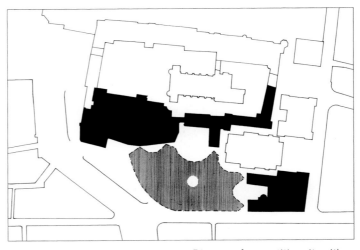

Diagram of competition site with existing Parliament buildings shown in black and proposed new building area hatched.

The Dutch government and the Dutch Parliament share a historic complex in the heart of The Hague—the Binnenhof, a rectangular fortress along a rectangular lake. Inside the fortress stands the Gothic Ridderzaal, or Hall of Knights; in front of the Ridderzaal, enclosed by the walls of the fortress, is the Binnenhof, or Inner Court. Connected to it by a narrow porch is the Buitenhof, or Outer Court.

Since the 13th century, the Binnenhof complex has undergone a continuous process of both architectural and programmatic transformation in which its defensive purposes have been replaced by governmental and symbolic functions. Over the centuries it has served as royal palace, archive, Republican headquarters, and once again, royal palace until it was completely taken over in the 19th century by various ministries and the apparatus of Parliament. These changes have provoked incremental adjustments to the fortress wall, generating an agglomeration of different historical styles.

Superimposed on these authentic changes is a layer of restorations intended to preserve the complex's historicity, but which only proves that each act of preservation embodies a revision, a distortion, even a redesign. The largest single block of fabricated history is the Ridderzaal itself, whose original Gothic architecture has been transformed into a 19th-century fantasy *à la* Viollet-le-Duc. There is very little *medieval* medieval architecture left; the Binnenhof complex has become a catalog of medievalnesses.

The situation is further blurred and complicated by an early-20th-century traffic cut conceived by Berlage that destroyed the spatial definition of the Buitenhof, cut away the original fabric around the fortress, and exposed facades never intended to be revealed. In a protorationalist gesture, the edges of this scar were lined with ersatz 17th-century structures that are now the most visible parts of the entire complex. In its layering of real and imagined histories, the complex unavoidably raises the issue of authenticity.

In addition to this overall complexity, government and Parliament are intertwined in this composition in a way that belies their political opposition. The governmental agencies occupy the water side; the Parliament, a guitar-shaped conglomeration in the southeast corner; the assembly, the former royal ballroom at the center.

In 1978 a competition was held. A roughly triangular area east of the Binnenhof was designated hooked in yet (it is neither in a here nor a there but is a continual articulation relentlessly boring through us), is, according to the slogan, "Where you are when you are talking on the telephone." In more precise terms, it is where your attention is within a promiscuous, multidimensional electromagnetic matrix, even when your body (for which there seems to be, yet again, no limit of protestant-capitalist contempt) is hopelessly fixed in viscous Euclidean "real" space.

D

DANCE[1]

Civilized men dance for pleasure, entertainment and social communication with the opposite sex. There is no limit to the use of dance in one's life.

DANCE[2]

The work of the Office for Metropolitan Architecture — named as if to confront the modern crisis fearlessly and head-on — has always resisted this great divide between program and form, between social text and artistic technique. From the first narrative paintings of Madelon Vriesendorp and their accompanying texts, the "conceptual project" of OMA at least has tried to weld text and image in a reciprocal dance, a dance that in its various steps mirrored the lusts, atavisms, hopes, and horrors of the modern metropolis par excellence — New York.

DANCING

Upstairs Beloved was dancing. A little two-step, two-step, make-a-new-step, slide, slide and strut on down. Denver sat on the bed smiling and providing the music.

DANGER

In 1992 there is a danger that the Dutch language will be lost in the melting pot of Europe.

DATE[1]

"He made me laugh! And I haven't laughed for such a long time." CAROL, a meat trader, widowed very young, found TED "made her feel so comfortable and happy," and "she made me feel alive!" Carol just knew it would work out for them. "We have such good fun together."

Colin Rowe, "Roma Interotta": forced to telescope vicissitudes of centuries into a single moment of conception?

as the site for a much-needed extension for parliamentary accommodation. The competition was also an occasion to restore symbolism — to separate conceptually the government from the representatives who are supposed to supervise its actions.

Contextualism, Rationalism, Structuralism

Both contextualist and rationalist doctrines claim the center of the historical city as their territory; in Holland this ground is further contested by a third, more local doctrine, that of so-called Dutch structuralism.

Contextualism

The central moment of the contextualist epiphany is the collision of a projected ideal with an empirical necessity. Insofar as the latter transforms the former and dampens its utopian tendencies, the contextualist derives not only aesthetic pleasure, but also — more importantly — a degree of antimetaphysical comfort.

A contradiction lies at the heart of contextualist design: in the contextualists' favorite examples, these collisions and aborted utopias are literally generated by the course of events over long periods of time; but the modern contextualist is forced to telescope vicissitudes of centuries into a single moment of conception. In an act of more-or-less inspired projection, the contextualist generates a scenario that simulates the history of the next 400 to 500 years. Through this extrapolation in the name of history, the contextualist short-circuits historical continuity.

A second problematic area is that of empirical necessity. In simulating the aesthetics of history single-handedly, the contextualist must impersonate — with equal conviction — both sides in the reenactment of the eternal battle between the ideal and the real, the Platonic and the circumstantial. The contextualist's search for empirical necessity — the circumstantial forces that will inflect the pure model — can become frantic. The existing is squeezed for its maximum potential to inspire imperfection and cause impurity; it is forced to carry assumptions and speculations that it can hardly support and is thus subjected to an *idealization in reverse*. The circumstantial becomes another utopia, with a subsequent loss of precisely that aura of concreteness and

Ted had always told himself he would never marry again (he'd always thought he would never join something like Dateline!) but he proposed to Carol in a matter of weeks.

DATE²

It is common practice in the frozen food industry to mark frozen foods with an expiry date. It is always quite difficult for manufacturers to decide what expiry date to put on a package.

DAY

For the visitor interested primarily in buildings, a whole day might be necessary to get an idea of Antoni Gaudí's work, although it would also be possible to visit the Barri Gòtic in the morning, and then the Pedrera, the Casa Batlló, the Sagrada Família and, at a pinch, the Parc Güell too, in the afternoon.

DECIDE¹

After the Thruway exit, the road took them through North Dudson, a very small town full of cars driven with extreme slowness by people who couldn't decide whether or not they wanted to make a left turn.

DECIDE²

Don't think! Decide now!

DECORATIVE

My skepticism about the deconstructivists is based on their presumption of this naive, banal analogy between a supposedly irregular geometry and a fragmented world or a world where values are no longer anchored in a fixed way. It is hopelessly visual, compositional and therefore, in a very traditional sense, architectural. And for me, that is ultimately decorative.

DEGLOVED

The chin is degloved subperiosteally through an inferior buccal sulcus incision. A good cuff of mucosa is left for later suturing. As much muscle attachment as possible is left on its posterior surface.

DEGRADATION

It is good to wander along lines of sea-coast, when formed of moderately hard rocks, and mark the process of degradation. The tides in most cases reach the cliffs only for a short time twice a day, and the waves eat into them only when they are charged with sand or pebbles... At last the base of the cliff is

Rob Krier, "Morphological Series of Urban Spaces": chaste economy of the imagination?

specificity that the contextualist doctrine set out to maintain. Finally, since the contextualist, a Popperian, does not *believe* in utopia, the contextualist's aesthetic lacks exactly that dourness that would make its violation a drama. In both its preemptive aspect and its perverse *idealization of the empirical*, contextualism actually precludes a series of more complex and precise choices that could bring the actual context into focus.

Rationalism

The appeal of rationalism lies in the chaste economy of the imagination that it postulates: it asserts that it is redundant and even dangerous to invent or replace forms of urban organization—the street, the plaza, etc.—that have been perfected over centuries. Within this restoration of sanity, it is disconcerting that everything the 20th century contributed to the historic sequence—new types that are demonstrably responses to authentic programmatic demands and inspirations—is excluded. Through this arbitrary closure, the infinitely reassuring dream of a world inhabited by a known series of typologies and morphologies, endowed with eternal life and capable of absorbing *all* programs, turns ominous when, for instance, Gunnar Asplund's Stockholm Public Library is shamelessly recycled in Luxembourg as the new European Parliament.

With such theories, culture is at the mercy of an arsenal of procrustean types who censure certain activities and expressions with the simple excuse that there is no room for them and at the same time proclaim the continuing validity of others simply because they do not disrupt the continuity of the urban texture. (In the Parliament competition, for instance, the program included a 5,000 m² conference center. For such elements, there is no typology.) With their obsessive legitimizations from history, both contextualism and rationalism are preemptive tactics that abort history before it can happen.

Structuralism

Over the last 20 years, large sectors of the architectural world in Holland have been in the grip of the local doctrine of Dutch structuralism. Claiming as its ancestors Aldo van Eyck's orphanage in Amsterdam and the allied research of the Dutch Forum group, the doctrine preaches, in the undermined, huge fragments fall down, and these remaining fixed, have to be worn away, atom by atom, until reduced in size they can be rolled about by the waves, and then are more quickly ground into pebbles, sand, or mud.

DELAY
In rush hours a double-parked car blocking one lane of a main road for 12 minutes can delay 2,800 other vehicles.

DEMENTED
The only kind of demented thing about him was that his ears hadn't grown. They were like those little pasta shells. It was as if his body had grown but his ears hadn't caught up yet.

DEMOLITION
This charge is intended for the demolition of reinforced concrete or steel structures and may also be used against underwater structures. It consists of a watertight plastic casing, a mechanical delayed arming device, an electrical timer and the HE explosive charge...The charge may be fired remotely by a standard electric exploder or by means of a built-in timer.

DENSITY[1]
The impression of declining densities would be incomplete, even misleading, if the special impact of multifamily dwellings upon the figures were not recognised. Density per acre of ground assumes a quite different significance when we begin to pile dwelling units on top of one another and give up the amenity of the individual yard.

DENSITY[2]
The density of human beings is matched by the density of cars: There are more cars per square mile in the Netherlands than in any other country.

DERIVE
A mode of experimental behavior linked to the conditions of urban society: a technique of transient passage through varied ambiances. Also used to designate a specific period of continuous dériving.

DESERT[1]
The desert fits the screen. It is the screen. Low horizontals, high verticals. People talk about classic westerns. The classic thing has always been the space, the emptiness. The

Aldo van Eyck, orphanage, Amsterdam, 1960: smaller components that re-establish the human scale?

name of humanism, that all larger institutions can and should be divided into smaller components that reestablish the human scale—as if each institution, whatever its nature, would become more transparent, less bureaucratic, less alienating, more understandable, and less rigid through the mere act of subdivision. But when van Eyck subdivided a large group of orphans into smaller "families," he at least created a metaphorical correspondence between those families and the "houses" they inhabited. In later manifestations of the theme, such a connection was completely lost; subdivision became a mere mannerism. Since Herman Hertzberger's celebrated subdivided offices for Centraal Beheer, this model has been exhausted and debased, reaching a phase of extreme decadence in which it has become responsible for an acute crisis of legibility. Today orphanages, dormitories, housing, offices, prisons, department stores, and concert halls all look the same.

The typical entry for the Parliament competition would follow this model, finally enlisting the Parliament itself in this humanist crusade. This solution would propose the *casbah-parliament*: a grid would subdivide the triangular site into smallish squares (their dimensions a reference to the mythical six-meter module of the Amsterdam canal house), each marking the location of a small tower that would be connected to other towers. Since the towers would differ in height, the roofscape would display all the spontaneity of planned irregularity. Thrown in as an extra measure of respect for history, colors and materials would reflect the existing patterns.

Tradition

In this project, the Binnenhof is seen as undergoing a permanent, slow-motion process of transformation in which democratic institutions invade and appropriate the feudal typology of the fortress. Only an architecture that is unapologetic about its modernity can preserve and articulate this tradition. In such an interpretation, all historicist doctrines represent, in fact, interruptions or even obstructions of this transformation. According to this reading, the conquest of the Binnenhof is made final with the introduction of the new Parliament, the architectural representation of the final push that creates a breach of modernity in the walls of the fortress. **1980**

lines are drawn for us. All we have
to do is insert the figures, men in
dusty books, certain faces. Figures
in open space have always been
what film is all about. American
film. This is the situation. People
in a wilderness, a wild and barren
space. The space is the desert, the
movie screen, the strip of film, however you see it. What are the people
doing here? This is their existence.
They're here to work out their existence. This space, this emptiness is
what they have to confront.

DESERT[2]

No more "likeness of reality," no
idealistic images — nothing but a
desert!

DESIRE[1]

Each evening the skyscrapers of
New York assume the anthropo-
morphic shapes of multiple gigantic
Millet's *Angeluses* ... motionless,
and ready to perform the sexual act
and to devour one another ... It is the
sanguinary desire that illuminates
them and makes all the central heating
and the central poetry circulate within their ferruginous bone structure.

DESIRE[2]

On one of the stained-glass windows
was a figure of the Prophet Elijah
and his raven. Outside, on the sill,
a pair of pigeons were billing and
cooing and pecking the pane.
The first hymn was "Guide Me,
O Thou Great Jehovah" and as the
voices swelled in chorus, Amos
caught her clear, quavering soprano
while she felt his baritone murmur-
ing like a bumblebee round the nape
of her neck. All through the Lord's
Prayer he stared at her long, white,
tapering fingers.

DESTRATIFICATION

The beauty of the concept of the
Vierendeel beam lies in the use of
structure as space, inverting the
traditional full/empty categories,
structurally using the *discontinuity
of matter*. The *Vierendeel beam* is
at the same time a real instrument
of *destratification* in the most literal
sense of the term: it is the mechanism capable of completely changing
the geological, gravitational, *natural*
order, shifting the material presence
of the structure from the base of the
building to its coronation, dissolving
the continuity of the lines of gravitational force.

Painting: Madelon Vriesendorp, "The Final Push."

OMA: the conquest of the Binnenhof is made final.

DETOURNEMENT

Short for: detournement of preexisting aesthetic elements. The integration of present or past artistic production into a superior construction of a milieu. In this sense there can be no situationist painting or music, but only a situationist use of these means. In a more primitive sense, detournement within the old cultural spheres is a method of propaganda, a method which testifies to the wearing out and loss of importance of those spheres.

DIARY

Dear Diary, each day I die.

DICHOTOMY

In retrospect, it is easy to understand the failure of modernism to accomplish a fundamental dislocation in architecture consistent with the revolution in man's condition of being. For the new dominant vector, science, harboured a profound and unresolvable dichotomy. On the one hand, through technology and the social sciences, it promised the realization of something that had always been a dream, a utopia of perfect certainty. On the other hand, in its deeper implications, it already anticipated both the impossibility of achieving that vision and its own fatal anthropocentrism.

DIMENSIONS

If DIMSAH is "on," DIMBLK1 and DIMBLK2 specify user-defined arrow blocks for the first and second ends of the dimension line. These variables contain the names of previously defined blocks (just as for DIMBLK). If either block name is unspecified, DIMBLK is used in its place; if DIMBLK is also unspecified, the regular arrowhead is drawn. (If DIMTSZ is nonzero, ticks are drawn regardless of the settings of DIMSAH, DIMBLK, DIMBLK1, and DIMBLK2.) Default values: None (draw regular arrows, ticks, or the arrow specified by DIMBLK).

DIRECTIONS

"Would you tell me, please, which way I ought to walk from here?"
"That depends a good deal on where you want to get to," said the Cat.

DIRTY REALISM

Dirty realism is ... a fiction of a different scope devoted to the local details, the nuances, the little disturbances in language and gesture ...

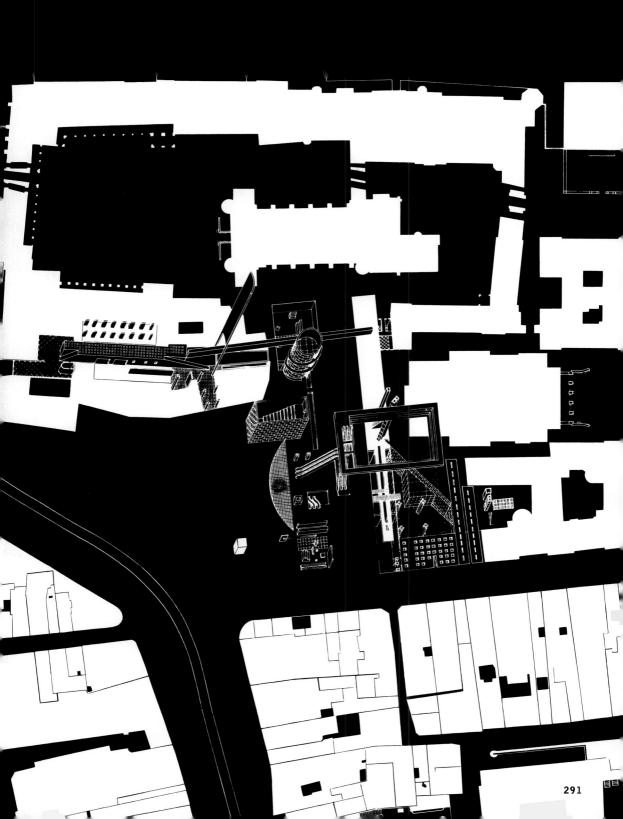

But these are strange stories: unadorned, unfurnished, low-rent tragedies about people who watch daytime television, read cheap romances or listen to country and western music. They're waitresses in roadside cafes, cashiers in supermarkets, construction workers, secretaries, and unemployed cowboys. They play bingo, eat cheeseburgers, and stay in cheap hotels, they drink a lot and are often in trouble for stealing a car or breaking a window, pickpocketing a wallet. They're from Kentucky or Alabama or Oregon. Mainly, they could be from just about anywhere — drifters in a world cluttered with junk food and the oppressive details of modern consumerism.

DISCIPLINE

Often a work is stylized in such a way that a degree of almost military-like discipline is necessary for effect (e.g. geometric spacing of performers, synchrony of movement — or absence of movement, as in a frozen tableau). In such a context, individual actors "feeling their parts" all over the stage are nothing but a nuisance to the director and other performers.

DISCOVER

Two possibilities: either to change basic urban structures which would be a very long-term venture, or to perceive differently, to enjoy these particular shortcomings in the city — to discover beauty where one would have never perceived it before.

DISLOCATION

An argument can be made that every stylistic innovation in architecture is, to some extent at least, a dislocation in the metaphysics of architecture. Thus the shifts from Renaissance to Baroque, from Baroque to Rococo, from Rococo to Neoclassical could be seen as dislocations. However, this argument takes for granted an error that has exerted great power over the arts in general and architecture in particular in the last century: the belief that whatever is new is necessarily a dislocation.

DISORDER

I think I like a certain kind of disorder, though connected to and contained within an area of order.

Organization

The program for the new parliamentary facilities had to be divided between existing structures and new building(s). It consisted of an assembly building with seating for 225 members, including government representatives, speakers, and stenographers, and a public gallery for 100 people; accommodations for the political parties (there are more than 13) to meet in committee; a vast conference center for events involving the press and the general public; 340 rooms for politicians and civil servants; accommodations for all services (stenographers, printing facilities, cleaners, police); and a complex of three restaurants.

In this scheme, the tradition whereby each age manifests itself inside the walls of the Binnenhof is maintained by transplanting a 17th-century structure to a position in front of the complex, where it partly undoes Berlage's traffic cut and restores some of the original definition of the Buitenhof. The breach created by this removal is then occupied by two slabs — one horizontal, one vertical — connected by the assembly.

The horizontal slab, a glass-brick podium, contains the conference center. Conceived as a covered forum for political activity, it is directly accessible to the general public from the adjoining plaza. The vertical slab accommodates the politicians. The assembly — a bridge between the amateurs in the podium and the professionals in the slab — frames

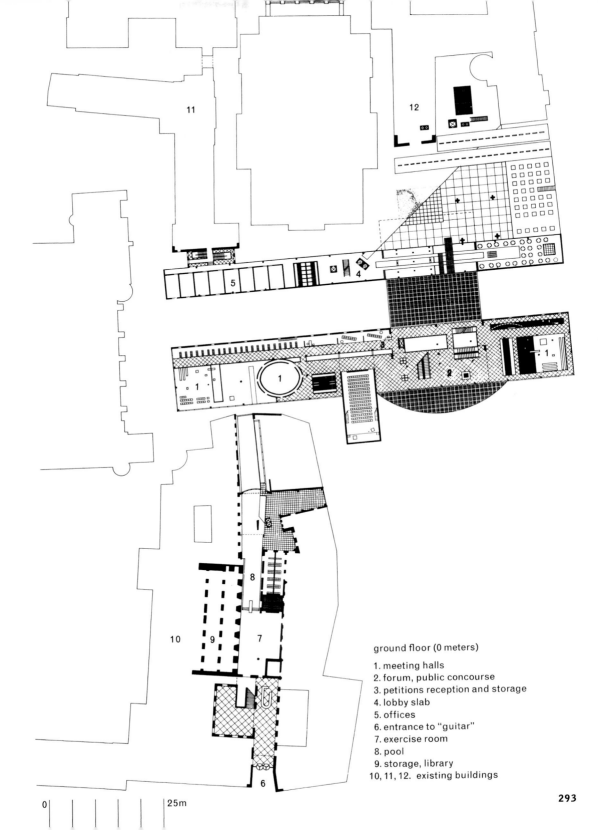

ground floor (0 meters)

1. meeting halls
2. forum, public concourse
3. petitions reception and storage
4. lobby slab
5. offices
6. entrance to "guitar"
7. exercise room
8. pool
9. storage, library
10, 11, 12. existing buildings

0 | | | | | | | 25m

293

DISORGANIZATION
Disorganization is a kind of anesthesia.

DISRUPTED
It was debatable in any case whether the library was actually a library anymore. The system of classification had been thoroughly disrupted, and with so many books out of order, it was virtually impossible to find any volume you might have wanted. When you consider that there were seven floors of stacks, to say that a book was in the wrong place was as much to say that it had ceased to exist. Even though it might have been physically present in the building, the fact was that no one would ever find it again.

DISTANCE[1]
Never in history has distance meant less. Never has man's relationship with place been more numerous, fragile, and temporary... In 1914, according to Buckminster Fuller, the typical American averaged about 1,640 miles per year of total travel, counting some 1,300 miles of just plain everyday walking to and fro... Today, by contrast, the average American car owner drives 10,000 miles per year — and he lives longer than his father or grandfather. "At 69 years of age," wrote Fuller a few years ago, "... I am one of a class of several million human beings who, in their lifetimes, have each covered 3,000,000 miles or more."

DISTANCE[2]
I took the subway down to the Village so I could walk all the way up Fifth Avenue to the zoo. It's one of those things a person has to do; sometimes a person has to go a very long distance out of his way to come back a short distance correctly.

DISTRACTED
He may need to flutter his wings in order to pull harder as her wet head, thorax, and wings come through the adherent surface film. She cannot escape the grip of the water without his help, yet if she takes her time, he may get distracted. Even though he can feel his mate's presence where his claspers hold her by the neck, he sees other females, as yet uncourted, winging past. They tempt him to let go and leave the immersed female to drown.

DIVORCE
The genius of Manhattan is the

a new entrance to the Binnenhof that reveals the Ridderzaal; its relationship to the new triangular plaza mirrors the relationship between the Ridderzaal and the Binnenhof. An ambulatory runs horizontally through the assembly toward the "smoke-filled room." Above the ambulatory are three floors where the political parties prepare their positions; from there they filter down to the ambulatory and the assembly. Below the ambulatory are three floors that accommodate the managers of parliamentary procedures.

A neo-Renaissance building houses all services required by the program; a stenographers' bridge connects the building to the backstage area of the assembly. Underneath the bridge, three restaurants are arranged around a sunken patio; its columns are remnants of an art deco hotel that was once on the site. The rooms for the members of Parliament and their assistants are placed in the existing structures along the Binnenhof.

Forum
The sixties and seventies saw an explosion of the volume of speech expended by the Dutch in the pursuit of politics. Not only are more than 13 parties represented in the Parliament, each asserting its position on every subject, but there has also been an increasing reluctance to make decisions unless elaborate consultation includes nearly all those affected. To an extent this phenomenon undermined the whole system of representation upon which

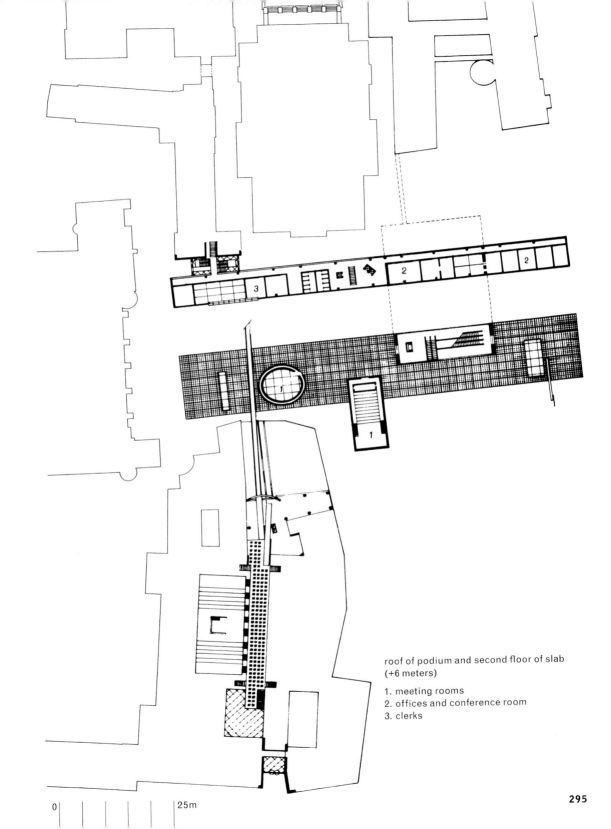

roof of podium and second floor of slab
(+6 meters)

1. meeting rooms
2. offices and conference room
3. clerks

0   25m

simplicity of this divorce between appearance and performance: it keeps the illusion of architecture intact, while surrendering wholeheartedly to the needs of the metropolis.

DOGMA[1]

The problem starts at the secondary level, not with the originator or developer of the idea but with the people who are attracted by it, who adopt it, who cling to it until their last nail breaks, and who invariably lack the overview, flexibility, imagination, and, most importantly, sense of humor, to maintain it in the spirit in which it was hatched. Ideas are made by masters, dogma by disciples, and the Buddha is always killed on the road.

DOGMA[2]

As for the dogma you were taught in the university — it's like having very strong parents ... part of education might be rejecting them.

DOLDRUMS

1. A spell of listlessness or despondency: BLUES. 2. A part of the ocean near the equator abounding in calms, squalls, and light shifting winds. 3. A state of inactivity, stagnation, or slump.

DOOMED

What could be culmination is doomed to become anti-climax.

DOOR

He dreams beyond exhaustion of a door
At which he knocked and entered years before,
But now no street or city comes to mind
Nor why he knocked, nor what he came to find.

DOUBLE

It is estimated that the world's great libraries are doubling in size every 14 years, a rate of 14,000 percent each century. In the early 1300s, the Sorbonne Library in Paris contained only 1,338 books and yet was thought to be the largest library in Europe. Today, there are several libraries in the world with an inventory of well over 8 million books each.

DOUGHNUT[1]

As you know, the French library competition was won by Dominique Perrault, a young and very intelligent French architect, and what we

parliamentary structure is based. An architectural fallout has been a mushrooming of the volumes needed for these consultation rituals — conference centers, meeting halls, forums, etc.

In this competition, the new area required for speech was as large as the entire area occupied by the present Parliament. Such unforeseeable programmatic explosions prove that typologies can no longer be stable; the program destroys the typology. Clearly there are no precedents for such orgies of speech in any culture, except perhaps the open-air agora.

In this scheme, the conference center was conceived as such a forum — a covered continuation of the plaza in front. If the total volume of speech diminishes, the building could dwindle with it; the roof, or parts of it, could be dismantled so that the individual conference buildings would stand as autonomous pavilions in front of the slab.

From the entrance, a system of escalators leads directly to the public gallery of the assembly hall, a rectangle that completely surrounds the parliamentarians. The entire mezzanine level contains facilities for the press: a linear beam of editorial offices and a suspended press plaza for more public events. Segments of the ground floor, which serves primarily as a lobby, are screened off for the more informal exchanges planned by the Parliament. The oval structure contains three superimposed conference rooms connected by a spiraling ramp.

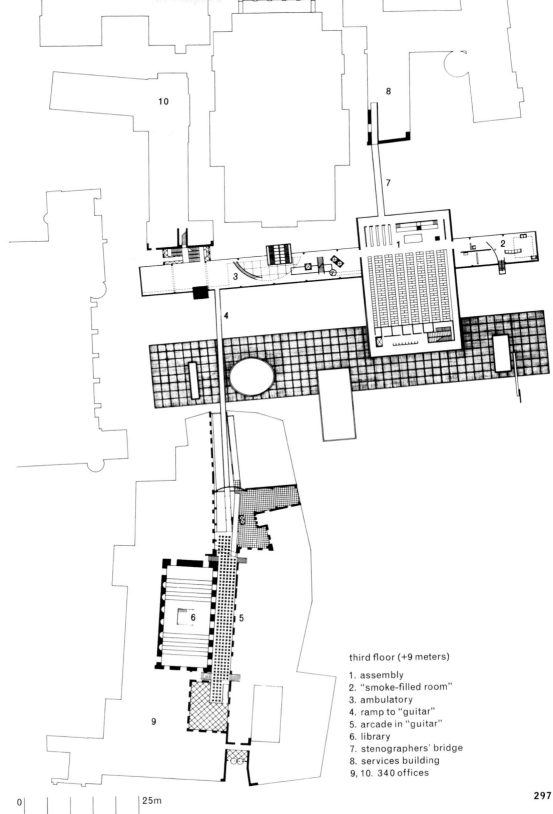

third floor (+9 meters)

1. assembly
2. "smoke-filled room"
3. ambulatory
4. ramp to "guitar"
5. arcade in "guitar"
6. library
7. stenographers' bridge
8. services building
9, 10. 340 offices

0   25m

especially admire in his project is, while we had been hesitating for a long time between a horizontal version and a vertical version, he had the ability to have it both ways, in the sense that his scheme is a doughnut, a kind of rectangular doughnut, the size of the Place de la Concorde.

DOUGHNUT²

The perfection of design that the modern doughnut represents has been overlooked by the academic world. One perfect circle of air-cushioned dough encircling another one of empty space. Few achievements in this century have equaled this level of form marrying function. It should also be noted that they taste damn good.

DRAG

But no bed, however unexpected, no matter how apparently gratuitous, is free from the de-universalising facts of real. We do not go to bed in simple pairs; even if we choose not to refer to them, we still drag in there with us the cultural impediments of our sexual and emotional expectation, our whole biographies — all the bits and pieces of our unique existences. These considerations have limited our choice of partner before we have even got them into the bedroom.

DRAMA

It often happens that the real tragedies of life occur in such an inartistic manner that they hurt us by their crude violence, their absolute incoherence, their absurd want of meaning, their entire lack of style. They affect us just as vulgarity affects us. They give us an impression of sheer brute force, and we revolt against that. Sometimes, however, a tragedy that possesses artistic elements of beauty crosses our lives. If these elements of beauty are real, the whole thing simply appeals to our sense of dramatic effect. Suddenly we find that we are no longer the actors, but the spectators of the play. Or rather we are both. We watch ourselves, and the mere wonder of the spectacle enthralls us.

DREAM

There he sat. His eyelids were closed, there was only a swift, sidelong glint of the eyeballs now and again, something between a question

Extrusion

Before the true skyscraper had been "invented" in New York, mutant buildings were generated, not designed, by replicating entire sites as found. In 1902, the triangular site of the Flatiron Building abruptly became an acute 23-story wedge; in 1915, the rectangle of the Equitable Building, a 39-story extrusion. In the case of less geometrical plots, this architecture-through-process generated mystifying images such as the 1908 City Investing Building, in which the brutality of the purely mechanical creation-through-extrusion acquired an aesthetic dimension.

In 1921–22, Mies van der Rohe invested the same irregularity with explicit intention in projects for two glass towers that define the essential difference between the built subconscious of America and the unbuilt consciousness of Europe.

In the "guitar," an extra 1,000 m² was needed; the plan of a star-shaped courtyard is extruded at the point where the surrounding building stops to form a small, irregular, five-story skyscraper.

Connections

In a project where a large number of programmatic elements is distributed among several structures, the quality of the connections determines the quality of the project. This scheme is based on two intersecting axes: one, the new arcade that runs north-south through the existing buildings; the other, the ambu-

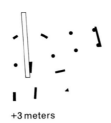

+3 meters

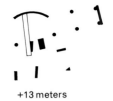

+13 meters

+16 meters

+19 meters

+21 meters

+24 meters

+27 meters

extruded skyscraper

and a leer; while the rouged and flabby mouth uttered single words of the sentences shaped in his disordered brain by the fantastic logic that governs our dreams.

DRESS
Dress designing ... is to me not a profession but an art. I found it was a most difficult and unsatisfying art, because as soon as the dress is born it has already become a thing of the past ... A dress has not life of its own unless it is worn, and as soon as this happens another personality takes over from you and animates it, or tries to, glorifies it or destroys it, or makes it into a song of beauty. More often it becomes an indifferent object, or even a pitiful caricature of what you wanted it to be — a dream, an expression.

DRESSING ROOM
From her dim crimson cellar Lenina Crowne shot up seventeen stories, turned to the right as she stepped out of the lift, walked down a long corridor and, opening the door marked GIRLS' DRESSING-ROOM, plunged into a deafening chaos of arms and bosoms and underclothing. Torrents of hot water were splashing into or gurgling out of a hundred baths. Rumbling and hissing, eighty vibro-vacuum massage machines were simultaneously kneading and sucking the firm and sunburnt flesh of eighty superb female specimens. Everyone was talking at the top of her voice. A Synthetic Music machine was warbling out a super-cornet solo.

DRIFT
See **DERIVE.**

DRIFTER
The drifter has no fixed itinerary or timetable and no well-defined goals of travel. He is almost wholly immersed in his host culture. Novelty is here at its highest, familiarity disappears almost completely.

DRIVE
Immediate proximity of related use, as on Main Street, where you walk from one store to another, is not required along the Strip because interaction is by car and highway. You drive from one casino to another even when they are adjacent because of the distance between them, and an intervening service station is not disagreeable.

latory, running east-west through the middle of the slab.

The guitar was originally generated by building extensions across the moat and connecting these new structures to the main building with a system of courtyards. Three of the five courtyards are aligned on the location of the former moat; they are connected to form an arcade that directs all traffic toward a split ramp, which in turn leads directly to the ambulatory and to the basement of the conference hall. Since the guitar is an agglomeration of separate buildings, it has a variety of different facades along its perimeter, ranging from authentic Renaissance fragments and neoclassical fronts to the ersatz 17th-century fantasies along Berlage's traffic cut. By cutting the arcade through its interior, the original facades along the moat are exposed. In a further clarification, a swimming pool replaces the original moat.

A second connection between old and new — between the slab and the preserved fragment of the Binnenhof wall — is the interior of a small 16th-century canal house that is completely filled with staircases to negotiate the different levels between the slab and its neighbors.

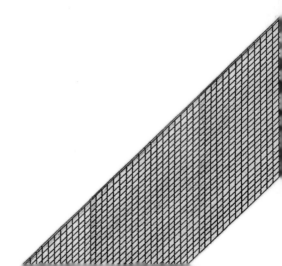

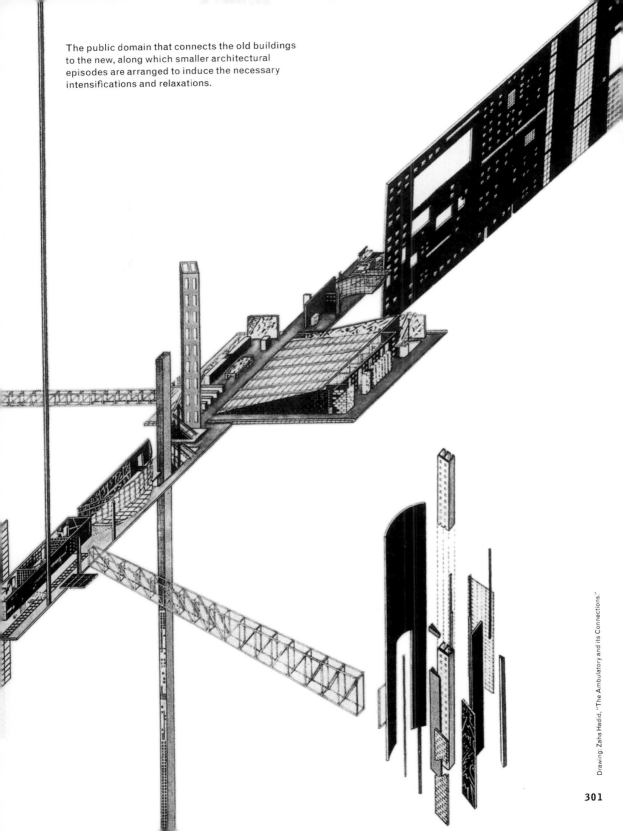

The public domain that connects the old buildings to the new, along which smaller architectural episodes are arranged to induce the necessary intensifications and relaxations.

Drawing: Zaha Hadid, "The Ambulatory and its Connections."

DRIVE-THRU

Road infrastructure cutting through the building as if it were a destructured, informal mass. No influence on the organization of form, no articulation with its material or spatial structures, but rather the intentional exploitation of penetration.

DRUNK

Les charmes de l'horreur n'enivrent que les forts ...

DUTCH[1]

The Netherlands is a constitutional monarchy. The Parliament, known as the States-General, consists of two Chambers, the first of 75 members, elected by the Provincial States for six years, and the second of 150 members, elected by universal suffrage for four years. The national language is Dutch.

DUTCH[2]

Therefore, in order to work, I had to develop a reaction to standard Dutch problems and issues. For me, the most attractive proposition was to build essentially very unpretentious, intelligent — I'm not saying the Dutch aren't like that, but this was our ambition in any case — relatively elegant, but also relatively neutral things.

DUTCH[3]

In Holland there are no mountains, just wind.

DUTCH GREY

A Dutch friend asked me if I would like to see the tulip fields. Inwardly I really did not want to see the tulip fields. For some reason I thought that seeing so many tulips — red, yellow, white, purple — would be too much. In any case I did not want to see the tulips. My friend persuaded me to go with him. I am glad that he did. He brought me into a deep view. When we rode along the roads which moved through the tulip fields I began to understand Mondrian. I always thought him to be an international painter; I found him to be a Dutch painter. It was not the color of the tulips but the density of the sand and earth where the bulbs were planted which reminded me of Mondrian. It was the atmosphere of opacity. The place, the land, the earth was dense opacification. The colored flowers were not the issue, it was the infinite penetration and the compaction of trapped light crystals

302

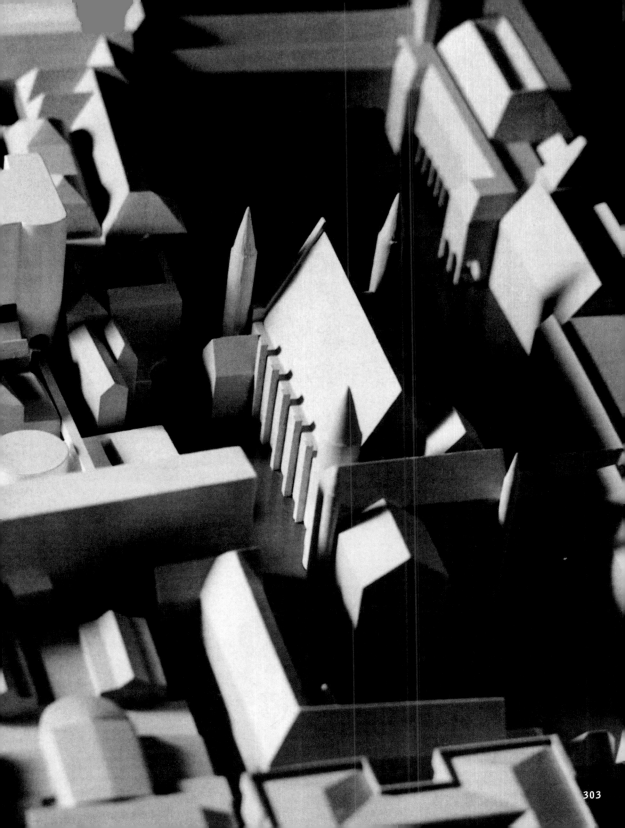

303

in the earth which illuminated the air into a grey solidity ... Dutch grey.

DUTCHNESS
To its first generation of patriotic eulogists, Dutchness was often equated with the transformation, under divine guidance, of catastrophe into good fortune, infirmity into strength, water into dry land, mud into gold.

DUTY
The duty of management is to make money, not steel.

E

EDIBLE
In this catalogue of the Exhibition of Edible Sculpture, you will be able to read tonight the original erotic-sentimental chatter which aroused in the artists certain seemingly incomprehensible flavours and forms. It is light, aerial art. Ephemeral art. Edible art. The fugitive eternal feminine imprisoned in the stomach. The painful, superacute tension of the most frenetic lusts finally gratified. You consider us wild; others think us highly compli-cated and civilized. We are the instinctive new elements of the great Machine future lyrical plastic architectonic, all new laws, all new instructions.

EDIT
We learnt where to edit. I think it was important that there were all these diverse things. We could take some of them with a pinch of salt and we could take others more seriously — you could choose.

EGG¹
"Bokanovsky's Process," repeated the Director, and the students under-lined the words in their little note-books.
One egg, one embryo, one adult — normality. But a bokanovskified egg will bud, will proliferate, will divide. From eight to ninety-six buds, and every bud will grow into a perfectly formed embryo, and every embryo into a full-sized adult. Making ninety-six human beings grow where only one grew before. Progress.

EGG²
Chaos, cosmic germ of the universe,

Battlefield

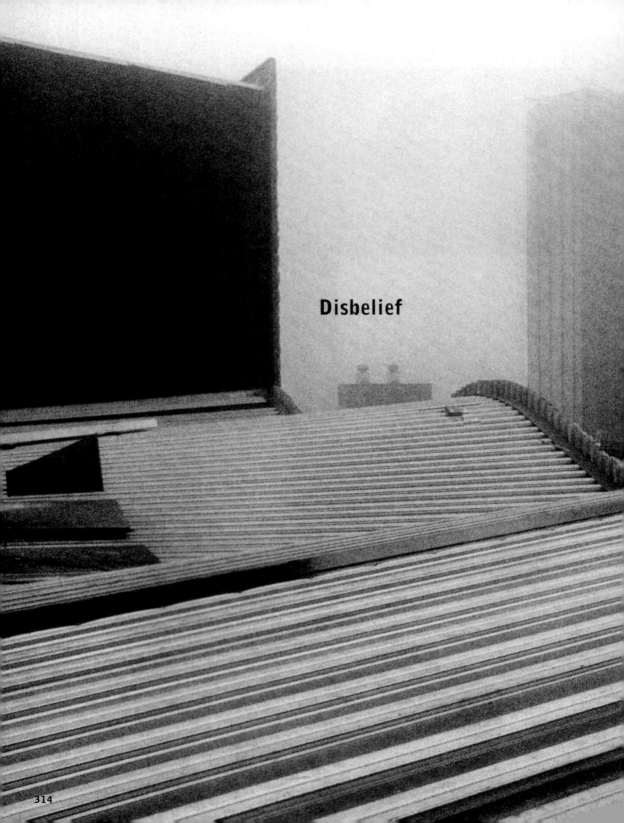

Disbelief

creation, germ of life, immortality, sun, triad. In some traditions, heaven and earth were developed from an egg-shaped chaotic mass; in others, earth formed from the egg which floated on the primeval sea; in still others, the sun came into being when an egg, tossed into the sky, burst.

ELEVATED
On our arrival in Denmark, we found the king and queen of that country elevated in two armchairs on a kitchen-table, holding a Court.

ELEVATOR
It is presented to the public as a theatrical spectacle.
Elisha Otis, the inventor, mounts a platform that ascends — the major part, it seems, of the demonstration. But when it has reached its highest level, an assistant presents Otis with a dagger on a velvet cushion.
The inventor takes the knife, seemingly to attack the crucial element of his own invention: the cable that has hoisted the platform upward and that now prevents its fall. Otis cuts the cable; it snaps.
Nothing happens, either to platform or to inventor.
Invisible safety catches — the essence of Otis' brilliance — prevent the platform from rejoining the surface of the earth.
Thus Otis introduces an invention in urban theatricality: the anticlimax as denouement, the non-event as triumph.

ELITISM
Architecture is not the satisfaction of the needs of the mediocre, is not an environment for the petty happiness of the masses ... Architecture is an affair of the elite.

EMEUTE
Right bank, left bank, on the quays, on the boulevards, in the Latin Quarter, in the region of the markets, breathless men, workingmen, students, sectionaries, read proclamations, cried: "To arms!" broke the streetlamps, unharnessed wagons, tore up the pavements, broke in the doors of the houses, uprooted the trees, ransacked the cellars, rolled hogsheads, heaped up paving stones, pebbles, pieces of furniture, boards, made barricades.

EMOTION
See **NEUTRALITY**.

Approach

317

EMPTY

And what would become of the
emptiness of space? Often enough it
appears to be a deficiency.
Emptiness is held then to be a failure
to fill up a cavity or gap.
Yet presumably the emptiness is
closely allied to the special character
of place, and therefore no failure,
but a bringing-forth. Again, language
can give us a hint. In the verb "to
empty" (leeren) the word "collecting"
(lesen), taken in the original sense of
the gathering which reigns in place,
is spoken. To empty a glass means:
to gather the glass, as that which can
contain something, into its having
been freed.
To empty the collected fruit in a bas-
ket means: to prepare for them this
place.
Emptiness is not nothing. It is also
no deficiency. In sculptural embodiment, emptiness plays in the manner
of a seeking-projecting instituting
of places.

ENERGY

Those two hemispheres, brimming
with mysterious energy, drew me
like a magnet.

ENGINEER

We know better now how to engineer
the creative processes and to create
the right conditions, the right mixture between panic and contemplation, the right incentive in terms
of competitive and supportive relationships, and in the end you could
even talk about the composition of
the office as a "design" issue, a composition of national accents and
complimentaries.

ENLIGHTENING

Held against the light, the contents
of both sides of the paper are visible
at once.

ENORMITIES

Pyramids, arches, obelisks, were
but the irregularities of vain-glory,
and wild enormities of ancient
magnanimity.

ENORMITY

1. A grave offense against order,
right, or decency. 2. The quality or
state of being immoderate, monstrous, or outrageous; esp: great
wickedness. 3. The quality or state
of being huge: IMMENSITY.

ENORMOUS

We are swimming on the face of
time and all else has drowned, is

Performance

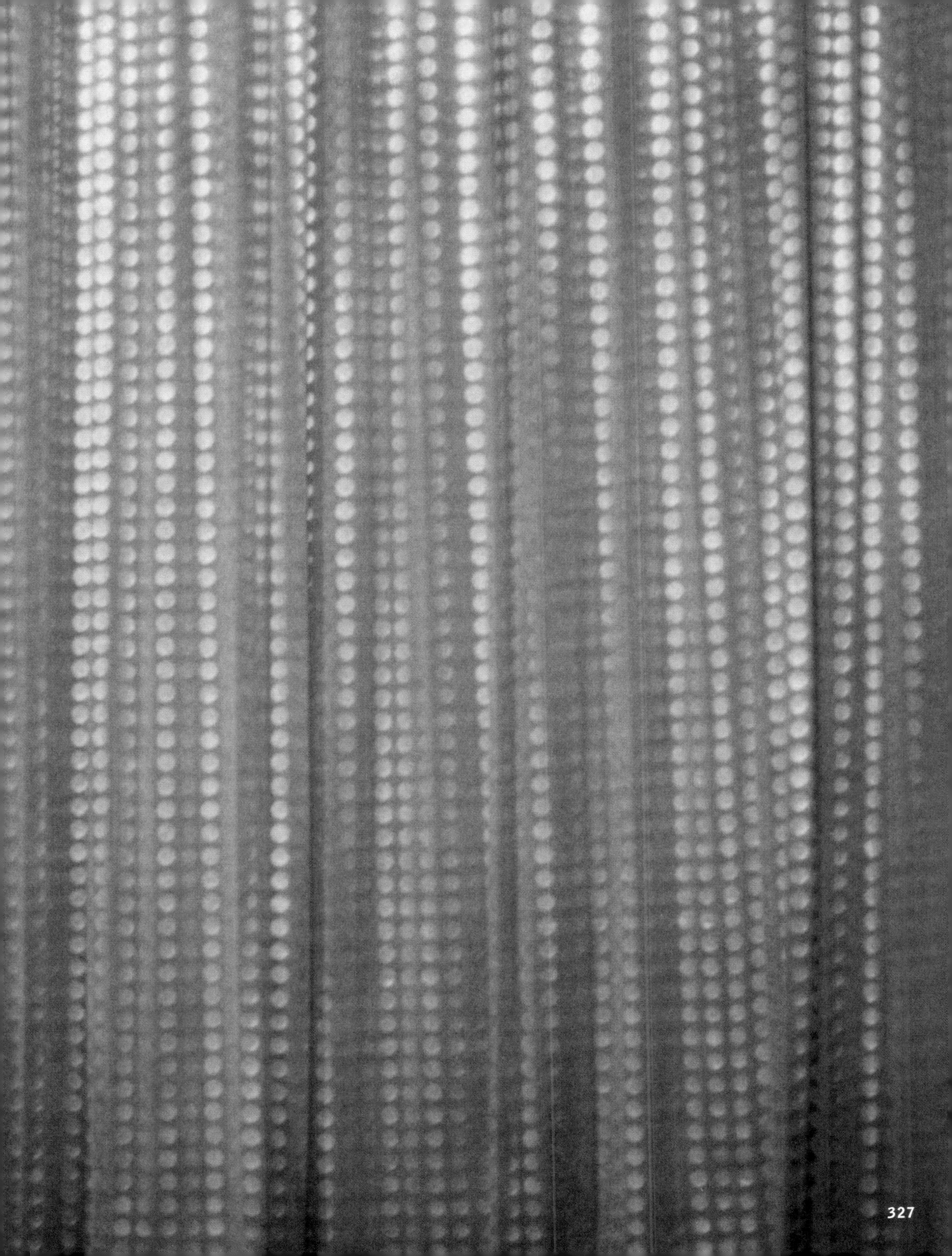

Chronology

1958 Carel Birnie, opera director, begins to go deaf. Becomes managing director of the National Ballet, then bolts with 16 dancers and assorted choreographers to form new contemporary company: Netherlands Dance Theater.

1959–78 NDT squats in various buildings in The Hague. Birnie, obsessed with improving accommodations, seeks "home" in factories, warehouses, schools, churches. Tries to convince bureaucrats that his company deserves funding. No interest. Starts foundation; regularly deposits profits; company prospers; saves.

1978 *Delirious New York* published in New York, London, Paris.

1979 Birnie has saved 13,000,000 guilders—enough to start thinking seriously about building. Carries pocket-sized model of studios and offices everywhere. Begins looking for sites.

Meanwhile, 1979 OMA's entry for the Dutch Parliament competition wins recognition in Holland but not the competition: "too inhuman." Jan Voorberg, architect from The Hague, is a lone lobbyist; continues to promote project regardless; almost turns tide.

Early 1980 Birnie approaches architects from three generations: Quist: safe; Weeber: rational; OMA: ?

Around the same time, 1980 NDT usually performs at Circus Theater, Scheveningen— semi-dilapidated seaside resort of The Hague. Birnie discovers previously unnoticed site between Circus Theater and nearby tramway. Dreams become rosier; updates mini-model accordingly.

Mid-1980 Convinces city—tied in public-private covenant with mammoth financial conglomerate—to let him build "26,000 m³ of culture," 10% of the total 230,000 m³ of new offices planned by conglomerate.

Soon, 1980 Job interview in schoolhouse: Koolhaas, Voorberg (now OMA partner in Holland), Birnie; sounds of dancers rehearsing. Architects recognize music: Cage; earn points.

Same day, 1980 Birnie presents equation: "Can you build it for: $\dfrac{\text{fl. } 13{,}000{,}000}{26{,}000 \text{ m}^3} = $ fl. 500 (\$250) per m³?" OMA—no phone, no office, no secretary: "Yes."

ASAP Location of first OMA office is ideological choice: Rotterdam.

1981 First OMA proposal: 34,000 m³ of studios and offices against tramway plus unexpected bonus: residual space becomes tent-covered auditorium (not included in Birnie's previous fantasies). But once alerted, Birnie wants more: asks for red velvet chairs and a gigantic Stopera stage tower (34 x 19 x 26 meters) adding impossible 16,796 m³ to equation. Political volume: 26,000 m³. Program volume: 50,000 m³. Conclusion: no possible architecture. "Objective" discovery: wall without roof or roof without wall = 0 m³; therefore, architecture of walls and roofs.

Later, 1981 OMA looks for structural engineer who can design floating roof. No luck in Holland. Mathias Ungers recommends "acrobat": German-Hungarian Stefan Polonyi. In first meeting, Professor Polonyi promises glass columns, if wanted.

Behind closed doors, 1982 City of The Hague studies possible cultural concentration in city center. Site designated on Spui for new concert hall and other yet to be specified buildings. "Someone" suggests NDT as candidate for the project.

June 23, 1983 Design documents completed for Scheveningen site.

September 30, 1983 City Council accepts design; gives green light. To celebrate, Jan Voorberg takes vacation in Brazil.

Tuesday, October 11, 1983 Voorberg murdered in Brazil.

Later that week, 1983 City announces plans to cancel Scheveningen building and move site to Spui; cultural complex to be shared by NDT, concert hall, hotel. New volume: 54,000 m³ (twice as large). Old budget: 13,000,000 guilders (still the same). Budget per m³: halved. Birnie: thrilled, bolts. OMA: despairing, stays.

November 1983 Site plan by Carel Weeber shows "urban square" with NDT cornered between future concert hall and 12-story hotel. OMA fights for another arrangement. Birnie agrees to Weeber plan while architects are out of town.

December 1983 According to OMA, site is sterile. Will not allow fertilization. Proposes therefore to transplant Scheveningen embryo to barren womb. Graft does not take. Dry spell.

1984 New start. Since money is halved, so is architectural potential. No money, no exterior; all invested in interior. Maybe that's all the site deserves.

Still 1984 Structural grid of parking garage below (architect: Weeber) limits possibilities.

Program divided into three zones: (1) performance: stage and auditorium; (2) rehearsal: studios; and (3) administration: offices, common rooms, etc. *Cadavre exquis* with concert hall (architect: van Mourik): void of demarcation line is inflated to become lobby; first use of nothingness.

One summer day, 1985 Final negotiation with contractor: Birnie's deafness strengthens negotiating position. Tense contractor squeezes metal eyeglass case in frustration; contract signed in blood, literally.

September 1985 Construction of parking garage begins.

December 1985 Dancers demand participation—want more privacy in dressing rooms. OMA had assumed American locker-room nakedness. Dressing rooms redesigned.

February 1986 Contractor complains about auditorium roof. Claims that flat roof would be 30% cheaper than OMA/Polonyi "wave." Birnie agrees; accuses OMA of profligacy.

March 1986 As in a fairy tale, OMA builds model big enough to imprison Birnie and choreographer Jiri Kylian. One Saturday morning, both are kidnapped and locked up in the model. They like it. Flat roof canceled; wave restored.

March 1986 Van Mourik complains about OMA's lobby balcony: because it touches "his" facade, it may transmit unwanted sound into auditorium. Balcony redesigned by Polonyi for zero interface with neighbor: it floats.

April 1986 Birnie "always" wanted auditorium with 18x9–meter stage opening—as big as the Amsterdam Stopera. Now he gets it.

May 1986 Wants more than 1,000 seats in auditorium. Gets 1,001.

May 1986 Wants 1,001 red seats in red auditorium with red velvet curtain. OMA proposes blue seats (with cowhide backs) in black auditorium with gold curtain. Rejected (cows too distracting, black too depressing, gold too expensive).

June 1986 Wants 1,001 red seats with individual lights. OMA develops LCD lighting system for chairs. Rejected (lights would make empty seats too noticeable).

Rest of 1986 Battles.

January 1987 Birnie separates.

February 2, 1987 His right hand quits.

February 4, 1987 Fires structural engineer.

February 5, 1987 Fires acoustical engineer.

February 6, 1987 Fires services engineer.

February 8, 1987 Fires OMA.

February 9, 1987 Birnie has heart attack; keeps working anyway.

March 1987 OMA keeps working anyway. Assembles team of friends/students/amateurs to finish building. No money, no details.

April 1987 Issue: color scheme for lobby. OMA asks van Mourik for color of *his* wall. Response: RAL 3015. Color chart shows bluish pink, white race at its worst. Model updated to show pink wall. OMA considers "tasteful" combinations, then proposes red (casting lively humanist glow over lifeless pink). Decision contains extra benefit: red foyer opens way for "un-red" auditorium: becomes black box with blue velvet chairs.

June 1987 German factory produces auditorium chairs. At 500 guilders per chair, Birnie can only afford 600.6 chairs. Germany donates the other 400.4.

(Hot) Summer 1987 Money runs out. No paint (backstage still half-bare). No furniture (OMA finds tree trunk instead). No blue astroturf on roof (heavy rain can still be heard). No lights for auditorium (extra stage lights used instead). No curtain, almost (sponsors pay cash for gold "coins" on gray velvet).

September 9, 1987 Opening. Koolhaas gives Birnie a gift—framed silk screen of Scheveningen project with dedication: "To Carel, for everything you made (im)possible."

1993 Carel Birnie calls OMA; wants more: a new opera in The Hague.

Typical Plan

Typical Plan is an American invention. It is zero-degree architecture, architecture stripped of all traces of uniqueness and specificity. It belongs to the New World.

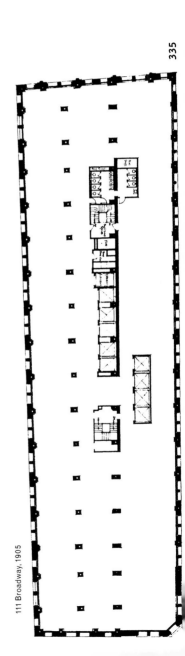

Photo: Berenice Abbott, 1932.

111 Broadway, 1905

The notion of the typical plan is therapeutic; it is the End of Architectural History, which is nothing but the hysterical fetishization of the atypical plan. Typical Plan is a segment of an unacknowledged utopia, the promise of a post-architectural future.

Just as *The Man Without Qualities* haunts European literature, "the plan without qualities" is the great quest of American building.

From the late 19th century to the early 1970s, there is an "American century" in which Typical Plan is developed from the primitive loft type (ruthless creation of floor space through the sheer multiplication of a given site) via early masterpieces of *smooth space* like the RCA Building (1933)—its escalators, its elevators, the Zen-like serenity of its office suites—to provisional culminations such as the Exxon Building (1971) and the World Trade Center (1972–73). Together they represent evidence of the discovery and subsequent mastery of a *new architecture* (often proclaimed but never realized at the scale of Typical Plan).

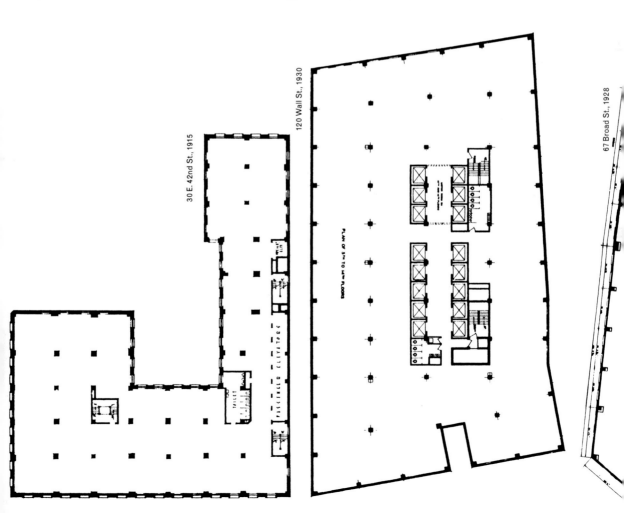

30 E. 42nd St., 1915

120 Wall St., 1930

67 Broad St., 1928

The ambition of Typical Plan is to create new territories for the smooth unfolding of new processes, in this case, ideal accommodation for business. But what is business? Supposedly the most circumscribed program, it is actually the most formless. Business makes no demands. The architects of Typical Plan understood the secret of business: the office building represents the first totally abstract program—it does not demand a particular architecture, its only function is to let its occupants *exist*. Business can invade *any* architecture. Out of this indeterminacy Typical Plan generates character.

Raymond Hood, one of its inventors, defined the typical plan with tautological bravura: "The plan is of primary importance, because on the floor are performed all the activities of the human occupants."

(Typical Plan provides the multiple platforms of 20th-century democracy.)

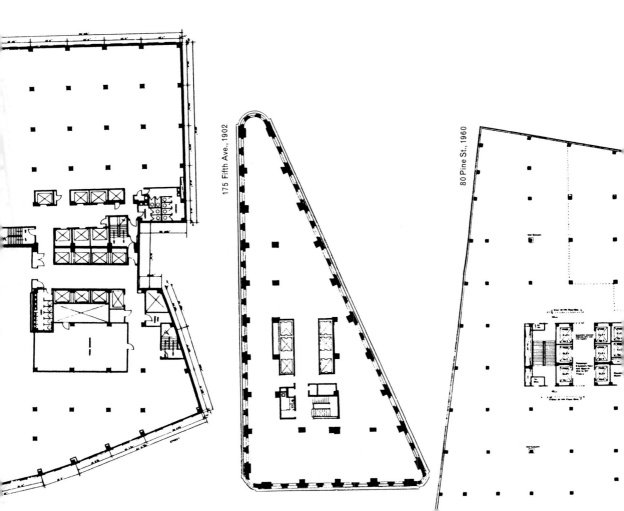

175 Fifth Ave., 1902

80 Pine St., 1960

Typical Plan is an architecture of the rectangle; any other shape makes it atypical — even the square. It is the product of a (new) world where sites are made, not found. At its best, it acquires a Platonic neutrality; it represents the point where pragmatism, through sheer rationality and efficiency, assumes an almost mystical status.

Typical Plan is minimalism for the masses; already latent in the first brutally utilitarian explorations, by the end of the era of Typical Plan, i.e., the sixties, the utilitarian is refined as a sensuous science of coordination — column grids, facade modules, ceiling tiles, lighting fixtures, partitions, electrical outlets, flooring, furniture, color schemes, air-conditioning grills — that transcends the practical to emerge in a rarified existential domain of *pure objectivity*.

You can only *be* in Typical Plan, not sleep, eat, make love.

338

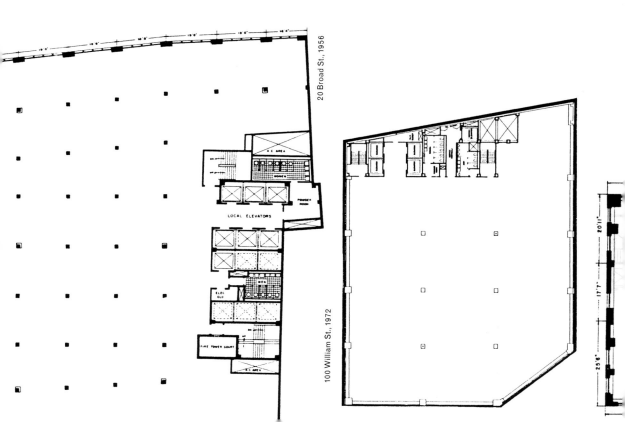

20 Broad St., 1956

100 William St., 1972

Typical Plan threatens the myth of the architect as demiurge, source of unlimited supplies of uniqueness.

As in the scene of a crime, the removal of all obvious signs of the perpetrator characterizes the true typical plan; its authors form an avant-garde of architects as *erasers*. Its unsung designers—Bunshaft, Harrison and Abramovitz, Emery Roth—represent vanishing acts so successful that they are now completely forgotten. These architects were able to create aleatory playgrounds (interior Elysian fields accessible in anyone's lifetime), i.e., perfection in quantities—trillions of acres—that have become, 25 years later, literally unimaginable.

Securely entrenched in the domain of philistinism, Typical Plan actually has hidden affinities with other arts: the positioning of its cores on the floor has a *suprematist* tension; it is the equivalent of atonal music, seriality, concrete poetry, art brut; it is architecture as mantra.

343

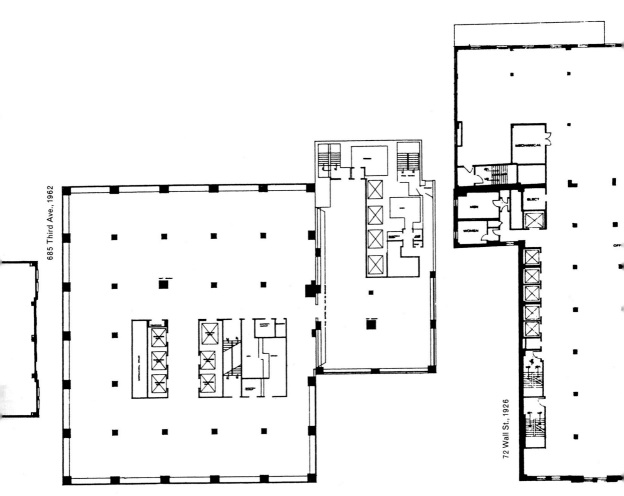

685 Third Ave., 1962

72 Wall St., 1926

Typical Plan is as empty as possible: a floor, a core, a perimeter, and a minimum of columns.

All other architecture is about inclusion and accommodation, incident and event; Typical Plan is about exclusion, evacuation, non-event.

Architecture is monstrous in the way in which each choice leads to the reduction of possibility. It implies a regime of either/or decisions often claustrophobic, even for the architect. All other architecture preempts the future; Typical Plan—by making *no* choices—postpones it, keeps it open forever.

344

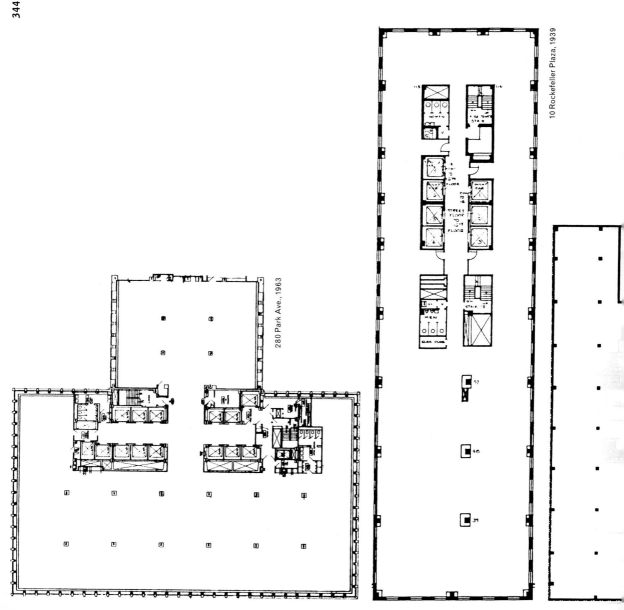

280 Park Ave., 1963

10 Rockefeller Plaza, 1939

The cumulative effect of all this vacancy—this systematic lack of commitment—is, paradoxically, density. The typical American downtown is a brute accumulation of Typical Plans, a *massif* of indetermination, hollowness as core.

Could the office building be the most radical typology? A kind of reverse type defined by all the qualities it does *not* have? As the major new program of the modern age, its effect is one of deprogramming. Typical Plan is the initial mutation in a chain that has revolutionized the urban condition. Concentrations of Typical Plan have produced the skyscraper: unstable monolith; accumulations of skyscrapers, the only "new" urban condition: downtown, defined by sheer quantity rather than as a specific formal configuration. The center is no longer unique but universal, no longer a place but a condition. Practically immune to local variation, Typical Plan has made the city unrecognizable, an unidentifiable object. Typical Plan is a quantum leap that provokes a conceptual leap: an *absence* of content in quantities that overwhelm, or simply preempt, intellectual speculation.

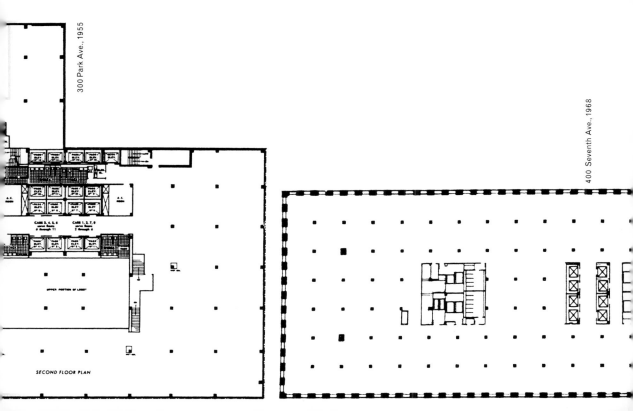

300 Park Ave., 1955

400 Seventh Ave., 1968

SECOND FLOOR PLAN

What insecurity triggered the crisis of Typical Plan? Where did the rot start? Was it its very apotheosis that turned neutrality into anonymity?

Did the plan without qualities create men without qualities? Was the space of Typical Plan the incubator of the man in the gray flannel suit?

Suddenly, the graph blamed the graph paper for its lack of character.

It was as if Typical Plan created the castrated white-collar caricature, suppressed family photos, frowned on the fern, resisted the personal debris that now—20 years later—makes most offices ghastly repositories of individual trophies, packed with the alarming assertions of millions of individual mini-ecologies.

An environment that demanded nothing and gave everything was suddenly seen as an infernal machine for stripping identity.

Nietzsche lost out to Sociology 101.

346

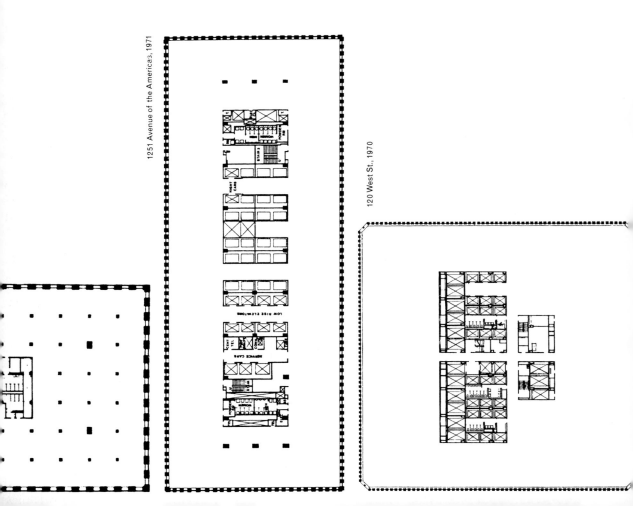

1251 Avenue of the Americas, 1971

120 West St., 1970

347

In Europe, there are no Typical Plans.

In the twenties, European architects fantasized about offices. In 1921, Mies imagined the ultimate atypical plan in Friedrichstrasse; in 1929, Ivan Leonidov proposed the first office slab for Moscow, a House of Industry. Its rectangles were conceived as socialist Typical Plans: a parallel zone reintroduced the full paraphernalia of daily life — pools, tanning beds, clublike arrangements, small dormitories — to create a compressed 24-hour cycle not of business-life, but of life-business. In 1970, Archizoom interpreted Typical Plan as the terminal condition of (Western) civilization, a utopia of the norm.

Since then, the one really new architectural subject this century has introduced has been endlessly denigrated in the name of ideology — its occupants "slaves," its environment "faceless," its accumulations "ugly." Europe has suffered from a catastrophic failure to accommodate — to "think" — the one typology whose emergence was architecturally and urbanistically irresistible. Typical Plan has been forced underground, condemned to the status of parasite — devouring larger and larger sections of historical substance, invading whole centers — or exiled to the periphery.

348

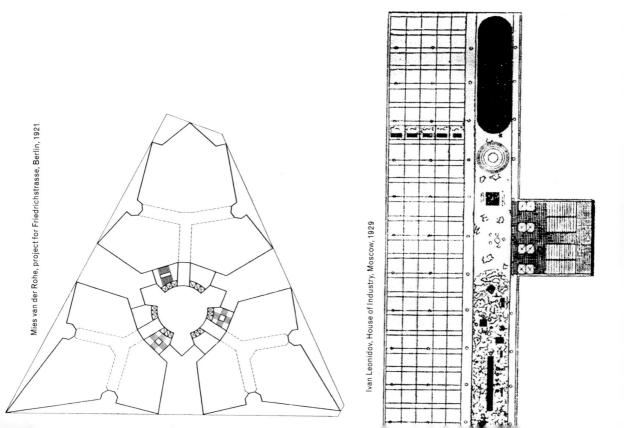

Mies van der Rohe, project for Friedrichstrasse, Berlin, 1921

Ivan Leonidov, House of Industry, Moscow, 1929

Amsterdam, 20 years after the sixties ... the city still firmly in socialist hands ... big dreams, no money ... So why not sell old power station downtown — near museums, fashionable shops, exciting conversions (prison turned into casino), and the park?

Mayor's brainwave: replace power plant with modern masterpiece!
Marry six architects to six developers; let them fight it out for the biggest gain in money and beauty.

Sorry, there's only one name left: OMA ...

Well, if there's no choice, I'll take them, I guess.

But the developer has a plan ...
Later, in another part of town, he reveals his "project" to his would-be competitors.
None of us can win alone. Let's make it a sure thing ... We'll win with YOUR architect and split the profit three ways ...
Sounds good to me, but what about OMA?
You mean sabotage through collaboration?

Next day, OMA is invited to meet one developer, but discovers a consortium of three ...
My company handles the parking. We like them with nothing on top.
We do housing — bungalows mostly.
We specialize in shops and offices. We like them freestanding.
I'm the architect. We believe in integration and complication.

Back in Rotterdam... 24-hour work day at the OMA office. Day and night shifts. How to create masterpiece from 10,000 m² housing, 5,000 m² offices, 2,500 m² shopping, 15,000 m² parking?

After three months of torturous labor, a project is born...

... only to be quickly dismantled.

Meanwhile, the power station is almost completely destroyed.

OMA talks to lawyer. All this interference raises issues of artistic integrity.

Final effort to break deadlock...
Man-to-man meeting with developer at his own castle, only days before deadline...

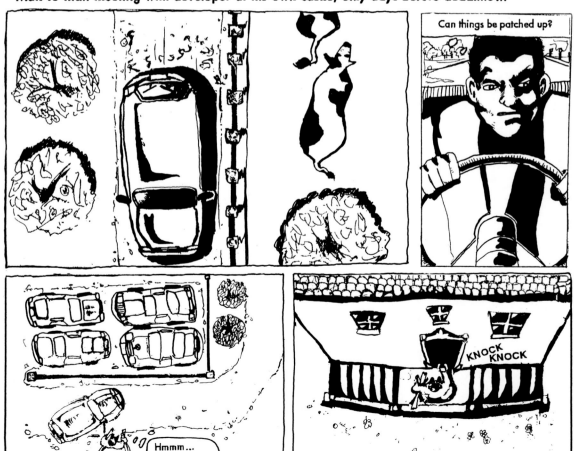

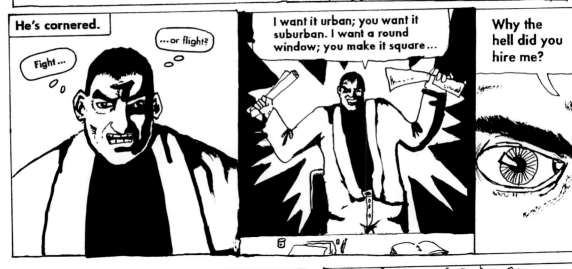

Competition deadline arrives. Five architects file in with their wares... At the last moment OMA appears, out of breath. Developers back scheme, believing it won't win anyway.

But public opinion mobilizes behind OMA... Critics and public unanimously endorse OMA's position... Somehow, to the developers' horror,

OMA WINS!!!

A victory for complication.

Globalization

According to myth, Wallace Harrison was the "bad" corporate architect—if not simply a hack—who stole Le Corbusier's design for the
United Nations building (1947–50) and made it mediocre reality.

This myth was sufficiently established to prevent anyone from taking a serious look at the building itself. But a closer inspection of the
dry theoretical pretension of Le Corbusier's proposition and the
polymorphously perverse professionalism with which Harrison realized it suggested, if not a reversal of the myth, a rewriting: the UN
was a building that an American could never have *thought* and a
European could never have *built*. It was a *collaboration*, not only
between two architects, but between cultures; a cross-fertilization
between Europe and America produced a hybrid that could not have
existed without their mating, however unenthusiastic.

The Seagram Building (1957) can be reread in the same way as the
UN, except that here the roles of Europe and America were enacted
by the same person: Mies had to "become" an American to realize his
European self. Without the combined intelligence of the two cultures,
the Seagram Building could not have been.

Some of Paul Rudolph's most impossible megastructural speculations for New York—concrete houses of cards in inexplicable states of suspense proliferating over half of Manhattan—stand, 25 years after their initial conception, marooned among the palms in Singapore. Is Singapore an accident or a symbol? Is Singapore now a destination where ambitions spawned elsewhere are realized? Has the terrain of possibility shifted?

There is an Aldo Rossi building in Fukuoka, the "deep south" of Japan. In pictures it looks like a caricature—red Persian travertine facades hermetically closed, overblown copper roofline. Il Palazzo dominates its surroundings like a samurai castle. It looks cynical—deliciously fascist. It is a hotel; some even say a love hotel. Rossi did not do the interiors or the nightclubs that invade the stoic exterior, but his envelope has a weird fascination. It is pure emblem, Rossi without ideological ballast: hyper-Rossi.

The Japanese have realized Rossi's poetry *on the surface*, with a density he seems incapable of on his own ground: a masterpiece unimaginable for the Japanese, unbuildable for Rossi. As a hybrid, it is fundamentally different from the Seagram Building or the UN: its fertilization not the result of fusion, but reminiscent of more contemporary forms of bioengineering. It is a gene splice: Rossi's poetry, first stripped of ideology, then boosted by Japanese ingenuity.

Beyond Florida, there is an entire "Michael Graves World" in Japan—more than 40 projects, from skyscrapers to city halls for small villages,

Vanishing Act

Biocenter, University of Frankfurt
Frankfurt, Germany
Competition, 1988

4. Extrapolation does not yield exhilarating prospects: eventually the entire hill will be covered with architecture. A second building is planned to contain more laboratories, offices, and public rooms for the dissemination of knowledge: lecture halls, a library, and a big room for what Hannes Meyer would call "carbohydrate administration."

5. OMA was invited to participate in the competition for this second building along with Peter Eisenman, Richard Rogers, and a handful of German architects. The site was strategic; located next to the existing eyesore, it was more or less at the center of the hill. A tall building here would condemn the surrounding fields to a premature status of residue.

6. The entire program could form a flat, double-height plate. Embedded in the hill, it would resemble a colossal step: one side exposed, the other half-buried.

7. The laboratories—the location of potentially dangerous processes—are placed in the buried side; six Zen-like patios provide daylight.

8. The public facilities are strung along an interior boulevard. Barely perceptible from the city, they offer a panoramic view of Frankfurt.

9. The patterns of the fields are reestablished in synthetic materials on the roof of the complex, each surface accommodating different open-air activities, including a lecture hall.

10. In the long term, an experimental greenhouse will represent the only connection to nature.

11. When the campus is finished and the hill is entirely covered with architecture, the half-buried building will appear as an absence: a miniature Central Park surrounded by efficient factories of learning.

373

FOREIGN NEWS

ALGERIA

The Pep Talk

Heading off for a tour of French army bases in Algeria, Charles de Gaulle kept his itinerary secret, took with him only a handful of aides and a single reporter—Agence France-Presse's Jean Mauriac, son of Novelist Francois Mauriac. In Paris, wags cracked that the general was traveling more like a spy than a head of state, and in Algiers, disgruntled European settlers jeered that he was afraid to face them. But within 24 hours, diehard French officers in Algeria were gleefully proclaiming: "We've got him!"

Traveling across Algeria's rugged countryside in helicopters and observation planes, De Gaulle ate in brigade messes, insisted on delivering a pep talk to the officers of each unit he visited. Over and over again, according to both Reporter Mauriac and army spokesmen, De Gaulle plugged a single theme: "Separated from France, Algeria would not be able to live; on the other hand, the Algerian Moslems cannot be Frenchmen from Provence or Brittany . . . The Algerian problem will not be solved for a long, long time . . . It will not be solved before the final victory brought about by French arms . . . France is determined to stay in Algeria . . . She must not leave. She will stay."

In Paris, downcast moderates puzzled over the apparent direct contradiction between these statements and De Gaulle's previous insistence that the Algerians must be allowed to choose by free vote anything from complete integration with France to complete independence. Socialist Leader Guy Mollet challenged the accuracy of Mauriac's stories, and right-wing Deputy Colonel Jean Robert ("Leather Nose") Thomazo incredulously remarked: "I was expelled from the [Gaullist] Party for saying less."

But nobody in authority (particularly in the army, delighted by the new stand) challenged Reporter Mauriac's ears. The general had long ago warned: "If the Algerian rebels persist in behaving stupidly, I will wage war." The recent equivocal response of rebel "Premier" Ferhat Abbas to De Gaulle's cease-fire offers is said to have convinced De Gaulle that the rebels are not interested in ending the Algerian war, but only in shifting blame for its continuance onto him. To unhappy Parisians, peace in Algeria seemed farther away than at any time since De Gaulle took power.

MOROCCO

The Dead City

Lying between sand-colored mountains and the blue rollers of the Atlantic, the Moroccan seaport of Agadir (pop. 48,000) felt a slight earth tremor one afternoon last week. It was strong enough to tilt the pictures in Room 6 of the Marhaba resort hotel, but Mrs. Philip Mole, a British tourist, decided against

mentioning it to her husband because he might worry. On the hilltop Casbah, a 16th century fortress, the tremor knocked over a slop pail in the mud-brick house of 16-year-old Hassan ben Mohammed, and he was scolded by his father for not having taken the pail outside. In a five-story apartment building in the European-style new city, the shock woke Mme. André Alabert from her siesta, and she called to her husband that someone was knocking at the door. He told her to go back to sleep.

Homage to Strength. Next day, life in Agadir* went on as usual. Moslem workers from the Casbah and the Talborjt quarter at the bottom of the hill traveled to their jobs in the mines, canneries and on the docks. Agadir's small Jewish colony (2,200) opened its shops and trucking offices.

Tourists Philip Mole and his wife had a swim at Agadir's superb beach, André Alabert was in the office of his prosperous electrical-equipment factory, and young Hassan took his father's three donkeys to pasture. That night at 10:50, Agadir was shaken again. Seventy-five Moslems from the Talborjt quarter hurried to their mosque confident that, on this third day of the holy month of Ramadan, Allah would "not strike us while we are paying homage to his strength, omnipotence and mercy."

Dust-Choked Dark. At 11:45 p.m., uncounted thousands of people and the entire city died. The great earthquake lasted only twelve seconds, and all of the damage was done in the two "center" seconds. In that catastrophic moment, the earth under Agadir moved 4 ft. and then wrenched back again, bringing down 70% of the city and burying its citizens in the rubble of their houses. A tidal wave from the Atlantic swept 300 yds. in from the shore. Lights went out, and the city's streets were flooded by bursting mains. Screams pierced the dust-choked dark, and fires began to flicker in the broken

---

* Known previously to aging history students as the site of a crisis that almost precipitated World War I. In 1911, as France was extending its influence over Morocco, Germany sent a small warship to Agadir to protect the "lives and property" of German merchants. British pressure finally produced a settlement.

---

city, but all of Agadir's fire engines were buried in the ruins.

In the Casbah, 98% of the buildings collapsed and nearly two-thirds of their 2,500 inhabitants died. Young Hassan saved himself and his baby sister but lost his parents and grandparents. The Talborjt quarter at the foot of the Casbah was 80% leveled. Only the minaret of the mosque remained standing: its roof and walls had fallen in, crushing the 75 worshipers. An estimated 1,500 of Agadir's 2,200 Jews perished in the night.

In the new city the ruin was not quite total. Philip Mole and his wife were playing bridge in the lobby of the Marhaba Hotel when the ceiling fell; they were even able to go to their rooms and pack their belongings before leaving the hotel. The other two tourist hotels in the city collapsed, and the wife of a vacationing U.S. Air Force lieutenant was pinned for 38 hours in the wreckage of the Hotel Saada before being rescued.

Rats & Jackals. The first help for Agadir came from the nearby French naval airbase, which sent trucks, stretchers and fire-fighting equipment. From three U.S. bases came 300 men with bulldozers, generators and portable operating rooms. Moroccan soldiers poured in the next day. The badly injured were flown out to Casablanca and Rabat 50 at a time, but the planes arrived with many dead. Other wounded lay on stretchers in the streets, calling for water during the stifling heat of day, moaning in the cold of the African night. Rats and jackals dug for food in the ruined city, and weakening voices still cried from the tumbled buildings in French, Arabic, German, Swedish and English. The exhausted rescue teams working under the blazing noonday sun wore wet handkerchiefs across the lower parts

MOROCCAN SOLDIERS LAYING OUT THE DEAD AT AGADIR
Catastrophe within the space of two seconds.

A. F. P.—Gilloon

of their faces in a futile effort to cut down the dreadful stench.

Sprinkled Lime. The recovered dead were put to rest in mass graves. A U.S. bulldozer scraped a trench 2 ft. deep, up to 100 ft. long and 10 ft. wide. Moroccan soldiers rolled the dead in, while their dazed relatives mourned in the background. When the ditch was filled with bodies, it was sprinkled with lime, and the bulldozer covered the open grave with tons of dirt. Religious scruples complicated the gravediggers' job. Imans insisted that Moslems be buried close to the surface in accordance with local tradition in Agadir, thus increasing the danger of plague. Jews begged that their dead fellow men be buried separately from the Moslems and Christians.

Few of the living could see any future for Agadir. King Mohammed V of Morocco pledged his personal fortune to start the rebuilding of the city. But one survivor said in anguish: "The only thing I'm thinking of is getting away, really away. The quicker they destroy this place the better. I doubt if they can ever get rid of the odor." At week's end, as it was feared that the toll of dead might mount above 10,000, a French café owner uttered Agadir's epitaph: "We were a peaceful union of Moslem and Christian, Arab and European. This was a prosperous city, and we had a future. We worked and behaved ourselves. We were growing. What in God's name do you suppose we did wrong?"

FRANCE

Les Téléfilles

Ever since the brothels of France were closed by law after the war, amorous Frenchmen and tourists have had to make do with the makeshift arrangement of picking up a prostitute in a bar or on the street, and then retiring to the sort of small hostelry often referred to as a *hôtel de vingt minutes*.

The system was much too crude to be Parisian, and Gabrielle Gaucher, 48, decided that the simplest solution was to introduce the call girl to France. Renting an office on Rue Laugier, not far from the Etoile, Gabrielle and a bookkeeper assistant soon assembled a list of some 400 personable girls. As the French once adopted the word "weekend," they borrowed "call girl," though some preferred to Frenchify it to *téléfilles*. When the clients came calling, Gabrielle had ready an album containing pictures of her *téléfilles*, and a brief paragraph that stated whether the girl was blonde, brunette or redheaded—and succinctly described other attributes. Sometimes Gabrielle would interview a client in depth before offering expert advice. On payment of a fee, varying from $20 to $60, the client received the telephone number of the Fifi or Gigi most suited to his taste.

The Spenders. Gabrielle usually divided the fee fifty-fifty with her girls, and had she confined her operations to supplying Paris with attractive *téléfilles*, she might never have run afoul of the law. But Gabrielle was greedy and sent some of her girls into service overseas in Casablanca, Dakar and Damascus, thus qualifying as a white-slave trafficker. Last week plump, double-chinned Gabrielle Gaucher was fined $3,600 and deprived of civil rights for ten years. Her husband Marcel, a gay boulevardier who had lived a happy, dronelike existence on his wife's earnings, could not stand the publicity, and killed himself.

Frenchmen, who delight in intellectualizing sex as much as they do politics, noted that the principal difference between the old-style *poule de luxe* and the new *téléfilles* was the elimination of the pimp, who has traditionally dominated Parisian prostitutes and exacted a brutal tribute from their earnings. In the opinion of Judge Marcel Sacotte, who has written a modest but informative monograph on the subject, the call girl is better educated than ordinary prostitutes. Gabrielle had insisted that each of her girls supply proof of her education, discretion and relatively amateur standing, and her list included teachers, artists, manicurists, models, a dentist, and a few young girls referred to as "starlets." An estimated 75% were divorcees, 20% unmarried, and only 5% wandering wives.

In Judge Sacotte's opinion, the call girls "have one feature in common: an extraordinary facility in spending money. As a consequence, their legitimate profession —if they have one—never earns them enough. Hence the necessity to obtain extra money through a partner of the moment, announced by telephone and furnished with discretion."

The Tolerance. Sacotte also finds that call girls often drop out of the business and then take it up again when in need of extra income. Thus, reasons the judge, there is more hope of eventually winning a call girl back to respectable life than is the case with common prostitutes, and more tolerance for the call girl from police and magistrates. In concluding his essay, Judge Sacotte gave generous and unstinted credit for this advance in "de luxe prostitution, perfected and modernized by the employment of the telephone," not to Gabrielle Gaucher but to its true innovator, the U.S.

GREAT BRITAIN

The Unhappy Memory

In London last week the bitterest and most divisive British political controversy of modern times flared into renewed life. Once again Englishmen argued in passionate detail the rights and wrongs of the Suez invasion of 1956. Cause of the furor: publication of *Full Circle*, the memoirs of former Prime Minister Sir Anthony Eden.

In the *Observer*, Sir William Hayter, who was Britain's Ambassador to Moscow at the time, wrote that Suez "was morally repulsive to many people (myself included)." After World War II, Sir William continues, Britain, though declining as a military power, was gaining a new reputation for "moderation, wisdom, respect for international law . . . Suez blew it all away," and Britain was made to appear "the same old grasping imperialist as ever, but toothless and rather incompetent." If Eden had not resorted to force, "some kind of international element in the control of the canal would have been preserved; the weakness of Great Britain and France would not have been so publicly demonstrated, and many people now dead would be alive."

Labor Pains. Labor Party Leader Hugh Gaitskell, plainly nettled by Eden's statement that he regarded Gaitskell's rise to leadership of the Labor Party as "a national misfortune," said that his own view of Eden as a Prime Minister was "even stronger," and bluntly called Eden's account of the Opposition's role during the

After the earthquake, Agadir was reconstructed in the 1960s as a typical New Town — mostly modern architecture by French architects in a kind of idyllic CIAM idiom, its post-Corbusian concrete cubes almost benign in the Moroccan sun. It is not grand; its only resemblance to a resort is the seemingly accidental fact that this small urban prototype confronts kilometers of impeccable tropical beach.

On the other side of town lives the Moroccan king, or at least a forbidden oasis there is the site of one of his five palaces. Comings and goings of helicopters are the only visible sign of his presence (or absence).

Between the invisible palace and the innocent town, a group of "friends of the king" is developing a "new" Agadir. A beaux-arts composition of boulevards, plazas, and axes defines individual plots the size of mini-palaces. Between this sector and the palace, a new 18-hole golf course ensures the king's privacy. For the launch of the new Agadir, the king and his party landed by Concorde at the otherwise unremarkable airport.

Islam After Einstein

Palm Bay Seafront Hotel and Convention Center
Agadir, Morocco
Competition, 1990

Two of the dominant axes of the new Agadir converge at a eucalyptus forest on the beach. This focal point is the obvious (too obvious?) site for the Palm Bay Seafront Hotel and Convention Center, which would remove definitively the stigma of sobriety that has clung to this city since the earthquake.

An international competition was held: from Japan, Kazuo Shinohara; from America, Antoine Predock (fresh from Euro Disney's Hotel Santa Fe); from France, Richard Simounet, architect of the Picasso Museum in Paris; from "Europe," OMA. Globalization reaches Agadir.

At first sight, the size of the program — its possible delusions of grandeur — seems overwhelmingly at odds with the fragrant, almost virginal beauty of the site. In a context of systematically compromised authenticity, it seemed cruel and unusual to destroy part of its remaining natural qualities. Were these boulevards and axes dreams of Africa? Should they be answered? What could be the status of projections in such a conceptual quicksand? Was there a way to escape the apparent necessity for a monument or a climax?

379

truth which the actual building expresses in material stuff.

EUGENIC

An agreeable group calling itself the Society for the Betterment of the Human Race picked three men and three women who have, it announced, the "natural endowments" to be the ideal "eugenic parents." The perfect ancestors turned out to be cinema actors Clark Gable and Burt Lancaster, radio singer Jack Smith and Hollywood's Jane Russell, Betty Grable and Linda Darnell.

EVERY

Rachmaninoff created enduring music at the Steinway, as did Paderewski, Berlioz, Gounod. Today virtually every great artist uses the Steinway: Brailowsky, Casadesus, Gorodnitzki, Hofmann, Horowitz, Kapel, Liszt, Mayner, Menuhin, Reiner, Artur Rubinstein, Rodzinski, Serkin, Wallenstein, Whitmore & Lowe, Zaremba, and many more . . . For the name of your nearest Steinway representative, consult your local classified telephone directory.

EVERYONE

Everyone changes in time.

EX

Look at it logically — an ex is usually an ex for good reason.

EXAGGERATION

In a certain kingdom once lived a poor miller who had a very beautiful daughter. She was moreover exceedingly shrewd and clever; and the miller was so vain and proud of her, that he one day told the king of the land that his daughter could spin gold out of straw.

EXCEPTIONS

"I have also thought of a model city from which I deduce all the others," Marco answered. "It is a city made only of exceptions, exclusions, incongruities, contradictions. If such a city is the most improbable, by reducing the number of elements, we increase the probability that the city really exists. So I have only to subtract exceptions from my model, and in whatever direction I proceed, I will arrive at one of the cities which, always as an exception, exists. But I cannot force my operation beyond a certain limit: I would achieve cities too probable to be real."

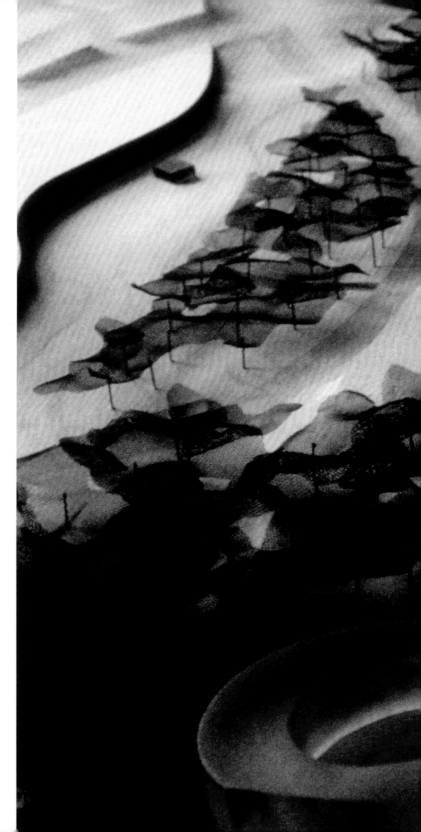

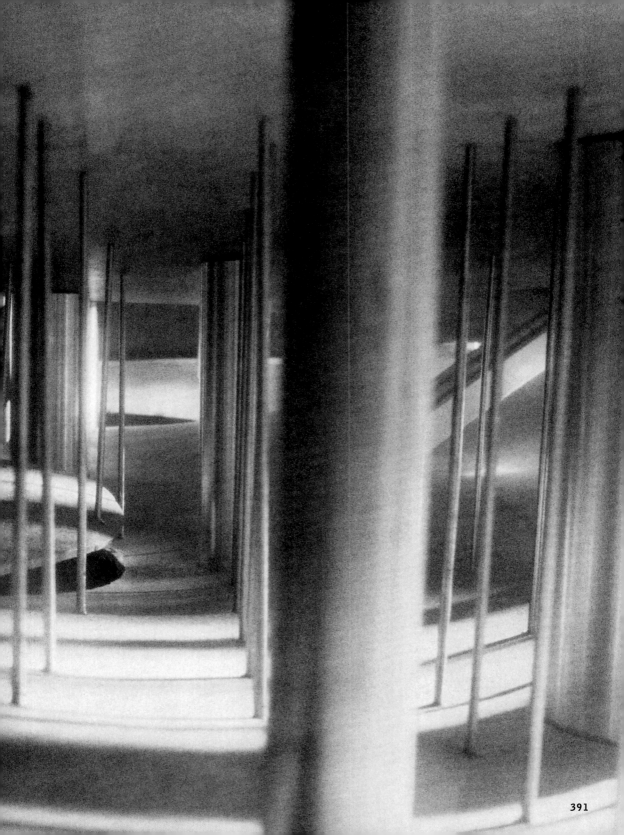

393

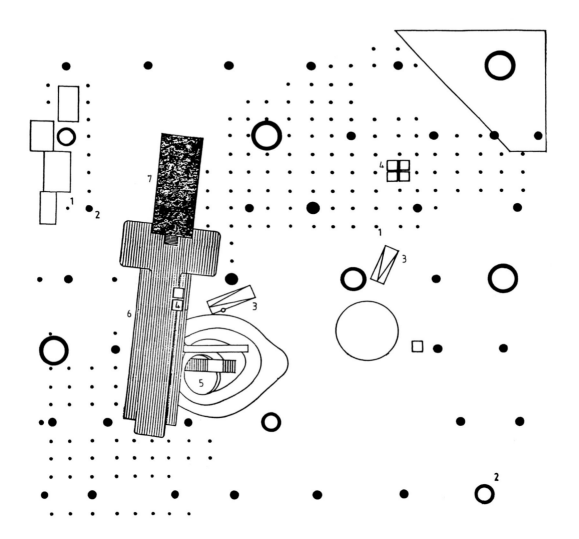

casino (+14 meters)

1. hanger
2. hollow column
3. escalator
4. elevator
5. void to basement
6. casino
7. bar

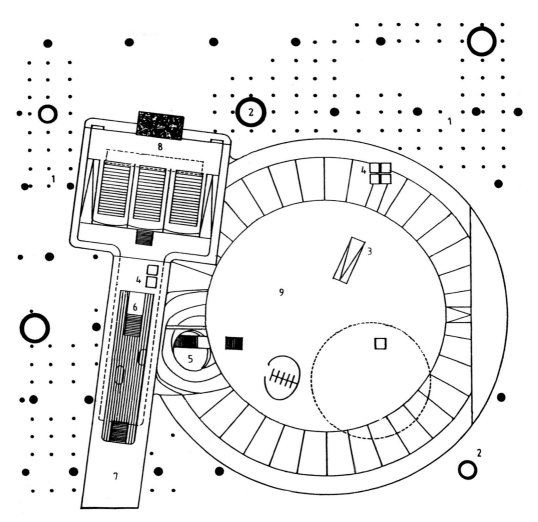

nightclub and royal chamber
(+17 meters)

1. hanger
2. hollow column
3. escalator
4. elevator
5. void to basement
6. void to casino
7. nightclub
8. cinemas
9. royal chamber

0   50m

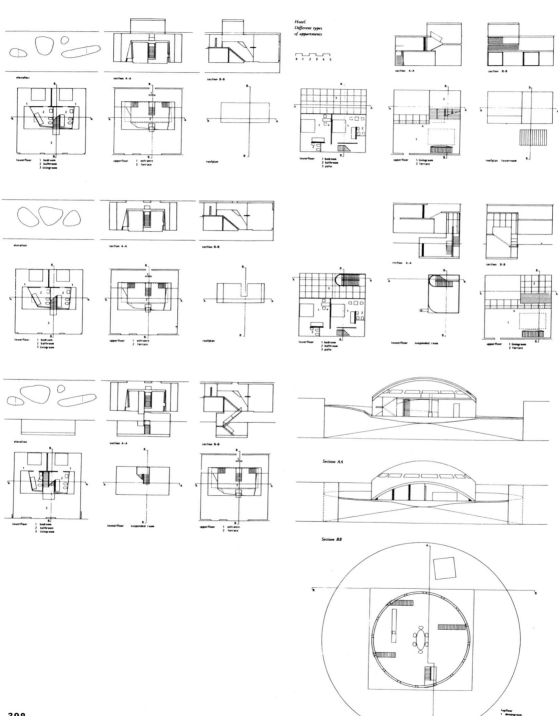

elevation

section A-A

section B-B

lowerfloor
1 bedroom
2 bathroom
3 livingroom

upperfloor
1 entrance
2 terrace

roofplan

Hotel.
*Different types
of appartments*

section A-A

section B-B

lowerfloor
1 bedroom
2 bathroom
3 patio

upperfloor
1 livingroom
2 terrace

roofplan towerroom

elevation

section A-A

section B-B

lowerfloor
1 bedroom
2 bathroom
3 livingroom

upperfloor
1 entrance
2 terrace

roofplan

section A-A

section B-B

lowerfloor
1 bedroom
2 bathroom
3 patio

lowestfloor
suspended room

upperfloor
1 livingroom
2 terrace

elevation

section A-A

section B-B

lowerfloor
1 bedroom
2 bathroom
3 livingroom

lowestfloor
suspended room

upperfloor
1 entrance
2 terrace

Section AA

Section BB

topfloor
1 diningroom

Royal Chambre

398

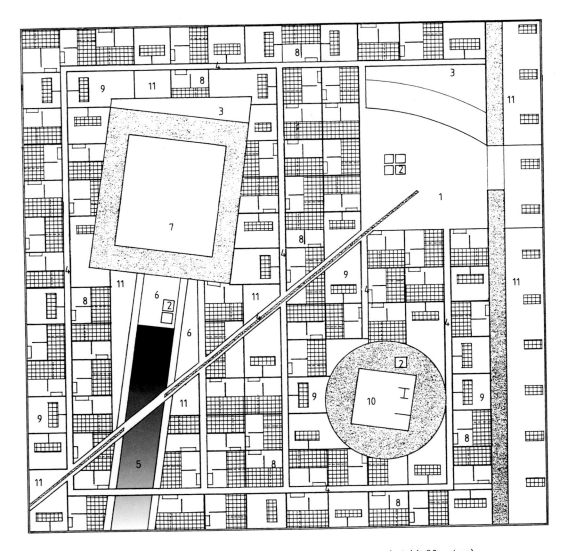

hotel (+20 meters)

1. lounge
2. elevator
3. void to veranda
4. alley
5. swimming pool
6. dressing rooms
7. gymnasium
8. hotel suite type 1
9. hotel suite type 2
10. royal chamber
11. service and technical rooms

0   50m

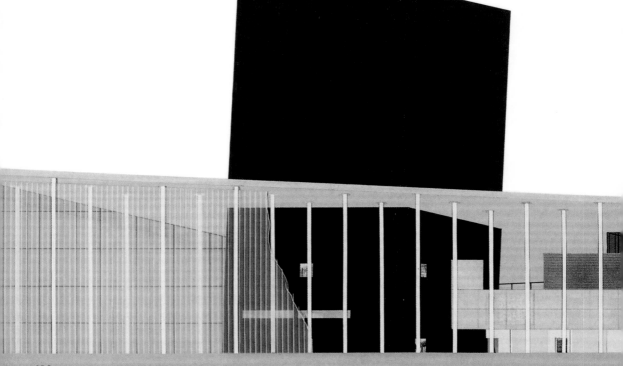

Key to Romantic Garden

- Spirea japonica "Snowmound"
- Spirea vanhouttei
- Viburnum plicatum "Mariesii"
- Hydrangea macrophylla "Veitchii"
- Viburnum tinus "Variegatum"
- Hamamelis japonica
- Hamamelis mollis
- Hamamelis virginiana
- Cornus mas
- Chimonanthus praecox
- Mahonia x wagneri "Undulata"
- Mahonia aquifolium
- Ilex aquifolium "Bacciflava"
- Amelanchier lamarckii
- Euonymus fortunei "Coloratus"
- Rosa virginiana
- Berberis thunbergii
- Rosa rugosa
- Rosa nitida
- Spirea x bumalda "Anthony Waterer"
- Ilex crenata
- Ilex crenata "Convexa"
- Hypericum "Hidcote"
- Potentilla fruticosa "Tangerine"
- Potentilla fruticosa var. rigida
- Rubus odoratus
- Cornus florida
- Cornus alba "Sibirica Variegata"
- Cornus stolonifera "Keysey's Dwarf"
- Salix alba "Vitellina"
- Prunus lusitanica
- Cotoneaster horisontalis
- Magnolia liliiflora "Nigra"
- Viburnum opulus
- Poncirus trifoliata
- Buddleja globosa
- Skimmia japonica "Thumb"
- Erica herbacea "Springwood White"
- Cytisus x kewensis
- Salix lanata
- Lonicera nitida "Baggesen's Gold"
- Salix viminalis
- Azalea mollis "Dr. M. Oosthoek"
- Acer palmatum "Atropurpureum"
- Rhododendron "Catawbiense Boursault"
- Carpinus betulus "Purpurea"
- Vinca minor
- Ajuga reptans "Atropurpurea"
- Asarum europaeum
- Viola labradorica
- Hedera helix "Glacier"

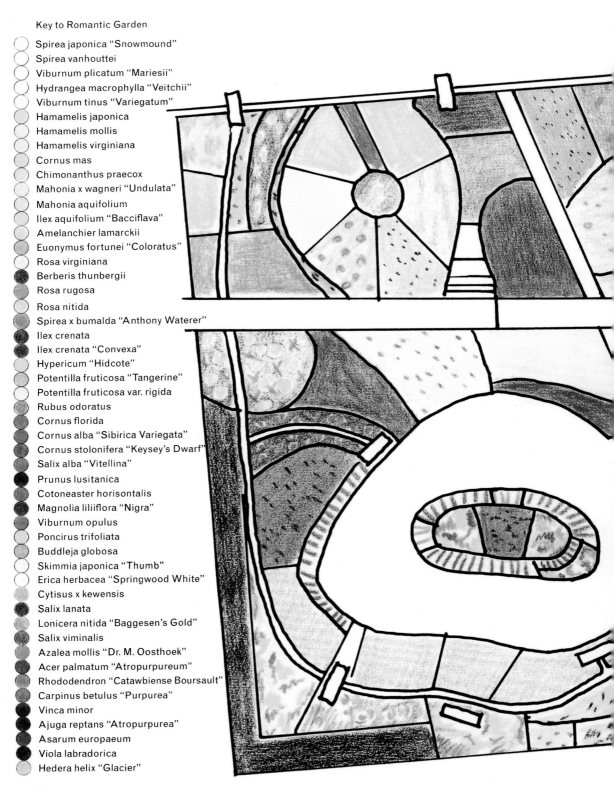

426

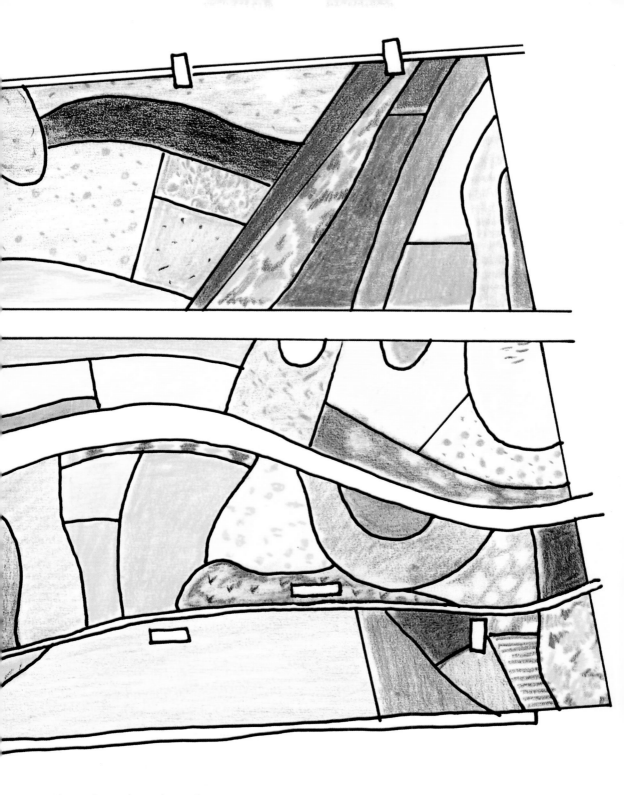

0   20m

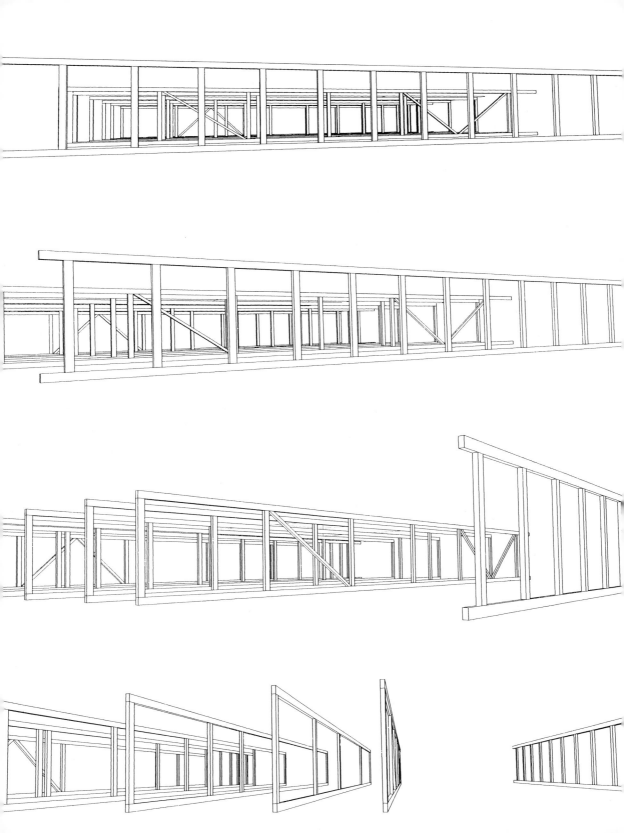

Kunsthal I

The Architecture Museum is a study in weight and heaviness; Kunsthal I floats above the park at the level of the dike. The core of the Architecture Museum is solid; the center of Kunsthal I is a void, a machine or robot that enables, like a stage tower, an endless series of permutations: walls, floors, slopes, sets, presence, absence, dry, wet—each condition contaminating the perimeter of the hall.

This 60x60–meter glass box is carried by vierendeel beams whose structural depth coincides with the usable depth of the building. The vierendeels form a catalog: each one is different, from the regular and closely spaced to a logarithmic sequence of ever-increasing intervals and structural dimensions. Since the horizontal sections of the vierendeels are accommodated in the floor and ceiling, the beams read as columns.

If in the Architecture Museum the regular grid of columns stabilizes an irregular form, in Kunsthal I the apparently chaotic aspect of the compressed perspective of the beams—a random anti-grid—destabilizes the regular form; its logic becomes apparent only in passing through the different planes of the structure.

Jo Coenen won the competition for the Architecture Museum and built it. With the demise of our museum, Kunsthal I became a pathetic remnant. But the future director's dislike for the design offered us a pretext to start all over again...

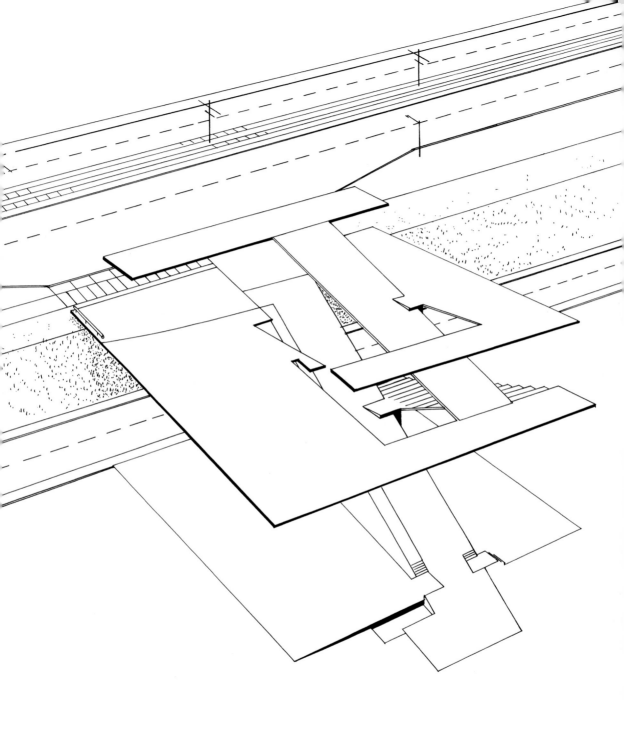

Life in the Box?

Kunsthal II
Rotterdam, Netherlands
Completed 1992

We would keep the same square as a general envelope.

The square would be crossed by two routes: one, the existing road running east-west; the other, a public ramp running north-south, the entrance to both the park and the Kunsthal.

These crossings would divide the square into four parts.

The question then became:

How to imagine a spiral in four separate squares?

I'm not
a historian.

Approach the building from the boulevard.

we embraced
we were happy...
happy... what do we do
ow that we're happy
...go on waiting...
waiting... let me think
...it's coming... go on
waiting... now that
we're happy... let me
see... ah! The tree!

The tree?

Do you not

It slopes down toward the park.

I'm tired.

Halfway down, enter the auditorium.

Look u

It slopes in the opposite direction.

In a single night.

Walk down.

It must be the
Spring.

Turn the corner.

But

a single night!

Enter the lower hall, facing the park.

I tell you
we weren't here
yesterday.
Another of your
nightmares.

It is dark, with a forest of five columns.

And where were we yesterday evening according to you?

To the right, a slender aperture opens to a narrow gallery.

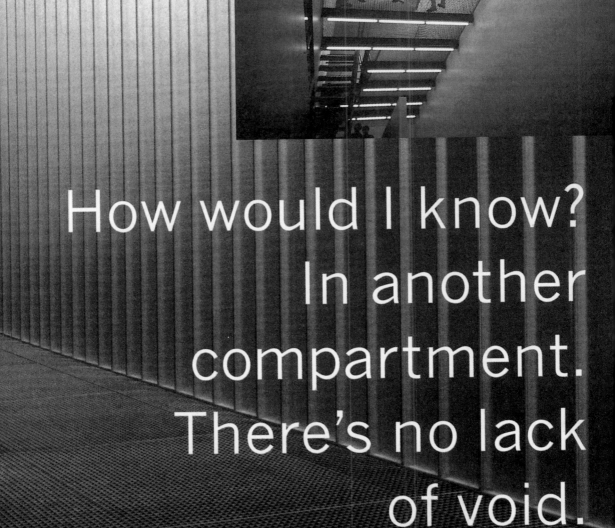

How would I know?
In another
compartment.
There's no lack
of void.

Look up.

Good.
We weren't here
yesterday evening.
Now
what did we do
yesterday evening?

Rediscover the ramp you used to enter. Walk up.

Do?

A glass wall separates the people outside.

Try and
remember.

At the top...

Do... I suppose
we blathered.

...turn left.

About what?

Enter the second hall. It is bright, with no columns.

Oh ... this and that I suppose, nothing in particular. Yes, now I remember, yesterday evening we spent blathering about nothing in particular. That's been going on now for half a century.

Look back...

You don't
remember
any fact, any
circumstance?

Don't torment
me, Didi.

Exit under the balcony.

The sun.
The moon.
Do you not
remember?

See the auditorium, but don't walk that far. Instead, turn and take a third ramp. Halfway up, grope through
a small dark room ...

They must have been there, as usual.

...and emerge on a balcony that penetrates the second hall.

u didn't notice
anything
out of the ordinary?

Return to the ramp, run up, and emerge on the roof. Look down.

Alas!

Spiral back down to the beginning.

Exit to the park.

What were you saying when?

Pause.

At the very
beginning.

Turn the corner.

The very beginning of WHAT?

Pass the restaurant underneath the auditorium.

KU

Hofcultuur
uit Indonesië

tot 17 januari '93

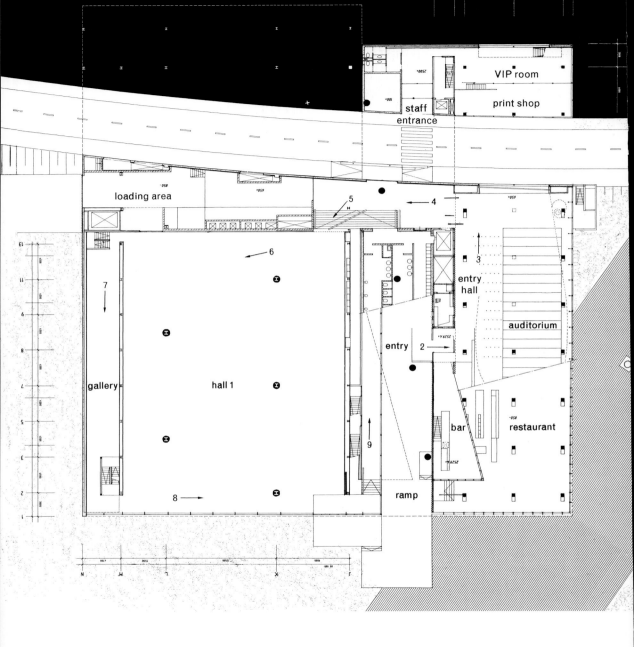

VIP room

print shop

staff
entrance

loading area

5

4

3

6

entry
hall

7

entry

2

auditorium

gallery

hall 1

9

bar

restaurant

8

ramp

park level

468

FRANKF...

Neue Sachlichkeit

bg.

Steinb.

Schwalb.

Esch- born

Hatters- hm.

erb.

Bütteborn E 451

Mörfldn.

USSELS- M.

Walldf.

Dreieich

Langen

Egelsb.

Erzhsn.

Weiterst. DARMSTADT

a. Main

Bad Vilbel

Maintal

ADAC

ADAC

OFF BA

Obertsh

15

Neu- Isenbg.

661

Dietzenb.

Langen

459

Röder- mark

Heuse stamr

12

14

Messel

45

E 42

Nidda

1991

9

11

6

2 5

3

2

8

8

6

7

8

9

8

8

22

20

1

2

14

17

10

16

11

4

6 12

14

7

4

5

9

4

4

16

475

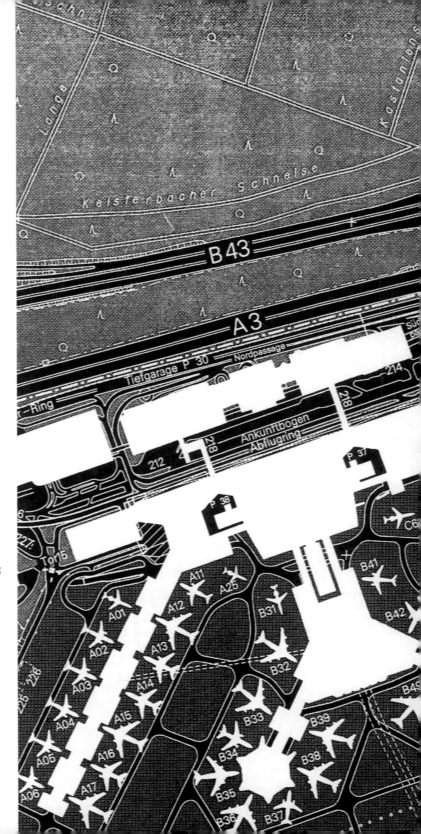

FAITH

The trouble with Mr. Cram is that
he has no faith in God. I will design
a church for you that will be the
greatest church in the world. It will
include all the hotels, swimming
tanks and candy stores you desire.
Furthermore, in the basement will
be the largest garage in Christendom
because I will build your church on
toothpicks and have faith enough in
God to believe it will stand up.

FAKERS

Unfortunately, I remember all too
well Colonial Williamsburg where
the authentic costumes were made
out of dacron and poly and the shoes
were naughahyde. I remember
exactly how much I detested seeing
these fakers in these clothes as I
was then very concerned with detail.
Even more than the outer garments, I
imagined that of course they weren't
wearing the right undergarments. I
knew in my heart that, for instance,
the person who was dressed up to
look like the 1790s blacksmith had
on modern Fruit of the Loom under-
pants. Hiding under colonial skirts
that the women wore were cheap
seventy-nine-cent nylon pantyhose
from Woolworth's. This bothered
me very much.

FAKES[1]

Fakes teach us many things, most
obviously perhaps the fallibility of
experts.

FAKES[2]

He possessed a wonderful collection
of tropical plants, fashioned by the
hands of true artists, following
Nature step by step... This admir-
able artistry had long enthralled
him, but now he dreamt of collecting
another kind of flora: tired of artificial flowers aping real ones, he
wanted some natural flowers that
would look like fakes.

FALSE-DAY

The technology of the VCR creates
a day, an additional "false-day";
you have a secondary day which
comes into being for you alone, just
as in the secondary residence whole
heating turns on of its own accord
when it gets cold. That's just like a
day that emerges for you, which is
staged; there is a sort of electronic
cosmography.

FAMOUS

If real, this set would cost $5,000.

But like the most famous women, you can have all six pairs (clip or pierced) for only $29.50. 30-day money-back guarantee.

FANATIC

Fanaticism is to superstition what delirium is to fever, and what fury is to anger. The man who has ecstasies and vision, who takes dreams for realities, and his imaginings for prophecies, is an enthusiast. The man who backs his madness with murder is a fanatic.

FANTASTIC

How can so many mediocre buildings together generate such a fantastic architectural spectacle? How can so much "badness" sometimes lead to a kind of intelligence?

FASHION

What goes out of fashion passes into everyday life. What disappears from everyday life is revived in fashion.

FATE

The challenging revealing has its origins a destining in bringing-forth. But at the same time Enframing, in a way characteristic of a destining, blocks *poesis*... technology is the fate of our age, where *fate* means the inevitableness of an unalterable course.

FATHER

The triumph over the Father must have been planned and fantasised through countless generations before it was realised.

FATHERS

Behind the superficial categories of "ancient" and "modern," of "classical" and "experimental," one can read a parallel history of the cinema where fathers do not always come before sons.

FAX

"Fax" is shorthand: It's a verb meaning to send a document from one facsimile machine to another, a noun meaning the document sent, and another noun for the machine itself. The facsimile machine is simply a photocopier that knows how to use the phone. So you can fax a fax from your fax to any other fax in the world—a miracle indeed.

FEATURED

My pregnancy was first announced on the "I Love Lucy" show December 8, 1952. From then until the day my son was born my condition was featured on a televised

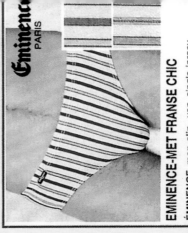

ÉMINENCE-MET FRANSE CHIC

ÉMINENCE men-slip, van single-jersey, van 100% gemerceriseerde katoen. Kl.: Vanaf (royalblauw) 15, (mint) 37, (seringen) 87.
N273/775 Mt.: 3, 4, 5   27.95
N273/775 Mt.: 6, 7   30.95

27

dorlastan
de elastische

EVERSIT-STERK IN STYLING

Set (=2 stuks) slips van EVERSIT. Van 100% gemerceriseerde katoen. Kl.: (wit) 09, (marine) 11, (rood) 65.
N269/336 Mt.: 4, 5   24.95
N269/336 Mt.: 6, 7   27.95

Vanaf 2495

ASCOT

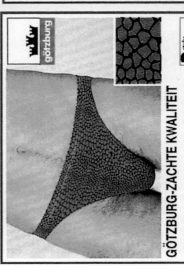

GÖTZBURG-ZACHTE KWALITEIT

Set (=2 stuks) slips van GÖTZBURG. Van single-jersey van 100% katoen. Kl.: (assorti) 99.
N269/913 Mt.: 4, 5   29.95
N269/913 Mt.: 6, 7   32.95

Vanaf 2995

ASCOT

AKTUELE SLIP-BOUTIQUE

SCHIESSER-VOOR SPORTIEVE MANNEN

SCHIESSER bluebird-slip in nauwsluitend model met platte boordjes. Van single-jersey van 95% Egyptische katoen, 5% Elasthan. **Kl.:** (wit) **09**, (gentiaan) **14**, (maïs) **42**.

N267/325 Mt.: 4, 5, 6, 7

27.95   20.75

20

GÖTZBURG-MARITIEME DESSINS

Set (= 2 stuks) mini-slips van GÖTZ-BURG met sportief scheepjesdessin. Single-jersey van 100% katoen. **Kl.:** (assorti) **99.**

| N269/050 | Mt.: 4, 5 | 27.95 |
| N269/050 | Mt.: 6, 7 | 29.95 |

Vanaf

2795

2 stuks verpakking

GLOBETROTTER-3X SPORTIEF

Set (= 3 stuks) slips van GLOBETROTTER met label en elastische band. Single-jersey van 100% katoen. **Kl.:** (assorti) **99.**

| N267/228 | Mt.: 4, 5 | 19.95 |
| N267/228 | Mt.: 6, 7 | 21.95 |

Vanaf

199

3 stuks verpakking

ASCOT-NIEUW GEMODELLEERD

Set (= 2 stuks) tanga-slips van ASCOT van single-jersey van 100% supergekamde, gemerceriseerde katoen. **Kl.:** (assorti) **99.**

| N269/905 | Mt.: 4, 5 | 27.95 |
| N269/905 | Mt.: 6, 7 | 29.95 |

Vanaf

2795

2 stuks verpakking

GÖTZBURG-KWALITEIT DIE MEN ZIET

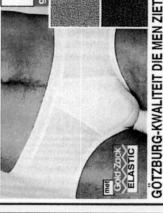

Men-slip van GÖTZBURG met Goldzack band. Fijne rib van 100% gekamde katoen, dus huidvriendelijk. **Kl.:** (wit) **09**, (marine) **11**, (blauw) **15.**

| N584/290 | Mt.: 4, 5 | 17.95 |
| N584/290 | Mt.: 6, 7 | 19.95 |

Vanaf

1795

IMPETUS-TEMPERAMENTVOLLE SLIP

Set (= 2 stuks) tanga-slips van IMPETUS met elastische band. Single-jersey van 100% katoen. **Kl.:** (assorti) **99.**

| N268/488 | Mt.: 4, 5 | 22.95 |
| N268/488 | Mt.: 6, 7 | 24.95 |

vanaf

2295

2 stuks verpakking

ASCOT-ORIGINELE, BONTE MOTIEVEN

Set (= 2 stuks) minislips van ASCOT van single-jersey van 100% katoen. **Kl.:** (assorti) **99.**

| N268/739 | Mt.: 4, 5 | 27.95 |
| N268/739 | Mt.: 6, 7 | 29.95 |

Vanaf

2795

2 stuks verpakking

EVERSIT-ONDERMODE MET "SCHWUNG"

Set (= 3 stuks) minislips van EVERSIT. Uitstekende pasvorm, opvallend dessin. Single-jersey van 100% katoen. **Kl.:** (assorti) **99.**

| N268/321 | Mt.: 4, 5 | 25.— |
| N268/321 | Mt.: 6, 7 | 27.50 |

Vanaf

25.-

3 stuks verpakking

ELZA-DE BRUTALE SLIP

Set (= 2 stuks) mini-stringtanga's in leder-look. Smal elastisch bandje achter. Van 100% Polyamide. **Kl.:** (assorti) **99.**

N585/742 Voor alle maten   19.95

vanaf

1995

2 stuks verpakking

483

west elevation

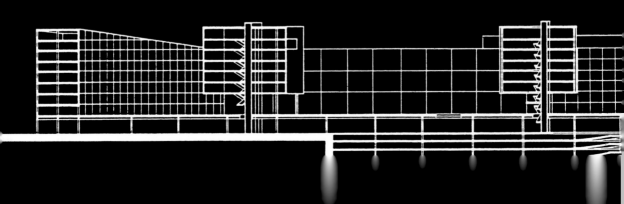

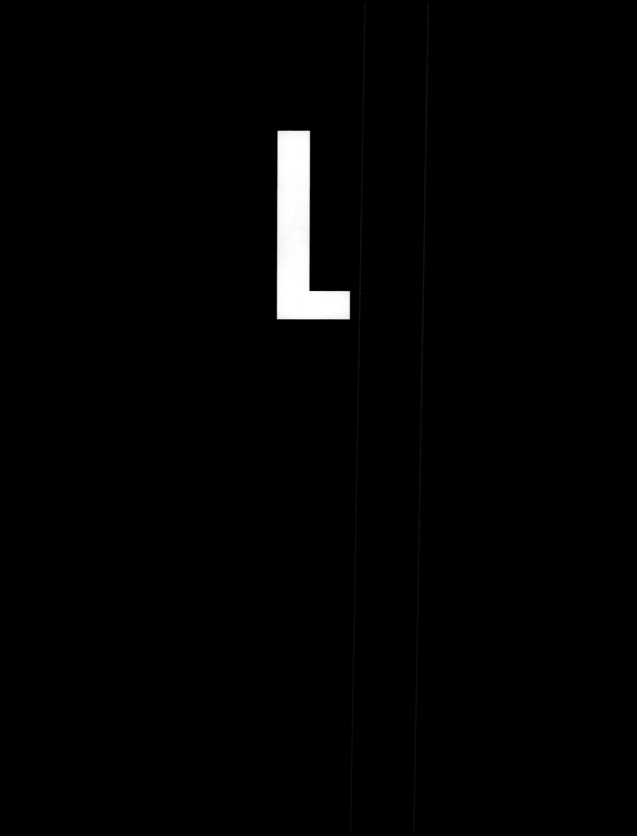

of a new wave of modernization that would engulf—in more or less camouflaged form—the Old World, provoking episodes of a new beginning even on the "finished" continent.

Against the background of Europe, the shock of Bigness forced us to make what was implicit in *Delirious New York* explicit in our work.

Bigness became a double polemic, confronting earlier attempts at integration and concentration *and* contemporary doctrines that question the possibility of the Whole and the Real as viable categories and resign themselves to architecture's supposedly inevitable disassembly and dissolution.

Europeans had surpassed the threat of Bigness by theorizing it beyond the point of application. Their contribution had been the "gift" of the megastructure, a kind of all-embracing, all-enabling technical support that ultimately questioned the status of the individual building: a very safe Bigness, its true implications excluding implementation. Yona Friedman's *urbanisme spatiale* (1958) was emblematic: Bigness floats over Paris like a metallic blanket of clouds, promising unlimited but unfocused potential renewal of "everything," but never lands, never confronts, never claims its rightful place – criticism as decoration.

In 1972, Beaubourg – Platonic Loft –

had proposed spaces where "anything" was possible. The resulting flexibility was unmasked as the imposition of a theoretical average at the expense of both character and precision—*entity* at the price of *identity*. Perversely, its sheer demonstrativeness precluded the genuine neutrality realized without effort in the American skyscraper.

So marked was the generation of May '68, *my* generation—supremely intelligent, well informed, correctly traumatized by selected cataclysms, frank in its borrowings from other disciplines—by the failure of this and similar models of density and integration—by their systematic insensitivity to the particular—that it proposed two major defense lines: dismantlement and disappearance.

In the first, the world is decomposed into incompatible fractals of uniqueness, each a pretext for further disintegration of the whole: a paroxysm of fragmentation that turns the particular into a *system*. Behind this breakdown of program according to the smallest functional particles looms the perversely unconscious revenge of the old form-follows-function doctrine that drives the content of the project — behind fireworks of intellectual and formal sophistication — relentlessly toward the anticlimax of diagram, doubly disappointing since its aesthetic suggests the rich orchestration of chaos. In this landscape of dismemberment and phony disorder, each activity is *put in its place*.

The programmatic hybridizations/

proximities/frictions/overlaps/super-positions that are possible in Bigness — in fact, the entire apparatus of *montage* invented at the beginning of the century to organize relationships between independent parts — are being undone by one section of the present avant-garde in compositions of almost laughable pedantry and rigidity, behind apparent wildness.

The second strategy, disappearance, transcends the question of Bigness — of massive presence — through an extended engagement with simulation, virtuality, nonexistence.

A patchwork of arguments scavenged since the sixties from American sociologists, ideologues, philosophers, French intellectuals, cybermystics, etc., suggests that architecture will be the first "solid that melts into air" through the combined effects of demographic trends, electronics, media, speed, the economy, leisure, the death of God, the book, the phone, the fax, affluence, democracy, the end of the Big Story…

Preempting architecture's actual disappearance, *this* avant-garde is experimenting with real or simulated virtuality, reclaiming, in the name of modesty, its former omnipotence in the world of virtual reality (where fascism may be pursued with impunity?).

Maximum

Paradoxically, the Whole and the Real ceased to exist as possible enterprises for the architect exactly at the moment where the approaching end of the second millennium saw an all-out rush to reorganization, consolidation, expansion, a clamoring for megascale. Otherwise engaged, an entire profession was incapable, finally, of exploiting dramatic social and economic events that, if confronted, could restore its credibility.

The absence of a theory of Bigness—what is the maximum architecture can do?—is architecture's most debilitating weakness. Without a theory of Bigness, architects are in the position of Frankenstein's creators: instigators of a partly successful experiment whose results are running amok and are therefore discredited.

Because there is no theory of Bigness, we don't know what to do with it, we don't know where to put it, we don't know when to use it, we don't know how to plan it. Big mistakes are our only connection to Bigness.

But in spite of its dumb name, Bigness is a theoretical domain at this *fin de siècle*: in a landscape of disarray, disassembly, dissociation, disclamation, the attraction of Bigness is its potential to reconstruct the Whole, resurrect the Real, reinvent the collective, reclaim maximum possibility.

Only through Bigness can architecture dissociate itself from the exhausted artistic/ideological movements of modernism and formalism to regain its instrumentality as vehicle of modernization.

Bigness recognizes that architecture as we know it is in difficulty, but it does not overcompensate through regurgitations of even more architecture. It proposes a new economy in which no longer "all is architecture," but in which a strategic position is regained through retreat and concentration, yielding the rest of a contested territory to enemy forces.

Beginning

Bigness destroys, but it is also a new beginning. It can reassemble what it breaks.

A paradox of Bigness is that in spite of the calculation that goes into its planning — in fact, through its very rigidities — it is the one architecture that engineers the unpredictable. Instead of enforcing coexistence, Bigness depends on regimes of freedoms, the assembly of maximum difference.

Only Bigness can sustain a promiscuous proliferation of events in a single container. It develops strategies to organize both their independence and interdependence within a larger entity in a symbiosis that exacerbates rather than compromises specificity.

Through contamination rather than purity

and quantity rather than quality, only Bigness can support genuinely new relationships between functional entities that expand rather than limit their identities. The artificiality and complexity of Bigness release function from its defensive armor to allow a kind of liquefaction; programmatic elements react with each other to create new events — Bigness returns to a model of programmatic *alchemy*.

At first sight, the activities amassed in the structure of Bigness *demand* to interact, but Bigness also keeps them apart. Like plutonium rods that, more or less immersed, dampen or promote nuclear reaction, Bigness regulates the intensities of programmatic coexistence.

Although Bigness is a blueprint for perpetual intensity, it also offers degrees of serenity and even blandness. It is simply impossible to animate its entire mass with intention. Its vastness exhausts architecture's compulsive need to decide and determine. Zones will be left out, free from architecture.

Team

Bigness is where architecture becomes both most and least architectural: most because of the enormity of the object; least through the loss of autonomy — it becomes instrument of other forces, it *depends*.

Bigness is impersonal: the architect is no longer condemned to stardom.

Even as Bigness enters the stratosphere of architectural ambition — the pure chill of megalomania — it can be achieved only at the price of giving up control, of transmogrification. It implies a web of umbilical cords to other disciplines whose performance is as critical as the architect's: like mountain climbers tied together by life-saving ropes, the makers of Bigness are a *team* (a word not mentioned in the last 40 years of architectural polemic).

Beyond signature, Bigness means surrender to technologies; to engineers, contractors, manufacturers; to politics; to others. It promises architecture a kind of post-heroic status — a realignment with neutrality.

Bastion

If Bigness transforms architecture, its accumulation generates a new kind of city. The exterior of the city is no longer a collective theater where "it" happens; there's no collective "it" left. The street has become residue, organizational device, mere segment of the continuous metropolitan plane where the remnants of the past face the equipments of the new in an uneasy standoff. Bigness can exist *anywhere* on that plane. Not only is Bigness incapable of establishing relationships with the classical city — *at most, it coexists*

— but in the quantity and complexity of the facilities it offers, it is itself urban.

Bigness no longer needs the city: it competes with the city; it represents the city; it preempts the city; or better still, it *is* the city. If urbanism generates potential and architecture exploits it, Bigness enlists the generosity of urbanism against the meanness of architecture.

Bigness = urbanism vs. architecture.

Bigness, through its very independence of context, is the one architecture that can survive, even exploit, the now-global condition of the tabula rasa: it does not take its inspiration from givens too often squeezed for the last drop of meaning; it gravitates opportunistically to locations of maximum infrastructural promise; it is, finally, its own raison d'être.

In spite of its size, it is modest.

Not all architecture, not all program, not all

events will be swallowed by Bigness. There are many "needs" too unfocused, too weak, too unrespectable, too defiant, too secret, too subversive, too weak, too "nothing" to be part of the constellations of Bigness. Bigness is the last bastion of architecture — a contraction, a hyper-architecture. The containers of Bigness will be landmarks in a post-architectural landscape — a world scraped of architecture in the way Richter's paintings are scraped of paint: inflexible, immutable, definitive, forever there, generated through superhuman effort. Bigness surrenders the field to after-architecture. 1994

1.

Late seventies dilemma: stay in **USA** or go back to Europe?

USA: postmodernism triumphant.

Europe: historicism on the rise—the "new" superseded, maybe forever?

USA: freedom from context.

Europe: context is all.

USA: everything big.

Europe: everything small.

OMA: only a front—in fact, we are teaching in London at the **AA**.

Paradox: *Delirious New York* generates "fame"—superimposed on complete inexperience. Postmodern combination.

Question (and doubt): is there "theoretical" architecture? Can architecture embody ideas? Or is it just space, a subject so far denied? (The book can be seen as an elaborate argument for its irrelevance.)

Then, one day in 1979, an event intervenes (and I realize that from now on, events will decide my dilemmas, instead of my dilemmas deciding the events).

518

Soft Substance, Harsh Town

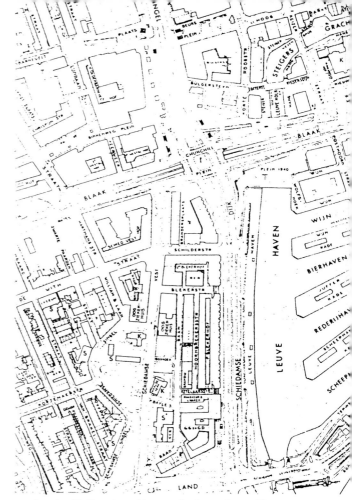

2.

A Rotterdam councillor (the vice mayor for building) calls me in London. He
wants to see me. When I meet him, he sits in front of a colossal plan of the city.
"Which site do you want?" he asks with un-Dutch generosity.

I point to an almost nonexistent speck, framed by obstacles. To the south:
the Maas Boulevard (four lanes) and Maas River (300 meters wide at that
point); to the north: a canal; to the east: a bridge—Willemsbrug—where in
1940 Dutch Marines made their last stand; to the west: a seven-story slab
(later OMA's office).

The site is 120 meters long; it tapers from 40 to 20 meters in width. It is a
residue, mostly grass. The city planning office has already imagined a program—housing—and a form for the site: a building that steps down from seven
stories to three, connecting to a future pedestrian level.

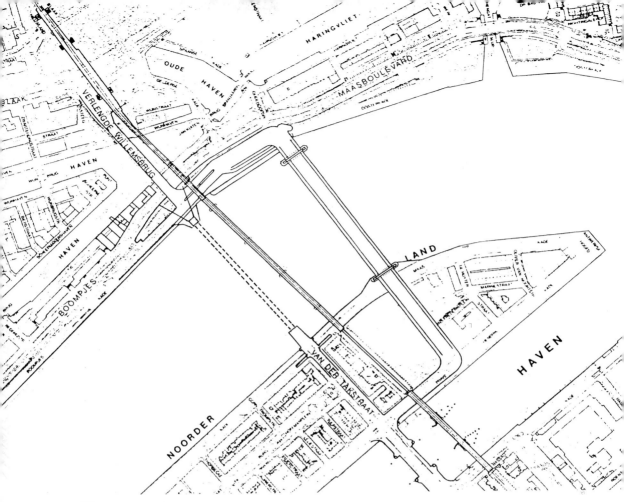

3.

A new suspension bridge is being built to replace the Willemsbrug, but instead of crossing the river in a straight line, it turns abruptly left just before it hits water, then turns again to cross, passes Noordereiland (northern island), and turns right and abruptly left again, finally realigning itself with its initial trajectory.

The multiplicity of seemingly inexplicable 90-degree turns and twists is emblematic of the Europe of the eighties: politics, no longer able simply to impose its will, surrenders to real and imagined resistance and carries everyone and everything with it in an avalanche of yielding.

4.

In the first week of the war, as an exercise in intimidation, the Germans bombed the center of Rotterdam. The city turned into a three-kilometer crater.

Life went on. On the site of the void, temporary accommodations in wood and canvas with occasional outlines in neon created a strangely American substitute (glamour out of the ashes?) — Hollywood mirage as pre-reconstruction.

In their studies, meanwhile, planners started the real reconstruction: they proposed a gridlike center of blocks and courtyards; the plan did not control heights.

After the war, the plan was kept, the city rebuilt, mostly with slabs and some impressively massive new blocks: Postkantoor, Groothandelsgebouw. To avoid the "mistakes of the past," open space was kept in the center and programmed with simple pleasures: parks, playgrounds, basins, fountains, shops. In the late fifties Bakema built the Lijnbaan, a linear shopping center conceived as Team X tissue, connecting the fragments of the modernist city.

The center became ever newer, therefore ever less European. Breuer built a department store. In the late fifties–early sixties, the city became an example: it generated its own tourism, mostly of planners. Did these innocents, inspecting one of the greatest success stories of their profession, realize its dependency on (German) bombs? No crater, no city.

BESTEMMIN
GLOBAAL OVERZICHT VAN DE

HERBOUW BINNENSTAD ROTTERDAM
MINGEN DER RUIMTEN OP DEN BEGANEN GROND IN DE NIEUWE BINNENSTADSBEBOUWING

5.

But hostility was brewing among new generations of architects.

Newness became sterility.

Space (good) became emptiness (bad).

Orthogonality became suspect. "What about 60 degrees, or 120 degrees? Even things in between! And why must a cube always be stable? It can 'dance' on an angle... "

The new center was "not really a city."

Revisionists first thought, "If we fill all that is empty, maybe we will have a city."

Modernity, once blessing, now curse. Oedipal drives trivialized as pendulum movement: new generation programmed to do the opposite of previous one.

To achieve urbanity planners now adopted a strategy of densification, filling the voids. The effect of the intellectuals' disapproval was negative proof of their power: even if the proposals hardly made sense, the rhetoric could at last spoil it for the survivors.

Inhabitants, meanwhile, had adjusted perfectly to new conditions. As if Rotterdam were a wind-tunnel test at the scale of a whole population, they had no problem with emptiness and occasionally exploited its virtues: freedom from architecture, from too many intentions, from rules, propositions, purpose...

The city became schizophrenic—condemned ideo-logically yet in every sense popular.

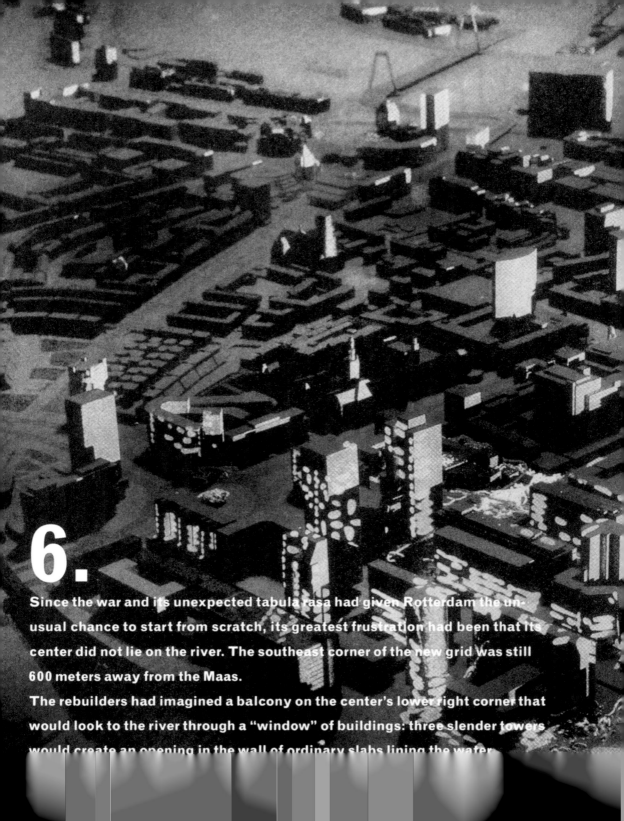

6.

Since the war and its unexpected tabula rasa had given Rotterdam the unusual chance to start from scratch, its greatest frustration had been that its
center did not lie on the river. The southeast corner of the new grid was still
600 meters away from the Maas.

The rebuilders had imagined a balcony on the center's lower right corner that
would look to the river through a "window" of buildings: three slender towers
would create an opening in the wall of ordinary slabs lining the water.

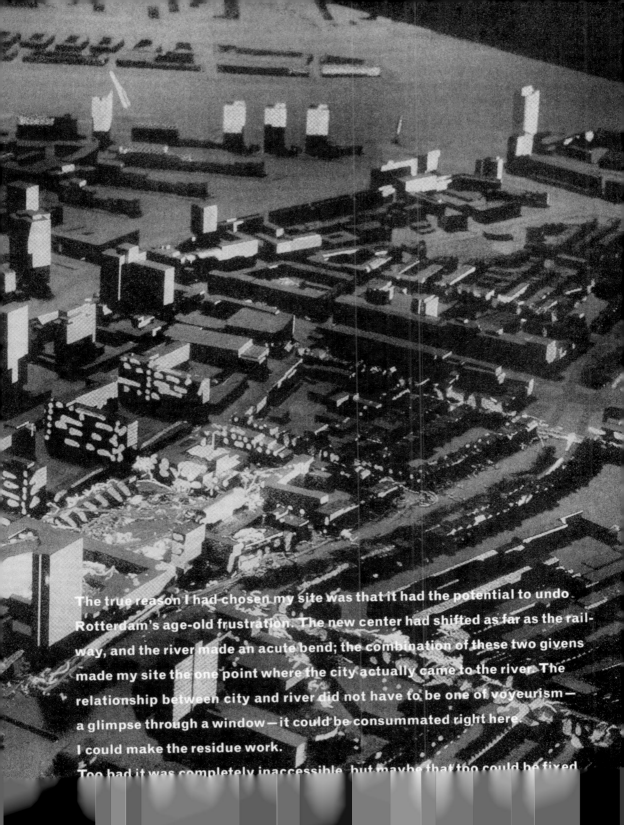

The true reason I had chosen my site was that it had the potential to undo Rotterdam's age-old frustration. The new center had shifted as far as the railway, and the river made an acute bend; the combination of these two givens made my site the one point where the city actually came to the river. The relationship between city and river did not have to be one of voyeurism— a glimpse through a window—it could be consummated right here. I could make the residue work.

Too bad it was completely inaccessible, but maybe that too could be fixed.

7.

While every New York project assumes an unstable context—an environment that could never be an argument for a specific configuration—back in Europe work had to begin with a careful reading and interpretation of what existed and would therefore probably stay.

East of the bridge: the "White House" (1898), once the tallest building in Europe; through a miracle it had survived the bombardment.

Beyond it, the concrete result of the sixties revision: a deliberate Gordian knot of conflicted geometries and metaphoric themes by Piet Blom. (At least *one* Dutchman had dared to be a postmodernist; all others would remain "forever" modern.)

In front: the vast space of the Maas River, with very dense ship traffic—poisonous loads (mostly from Switzerland) at frightening speeds.

Then Noordereiland: completely intact 19th-century idyll. Then de Hef (the lift)—Millet's *Angélus* made out of metal—two skeletal silhouettes connected by a third element that moves up and down to let ships pass. Since Rotterdam is a harbor, it is usually up, paralyzing train traffic between north and south.

Parked on the quay side: enormous 80-meter-high floating cranes that are summoned worldwide whenever there is a shipping disaster.

Behind: the unbuilt tip of a triangular island of offices ending in three harbor piers.

Then the old new city.

On the riverfront, room was left for four new buildings in the gaps between the original slabs. Here, the planning office proposed 20-story towers, art deco skyscrapers for Holland; they even had tops. For my site, not sure what it could take or even that it was there, they imagined a more "sensitive" volume.

8.

First investigation: our project as skyline. Next to the four new towers, the step-down to the more humanist level proposed by the planners would look pathetic. It has to be higher.

We make a clay slab, the maximum height of the proposed towers.
It looks inert.

We then make a row of five towers at right angles to the water. They look too thin. But the slits between the towers work; they deliver more than openness; the experience of passing the slab shows stroboscopic flashes of city...

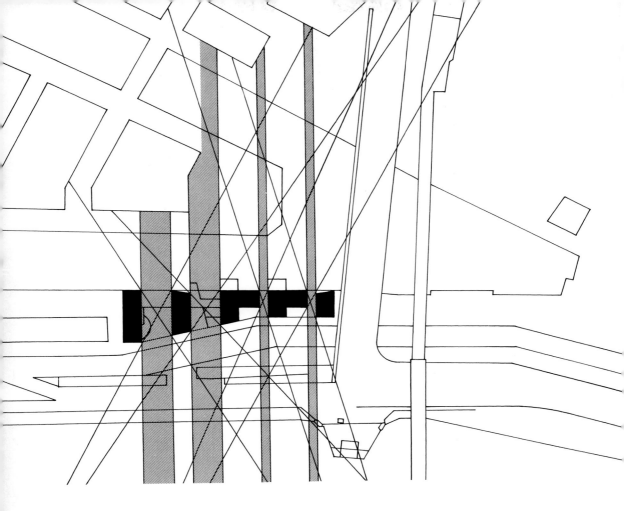

9.

For the Rotterdam building, as for any large building proposed in Europe in
the early eighties, the issue is how to combine transparency with density or,
better still, presence with nonexistence.

If the concept of the building is a row of towers with slots between them,
engaged at the top to form a slab, the slots deliver transparency but eliminate
volume; how to restore it? The towers cannot become wider—the slots
would close up; they can only become deeper. But the potential for additional
depth is thwarted by the boulevard in front and the canal in back.

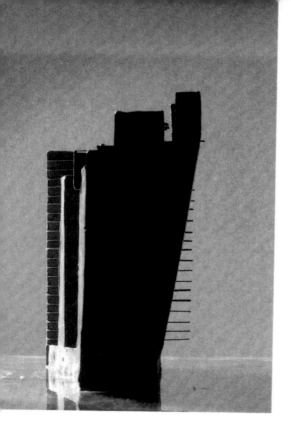

10.

Must the footprint always be where a building is largest? Imprisoned in
obstacles on the ground, it can still expand anywhere else.

In films, one of the surest signs of architectural genius—featured in
The Fountainhead, among many others—is the shape of an upside-down
pyramid, a minimal base widening upward, claiming maximum psychic
volume: the Mayans improved. It's everyone's idea of unusual, difficult,
implausible, impossible; therefore, brilliant.

First one, and finally two of the towers begin to "fall" forward over the
water toward the city, dissociating themselves from the slab.

Density is increased, inertness diminished.

14.

It was **OMA**'s first *retroactive* concept, the beginning of an exhausting
bombardment of idealization with which we tried to maintain a marginal
advantage vis-à-vis our own increasing revulsion.

The politicians' **P**andora's box infinite, our reservoirs finite?

Indeterminate Specificity

The Hague City Hall
The Hague, Netherlands
Competition, 1986

brought up for the head cook's inspection, he does not handle it with a fork. He picks it up in his fingers and slaps it down, runs his thumb round the dish and licks it to taste the gravy, runs it round and licks again, then steps back and contemplates the piece of meat like an artist judging a picture, then presses it lovingly into place with his fat, pink fingers, every one of which he has licked a hundred times that morning. When he is satisfied, he takes a cloth and wipes his fingerprints from the dish, and hands it to the waiter. And the waiter, of course, dips *his* fingers into the gravy — his nasty, greasy fingers which he is forever running through his brilliantined hair.

FIRE-FIGHTING
In buildings over 18.3 m high some staircases should be constructed as fire-fighting staircases with smoke outlets, vents and fire-resisting, self-closing doors.

FIRES
In the heart of the void, as well as in the heart of man, there are burning fires.

FISHERMAN
Then Rem appeared on a Monday from London with a few scratches on an envelope ... and it was all there, the concept and the *image* of this large building as a collection of buildings or a city on its own. It was amazing to watch — almost like a fisherman letting his line out ... the fish has it ... it keeps going out ... and at a certain point he starts reeling it in. Sometimes it takes a fisherman's patience to get an idea going. And when he got it going so brilliantly, everyone set about producing it.

FIZZ
I must clean the house. No-one else'll do it. Your financial adviser is coming to breakfast. I've got to think about that. His taste changes from day to day. One day he wants boiled eggs and toast, the next day orange juice and poached eggs, the next scrambled eggs and smoked salmon, the next a mushroom omelette and champagne. Any minute now it'll be dawn. A new day. Your financial adviser's dreaming of his breakfast. He's dreaming of eggs. Eggs, eggs. What kind of eggs? I'm exhausted. I've been up all night.

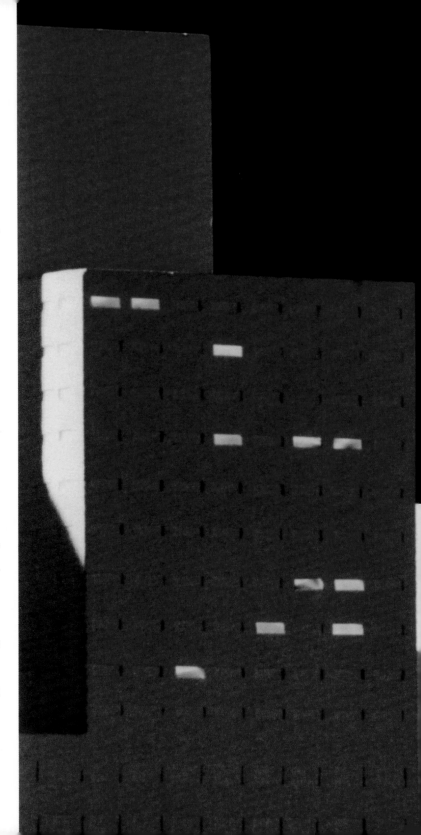

But it never stops. Nothing stops. It's
all fizz. This is my life. I have my
brief arousals. They leave me panting.

FLANEURS[1]

A pedestrian knew how to display
his nonchalance provocatively
on certain occasions. Around 1840
it was briefly fashionable to take
turtles for a walk in the arcades.
The "flâneurs" liked to have turtles
set the pace for them. If they had
had their way, progress would have
been obliged to accommodate
itself to this pace. But this attitude
did not prevail; Taylor, who popu-
larised the watchword, "Down with
dawdling!" carried the day.

FLANEURS[2]

Toni and I were strolling along
Oxford Street, trying to look like
flâneurs. This wasn't as easy as it
might sound. For a start, you usually
needed a *quai* or, at the very least,
a boulevard; and, however much we
might be able to imitate the aimless-
ness of the *flânerie* itself, we always
felt that we hadn't quite mastered
what happened at each end of the
stroll. In Paris, you would be leaving
behind some rumpled couch in a
chambre particulière; over here, we
had just left behind Tottenham Court
Road Underground station and were
heading for Bond Street.

FLAT[1]

As the plane glides in towards
Schiphol, the rectangular fields
stretch like quiltwork beneath one.
Columns of birch trees march away

along the canals. Long greenhouses
sparkle in the sun. Flatness is all.

FLAT²

People and things in flat landscapes
are forced to be really honest
because there's nothing to hide
behind … If somebody stands out
there they just kind of poke right up.
If you can stand being like that, then
you can stand just about anything.

FLEETING

My shoes aren't fashion, really.
They're just little fleeting moments.

FLUX¹

Yet he is aware that everything is in
a state of flux. A strong wind can
change the shape of a cloud, a tumbling river the shape of a river bank,
the process of changes in the earth's
crust the shape of mountains.

FLUX²

Ensure that your life stays in flux.

FLUX³

The flux of capital produces an
enormous channel, a quantification
of power with immediate Quanta,
in which everyone takes profit in his
own way of the circulation of the
money-flux.

FOOD

Indeed, Garrick's comment that a
good actor could as easily make love
to a wooden table as a beautiful
woman gave Diderot food for thought.

FOREIGN[1]
Confronted with a foreign face, they did not recognise their own language, as if momentarily they had been disabled by some kind of neurological short-circuit.

FOREIGN[2]
Everything's foreign.

FORGET
The beginner who has learned a new language always retranslates it into his mother tongue: he can only be said to have appropriated the spirit of the new language and to be able to express himself in it freely when he can manipulate it without reference to the old, and when he forgets his original language while using it.

FORMULA[1]
I think everything now is so indeterminate that it's an illusion to believe you have a theory. So, I've tried to devise formulas that combine architectural specificity with programmatic instability. I think this is terribly important to try to do.

FORMULA[2]
That's why Allen urges we close interviews with the flip side of his formula for hello, "The Magic Four Goodbye": smile; direct eye contact; a good handshake; and the words "It sounds like a great opportunity. I look forward to hearing from you."

FRACTAL
See **ZOOM**.

FRAGMENTS[1]
Architecture must always have as its goal the whole, the complete, remaining fully aware of the fact that a total transformation lies within the sphere of the Utopian, and that only fragments of a complete idea are ever executed.

FRAGMENTS[2]
Tremendous fragments of meaning.

FRICTION
I had enormous influence. He had the power and the craft to shape. When he only had the right to come to conclusions, when I *only* had the power to fulfill my ideas, nothing. But constant friction gave constant solutions.

FRIENDLY
Place oysters on the half shell in preheated deep dishes filled with sand (silver sand glistens prettily). Cover the oysters thickly with ¼ chopped parsley, ¼ finely chopped raw spinach, ⅛ finely chopped tarragon,

556

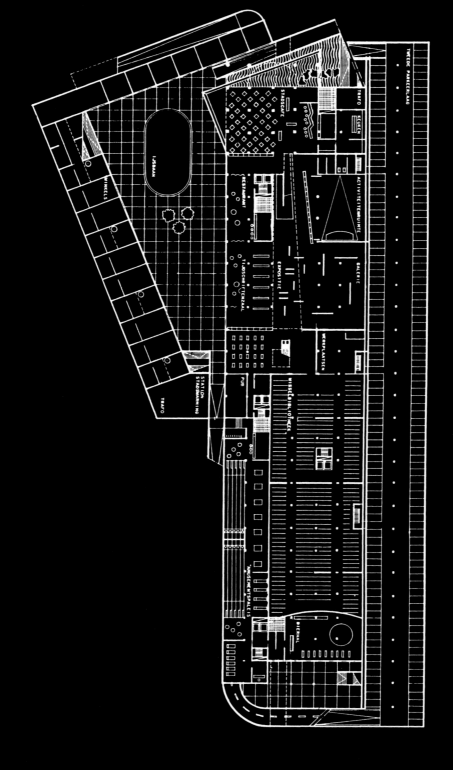

basement

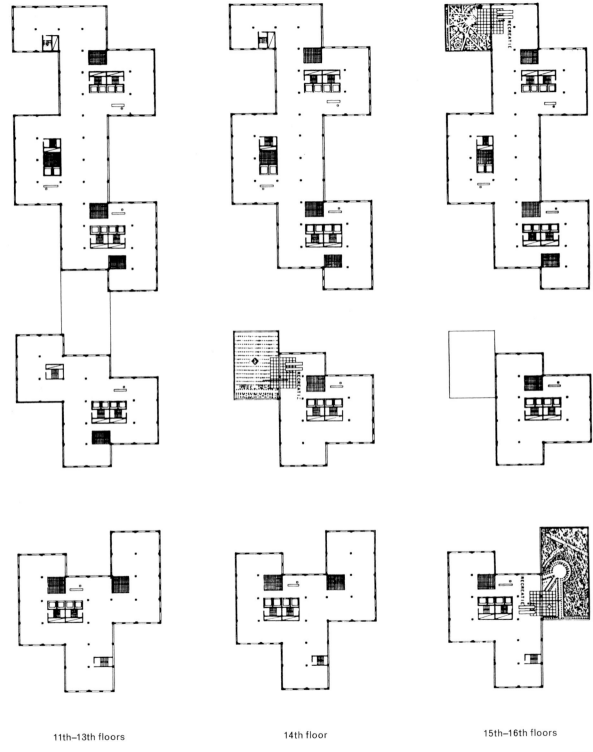

11th–13th floors   14th floor   15th–16th floors

0   50m

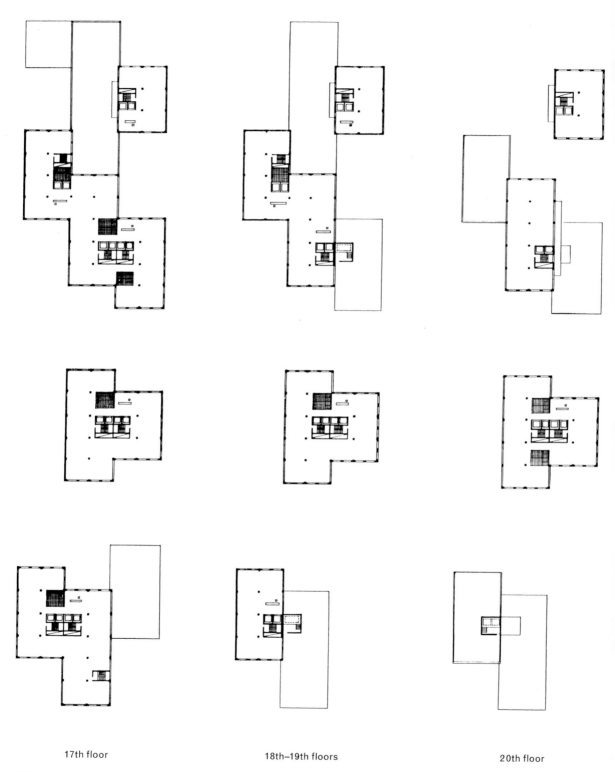

17th floor

18th–19th floors

20th floor

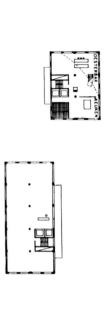

21st–23rd floors   24th floor

0   50m

¼ finely chopped chervil, ⅛ finely
chopped basil and ¼ finely chopped
chives. Salt and pepper some fresh
breadcrumbs, cover the herbs completely, dot with melted butter and
put for 4 or 5 minutes in a preheated
450° oven. Serve piping hot.
This dish is an enormous success
with French gourmets. It makes
more friends for the United States
than anything I know.

FROZEN
Not long ago, in the icy Siberian
plains, a few hard-frozen mammoths
were discovered. The discoverers
were astonished to find chamomile
flowers inside their bellies.

FRUGAL
Frugal doesn't mean cheap, it simply
means you don't waste anything.

FUKUOKA[1]
Seaport city on Hakata Bay; pop.
(1970c) 853,270; manufactures iron
and steel, electrical equipment;
fishing, shipbuilding; Kyushu Univ.
(1910). In ancient times one of the
three trade ports of Japan; at time
(1274–81) of attempted invasions
of Kublai Khan, the scene of much
fighting; heavily bombed 1945.

FUKUOKA[2]
Fukuoka is a city that has developed
toward the sea around Hakata Bay.
It is surrounded by mountains in the
background, and since its airport
is close to the city center, high-rise
buildings cannot be constructed
there. Thus there has been nowhere
for it to expand except forward,
into Hakata Bay.

FUMES
In Athens, where car ownership
has risen more than eightfold since
the mid-1960s, and could double
again by 2000, traffic fumes are
reckoned to cause 85% of the air
pollution that is eating the
Parthenon away.

FURNITURE
A door in the passage was ajar and
odd sounds came through it as
though someone were alternately
whistling and sighing, but nothing to
the page seemed strange. He just
went on: he was a child of this building. People of every kind came in
for a night with or without luggage
and then went away again; a few died
here and the bodies were removed
unobtrusively by the service.
Divorce suits bloomed at certain

three riddles…

Nervi's scheme…

Dutch economy…

570

Dirty Realism

A Mini-Farce

Rarely has an arbitrary section of road been bombarded by a single office with so much architectural consideration as the Spui (the Sluice) in The Hague by **OMA**.

It was as if some kind of bizarre architectural fates had condemned us to confront systematically, in this length of 200 meters of asphalt, the three major riddles of the European city: how to intervene in historical substance (**Dutch Parliament**), how to deal with the strictly contemporary (**Netherlands Dance Theater**), and finally, how to negotiate their interface (**Hague City Hall**). Certainly not through their once-vaunted powers of foresight, the Dutch, masters of miniature, had managed to turn this part of the city into a museum-quality display of the successive urban paradigms of the second half of the 20th century.

In the *sixties*, in an ambitious enterprise of modernization, the city "fathers" confided to the Italian architect **Pier Luigi Nervi** the task of planning a new center—a city of towers—on the site of the old. Then they razed the old center, but somehow never asked him to build the new.

When, in the *seventies*, the embrace of modernity became less enthusiastic, a new highway, intended to connect the major Amsterdam–The Hague–Rotterdam motorway with the coast, was stopped here abruptly, creating a bizarre enclave of abandoned highway and razed site. Slowly this dubious void was filled, mostly with ministries (foreign affairs, justice). They were high-rises built by Dutch architects, strong evidence of Dutch economy, notably that of the imagination.

seasons; co-respondents gave tips and detectives out-trumped them with larger tips — because their tips went on the expense account. The page took everything for granted.

FUTURE[1]

We were seeing the future and we knew it for sure. I saw people walking around in it without knowing it, because they were still thinking in the past, in references of the past. But all you had to do was *know* you were in the future, and that's what put you there.

The mystery was gone, but the amazement was just starting.

FUTURE[2]

Cyberspace will provide not only a one-way path into screenland but special effects at your table. The future is here, it just hasn't been evenly distributed (yet).

FUTURE[3]

But the future comes not by itself. Only if we do our work in the right way will it make a good foundation for the future. In all these years I have learned more and more that architecture is not a play with forms. I have come to understand the close relationship between architecture and civilization. I have learned that architecture must stem from the sustaining and driving forces of civilization and that it can be, at its best, an expression of the innermost structure of its time.

FUTURE[4]

Imagine the person you love saying to you, "Ten minutes from now you are going to be poked with a sharp stick. The pain will be excruciating and there isn't a single thing you can do to prevent it." Well then — the next ten minutes would be next to unendurable, would they not? Maybe it's good we can't see the future.

FUZZY

Fuzzy logic is an esoteric computer reasoning system — an algorithmic hybrid of conventional binary logic and artificial intelligence. Unlike binary logic, which uses precise "yes/no" or "zero/one" programming rules, fuzzy logic uses approximate or inferential reasoning to solve problems. It enables programmers to use ambiguous input language — such as "a little," "about 50," "most," and "often" — in much the way that

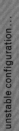

By the early *eighties*, the decision to create a modern center was declared
a mistake; a new master plan proposed a more historical morphology of low
urban blocks to surround the now dominant towers. The Dance Theater was
transplanted from its original site at the seacoast to inject a cultural presence
into such a block, to be shared with a concert hall in an uneasy *cadavre exquis*.
Since all buildings in Holland have to be cheap in the name of a Calvinist
afterburn, we decided to invest only in its interior identity and to contribute
an anonymous exterior to the accidental richness of the cityscape.

By the year the theater opened, 1987, the city was controlled by a fragile
socialist regime. A newly identified "need" for a colossal city hall—150,000 m²
(with additional space for parking)—once again burst the confines of dogma,
this time the politically correct, Barcelona-inspired city of blocks.

A competition was held for the building on a narrow rectangular site on the
fault line between the old and new towns, confronting the "old" city with an
unprecedented mass, this time in the name of socialism.

An emblematic standoff developed.

An activist councillor had developed a passion for Richard Meier (it was
enough to propel him to the directorship of the Netherlands Architecture
Institute). According to Meier's introductory video, he was willing to "repair
the city in the spirit of Berlage," to undo—like other major American contextualists of the eighties—the damage the Europeans had done to their cities
themselves.

OMA, on the other hand, interpreted both size and location as symptomatic of
the appearance of a new scale in Europe, one confronting its cities not so
much with a dilemma—for or against modernism—but rather with the manifestation of the *n*th wave of modernization and concentration that, while
potentially terminal, was also a condition for their survival.

With scrupulous attention to European sensibilities—daylight, privacy, even
context—we developed the city hall as an assembly of three slabs that accommodated in its lower regions the advantages of an American depth and evaporated toward the higher regions to avoid a too brutal confrontation with the

people process subjective information
before making decisions.

G

GENEALOGY

The history of architecture is not
the chronology of architectural form
but the genealogy of architectural
will.

GENESIS

The figure with the urn has disappeared. But by now my eyes are
rewarded by a more satisfying sight.
It is as if I had arrived at the very
end of this habitable earth, at that
magic fringe of the ancient world
where all the mysteries and gloom
and terror of the universe are
concealed.

GEOMETRY

A woodpecker's movement around
a tree trunk defines a perfect spiral.
To connect the hoppity helix of
the woodpecker to the macrocosmic
spiral of our stellar system or to
the microcosmic spiral of the DNA
molecule or, for that matter, to
the hundreds of natural spirals in
between—snail shells, crowns
of daisies and sunflowers, fingerprints, cyclones, etc.—may be
assigning to geometry more meaning than the mundane can abide.
Suffice to say that a woodpecker is
first on one side of a tree and then
the other; disappearing, then re-
appearing at a point slightly higher
up on the trunk.

GLANCE

One glance can annihilate the void
dance. Looking away is the passion
day by day, year by year the imita-
tive act hot from the mould of the
original fact, until we can no longer
contain the cry or live untouched in
the house of replicas.

GLIDE

The lights grow brighter as the earth
lurches away from the sun, and now
the orchestra is playing yellow cocktail music, and the opera of voices
pitches a key higher. Laughter is
easier minute by minute, spilled
with prodigality, tipped out at a new
cheerful word. The groups change
more swiftly, swell with new arrivals,
dissolve and form in the same breath;
already there are wanderers, confident

a new scale…

one of the best…

symbol of *civitas*…

last-ditch attempt…

574

delicate skyline of the historical center. Its unstable configuration allowed us to begin to dismantle our own increasingly embarrassing dependency on 1920s and 1930s precedents and, after our project for Parc de la Villette, to reexperiment with the relationship between specificity and indeterminacy, this time in a building. Meier's scheme, "as low as possible" at 14 stories, and introducing the atrium—that cornerstone of American urbanism—as a symbol of *civitas*, was chosen. It will probably be one of the best buildings in Holland. Meier's insistence on (his) quality first astonished, then pained the Dutch clients—a diffuse consortium that probably also owns half of Manhattan—but they surrendered and are now building to his specifications. After this denouement, it seemed that our role had been played out at the Spui; it was perfect: a new parliament (by Pi de Bruyn), a new city hall (by Richard Meier), a cultural block (50% OMA).

But in an ironic twist, the city asked us at the beginning of the *nineties* to "rescue" the center, to develop there our largest project to date, the Souterrain: a totally underground—invisible—system of federated parking garages, subway stations, sunken roads, etc., that would mine the entire center, invade, connect, and consolidate existing garages, including those of Dance Theater and City Hall—a proliferating parking gulag. With hopes of saving entire chains of department stores, it was a last-ditch attempt to restore the center's accessibility, which had been progressively compromised by the serial dogmas of the past decades that, in a Vietnam-like paradox, had suggested that in order to save the European city its arteries had to be blocked. Masters finally of our own hades, we quietly savored our triumph: staring down the future, underground. 1993

proliferating parking gulag...

girls who weave here and there among the stouter and more stable, become for a sharp, joyous moment the centre of a group, and then, excited with triumph, glide on through the seachange of faces and voices and colour under the constantly changing light.

GLITTER
What attracts the public? Hans Boot won the popular vote for his City Hall project, which was probably the last of the judges' recommendations. He had a sleek model made of silver mirrored plastic. It was glittering, and all the people were crowded around it — like these birds that collect shiny things. One guy who was looking at it said, "It's just like the building in 'Dallas.'" That's what drew the popular interest — the idea that the City Hall in The Hague could have the allure of what they see on TV — the glamour and intrigue of what they see on "Dallas."

GLOBAL[1]
As CNN marks its 10th birthday this month, the air is thick with metaphors. "The world's intercom," says National Public Radio's Daniel Schorr, a former CNN senior correspondent who was present at the creation. "Video valium," says Frank Radice, a onetime producer of the network's showbiz program, recalling all the celebrities who told him that CNN eased their homesickness in faraway lands. CNN founder Ted Turner's pet metaphor was coined by the media theorist Marshall McLuhan. "I was on a panel with McLuhan at a cable convention when we had just started to globalize and he said, 'Turner, you are creating the global village.' It's exciting because it has really happened."

GLOBAL[2]
I think of myself being global. I see myself participating in global activities: sitting in jets, talking to machines, eating small geometric food, and voting over the phone.

GLOBALIZATION
One of the key questions of our time is that there is globalization. One particular country is extremely aggressive in that pursuit, and that is Japan. An enormous amount of work in American firms is for

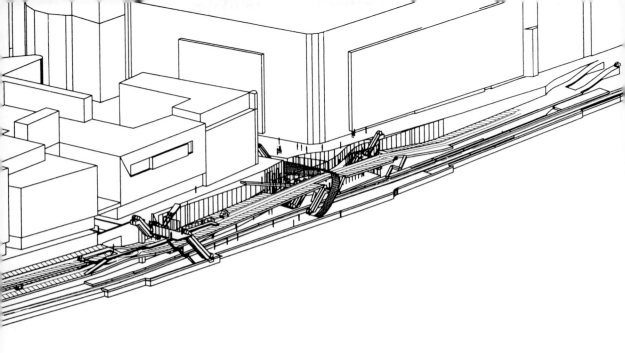

Japan. That confronts us with an
incredible dilemma, or an accumulated cluster of dilemmas which
have to do with scale, program,
articulation, strangeness, and alienation from origins. These are
phenomenally complex; do any of
us have terms of reference to really
judge their success or failure?
I don't think so.

GLOCAL

Glocal marries the words global and
local to describe the fine balance
between the two approaches in international management.

GO

Get away from Paris and Amsterdam and go see Atlanta; go straight-
away and without any preconceived
ideas. That's all I can say.

GOODNESS

The poor audience has so little
understanding of goodness that even
when it is being helped it thinks it
is being tortured. Poor soul, relax,
we really are trying to help.

GOPLACIA

NOPLACIA was once my name,
That is, a place where no one goes.
Plato's *Republic* now I claim
To match, or beat at its own game;
For that was just a myth in prose,
But what he wrote of, I became,
Of men, wealth, laws a solid frame,
A place where every wise man goes:
GOPLACIA is now my name.

GORDIAN KNOT

A difficult, almost insoluble problem. Gordius tied a knot in such a
manner it was impossible to unloose
it. The legend circulated that he who
could solve the problem would rule
all Asia. Alexander cut the knot
with one stroke of his sword, and
when he captured Asia, he was said
to have fulfilled the prophesy. Thus
to cut the Gordian knot is to get out
of a difficult situation by one bold
decisive step.

GRACE[1]

Selon ces théologiens, la compétitivité est comme la grâce: on l'a ou
on ne l'a pas. Elle n'est pas divisible. Ceux qui l'ont seront sauvés.
Ceux qui commettront le péché de
ne pas être compétitifs sont con-
damnés à disparaître.

GRACE[2]

Having already thought a great deal
about how this grace is acquired,
and leaving aside those who are

Working Babel

To stay viable after the opening of the tunnel
between England and the continent,
the ferry companies operating across the channel
propose to make the crossing
more exciting.
Not only would the boats turn into
floating entertainment worlds,
but their destinations — the terminals —
would shed their utilitarian character
and become attractions.
The original Babel was a symbol
of ambition, chaos, and ultimately failure;
this machine proclaims
a working Babel that effortlessly swallows, entertains,
and processes the travelling masses.
The theme reflects Europe's new ambition:
it's different tribes — the users of the terminal —
embarking on a unified future.

How to inject a new "sign" into a landscape that —
through scale and atmosphere alone — renders any object
both arbitrary and inevitable?

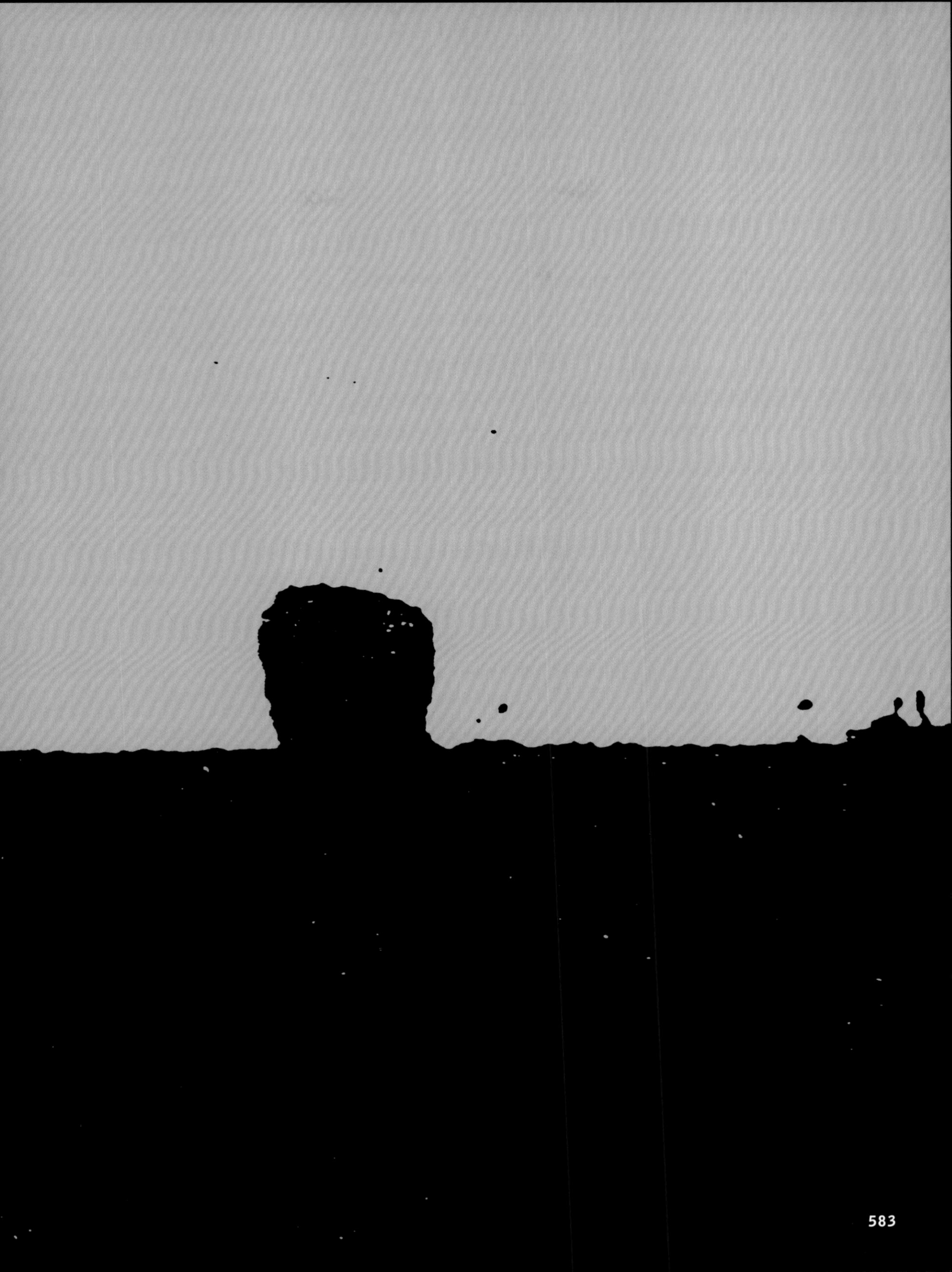

To become a landmark,
this project adopts a form that resists
easy classification
to free-associate with successive moods —
the mechanical, the industrial,
the utilitarian, the abstract, the poetic, the surreal.
It combines maximum artistry
with maximum efficiency.

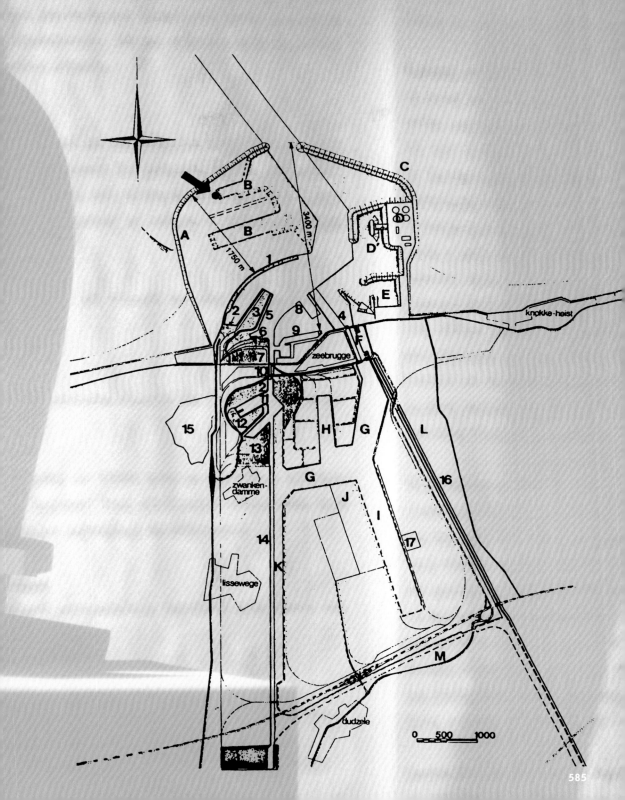

The building
crosses a sphere with a cone.
The two lowest floors
organize traffic to and from the ferries:
four ships can load and unload simultaneously
without interrupting traffic flow.
A bus station is
projected above this sorting machine;
pedestrian access is through
a separate external loop.
Above, two floors of parking wind in
an ascending spiral
culminating in a great public hall
where the panorama
of sea and land
is revealed for the first time.

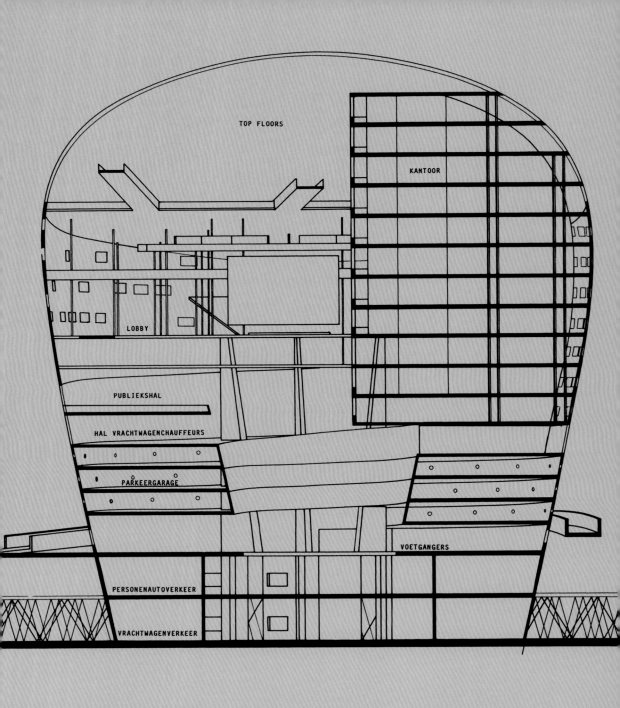

TOP FLOORS

KANTOOR

LOBBY

PUBLIEKSHAL

HAL VRACHTWAGENCHAUFFEURS

PARKEERGARAGE

VOETGANGERS

PERSONENAUTOVERKEER

VRACHTWAGENVERKEER

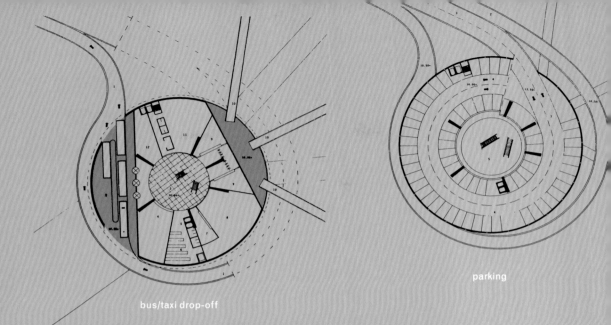

bus/taxi drop-off

parking

Then the cone splits into vertical segments:
a wedge of offices divides the sphere into
hotel and promotional sections.
The void between these two parts offers an upward
view to the sky and a downward view,
through a glass floor,
to the depths of the parking garage.

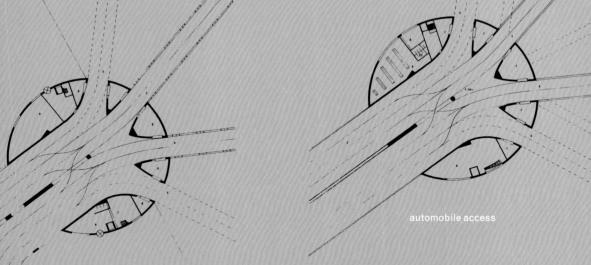

truck access

automobile access

0   30m

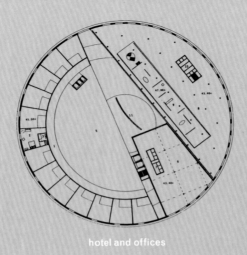

hotel and offices

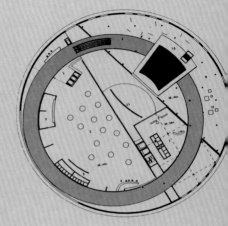

hotel lobby, restaurant, cinema

The entire building is capped by a glass dome.
Under the dome, the two halves
are connected by ramps and bridges.
The hotel roof accommodates
the ultimate "North Sea Casino";
an amphitheater that slopes down toward the
sea can be used as a conference center.

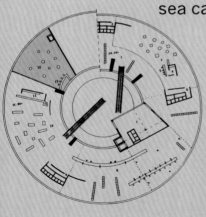

public lobby

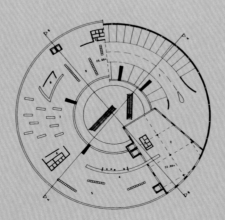

driver facilities, cafeteria

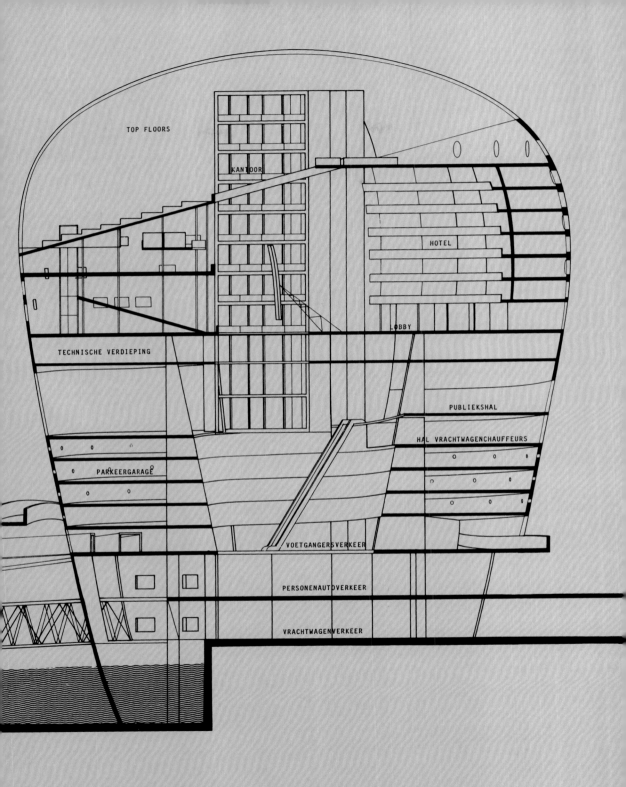

TOP FLOORS

KANTOOR

HOTEL

LOBBY

TECHNISCHE VERDIEPING

PUBLIEKSHAL

HAL VRACHTWAGENCHAUFFEURS

PARKEERGARAGE

VOETGANGERSVERKEER

PERSONENAUTOVERKEER

VRACHTWAGENVERKEER

0   20m

591

endowed with it by their stars, I have
discovered a universal rule which
seems to apply more than any other
in all human actions or words:
namely, to steer away from affect-
ation at all cost, as if it were a rough
and dangerous reef.

GRAFT

And they themselves can only be
read within the operation of their
reinscription, within the graft. It is
the sustained, discrete violence of
an incision that is not apparent in the
thickness of the text, a calculated
insemination of the proliferating
allogene through which the two texts
are transformed, deform each other,
contaminate each other's content,   .
tend at times to reject each other, or
pass elliptically one into the other
and become regenerated in the repetition, along the edges of an overcast
seam. Each grafted text continues
to radiate back toward the site of its
removal, transforming that too, as
it affects the new territory.

GRASP

As the meaning of a whole sentence
is different from the meaning of the
sum of single words, so is the creative vision and ability to grasp the
characteristic unity of a set of facts,
and not just to analyse them as
something which is put together by
single parts.

GREAT

I'm so great, I even impress myself ... It's hard to be modest when
you're as great as I am.

GREED

Greed is all right. Greed is healthy.
You can be greedy and still feel
good about yourself.

GREEN

These smart and fashionable salad
bowls and servers are also environ-
mentally friendly.

GREW

At once Goldmund thought of a certain dream, dreamed by him a long
while since, when he had made little
clay men and women that rose up
and grew into giants. But he did not
tell it, only saying humbly that he
had never tried such a work.

GRID

The *Grid* — or any other subdivision
of the metropolitan territory into
maximum increments of control —
describes an archipelago of "Cities
within Cities." The more each

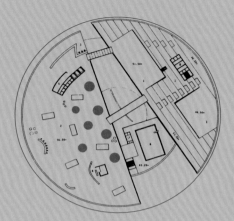

casino, pool, auditorium

30m

0

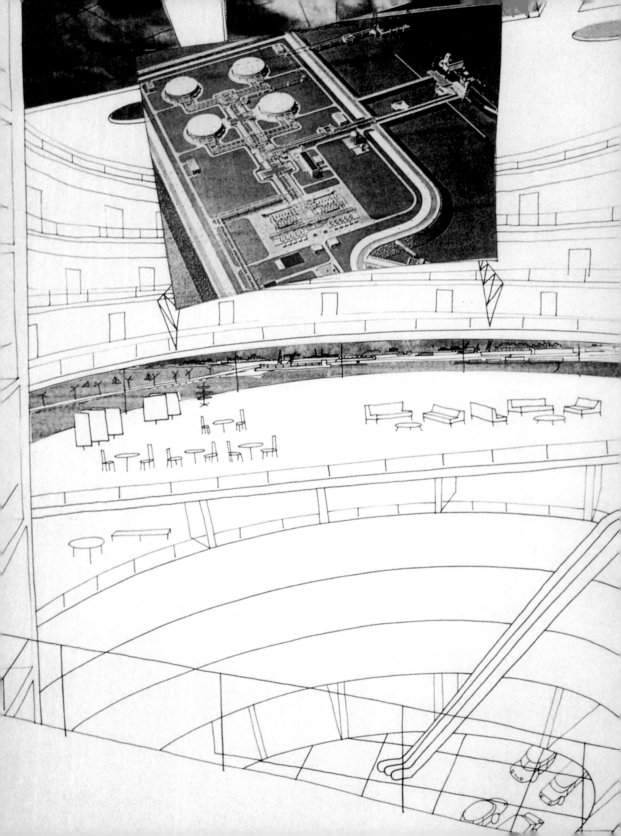

"island" celebrates different values, the more the unity of the archipelago as system is reinforced. Because "change" is contained on the component "islands," such a system will never have to be revised.

GROOVE
I'm just an ordinary teacher who got in a rut 22 years ago and has been polishing the groove ever since.

GROTESQUE
In the weak sunlight between autumn showers it was a queer looking city, all blank stone walls with a few narrow windows set too high, wide streets that dwarfed the crowds, street-lamps perched on ridiculous tall posts, roofs pitched steep as praying hands, shed roofs sticking out of house walls eighteen feet above the ground like big aimless bookshelves — an ill-proportioned grotesque city, in the sunlight. It was not built for sunlight. It was built for winter. In winter, with those streets filled ten feet up with packed, hard-rolled snow, the steep roofs icicle-fringed, sleds parked under the shed-roofs, narrow window-slits shining yellow through driving sleet, you would see the fitness of that city, its economy, its beauty.

GROVEL
But finally you'll get into a man's office with your drawing, and you'll curse yourself for taking so much space of his air with your body, and you'll try to squeeze yourself out of his sight, so that he won't see you, but only hear your voice begging him, pleading, your voice licking his knees; you'll loathe yourself for it, but you won't care, if only he'd let you put up that building, you won't care, you'll want to rip your insides open to show him, because if he saw what's there he'd have to let you put it up.

GUARANTEE
Crescourt Loft Conversions, recommended by Local Authorities and Building Societies, are guaranteed for a full five years.

GUIDANCE
My dear Rabbi:
Do cheer up! All is not lost.

GUZZLERS
How fickle is art and the art world. In a state of political stagnation such as this, the work has no option but to be ridiculous, because it is handed

Bifurcation

The Zeebrugge terminal was an early warning about
the impact that structure (and to a less visible extent, services)
would have on the series of "large" buildings:
Très Grande Bibliothèque, ZKM, Jussieu.

Different structural concepts for each project were
elaborated in tandem by OMA and Ove Arup; each time
they would result in fundamentally new buildings.
Decisions in one area had radical repercussions in the other.

Arup imagined two construction scenarios for
the Zeebrugge client that, as in a road bifurcation,
led to absolutely different destinations.

The first, guided by speed, suggested the establishment of
an initial base, then the rapid assembly of prefabricated elements,
which would finally be cloaked in a balloon of
ferroconcrete foam sprayed on formwork of chicken wire.
In the second scenario, the building became hyper-substantial:
it would be built in reinforced concrete by
a handful of workers at the enormous expense of time.

In the first case, sudden erection would become *spectacle*;
in the second, almost imperceptible progress
a potential source of *suspense*: the workers would visibly age during
the course of construction; children would become adults
as the building remained stubbornly unfinished.

More disturbing, the first building would be instant but immaterial;
the second, slowly (if ever) completed, but "authentic": opposites
ostensibly based on the same plans, sections, architecture.   **1993**

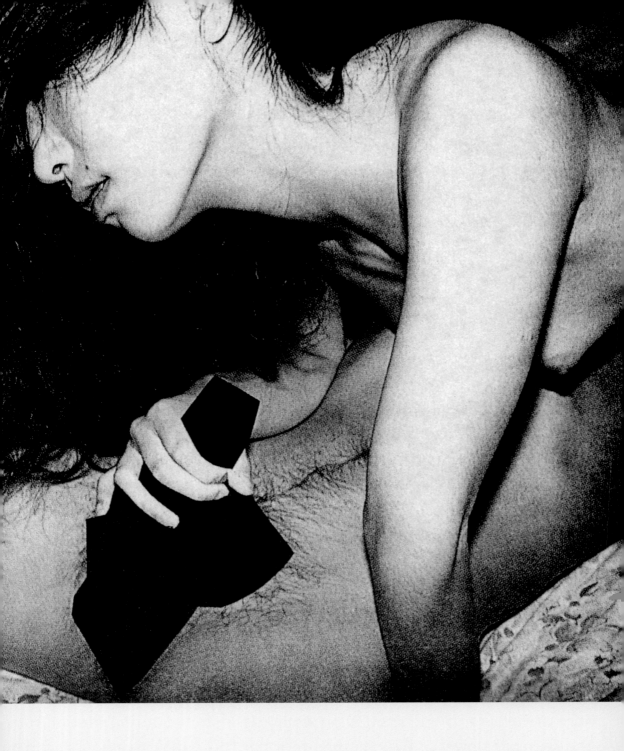

Strategy of the Void

The ambition of this project is to rid architecture of responsibilities it can no longer sustain and to explore this new freedom aggressively. It suggests that, liberated from its former obligations, architecture's last function will be the creation of the symbolic spaces that accommodate the persistent desire for collectivity.

Weird Science: Excerpts from a Diary

April 29, 1989

Dear Diary,

Do we want to win this competition or not?

Of course, juries, not architects, decide competitions, but first there is our own, invisible judgment: for each project there is a beyond — a domain where no jury will follow.

Greater than the total loss to all the conspiracies, political pressures, blatant corruption — all those "masterworks" that *they* didn't give first prize — is the tragedy of the even more brilliant works that *we* didn't dare to imagine.

Wanting to win a competition is not the same as wanting to do your best possible work.

Anyway, don't be paranoid; forget names, juries are a mere statistical sample, their "plots" just a message from the real world (you don't kill the messenger)...

604

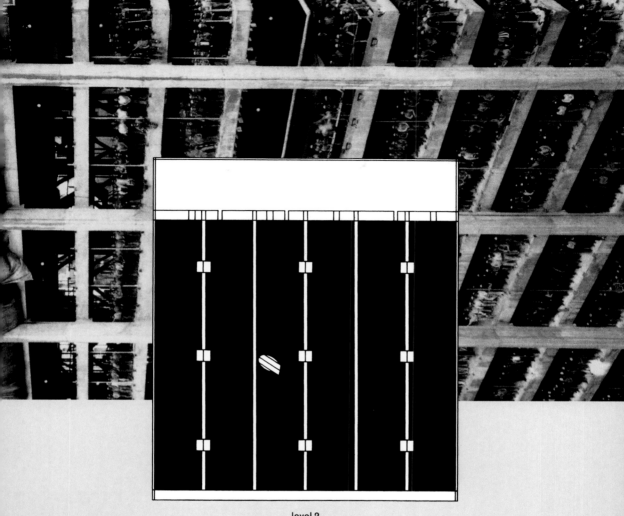

level 2
storage

0 | | | | 20m

Since they are voids — they do not have to be "built" — individual libraries can be shaped strictly according to their own logic, independent of each other, of the external envelope, of the usual difficulties of architecture, even gravity.

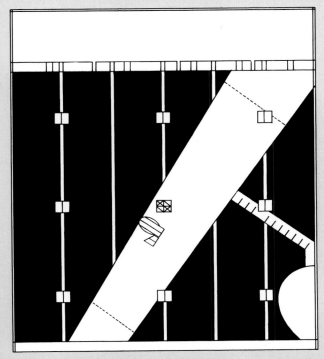

level 3

Intersection

Recent Acquisitions Library: two voids that cross—a horizontal
reading room and an auditorium that slopes toward the river.
The walls are lined with transparent viewing booths.

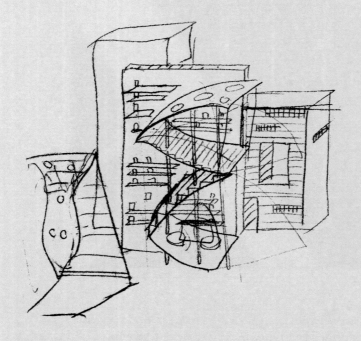

May 12

"Scientific" day.

Take:

    1 slab of storage

    1 slab of administration/offices

    1 slab of circulation/elevators

Laminate them together to form a single large block. Pull string of folded reading rooms
upward like a limp Tower of Babel facing the Seine. Now slice horizontally through the block:
each cut statistically mimics the program. You can't go wrong. The plan = the section.

622

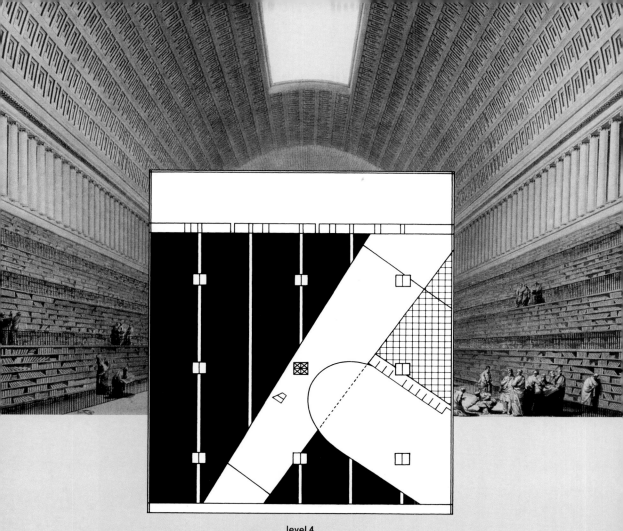

level 4
Recent Acquisitions Library: audio, booths, plant, storage

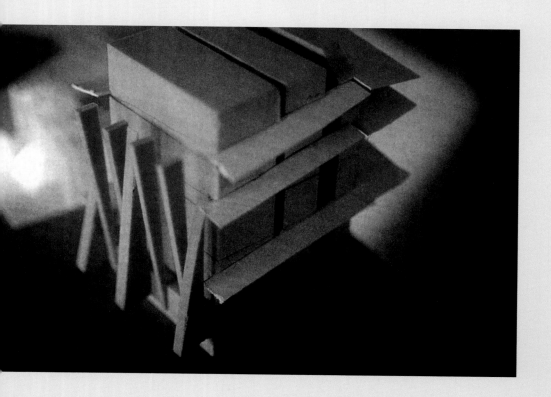

May 13

The core of three slabs now surrounded by a spiral of reading rooms. No more focus
on the river; in this way they will see everything: the center, the Périphérique,
the periphery, the XVIth, the good, the bad, and the ugly ... ugly but promising?

624

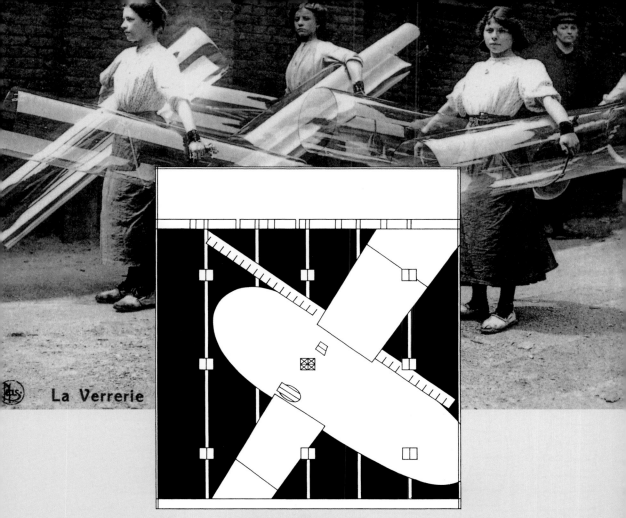

La Verrerie

level 5
Recent Acquisitions Library: audiovisual, auditorium

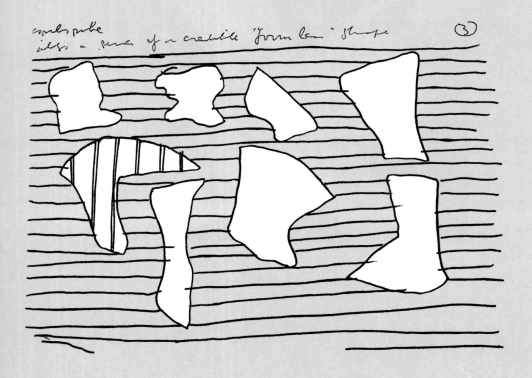

May 15

An old sketch for ZKM, suddenly pregnant.

Imagine a building consisting of regular and irregular spaces, *where the most important parts of the building consist of an absence of building*.

The regular here is the storage; the irregular, reading rooms, not designed, simply carved out.

Could this formulation liberate us from the sad mode of simulating invention?

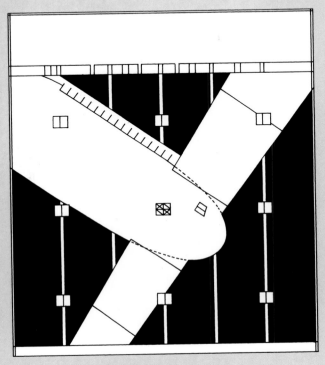

level 6
Recent Acquisitions Library: video, booths, storage

0 | | | | | 20m

May 19

The TGB is a cube.

It is solid storage with the reading rooms — voids — excavated where efficient.

Dark in the center, daylight on the perimeter.

Crowds below, empty chambers above for reflection.

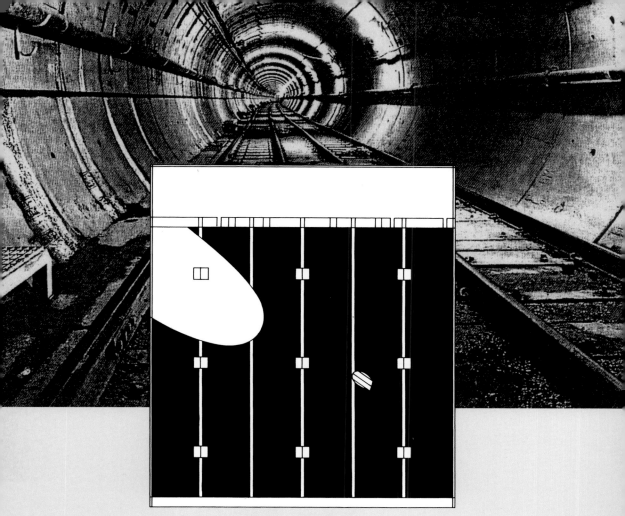

level 7
video, storage

0 | | | | | 20m

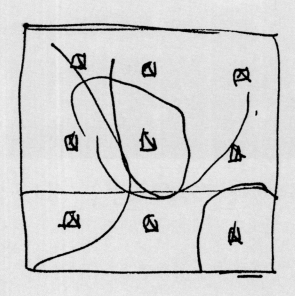

May 20

Cube pierced by nine shafts of vertical movement. As long as a void surrounds one of the
elevator squares, it's accessible.

630

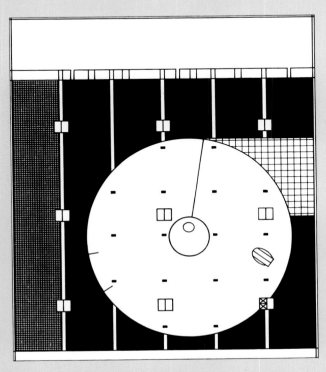

level 10
Reference Library: reading room, open storage, carrels,
robotized storage, plant

May 25

Only anxiety, amid early symptoms of exhilaration: it's an idea, we know, but it is absolutely unclear at this point whether it's a good or a bad one.

Model, intended to clarify, prolongs uncertainty…

We suspend judgment; it needs time.

A cube. All the "deductions" have been performed: the building as residue of process of elimination. We are dealing not with aesthetics here, but with quantities.

We only add and subtract.

636

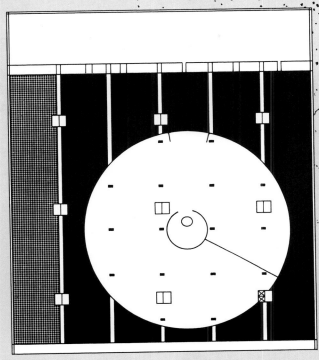

level 11
Reference Library: reading room, storage

0 | | | | | 20m

May 26

Portrait of all the libraries the way they will never be seen: as shapes, as objects.

If all goes according to plan, we will have taken that status away from them.

Formless architecture.

638

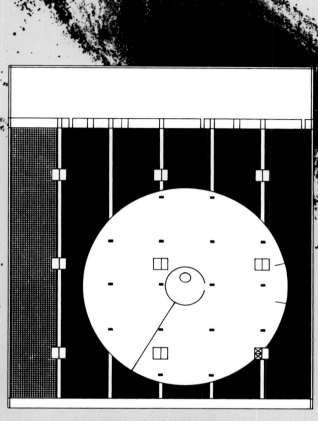

level 12
Reference Library: reading room, plant, storage

0   20m

May 30

Not looking for differences, the project has become "different."

First "ghost" of the eventual project, on site.

Somehow, presence of cube — unstable through its multiple erosions — seems only way to respond to the surrounding "neatness" of the new architectural landscape (nothing older than ten years).

But can such a container still have a relationship with the city? Should it? Is it important?

Or is "fuck context" becoming the theme?

Beginning to note signs of conviction.

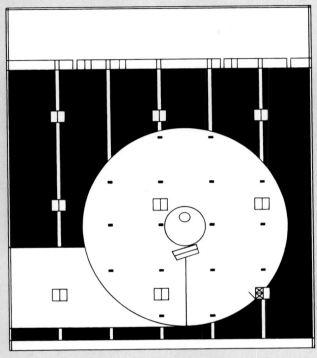

level 13
Reference Library: lounge, conference rooms, storage

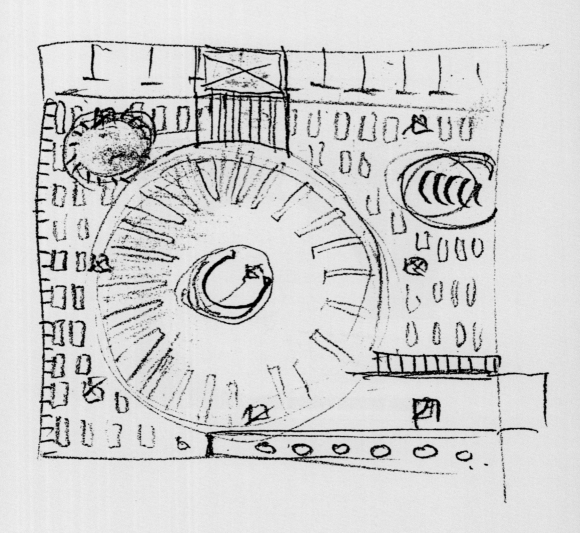

May 31

We begin to "think" the plans. There is nothing to think.

Is it that Bigness alone makes everything easy to the point of automatism? If the storage

pattern is wallpaper, planning is like tearing the wallpaper off the wall.

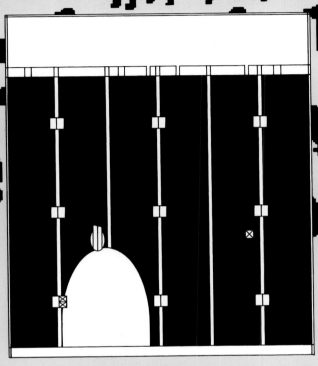

level 16
Catalog Room, storage

0   20m

June 9

Prepare intermediate presentation for colleagues, critics, intellectual friends.

Make a reverse model: what is solid has melted, what is void floats as object in nothingness.

Sparkling explanation followed by uneasy silence.

Is this the "beyond"?

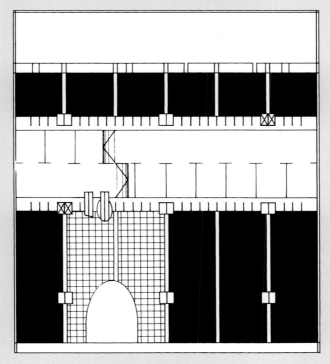

level 17
Loop
Research Library: a "scientific" interior where floor becomes
wall becomes ceiling becomes wall — a Möbius strip that performs
a loop-the-loop across the depth of the building.

June 24

Have to go on. We have no choice.

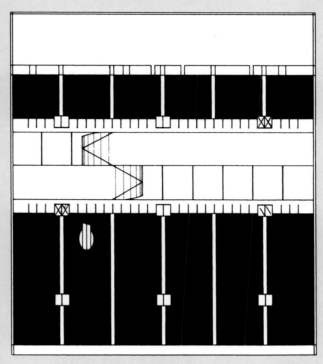

level 18
Research Library: conference rooms, storage

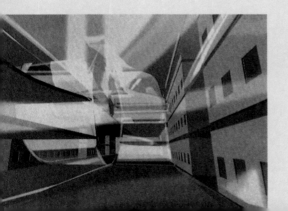

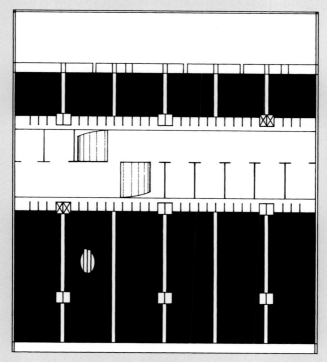

level 19
Research Library: reading room, storage

0   20m

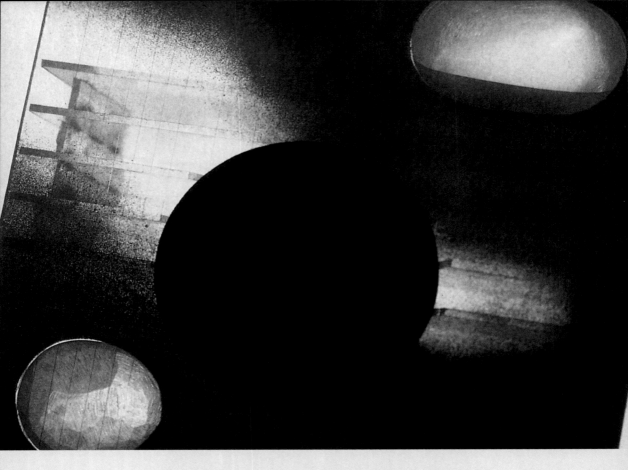

July 2

Dear Diary,

Final moment of relief: first test for facade... simulating the impossible.

A plane, sometimes transparent, sometimes translucent, sometimes opaque; mysterious, revealing, or mute...

Almost natural—like a cloudy sky at night, like an eclipse...

654

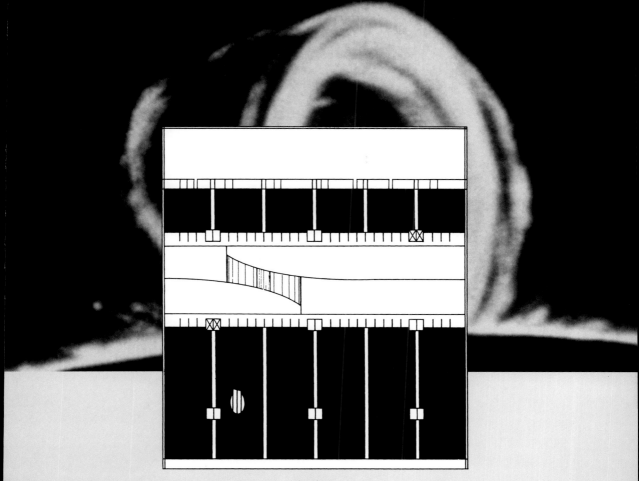

level 20
Research Library: café, lounge, storage

0 | | | | |20m

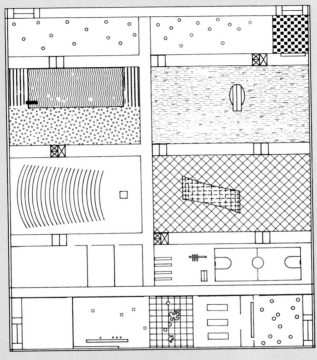

roof
restaurant, gymnasium, garden, swimming pool

0 | | | | |20m

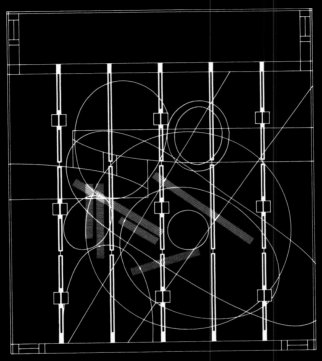

superimposition of voids

plines—in fact, a mutual invasion of territory—and the correspond-
ing blurring of specific professional identities (not always painless)
allowed us, at the end of the eighties—when, to our own consterna-
tion, Bigness emerged like a sudden iceberg from the mist of deconstructivist discourse and imposed itself as a political, economic,
artistic necessity—to defrost earlier ambitions and to explore the
redesign and demystification of architecture, this time experimenting
on ourselves.

With the cluster of the Very Big Library (250,000 m²), ZKM (two laboratories, a theater, two museums), and the Zeebrugge terminal, it
seemed that the impossible constellation of need, means, and naïveté
that had triggered New York's "miracles" had returned.

The simultaneous work in the summer of 1989 on these three competitions forced us to explore the potential of building Big in Europe,
with repercussions equally architectural and technical. They were
treated, in the newly bonded OMA-Arup team, as aggressive confrontations with the survival of earlier regimes. While other disciplines were gloating over their new freedoms—the hybrid, the local,
the informal, chance, the singular, the irregular, the unique—architecture was stuck in the consistent, the repetitive, the regular, the grid-
ded, the general, the overall, the formal, the predetermined. The work
became a joint campaign to explore these freedoms for architecture
and engineering, to reconquer the section, to address our shared dis-
comfort with services as the sprawling coils of a proliferating uncon-

scious, to abolish the single grandiose solution integrating structure and services. It was also, more secretly, a search for ways to make buildings that would *look* completely different: for genuine newness. This exploration allowed us to explode other unquestioned assumptions, for instance, that the so-called facade is of particular importance in architecture just because it is the interface between the building and the "natural" world (which explains the humiliating fact that across a 70-year gap in a century marked by incredible change, the *look* of architecture has barely changed).

In these projects—some of them more than 100 meters deep—the facades merely represent four out of an endless series of possible cuts, most of them vastly more important for the building and its performance as a collective object.

As we concentrated on the "settlement" of the program on these unusual territories, their very unnaturalness opened up more new possibilities: we were forced, for the first time, to explore new potentials for the formation of space.

When we realized that we identified 100% with these programmatic enterprises that intervene drastically in the cultural and political landscape of Europe, we wondered whether—paradoxically by playing with the real fire of Bigness, even in Europe—it could be again possible to become innocent about architecture, to use architecture to articulate the new, to imagine—no longer paralyzed by knowledge, experience, correctness—the end of the Potemkin world.   **1993**

Initially, we simply assume that the weight of the TGB will be supported by columns in a regular grid. The disadvantage is that the void spaces—the whole point of the building—would be skewered. Also, in the lower regions, the columns would get horribly fat. The entrance level would be stunning—a forest of at least 225 gigantic pillars—but not very efficient. Nobody would know where to go. And it would be impossible to excavate larger spaces below for the auditoriums.

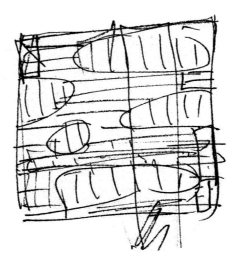

In the next step, we imagine that the outside carapace of the voids is strong enough to replace any structures inside, like a submarine resisting the pressure of the deep sea. But this would demand too many pyrotechnics: grottoes supporting the weight of 30 stories.

over to the indifference of the spectators who are indifferent candy guzzlers.

H

HABITAT

If only I was rich enough to purchase a stuffed warthog. I would have built a room just like one of these for it. Only I would not stick to re-creating perfectly the animal's natural environment, but would add laser guns and flying horses and all the rest of modern world to the background.

HALLUCINATION

Pompeii: we are indebted to a catastrophe for having preserved the most extraordinary piece of our classical heritage. But for Vesuvius we would not have had this living hallucination of Antiquity — as we owe the preservation of mammoths to the sudden onset of the Ice Age. Today, it is all our artificial memory systems that play the museum-building role of natural disasters.

HANDWRITING

He had begun to find "notes," unmistakably in his wife's handwriting, exceedingly small, but very clear, so that if one held a magnifying glass to the page on which she wrote, the letters were perfectly formed, remarkably easy to read, round and clear, the kind of handwriting one would expect from a personality without convolution or complexity.

HAPPEN

You're missing the point. We don't arrange things in an order (that's the function of the utilities). Quite simply, we are facilitating the processes

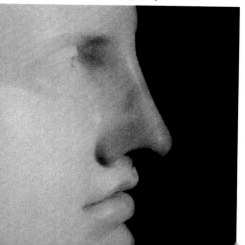

Then we look at Beaubourg: no columns at all, but 84 trusses that span the 48 meters between sides. At these distances, the trusses are three meters deep; ominously, they already consume 43% of the section—space lost? Projected on the library, where trusses would have to span 100 meters, this strategy becomes absurd; they would have to be deeper than the floors they are supposed to liberate from the presence of structure.

But could a floor become an inhabited truss? We could occupy the entire depth of a floor with a vierendeel beam (see Kunsthal I) to create "even" floors dominated by structure alternating with "odd" floors totally free from any structural presence.
The vierendeels could be manipulated to accommodate or disturb program or reason, or simply for tectonic effect. They could form series or catalogs, or they could be identical. But this solution is too subtle for the library; to span 100 meters the vierendeels would have to "crash" through three floors and transgress the space of the voids.

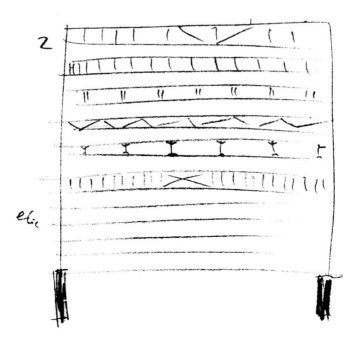

Span

The temple pillars of classical times are spanned by horizontal slabs of stone. Through material change, from stone, to timber, to steel and to reinforced concrete, the journey of span to support remains short & simple; solid beam elements carrying load by internal distribution of bending moment and shear forces.

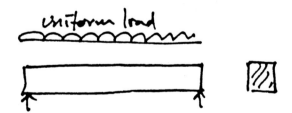

Scaling this concept to cover greater distance does not work — a truss is needed. The lattice framework of diagonals and horizontals booms supporting load by axial force only. The solution is efficient;

Now the plan is divided into parallel zones, 12.5 meters each, separated by walls of concrete; the walls are 100 meters high and act as "deep beams" of theoretically infinite strength. Where the voids occur, they simply punch holes in the beams. In the Great Hall of Ascension, the beams are supported on two opposite sides to create a column-free square of 70 x 70 meters.

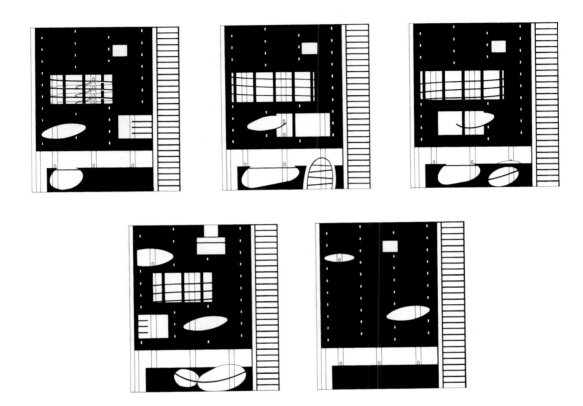

Because the building is colossal, almost a cube, and entirely public, its demands for "conditioning" are massive, its artificiality total. Yet, its 100-meter height (three times the limit specified for the competition) means its relationship with the skyline of Paris is critical. If its section expands like a soufflé through the additional demands of structures and services, the cube (now it fits *inside* the Grande Arche at La Défense) will turn into a tower.

The building simply cannot afford to have ducts. If it turns "zebra," it will never exist. Services must be exiled from the section.

So the walls are made hollow—even stronger—and are subdivided into vertical shafts— plenums—that supply and extract. To service the 12.5 meters in between, they merely have to be punctured. The void spaces each have their own plant rooms: five technological placentas.

Barns, factories, stadia proliferate with them — Railway bridges are dominated by them.

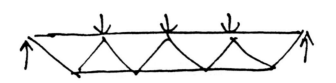

Vierendeel, a Belgian engineer, working at the turn of the century thought the monotony of the diagonals too much. To create a better aesthetic, one that freed the vision, he proposed an open configuration of vertical chords only attached to horizontal booms. The diagonal disappeared and with it the limitations of space.

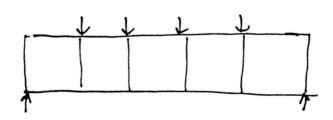

Vierendeel offered the idea to architects. He thought the possibilities of his 'beam' gave more opportunity for design. The Vierendeel girder as it became known, acts

Just as the initial sketches for ZKM trigger the TGB, the vierendeel concept, which doesn't work for the library, forms the basis for the project in Karlsruhe. Its six-meter stories are deep enough for vierendeels to span the 30-meter distance between walls; two walls and nine beams create a "rack," 58 meters tall; the alternation of structurally "marked" and liberated floors allows the sheer superposition of program and architecture—theater on top of laboratory, museum on top of theater, etc.

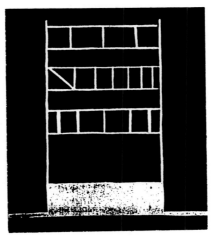

The vierendeels, either through their absence or their presence, become the major instruments that characterize the interior. In Germany, as in Paris, where height is in itself a reason for suspicion, it is equally important to "repress" the section.

The technological placentas of the Bibliothèque become ZKM's atomized plant rooms, which service, from the side, their designated horizontal compartments as directly as possible. Because connections are horizontal, not vertical, "atomizing" and distributing the plant rooms allow us in Karlsruhe to avoid the maddening expansionism of vertical shafts (ultimately to a terminal point where they squeeze all program out of the plan). But actually, that nightmare— the building as shaft—seemed a pregnant formula too, applied three years later in Jussieu.

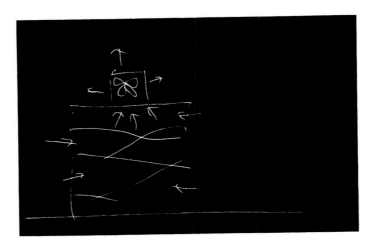

by bringing back bending and shear into the
elements, distributing them throughout the framework.
There are no diagonals. As a result more
material goes into their make up than a truss
but the 'openess' remains a worthwhile
challenge. ~~to take up~~.

The idea never caught on with
the architects of that time and the
Vierendeel remained a civil engineering
concern. Due to the extra material
needed over a truss and the avg
for efficiencies, it has not been popular.

Measure for measure on weight and
strictly engineering parameters the truss is
hard to beat. However if a Vierendeel
is used in a context of penetrability,
where the freedom of the elevation cross
section is important, then it is a good
solution for long span.

In buildings, utilising the storey height,
mobilising lines in the floor and in the
ceiling in conjunction with given columns

in the space, yields a Vierendeel girder.
It offers itself, as it were, for nothing;
but even more spectacular is the gain,
for the area beneath this floor or ~~above~~ above
the ceiling, ~~could~~ need have no columns.

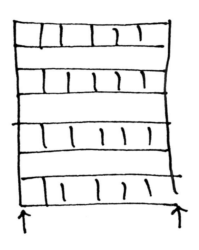

The solution is compact and no disruption
to occupants with a rigid geometry of
diagonals, carving space triangles of limitation.

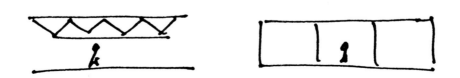

Column placement in a building follows
one above the other in a conventional building.
The foundation sits way below to collect the
regular grid of load. A vierendeel changes
that within the internal confines of a building.

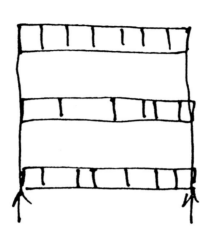

Within the storey, that a vierendeel works,
columns may be adjusted to suit, as
they are only part of a beam system
that can be proportioned and designed
as any other structural component. Its
logic of placement is only relative ~~within~~ to that
storey not the one above or ~~below~~.

In fact, arranging the 'columns'
in equal spacing is not
the best of options.

The Vierendeel works hardest near the supports and more material is needed there.

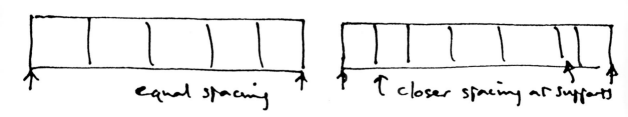

equal spacing   closer spacing at supports

Spacing the columns closer together near the support helps. Placing a wall, that 'joins' up two closely spaced columns is another device.

Boldly compromising the purity of the concept and putting in a diagonal, only in the end bay, solves the support problem at a stroke.

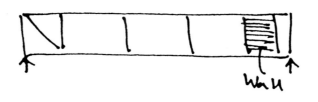

Wall

Using fat column/walls near the edge and using thinner ones near the centre of span is yet another device.

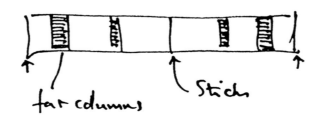

fat columns

Sticks

Playing with the make up of the columns to increase/vary stiffness leads to endless variation.

Thus the make up of a Vierendeel girder becomes an excursion into the science of material, proportion and aesthetics. The efficiency tag of a truss becomes distant, an industrial echo.

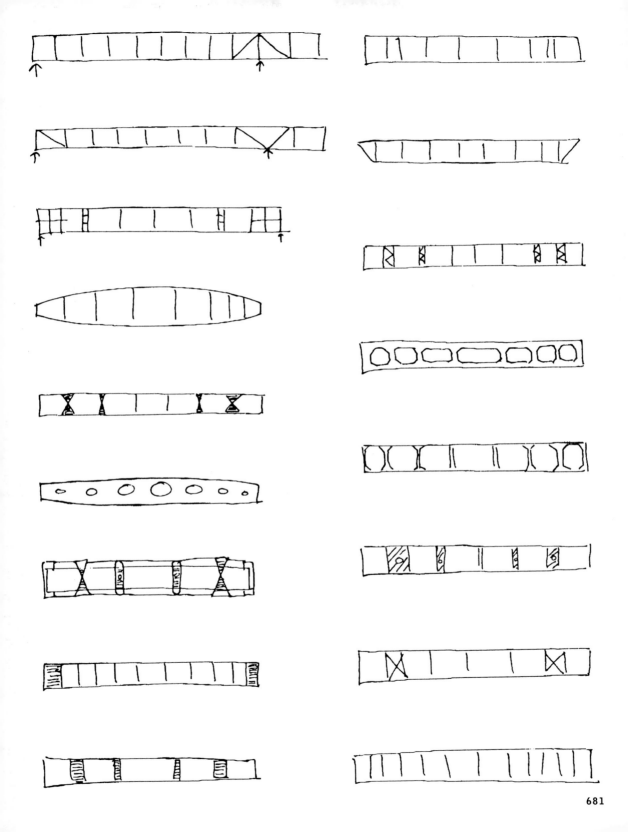

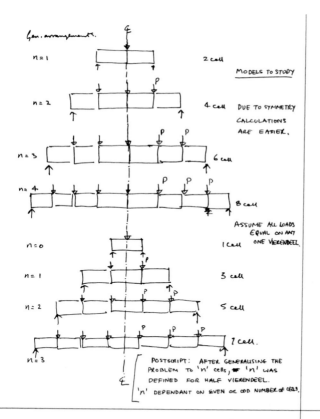

Gen. arrangement.

n = 1 — 2 cell

MODELS TO STUDY

n = 2 — 4 cell — DUE TO SYMMETRY CALCULATIONS ARE EASIER.

n = 3 — 6 cell

n = 4 — 8 cell

ASSUME ALL LOADS EQUAL ON ANY ONE VIERENDEEL.

n = 0 — 1 cell

n = 1 — 3 cell

n = 2 — 5 cell

n = 3 — 7 cell.

POSTSCRIPT: AFTER GENERALISING THE PROBLEM TO 'n' CELLS, 'n' WAS DEFINED FOR HALF VIERENDEEL. 'n' DEPENDANT ON EVEN OR ODD NUMBER OF CELLS.

Investigate action of open cell Vierendeel structures.

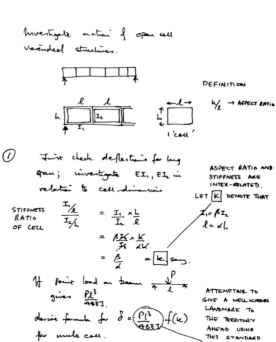

DEFINITION

$h/l \rightarrow$ ASPECT RATIO

1 'cell'

① First check deflections for long span; investigate EI_1, EI_2 in relation to cell dimensions.

ASPECT RATIO AND STIFFNESS ARE INTER-RELATED. LET $\boxed{K}$ DENOTE THAT

$I_1 = \beta I_2$
$l = \alpha h$

STIFFNESS RATIO OF CELL

$$\frac{I_1/l}{I_2/h} = \frac{I_1}{I_2} \times \frac{h}{l}$$

$$= \frac{\beta I_2}{I_2} \times \frac{h}{\alpha h}$$

$$= \frac{\beta}{\alpha} = \boxed{k} \text{ say.}$$

If point load on beam $\xrightarrow{P}{l}$ gives $\frac{Pl^3}{48EI}$

derive formula for $\delta = \boxed{\frac{Pl^3}{48EI}} f(k)$ for multi cell.

$f(k)$ IS THE AREA OF UNCERTAINTY.

ATTEMPT TO GIVE A WELL KNOWN LANDMARK TO THE TERRITORY AHEAD USING THIS STANDARD SOLUTION.

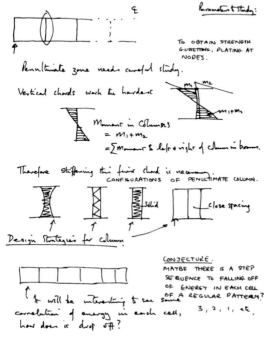

Parameters to study:

TO OBTAIN STRENGTH GUSSETING, PLATING AT NODES.

Penultimate zone needs careful study.

Vertical chords work the hardest

Moment in Columns = $m_1 + m_2$ = Σ Moment to left + right of column in beams.

Therefore stiffening this final chord is necessary.

CONFIGURATIONS OF PENULTIMATE COLUMN.

Solid | Close spacing

Design Strategies for column.

CONJECTURE. MAYBE THERE IS A STEP SEQUENCE TO FALLING OFF OF ENERGY IN EACH CELL OF A REGULAR PATTERN? 3, 2, 1, etc.

It will be interesting to see some correlation of energy in each cell, how does it drop off?

② Check joint behaviour

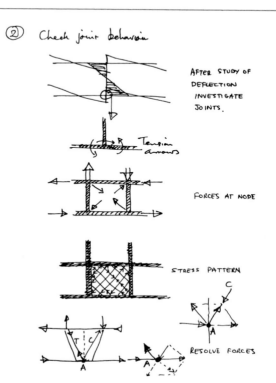

AFTER STUDY OF DEFLECTION INVESTIGATE JOINTS.

Tension arrows

FORCES AT NODE

STRESS PATTERN

RESOLVE FORCES

682

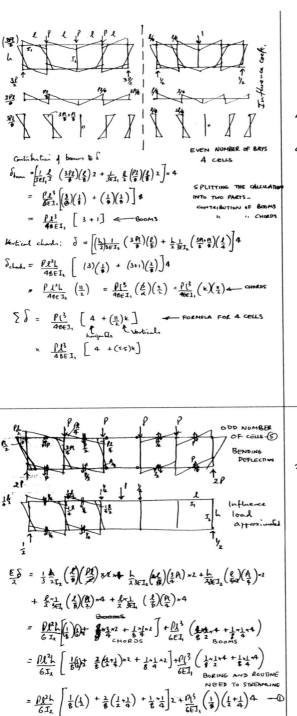

Top-left quadrant:

Bending Moment (vertical label) Influence coeff. (vertical label)

$\left(\tfrac{3P\ell}{8}\right)$ h

$\tfrac{3P}{2}$ $\tfrac{3}{2}$

$\tfrac{3P\ell}{8}$ $\tfrac{3P\ell}{8}+P\ell$ 0

EVEN NUMBER OF BAYS
4 CELLS

Contribution of booms to δ

$$\delta_{boom} = \left[\frac{1}{3EI_1}\frac{\ell}{2}\left(\frac{3P\ell}{8}\right)\left(\frac{\ell}{8}\right)2 + \frac{1}{3EI_1}\frac{\ell}{2}\left(\frac{P\ell}{8}\right)\left(\frac{\ell}{8}\right)2\right]\times 4$$

$$= \frac{P\ell^3}{8EI_1}\left[\left(\frac{3}{8}\right)\left(\frac{1}{8}\right)+\left(\frac{1}{8}\right)\left(\frac{1}{8}\right)\right]8$$

$$= \frac{P\ell^3}{48EI_1}\;[\,3+1\,]\;\longleftarrow\;\text{BOOMS}$$

SPLITTING THE CALCULATION INTO TWO PARTS –
CONTRIBUTION OF BOOMS
      "   "   CHORDS

Vertical chords: $\delta = \left[\left(\frac{h}{2}\right)\frac{1}{3EI_2}\left(\frac{3P\ell}{8}\right)\left(\frac{\ell}{8}\right)+\frac{h}{2}\frac{1}{3EI_2}\left(\frac{3P\ell+P\ell}{8}\right)\left(\frac{1}{4}\right)\right]4$

$$\delta_{chords} = \frac{P\ell^2 h}{48EI_2}\left[(3)\left(\frac{1}{8}\right)+(3+1)\left(\frac{2}{8}\right)\right]4$$

$$\rightarrow \frac{P\ell^2 h}{48EI_2}\left(\frac{11}{2}\right) = \frac{P\ell^3}{48EI_1}\left(\frac{h}{\ell}\right)\left(\frac{I_1}{I_2}\right)= \frac{P\ell^3}{48EI_1}\left(k\right)\left(\frac{11}{2}\right)\;\longleftarrow\;\text{CHORDS}$$

$$\sum\delta = \frac{P\ell^3}{48EI_1}\left[\,4+\left(\frac{11}{2}\right)k\,\right]\;\longleftarrow\;\text{FORMULA FOR 4 CELLS}$$

horizontals verticals

$$= \frac{P\ell^3}{48EI_1}\left[\,4+(5.5)k\,\right]$$

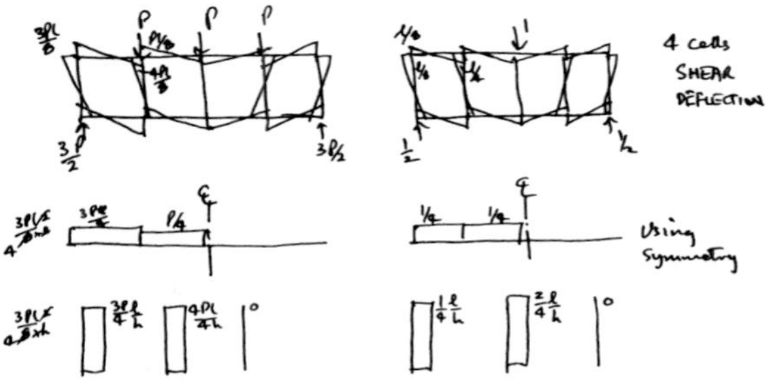

Top-right quadrant:

$\tfrac{3P\ell}{8}$ P P P 4 cells SHEAR DEFLECTION

$\tfrac{3P}{2}$ $\tfrac{3P}{2}$ $\tfrac{1}{2}$ $\tfrac{1}{2}$

$\tfrac{3P\ell}{4\times h}$ $\tfrac{3P\ell}{4h}$ $\tfrac{P\ell}{4}$ Using Symmetry

$\tfrac{3P\ell}{4\times h}$ $\tfrac{3P\ell}{4L}$ $\tfrac{9P\ell}{2L}$ 0 $\tfrac{1\ell}{4L}$ $\tfrac{2\ell}{4L}$ 0

$$\delta_{booms} = \frac{\ell}{GA_1}\left[\left(\frac{3P}{4}\right)\left(\frac{1}{4}\right)+\left(\frac{P}{4}\right)\left(\frac{1}{4}\right)\right]\times 2\times 2$$

$$= \frac{\ell}{GA_1}\left[\frac{3P}{4}+\frac{P}{4}\right] = \frac{P\ell}{4GA_1}\,(3+1)=\frac{P\ell}{4GA_1}[4]$$

$$\delta_{vertical\;chords} = \frac{h}{GA_2}\left[\left(\frac{3P\ell}{4L}\right)\left(\frac{1}{4}\frac{\ell}{L}\right)+\left(\frac{4P\ell}{4L}\right)\left(\frac{2}{4}\frac{\ell}{L}\right)+0\right]\times 2$$

$$\delta_{vert.\;chords} = \frac{h}{4GA_2}\left[\left(3P\frac{\ell^2}{h^2}\right)\frac{1}{4}+\left(8P\frac{\ell^2}{h^2}\right)\frac{1}{4}\right]\times 2$$

$$= \frac{P h}{4GA_2}\left(\frac{\ell^2}{h^2}\right)\left(\frac{3+8}{2}\right)$$

$\frac{\ell}{h}=\alpha$ $\frac{A_1}{A_2}=\beta$

$A_2 = \frac{A_1}{\beta}$ $h=\frac{\ell}{\alpha}$

$$= \frac{P}{4G}\left(\frac{\ell}{\alpha}\right)\left(\frac{1}{A_1/\beta}\right)(\alpha^2)\left(\frac{11}{2}\right)$$

$$= \frac{P\ell}{4GA_1}\left(\frac{\beta}{\alpha}\right)(\alpha^2)\left(\frac{11}{2}\right)$$

$$= \frac{P\ell}{4GA_1}(\alpha\beta)\left(\frac{11}{2}\right)$$

$$\delta_{Total}\;shear = \frac{P\ell}{4GA_1}\left[\,4+(\alpha\beta)\frac{11}{2}\,\right]\;\;\text{Deflection due to shear.}$$

Bottom-left quadrant:

ODD NUMBER OF CELLS (5)
BENDING DEFLECTION

Influence load approximated

$\tfrac{P\ell}{2}$ ... $2P$ ... $\tfrac{\ell}{I_1}$ ... I_2 h

$\tfrac{1}{2}$ ... $\tfrac{1}{2}$

$$\frac{E\delta}{2}=\frac{1}{3}\frac{h}{2I_2}\left(\frac{\ell}{8}\right)\left(\frac{P\ell}{2}\right)\times\alpha + \frac{h}{2\cdot3EI_2}\left(\frac{h\ell}{8}\right)\left(\frac{3P\ell}{8}\right)\times 2+\frac{h}{2\cdot3EI_2}\left(\frac{\ell}{8\cdot2}\right)\left(\frac{P\ell}{4}\right)\times 2$$

$$+ \frac{\ell\cdot\frac{1}{2}}{3EI_1}\left(\frac{\ell}{8}\right)\left(\frac{P\ell}{2}\right)\times 4+\frac{\ell}{2}\frac{1}{3EI_1}\left(\frac{\ell}{8}\right)\left(\frac{P\ell}{4}\right)\times 4$$

$$= \frac{P\ell^2 h}{6I_2}\left(\frac{1}{8}\right)\left(\frac{1}{2}\right)+\left[\frac{3}{8}\times 2+\frac{1}{8}\times 2\right]+\frac{P\ell^3}{6EI_1}\left(\frac{1}{8}\cdot\frac{1}{2}\times 4+\frac{1}{8}\cdot\frac{1}{4}\times 4\right)$$

CHORDS   BOOMS

$$= \frac{P\ell^2 h}{6I_2}\left[\frac{1}{8}\left(\frac{1}{2}\right)+\frac{3}{8}\left(\frac{1}{2}+\frac{1}{4}\right)\times 2+\frac{1}{8}\times\frac{1}{4}\times 2\right]+\frac{P\ell^3}{6EI_1}\left(\frac{1}{8}\right)\left(\frac{1}{2}+\frac{1}{4}\right)4$$

BORING AND ROUTINE NEED TO STREAMLINE

$$= \frac{P\ell^2 h}{6I_2}\left[\frac{1}{8}\left(\frac{1}{2}\right)+\frac{3}{8}\left(\frac{1}{2}+\frac{1}{4}\right)2+\frac{1}{8}\cdot\frac{1}{4}\right]2+\frac{P\ell^3}{6EI_1}\left(\frac{1}{8}\right)\left(\frac{1}{2}+\frac{1}{4}\right)4 \quad\longrightarrow\;①$$

$$= \frac{P\ell^3}{6I_2}\left(\frac{1}{2}\right)\left[\left(\frac{1}{8}\right)\left(\frac{1}{2}\right)+\left(\frac{3}{8}\right)\left(\frac{1}{2}+\frac{1}{4}\right)+\frac{1}{8}\frac{1}{4}\right]2+\frac{P\ell^3}{6EI_1}\left(\frac{1}{8}\right)\left(\frac{1}{2}+\frac{1}{4}\right)4$$

$$= \frac{P\ell^3}{6I_2}\left(\frac{2}{8}\right)\left[\left(\frac{1}{8}\right)\left(\frac{1}{2}\right)+\left(\frac{3}{8}\right)\left(\frac{1}{2}+\frac{1}{4}\right)+\frac{1}{8}\left(\frac{1}{4}\right)\right]+\left(\frac{4}{8}\right)\left[\left(\frac{1}{2}\right)\left(\frac{1}{2}+\frac{1}{4}\right)\right]$$

$$= \frac{P\ell^3}{48EI_1}\,(6+9k)$$

$k=\frac{\beta}{\alpha}=\frac{I_1/\ell}{I_2/h}=$ Stiffness ratio

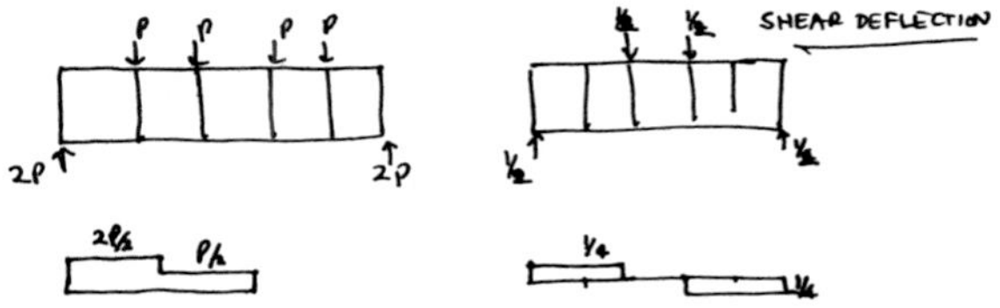

Bottom-right quadrant:

P ... P ... SHEAR DEFLECTION

$2P$ ... $2P$

$\tfrac{2P\ell}{2}$ $P\ell$ $\tfrac{V}{4}$

$$\delta_{booms} = \frac{\ell}{GA_1}\left[\left(\frac{2P}{2}\right)\left(\frac{1}{4}\right)+\left(\frac{P}{2}\right)\left(\frac{1}{4}\right)\right]\times 4$$

$$= \frac{P\ell}{GA_1}\left(\frac{1}{4}\right)\left(\frac{2}{2}+\frac{1}{2}\right)\times 4 \qquad\text{DEFLECTION OF BOOMS}$$

$$= \frac{P\ell}{4GA_1}\left(\frac{4}{2}\right)(2+1)=\frac{P\ell}{4GA_1}(6)$$

Chords:

$\tfrac{2P\ell}{2h}$ $\tfrac{3P\ell}{2h}$ $\tfrac{P\ell}{2h}$ $\tfrac{\ell}{4h}$ $\tfrac{2\ell}{4h}$ $\tfrac{\ell}{4h}$

CALCULATION STREAMLINED

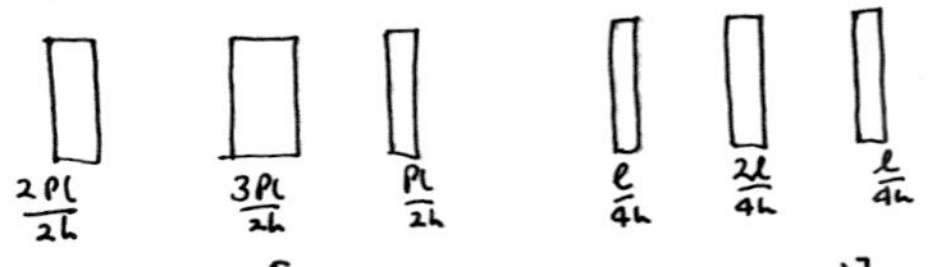

$$\delta_{chords} = \frac{h}{GA_2}\left[\left(\frac{2P\ell}{2L}\right)\left(\frac{\ell}{4L}\right)+\left(\frac{P\ell}{2L}\right)\left(\frac{\ell}{4L}\right)+\left(\frac{3P\ell}{2L}\right)\left(\frac{2L}{4L}\right)\right]\times 2$$

$$= \frac{Ph}{GA_2}\left(\frac{\ell^2}{h^2}\right)\left(\frac{1}{4}\right)\left[\frac{2}{2}+\frac{1}{2}+\frac{3}{2}\times 2\right]\times 2$$

$$= \frac{P\ell}{GA_2}\left(\frac{\ell^2}{h^2}\right)\left(\frac{1}{4}\right)[9] \qquad\text{DEFLECTION DUE TO CHORDS}$$

For $n=2$ Coeffs. [6] for booms, [9] for chords.
For $n=1$ Coeffs. [2] for booms, [4] for chords.

SAME COEFTS. AS FOR BENDING !!

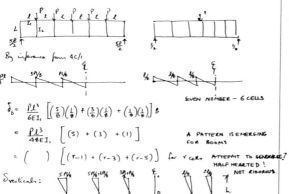

By inference from 4C/1

EVEN NUMBER – 6 CELLS

$$\delta_b = \frac{P\ell^3}{6EI_1}\left[\left(\frac{5}{8}\right)\left(\frac{1}{8}\right)+\left(\frac{3}{8}\right)\left(\frac{1}{8}\right)+\left(\frac{1}{8}\right)\left(\frac{1}{8}\right)\right]8$$

$$= \frac{P\ell^3}{48EI_1}\left[(5)+(3)+(1)\right]$$

$$= (\quad)\left[(r-1)+(r-3)+(r-5)\right] \text{ for } r \text{ cells}$$

A PATTERN IS EMERGING FOR BOOMS

ATTEMPT TO GENERALISE? HALF HEARTED! NOT RIGOROUS

$\delta_{verticals}:$

$$\delta_v = \frac{h}{2}\frac{1}{3EI_2}\left[\left(\frac{5P\ell}{8}\right)\left(\frac{\ell}{8}\right)+\left(\frac{5P\ell+3P\ell}{8}\right)\left(\frac{2\ell}{8}\right)+\left(\frac{3P\ell+P\ell}{8}\right)\left(\frac{2\ell}{8}\right)+0\right]4$$

$$= \frac{P\ell^2}{48EI_1}k\left[(5)+(5+3)(2)+(3+y)(2)+\right]\frac{4}{8}$$

$$= (\quad)\left[5 + 16 + 8\right]\frac{1}{2}$$

LITTLE MORE HOPE – MAYBE ?

$$\sum\delta = \frac{P\ell^3}{48EI_1}\left[9 + \left(\frac{29}{2}\right)k\right]$$
↑horiz ↑verticals

BUT ODD LOOKING NUMBERS.

PREVIOUS SHEET GAVE 11

THERE IS A PATTERN HERE SIMPLY HAVE TO LIST POSSIBLE VARIATIONS BY EXTRAPOLATING AND ATTEMPT ANALYSIS.

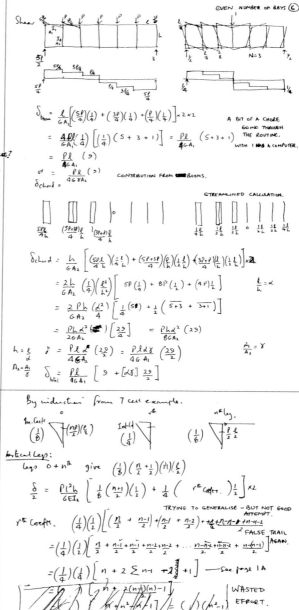

Shear

EVEN NUMBER OF BAYS (6)

N=3

$$\delta_{boom} = \frac{\ell}{GA_1}\left[\left(\frac{5P}{4}\right)\left(\frac{1}{4}\right)+\left(\frac{3P}{4}\right)\left(\frac{1}{4}\right)+\left(\frac{P}{4}\right)\left(\frac{1}{4}\right)\right]\times2\times2$$

A BIT OF A CHORE GOING THROUGH THE ROUTINE. WISH I HAD A COMPUTER.

$$= \frac{4P\ell}{GA_1}\left(\frac{1}{4}\right)\left[\left(\frac{1}{4}\right)(5+3+1)\right] = \frac{P\ell}{4GA_1}(5+3+1)$$

$$= \frac{P\ell}{4GA_1}(9)$$

$$\sigma = \frac{P\ell}{4G\cdot 8A_1}(9)$$ CONTRIBUTION FROM BOOMS.

$\delta_{chord} =$ STREAMLINED CALCULATION.

$$\delta_{chord} = \frac{h}{GA_2}\left[\left(\frac{5P\ell}{4h}\right)\left(\frac{1}{4}\frac{\ell}{h}\right)+\left(\frac{5P+3P}{4}\right)\left(\frac{\ell}{h}\right)\left(\frac{1}{2}\frac{\ell}{h}\right)+\left(\frac{3P+P}{4}\right)\left(\frac{\ell}{h}\right)\left(\frac{1}{2}\frac{\ell}{h}\right)\right]\times2$$

$$= \frac{2h}{GA_2}\left(\frac{1}{4}\right)\left(\frac{\ell^2}{h^2}\right)\left[5P\left(\frac{1}{4}\right)+8P\left(\frac{1}{2}\right)+(4P)\frac{1}{2}\right]$$

$$= \frac{2Ph}{GA_2}\left(\frac{\ell^2}{h^2}\right)\frac{1}{4}\left[\frac{1}{4}(5P)+\frac{1}{2}(\overline{5+3}+\overline{3+1})\right]$$

$$= \frac{P\ell}{2GA_2}\left(\frac{\ell}{h}\right)\left[\frac{23}{4}\right] = \frac{Ph\ell^2}{8GA_2}(29)$$

$h=\frac{\ell}{\alpha}$, $\delta = \frac{P\ell\alpha}{4G A_2}\left(\frac{29}{2}\right) = \frac{P\ell\gamma}{4G A_1}\left(\frac{29}{2}\right)$

$h=\frac{\ell}{\alpha}$

$A_2=\frac{A_1}{\gamma}$

$\frac{A_1}{A_2}=\gamma$

$$\delta_{total} = \frac{P\ell}{4GA_1}\left[9+\left[\alpha\gamma\right]\frac{29}{2}\right]$$

$$\frac{3P\ell}{2}\cdot\frac{\ell}{2}$$

INFLUENCE LOAD SPLIT $\frac{1}{2}$, $\frac{1}{2}$

Vert. legs. $$\frac{\delta}{2} = \frac{h}{2}\frac{1}{3EI_2}P\ell\alpha\left[\frac{1}{8}\times\frac{3}{2}\times\frac{1}{2}+\frac{1}{8}\left(\frac{3}{2}+\frac{2}{2}\right)\frac{1}{2}+\frac{1}{4}\left(\frac{2}{2}+\frac{1}{2}\right)\left(\frac{1}{2}\right)+\frac{1}{8}\left(\frac{1}{2}+0\right)\left(\frac{1}{2}\right)\right]\times2$$

$$\frac{\delta}{2} = \frac{P\ell^2 h}{6EI_2}\left[\frac{1}{8}\times\frac{3}{4}+\frac{1}{8}\left(\frac{3}{2}+\frac{2}{2}\right)+\frac{1}{2}\left(\frac{2}{2}+\frac{1}{2}\right)+\frac{1}{8}\left(\frac{1}{2}\right)\left(\frac{1}{2}\right)\right]\times2$$

$$= (\quad)\frac{1}{8}\left[\frac{3}{4}+\frac{1}{4}+\frac{1}{2}\left(3+2+1+1\right)\right]\times2$$

DEFLECTION VERTICAL CHORDS

$$= (\quad)\frac{1}{8}\left[1+4\right] = \left(\frac{5}{8}\right)\left[\frac{P\ell^2 h}{6EI_2}\right]\times2$$

Horiz. $$\frac{\delta}{2} = \frac{\ell}{2}\frac{1}{3EI_1}P\ell\alpha\left[\frac{3}{2}\times\frac{1}{2}\times\frac{1}{8}+\frac{2}{2}\times\frac{1}{2}\times\frac{1}{8}+\frac{1}{2}\times\frac{1}{2}\times\frac{1}{8}\right]\times4$$

$$= \frac{P\ell^3}{6EI_1}\left[\frac{1}{8}\times\frac{1}{2}\left(\frac{3}{2}+\frac{2}{2}+\frac{1}{2}\right)\right]\times4$$

CONTRIBUTION FROM BOOMS

$$= \frac{P\ell^3}{6EI_1}\left[\frac{1}{8}\times\frac{1}{2}\times3\right]\times4 = \frac{P\ell^3}{48EI_1}\times\left(\frac{6}{2}\right)4$$

$$\sum\delta = \frac{P\ell^3}{48EI_1}\left[\left(\frac{\beta}{\lambda}\right)\times10+\frac{3}{2}\times4\right] = \frac{P\ell^3}{48EI_1}\left[10k+6\right]\times2$$

SUFFICIENT MODELS TO DETERMINE COEFFICIENTS OF A GENERAL EXPRESSION

$$= \frac{P\ell^3}{48EI_1}\left[20k+12\right]$$

By induction from 7 cell example.

In. Cells $\left(\frac{1}{8}\right)$ $\left(\frac{nP}{2}\right)\left(\frac{\ell}{4}\right)$ Intld $\left(\frac{1}{4}\right)$ nth leg. $\left(\frac{1}{8}\right)$ $\frac{P}{2}\frac{\ell}{2}$

Vertical Legs:

legs $0+n^{th}$ give $\left(\frac{1}{8}\right)\left(\frac{n}{2}+\frac{1}{2}\right)\left(P\ell\right)\left(\frac{\ell}{2}\right)$

$$\frac{\delta}{2} = \frac{P\ell^2 h}{6EI_2}\left[\frac{1}{8}\left(\frac{n+1}{2}\right)\left(\frac{1}{2}\right)+\frac{1}{4}\left(r^{th}\text{ Coeffs.}\right)\frac{1}{2}\right]\times2$$

TRYING TO GENERALISE – BUT NOT GOOD ATTEMPT

r^{th} Coeffs. $\left(\frac{1}{4}\right)\left(\frac{1}{2}\right)\left[\left(\frac{n}{2}+\frac{n-1}{2}\right)+\left(\frac{n-1}{2}+\frac{n-2}{2}\right)+\frac{n-2}{2}\frac{n-3}{2}\cdot\cdot\cdot\frac{n-4-2}{2}\right]$

FALSE TRAIL AGAIN.

$$= \left(\frac{1}{4}\right)\left(\frac{1}{2}\right)\left[\frac{n}{2}+\frac{n-1}{2}+\frac{n-1}{2}+\frac{n-2}{2}+\frac{n-2}{2}+\ldots+\frac{n-\overline{n-2}}{2}+\frac{\overline{n-n}}{2}+\frac{n(n-1)}{2}\right]$$

$$= \left(\frac{1}{4}\right)\left(\frac{1}{4}\right)\left[n+2\sum_{n-1}+2\frac{1}{2}+1\right] \longrightarrow \text{See page 1A}$$

WASTED EFFORT.

$$\frac{1}{2}\left[n+2\frac{(n-1)(n)}{2}-1\right] = \frac{n+n^2-n}{2}-1 = \frac{n^2}{2}-1$$

$$\frac{\delta}{2} = [fP]\left[\frac{1}{8}\times\frac{1}{2}\left(\frac{n+1}{2}\right)+\frac{1}{4}(n^2-1)\right]\times2 \qquad \times\text{ FAILED }\times$$

$$= [fP]\frac{1}{16}\left[\frac{n+1}{2}+2n^2-2\right]\times2$$

$$= [fP]\frac{1}{16}\left[\frac{2n^2+n-1}{2}\right]\times2 = \frac{P\ell^2 h}{48EI_2}\left[2n^2+n-1\right]$$

$n=2$, $[\quad] = 2+4+2-1 = 9$

$n=3$, $= 2\times9+3-1 = 20$ etc.

684

Shear:

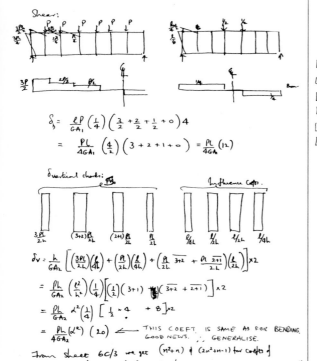

$$\delta_b = \frac{\ell P}{GA_1}\left(\frac{1}{4}\right)\left(\frac{3}{2}+\frac{2}{2}+\frac{1}{2}+0\right)4$$

$$= \frac{PL}{4GA_1}\left(\frac{4}{2}\right)(3+2+1+0) = \frac{PL}{4GA_1}(12)$$

Svertical chords:

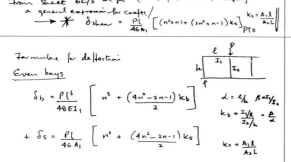

Influence coeffs.

$$\delta_v = \frac{h}{GA_2}\left[\left(\frac{3PL}{2L}\right)\left(\frac{L}{4L}\right)+\left(\frac{PL}{2L}\right)\left(\frac{L}{4L}\right)+\left(\frac{PL}{2L}\overline{\frac{3+2}{}}\right)+\left(\frac{PL}{2L}\overline{\frac{2+1}{2L}}\right)\left(\frac{L}{2L}\right)\right]\times 2$$

$$= \frac{Ph}{GA_2}\left(\frac{L^2}{L^2}\right)\left(\frac{1}{4}\right)\left[\left(\frac{1}{2}\right)(3+1)+(\overline{3+2}+\overline{2+1})\right]\times 2$$

$$= \frac{Ph}{GA_2}\alpha^2\left(\frac{1}{4}\right)\left[\frac{1}{2}\cdot 4 + 8\right]\times 2$$

$$= \frac{Ph}{4GA_2}(\alpha^2)(20) \longleftarrow \text{THIS COEFT. IS SAME AS FOR BENDING. GOOD NEWS. } \therefore \text{ GENERALISE.}$$

From sheet 6C/3 we get (n^2+n) & $(2n^2+n-1)$ for coefts of a general expression for coefts/

$$\longrightarrow \text{\Large\textasteriskcentered} \quad \delta_{shear} = \frac{PL}{4GA_1}\left[(n^2+n)+(2n^2+n-1)k_s\right] \quad k_s=\frac{A_1\ell}{A_2L} \quad \text{PTO}$$

Formulae for deflection

Even bays

$$\delta_b = \frac{P\ell^3}{48EI_1}\left[n^2+\left(\frac{4n^2-2n-1}{2}\right)k_b\right]$$

$$+\ \delta_s = \frac{PL}{4GA_1}\left[n^2+\left(\frac{4n^2-2n-1}{2}\right)k_s\right]$$

$$\alpha = \ell/h \quad \beta = I_1/I_2$$
$$k_b = \frac{I_1/\ell}{I_2/h} = \frac{\beta}{\alpha}$$
$$k_s = \frac{A_1\ell}{A_2h}$$

Odd bays

$$\delta_b = \frac{P\ell^3}{48EI_1}\left[(n^2+n)+(2n^2+n-1)k_b\right] \quad k_b=\frac{I_1/\ell}{I_2/h}$$

$$\delta_s = \frac{PL}{4GA_1}\left[(n^2+n)+(2n^2+n-1)k_s\right] \quad k_s=\frac{A_1\ell}{A_2h}$$

IT IS SATISFYING THAT THE COEFTS. FOR BENDING AND SHEAR DEFLECTION ARE THE SAME.

NOTE:

① δ_b = deflection due to bending in elements
   δ_s = deflection due to shear } deflection due to axial needs to be looked at.

② For even bays ▨▢▢▢ n = half no. of bays
   for 6 bays n=3.
   For odd bays ▨▨▢▢ 5 is bays n=2
   7 bays n=3 etc.

   MORE WORK NEEDED ON AXIAL COMPONENT. ++ IRREGULAR BAYS!

③ For odd bays deflection is underestimated by about 10% - better as no. of bays increases. Coeft affected $\boxed{2n^2+n-1}$ ⟵ needs improving

④ Equations in form $\delta = \left[f(P)\right]\left[C_1 + C_2 k\right]$

From 6C/1
Extrapolate coeffs:

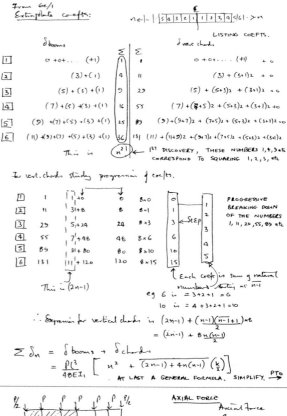

$$\Sigma \delta_n = \delta_{booms} + \delta_{chords}$$
$$= \frac{P\ell^3}{48EI_1}\left[n^2 + \overline{(2n-1)+4n(n-1)}\left(\frac{k_s}{2}\right)\right]$$
AT LAST A GENERAL FORMULA. SIMPLIFY. PTO ⟶

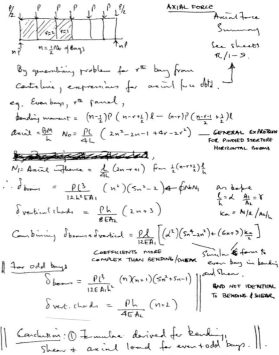

AXIAL FORCE
Axial Force Summary
See sheets R/1-9.

By generalising problem for rth bay from Centreline, expressions for axial force obtained.

eg. Even bays, rth panel,

bending moment = $(n-\frac{1}{2})P(n-r+\frac{1}{2})\ell - (n-r)P(\frac{n-r-1}{2}+\frac{1}{2})\ell$

Axial = $\frac{BM}{h}$ $N_0 = \frac{PL}{4L}(2n^2-2n-1+4r-2r^2)$ ── GENERAL EXPRESSION FOR PINNED STRUCTURE HORIZONTAL BOOMS

N_1 = Axial influence = $\frac{\ell}{4L}(2n-r+1)$ for $\frac{1}{2}(n-r+\frac{1}{2})\ell$

$\therefore \delta_{booms} = \frac{P\ell^3}{12L^2EA_1}(n^2)(5n^2-2)$ ⟵ $\oint N_0 N_1$ as before $\frac{\ell}{L}=\alpha$ $\frac{A_1}{A_2}=\gamma$

$\delta_{vertical\ chords} = \frac{Ph}{8EA_2}(2n+3)$ $k_a = \frac{A_1\ell}{A_2h}$

Combining $\delta_{booms}+\delta_{vertical} = \frac{P\ell}{12EA_1}\left[(\alpha^2)(5n^4-2n^2)+(6n+3)\frac{k_a}{2}\right]$

COEFFICIENTS MORE COMPLEX THAN BENDING/SHEAR Similar in form to even bay in bending and shear.

For odd bays
$$\delta_{booms} = \frac{P\ell^3}{12EA_1L^2}(n)(n+1)(5n^2+5n-1)$$
$$\delta_{vertical\ chords} = \frac{Ph}{4EA_2}(n+2)$$

AND NOT IDENTICAL TO BENDING & SHEAR

Conclusion: ① Formulae derived for bending, shear + axial load for even + odd bays.
Also ② Test formulae against computer models. ③ Study irregular bay spacing!

685

Darwinian Arena

Zentrum für Kunst und Medientechnologie
(Center for Art and Media Technology)
Karlsruhe, Germany
Competition, Design Development
1989–92

Karlsruhe is a city in denial.

While, with the imminence of a united Europe, each city positions itself by claiming — and if necessary constructing — maximum centrality, Karlsruhe *is* Europe's geographical middle, a condition it can therefore afford to ignore. It prefers the oblivious pose of "typical West German city at the end of the 20th century." Its citizens serenely inhabit the baroque idyll of their reconstructed townscape, united in their determination to resist unpleasantness from wherever it may come.

It matters little that, like each historical city in Europe, their town has been thoroughly modernized: on top of a new parking garage, its train station is being extended to receive the IDZ, Germany's (slower) equivalent of the French TGV. Surrounded by twenties *Siedlungen*, suburbs, shopping centers, and other emblems of the nonhierarchical world, the city is dwarfed by its own periphery. But conceptually its "heart" will always remain the center: Kaiserstrasse, its main pedestrian shopping street; town square; *Schloss*; university; the surrounding *Wälder*.

Take a futuristic institution—ZKM, Zentrum für Kunst und Medientechnologie, also known as Electronic Bauhaus—and place it in this
context! Projected on the perimeter of the baroque town, on a narrow
strip of land on the wrong side of station and tracks, it faces on- and off-
ramps of the *Autobahn*.

Its program amalgamates a museum of media art; a museum of contemporary art; research and production facilities for music, video, and virtual
reality; a theater for media; lecture hall; media library (a future Hoch-
schule für Media); etc. It represents a laboratory open to the public—a
huge apparatus to investigate, once and for all, the elusive connection
between *Kunst* and technology, a Darwinian arena where classical and
electronic media can compete with and influence each other.

To generate density, exploit proximity, provoke tension, maximize friction, organize in-betweens, promote filtering, sponsor identity *and* stimulate blurring, the entire program is incorporated in a single container, 43 x 43 x 58 meters.

The container is pushed bluntly against the railway embankment, then coupled with the station circulation to form a new, two-faced entity: to the city, it is BAHNHOFMUSEUM, to the periphery MUSEUMBAHNHOF.

On the south is the "robot," an adaptation of the fly tower of a conventional theater: a void space that runs the entire height of the building to allow stage sets, electronic devices, projectors, art, containers, capsules to move up and down or to be locked in place to create new conditions on particular floors. Behind a corrugated polyester skin, these movements become signals of activity to the *Autobahn* traffic.

The west zone, clad in giant glazed bricks, contains offices and individual plant rooms for each major program, to provide the most specific, direct, precise servicing.

B A H

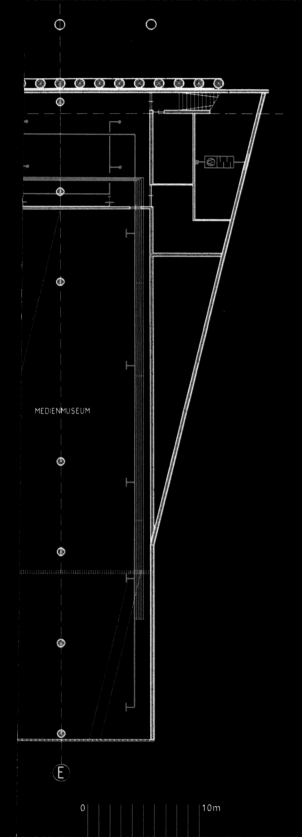

MEDIENMUSEUM

E

0 |||||||||||| 10m

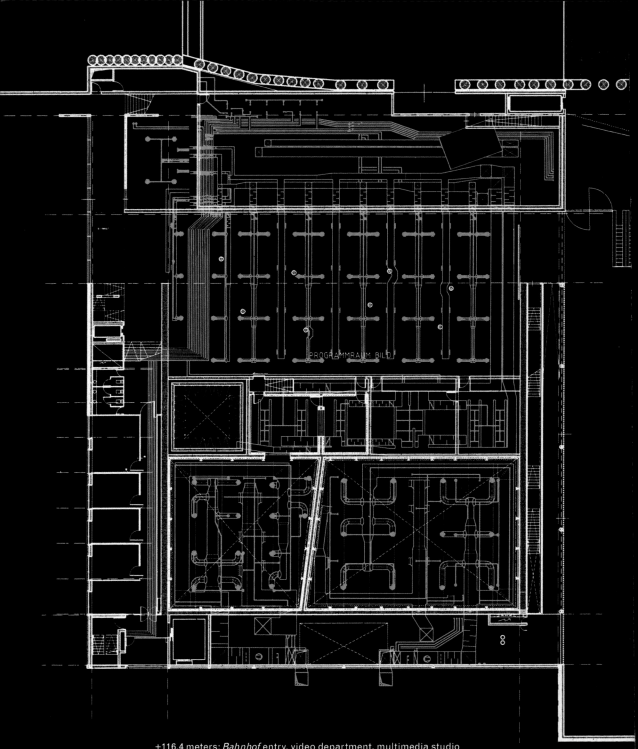

PROGRAMMRAUM BILD

+116.4 meters: *Bahnhof* entry, video department, multimedia studio.

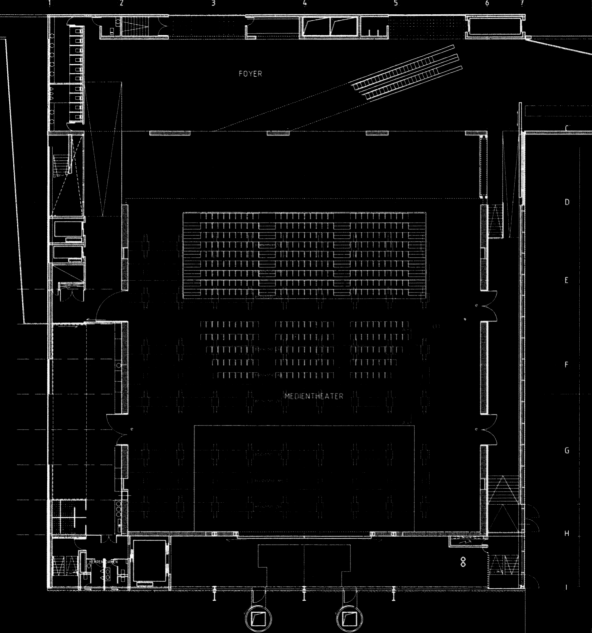

FOYER

MEDIENTHEATER

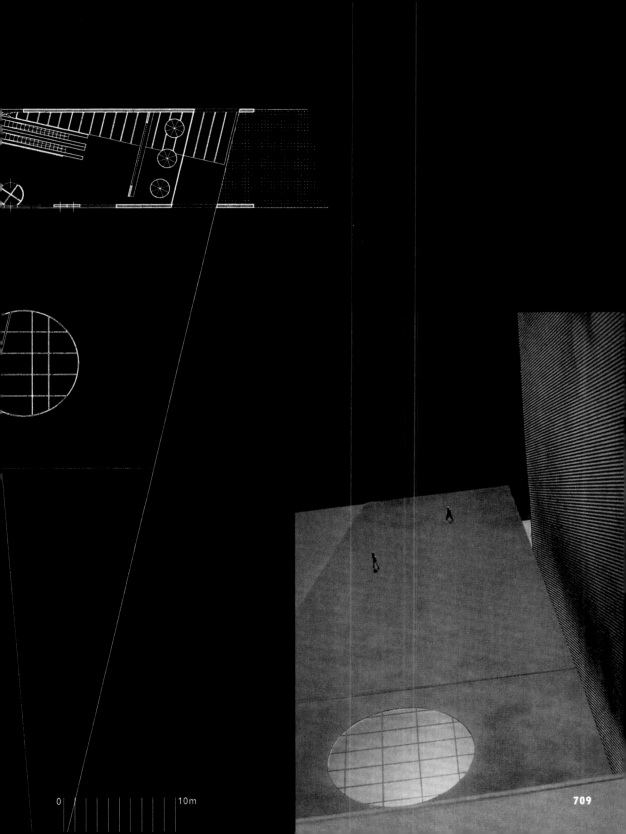

0 | 10m

709

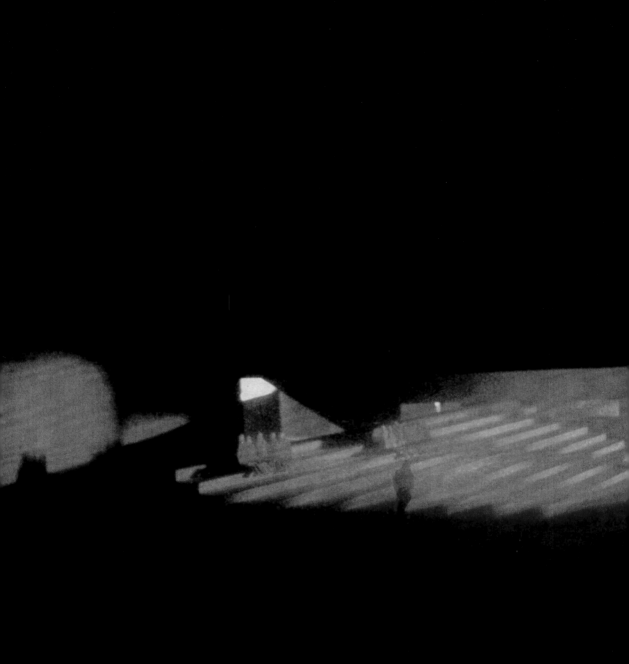

712

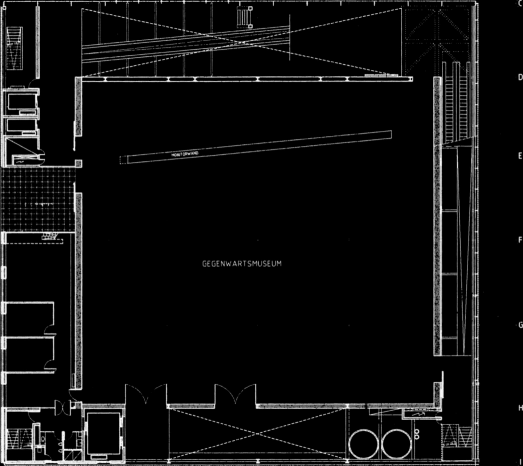

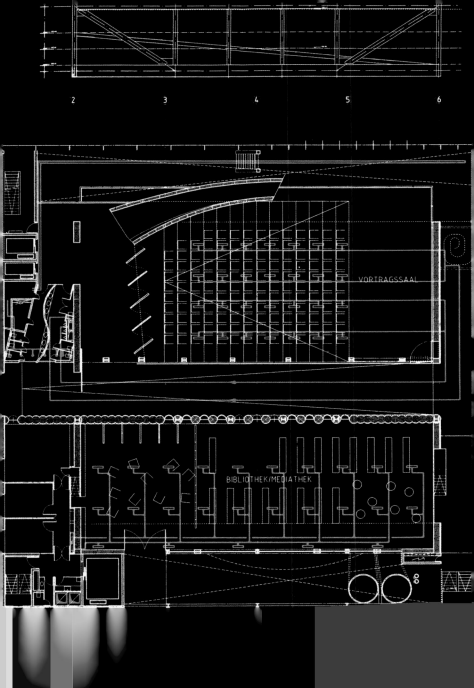

2　　　　3　　　　4　　　　5　　　　6

VORTRAGSSAAL

BIBLIOTHEK/MEDIATHEK

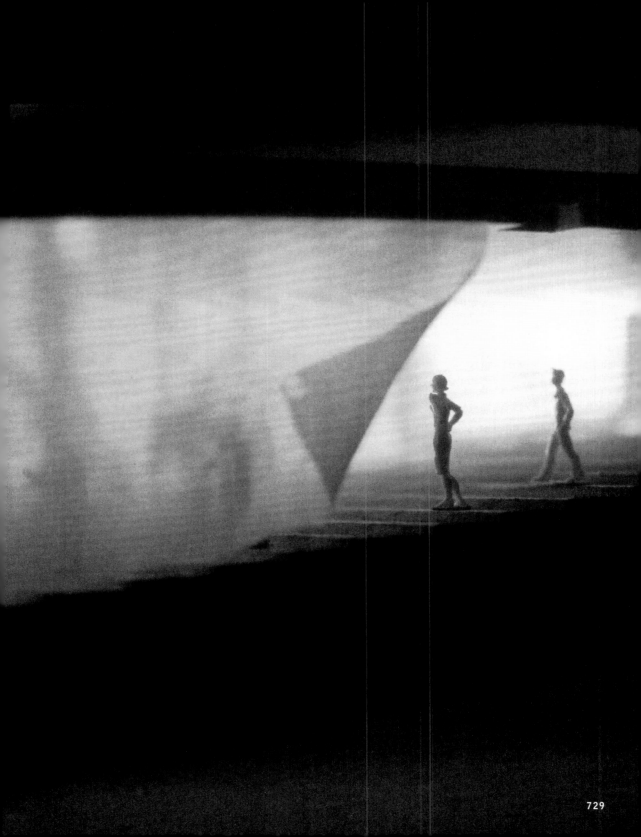

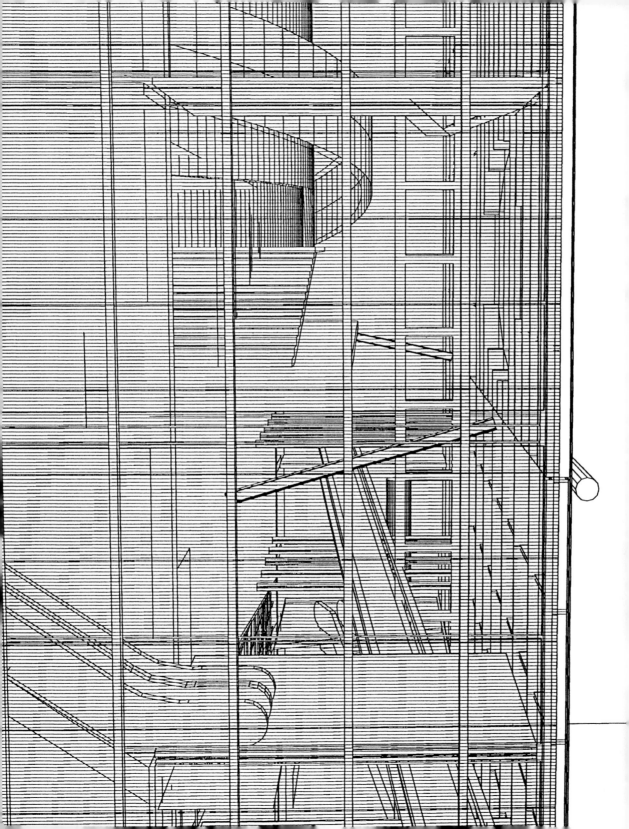

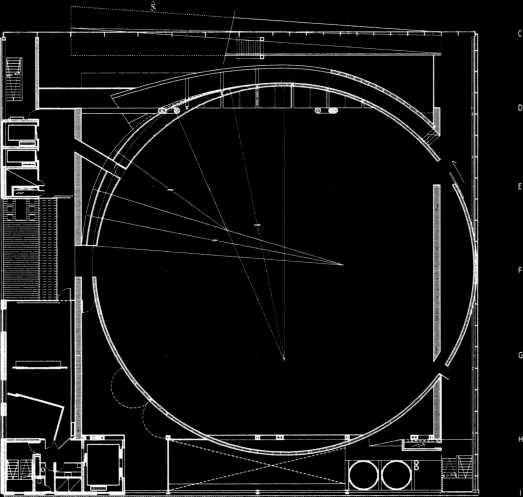

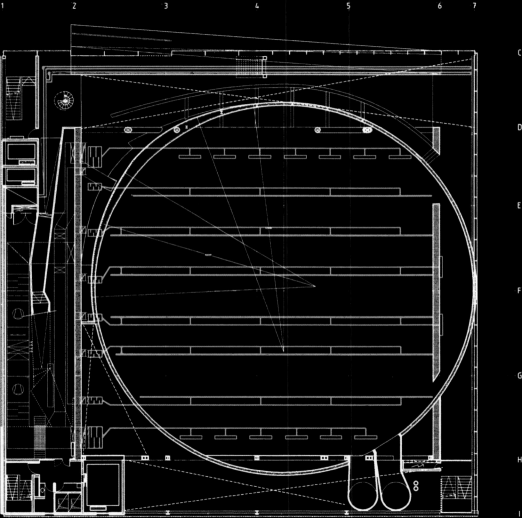

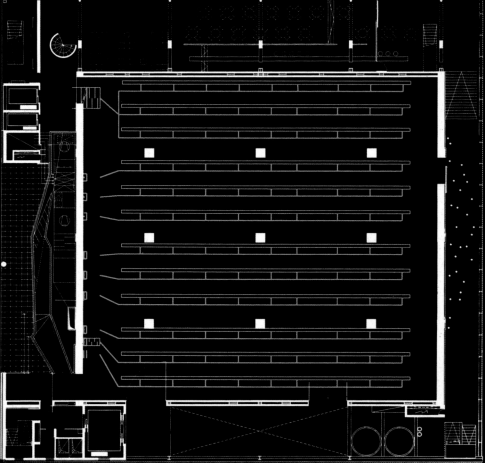

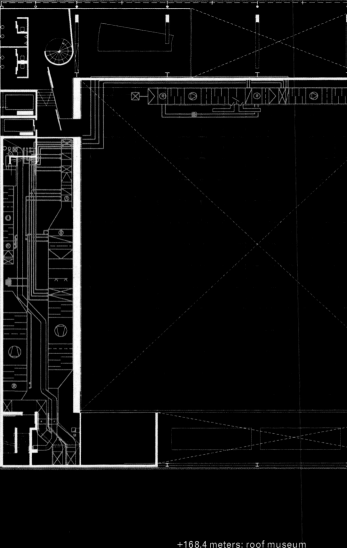

+168.4 meters: roof museum

743

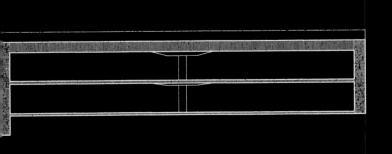

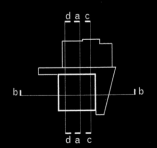

d a c

b | | b

d a c

0 |||||||||| 10m

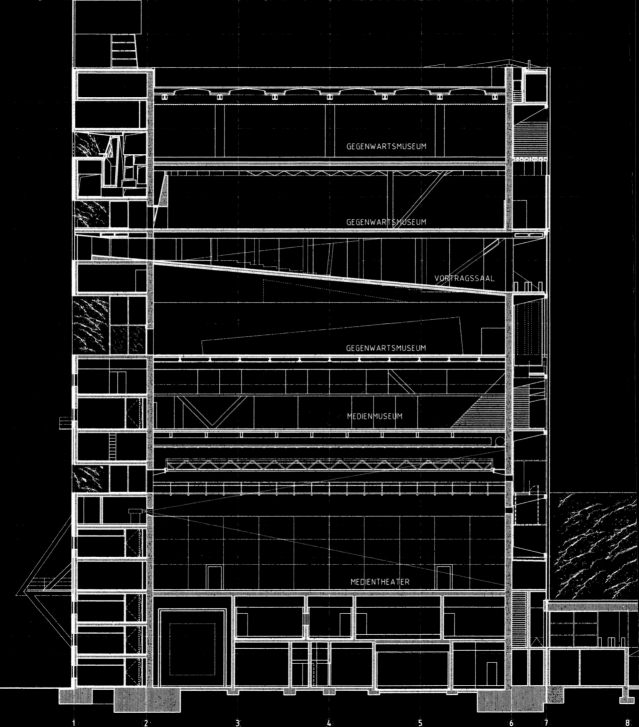

GEGENWARTSMUSEUM

GEGENWARTSMUSEUM

VORTRAGSSAAL

GEGENWARTSMUSEUM

MEDIENMUSEUM

MEDIENTHEATER

1   2   3   4   5   6   7   8

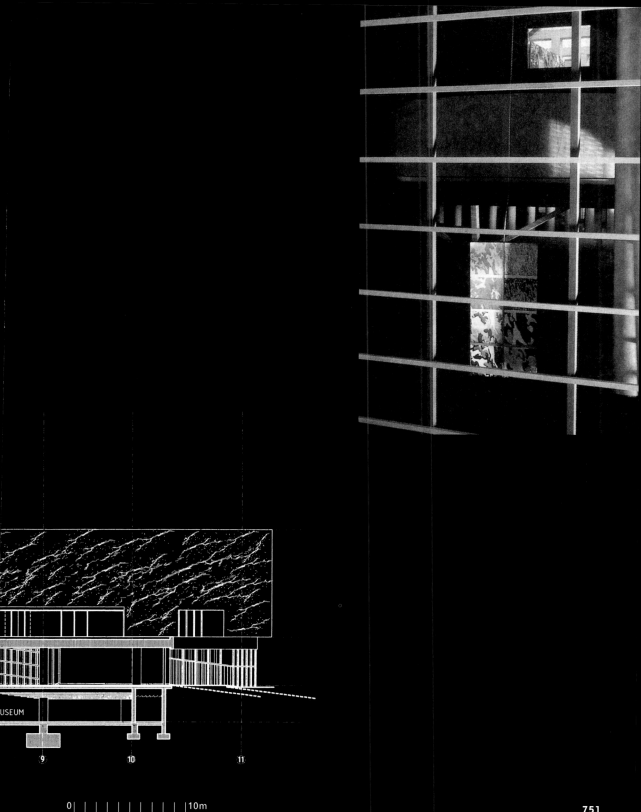

USEUM

9   10   11

0   10m

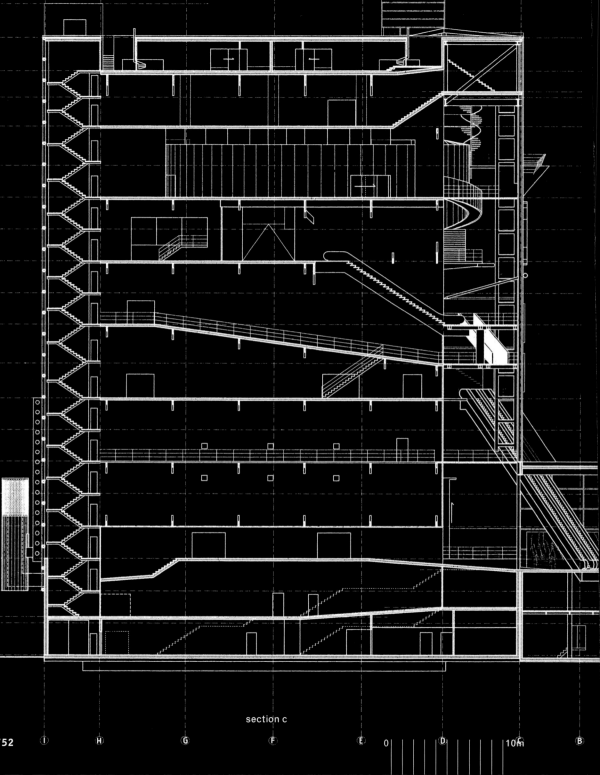

section c

Ⓘ   Ⓗ   Ⓖ   Ⓕ   Ⓔ   0   Ⓓ   10m   Ⓑ

762

Passion Play On June 16, 1992, the city council of Karlsruhe (provincial south German city; 293,854 God-fearing, mostly Roman Catholic inhabitants; center of German high-tech activity; Europe's hidden equivalent to Silicon Valley) voted (42 to 25) to abandon the project for a new Zentrum für Kunst und Medientechnologie — the implausible implantation of an avant-garde institution deep in the German province — for which, three years earlier, OMA had been appointed architect after winning an international competition. It was going to be OMA's first demonstration of Bigness.

ZKM was an experimental building for a culture that only registers what is (presented as) conventional. Its fiasco showed that even where such a culture needs *recombinations*, the inevitable slowness of architecture — its inability to embody experiments *quickly* — tends to obliterate the fragile opportunities that occur in the unstable constellations of political and economic forces that indeed seal our fate.

The vote was the final episode in a slow unraveling of the project's feasibility that shockingly exposed the fundamental inequality of the forces at work: on one side, the best efforts of the architect — the conception of the project itself, three years of weekly visits to Germany, 300 flights, 30,000 kilometers of *Autobahn* risk, 150 German meals, the assembly of a brilliant team of advisers, the transplant of a considerable part of the office to the "deep south" of another country, the production of full working drawings; on the other side, a chain of unpredictable events that started with Germany's sudden unification (which made vast ambitions in the former west almost suspect), was accelerated by the fall from grace of a key politician for allegedly accepting a free vacation in Thailand (or was it Trinidad?), and ended at the municipal level with the mayor's brainchild: to put the new museum in an abandoned munitions factory which was first supposed to be demolished, then almost turned into a shopping center with Taiwanese money, and finally declared a national monument, all in the space of three years.

The structural disproportion between the energy invested and the pleasure (and money) derived from architecture left a malaise beyond a normal period of mourning: the architect is prisoner of an infernal equation in which passion undermines best interests. Local regimes need special projects to demonstrate their "modernity" but are finally unwilling to assume their radicalism, conceiving then aborting successive "could have beens" to prove first their adventurousness, then their sobriety.

The problem with Bigness is that it delivers more at a time, but also takes more time to deliver. In the absence of an implacable urgency — real or invented — the rush of modernization outruns its own potential implementations, another mother eating her chidren.

1992

Organization of Appearances

Congrexpo (Lille Grand Palais)
Lille, France
Completed 1994

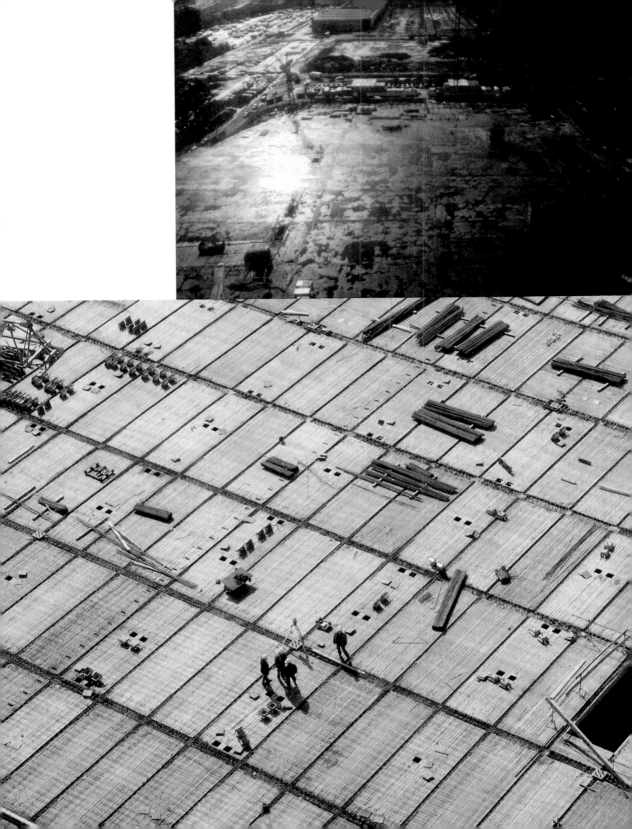

smoothly for decades thanks to a social hierarchy as rigid and as formal-
ized as an anthill's, with an incidence
of crime, social unrest, and petty
misdemeanors that was virtually nil.

HIGHFALUTIN

1. PRETENTIOUS. 2. Expressed in
or marked by the use of high-flown
bombastic language: POMPOUS.

HISTORICAL

Any group of buildings may be
classified as historical whose homo-
geneity, and historical, archaeological,
aesthetic and picturesque qualities
are sufficient to justify preserving it
and displaying it to advantage.

HISTORY

This is what you get as a result of this
belief in history: a building that mimics history, but through its scale and
volume alone radically breaks through

the scale of history and is neither
really new, nor really historical.

HOLE[1]

The first hole made through a piece
of stone is a revelation. The hole
connects one side to the other, making

malchick in the chair of torture
while they flashed nasty bits of
ultra-violence on the screen, my
glazzies clipped open to viddy all,
my plott and rookers and nogas
fixed to the chair so I could not get
away. What I was being made to
viddy now was not really a veshch
I would have thought to be too bad
before, it being only three or four
malchicks crasting in a shop and filling their carmans with cutter, at the
same time fillying about with the
creeching starry ptitsa running the
shop, tolchoking her and letting the
red red krovvy flow. But the throb
and like crash crash crash in my gul-
liver and the wanting to be sick and
the terrible dry rasping thirstiness
in my rot, all were worse than yesterday. "Oh, I've had enough," I
cried. "It's not fair, you vonny sods,"
and I tried to struggle out of the
chair but it was not possible, me
being as good as stuck to it.

HOTELS
I like hotels because in a hotel room
you have no history, you have only
an essence. You feel like you're all
potential, waiting to be rewritten,
like a crisp, blank sheet of 8½-by-
11-inch white bond paper. There is
no past.

HUMAN
In the same way that surplus values
are increasingly independent of man-
power in the post-capitalist technological environment, the human
scale ceases to be applicable to a
topography implemented mechani-
cally: the *phenomenological* relationship between the human body and
constructed space loses its sense.

HUMANITY
The majority of people are a fragmentary, exclusive image of what
humanity is: you have to add them
up to get humanity. In this sense,
whole eras and whole peoples have
something fragmentary about them;
and it may be necessary for humanity's growth for it to develop only
in parts. It is a crucial matter therefore to see that what is at stake is
always the idea of producing a synthetic humanity and that the inferior
humans who make up a majority of
us are only preliminaries, or prepar-
atory attempts whose concerted play
allows a *whole human being* to
appear here and there like a military

IMAGES²

Images have become our true sex object, the object of our desire. The obscenity of our culture resides in the confusion of desire and its equivalent materialized in the image; not only for sexual desire, but in the desire for knowledge and its equivalent materialized in "information," the desire for fantasy and its equivalent materialized in the Disneylands of the world, the desire for space and its equivalent programmed into vacation itineraries, the desire for play and its equivalent programmed into private telematics. It is this promiscuity and the ubiquity of images, the viral contamination of things by images, which are the fatal characteristics of our culture.

IMAGINE

Imagine that there's a war … and no one is watching television.

IMPORT

Cod roe with red peppers is one of Hakata's most famous products. However, it is not actually a traditional food of Hakata, rather it originally came from Korea. It is a mixture of cod roe (walleye pollack eggs) from Hokkaido with red

peppers from Kyoto, prepared in
Korean style.

IMPORTANT

It was the most important event of
my professional life.

IMPOSSIBILITIES

A creator is someone who creates
his own impossibilities, and thereby
creates possibilities. It's by banging
your head against the wall that you
find an answer. You have to work
on the wall, because without a set of

impossibilities, you won't have the
line of flight, the exit that is creation,
the power of falsity that is truth.
You have to be liquid or gaseous,
precisely because normal perception
and opinion are solid, geometric.

IMPOSTER

And when I put that name "Architect" on a glass door, which by the
way was about the first glass door
ever done, [it] came crashing down
the first week after it was put up
because somebody slammed it too
hard — and the letters came down
with it. Gold letters. I sit out there
in the hall looking at it, and I
thought I had a terrible nerve to put
that thing up there, you know. I felt
kind of like an imposter. That's the
feeling I had about architecture
when I went into it. Well, that's
what it is, too.

IMPUTETH

It were good, therefore, that men in their innovations would follow the example of time itself; which indeed innovateth greatly, but quietly, by degrees scarce to be perceived. For otherwise, whatsoever is new is unlooked for; and ever it mends some and pairs others; and he that is holpen, takes it for a fortune, and thanks to the time; and he that is hurt, for a wrong, and imputeth it to the author.

INCOHERENCE

Incoherence seems to me preferable to a distorting order.

INDECISION

It is a pleasant thought to imagine a mind exactly poised between two parallel desires, for it would indubitably never reach a decision, since making a choice implies that there is an inequality of value; if anyone were to place us between a bottle and a ham when we had an equal appetite for drink and for food there would certainly be no remedy but to die of thirst and of hunger.

INDUSTRY

We make no distinction between man and nature: the human essence of nature and the natural essence of man become one within nature in the form of production or industry, just as they do within the life of man as species. Industry is then no longer considered from the extrinsic point of view of utility, but rather from the point of view of its fundamental identity with nature as production of man and by man. Not man as the king of creation, but rather as the being who is in intimate contact with the profound life of all forms or all type of beings, who is responsible for even stars and animal-life, and who ceaseless plugs an organ-machine into a energy-machine, a tree into his body, a breast into his mouth, the sun into his asshole; the eternal custode of the machines of the universe.

INFERNO

And Polo said: "The inferno of the living is not something that will be; if there is one, it is what is already here, the inferno where we live every day, that we form by being together. There are two ways to escape suffering it. The first is easy for many: accept the inferno and

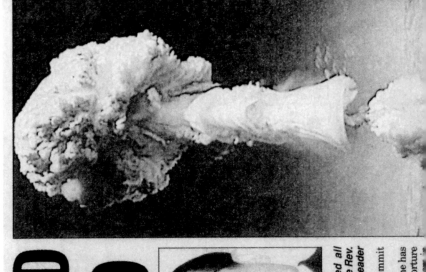

THE WORLD ENDED EIGHT YEARS AGO

We are all in the afterlife, says top researcher

by BILL ISLAND

ALL OF THE end-of-the-world predictions are nothing but hogwash – because they're all eight years too late, says a Midwest preacher.

This astounding claim by comes from the Rev. Jean Woolf of the Church of the Seekers for Truth and Penitence, a small but growing cult headquartered outside North Burrington, Illinois.

Locked horns

"Almost a decade ago, the United States and the Soviet Union locked horns over a volatile situation in the Middle East," explains Woolf. "This eventually culminated in a worldwide nuclear war.

material plane. God has mercifully erased all memories of this nuclear catastrophe from our minds. In other words, we're all dead but we don't know it.

"The only reason I know about this is because the dison, a noted sociologist and cult expert, isn't so sure.

"All cults like to encourage a feeling of persecution among their followers," says Dr. Eddison.

"It's a very good way to keep their membership tightly knit and immune to outside influences.

Justify harming

●GOD HAS erased all memories, says the Rev. Jean Woolf, a cult leader

it's impossible to commit murder, right?"

Dr. Eddiso says he has received repo s of torture

Women are the hunters now

THE NUMBER OF women involved in sport shooting has grown to ten percent of all American hunters, the government estimates.

Merchandisers are starting to make hunting gear designed for women and some are targeting females for specialized hunts.

Studies show women are more likely to pursue instruction in hunting and shooting, and the average age is lower than that of male hunters.

Evidence suggests that women cite getting in touch with nature or getting outdoor exercise as more important than the typical male pursuits of acquiring trophies or demonstrating marksmanship.

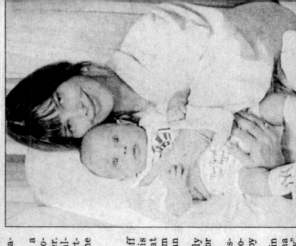

LENIN WAS JUST AN ORDINARY GUY

LENIN'S BRAIN is much like anyone else's, Russian scientists have concluded after 70 years of secret research.

"In the anatomical structure of Lenin's brain, there is nothing sensational," says Oleg Adrianov, director of the Moscow Brain Institute.

Experts at the institute have spent much of this century delving into the

secret of the Bolshevik leader Vladimir Ilich Lenin's genius.

But he concedes the brain was "undoubtedly the brain of a talented man."

Studies showed that the right side of his brain was slightly bigger than average.

Lenin's brain now lies in thousands of slices in the secretive institute.

EROTIC FATHER CHARGES:

PORN STAR RAISING X-RATED BABY

STORY by JENNY LYNN

A BABY BOY is being bounced around by his porn star mom and her erotic artist ex-husband. Both halves of the kinky couple want custody of little Ludwig, but dad gained the upper hand by whisking the child from Italy to America.

But the miffed mom isn't giving up without a fight. Ilona Staller, who prefers her stage name of La Cicciolina, once held a seat in the Italian parliament.

The X-rated actress remains bet-

ter known for her steamy sex scenes than her parliamentary professionalism. And it's the kind of wild lifestyle that surrounds sex stars which led Jeff Koons to kidnap his son and jet him to New York.

The angry American artist ignored an Italian court order so that he could save his son from "pornography, prostitutes, procur-

ers and members of the pornography industry."

At least that's what he told a judge while painting a not-too-pretty picture of his former lover. He added sordid details of a phallic-shaped fountain in her apartment and a glass sex toy that the baby boy played with.

Turned her back

"The feeling here is that Jeff Koons is a hero for rescuing his son from the environment that this porno star had placed him in," says Dan Klores, a spokesman for Koons.

The mad mom has supposedly turned her back on politics in favor of a born-again porn career.

Manhattan Supreme Court Justice David Saxe has granted temporary custody of the 13-month-old boy to his protective papa.

But things are sure to heat up in this kinky case when La Cicciolina gets a chance to present her "bawdy"

Hair loss linked to success

WOMEN WHO ARE successful in business are more likely to lose their hair, say researchers.

Climbing the ladder of success can increase the levels of the male hormone testosterone, which causes hair loss.

"The male hormones are naturally present in women, but at a much lower level than in men," says professor Onorio Carlesimo, a skin specialist who conducted his research in Rome, Italy.

"The stresses of a career can boost these levels, bringing on male-pattern baldness. The price women pay for success is stress and

---

seems identical to our peaceful and tolerant previous existence on the lifestyle, but Dr. Arlen Ed-

mies. After all, if every- one is already dead, then

described with a similar system of differentiation.

INTERRUPT[1]

Buckminster Fuller paused dramatically. His voice in the small room had risen to a boom not far short of lecturing strength. His fruit salad was unfinished, his tea undrunk, and mine too. Whenever I interjected, he seemed to get more angry: but if I did not interrupt him there was no telling where all this might lead.

INTERRUPT[2]

Well, you shouldn't interrupt my interruptions: That's really worse than interrupting. Now my head's fairly spinning. I must have a cocktail.

INTIMACY

And what does getting intimacy out of space mean, if not miniaturizing it?

INTO

But recent spatial transformation has brought about an unforeseen difficulty: it is no longer possible to see the entire text from one position. It seems that the characters suspended in the foreground obstruct our view of the characters located behind them. So, in order not to miss relationships that could provide the key to understanding this language, let us move into the text.

INTUITION

We were working very hard on the neutron-induced radioactivity and the results we were obtaining made no sense. One day, as I came to the laboratory, it occurred to me that I should examine the effect of placing a piece of lead before the incident neutrons. And instead of my usual custom, I took great pains to have the piece of lead precisely machined. I was clearly dissatisfied with something: I tried every "excuse" to postpone putting the piece of lead in its place. When finally, with some reluctance, I was going to put it in its place, I said to myself, "No: I do not want this piece of lead here; what I want is a piece of paraffin." It was just like that: with no advance warning, no conscious prior reasoning. I immediately took some odd piece of paraffin I could put my hands on and placed it where the piece of lead was to have been.

INVALID

The Chairman of the Board of Appeals, when we had made our

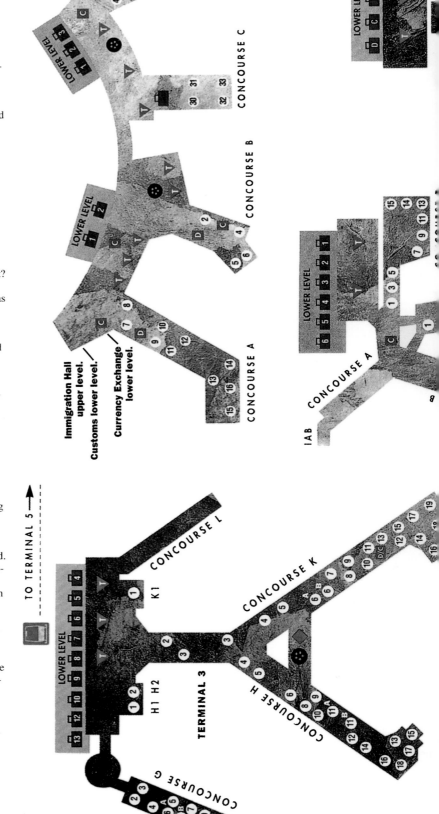

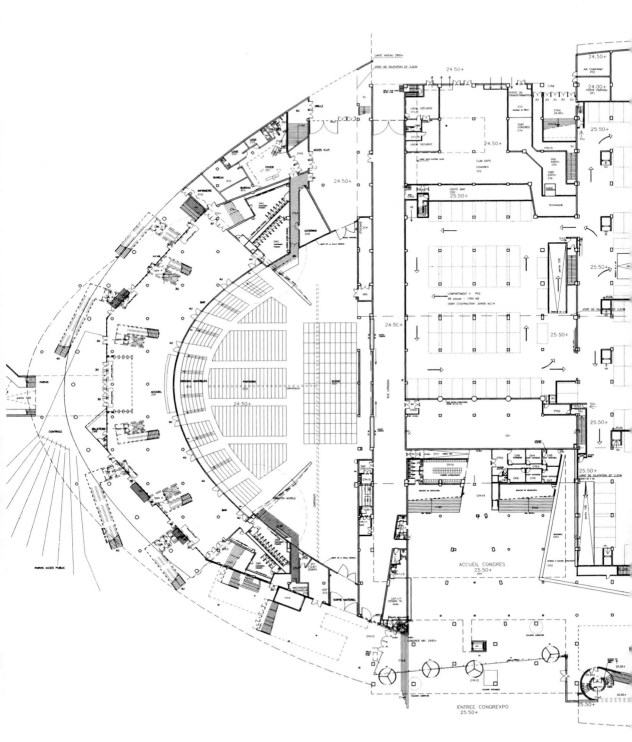

ground entrance level +24.5 m

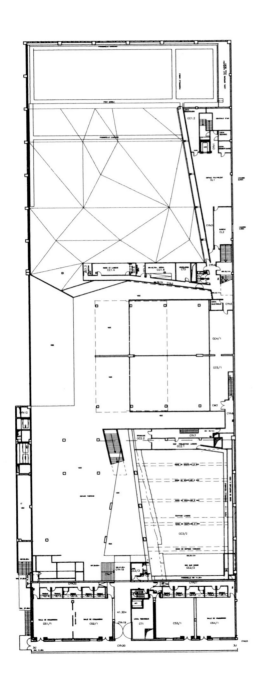
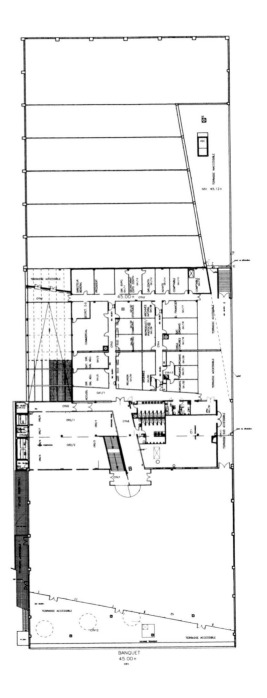

BANQUET
45.00+
CR1

0   20m

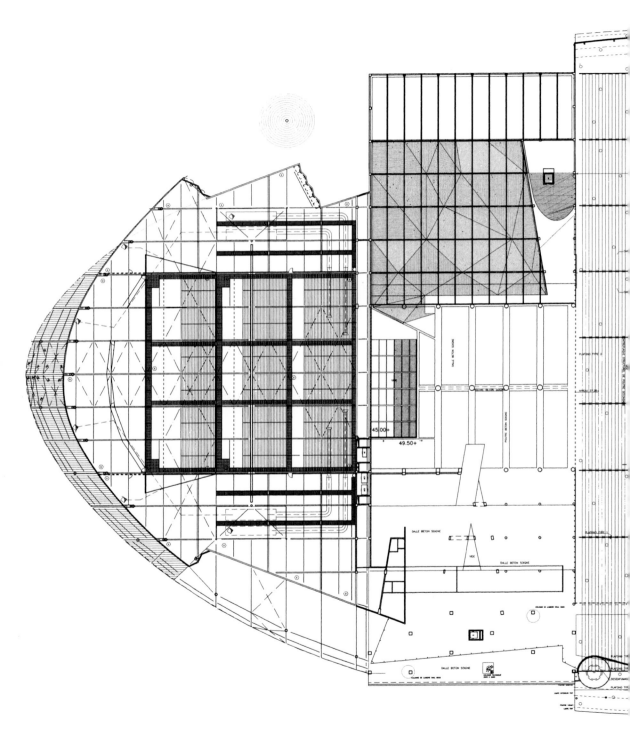

reflected ceiling plan

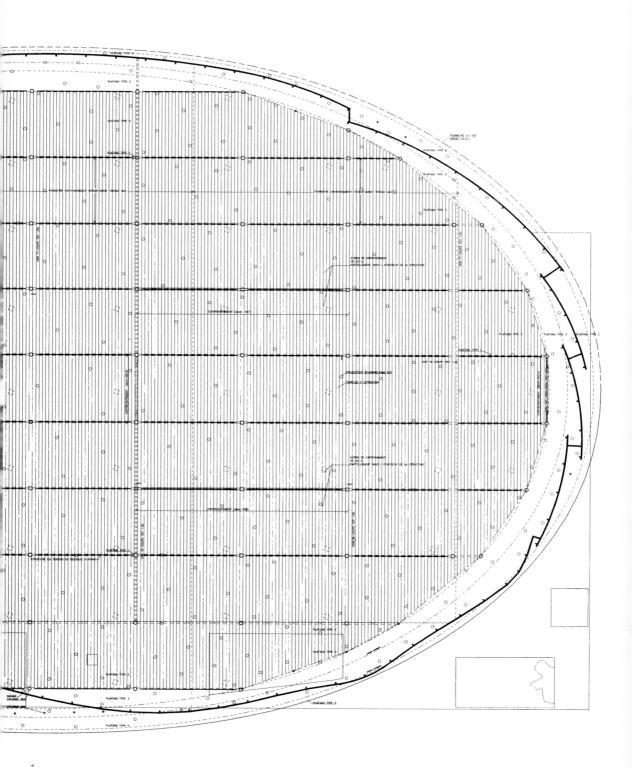

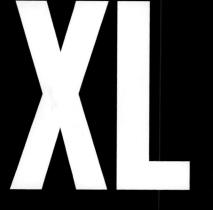

The White Sheet (A Dream)

I was walking with Jan Voorberg, my partner at the time. He was an architect from The Hague, exactly my age, but small and blond.

We were walking together along the edge of a river on a kind of sinking boardwalk.

That typified our situation — every moment of the week, our position was slowly sinking in the general swamp, and we constantly had to try to uplift and inspire each other.

So, half sinking, I said, "Well, in a way it's *interesting* to walk along a river on a sinking boardwalk — don't you think?"

We were both wearing shorts and were wet to our waists.

"Yes," he said. "It *is* interesting… but it's completely different from taking a dry walk."

When we got to the end of the river, there was an enormous abyss. Hesitantly, we both looked over the edge.

"Well, it's not that deep," I said.

"No," he said, "it's not. And the wall isn't all that steep. I think if we're really careful, we can almost walk down. Yeah, we may have to walk kind of diagonally, but I think we can do it."

So, encouraging each other, we started our descent. And of course, before we knew it, we were falling. Tumbling down this cliff, I could see that we were going to crash over a small meadow, where, on a tiny piece of green grass, there was an enormous group of people having a picnic. I knew right away it was a picnic — there was a large white sheet and the entire group was sitting around it.

So, still falling, I thought, "How should I land? How can I maneuver to avoid the people? How can I crash without making a desperate mess of this picnic?" I worked out a trajectory in my mind. I thought it would work amazingly.

I hit the ground and made a few leaps, successfully avoiding everybody. But then, at the very last moment, there was a sick, soft feeling in my heel.

"My God, Jan, I hit it!" I hardly dared to touch it. When I felt my heel, there was a bloody mush on my fingers. Then I turned around and saw a small gap in the ground, with a baby whose head I had smashed.

1981

Las Vegas of the Welfare State

Bijlmermeer Redevelopment
Amsterdam, Netherlands
Project, 1986

5000m

0

852

What Las Vegas is to late capitalism, the Bijlmermeer is to the Welfare State.

Like Las Vegas, the Bijlmer is essentially a *strip*. But instead of Las Vegas's sensual overkill of meaning and information—however trivial—the Bijlmer represents the signs and language of socialism: elevated highways reveal identical housing slabs of gray concrete bent into colossal hexagons. The slabs are embedded in a park for pedestrians, still in its infancy, with an elaborate system of bicycle paths. Abutting the road are the concrete blocks of multilevel parking garages.

The themes—however latent—displayed along the Bijlmer strip are *equality, puritanism, physical and mental health, a New Age.*

Panic

Since its completion five years ago, this socialist Las Vegas has provoked fear and loathing, almost panic, in Holland's intelligentsia—anxieties exemplified when some of the country's most famous architects (Aldo van Eyck among them) were seen on national television, driving on the brand-new highway, literally crying over this inhuman outrage, tears streaming down their hollow cheeks against the impassive gray backdrop of the buildings.

Complication

With its segregation of traffic, its elevated highway, metro, green grounds, rational apartments, the Bijlmer represents a particular architectural doctrine—codified most memorably by CIAM in the thirties—*realized in retrospect.* As such, it injects an unusual complication into the architectural debate—one which, due to the increasingly erratic and vulnerable channels whereby architectural ideologies are implemented, is bound to become more common: the appearance of the discrete episodes that together constitute architectural history *out of their original chronological sequence.*

Even more than, for instance, Beaubourg—the liberating sixties realized in the conservative seventies—this aberrant timing

So near and yet so far: Amsterdam center (top) and Bijlmer (bottom) connected by highway, tram, metro. Prewar CIAM urbanism realized in the late sixties: original project of hexagonal slabs encircled by varied afterthoughts, all referring to the "traditional city."

...tears streaming down their hollow cheeks against the impassive backdrop of the buildings...

Bijlmermeer

Congestion Without Matter

Parc de la Villette
Paris, France
Competition, 1982

and Spain but soon recaptured by
Louis XIV 1667; captured again in
1708; restored to France 1713; occupied by Germans October 1914 –
October 1918; occupied again by
Germans June 1940 – September
1944; to date occupied and governed
by the French.

LILLE[3]
Amongst other things, the Lille
metropolis has 6 golf courses. It is
also possible to go sailing, wind-
surfing, horse-riding, and gliding as
well as play tennis and plan walks
and cycling outings near Lille.

LILLE[4]
In the case of Euralille — a name
which expresses Lille's desire to
situate itself firmly at the centre of
an increasingly homogenous continent — the site plan encompasses
the neighbouring cities of London,
Brussels and Paris. Euralille could
be a monster.

LIMINAL
The liminal period is that time and
space betwixt and between one context of meaning and action and
another. It is when the initiand is
neither what he has been nor is what
he will be.

LIQUEFACTION
The latest generation of OMA buildings is probably explained better as
a collection of containers of gel or
hydropneumatic mechanisms rather
than a series of geological formations or piles.

LITE
Welcome to rich cocoa flavor at its
peak … with one-third less calories.
One delicious sip of Swiss Miss®
Lite Hot Cocoa, and you're snug-
gling by a fireplace in a cozy chalet
nestled in beautiful, snow-covered
mountains. Just add hot water and
your wholesome treat is ready with
all the chocolatey goodness you've
come to expect from Swiss Miss®.
And with one-third less calories
than our regular hot cocoa mix.
Whether you're out for a brisk tobog-
gan run, or just huddled around the
TV, your family will love the chocolatey goodness of Swiss Miss® Lite
Hot Cocoa Mix. For rich cocoa
flavor at its peak, with one-third less
calories.

LITE CITY
It is clear on any drive through Houston that what is needed is a science

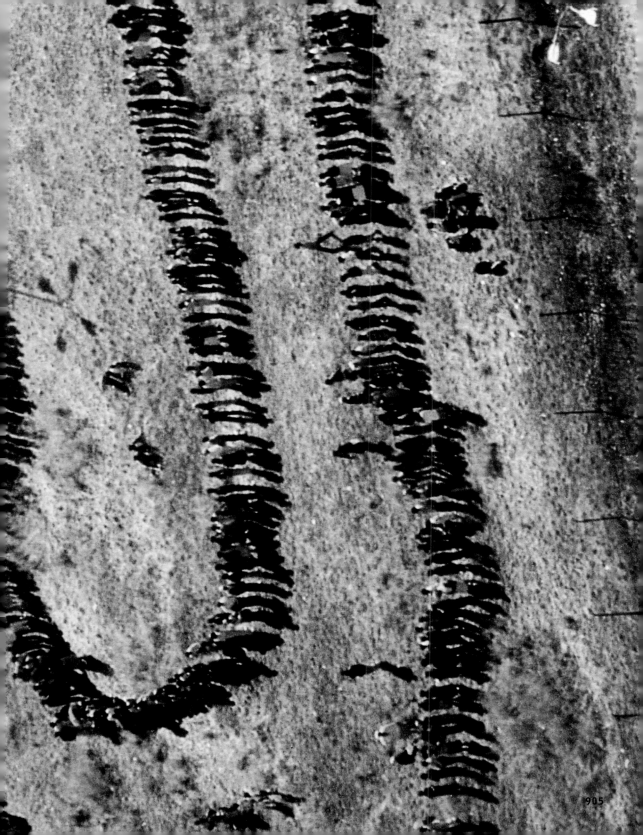

1905

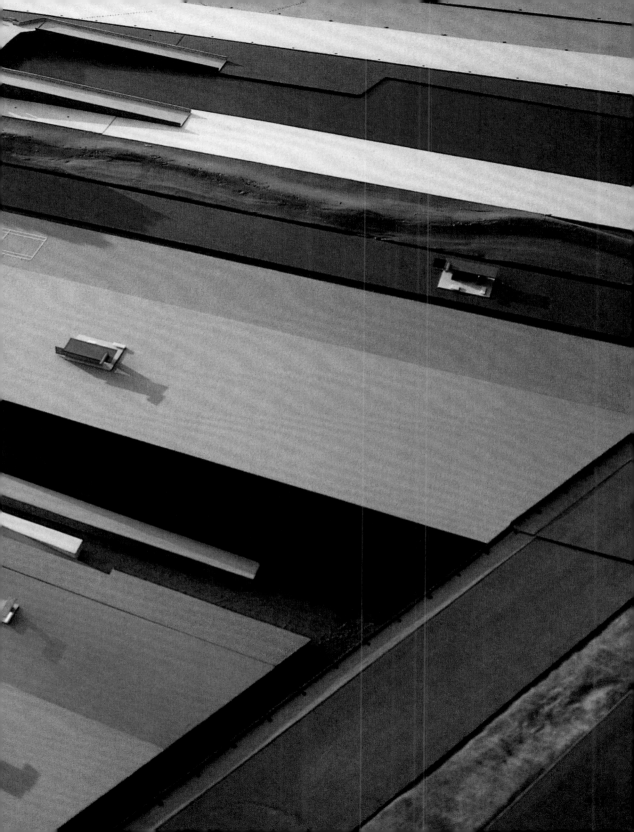

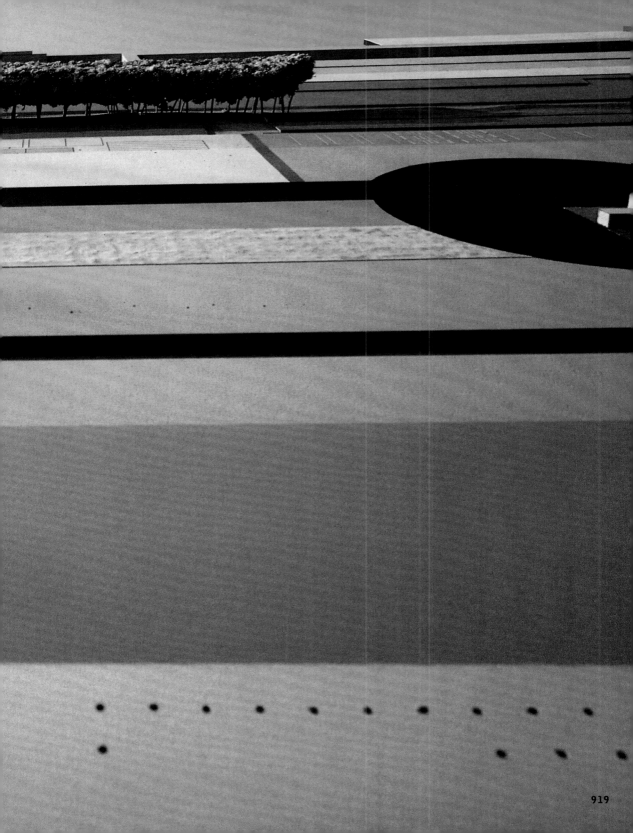

of desettlement — an art of erasure —
the development of "occupying" formerly urban territory (park is not by
any stretch of the imagination the
right word) but with a less substantial,
therefore less oppressive and less
vulnerable kind of urban condition
that offers the benefits of the urban
condition — catalytic chains and
patterns of unpredictible events —
without the weight of matter — call
it Lite City.

LITERATURE
Now everyone seems, and seems
to themselves, to have a book in
them, just by virtue of having a particular job, or a family even, a sick
parent, a rude boss. A novel for
everyone in the family or the business... It's forgotten that for anyone,
literature involves a special sort of
exploration and effort, a particular
creative purpose that can be pursued
only within literature itself, whose
job is in no way to register the
immediate results of very different
activities and purposes. Books
become "secondary" when market-
ing takes over.

LITTLE STONES
When you look at hardened concrete

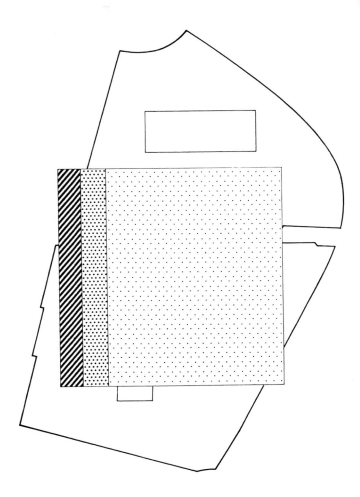

1. Initial Hypothesis

As the diagram reveals, the site of La Villette is too small, and the program too large, to create a park in the recognizable sense of the word. A conventional park is a replica of nature serviced by a minimal number of facilities that ensure its enjoyment; the program of Parc de la Villette extends like a dense forest of social instruments across the site.

At this stage it would be nonsense to design a detailed park. We have read the program as a suggestion, a provisional enumeration of desirable ingredients. It is not definitive: it is safe to predict that during the life of the park, the program will undergo constant change and adjustment. The more the park works, the more it will be in a perpetual state of revision. Its "design" should therefore be the proposal of a method that combines architectural specificity with programmatic indeterminacy.

In other words, we see this scheme not simply as a design but mostly as a tactical proposal to derive maximum benefit from the implantation on the site of a number of activities — the use of nature among them — in the most efficient and explosive manner, while at the same time offering a (relatively) stable aesthetic experience. The underlying principle of programmatic indeterminacy as a basis of the formal concept allows any shift, modification, replacement, or substitution to occur without damaging the initial hypothesis.

The essence of the competition therefore becomes: how to orchestrate on a metropolitan field the most dynamic coexistence of activities x, y, and z and to generate through their mutual interference a chain reaction of new, unprecedented events; or, how to design a *social condenser*, based on horizontal congestion, the size of a park. To do this we propose the following projections that, superimposed on the site, constitute the park.

you do not normally see which aggregate has been used because a film of cement covers every one of the little stones in it. But sometimes the surface film is specially removed in order to expose the natural stone and give the building a richer appearance. In this way, concrete can display a whole variety of textures and colours.

LIVERS

The construction of situations begins on the ruins of the modern spectacle. It is easy to see the extent to which the very principle of the spectacle — nonintervention — is linked to the alienation of the old world. Conversely, the most pertinent revolutionary experiments in culture have sought to break the spectator's psychological identification with the hero so as to draw him into activity … The situation is thus made to be lived by its constructors. The role played by a passive or merely bit-part playing *public* must constantly diminish, while that played by those who cannot be called actors, but rather, in a sense of the term, livers, must constantly increase.

LOBOTOMY

In the deliberate discrepancy between container and contained New York's makers discover an area of unprecedented freedom. They exploit and formalize it in the architectural equivalent of a lobotomy — the surgical severance of the connection between the frontal lobes and the rest of the brain to relieve some mental disorders by disconnecting thought processes from emotions. The architectural equivalent separates exterior and interior architecture.
In this way the Monolith spares the outside world the agonies of the continuous changes raging inside it. It hides everyday life.

LOGIC

1. The science of reasoning by formal methods. 2. A way of reasoning. 3. Reasonable thinking.

LONGER

And, because it keeps its texture longer, the beauty lasts up to twice as long as many other carpets.

LOOK-ALIKE

In the "look-alike" phenomenon, the subject duplicates the early narcissistic identification with the mirror image; only now, the Ideal-Imago structure is projected into desire to look like some rock star. Different from the familiar Hollywood star fetish is that the market now makes available clothes associated with particular highly successful rock stars, like Madonna. Hence, in 1986, Macy's ran a whole campaign around its stocks of Madonna look-alike clothes, with a prize going to the woman who came closest to the Madonna image. Look-alike performance contests encourage the same consumption.

LOVE

The tender soul has fixed his love on one spot in the world; the strong man has extended his love to all places; the perfect man has extinguished his.

LULLABY

Sunray sat under a golden lantern and listened to the musician and watched his nimble hands, but Sarnac was more deeply moved. He had not heard much music in his life, and the player seemed to open shutters upon deep and dark and violent things that had long been closed to mankind.

LUMBER

In the Yellow Pages of Garp's phone directory, Marriage was listed near Lumber. After Lumber came Machine Shops, Mail Order Houses, Manholes, Maple Sugar, and Marine Equipment; then came Marriage and Family Counselors. Garp was looking for Lumber when he discovered Marriage.

LURID

By artificial light the colours were lurid and unconvincing, as though the flowers had been made of bright paper and gleaming.

M

MA

Ma is all of the following: a slit, a distance, a crack, a difference, a split, a disposition, a boundary, a pause, a dispersion, a blank, a vacuum. One can say that its function is infinitely close to Derrida's espacement = becoming space.

MAD

We all go a little mad sometimes. Haven't you?

MADNESS

Off in the distance she could make out the shape of cities. These were cities that she might have seen before but couldn't name. As she continued to look, they ran together. First appearing in one way, then another. Sometimes a part of a building, then a window, then a whole street. And then the perspective shifted as well, dipping and whirling about in a mad kind of dance. Depositing building parts around for them to see and then casually dissolving them into something else. What she could not be sure.

MAINTENANCE

Servicing a scraper can be a dangerous business, unless the operator or mechanic knows what he is doing, and takes proper precautions. When changing blades or doing other work under the scraper, both the bowl and the apron should be blocked, so that they cannot come down if the supporting cables break or are accidentally released.

MAKE

And right now it is ten times more interesting to make things than to explode things … Explosion lasts one moment, but making takes much longer. In that sense, deconstruction has done everything it could do in architecture. It might have been an important way of analyzing things, to experiment, but I do not see any future for it within architecture.

MAKE-UP

In every 100 men, 95 weigh between 127 and 209 lb. (for women it is 95 and 195 lb.). In the average 162 lb. man, about 43% of the weight is muscle, 14% is fat, 14% bone and marrow, 12% internal organs, 9% connective tissue and skin, and 8% blood. The weight distributes: 47% in the trunk and neck, 34% in the legs, 12% in the arms, and 7% in the head. Broken down into his elements, man is 65% oxygen, 18.5% carbon, 9.5% hydrogen, 3.3% nitrogen, 1.5% calcium, 1% phosphorus, 0.35% or less each of potassium, sulphur, chlorine, sodium, and magnesium, with traces

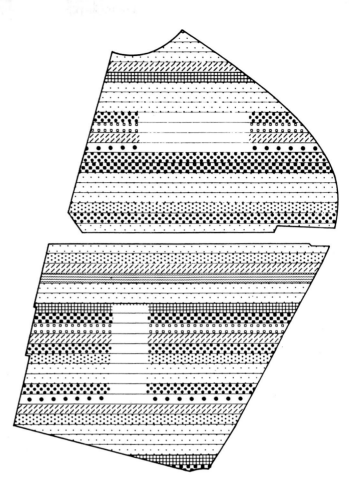

2. The Strips

In the first primordial gesture the whole site is subdivided in a series of parallel bands — running east-west — that can accommodate, in principle, zones of the major programmatic categories: the theme gardens, the playgrounds (50%), the discovery gardens, etc.

In this way, concentration or clustering of any particular programmatic component is avoided; the bands can be distributed across the site partly at random, partly according to a logic derived from the characteristics of the site.

This tactic of layering creates the maximum length of "borders" between the maximum number of programmatic components and will thereby guarantee the maximum permeability of each programmatic band and — through this interference — the maximum number of programmatic mutations.

The direction of the bands is chosen so that the dominant elements already on the site — the Science Museum and the Grande Halle — are incorporated into the system: the museum as an extrawide band (that could itself be divided in analogous thematic bands), the Grande Halle as an incidental covered part of another series of bands running through it.

The strips are based on certain standard dimensions — a basic width of 50 meters divisible into increments of 5, 10, 25, or 40 meters — to facilitate change and replacement without disruption and to create fixed points for the infrastructure.

Nature — whether the thematic/discovery gardens, or "real" nature — will also be treated as program. Blocks or screens of trees and the various gardens will act like different planes of a stage set: they will convey the illusion of different landscapes, of depth, without offering, in passing, the substance.

The layering is not unlike the experience of a high-rise building, with its superimposed floors all capable of supporting different programmatic events, yet all contributing to a summation that is more than the accumulation of parts.

of iron, iodine, zinc, fluorine, and other elements. This gives him enough water to fill a 10-gallon barrel, enough fat for 7 bars of soap, enough phosphorus for 2,200 match heads, and enough iron for a 3 in. nail.

MAMMALS
Do suburbs represent the city's convalescent zone or a genuine step forward into a new psychological realm, at once more passive but of far greater imaginative potential, like that of a sleeper before the onset of REM sleep? Unlike its unruly city counterpart, the suburban body has been wholly domesticated, and one can say that the suburbs constitute a huge petting zoo, with the residents' bodies providing the stock of furry mammals.

MANEUVER
In me grows a tiny feeling against dichotomies (strong-weak; big-small; happy-unhappy; ideal–not ideal). It is so only because people cannot think more than two things. More does not fit into a sparrow's brain. But the healthiest thing is simply: maneuver.

MANUSCRIPTS
Deep beneath the grimy surface of Manhattan, in a shimmering white vault cooled to 68 degrees, lie 20,000 linear feet of manuscripts — from Truman Capote's notebooks to George Washington's handwritten recipe for beer.

MAP[1]
"Hey Pal! How do I get to town from here?"
And he said: "Well, just take a right where they're going to build that new shopping mall; go straight past where they're going to put in the freeway; take a left at what's going to be the new sports center; and keep going until you hit the place where they're thinking of building that drive-in bank. You can't miss it."

MAP[2]
Principle of cartography or decalomania: A rhizome is not amenable to any structural or generative model. It is a stranger to any idea of genetic axes or deep structure. A rhizome is a map, not a tracing. It does not follow the tree logic, oriented to reproduction and establishment of competences, but a rhizomatic logic, drawn to experi-

mentation and performance. It has multiple entrances rather than a single viewpoint.

MAQUILLAGE
Europe now bears a paradoxical resemblance to exactly what it claims to despise across the Atlantic Ocean. Once unique, its forms have been diluted or, worse, survive under the cover of *maquillage*. We can ridicule Twentynine Palms, California; Bismarck, North Dakota; Saint Cloud, Minnesota; Murfreesboro, Tennessee; Pocomoke City, Maryland; Holbrook, Arizona; and a thousand other cities, which Lewis Mumford referred to as no more than postal addresses, but only on condition that we do the same thing with obscure French villages like Cergy-Pontoise, Saint-Quentin-en-Yvelines, L'Isle-d'Abeau, and indeed even Maubeuge or Annemasse.

MARBLE
I went into Italian churches a great deal then and I began to be very much interested in black and white marble. Even other colored marbles. I went in Rome to Saint John without the walls and I did not like the marble and then I looked at the marble I did like and I began to touch it and I found gradually that if I liked it there was always as much imitation oil painted marble as real marble. And all being mixed together I liked it. It was very hard to tell the real from the false. I spent hours in those hot summer days feeling marble to see which was real and which was not.

MASKS[1]
Every day of our lives the masks go off and on, donned, discarded, exchanged, as we move from obligation to obligation and from friend to friend. Never mind that the masks are invisible, being facial expressions, the stance, the vocabulary, attitudes, even the tone of voice appropriate to each position, each condition of life. We wear them all the same.

MASKS[2]
Many of the caresses had already begun in the crowded automobiles. The masks gave people a liberty that turned the most refined ones into hungry animals. Hands ran under the sumptuous evening dresses to touch what they wanted to

touch, knees intertwined, breaths came quicker.

MASTERPIECE
MOVED IN YESTERDAY. YOU HAVE MADE ANOTHER MASTERPIECE. THRILLING BEYOND WORDS.

MATADOR
If he was so short he should not have tried to be a matador.

MAY
It's not the work of an architect, yet he may become an architect.

ME
As soon as my glance met theirs, they began to applaud. And I realized that my *Faust* didn't interest them at all and that the show they wished to see was not the puppets I was leading around the stage, but me myself! Not *Faust*, but Goethe! And then I was overcome by a sense of horror very similar to what you described a moment ago.

MEDIA[1]
The media are nothing else than a marvellous instrument for destabilizing the real and the true, all historical or political truth … And the addiction that we have for the media … is not a result of a desire for culture, communication, and information, but of this perversion of truth and falsehood, of this destruction of meaning in the operation of the medium.

MEDIA[2]
In 1980 there were 23.3 million radio and 21.2 million television receivers registered in the Federal Republic of Germany. 93.9% of all households had radio and 85.4% television. More than 20 million newspapers were sold every day. Three out of four West Germans read a newspaper daily. Only about 5% of the population are reached by no medium at all.

MEDIATORS
Mediators are fundamental. Creation is all about mediators. Without them, nothing happens … Whether they're real or imaginary, animate or inanimate, one must form one's mediators. It's a series: if you don't belong to a series, even a completely imaginary one, you're lost. I need my mediators to express myself, and they'd never express themselves without me: one is always working in a group, even when it doesn't

939

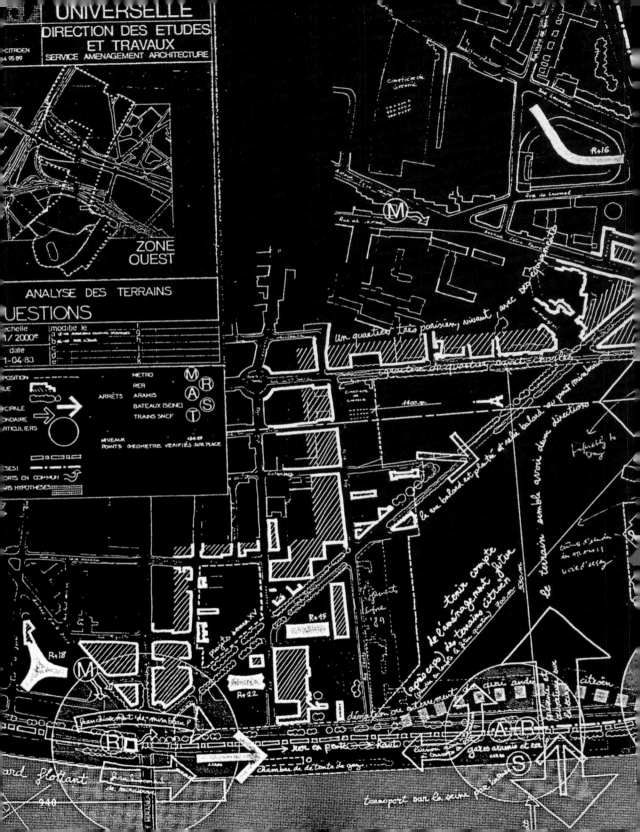

953

1954

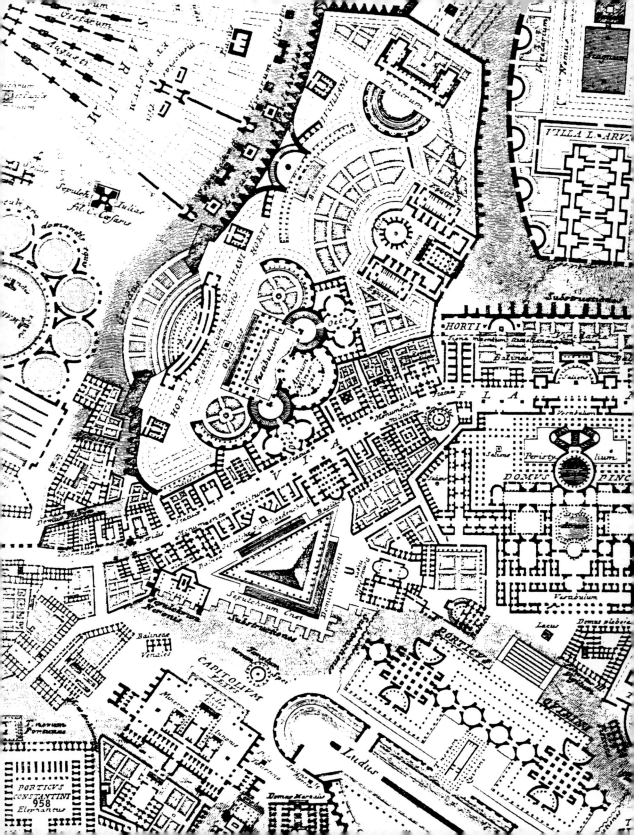

outwits all attempts at capturing the city, exhausts all ambitions of its definition, ridicules the most passionate assertions of its present failure and future impossibility, steers it implacably further on its flight forward. Each disaster foretold is somehow absorbed under the infinite blanketing of the urban.

Even as the apotheosis of urbanization is glaringly obvious and mathematically inevitable, a chain of rear-guard, escapist actions and positions postpones the final moment of reckoning for the two professions formerly most implicated in making cities — architecture and urbanism. Pervasive urbanization has modified the urban condition itself beyond recognition. "The" city no longer exists. As the concept of city is distorted and stretched beyond precedent, each insistence on its primordial condition — in terms of images, rules, fabrication — irrevocably leads via nostalgia to irrelevance.

For urbanists, the belated rediscovery of the virtues of the classical city at the moment of their definitive impossibility may have been the point of no return, fatal moment of disconnection, disqualification. They are now specialists in phantom pain: doctors discussing the medical intricacies of an amputated limb.

The transition from a former position of power to a reduced station of relative humility is hard to perform. Dissatisfaction with the contemporary city has not led to the development of a credible alternative; it has, on the contrary, inspired only more refined ways of

NEW YORK[1]

Ten years ago, I wrote a book about
New York which was an investigation
into another kind of modernity —
not the European modernity of
the twenties and thirties which consisted of a dream that was not realized. What fascinated me about
New York was that in the twenties
and thirties, buildings like
Rockefeller Center were as revolutionary as the architecture in Europe,
but built, realized, and maybe more
important — popular. So New York's
great virtue, in my eyes, is that it
presents a modernity that is not
alienated from the population but is
in fact, populistic.

NEW YORK[2]

The other areas of Manhattan such
as Lower East Side and The Bowery
offer discount bargains, unusual
trendy restaurants, and great buys
in lighting and kitchen equipment.
However, it's best to avoid them at
night. Northern parts of Manhattan,
such as Harlem, are worth exploring
with an organized tour.

NICE

This time I was nice, braked in time
and moved out of his way. Next time
I may not be so nice. Perhaps I may
not be able to brake in time.

NICER

Buildings under construction look
nicer than buildings finished.

NIGHTCAP

From the stairwell came the sound
of rather beautiful singing. A Welsh
guest, very drunk, was wishing
everyone goodnight.

NIGHTMARES

"Grunder," "Fleerde," "Egeldonk"
were the barbaric names of the nightmares to which architects, with hollow laughter, had here given shape.

NOMAD

I can't feel pity for you in Manhattan's
grid: a good nomad carries his identity on his back, wherever he is, even
in the Waldorf.

NON-CAPTIVE

Whoever you are, come out. You are
free. The people who held you are
captives themselves. We heard you
crying and we came to deliver you.
We have bound your enemies upstairs
hand and foot. You are free.

NONSTOP

Ships are virtually floating resorts.
Ships now have domed indoor/

articulating dissatisfaction. A profession persists in its fantasies, its ideology, its pretension, its illusions of involvement and control, and is therefore incapable of conceiving new modesties, partial interventions, strategic realignments, compromised positions that might influence, redirect, succeed in limited terms, regroup, begin from scratch even, but will never reestablish control. Because the generation of May '68 — the largest generation ever, caught in the "collective narcissism of a demographic bubble" — is now finally in power, it is tempting to think that it is responsible for the demise of urbanism — the state of affairs in which cities can no longer be made — paradoxically *because* it rediscovered and reinvented the city.

Sous le pavé, la plage (under the pavement, beach): initially, May '68 launched the idea of a new beginning for the city. Since then, we have been engaged in two parallel operations: documenting our overwhelming awe for the existing city, developing philosophies, projects, prototypes for a preserved *and* reconstituted city and, at the same time, laughing the professional field of urbanism out of existence, dismantling it in our contempt for those who planned (and made huge mistakes in planning) airports, New Towns, satellite cities, highways, high-rise buildings, infrastructures, and all the other fallout from modernization. After sabotaging urbanism, we have ridiculed it to the point where entire university departments are closed,

outdoor centers for nonstop entertainment, dining, and dancing, health
facilities, spas, computer centers
with instructors, and fitness programs.

NOODLES
The Japanese love noodles, especially
instant noodles that can be heated
and slurped down in minutes. They
bought $4 billion worth of them last
year, and almost certainly will consume even more in the years ahead.
Companies keep coming up with
easier ways for hurried people to eat
them. First came noodles in bags,
then noodles in cups. Now the giant
Nissin Food Products Co. has conceived of noodles in self-heating
cans that can be taken anywhere;
no cooking is necessary.

NORMAL
In this "normal" house, the couple
never sit or sleep together. They
quarrel standing up, and always
leave the house separately. It is as
if they want to say that they cannot
go on living together, because their
house is so normal, and therefore
they have to look for lovers outside.

NOT
Le futur de l'architecture n'est pas
architectural.

NOVELLA
It depends on how you perceive it;
to some people, Soviet Power is not
power, but a novella.

NUMBER
The pleasure of being in crowds is
a mysterious expression of sensual
joy in the multiplication of Number.
All is Number. Number is in all.
Number is in the individual. Ecstasy
is a Number.

OBJECTLESSNESS
Thus when man, investigating,
observing, ensnares nature as an area
of his own conceiving, he has already
been claimed by a way of revealing
that challenges him to approach
nature as an object of research, until
even the object disappears into the
objectlessness of standing-reserve.

OBJECTS[1]
Our plan is to drop a lot of odd objects
onto your country from the air. And
some of these objects will be useful.
And some will just be … odd.

not only, or mostly, be a profession, but a way of thinking, an ideology: to accept what exists. We were making sand castles. Now we swim in the sea that swept them away.

To survive, urbanism will have to imagine a new newness. Liberated from its atavistic duties, urbanism redefined as a way of operating on the inevitable will attack architecture, invade its trenches, drive it from its bastions, undermine its certainties, explode its limits, ridicule its preoccupations with matter and substance, destroy its traditions, smoke out its practitioners.

The seeming failure of the urban offers an exceptional opportunity, a pretext for Nietzschean frivolity. We have to imagine 1,001 other concepts of city; we have to take insane risks; we have to dare to be utterly uncritical; we have to swallow deeply and bestow forgiveness left and right. The certainty of failure has to be our laughing gas/oxygen; modernization our most potent drug. Since we are not responsible, we have to become irresponsible. In a landscape of increasing expediency and impermanence, urbanism no longer is or has to be the most solemn of our decisions; urbanism can lighten up, become a *Gay Science* — Lite Urbanism.

What if we simply declare that there *is* no crisis — redefine our relationship with the city not as its makers but as its mere subjects, as its supporters?

More than ever, the city is all we have.   **1994**

It was heartbreaking, if not obscene ...

We took a careful inventory of the situation:

There was a highway across the site; there were old villages; there were two enormous forests, farmland, a future campus, and a very beautiful area of landscape between the forests where French kings chased deer from one mini-forest to another, and shot them as they ran for cover.

And we began to analyze by reverse logic:

Instead of starting the competition by saying "this is what we want to do," we defined very carefully what we did *not* want to do; we asked not "where to build?" but "where not to build? How to *abstain from architecture*?"

Instead of projecting onto the landscape, we deducted from it, hoping that we could invent a reverse argument. Through this process of elimination, we arrived at an almost Chinese figure of void spaces that we could protect from contamination by the city — a new controlling element that would give the city, which was obviously not a classical city, but maybe a contemporary city, a form of coherence and conviction.

And then we said, "the rest we will surrender to chaos." We will abandon the residue — the terrains around and between the Chinese figure — to what the French call *merde* — to the average-contemporary-everyday ugliness of current European-American-Japanese architecture, and generate, through that ugliness, a potentially sublime contrast between the empty areas of the site — those we had protected from building — and the uncontrollable, almost cancerous chaotic growth of the city as a whole.

977

OPPORTUNITY
Once a moment's passed, you've missed the opportunity to preserve it forever.

OPPOSITE
The surgeon represents the polar opposite of the magician. The magician heals a sick person by laying on of hands; the surgeon cuts into the patient's body. The magician maintains the natural distance between the patient and himself ... The surgeon does exactly the reverse; he greatly diminishes the distance between himself and the patient by penetrating into the patient's body.

ORDER
There must be an order of movement, an order of winds, an order of light.

OTHER[1]
The now obligatory Japanese reference also marks the obsession with the great other who is perhaps our own future rather than our past, the punitive winner in the coming struggle, whom we therefore compulsively imitate, hoping that thereby the inner mindset of the victorious other will be transferred to us along with the externals.

OTHER[2]
To claim yourself something is always at the behest of a vengeful Other, to enter into his discourse, to argue with him, to seek from him a scrap of identity.

OXYGEN
The blessed torrent of cool, pure oxygen poured into his lungs. For long moments he stood gasping, while the pressure in the closet-sized chamber rose around him. As soon as he could breath comfortably, he closed the valve. There was only enough gas in the cylinder for two such performances; he might need to use it again.

OXYMORON
A combination of contradictory or incongruous words.

P

PAID
My sister was a tomboy and had a very high IQ, higher even than mine. Even though her IQ was high, she couldn't understand how a high IQ

Phasing

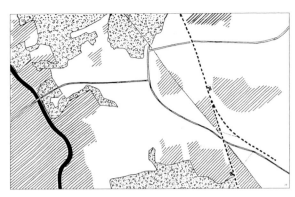

Phase 0: Inventory
The Seine, two forests, existing villages, motorway, TGV line.

Phase 1
Minimum public investment for maximum preservation of existing qualities.

Phase 2: First programmatic reservations
East/west: campus strip; north/south: nature/leisure; beginning of business band along motorway.

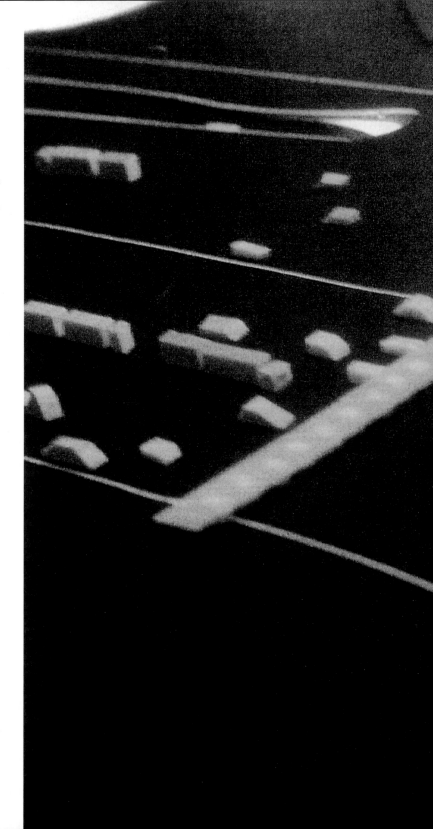

and the desire to be loved as a female could exist together in one body. Since her body thus had to be monstrous, she refused to go out of our parents' house. She knew who she was: since she was a freak, she was unlovable. She had to and did pay, rather my parents paid, someone to love her. She loved this paid companion because the paid companion loved her and at the same time she detested the paid companion because, since the paid companion loved her only for economic reasons, she was proved to be unlovable.

PANIC

Long ago (1968), in the days before fax, cable TV and personal computers, Marshall McLuhan noted that innumerable confusions and a profound feeling of despair invariably emerge in periods of technological and cultural transitions. As a result of trying to do today's job with yesterday's tools and concepts, he said, we were living in an Age of Anxiety.

Today, that same technological and cultural transition is intensified dramatically. Conflict between old and new is increasing at the same rate as communications networks are decreasing our ability to escape knowing so. Confusion and despair are old hat in the new Age of Panic.

PARANOIA

In fact, paranoia is a *delirium of interpretation*. Each fact, event, force, observation is caught in one system of speculation and "understood" by the afflicted individual in such a way that it absolutely confirms and reinforces his thesis — that is, the initial delusion which is his point of departure. *The paranoiac always hits the nail on the head, no matter where the hammer blows fall.*

PARASITE

What happens when a critical essay extracts a "passage" and "cites" it? Is this different from a citation, echo, or allusion within a poem? Is a citation an alien parasite within the body of its host, the main text, or is it the other way around, the interpretative text the parasite which surrounds and strangles the citation which is its host?

PARIS

Thé Cool: 10, rue Jean-Bologne,

t some point, through erratic mixtures of intense tivity and political inertia, whole European egions grind to a halt. Holland — the Randstad — is ne of the first. It has distributed its inhabitants cross its entire territory — at least as big as Los ngeles, in spite of its self-image of smallness — by scouraging density and concentration, neglecting etworks, leaving bottlenecks, aborting highway idenings, stimulating car ownership, proclaiming ne undying appeal of the city (when will anyone tart to sing the appeal of the new?), suffering the umulative brutality of a daily invasion of post-urban ordes. The smelly train systems are always too ll; buses crisscross the country without rhyme or eason; roads in all directions clog to suffocation ith a conveyor belt of trucks proving that no one where he should be; all goods are delivered to ne wrong place.

evitably, this motion convulses to a sudden death – n unexpected outburst of serenity, a collective, voluntary mini-vacation; *Le Weekend* (Godard!) as weeklong experience, as a sentence, as life ... he brazen shamelessness with which democratic gimes engineer this Luddite experience — they eal our time and even pretend that it is the result foresight or deliberate policy — appalls ... Why e we taking this?

is project is based on a counter-possibility. What those millions that now in their innocence strangle hole regions with the dumb fact of their simple istence could, instead of being mar ed in t

erversely flexible labyrinth of late-20th-century
ulture — you never know where the next blockage
ccurs — actually be *accommodated*?
Vhy not conceive vast bastard cities: gigantic
rchitectural accumulations, huge buffer buildings,
rban outposts beyond the city, urban obstacles
nat simply absorb all the flows, swallow the goods,
ne cars, the people from wherever they come?
ighways could suddenly terminate in them; they
night be used to park cheaply, then to take trains,
ams, buses, or whatever survivors of a more
ollective period, to the center — to transfer from
hatever to wherever...
hese buildings would be, by definition, most
fficient, in places where people least want to go.
oth obstacles and facilitators, using unexpected
ack within seemingly exhausted infrastructural
piderwebs, combining promiscuous access with
heap, almost Indian density, they would be places
ith infinite capacity for the absorption of bridge-
nd-tunnel people; mutt buildings that would quickly
ecome ersatz cities, spontaneously develop para-
rbanistic mutations, forms of urban life like home-
ss beggars at the automated tellers; buildings
nat would turn into self-regulating programmatic
umps, would be infiltrated by commerce, day-care
nters for the unfaithful, endlessly proliferating
neplexes, certainly water parks, maybe drive-in
niversities; mosques invading the endlessness of
ne concrete decks ... Buildings that in their very
utality might save civilization as we know it.

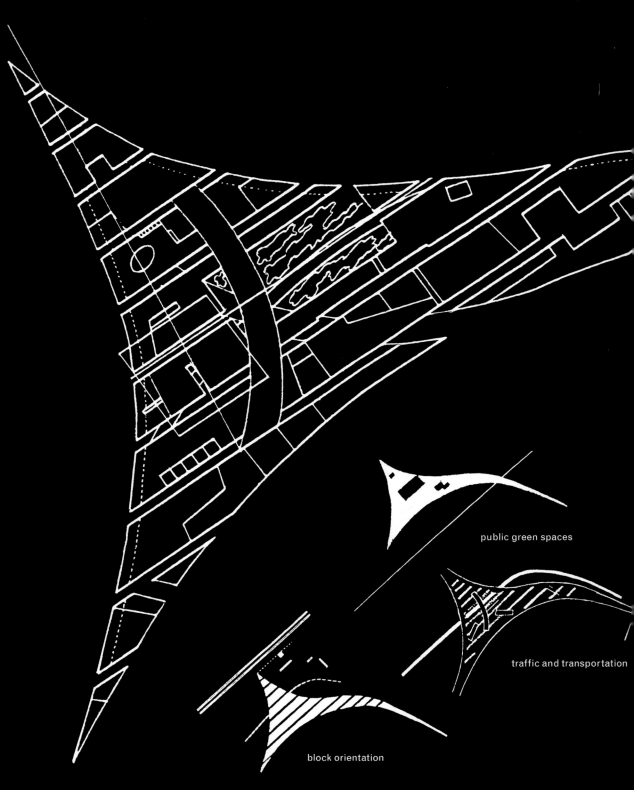

public green spaces

traffic and transportation

block orientation

Singapore

Portrait of a Potemkin Metropolis

Songlines

. . . or Thirty Years of Tabula Rasa

1995

Rem Koolhaas

Singapore can be weird. Five years ago it became clear that the upward curve of tourism was about to intersect the downward graph of historical presence—in the rush for development, history had been almost completely erased. On the exact site that had been known in the now-laundered past for its extensive and varied sexual options—the splendor of its transvestites—the state sponsored Bugis, a brand-new intersection of two "traditional" streets, framed by entirely new Chinese shophouses. One of the streets was declared "market"; the other accommodates a systematic variety of restaurants. On the upper level are clubs, one—the Boom Boom Club—discreetly anticipating the possible resurrection of the transvestite in the form of *female* female impersonators.

The block is hypermodern. The seemingly individual food stalls are connected by a single huge dishwasher-conveyor; on our first visit we are invited to the control room, a wall of monitors connected to hidden cameras that allows supervisors to zoom in on each table, watch each transaction at every stall.

It is shown with pride, not shame.

They think there will be no crime.

We think there can be no pleasure.

Singapore is clearly not free, but at the same time it is difficult to identify *what* precisely is unfree, how and where the exact repression occurs, to what extent its magnetic field—the unusual cohesion of its inhabitants—is imposed or, more ambiguously, the result of a "deal," a perceived common interest: liberties suspended in return for the unlimited benefits of a roller-coaster of development that, in 30 years, has only gone up.

Singapore stands out as a highly efficient alternative in a landscape of near universal pessimism about a makable future, a pertinent can-do world of clearly defined ambitions, long-term strategies, a ruthless determination to avoid the debris and chaos that democracy leaves in its wake elsewhere.

1

2

1 a hard-core Confucian shamelessness
2 the unusual cohesion of its inhabitants—imposed or the result of a "deal"?

The next round of East-West tension will be fought over this question: whether democracy promotes or erodes social stability; whether free speech is worth the cultural trash it also produces; whether the health of a collective matters more than the unfettered freedom of the individual. To the West this authoritarianism seems a temporary aberration, a deviation from the norm; but it is more likely that a new norm is being synthesized in Singapore: a hard-core Confucian shamelessness, a kind of ultimate power of efficiency that will fuel Asian modernization. "The American view that out of contention, out of the clash of ideas and ideals, you get good government and a healthy economy...that view is not shared in Asia."[4] Singapore has developed its own way. "The tenacious vitality of Confucianism lies in its combination of the dross of feudalism and the cream of democracy."[5]

Singapore seems a melting pot that produces blandness and sterility from the most promising ingredients. I have tried to decipher its reverse alchemy, understand its genealogy, do an architectural *genome project*, re-create its architectural songlines.

An analysis of Singapore is also, inevitably, a close-up of the mid-sixties, revealing once unassailable demographic urgencies—the brutal evidence of numbers that, on all continents, presented an overwhelming need to construct unprecedented quantities of new urban substance and offered compelling arguments for the discipline of urbanism and the notion of urban renewal that have completely unraveled in the past 30 years (or were successfully repressed).

It seems as if, in the world, only Singapore heeded these alarms *and* dealt with them, developed a solution. Singapore is an apotheosis of urban renewal, a built answer to the shift from country to city which was thought, 30 years ago, to force Asia to construct in 20 years the same amount of urban substance as the whole of Western Europe.

In unearthing its brand new archaeology, the most disconcerting question is: Where are these urgencies buried?

After 140 years of British rule **1** overcrowded Chinatown **2** stylish colonial clumps **3** neglected hinterland
4 port **5** mess **6** the island "denatured": first industrial estates **7** multilevel factories **8** new harbor facilities

Intermezzo

In 1959 Singapore—a British colony—becomes self-governing. The first full elections sweep Lee Kuan Yew to power with his People's Action Party (PAP—subliminally close to PAPA, DAD?). Nixon describes Lee as an Asian Churchill: "talking left and walking right";[6] at 35 he already has a number of tactical identities behind him, all later consolidated under the ideological umbrella of neo-Confucianism.

The island he and his party inherit after 140 years of British rule is a mess: clumps of stylish colonial enclave (it had been settled in 1819 by Sir Stamford Raffles), shabby military bases, a port, embedded in a huge, overcrowded Chinatown with a neglected hinterland of marsh, jungle, incidental farming, largely covered by squatter encampments.

"During the fifties all visitors were struck by the extreme precariousness of living conditions, the misery of the vast majority...What is more, conditions were constantly worsening: a galloping demography, pervasive tuberculosis, escalating joblessness, overcrowding in inhabitable housing, all this against a background of economic stagnation..."[7]

The very direness of the situation—its unpromising ingredients—provides the underpinnings for the program of the incipient city-state in the form of an undeniable crisis. "The general features of the PAP's ideological system unfold from a central concern... the survival as an independent island nation. Survival has been the structuring and rationalizing centre for the policies by which Singapore [has been] governed since it gained the right to self-government in 1959... The result was, and continues to be, an ideology that embodies a vigorous *developmentalist* orientation that emphasizes science, technology, and centralized public administration as the fundamental basis for an export-oriented industrialization programme, financed largely by multinational capital."[8]

For Lee, advised by Western thinkers/futurologists of the caliber of Herman (*The Next Two Hundred Years*) Kahn and Alvin (*Future Shock*) Toffler, the post-colonial period is in *every* sense a new beginning, a stunning overdose of newness. With unparalleled zeal, Lee's regime embarks on a campaign of modernization.

Immediately, a considerable section of the island is "denatured" to become a platform for industry; at Jurong, in the southwest, preparations are made for a huge industrial city of "flatted" (multilevel) factories connected to vast new harbor facilities.[9]

1 plan of Queenstown
2 colossal accumulations of slabs
3 before and after: living rooms
4 before and after: kitchens
5 "Town Centre" surrounded by slabs

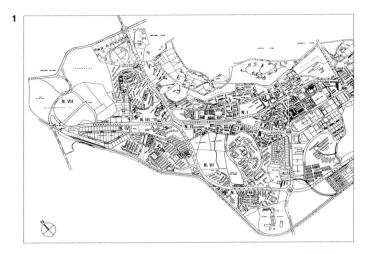

In 1960 the Housing and Development Board (HDB) is created. It will be the major vehicle for Singapore's future overhaul. Within months, construction of Queenstown (160,000 inhabitants) is begun on "virgin" land (liberated from squatters) outside the center: colossal accumulations of slabs seemingly without architectural qualities, their only concession to tropicality continuous balconies, stand in militaristic formation (with an occasional incomprehensible exception, conspicuous like a fainted soldier). They impassively surround communal areas that frantically attempt to discharge the neglected semantic duties of *interest* and *life*: shopping centers, playgrounds, places of worship.

Queenstown "reflects the policy of...the so-called '*Total Environment*' ... A shopping centre...for each Neighbourhood...Town Centre with cinemas, emporium, restaurants, night-club, Japanese Garden...A sports complex is under construction in neighbourhood VI...Focal areas and open spaces around the housing blocks have been landscaped... The high-rise blocks...located near primary and secondary schools... Frequent and efficient bus service criss-crosses the neighbourhood... A vigorous social atmosphere is already evident...Queenstown can be said to have been 'lived in.'"[10]

Years later—in 1985—the HDB admits: "In the first stage of public housing development, urgency to find a solution to the problem of housing shortage in Singapore did not allow time for research. Pragmatism prevailed..."[11]

To the extent that pragmatism has a look it is utilitarian, Anglo-Saxon: the slabs are purely quantitative emblems—modernity stripped of ideology, like the notorious English council estates. If the transition from the English slum to the estate was traumatic, the leap from the Chinese shophouse—typology that packs store, factory, family living quarters together in a single block around a courtyard—to Singapore's high-rise containers is even more merciless, not only in terms of material difference—from the Asian to the Western—but because the new inhabitants, cut off from connective networks of family relationships, tradition, habits, are abruptly forced into another civilization: the slab as time machine.

A second New Town, Toa Payoh, is launched for 1966. "Built on virtually virgin land, the whole town was conceived in its entirety: the Road System, Neighbourhood Precincts, the Shopping, Town Centre, and Sports Complexes, and a Town Park."[12]

knowledge based on the critical and systematic objectifications of delirious associations and interpretations."

PC/VME

The PC expansion card is not only standard to most DSPs; VME boards have also proved to be a popular choice with several manufacturers. Of course, they represent a greater investment than PC cards. But flexibility of the VME standards does have its advantages especially if previously designed systems were based on it.

PERCEPTION

Now since we perceive that we are seeing or hearing, it must either be by sight that something perceives that it is seeing or by some other sense. But given the consequent identity of the sense that perceives sight and that which perceives the colour that is the object of sight, there will either be two senses with the same object or the one sense will perceive its self. Further, if the sense that perceives sight were some other sense than sight, [the] only alternative to an infinite regress will be that there be some sense that perceives its self.

PERFECT

I get so sentimental when I see
How perfect perfection can be.

PERISHABLE

It was current consumer preference which determined product design and not any Platonic categories; it was a full-blown, emphatic style banking on the assets of competitive sex and as quickly perishable as the obsolescing product it wrapped.

PERMANENT

The rites of passage are no longer intermittent—they have become permanent.

PHILOSOPHERS

A couple of hundred years from now, maybe Isaac Asimov and Fred Pohl will be considered the important philosophers of the twentieth century, and the professional philosophers will almost all be forgotten…
Whenever Pohl or Asimov writes something, I regard it as extremely urgent to read it right away. They might have a new idea. Asimov has been working for forty years on this problem: if you can make an intelligent machine, what kind of relations will it have with people? How do you

Scenes from Toa Payoh

has been told that Singapore needs 'a more flexible plan...a more positive approach.'"[17]

What the transformation of the island needs is a manifesto. Instead of the master plan, with its rigid procedures and emphasis on controlling the built, the UN experts propose to "guide, accelerate, and coordinate public development" under the umbrella of a more fuzzy *guiding concept*, which will be decomposed in *action programs*[18] "comprehensive insofar as they should deal with *all* aspects of urban life: employment, shelter, communications, traffic, education, welfare, capital formation, stimulation of savings, community development, and public relations," finally translated in "a mosaic of *action maps* which will eventually cover the whole island..."

Once the tripartite planning vehicle is defined—guiding concept, action program, action map—they look for targets: "The central business district is flanked by mixed commercial and residential zones"—the Chinese shophouses that form the vast majority of the city's substance—"of spectacularly high density. Overcrowding of buildings and streets reaches proportions known in few other cities of the world... An earlier report by a UN expert found that substantial sections were ripe for demolition and rebuilding."

Probably aware that they are about to unleash a bureaucracy of almost communist omnipotence, the experts see it tempered and complemented by private enterprise: "Performance standards or social principles are needed to ensure a healthy and pleasant urban environment for all Singaporeans...without stifling the initiative of the developer or the inventiveness of the designer..."

They extend the reach of the guiding concept over the whole island: "The first principle should be the acceptance of Singapore island and Singapore city as one unit. We must look at the island as an *urban complex* which includes essential open spaces rather than as a province or county containing 2 different elements, a town and its rural hinterland."[19]

Then, daringly, they project—*ex nihilo*—the Dutch model, "the Ring City idea," on the newly prepared planning canvas: "A chain or necklace of settlements around a central open area has been called a 'ring city.' The idea comes from Holland where a group of major towns including Amsterdam, Haarlem, Utrecht, Delft, The Hague, Leiden, Dordrecht, and Rotterdam forms a large circle around a central stretch of open country. This constellation is the result of historic forces rather than of deliberate planning. Yet it

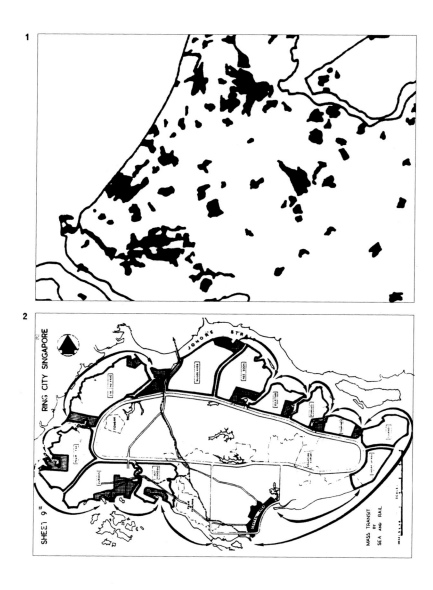

1 Ring City, Holland: Amsterdam, Utrecht, Rotterdam, Delft, The Hague, Leiden, Haarlem (clockwise from north) encircle so-called Green Heart — the void as center
2 projection of Ring City model on Singapore island (UN Report)

where what is given is taken away in a convulsion of uprooting, a state of permanent disorientation.

All the new housing, accommodated in high-rises, close together, entirely devoid of the centrifugal vectors of modernism, obscuring both sky and horizon, precludes any notion of escape. In Singapore, each perspective is blocked by good intentions.

"The overwhelming presence of more than half a million completed dwelling units is a constant reminder...of the government's achievement. The extensive public housing programme is symbolically, hence ideologically, a powerful sign of the existing regime's ability to fulfil its promises to improve the living conditions of the entire nation."[30]

How can the republic now known for establishing the ultimate capitalist environment begin with a quasi-socialist transformation of its entire territory? Turning the island into one huge housing project created the most brutal evidence of its "taking care" of its people, proof of the Confucian dictum "to give extensively to the common people and bring help to the multitude."[31]

The mystery of how—on an island almost antipodal to its geographical origins, for a people completely removed from its implied scenarios—the strategy of modern housing that failed in much more plausible conditions could suddenly "work" is left suspended between the assumption of greater authoritarianism and the inscrutable nature of the Asian mentality.

Empire of Semantics I **1, 2** "Asian" Village **3** "Chinese" garden
4 Chinatown— authentic subversiveness **5** respect... **6** given to... **7** each specific culture...

Barthian Slate

In 1967 Roland Barthes publishes *Système de la Mode*, an analysis of the system of signification created by the seemingly arbitrary manipulations of fashion designers—the up-and-down journey of the hemline, the present or absent waist, the roughness or luxury of fabrics. In 1970 he publishes *Empire des Signes*; it decodes the signs of Japanese culture. Both are unmaskings of the seemingly inscrutable—or rather, his method describes inscrutability *itself*, finally, as a sign.

Singapore is perhaps the first semiotic state, a Barthian slate, a clean synthetic surface, a field at once active and neutralized where political themes or minimal semantic particles can be launched and withdrawn, tested like weather balloons. Singapore is run according to Machiavellian semantics—not in an attempt to decode what already exists but as a prospective construction of political meaning. The resulting realm is not an "empire of signs" but an "empire of semantics."

America adopted the metaphor of the melting pot; Singapore is an ethnic "cuisine" where ingredients are kept separate, contamination is avoided. In its place is the manipulation of identities, through which the respect given to each specific culture—its ethnic, religious heritage—is an alibi for avoiding the serious demands—for more and more freedoms—of modern culture.

Each identity is a vessel carefully emptied through the efficiency of earlier cultural uprooting. (It is shocking to experience the authentic *subversiveness*—one of the most debased signifiers, resemanticized here through savage recontextualization—of life in one of the "streets the bulldozer forgot" in what remains of Chinatown against the overwhelming quantity of hygienic newness around it. Like an overdone film set, it seems "tropical" in its sense of dirty, lazy, corrupt, drugged—absolutely other.)

Education is enlisted in the creation of semantic orphans: there is a tabula-rasa quality even about the language ("I cry when I think that I cannot speak my own mother's tongue as well as I can speak the English language…"),[32] a sense that no one in Singapore speaks *any* language perfectly. But in the interest of global communication, the erasure continues. "Since 1987 English is the first language in all schools, with Chinese or another mother tongue as a second language…"[33]

1

2

Empire of Semantics II **1** seemingly unserious interdictions **2** very effective advertising

Even Singapore's notorious system of seemingly unserious interdictions (chewing gum) and serious penalties (death, caning) has to be seen as a sign. While Nevada once achieved identity through suspending a maximum number of laws to establish a climate of licentiousness, Singapore performs a legalistic redesign in the opposite direction—severity—that plays the role of very cheap and very effective worldwide advertising.

In Singapore—modernization in its pure form—the forces of modernity are enlisted against the demands of modernism. Singapore's modernism is lobotomized: from modernism's full agenda, it has adopted only the mechanistic, rationalistic program and developed it to an unprecedented perfection in a climate of streamlined "smoothness" generated by shedding modernism's artistic, irrational, uncontrollable, subversive ambitions—revolution without agony.

1

2

3

The sixties: anxieties and inspirations **1** "we may be turning the world into a place peopled only by little glass and concrete boxes…" (drawing, Saul Steinberg) **2** the injection of non-Western sources (Bernard Rudofsky, *Architecture Without Architects*) **3** Kenzo Tange, Tokyo Bay project

Architectural Context

The mid-sixties are maybe the last moment of architectural confidence. Urban renewal, ostensibly at its zenith, has exponentially expanded the scope of the urbanist. By consensus, the urban designer is "charged with giving form, with perceiving and contributing order."[34] At the same time there is a gnawing doubt about urban renewal's assumptions, a feeling that the entire thrust of its performance could be flawed. In the words of Christopher Alexander, "The prospect that we may be turning the world into a place peopled only by little glass and concrete boxes has alarmed many architects too…"[35]

Team X makes an effort to humanize the central vision/model of CIAM, partly through the injection of non-Western sources—African villages, Yemenese desert towns—and other foreign associations. Rumblings are heard from Egypt; Christopher Alexander tests his theories on Indian villages.[36]

The ideological foundations are prepared for a critical reverse idealization in which the inarticulate masses of the Third World are felt to offer an antidote to the sterility of modernization: the "values" of underdevelopment are presumed to incorporate an anti-materialist ideology; lessons are extracted from "unspoiled" lands like China, Vietnam, India, Africa—cultures more collective than those of the individualistic, atomized West; new concepts are harvested from Asia, presumably of greater subtlety, inscrutability, stoicism.

The mid-sixties are also the moment when, for the first time in the male whiteness of prewar modernism, "other" architects emerge from their "exotic" cultures to participate in the Oedipal skirmishes that have developed around the central dogmas of modernism. On its way to ultimate globalization, Western civilization creates and must recognize thinkers at the periphery.

The most exciting movement of the early sixties is Japanese. The new awareness of huge quantitative obligations that have to be discharged in a climate of acceleration and instability has sponsored the metabolist movement, a loose federation of Japan's thinking elite—Tange, Kurokawa, Maki, Isozaki—combining organic, scientific, mechanistic, biological, and romantic (sublime) vocabularies. Kenzo Tange's Tokyo Bay project stuns in the way an entirely new doctrine seems immediately convincing. It is the first time in over 3,000 years that architecture has a non-white avant-garde.

What makes these architects exciting—and maybe what makes them Asian—is that they do not avoid, like their European contemporaries, the central issue of quantity—the masses—that had propelled the prewar modernists.

European cousins refine, rediscover the small scale; metabolist Asians—conscious of, even inspired by, demographic pressure—imagine other richer, more spontaneous, freer ways of organizing congestion. (Paradoxically, Singapore's pragmatic, thoughtless HDB New Towns, with their absence of detail, their sheer pileups of numbers, can be read simultaneously as decadent modernism and as proto-metabolism produced by the regime's almost biological thyroid overdrive.)

With his *Investigations in Collective Form*, Maki—educated and frequently teaching in the US—asserts an explicitly Asian presence. Like so many architecture books of the period, Maki's brochure is an amalgam of more or less coherent theoretical insights, illustrated by more or less theoretical projects. Which came first—theory or illustration— is ambiguous.

As a Japanese Harvard graduate, Maki straddles two worlds. His treatise is a knowing exploitation of the slack in between. Unlike the "original CIAM theorists," he suggests, "we must now see our urban society as a dynamic field of interrelated forces. It is a set of mutually independent variables in a rapidly expanding infinite series. Any order introduced within the pattern of forces contributes to a state of dynamic equilibrium— an equilibrium which will change in character as time passes…

"Our cities are fluid and mobile. It is difficult to conceive of some of them as places, in the real sense of that word. How can an entity with no discernible beginning or end be a place? It is certainly more apt to think *of a particular part of a city as a place*. If it were possible to articulate each of the parts of the city more adequately, to give qualities of edge and *node* to now formless agglomerates, we would have begun to make our large urban complexes at least understandable, if not 'imageable.'"

The rigidities of early modernism are now undermined by the instability that it itself has proclaimed: "The reason for searching for new formal concepts in contemporary cities lies in the magnitude of…recent change in those very problems. Our urban society is characterized by: (1) coexistence and conflict of amazingly heterogeneous institutions and individuals; (2) unprecedented rapid and extensive transformation in the physical structure of the society; (3) rapid communications methods; and (4) technological progress *and its impact upon regional cultures.*"

In those conditions, the instrumentality of urbanism, obsessed with fixity, is obsolescent, as the UN experts had also suggested: "Our concern here is not, then, a 'master plan,' but a 'master program'... As a physical correlate of the master program, there are 'master forms' which differ from buildings in that they... respond to the dictates of time."

Out of this interpretation, Maki produces "collective form"—its name alone a hidden rebuke to the individualism of Western practice. "Collective form represents groups of buildings and quasi-buildings—the segment of our cities. Collective form is, however, not a collection of unrelated, separate buildings, but of buildings that have reasons to be together."

For Maki, it exists in three kinds: *compositional form*, *megastructure*, and *group form.*

Obviously bored by compositional form ("commonly accepted and practiced concept in the past and at present"), he is fascinated by megastructure and group form. "The megastructure is a large frame in which all the functions of a city or part of a city are housed... It is a manmade feature of the landscape... Urban designers are attracted to the megastructure... because it offers a legitimate way to order massive grouped functions." But Maki is skeptical: "If the megaform becomes rapidly obsolete... it will be a great weight about the neck of urban society."[37]

Maki's real affinity is with group form, where "the elements create extremely well-differentiated communal formal and functional factors, which are then developed in connectors. The elements do not depend on the framework; instead they establish a group in which an organic interdependence exists between them and the framework..."[38]

The coexistence of these categories is conceived as a new urbanism, a new city: "The ideal is a kind of master form which can move into ever new states of equilibrium and yet maintain visual consistency and a sense of continuing order in the long run."

POLES[2]

Why settle for lighting pole function alone? You can also have lighting pole *personality*—to complement, contrast, or signature—the exterior lighting for your next project! Whether you require historic period lighting, environmental sensitivity, or 21st century flash, Union Metal has the poles you want.

PONTIFICATE

"Ah!" said the fisherman, "my wife wants to be pope."

"Go home," said the fish, "she is pope already."

POODLE

If it's not true that art has become a trained poodle of the techno social elitethen how do you explain Wayne Thiebaud's oils of pastry in *The Chez Panisse Dessert Cookbook*? a coming together of art as culturescape and food-as-meaning-of-life into a chocolate cream pie of kitsch of which each consumer will get an equal slice.

POOL[1]

In Tokyo there is a new indoor swimming pool equipped with a basin of intensely undulating water in which the swimmers remain on the same spot. The turbulence prevents any attempt to move forward, and the swimmers must try to advance just to hold their position. Like a kind of home-trainer or conveyor belt on which one moves in the direction opposite that of the belt, the dynamics of the currents in this Japanese pool have the sole function of making the racing swimmers struggle with the energy passing through the space of their mutual encounter, and energy that takes the place of the dimensions of an Olympic pool just as the belts of the home trainer have been replacing stadium race tracks.

POOL[2]

One day they discovered that if they swam in unison—in regular synchronized laps from one end of the pool to the other—the pool would begin to move slowly in the opposite direction.

POOL[3]

They wanted a swimming pool on the roof, which I found very unpleasant because I wanted to do a project without a swimming pool for once.

Golden Mile Complex: Singapore theorized

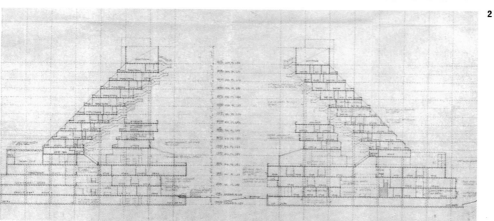

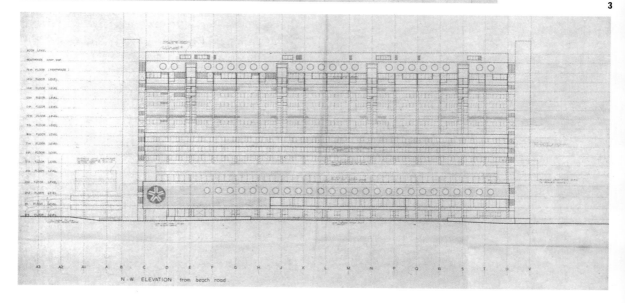

N-W ELEVATION from beach road

1 Golden Mile Complex, looking up, November 1993 **2, 3** Golden Mile Complex, sections and elevation

In the tropics, this prying open can be seen as a genuine, almost ecological wish to expose the hidden interior to the breezes of a beneficial climate. There is no segregation of the interior but a condition of mutual exposure and utmost urban permeability.

In these projects, Singapore's center is theorized as a prototype of the modern Asian metropolis: the city as a system of interconnected urban chambers. The climate, which traditionally limits street life, makes the interior the privileged domain for the urban encounter. Shopping in this idealized context is not just the status-driven compulsion it has become "here" but an amalgam of sometimes microscopic, infinitely varied functional constellations in which each stall is a "functoid" of the overall programmatic mosaic that constitutes urban life.

In the late sixties, Singapore architects—savagely synthesizing influences of Le Corbusier, the Smithsons/Team X, self-consciously Asian speculations derived from Maki, a new Asian self-awareness and confidence—crystallized, defined, and built ambitious examples of vast modern socles teeming with the most traditional forms of Asian street life, extensively connected by multiple linkages, fed by modern infrastructures and sometimes Babel-like multilevel car parks, penetrated by proto-atriums, supporting mixed-use towers: they are containers of urban multiplicity, heroic captures and intensifications of urban life in *architecture*, rare demonstrations of the kind of performance that could and should be the norm in architecture but rarely is, giving an alarming degree of plausibility to the myths of the multilevel city and the megastructure that "we," in infinitely more affluent circumstances, have discredited and discarded.

1 Singapore now: tenuous quality of a freeze-frame… **2** that can be set in motion again at any time…

Promethean Hangover: The Next Lap

From one single, teeming Chinatown, Singapore has become a city *with* a Chinatown. It seems completed.

But as a (former) theater of the tabula rasa, Singapore now has the tenuous quality of a freeze-frame, of an arrested movement that can be set in motion again at any time on its way to yet another configuration; it is a city perpetually morphed to the next state.

The curse of the tabula rasa is that, once applied, it proves not only previous occupancies expendable, but also each *future* occupancy provisional too, ultimately temporary. That makes the claim to finality—the illusion on which even the most mediocre architecture is based—impossible. It makes Architecture impossible.

The anxiety induced by the precarious status of Singapore's reality is exacerbated by the absence of a geometric stability. Its courage to erase has not inspired a new conceptual frame—*guiding concept?*—a definitive prognosis of the island's status, an autonomous identity independent of infill, such as the Manhattan grid. Singapore's proliferating geometry is strained beyond its breaking point when it has to organize the coexistence of the strictly orthogonal super-blocks of average modernity that comprise the vast majority of its built substance. Singapore's "planning"—the mere sum of presences—is formless, like a batik pattern. It emerges surprisingly, seemingly from nowhere, and can be canceled and erased equally abruptly. The city is an imperfect collage: all foreground, no background.

Maybe this lack of geometry is typically Asian; Tokyo is the eternal example. But what does that make the present, almost worldwide condition? Is Paris encircled by an Asian ring? Is Piranesi's Roman Forum Chinese? Or is our tolerance for the imperfection of "other" cultures, "other" standards a camouflaged form of post-colonial condescension?

The resistance of these assembled buildings to forming a recognizable ensemble creates, Asian or not, a condition where the exterior—the classic domain of the urban—appears residual, leftover, overcharged with commercial effluence from hermetic interiors, hyper-densities of trivial commandments, public art, the reconstructed tropicality of landscaping.

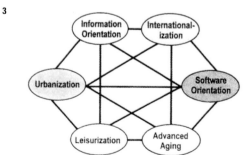

1 Lee Kuan Yew, former prime minister, and his successor, Goh Chok Tong **2** a more relaxed version of Sparta
3 "New Orientations" diagram

As a manifesto of the quantitative, Singapore reveals a cruel contradiction: huge increases in matter, the overall effect increasingly unreal. The sinister quality of the windows—black glass, sometimes purple—creates, as in a model-railroad landscape, an additional degree of abstraction that makes it impossible to guess whether the buildings are empty or teeming with transplanted Confucian life...

In spite of its colossal substance, Singapore is doomed to remain a Potemkin metropolis.

That is not a local problem. We can *make* things, but not necessarily make them real. Singapore represents the point where the volume of the new overwhelms the volume of the old, has become too big to be animated by it, has not yet developed its own vitality. Mathematically, the third millennium will be an experiment in this form of soullessness (unless we wake up from our 30-year sleep of self-hatred).

After its monumental achievement, Singapore now suffers a Promethean hangover. A sense of anticlimax is palpable. The "finished" Barthian state is grasping for new themes, new metaphors, new signs to superimpose on its luxurious substance. From external enemies, the attention has shifted to internal demons, of which doubt is so far the most unusual.

Lee resigned in 1990 but remains prominently in the background as an éminence grise. His successor, Goh Chok Tong, must assure the transition from a hyper-efficient garrison state to a more relaxed version of Sparta.

It is a period of transition, revision, marginal adjustments, "New Orientations"; after urbanization comes "leisurization." "Singaporeans now aspire to the finer things in life—to the arts, culture, and sports..."[50]

The recent creation of a Ministry for Information and the Arts is indicative. As Yeo, its minister, warns, "It may seem odd, but we have to pursue the subject of fun very seriously if we want to stay competitive in the 21st century..."

Singapore is a *city without qualities* (maybe that is an ultimate form of deconstruction, and even of freedom). But its evolution—its songline—continues: from enlightened postwar UN triumvirate, first manifestation of belated CIAM apotheosis, overheated metabolist metropolis, now dominated by a kind of Confucian postmodernism in which

5

6

1, 2 Confucian postmodernism: early housing slabs rehabilitated **3** shopping center atrium, Orchard Road
4 city as shopping center **5** global consumer frenzy **6** Nge Ann City, roofscape

the brutal early housing slabs are rehabilitated with symmetrical ornament.

In the eighties, the global consumer frenzy perverted Singapore's image to one of repulsive caricature: an entire city perceived as shopping center, an orgy of Eurasian vulgarity, a city stripped of the last vestiges of authenticity and dignity. But even in a terminal project such as Nge Ann City, the elements of former ideological life are present, latent under the sheen of garish postmodernity (granite, brass, brick) which, in the new rhetoric, is based not only on Asian life but on the resurrection of Asian aesthetics: the Chinese Wall, pagodas, the Forbidden City, etc. Under the forms and decorations it is still a stunning urban machine, with its lavish parking decks on the 11th floor, the diversity of its atriums, the surprising richness of its cellular department stores, mixing Nike with Chanel, Timberland with Thai food: Turbo-Metabolism.

History, especially colonial history, is rehabilitated, paradoxically because it is the only one recognizable *as* history: the Raffles Hotel, painstakingly restored in the front, is cloned in the back to accommodate a shopping-center extension that far exceeds the original in volume.

Paul Rudolph reemerges from limbo. Somewhere in the city one of his American prototypes—it started its conceptual life in the sixties as a stack of mobile homes hoisted in a steel skeleton—stands realized in concrete.

In 1981 he had been part of the Beach Road experiment—presumably unknowingly. For a developer, and without contact with his Singaporean colleagues, the American designs a metabolic project: a rotated concrete tower next to a deformed bulge of a podium, one of the first manifestations of the independent atrium. Thirteen years later, it too stands realized, but in aluminum, the rotation of the tower replaced by indentation, a metallic corncob, its "American atrium" more hollow than its Asian counterparts.

Singapore's center will be hyper-dense; a massive invasion of stark, undetailed forms crowds the city model on the top floor of the planning office. On newly reclaimed land, the last center pieces are being fitted with contextual masterpieces: a "Botta," a posthumous "Stirling." But how can buildings be sympathetic to their environment if there *is* no environment?

Various anxieties (repressed? imported?) come gingerly to the surface, most insidi-

1, 2 the center will be hyper-dense: city model at Urban Redevelopment Authority, top floor, November 1993
3 "all of our efforts are marked by the desire to balance development with nature"
4 Lee Kuan Yew launches tree-planting campaign, 1963 **5** after development, Eden…

ously about the disappearance of history. "There is a call to preserve and explore our rich cultural heritage..."

Goh has identified his reign as the Next Lap (it supersedes Vision 1999). At his November 1990 swearing-in he proclaims, "Singapore can do well only if her good sons and daughters are prepared to dedicate themselves to help others. I shall rally them to serve the country. For if they do not come forward, what future will we have? I therefore call on my fellow citizens to join me, to run the next lap together..."[51]

But the name alone betrays an inbuilt fatigue, like a marathon run around a track. Goh's Next Lap is like an invitation to join him on a treadmill.

Mostly, the Next Lap represents further work on Singapore's identity. "Our vision is... an island with an increased sense of 'island-ness'—more beaches, marinas, resorts, and possibly entertainment parks as well as better access to an attractive coastline and a city that embraces the waterline more closely as a signal of its island heritage. Singapore will be cloaked in greenery, both manicured by man and protected tracts of natural growth and with waterbodies woven into the landscape."[52] Altogether, Singapore is poised to evolve "Towards a Tropical City of Excellence."

In this climate of relative reconsideration, if not contemplation, nature itself is a prime candidate for rehabilitation, sometimes retroactively. "All of our efforts are marked by the desire to balance development with nature... Sometimes, as elsewhere around the world, we have tended to over-develop a few. In some such cases, there is a need to roll back time, remove the buildings and rehabilitate the old vegetation." Almost ominously, it even seems as if nature will be the next project of development, throwing the mechanics of the tabula rasa into a paradoxical reverse gear: after development, Eden.

Already in 1963, Lee Kuan Yew "personally launched a tree-planting campaign" as prophylactic compensation for the urban renewal programs that were to be initiated. "Active tree planting was carried out for all roads, vacant plots, and new development sites."

Parallel to the intensification of urban renewal, a "garden city" campaign was started in 1967, "a beautification programme that aims to clothe the republic in a green mantle resplendent with the colors of nature..."[53]

1 "Tropical Excellence" **2**, **3** outdoors: Potemkin nature
4, **5** indoors: shopping Eden, Raffles City, 1993

Now the state is about to complete a "park network," an ambitious web implemented through a "park connector system" that will convert Singapore into a "total playground."

Worldwide, landscape is becoming the new ideological medium, more popular, more versatile, easier to implement than architecture, capable of conveying the same signifiers but more subtly, more subliminally; it is two-dimensional rather than three-dimensional, more economical, more accommodating, infinitely more susceptible to intentional inscriptions.

The irony of Singapore's climate is that its tropical heat and humidity are at the same time the perfect alibi for a full-scale retreat into interior, generalized, non-specific, air-conditioned comfort—*and* the sole surviving element of authenticity, the only thing that makes Singapore tropical, still. With indoors turned into a shopping Eden, outdoors becomes a Potemkin nature—a plantation of tropical emblems, palms, shrubs, which the very tropicality of the weather makes ornamental.

The "tropical" in "tropical excellence" is a trap, a conceptual dead end where the metaphorical and the literal wrestle each other to a standoff: while all of Singapore's architecture is on a flight *away* from the heat, their ensemble is supposed to be its apotheosis.

The only tropical authenticity left is a kind of accelerated decay, a Conradian rot: it is the resistance to *that* tropicality that explains Singapore's uptightness. "It corresponds to a deep primordial fear of being swallowed up by the jungle, a fate that can only be avoided by being ever more perfect, ever more disciplined, always the best..."[54]

1 Liu Thai Ker interviewed **2** "after the pavement, beach" —move beyond irony…

1

2

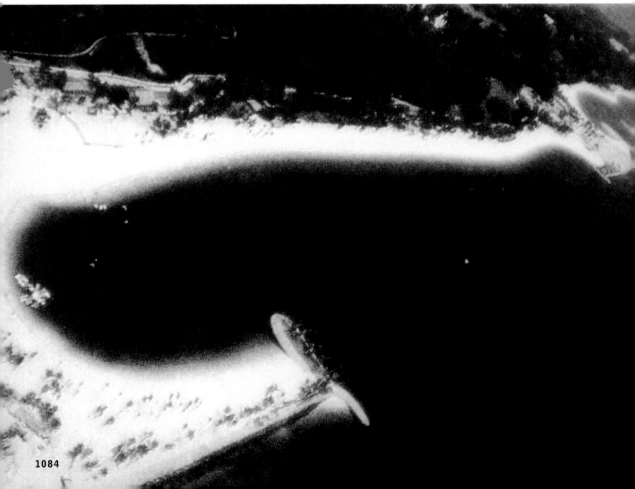

Finally, in a move beyond the reach of irony, the island is now being outfitted with a perimeter beach. "By the year x, through reclamation and replanning, the amount of accessible shoreline is almost doubled, while the inaccessible areas are correspondingly reduced. There are ample opportunities for us to create beaches, promenades, marinas, resorts, etc."

Singapore now becomes a willed idyll—"like in May '68," the former chief planner, Liu Thai Ker, whispers to me. It is a subtle revision. Not "under the pavement, beach," but "after the pavement, beach."

thermal insulation is to control heat transfer and thereby protect a building from excessive heat loss during cold seasons and heat gain during hot seasons.

PROVOCATEUR
The architect proceeds as the avant-garde does in any battle, as a provocateur. He saps the edges of taste, undermines the conventional boundaries, assaults the thresholds of respectability and shocks the psychic stability of the past by introducing the new, the strange, the exotic and the erotic.

PROXIMITY[1]
Anyway, these two nuns were sitting next to me, and we sort of struck up a conversation.

PROXIMITY[2]
As long as two buildings share the same space or are in each other's proximity, whether the architect wants it or not, or whether anybody cares, they do have a relationship. It is an enormous farce to believe that to create a relationship, one thing has to be like another thing, or one thing has to adjust to another thing. As anybody who shares the world with anybody else knows, the simple proximity—the simple juxtaposition of things—creates a relationship that is there, almost independent of the mutual will of the people who created these objects.

PSEUDONYM
No, I'm not Thomas Pynchon. I am, however, John Fowles, uh, I'm John Barth, and I used to be Flannery O'Connor—but I killed that one off.

PSYCHOGEOGRAPHY
Psychogeography is the study of the specific effects of the geographical environment, consciously organized or not, on the emotions and behavior of individuals.

PURGE
I felt stifled. Everything I looked at reminded me of myself. I opened wide the doors of my wardrobe and threw in all the debris from the floor. I pulled the sheets, blankets and pillows off my bed and put those in too. I ripped down pictures from the wall that I had once cut out of magazines. Under the bed I found plates and cups covered in green mold. I took every loose object and put it in the wardrobe till the room was bare. I even took down the light bulb and

Postscript: Metastasis

As it stands, the Singapore model—sum, as we have seen, of a series of systematic transubstantiations which make it, in effect, one of the most ideological of all urban conditions—is now poised to metastasize across Asia. The sparkle of its organization, the glamour of its successful uprooting, the success of its human transformation, the laundering of its past, its manipulation of vernacular cultures present an irresistible model for those facing the task of imagining—and building—new urban conditions for the even more countless millions. More and more, Singapore claims itself a laboratory for China, a role that could lift its present moroseness.

The sums are stark: "Eighty percent of China's population is still rural," argues Liu Thai Ker, former head of the URA, now in private practice. "The mere shift of one fourth of them to the city over the next 20 years—an implausibly low figure—would imply a doubling of all their urban substance."

It is unlikely that the deconstructivist model, or any of the other respectable contemporary propositions (what are they anyway?), has a great attraction in these circumstances. Singapore represents the exact dosage of "authority, instrumentality, and vision" necessary to appeal. In numerous architectural offices in Singapore, whose names few of us have ever heard, China's future is being prepared. In these countless new cities the skyscraper is the only surviving typology. After the iconoclasm of communism there will be a second, more efficient Ludditism, helping the Chinese toward the "desired land": market economy—but minus the decadence, the democracy, the messiness, the disorder, the cruelty of the West.

Projecting outward from Singapore, an asymmetrical epicenter, there will be new Singapores across the entire mainland. Its model will be the stamp of China's modernization.

Two billion people can't be wrong.

Exit

Singapore mantra: don't forget to confirm your return flight.

light shade. Then I took my clothes off, threw them in and closed the doors. The room was empty like a cell. I lay down on the bed again and stared at my patch of clear sky till I fell asleep.

Q

QUANTITY
Mies van der Rohe said, "The least is the most." I agree with him completely. At the same time, what concerns me now is quantity.

QUASI-HISTORICAL
But of course, the modern architecture in OMA's scheme of things is not Ville Radieuse rationality, nor Hilberseimerian sobriety, nor megastructural systematicity. It is already a quasi-historical modernity which harks back to the decade of the twenties in Russia and in America. It recalls the abstractions of Malevich and Lissitzky, the idealities of Chernikov and Leonidov, the sensuous, wayward and episodic in a way which has not been seen since the early days. All that strange variety of modern architecture in the days before Pavillon Suisse defined the canon of rationality and commercial expediency once and for all, returns now in OMA to haunt us with the possibilities of a future which we had already thought was over.

QUERY
Dame Mouse went to the Sun and said to him,
"Sun, do you know why I have come to you?"
"How should I know?"

QUOTE¹
I hate quotations.

QUOTE²
I am a foreigner to myself in my own language and I translate myself by quoting all the others.

R

RADIUS
Since the internal radius of turn of a commercial vehicle is about 8m,

Notes

The author gratefully acknowledges William S. W. Lim, Tay Kheng Soon, Chua Beng Huat, and Liu Thai Ker for contributing their time and insights; nevertheless, the ideas and opinions expressed in this text are those of the author.

1. William Gibson, "Disneyland with the Death Penalty," *Wired* (Sept.–Oct. 1993).

2. Deyan Sudjic, "Virtual City," *Blueprint* (February 1994).

3. Official slogan.

4. Lee Kuan Yew.

5. Lim Chee Then, "The Confucian Tradition and Its Future in Singapore: Historical, Cultural, and Educational Perspectives," in Yong Mun Cheong, *Asian Traditions and Modernization* (Times Academic Press, 1992), p. 214.

6. Richard Nixon, *Leaders* (New York: Warner Books, 1982), p. 311.

7. Jean Louis Margolin, 1989, as quoted in Rodolphe de Koninck, *Singapour/re: An Atlas of the Revolution of Territory* (Montpellier: Reclus, 1992), p. 25.

8. Chua Beng-Huat, "Not Depoliticized But Ideologically Successful: The Public Housing Programme in Singapore," *International Journal of Urban and Regional Research* 15, no. 1 (1991), p. 27.

9. At the moment of writing, Singapore is poised to overtake Rotterdam as the largest harbor in the world. It is already the most efficient.

10. *First Decade in Public Housing* (Singapore: Housing and Development Board, 1969), p. 18.

11. Aline K. Wong and Stephen H. K. Yeh, eds., *Housing a Nation: 25 Years of Public Housing in Singapore* (Singapore: Housing and Development Board/Maruzen Asia, 1985).

12. *First Decade in Public Housing,* p. 26.

13. Wong and Yeh, *Housing a Nation,* p. 95.

14. Charles Abrams, Susumu Kobe, and Otto Koenigsberger, "Growth and Urban Renewal in Singapore" (report to the UN, 1963), pp. 7, 109.

15. Abrams, Kobe, and Koenigsberger, "Growth and Urban Renewal in Singapore," pp. 121–22 (italics added).

16. Abrams, Kobe, and Koenigsberger, "Growth and Urban Renewal in Singapore," pp. 9, 10 (italics added). In 1994, Singapore has 2.7 million inhabitants.

17. Abrams, Kobe, and Koenigsberger, "Growth and Urban Renewal in Singapore," pp. 10, 11, 45 (italics added). In the subsection "The Silent Assumption of British Planning," the tone is surprisingly anti-colonial/anti-English.

18. Political name under People's Action Party.

19. Abrams, Kobe, and Koenigsberger, "Growth and Urban Renewal in Singapore," pp. 59, 16, 12, 61.

20. As noted in "Growth and

Urban Renewal in Singapore," the term Ring City was coined by Professor Jacobus P. Thijsso in his paper "Metropolitan Planning in the Netherlands" (Conurbation Holland, UN, 1959). In Holland, the "central stretch of open country" is called its Green Heart. Abrams, Kobe, and Koenigsberger, "Growth and Urban Renewal in Singapore," p. 63.

21. Chua, "Not Depoliticized But Ideologically Successful," p. 29.

22. De Koninck, *Singapour/re,* pp. 84, 37.

23. "At the turn of the sixties, the Jurong district was still covered with hills…30 to 40 meters high…By the early eighties, the hills have nearly all been leveled." De Koninck, *Singapour/re,* p. 44.

24. De Koninck, *Singapour/re,* p. 88.

25. World Health Organization, in Donald Canty, "Architecture and the Urban Emergency," *Architectural Forum,* Aug.–Sept. 1964, p. 173.

26. President Lyndon Johnson, in Canty, "Architecture and the Urban Emergency."

27. Fumihiko Maki, *Investigations in Collective Form* (St. Louis: Washington University School of Architecture, 1964), p. 34.

28. Chua, "Not Depoliticized But Ideologically Successful," p. 26.

29. Confucius, *The Analects,* VIII/9, trans. D. C. Lau, in Lim, "Confucian Tradition."

30. Chua, "Not Depoliticized But Ideologically Successful," pp. 35–36.

31. Confucius, *The Analects,* VI/30, in Lim, "Confucian Tradition."

32. Lee Kuan Yew, as quoted in Ian Buruma, "Singapore," *New York Times Magazine,* June 12, 1988, p. 58.

33. "Many traditional Chinese language textbooks are no longer suitable for use because of the students' lower level of proficiency in the language." Lim, "Confucian Tradition," p. 215.

34. Maki, *Investigations in Collective Form,* p. 3.

35. Christopher Alexander, "A City Is Not a Tree," *Architectural Forum,* April 1965.

36. In the introduction to "Notes on the Synthesis of Form," Peter Blake writes that Alexander "spent several months in India planning the development of a small village, which he now admits to having organized as a tree."

37. Maki, *Investigations in Collective Form,* pp. 3, 34, 4, 5, 6, 8–11 (italics added).

38. Fumihiko Maki, "The Theory of Group Form," *Japan Architect,* Feb. 1970, pp. 39–40.

39. Maki, *Investigations in Collective Form,* pp. 11, 27–35.

40. Maki, "Theory of Group Form," p. 40.

41. Maki, *Investigations in Collective Form,* pp. 82, 84, 85, 23, 21.

42. *SPUR 65–67,* pp. 1–2, 29, 34, 38, 52.

43. "The Future of Asian Cities," *Asia Magazine,* May 1966, pp. 5, 7, 8.

44. Lee Kuan Yew, lecture, in *SPUR 65–67,* p. 58.

45. Chua, "Not Depoliticized But Ideologically Successful," p. 30.

46. Its distance from the coast has increased since, through additional land reclamation.

47. William Lim, *Cities for People* (Singapore: Select Books, 1990), p. 8.

48. Urban Redevelopment Authority, *Chronicle of Sale Sites,* 1967, p. 25.

49. Urban Redevelopment Authority, *Chronicle of Sale Sites,* p. 30.

50. *The Next Lap* (Singapore: Times International Press, 1991), p. 101.

51. *The Next Lap,* p. 3.

52. Urban Redevelopment Authority, *Living the Next Lap: Towards a Tropical City of Excellence,* 1991.

53. Lee Sing Keng and Chua Sian Eng, *More Than a Garden City* (Singapore: Parks and Recreation Department, 1992), p. 8.

54. Buruma, "Singapore." In some cases, through the pervasiveness of the interior conditions, there is an acute point of reversal: it is as if the exterior is the unusual condition, seen through plate glass like a window display.

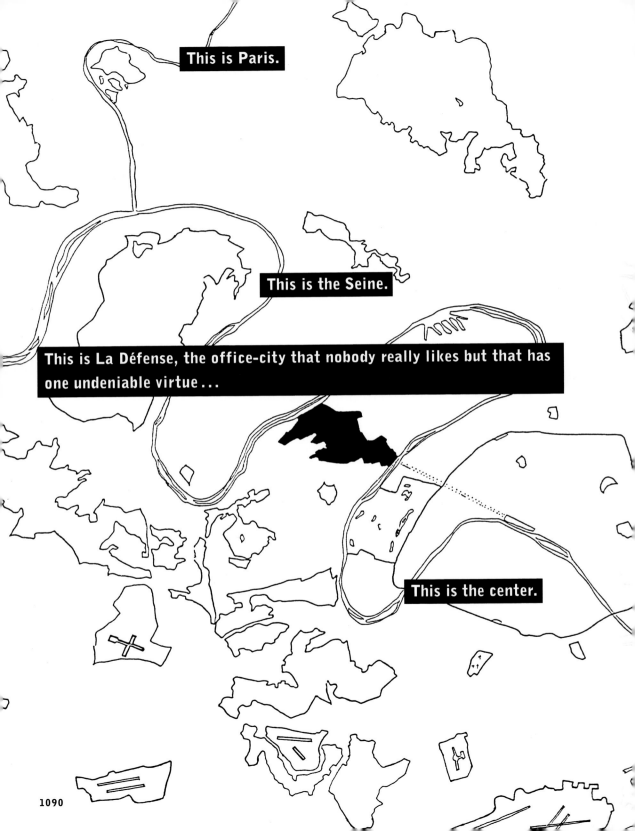

This is Paris.

This is the Seine.

This is La Défense, the office-city that nobody really likes but that has one undeniable virtue...

This is the center.

Tabula Rasa Revisited

Mission Grand Axe
La Défense, Paris, France
Competition, 1991

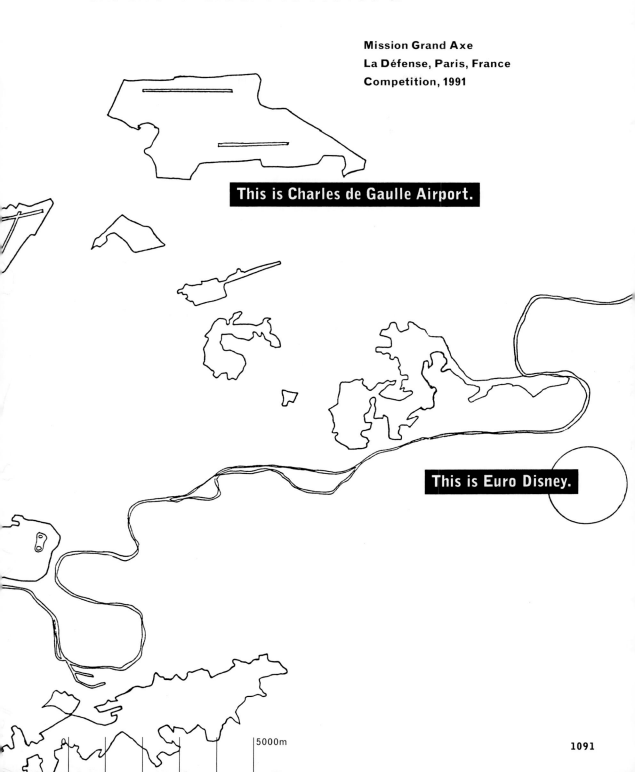

This is Charles de Gaulle Airport.

This is Euro Disney.

5000m

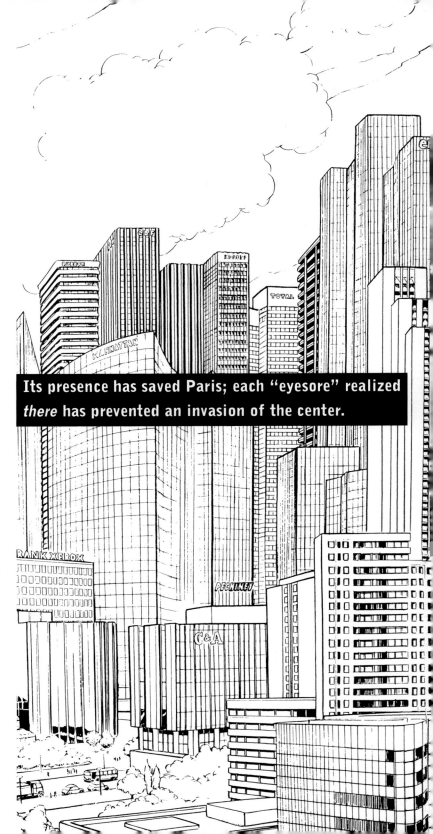

RAIN

The rain everyone was waiting for did not come.

RAINED

It rained all that day, and the next.

RANDOM

Like any story that hangs on suffering, chance, whim, stupidity in the right quarters, mercy and money, there was something random to it — a randomness that swelled and swelled like an abscess.

RAPSODES

De même que l'intarissable des rapsodes nécessite des accommodements avec la cheville et le bouchetrou, le fulgurant des moralistes a pour postérité le formel des verroteries.

RATIONALITY

Its rationality is the most interesting feature of the constructive approach; without that characteristic it is inconceivable.

RC

Film began to die the moment remote control became a household standard and subsequently evolved itself into the main item. Citizens went out and bought remote control units and were given free television sets for their troubles.

REACHABLE

In the old days the sky was not as high as it is today. It was very low and people could reach it. A man had only to stretch his arm and touch it. Once a woman, who washed her baby's diapers, stretched her arms and wiped her hands on the hanging sky. Another woman wiped her hands on the moon.

REASON

It is for this reason that we have dedicated our hands, legs, pens, speech and our own dear heads to progress and understanding in art.

REBEL

Permanently infecting the maternal sources which render identity, technique itself contaminates the sense of dwelling across language, introduces mechanisms of transference between architecture and subject,

it will be seen that a kerb radius of 10m will be needed for such vehicles to maintain a constant distance from the kerb while turning the corner, while allowing some spare for the distance covered while turning the steering wheel.

Its presence has saved Paris; each "eyesore" realized *there* has prevented an invasion of the center.

The competition called for an extension of La Défense, which starts at the Seine, to another loop of the Seine, so it would start at the Seine and end at the Seine. The French, with their eternal optimism about the significance of axes, had already decided that the only meaningful gesture would be to extend the famous axis that starts at the Louvre and continues, via the Arc de Triomphe, to the Grande Arche at La Défense, and to charge this unglamorous line with meaning.

reprieves fatherhood in the sense of conscious begetting.

RED

Red is the most joyful and dreadful thing in the physical universe; it is the fiercest note, it is the highest light, it is the place where the walls of this world of ours wear the thinnest and something beyond burns through.

REDOUBT

Want to add a serene, Eastern touch to your house or apartment? A Japanese company has started selling a build-it-yourself tearoom that can function as a redoubt from the stress of urban (or suburban) living. Called Space of Nippon, the tearoom comes in a kit — crates of "natural" wood from Japan (cypress and cedar) that the buyer assembles into a traditional Japanese room.

REFLECTION

I know very well that I am an ugly, wrinkled old man. When I look in the mirror at bedtime after taking out my false teeth, the face I see is really weird. I don't have a tooth of my own in either jaw. I hardly even have gums. If I clamp my mouth shut, my lips flatten together and my nose hangs down to my chin. It astonishes me to think that this is my own face. Not even monkeys have such hideous faces. How could anyone with a face like this ever hope to appeal to a woman?

REFRACTION

He opened his eyes and found that he was looking away from the tower and out into the world: and it had changed in nature. It had bent itself into a sort of bowl, detailed here, sweeping up beyond that to a blue rim.

REFUGE

They were down in the Cold War dream, the voices fading from the radios, the unwatchable events in the sky, the flight, the long descent, the escape to refuge deep in the earth, one hatchway after another, leading to smaller and smaller volumes. Sleeping compartments, water, food, electricity, curtailed possibilities, and extension to life in a never-ending hum of fluorescent light and recycled air. And right now, still this side of the Unimagined, also offering deep privacy for whatever those in

But when we looked at the rear of La Défense,

we were not very optimistic about our ability to charge this line with meaning.

command might wish to do to people they brought down here.

REFUSE
The challenge to our generation is to refuse to build now.

REGENERATION
The Americans ... have a blind faith in their own history — so blind in fact that Hollywood just keeps rehashing the same history. The American cinema of today regenerated itself almost exclusively, and deals with experiences which were had only in other films. In other words, the thread that ties cinema to life, that lets film have something to do with "real life," has been cut.

REGULATED
If your question is: to what degree *should* architecture regulate "human life," I can only answer that it doesn't; or at least not a single "human life" — those times are passed forever — now there are only multiple, fragmented, atomized human live*s* that actually need a multiplicity or maybe strong, maybe extreme, maybe *regulated* contexts, all "regulated" to a particular pitch, like the different speeds of a pitching machine.

REINCARNATION[1]
When I die and if I come back again, I'd like to be an architect or engineer. Build things up for a change. Build things like houses and museums and bridges. It's better than bombing, I think.

REINCARNATION[2]
Shortly after his reincarnation, the butcher opened his eyes and discovered that he was hanging with one leg on a hook in his own shop that by that time had been taken over by his son.

RELOCATED
The Archeological Museum, which contains finds from around the island, is being relocated somewhere in the park; ask at the tourist office for an update on its progress.

REMINDER
"Always remember," his mother reminded him frequently, "that you are a Nately. You are not a Vanderbilt, whose fortune was made by a vulgar tugboat captain, or a Rockefeller, whose wealth was amassed through unscrupulous speculations in crude petroleum; or a Reynolds or Duke, whose income was derived

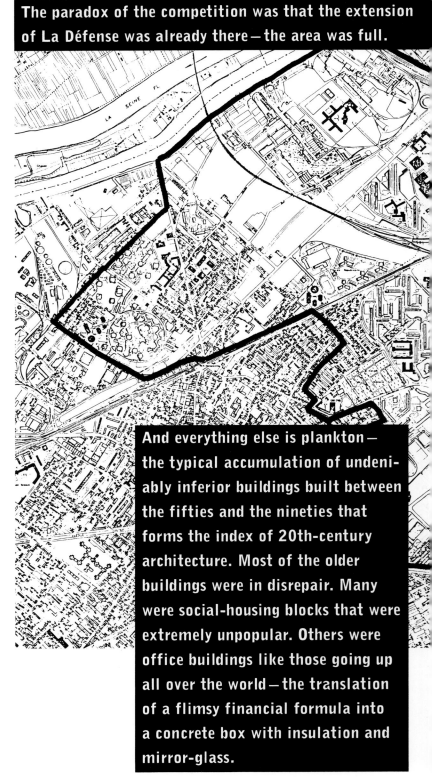

The paradox of the competition was that the extension of La Défense was already there — the area was full.

And everything else is plankton — the typical accumulation of undeniably inferior buildings built between the fifties and the nineties that forms the index of 20th-century architecture. Most of the older buildings were in disrepair. Many were social-housing blocks that were extremely unpopular. Others were office buildings like those going up all over the world — the translation of a flimsy financial formula into a concrete box with insulation and mirror-glass.

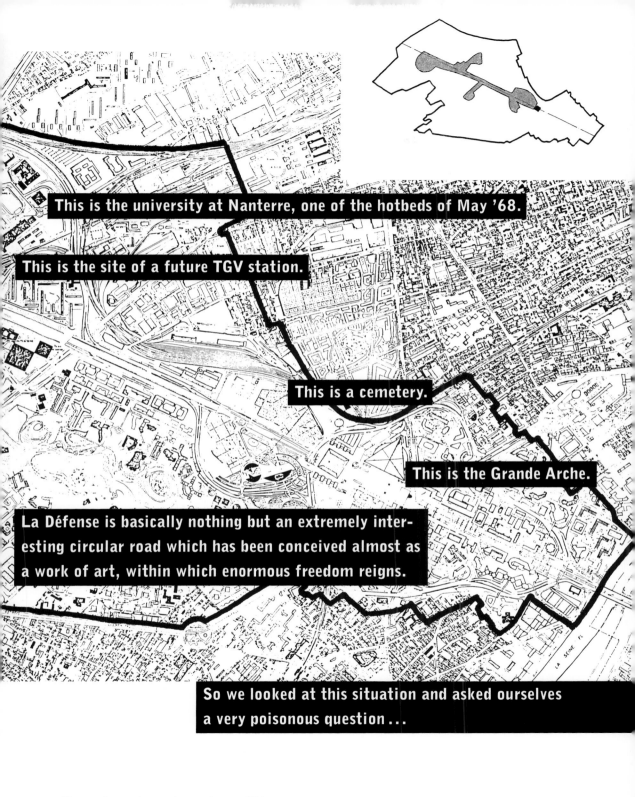

This is the university at Nanterre, one of the hotbeds of May '68.

This is the site of a future TGV station.

This is a cemetery.

This is the Grande Arche.

La Défense is basically nothing but an extremely interesting circular road which has been conceived almost as a work of art, within which enormous freedom reigns.

So we looked at this situation and asked ourselves a very poisonous question...

0   500m

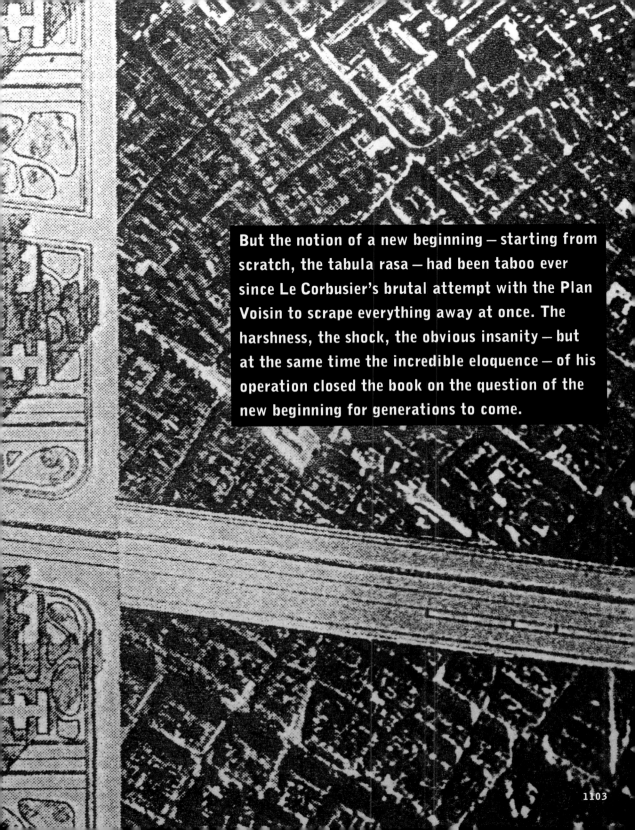

But the notion of a new beginning — starting from scratch, the tabula rasa — had been taboo ever since Le Corbusier's brutal attempt with the Plan Voisin to scrape everything away at once. The harshness, the shock, the obvious insanity — but at the same time the incredible eloquence — of his operation closed the book on the question of the new beginning for generations to come.

and it stops with some sort of
dictatorship.

REVOLUTION²

The burning question, then, becomes
this: Why have the immense proces-
sual potentials brought forth by the
revolutions in information processing,
telematics, robotics, office automa-
tion, biotechnology and so on up to
now led only to a monstrous re-
inforcement of earlier systems of
alienation, an oppressive mass-media
culture and an infantilizing politics
of consensus: What would make it
possible for them finally to usher in
a postmedia era, to disconnect themselves from segregative capitalist
values and to give free reign to the
first stirrings, visible today, of a revolution in intelligence, sensitivity
and creativity?

RHIZOME

The rhizome is an anti-genealogy,
a short-term memory or anti-
memory. The rhizome operates by
variation, expansion, conquest, capture, offshoots. Unlike the graphic
arts, drawing or photography, unlike
tracings, the rhizome pertains to
a map that must be produced,
constructed, a map that is always
detachable, connectable, reversible,
modifiable, and has multiple entry-
ways and exits, and its own lines
of flight. It is tracings that must be
put on the map, not the opposite.
In contrast to centered (even poly-
centric) systems with hierarchical
modes of communication and pre-
established paths, the rhizome is an
acentered, nonhierarchical, non-
signifying system without a General
and without an organizing memory
or central automaton, defined solely
by a circulation of states.

RHIZOMORPHS

The air in the room was getting
purer, and soon, in a dark corner,
down by the floor, a soft white
light appeared. He went up to it
and discovered that it came from a
clump of Rhizomorphs which, as
they breathed, shone like tiny
night-lights.
"These plants are really astounding," he said to himself, stepping
back to appraise the entire collection. Yes, his object had been
achieved: not one of them looked
real; it was as if cloth, paper, porce-
lain, and metal had been lent by man

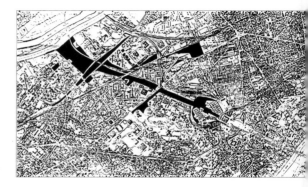

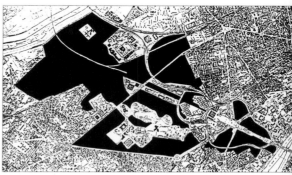

So we looked at La Défense
with, on the one hand, the
unpleasant and absurd
burden of having to invent
a concept for an area that
was already filled and, on
the other hand, the knowledge that there is one
major limit to our imagi-
nation — the limit of a new
beginning — and wondered ...

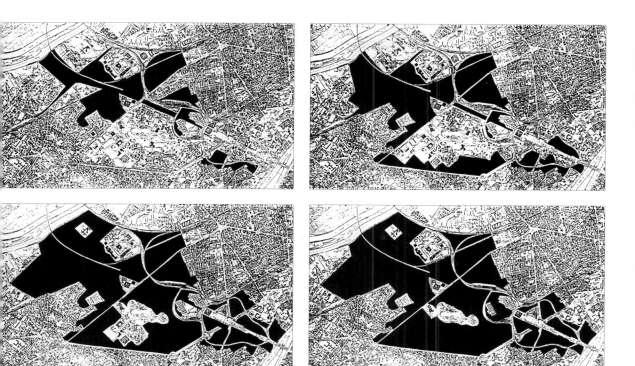

What would happen if, even in Europe — especially in Europe — we declare every building in the entire zone that is older than 25 years worthless — null and void — or at least potentially removable? How does such a question change the parameters and interpretation of this project, which we found intolerably sad with this tenuous axis supposedly giving coherence and quality to this zone?

We analyzed this question in numerical terms and discovered that if we laundered the site in five-year increments by simply erasing all buildings over the age of 25, vast areas would gradually be liberated.

We would preserve buildings of merit, or buildings of sentimental value — Nanterre, a very beautiful courthouse, a park, a station — and of course we would keep the Grande Arche, the CNIT, and the Tour Fiat as a kind of 20th-century acropolis.

to Nature to enable her to create these monstrosities.

RIGHT
Someone, at the end of the day, has to decide what's right and generally that's me.

RINGING
I came to the house ... and it was completely leveled. I mean, only two walls were standing ... I walked around back and the phone was ringing.

RIP-OFF
Here the question is, "Can a rip-off be beautiful?" I think the answer should be yes.

RISK
The moment the calligraphist set his brush to the page he was committing himself to something hazardous. However good he might be he was always taking a risk.

RIVER
The river of irises: instead of a river flowing along bordered by irises, it is the irises which flow between two banks of water.

ROAR
The first time I read *Delirious New York* was by listening to Rem talk about it. He tested it out on people. I was sitting next to Terry Smith — a former student of Rem's — at one of these lectures, and every once in a while this big English guy in front of us would roar with laughter. Terry was really getting upset; this guy was spoiling his listening pleasure. At the end of the lecture, Terry said, "Who is this guy? I want to beat him up!" And someone said, "Watch out, that's James Stirling."
Stirling came to every lecture on *Delirious New York* — he really loved it. He seemed to get the most enjoyment from Rem's description of the London Bridge being sold to the Americans and reconstructed in Arizona over a dry river bed, and then, the people who bought it being outraged because they thought they were buying Tower Bridge, which is the classic image of the Thames. They were disappointed because they got this very normal stone bridge. That sent Stirling into outrageous laughter — rightly so.

ROOM SERVICE
My life had turned into a total nightmare. The hotel was impossible: no

HIEREMIAS

The process of erasure could be spread over time in a surreptitious way — an invisible reality. We could gradually scrape ...

...whole areas of texture off the map...

air to breathe, plus all those insects, and, on top of it, no light, because as the duty woman told me, I had no lighting needs. And, in fact, I had none, because although I usually use light to read, there was nothing to read here except for that miserable newspaper, pieces of which were still slipped under my door even though my need for them had entirely vanished.

ROTTERDAM¹
Rotterdam derives its name from the little river of Rotte. In the 13th Century a fishing village was built on the dam across the river. The village was granted a charter in 1340 and was a prosperous trading town in the 16th and 17th Centuries.

ROTTERDAM²
Rotterdam will pursue the way to true construction with a deathly chill in its veins and Amsterdam will be destroyed by the fire of its own dynamism.

ROTTERDAM³
In Rotterdam, the bombs voided the center: it was replaced by an artificial heart that has emptiness as its core.

ROTTERDAM⁴
The new city has life, vitality, and ample growth potential.

RUG
Speak up for yourself, or you'll end up a rug.

RUINS
People visit us as if we were a museum or the site of ancient ruins. We are thinking of keeping some of the destruction as it is and using it to attract clients.

RULE
Astonish me!

RUNNING BARNS
Then the barn wasn't there and we had to wait until it came back. I didn't see it come back. It came behind us and Quentin set me down in the trough where the cows ate. I held on to it. It was going away too, and I held to it. The cows ran down the hill again, across the door.

RUSH
I had a friend who wanted to rush it, because he was going into the army and he'd never been punched out. So he went to his friend Paul and said, "Paul, I've never been punched out. But I'm drafted, I'm going into the army. Please punch

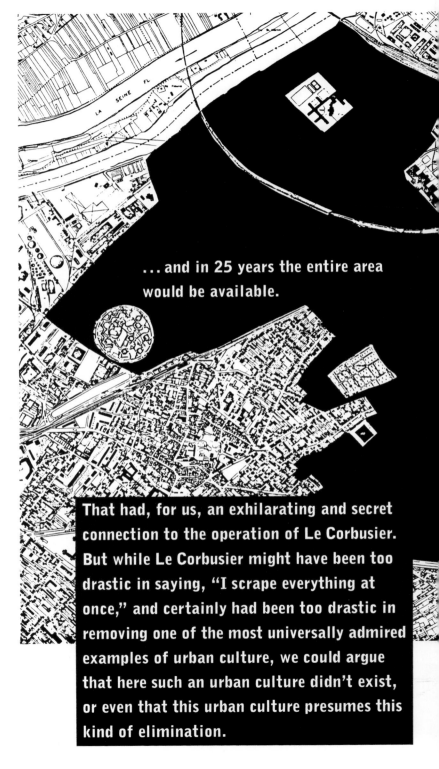

... and in 25 years the entire area would be available.

That had, for us, an exhilarating and secret connection to the operation of Le Corbusier. But while Le Corbusier might have been too drastic in saying, "I scrape everything at once," and certainly had been too drastic in removing one of the most universally admired examples of urban culture, we could argue that here such an urban culture didn't exist, or even that this urban culture presumes this kind of elimination.

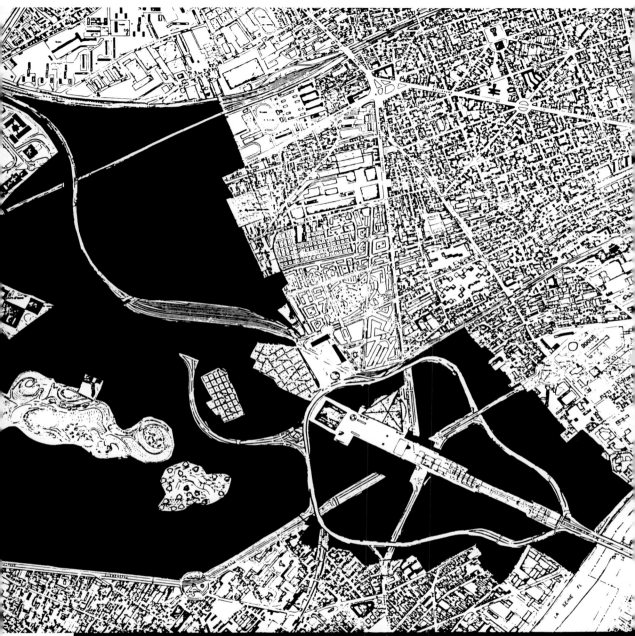

We looked at this newly liberated area, and asked an even more
frightening question...

me out Paul, quick." And Paul
knocked him out.

RUSHED
Nothing can be rushed. It must grow,
it should grow of itself, and if the
time ever comes for that work —
then so much the better!

S

SAME
When I went home that night, everything was the same.

SANK
Le Corbusier also made a disgraceful
mistake: never will reinforced cement
be used on other planets. Le Corbu,
Le Corbubu, Le Corbi, Le Corba,
Le Corbo dead, Le Corbousier died
by drowning. Yes! Yes and yes, he
sank like a stone, the weight of his
own reinforced cement pulling him
down like a masochistic Protestant
Swiss cheese.

SAPPHIC
Obsessed! — Barbara Dare, Sheena
Horne, Cara Lott and more. Barbara
and Cara shoot more than pool
with two hot hunks … Krista Lane
works up a real sweat with her
gym instructor … Sheena Horne and
Barbie Balke share a steamy bubble
bath with a wet and willing dude …
and three gorgeous babes explore
the forbidden world of sapphic sex.

SATISFACTION
I have CNN. I have MTV. I have chips.
What more do I need?

SAW
Of course. How could I know it was
real unless someone saw?

SCALE
I think working with scale puts
you in an almost godlike position,
like "You're in good hands with
Allstate," that ad on TV. You can
hold a piece of turf in your hand,
or a house, and you can plant it
somewhere, or you can crush it,
smash it.

SCATTERBRAIN
Yahweh came down to watch the
city and tower the sons of man
were bound to build. "They are one
people, with the same tongue,"
said Yahweh. "They conceive this
between them, and it leads up
until no boundary exists to what
they will touch. Between us, let's

What to do with this new territory?

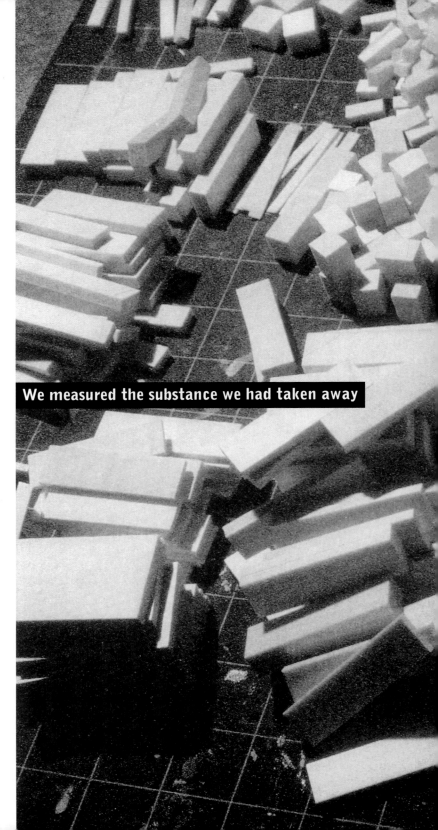

descend, baffle their tongue until each is scatterbrain to his friend."

SCENT

And suddenly I see him gripped, as it were, body and soul, his stump of tail switching furiously, erect in the air. His head goes forward and down, his body lengthens out, he makes short dashes in several directions, and then shoots off in one of them with his nose to the ground. He has struck a scent. He is off after a hare.

SCHISM

There is to be no seepage of symbolism between floors. In fact, the schizoid arrangement of thematic planes implies an architectural strategy for planning the interior of the Skyscraper, which has become autonomous through the lobotomy: the Vertical Schism, a systematic exploitation of the deliberate disconnection between stories.

SCOPOPHILIAC

Not a hot war either, but a new form of cold war. A virtual war fought, almost in its entirety, with cruise missiles which are heat seeking, but which themselves give off no traces of heat; seen not with normal ocular vision, but with optical scanners which magnify star light from the cold depths of outer space; missiles with fighter pilots themselves telematic spectators to their own acts of destruction. A scopophiliac war fought without depth, but always on the surfaces of the screen and the network, and always under the sign of the ecstasy of catastrophe. Or as Nietzsche has said: *Truth is dead; everything is permitted.*

SCREEN

One of the most famous images of contemporary Tokyo is the huge screen on the Alta Building in Shinjuku. It presents nonstop images, taken mainly from TV news and music advertising. Up-and-coming rock groups and the latest CDs for teenyboppers are often featured … Nobody watches or even notices the content. For the tribe of teenagers it is enough that there *is* "visual"; and for the brilliant technocrats, that there *is* "high-tech." The presence of such devices reminds me of a scene from *Blade Runner*: the image of an immense *kimono* lady publicizing *sake* on the entire wall

We measured the substance we had taken away

and the new program we had to add.

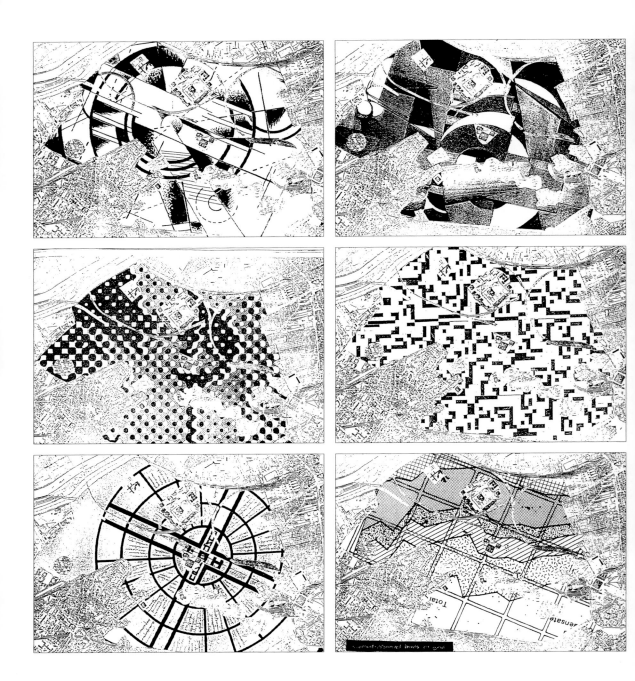

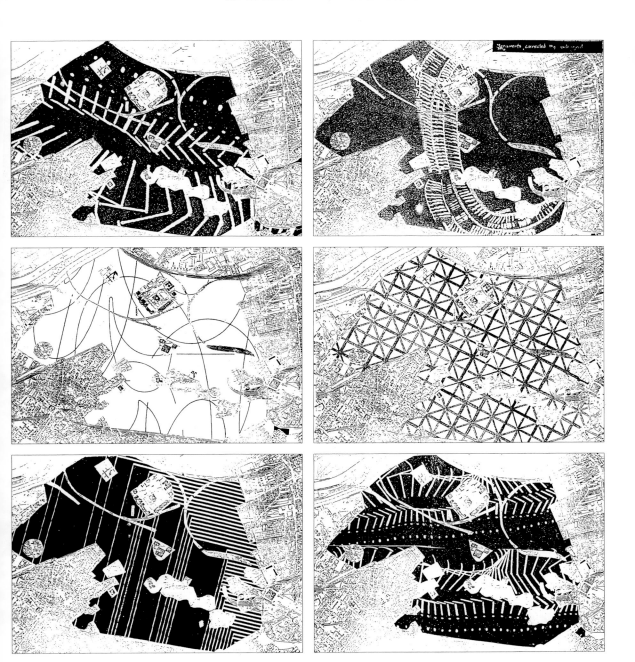

We made a series of studies to try to imagine an urban plan for this area.

0 | | | | 2000m

Do we make it "interesting"? "Dynamic"?

Do we make a plan that is connected to present investigations of chaos theory, or some analogy — it can never be more than an analogy — to parallel developments in other disciplines?

Or what happens if we simply take the method that is least limiting and most enabling — the Manhattan grid, a combination of two-dimensional discipline and an almost independent potential freedom of expression in the third dimension — and turn this into a kind of utilitarian polemic?

of a Los Angeles skyscraper in 2020.

SCULPTURE

The base is a disc of cherry-flavoured caramel.

The large cylinder: three leaves of puff pastry stuffed with tamarind pulp and covered with chocolate fondant.

The small cylinder: crowns of meringue one on top of the other covered in mandarin-flavoured fondant.

The centre of the upper cylinder contains whipped cream with tamarind pulp and shelled pistachios. The wing is mandarin-flavoured caramel.

Shortly before bringing it to the table the pudding should be covered with threads of green spun sugar.

SEALED

Yet, when he entered, there was only darkness and an open suitcase where Ya'ara had lain the last time. The apartment was chilly, perhaps because the windows and shutters had been closed against the sun all day long, and smelled as if the Sabbath, trapped between its walls for twenty-four hours, had begun to go bad.

SEARCH

To become aware of the possibility of the search is to be onto something. Not to be onto something is to be in despair.

SEARCHING

I am searching ... and when I've found something I'll tell you.

SECRETS¹

I think one of the most fatal things that occurs in an architect's career is the moment when he begins to take himself too seriously — where his idea of himself coincides with what the others think of him — when he runs out of secrets. I've always tried to find means and tactics with which to avoid this.

SECRETS²

The most you can hope for is to break even. The tactic of choice? Preemptive boringness. Being one-dimensional is the most satisfying method of coping with out-of-control people — with any situation that's out of control. Keep your face like a screen-saver software program. Don't let people know the ideas you love, the games you've

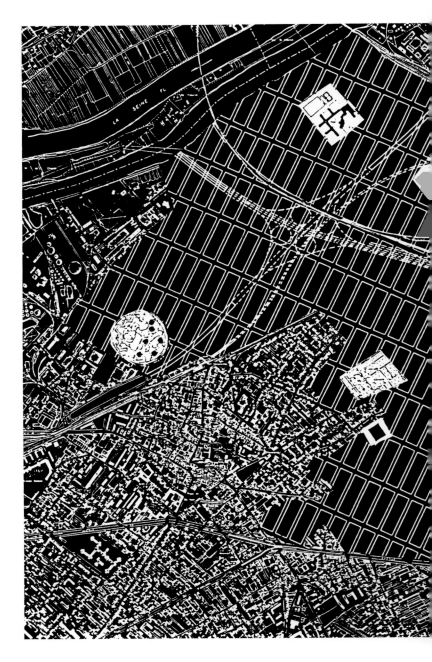

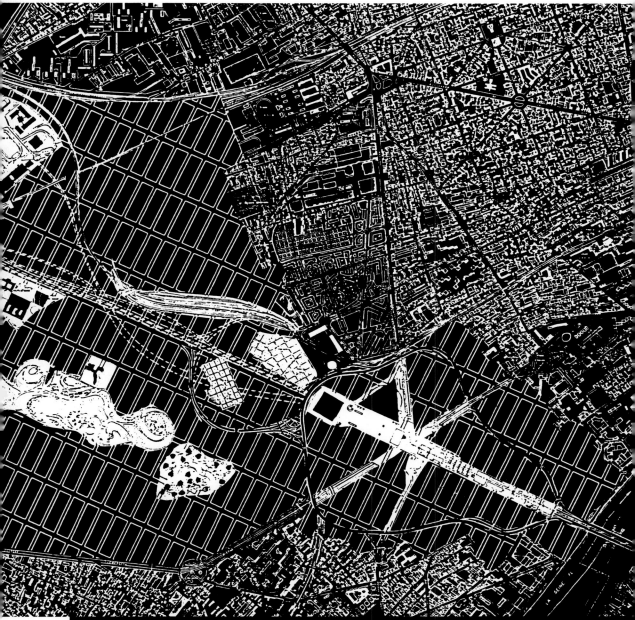

We projected the grid on the site. (Coincidentally, one of the grid lines happened to correspond with the axis.)

0   500m

Then we made a strict inventory of contemporary typologies with which we could plan the city.

TYPOLOGIES DES
TRAMES URBAINES

100m x 100m
BARCELONE

272m x 60m
MANHATTAN

66m x 108m
VILLES NOUVELLES

400m x 400m
VILLE RADIEUSE

TRAMES DÉRIVÉES DES
TYPOLOGIES D'IMMEUBLES
DE LOGEMENTS

104m x 108m
VILLA

120m x 150m
UNITÉ

40m x 108m
MAISONS EN BANDE

52m x 111m
TOUR DE LOGEMENTS

TRAMES DÉRIVÉES DES
TYPOLOGIES DES IMMEUBLES
DE BUREAUX DE TAILLE
MOYENNE (40.000m²)

120m x 36m
BARRE

150m x 104m
FORME

64m x 64m
COUR INTÉRIEURE

50m x 50m
TOUR DE BUREAUX

played, the places you've visited in your mind. Keep your treasure to yourself.

SECURITY
For man to be able to live with a feeling of security, the existence of some kind of boundary in space is a necessity.

SEDUCTION¹
This is what you have to do. Put some scent behind your ears, on your collar or under your arms. Approach the person you want to seduce and start talking to them, using any pretext ... and write to us right away to tell us what happened. If three people out of four have not said YES, if three out of four have not surrendered to your caresses, then your SexScent will cost you absolutely nothing.

SEDUCTION²
Distinctive signs, full signs, never seduce us. Seduction only comes through empty, illegible, insoluble, arbitrary, fortuitous signs, which glide by lightly, modifying the index of the refraction of space ... As such the signs of seduction do not signify; they are of the order of the ellipse, of the short circuit, of the flash of wit (le trait d'esprit).

SEEMED
So it is not at all strange that my square seemed empty to the public.

SEEMS
I know not seems.

SEEN
Honey, you ain't seen nothin' yet. Wait till tonight.

SEMI-MYTH
Architects do it all night.

SENSIBILITY
The first sensibility, that of high culture, is basically moralistic. The second sensibility, that of extreme states of feeling, represented in much contemporary "avant garde" art, gains power by a tension between moral and aesthetic passion. The third, Camp, is wholly aesthetic.

SENSITIVE
Deer are sensitive creatures which have to be handled carefully and kept free from stress.

SENTENCES
Sentences will be consigned to museums if the emptiness in writing persists.

SERENDIPITY
The faculty of finding valuable or

How to make a new beginning in Europe? *With* Europe?

La Défense (the territory of EPAD)* is a strategic reserve that has so far kept Paris intact (each tower built there "spares" the center an invasion), a privileged expansion zone that enables the city — even the country — to modernize itself constantly, to make the tactical adjustments necessary to compete with other world capitals — London, New York, Tokyo. It is a theater of progress.

Now that the first sector is "finished" — the original La Défense inside its elegant fifties *ceinture*, a success after decades of doubt — the question of its expansion becomes acute.

On the "other" side of the Grande Arche is an unfamiliar "beyond": cemeteries, some old villages, beginnings of city, Nanterre, a vast terrain of mostly postwar urban substance. Having endowed the line — the Grand Axe — that runs from the Louvre via the Arc de Triomphe to dead-end at the bigger arch with urbanistic magic, it seems inevitable to the French to extend it through this urban plane until it hits the Seine again.

The existing is, in Europe, an ambiguous condition. Because Europe is the Old World, the "continent of history," there is an unspoken assumption that all its substance — even the most mediocre — is historic, and *therefore* has a right to permanence. The idea of a new beginning is now, in Europe, literally unthinkable; the dream/nightmare of the tabula rasa is dead — completely abandoned.

Yet the average contemporary building has a paradoxically short life expectancy. It is built of materials unsuited for eternity. Architecture is now little more than a thermal barrier — against the *cold* in the north, against the *heat* in the south — its mirror-glass facades a perverse premonition of future nonexistence. The "modern" building has become the momentary embodiment of an opportunistic financial envelope that after 20, 25, at the most 30 years, simply expires — all within a single generation. Modern building is literally written off.

These three conditions:
• the assumption of European permanence;
• the ontological reality of its provisional substance;
• the impossibility of a new beginning;
form a claustrophobic triple impasse.

But if the existence of any contemporary building is fundamentally precarious, then, in fact, the entire substance of the contemporary city represents, at most, a temporary occupation. Inaction — one of the most difficult actions today — is all that is needed for these buildings' financial raison d'être to evaporate. Paradoxically, their redundancy

*EPAD (Etablissement Public d'Aménagement de la Région de La Défense) is the 760-hectare zone that falls under the direct control of the French prime minister, regardless of municipal borders, of which the present La Défense is only the first phase. The competition was held for the *entire* territory.

It was an immodest echo at the end of this century of how architecture could have been interpreted at the beginning of this century.

Momentary exhilaration as we reconquer the profession of urbanists...

1131

agreeable things not sought for.

SERVICE

I'm here to serve the public. I can print anything you want. If you prefer to have your work done on a German machine, I can arrange that too. My neighbour has an original Heidelberg, and we are like brothers.

SEVEN THOUSAND

If you dream of treasures, a visit to the Prado in Madrid is a must. There you'll find more than 7,000 works of fine art and the largest collection of Spanish masters found anywhere in the world.

SEWER

It was in the sewer of Paris that Jean Valjean found himself.
Further resemblance of Paris with the sea. As in the ocean, the diver can disappear.
The transition was marvelous. From the very center of the city, Jean Valjean had gone out of the city, and, in the twinkling of an eye, the time of lifting a cover and closing it again, he had passed from broad day to complete obscurity, from noon to midnight, from uproar to silence, from the whirl of the thunder to the stagnation of the tomb, and, by a mutation much more prodigious still than that of the rue Polonceau, from the most extreme peril to the most absolute security.

SHACKS

The permanent houses of the village were of brick with black stove pipes and a tangle of electric wires above. Where the brick houses gave out, the shacks of the Indians began. These were patched out of packing cases, sheet plastic and sacking.

SHOCKING

He stood up on the platform at Yale University, and said to a shocked hush across the room, "I would rather sleep in the nave of Chartres Cathedral with the nearest John two blocks down the street than I would in a Harvard House with back to back bathrooms"... I remember students saying to me, "He's talking about architecture as an art." And suddenly I realized that that is what it was all the time.

SHODDINESS

I can still remember quite well us standing as small children, scarcely sure on our feet, in our teacher's

will be liberating: underneath the thinning crust of our civilization a hidden tabula rasa lies in waiting.

In fact, such a renewal resumes the perpetual cycle of construction, deconstruction, reconstruction that has been suspended out of fear of our own inferiority.

We have used this competition to generate a critical mass of urban renewal, to imagine an anti-utopian strategy that would transform, beyond the tabula rasa, the most banal economic givens into a utilitarian polemic, to interpret the extension of La Défense as the gradual, progressive transformation of this chaotic "beyond" into a new urban system.

Assuming a maximum economic viability of 25 years, we have made an inventory, beginning with the sites available today, of subsequent redundancies in five-year increments to discover a gigantic domain of theoretical vacancy.

We propose to project a grid across the entire field of the competition area—over all that exists including the present enclave of La Défense—and to expose progressively this new system as buildings meet their successive expiration dates.

The grid proposed here is at the same time conceptual and operational; it will not subject everything in its way to its discipline but will act as a filter to absorb those entities whose right to survive is not contested—the university at Nanterre, Wogensky's prefecture, the new Parc André Malraux—accommodating the misfit of their anterior geometries. Along its entire perimeter it will generate a string of hybrids. To achieve its ultimate coherence, it will invest the so far isolated fragments with a premonition of identity.

The theoretical omnipresence of the grid does not imply homogeneous density: it will organize the coexistence of solid and void, density and emptiness. In the near future, it will become even more charged with potential and difference through new infrastructural connections, motorways, the TGV, connection to the hyper-Périphérique. Around these injections, the grid will allow different intensifications.

The Grand Axe itself will become almost incidental, just one of its orthogonal coordinates.

La Défense as we know it will be liberated from its condition of enclave, will dissolve over time to become simply part of the system. Some of its present masterpieces—CNIT, the Grande Arche, Tour Fiat—will remain to form a Parisian acropolis of the 20th century.

. . . and reinhabit . . .

1133

garden, and being ordered to build a sort of wall out of pebbles; and then the teacher, girding up his robe, ran full tilt against the wall, of course knocking it down, and scolded us so terribly for the shoddiness of our work that we ran weeping in all directions to our parents.

SHOPPER
He entered shop after shop, priced nothing, spoke no word, and looked at all objects with a wild and vacant stare.

SHOPPING
Shopping is an activity that consists of predictable yet indeterminate activities, where, as in the cinema, what we go to see, what we experience over and over again, is our own desire.

SHORT
Paris reckons it is short of 700,000 parking spaces for the 1.3 million cars entering the city each day.

SHOWROOM
Shop all of Europe in one showroom!

SIGNATURE[1]
Today, the signature is the mask; the falsification of a difference in work that is absolutely the same, in which there are no more differences or in which the differences are unsubstantial. It follows that we have lost the capacity to know what is real. When we need the signature, when we see that our glass boxes are absolutely identical in reality, the signature produces a lie.

SIGNATURE[2]
The signature was another source of marvelling; across the lined page it looked like an ornamented cluster of music notes, appropriately perhaps, since music, like gardening, was one of his passions.

SIGNATURE[3]
I think the architects of tomorrow will not be personae; they will not be anonymous, the singular signature will not be erased.

SIMPLE
The feeling toward life in the present-day intelligentsia is that of people who cannot grasp the morality of immorality because then everything would be "far too simple."

SIMULACRUM
These would be the successive phases of the image: 1/ it is the reflection of a basic reality 2/ it masks and

How to intervene in the robust chaos of La Défense?

How to "be" near the Grande Arche?

How to build next to Jean Nouvel's Tour Sans Fin, Europe's eventual seventh wonder?

By definition, it is impossible to compete with Nouvel's cylinder. The only possible contrast is between the sublime and the banal.

The client wanted standard office space. Therefore, this is a minimalist project: maximum repetition, minimum manipulation.

La Défense is full. To open up the west—l'Après la Défense— a motorway disengages from the central loop, eventually to continue the Paris axis; to the south: a cemetery—in its regularity a silent rebuke to the tortured mirror-clad shapes massed around it; in the armpit of the highways: Jean Nouvel, maybe; to the north: a business school and two office buildings, one tall, one low and prowlike.

The Zac Danton tower is superimposed on a socle. In the socle: motorway, metro station, parking. On the socle: pedestrian level with restaurants.

The building is a rectangular floorplate repeated 28 times, connected by ramp to the motorway. Two thirds of the way up, the upper part of the slab disengages and moves "closer" to Paris (persistent attraction of the center?). At the break, a floor is pulled toward the Grand Axe, invading the hallowed perspective. It will be covered in lights, emitting situationist messages.

On the south facade, shards of broken glass create a horizontal brise-soleil: assertion of messy vitality vis-à-vis Nouvel's dissolving perfection.

1134

... the formerly megalomaniacal ambitions of our predecessors.

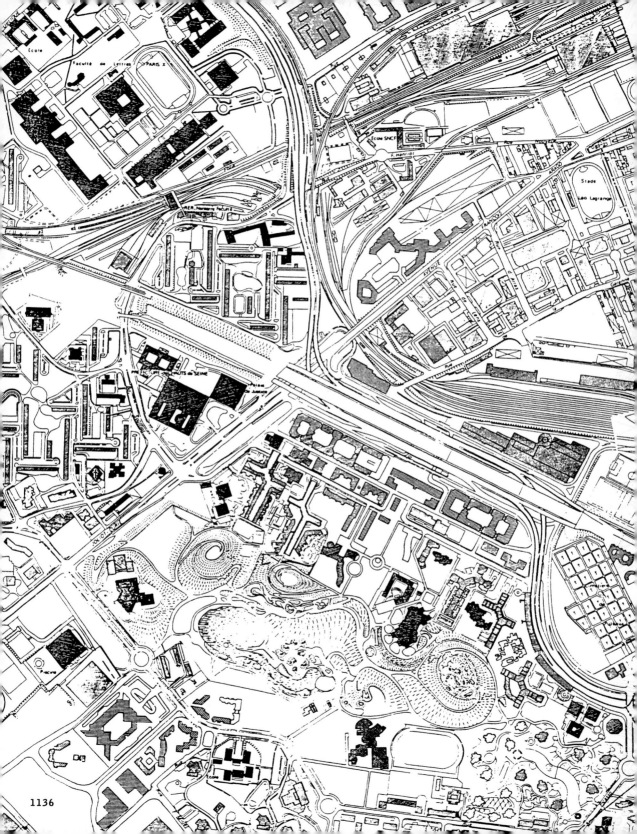

Side Show

**Zac Danton Office Tower
La Défense, Paris, France
Competition, Design Development
1991–93**

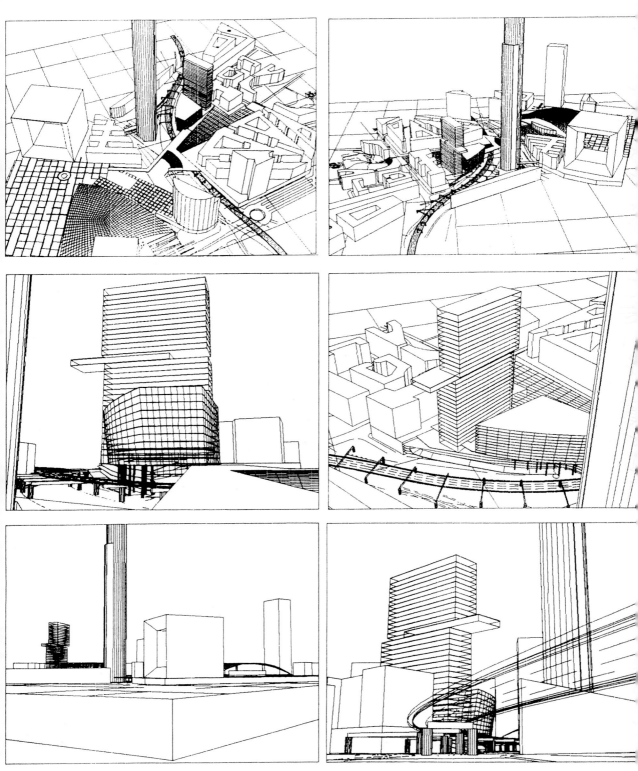

1138

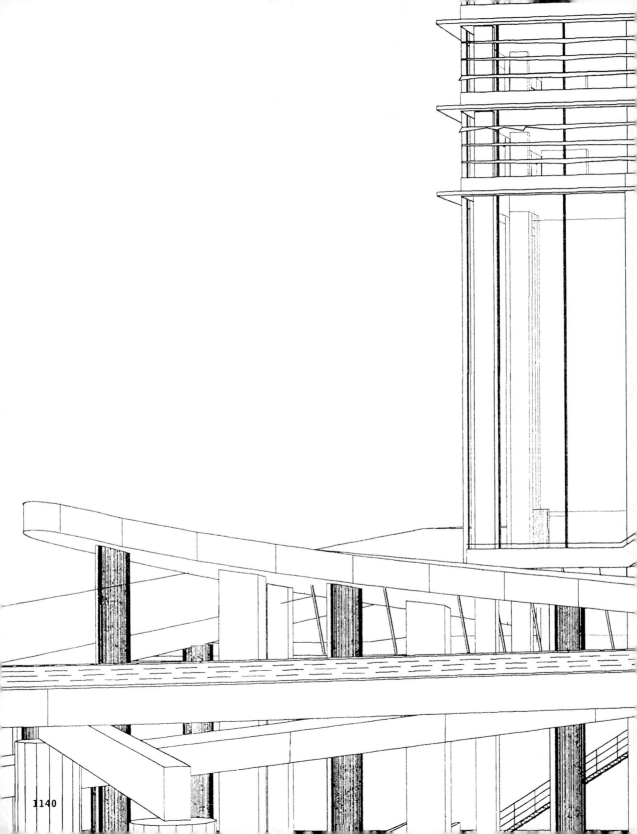

1140

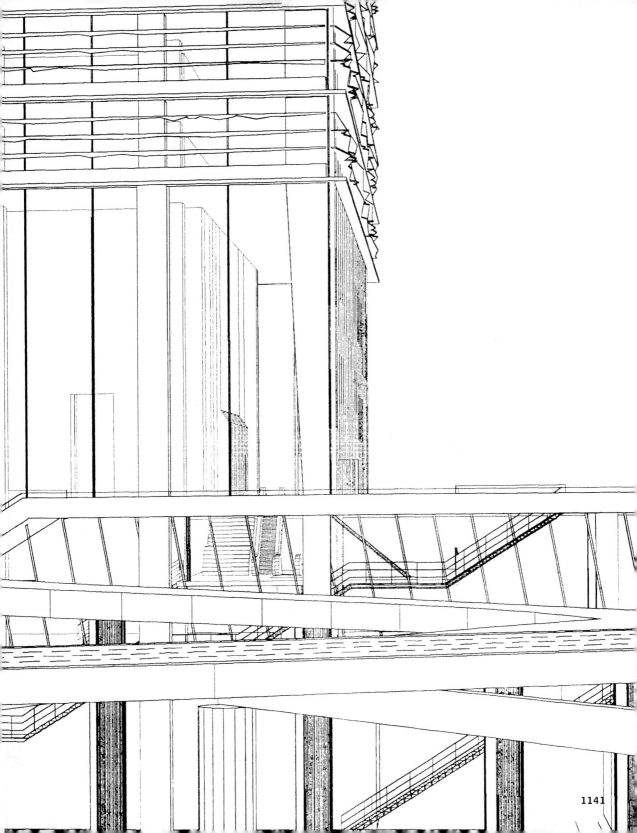

1141

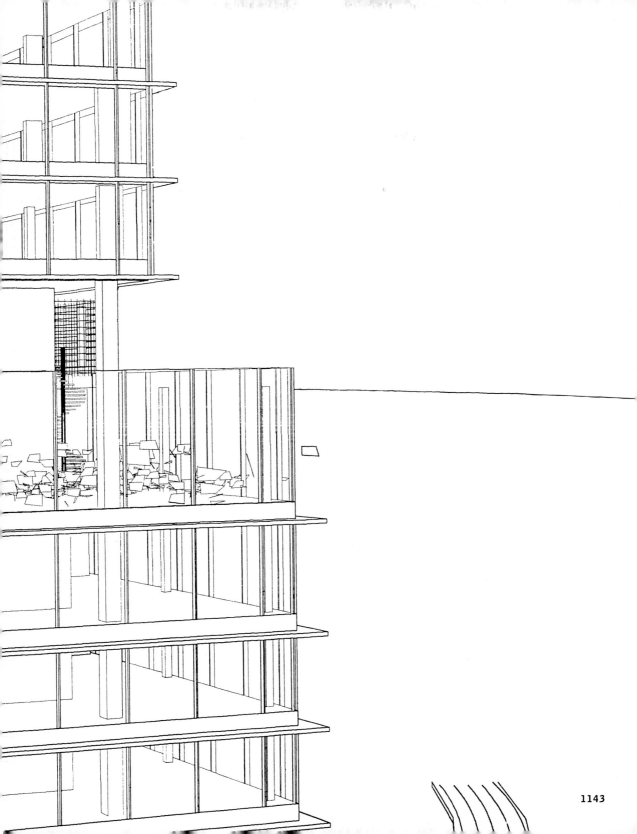

1143

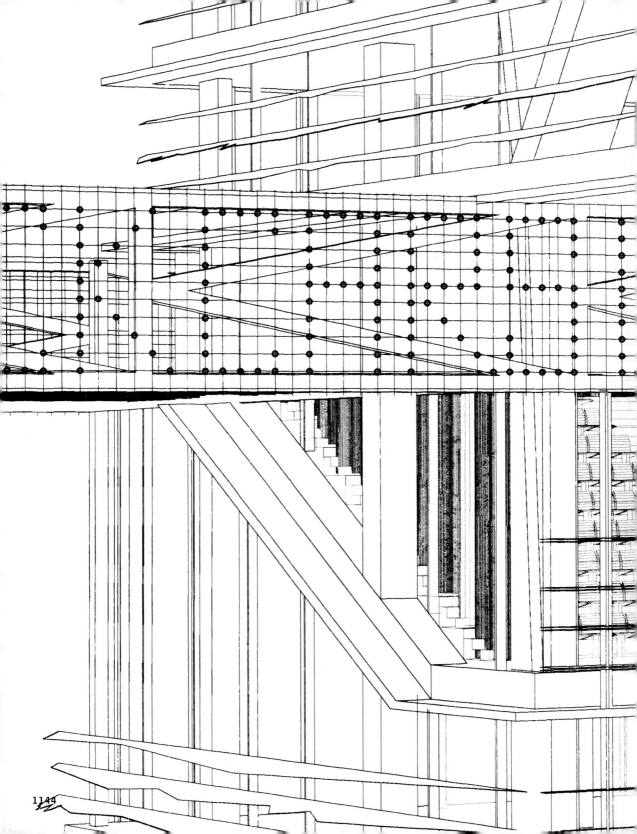

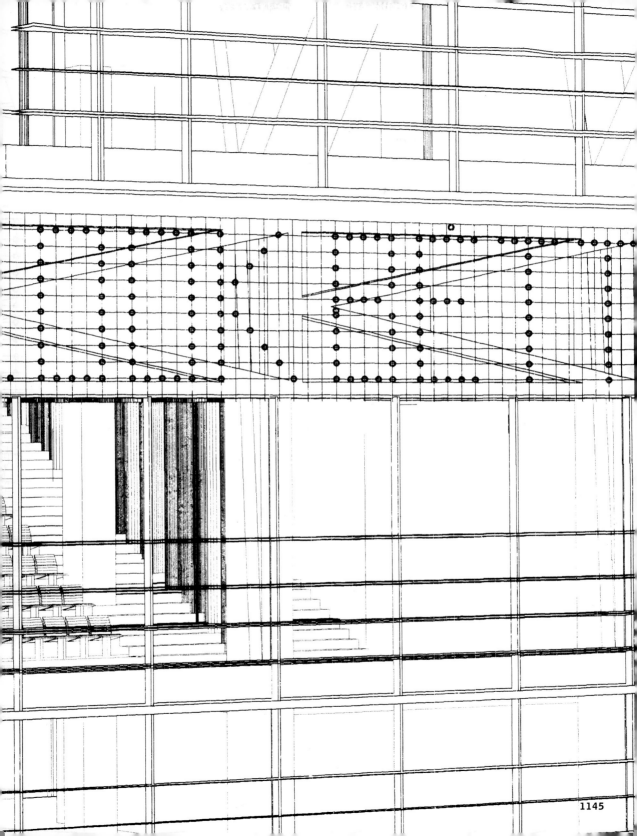

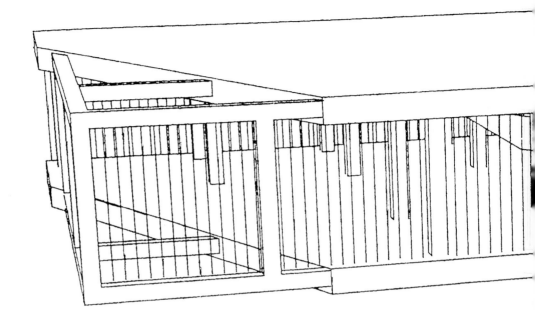

1147

1148

1155

Quantum Leap

Euralille: Centre International d'Affaires
Lille, France
Phase I Completed 1994

HYPOTHESIS
Until recently, Lille (pop. 1,000,000), a formerly significant
city, was leading a slightly melancholy existence. Once a
mining and textile town, it had fallen on hard times. But two
new givens—the tunnel between England and the continent
and the **TGV** network (the French superfast train that will
run through it)—will transform Lille as if by magic and
make it important in a completely synthetic way.

FRANCE

1993

ROTTERDA

ANTWERP

ZEEBRUGGE

LONDON

7 KRS → 1.10 m

B. / 1.30 → 18 m   BRUX

FR

LILLE   5h

2.30 → 50 m

DISNEYLAND

PARIS

perverts a basic reality 3/ it masks
the *absence* of a basic reality 4/ it
bears no relation to any reality
whatever; it is its own pure simulacrum.

SIMULATION

Patriot missiles, infrared sights for
night warfare and other inventions
of the Star Wars era are assembled
only a few kilometers from the site
where tourists board fantasy rocket
rides based on George Lucas' *Star
Wars*. Disney World has the Space
Mountain roller coaster; Orlando has
FreeFlight Zephyrhills, a firm that
is experimenting with wind-tunnel
technology to simulate a sky-diving
experience on the ground. Disney's
Epcot Center has Michael Jackson
in 3-D as Captain Eo; Orlando created the simulators on which allied
pilots learned to aim their smart
bombs.

SINCERITY

The most important thing about an
actor is his sincerity. If he can fake
that, he's made.

SING

And without a word, he began to
sing. And the sun came up, and the
sun came up.

SKELETON

It used to be different, but not any
more. Holland is now nothing but
a burned-out skeleton of a culture
which was once ambitious, critical,
and devoted to a kind of modernism.

SKELETONS

For decades India was the world's
main supplier of skeletons.
However in August 1985 the Indian
government banned the sales amid
rumors of grave robbing.

SKIMPY

Go into one of the skimpy Dutch
woods and there is always somebody
among the trees.

SKINNY

Lives which end like literary articles
in newspapers and magazines, so
pompous on page one and ending up
in a skinny tail, back there on page
thirty-two, among advertisements
for second-hand sales and tubes of
toothpaste.

SKI SLOPE

For outdoor purposes, staple *12* may
be used to secure the surface to the
side of a mountain. It is preferable
that the staple *12* be driven well into
layer *4* so that it will not protrude

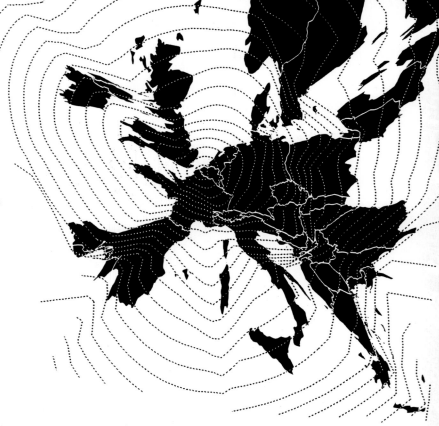

Above: Europe transformed.
Opposite: Lille 1984; yellow line: projected TGV trajectory.

**Not only will it become the intersection of major north-
south and east-west axes, but reduced travel times, through
train and tunnel combined, will minimize the importance
of distance and suddenly give Lille a strategic position: it
will become the center of gravity for the virtual community
of 50 million Western Europeans who will live within a 1¹/₂-
hour traveling distance.**

Far can be near now. So if you ever want to organize a Frank
Sinatra concert in Europe, it has to be in Lille, because in Lille,
anyone from London, Paris, or Brussels can attend. And if you
are a Japanese company and you want to conquer Northern
Europe, Lille is the place to start. And even if you are an English
company and can't afford to establish yourself in London, you
could set up an office in northern France and be "closer" to the
city of London than you would be in some parts of greater London
itself. The English are buying houses nearby because Lille-
London will be faster than Kent-London.

1000m

0

upwardly in such a manner as to interfere with skiing or constitute a safety hazard in the event of a fall. In outdoor applications, the surface is preferably cut in a geometrical pattern permitting air and sunlight to reach the mountainside. Of course, for indoor applications, the surface may be used without openings.

SLAVES

Most of the visual images that are being made in the world are slaves to text.

SLEDGEHAMMER

Lady Webster took a Sledgehammer to her cottage when she bought it, suspecting that behind the grey pebble dash there was a Georgian cottage trying to get out.

SLOW

Rush-hour speeds often fall below 10 mph in the busiest corridors of Los Angeles, despite its 4,000 miles of freeways, expressways and super-highways.

SLOWLY

Many of the watchers were still trapped in traffic, miles away, when the shuttle lifted off, and they were still there when traffic began to flow, ever so slowly, the other way. By then, the shuttle had passed completely around the earth and back almost overhead, and the astronauts could watch the traffic creeping along.

SMALL

The trouble with New York is that its skyscrapers are too small.

SMOKER

I had a package of gum cigarettes in my pocket and I extracted one carefully and placed the end in my mouth. I held the elbow of my right arm with my left hand and smoked the cigarette for a long time and then I folded it up in my mouth and I chewed it for a while.

SOBER

In 1980 or '81, Rem wrote a manifesto called "Our New Sobriety." It was delightful to read, but I wasn't totally convinced about the word "sobriety" in the context of the work OMA was producing. It had a lot of style, a lot of flair. Look at Parliament — those facades of Zaha's — if that's sober, I don't know what sober is. But then the Morgan Bank came along. That was sober.

Right: Pierre Mauroy, prime minister of France (1981–83), mayor of Lille.

Opposite: Euralille site/Manhattan comparative scale.

500m

0

PROGRAM

Based purely on this hypothesis, Euralille, a public-private partnership — Pierre Mauroy, former prime minister of France and mayor of Lille, is its president; Jean-Paul Baietto, *aménageur*, its director — conceived a vast program that will ultimately consist of ±800,000 m² of urban activities — shopping, offices, parking, a new TGV station, hotels, housing, a concert hall, congress accommodation — to be built on 120 hectares on the site of the former city fortifications by Vauban.

The program will enrich life in Lille but is at the same time autonomous: it equips Lille for its role as headquarters of the theoretical community generated by the new infrastructures.

In 1989 OMA was selected to be master planner of this speculative enterprise. There was not a competition; instead, eight architects were each interviewed for an entire day, then they made a decision.

We had to insert an entirely new city — a program of one million square meters — in a complicated urban condition. This synthetic new city is and isn't part of the old town. That was the hardest thing to explain. It has not been spawned by Lille; it has landed there.

VOLUME BATI 4.000.000 M³

SO FAR

So far, my career has gone well
and the success I have achieved has
meant a lot to me.

SOLUTION

Idea is: take one I-beam, put it in
the middle, cut it, and increase the
distance between the two halves to
articulate structural needs. All other
solutions are not compatible with
the concept. The present dimensions are monstrous. Dimensions
are unacceptable.

SOMETIMES

Sometimes — not often, but sometimes — less is more.

SOUL[1]

It was a face in which an excess of
soul was laid bare, causing the
onlooker to shrink from looking at
it directly, as if it talked too openly
of private things.

SOUL[2]

And if the body were not the soul,
what is the soul?

SPACE

She was sitting in the window seat,
staring out. She kept talking about
the Big Dipper and the Little Dipper
and pointing. Suddenly I realized
she thought we were in Outer Space,
looking down at the stars. I said,
"I think those lights down there are
the lights from little towns."

SPACE-TIME

The representation of the contemporary city is thus no longer determined
by a ceremonial opening of gates,
by a ritual of processions and
parades, nor by a succession of
streets and avenues. From now on,
urban architecture must deal with
the advent of a "technological
space-time." The access protocol of
telematics replaces that of the door-
way. The revolving door is succeeded by "data banks," by new rites of
passage of a technical culture
masked by the immateriality of its
components: its networks, highway
systems and diverse reticulations
whose threads are no longer woven
into the space of a constructed
fabric, but into the sequences of an
imperceptible planning of time in
which the interface man/machine
replaces the facades of buildings
and the surfaces of ground on which
they stand.

SPEAK

Science and technology multiply

GORDIAN KNOT

**OMA's first task was to undo a Gordian knot of infrastruc-
ture. On the site of the former fortifications was now a circular highway; it competed for space with rivers of railway
and the projected underground TGV trajectory, a yellow line
that thickened at the proposed site for the new station and
continued on to London, and surely one day — via Berlin,
Moscow, Korea — to Japan.**

We were surrounded by a group of people who said, "Please solve
this!" There is an *ur*-scene at the beginning of every architectural
enterprise: the architect, knowing almost nothing about the situation into which he is dropped, has to convince those who know
everything, who have wrestled sometimes for years with the same
issues — the most ignorant must persuade the most skeptical. It
requires suspension of disbelief from which, sometimes, neither
side recovers.

**Two important parameters had already been established:
the TGV line — running through a concrete tunnel to protect
the city from noise — and the site of the new station — in an
oblique relationship to the existing Gare Lille-Flanders, the
largest station in France after Paris.**

At first, it was very scary.

In the intimacy of my mind, I realized with a shock that we had
never expected to deal with such serious issues. We had always
assumed a pre-Oedipal safety net — fathers, uncles, cousins —
a reservoir of people, either much older or much younger than we,
with steadier nerves and more brutal instincts, who could deal
with the design of highways, flyovers, intersections, infrastructures; people less thoughtful, because we — in our very thought-
fulness — see too many nuances and complications to make such
serious decisions.

Either the highway or the tunnel had to move.

In trying to disentangle this Gordian knot, it felt like our parents
had gone out and, instead of forbidding us to play with fire, had
given us matches and insisted on it.

50m

0

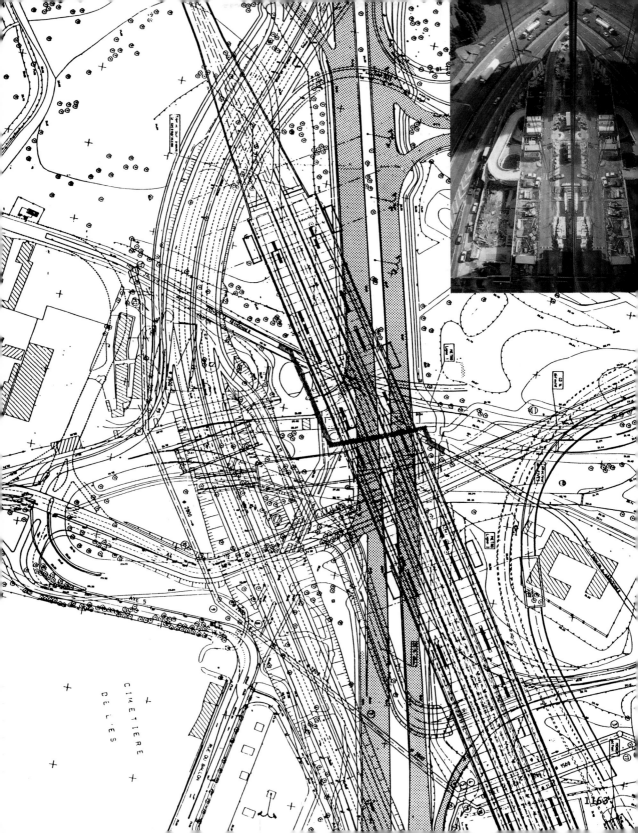

CIMETIERE DELÈS

around us. To an increasing extent they dictate the languages in which we speak and think. Either we use those languages, or we remain mute.

SPECIES
Slick, horny, quick, supple, fashionable, hyperactive and hyperattractive; these are the new species characteristics.

SPEECH
In speech the function of reference is linked to the role of the situation of discourse within the exchange of language itself: in exchanging speech, the speakers are present to each other, but also to the circumstantial setting of discourse, not only the perceptual surroundings, but also the cultural background known by both.

SPEED[1]
He couldn't stop; he didn't know yet even how to turn at that speed. Collision would be instant death. And so he shut his eyes.

SPEED[2]
Traffic speeds, like the capacity to duplicate both the written and the spoken word, have outstripped human needs. The energies that technology develops beyond the threshold of those needs are destructive. They serve primarily to foster the technology of warfare, and of the means used to prepare public opinion for war.

SPEED[3]
It is thus necessary to make a distinction between speed and movement: a movement may be very fast, but that does not give it speed; a speed may be very slow, or even immobile, yet it is still speed. Movement is extensive, speed is intensive. Movement designates the relative character of a body considered as "one," and which goes from point to point; *speed, on the contrary, constitutes the absolute character of a body whose irreducible parts (atoms) occupy or fill a smooth space in the manner of a vortex*, with the possibility of springing up at any point.

SPEED[4]
My car eats up the tarmac of crazed streets, lampposts and eucalyptus trees flying past in the opposite direction. Pure speed revives the heart, sweeping boredom away,

First notion of underground socle: sunken TGV tunnel, parking, highway.

SOCLE
In the early stages, the entire venture seemed overambitious, its realization unlikely. That was, paradoxically, liberating.
The only reason we were not completely paralyzed was that we never believed the project would actually happen.
So we approached it by saying, "Okay, we're shocked. We're surprised. So let's be hyper-shocked and hyper-surprised and take this as the pretext for a Freudian flight forward. This thing is so complicated that we are going to exacerbate the complication to reach incredible levels of complexity. Then, either the project won't happen, or we'll be fired."
OMA's first idea was to reroute the highway and project it underground, parallel to the TGV line, and to position between them — as a short circuit of the two major infrastructural flows — a huge multilevel parking garage: to create an underground socle that would support the new program close to the city but not part of it, buried, so that its mass would not overwhelm.
We thought, "Since the TGV station is underground, we'll also run this part of the highway underground, so that for the first time since the fortifications and then the highway isolated the center, there can be an easy connection between the city and its periphery. And in between these two infrastructures, we'll imagine the biggest parking garage in European history — for 10,000 cars — an underground podium of maximum modernity on which we can concentrate our enormous program."
To our surprise the client said, "Let's do it."

100m

0

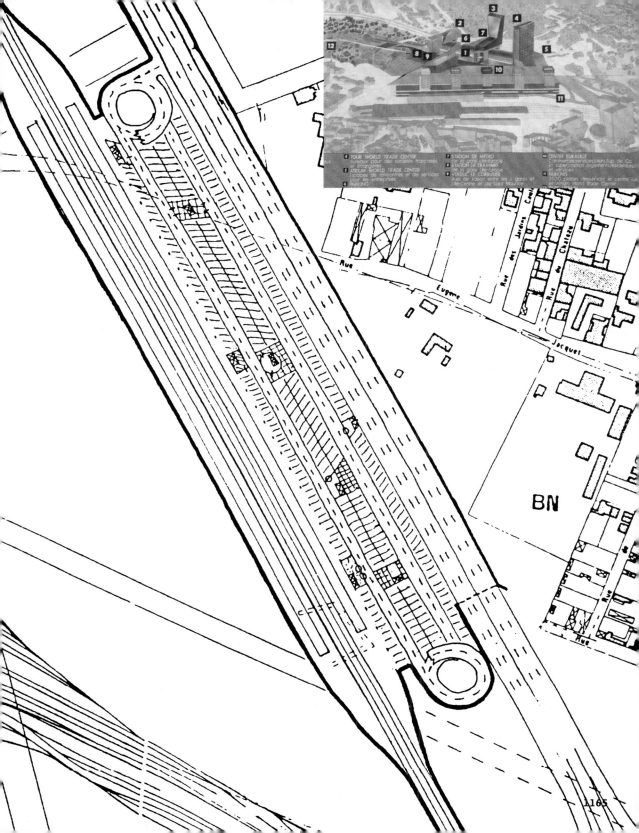

while the wind howls like a maniac,
rattling the branches and leaves of
trees, and rain beats down, washing
the fields bright green.

SPIRAL

I see the exploration with Rem — the
work we're doing — as more like an
Archimedean spiral — it goes round
but it gradually widens. It is an
open-ended exploration. Otherwise
you end up converging back into
yourself.

SPLODGY

Esther's gynaecologist, when she
went to see him, had changed. He
was no longer the grey-haired
respectable Englishman she remembered. He was bronzed, buoyant,
slim-hipped, crew-cut, and wore a
flowered shirt. The medical books
that had once lined the walls had
been swept away, and replaced by
splodgy paintings.

SPOONFED

They used to say that film was the
art of the dark room, but nowadays
the audience is dissatisfied if you
don't express everything in words
or show it directly. They insist on
seeing it all. In the meantime they
lose their contemplative power and
imagination.

SQUARE

A square is the opposite of a monument: it has no solidity, no volume.
In fact it is a kind of pure space with
no event, almost nothing to name
about it.

SQUASHED

The floor had been raised one foot.
Beneath it ran enough cables and
wires to electrify Guatemala. The
wires provided the power for the
computer terminals and telephones
of the bond trading room. The ceiling had been lowered one foot, to
make room for light housings and
air-conditioning ducts and a few
more miles of wire. The floor had
risen; the ceiling had descended;
it was as if you were in an English
mansion that had been squashed.

SQUAT

The repair men were always just
about to come, but somehow they
never did, and for over three months
that telephone had squatted on his
desk like a toad, symbol of a curse
that would never be lifted.

SQUIRREL

I own an animal; not a false one but

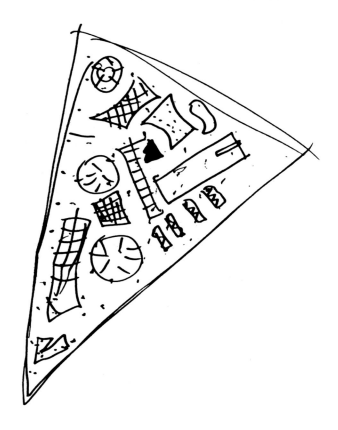

TRIANGLE

**The next problem was that the TGV would be hidden in a
tunnel — invisible.**

We felt it was important to make the TGV visible so that the people
of Lille would be able to inspect the event that would completely
transform the fate of the city...

**Initially, the residual triangle between the old and new sta-
tions was imagined, simply, as a plaza, or covered deck with
commercial activity. But if it was interpreted as a plane that
could rotate along an axis, one part would emerge from the
ground to become building while the other would descend
far enough to expose the flank of the TGV tunnel: the train
could be revealed through a 300-meter-long "window." The
TGV would assume a physical presence in the city, and the
two stations would be visually connected.**

If you pushed one edge of the plane down, another part would
come up, and if you tilted the plane in a certain way, you could
remove the side of the tunnel, exposing the trains.

And even that operation was not rejected by the client. So we
became even more daring in our speculations...

First working model: chaotic towers on socle, triangular plane (to be tilted), Congrexpo as bridge.

1168

the real thing. A squirrel. I love the squirrel, Deckard; every goddam morning I feed it and change its papers — you know, clean up its cage — and then in the evening when I get off work I let it loose in my apartment and it runs all over the place. It has a wheel in its cage; ever seen a squirrel running inside a wheel? It runs and runs, the wheel spins, but the squirrel stays in the same spot.

STAB

The stabbing, she discovered, was something strangely intimate. It took a tender touch to place the knife so neatly. To stab him, she discovered, was to know him. You have to get so close to stab. You can't be stand-offish, when you stab. Put your trust in your sword, and the sword in his side. But quickly, cleanly, nothing nasty. You jab-jab here, you stab-stab there. You put it in. You take it out. You put it in again.

STADIUM

Stadiums are about obsessions. In the stadium the masses gather to watch the few. The masses are reduced and multiplied individuals; the few are individuals blown up, magnified.

STAFF

The high-rise was a huge machine designed to serve, not the collective body of tenants, but the individual resident in isolation. Its staff of air-conditioning conduits, elevators, garbage-disposal chutes, and electrical switching systems provided a never-failing supply of care and attention that a century earlier would have needed an army of tireless servants.

STAND-IN

I heard rumors that OMA had started an office in Rotterdam. I tried to find the office, but it was so new that it wasn't in the telephone book, and nobody seemed to know exactly where it was. So I spent an entire day just wandering around the neighborhood looking for it. Then I found it. It was very small, and almost empty — with one drafting board in the corner and four people. I asked to work there. At first they didn't want me, but about a month later I called, just at the right moment — they needed more people to make the office look bigger because there

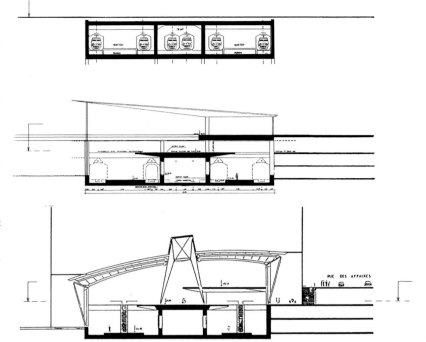

Above: From tunnel to station: evolution of TGV section.
Opposite: Towers superimposed on TGV station, window opened to city.

SUPERIMPOSITION

Lille would redefine the idea of "address." The site was important not because it was there — part of the city — but because it would be only an hour from both London and Paris. Lille itself would be an accidental appendix — almost a decor.

To articulate this condition, this new form of attraction, some buildings would be constructed over the tracks to become part of the TGV network: building and train would become different states of the same system.

What is important about this place is not where it *is* but where it *leads*, and how quickly. We imagined a series of skyscrapers straddling the station, towers that would suggest not a *place*, but a distance in *time* from various cities. The address would be defined as "70 minutes from London," "50 minutes from Paris," "18 minutes from Brussels."

Anywhere but France, such an idea would have been met with derision. Here, the client calculated the additional cost of building over the tracks — between 8 and 10% — and decided it was an acceptable investment in pure symbolism. Again, the client didn't say no.

1172

1155

was a client coming. So I stood there all day, just acting like I worked there! That's how I got the job.

STARS

I am attracted to movie stars but not for the usual reasons. I have no desire to speak to Holden or get his autograph. It is their peculiar reality which astounds me. The Yankee boy is well aware of it, even though he pretends to ignore Holden. Clearly he would like nothing better than to take Holden over to his fraternity house in the most casual way. "Bill, I want you to meet Phil. Phil, Bill Holden," he would say and go sauntering off in the best seafaring style.

STATISTIC

And the machines could have made an educated guess that, since Hagstrohm had gone that far in being average, he had probably been arrested once, had had sexual experience with five girls before marrying Wanda (only moderately satisfying) and had had two extramarital adventures since (one fleeting and foolish, the other rather long and disturbing), and that he would die at the age of 76.2 of a heart attack.

STIFLIN'

Gooper, will y'please open that hall

WE STEP INTO THE RESPONSIBILITY SUITS OF OUR ART.   THE GENERAL ANGLE

Euralille, first and second phases: sequence of large elements (park, triangle, Congrexpo mediating between city and towers).

WORKING IN FRANCE

Work on the Euralille project was a confrontation with a state — France — that operated, compared to other cultures, with a high degree of coherence and efficiency over a very long time, maybe as a residue of its former overcentralization; a confrontation with power and the uninhibited will to exercise it.

From Mitterrand's and Thatcher's "yes" to the tunnel, Mauroy's success in convincing the state to have a station *in* the city instead of on its periphery, to Baietto's creation of a spiderlike web of potential possibilities, the elaborate but highly disciplined consultations of the local populations, the construction of the vast edifices for limited budgets — the enterprise represents an awesome demonstration of continuity and concentration in the margin of the even vaster operation of the tunnel.

Compared to the anxious search for certainties that defines German and Japanese culture, here the degree of mobilization seemed directly proportional to the ultimate uncertainty of the enterprise, to its profoundly hypothetical nature; suddenly we were part of an army enlisted to prove a hypothesis.

The developer-driven architecture of the seventies and eighties had led to total resistance to anything complex, to a pulling apart of all the components that together form cities — a dismantlement infinitely more drastic than the one imagined in unfortunate parallel by the architectural avant-garde; here, montage of program and superimposition of building could restore both density and continuity — the return of complexity as a sign of the urban.

1000m

0

door—an' let some air circulate in
this stiflin' room?

STOLEN

One fine day, August 22, 1911, the
Mona Lisa was stolen from the
Louvre. They combed the national
museum; they searched high … and
… low. Dogs were brought in but to
no avail. She was in neither place.
She was loose. The theft made it
possible for everyone to see that
immortality did not hold an image
still, any more than it could spare
an image from modernity. And yet
when the Mona Lisa fell into the
hands of a robber, she did not fall
in any other sense. She showed that
she was alive, a rhizome, a hello.
By 1914 she would go under several
names. Brot. Zig-zag. Cubiste.

STORIES[1]

I have always wondered why layers
of a building are called stories.

STORIES[2]

Two great stories have been sex and
death.

STORM

The Angel of History does not move
dialectically into the future, but has
his face turned towards the past.
Where a chain of events appears to
us, he sees one single catastrophe
which keeps piling wreckage upon
wreckage and hurls it at his feet.
The angel would like to stay, awak-
en the dead, and join together that
which has been smashed to pieces,
but a storm is blowing from paradise
and irresistibly propels him into
the future to which his back is
turned, while the pile of ruins before
him grows skyward. What we call
progress is this storm.

STRANGER

I woke up as the sun was reddening;
and that was the one distinct time in
my life, the strangest moment of all,
when I didn't know who I was—
I was far away from home, haunted
and tired with travel, in a cheap hotel
room I'd never seen, hearing the
hiss of steam outside, and the creak
of the old wood of the hotel, and
footsteps upstairs, and all the sad
sounds, and I looked at the cracked
high ceiling and really didn't know
who I was for about fifteen strange
seconds. I wasn't scared; I was just
somebody else, some stranger, and
my whole life was a haunted life,
the life of a ghost.

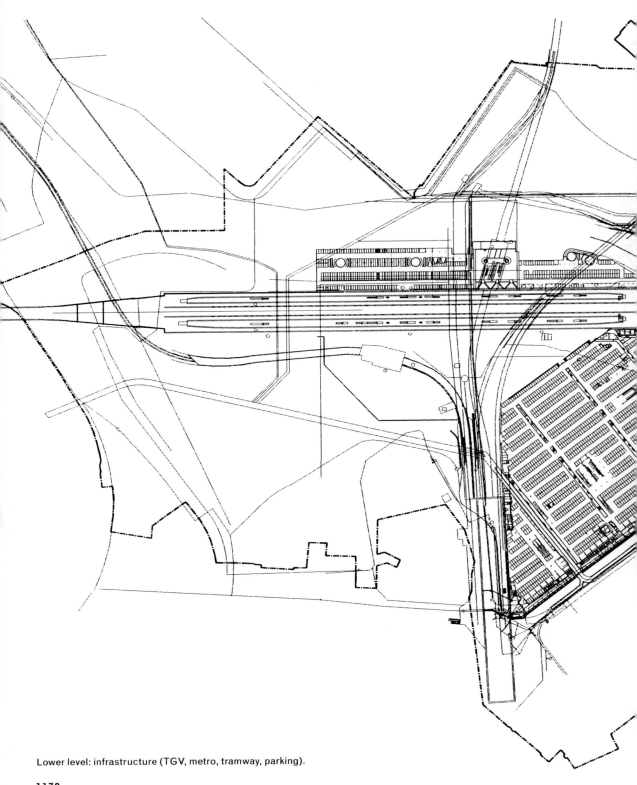

Lower level: infrastructure (TGV, metro, tramway, parking).

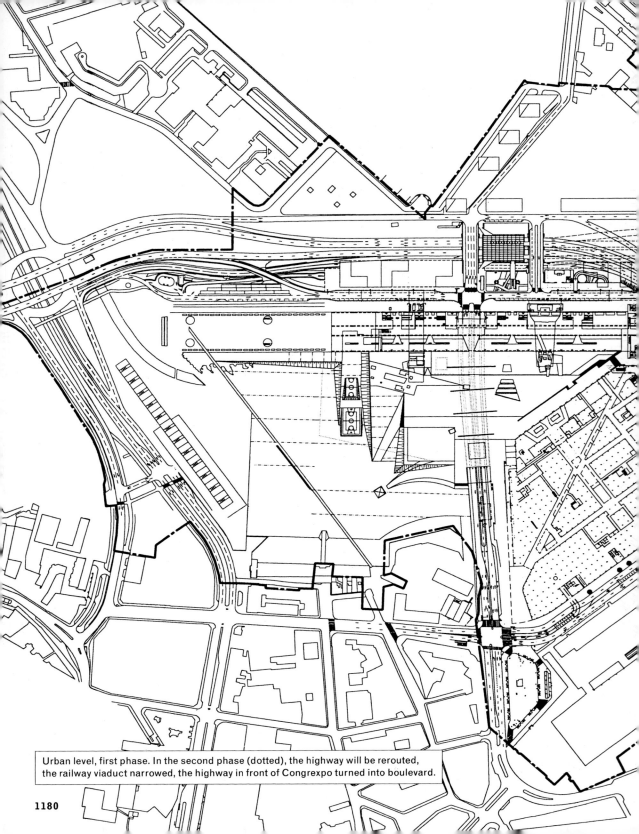

Urban level, first phase. In the second phase (dotted), the highway will be rerouted, the railway viaduct narrowed, the highway in front of Congrexpo turned into boulevard.

1180

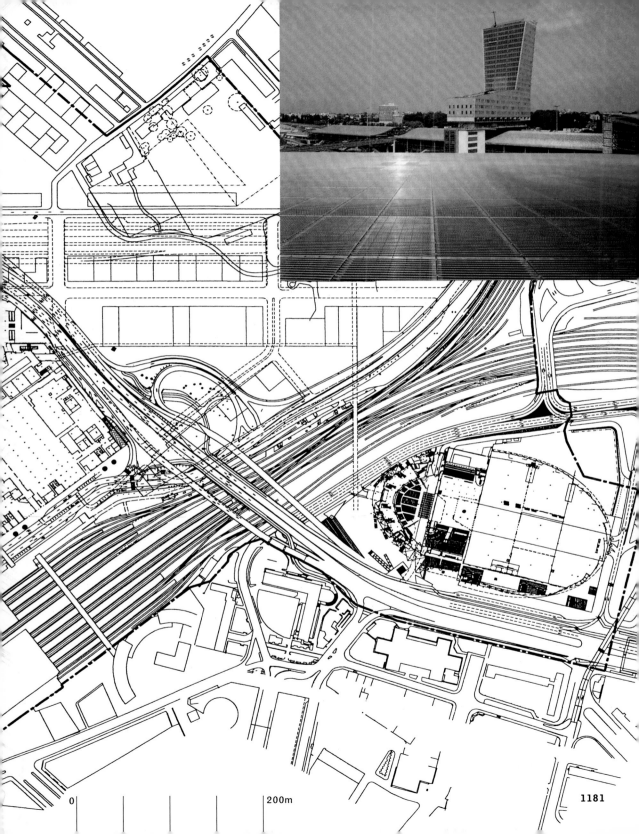

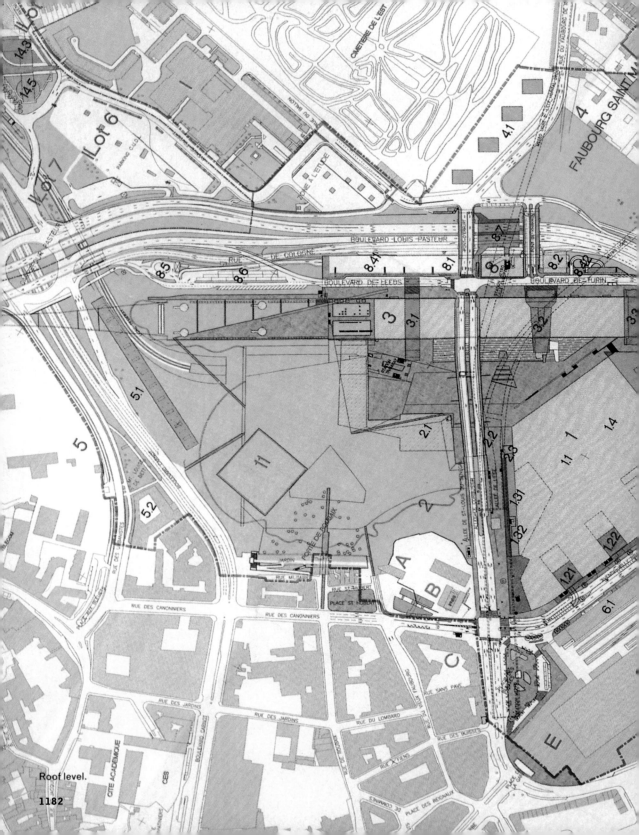

Roof level.

1182

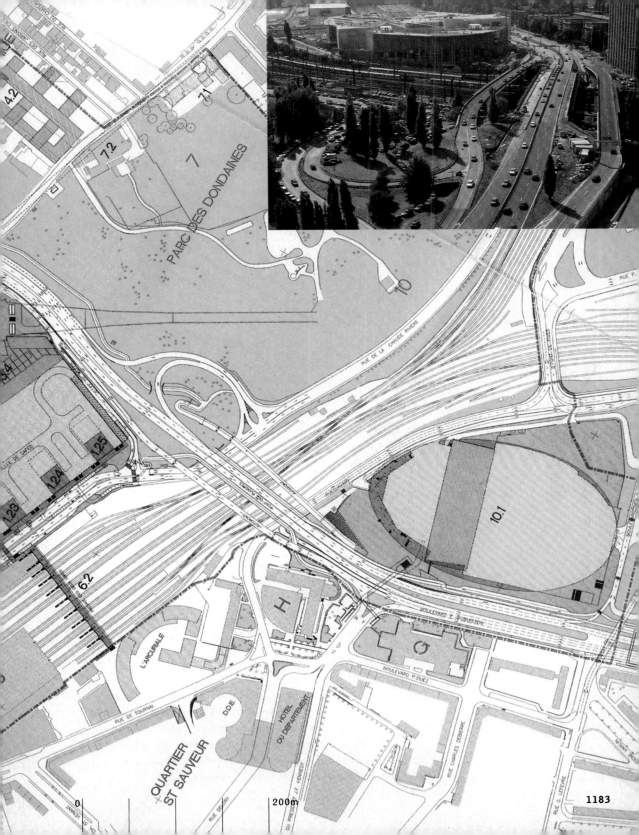

PARC DES DONDAINES

7

7.1

7.2

42

QUARTIER
ST SAUVEUR

L'ARCURIALE

RUE DE TOURNAI

HOTEL
DU DEPARTEMENT

D.D.E

RUE DE LA CHAUDE RIVIERE

BOULEVARD P. DUEZ

10.1

6.2

A25

A24

A23

H

0

200m

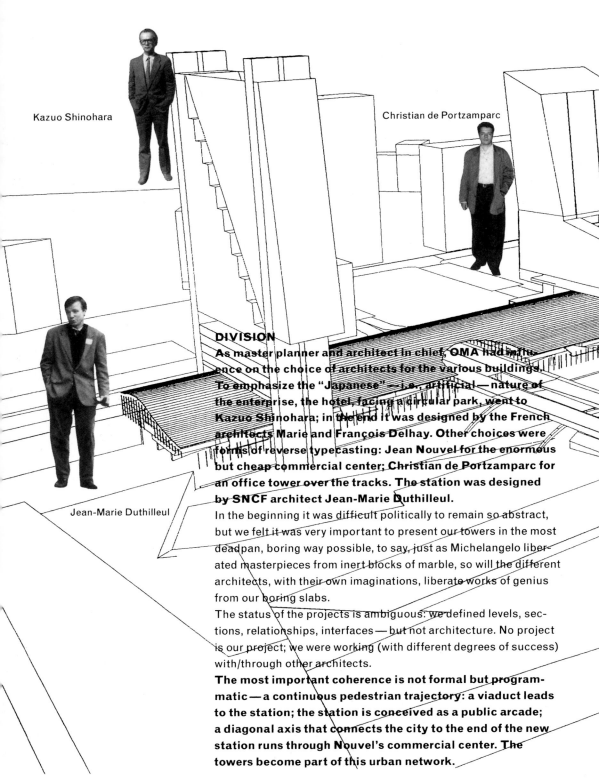

Kazuo Shinohara

Christian de Portzamparc

Jean-Marie Duthilleul

DIVISION
As master planner and architect in chief, OMA had influence on the choice of architects for the various buildings. To emphasize the "Japanese"—i.e., artificial—nature of the enterprise, the hotel, facing a circular park, went to Kazuo Shinohara; in the end it was designed by the French architects Marie and François Delhay. Other choices were forms of reverse typecasting: Jean Nouvel for the enormous but cheap commercial center; Christian de Portzamparc for an office tower over the tracks. The station was designed by SNCF architect Jean-Marie Duthilleul.

In the beginning it was difficult politically to remain so abstract, but we felt it was very important to present our towers in the most deadpan, boring way possible, to say, just as Michelangelo liberated masterpieces from inert blocks of marble, so will the different architects, with their own imaginations, liberate works of genius from our boring slabs.

The status of the projects is ambiguous: we defined levels, sections, relationships, interfaces — but not architecture. No project is our project; we were working (with different degrees of success) with/through other architects.

The most important coherence is not formal but programmatic—a continuous pedestrian trajectory: a viaduct leads to the station; the station is conceived as a public arcade; a diagonal axis that connects the city to the end of the new station runs through Nouvel's commercial center. The towers become part of this urban network.

asconi

Jean Nouvel

Marie and François Delhay

STRANGLED

Creation takes place in strangled channels.

STRATEGY

Strategy of absence, of evasion, of metamorphosis. An unlimited possibility of substitution, of concatenation without reference. To divert, to set up decoys, which disperse evidence, which disperse the order of things, the order of desire ... to slightly displace appearances in order to hit the empty and strategic heart of things. This is the strategy of oriental martial arts: never aim straight at your adversary or his weapon, never look at him, look to the side, to the empty point from where he rushes and hit there, at the empty center of the act, at the empty center of the weapon.

STRATUM

Every building has its position in a stratum — every building is not a cathedral.

STRESS

When an object, be this a building, a rail leading into an underground tunnel or an aircraft in flight, is struck by lightning the stresses to which it is subjected are determined by the current discharged into it.

STUDIO

[The Manhattan skyline] is my studio! Nothing has been fixed beforehand, nothing is rigid. All these blocks, all these forms, can be interchanged as the experiment unfolds.

STUPID

Tourism is the march of stupidity. You're expected to be stupid. The entire mechanism of the host country is geared to travelers acting stupidly. You walk around dazed, squinting into fold-out maps. You don't know how to talk to people, how to get anywhere, what the money means, what time it is, what to eat or how to eat it. Being stupid is the pattern, the level and the norm. You can exist on this level for weeks and months without reprimand or dire consequence. Together with thousands, you are granted immunities and broad freedoms. You are an army of fools, wearing bright polyesters, riding camels, taking pictures of each other, haggard, dysenteric, thirsty. There is nothing to think about but the next shapeless event.

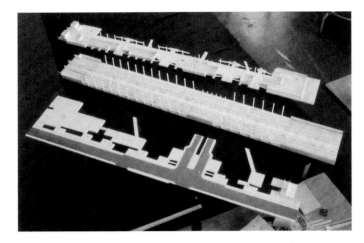

STATION

The station becomes an urban artery. The section was developed to be permeable from many points so that it performs as a connector.
Initially, it was conceived by the railway as a closed concrete box; the station itself would have been a pavilion on top. It has become, rather, a mutual exposure of the TGV and the city; the new section — two platforms on either side of an almost Roman viaduct for the trains that don't stop — is completely public and transparent. It connects the various components of the new city: parking, towers, metro, commercial center. The roof structure is one of Peter Rice's last works.

STYLES[1]

In architecture, as in art, there
seems to be a constant fluctuation
of styles. In art this is justified in
the basis of personal evolution and
the response on the part of the
artist, etc. In architecture there is
the rationale that the social fabric
is changing and creates new
requirements or else that new intellectual conclusions have been
reached concerning human needs,
etc. Change of style is exciting in rt.
In architecture where the responsibility is social, the situation is
somewhat different.

STYLES[2]

The "styles" are a lie.

SUICIDE

A b c d e f
g h i j k l
m n o p q r
s t u v w

x   y   z

SUITS

We step into the responsibility suits
of our art.

SUPPLANTATION

When a new and slightly improved
variety has been raised, it at first
supplants the less improved varieties

THE HEAD AFLOAT ON TOP LEVELS ON THE HORIZON OF OUR THOUGHT.

THE GENERAL ANGLE

in the same neighbourhood; when much improved it is transported far and near, like our short-horn cattle, and takes the place of other breeds in other countries. Thus the appearance of new forms and the disappearance of old forms, both natural and artifical, are bound together.

SURPASS
To deny worth, but to do what surpasses all praise or (for that matter) understanding.

SURPRISE
As Gregor Samsa awoke one morning from uneasy dreams he found himself transformed in his bed into a gigantic insect.

SURPRISED
He himself was surprised. He had acted against his principles.

SURREAL
I'm always very fond of your projects, you know. I'm predisposed. And that's why I'd probably be one of its most ardent critics. I have a sense that your work falls into the surreal category. It's my use of the term; I don't suggest that you even think your work is surreal, but if I were to categorize it — and I'm prone to make these overgeneralizations, and I apologize for the apology, but it seems necessary — I would say it's surreal.

SURREALISM
I have had a longstanding interest in surrealism, but more for its analytical powers than for its exploitation of the subconscious or for its aesthetics … I was most impressed by its "paranoid" methods, which I consider one of the genuine inventions of this century, a rational method which does not pretend to be objective, through which analysis becomes identical to creation.

SUSPENSE
This suspense is terrible. I hope it will last.

SWALLOWED
McDonald's committed to the mansard in 1968, after having turned its arches from an architectural element into an icon. In some cases, the mansard grew so huge as to virtually swallow the building it roofed, like a too-big hat settling down on a shorteared head.

SWARM
Mercedeses and BMWs now swarm

Opposite: Shinohara hotel, second version.
Above and inset: Smaller hotel for same site by François and Marie Delhay.

HOTEL
The original project for the hotel, by Kazuo Shinohara, evolved in two stages to accommodate financial and technical demands, until finally a new program for a smaller hotel was given to the Delhays.
The row of towers was abandoned. The station, bisected by the Viaduct Le Corbusier, faced two conditions — the vegetal and the mineral. The smaller hotel forms a more direct connection between the station and the park and its future facilities.

Shinohara's hotel was the first tower that demonstrated the potential of our "boring" blocks. It was beautiful: over the railway a block of public facilities, then a cylindrical health club — the waves of the pool readable on the facade — then an animated volume of rooms. But each project evolves in terms of commercial, technical, ideological, and time pressures; concepts are continually modified, or in some cases abandoned. After Shinohara's first version, the clients wanted a half-hotel, half-office building. He made another version — two sliding volumes. Then the economy dictated a smaller hotel still. That version was designed by the Delhay office in Lille. It will form a more direct relationship with the park and the public domain.

So we try to be very flexible in terms of accommodating the changes. Shinohara's hotel was a great loss: it would have been the most important Japanese building in Europe.

all over Tokyo's choicest neighborhoods. In 1989, Mercedes's sales were up 40 percent (31,511 vehicles registered) while BMW's rose 23 percent.

SWEAT SUIT
In September, he decided to alter his system of dressing. If he wore sweat suits at home — the zipper-free kind, nothing to scratch or bind him — he could go from one shower to the next without changing clothes. The sweat suit would serve as both pajamas and day wear.

SWING
To practice simulated iron shots with the described device, the golfer stands on simulated turf section *27* and addresses himself to one of the simulated golf balls *28*. He then swings at the simulated ball as he would at a real ball, and the motion of his club bends the ends of the bendable turf elements into an accurate simulation of the divotal depression that would have been produced thereby in a section of real turf.

SWISH
"Holland's great for driving fast, you know," Charles says with a smirk. "The Rotterdam ring road is long, oval and flat. You just go out there and hack it! It's really fun. It's sort of like a movie or something. Like the way gas stations are — bright and shiny. The roads are so direct and you look out at the flat fields. [He makes noises of cars swishing past in the manner of a movie soundtrack.] That's my ambition, you know, to make a cyberpunk movie. That's my dream."

SYNTHETIC
Max Headroom ... is digital personification of this image. While "pulsating flesh" (the actor Matt Frewer's) may have provided the basic stuff for the face of the successful VJ, for the rest, everything's synthetic: his skin, to which an unreal gloss layer has been applied, his glance, which is irregular and cold, his hair, which has a sculpted quality, and his jacket, which seems as though it was coloured with automobile lacquer. While Max Headroom is a portrayal of a human figure, he represents effortlessly the digital image in general: an image from which the human hand, the human factor has been eliminated

Christian de Portzamparc, Tour Crédit Lyonnais, section, details.

CREDIT LYONNAIS

First a famous English architect designed a fragment of high-tech here, the entire building proclaiming its status as bridge. When it was found to be too expensive, he first blamed the master plan, then offered to build a cheaper building parallel to the tracks, then withdrew.

Portzamparc was in a difficult situation: we had proposed a full tower; his client counter-proposed what we considered a "camel" — a kind of huge chair over the railway — as a cheaper solution. We thought of Christian de Portzamparc because he is extremely artistic, sensitive, poetic. He had done mostly cultural programs, but we felt that there was a possibility that someone like him could deal with the brutal demands of the client, and that somehow, by going ostensibly with the flow of events, the intersection of the client and Portzamparc could generate another interesting fragment, and that maybe a camel designed by Portzamparc could be a really beautiful camel.

1193

entirely, an image which André Bazin may have waxed enthusiastic about if he were alive today.

SYSTEMATIZE
I believe that the moment is at hand when by a paranoid and active advance of the mind, it will be possible to systematize confusion and thus help to discredit completely the world of reality.

SYSTEMATIZERS
I mistrust all systematizers and avoid them. The will to a system is a lack of integrity.

T

TACTICS
That turned the conversation, and they all began discussing dragon-slayings historical, dubious, and mythical, and the various sorts of stabs and jabs and undercuts, and the different arts, devices and stratagems by which they had been accomplished. The general opinion was that catching a dragon napping was not as easy as it seemed, and the attempt to stick one or prod one asleep was more likely to end in disaster than a bold frontal attack.

TALENT[1]
A third theory is that colour in dreams is related to the dreamer's artistic talent.

TALENT[2]
Even with the severest judgement, the danger is ever present of mistaking for creative talent what is only a gift for adroit imitation or " a highly developed skill in compilation.

TALL
Well now, they've been fooling around with tall buildings long enough. Why don't they build a tall one? That's all. There's no reason why they shouldn't, you know. When the man — who was it invented the elevator? — nobody knows. I guess he's lost in perspective. But the man, when he invented the elevator, made the upended street, and when the street became upended, who should say where it should stop?

TAXI
There are 17,000 taxis in Hong Kong.

TBMS
The answer to this logistical challenge

WORLD TRADE CENTER
Here we worked with the French architect Vasconi, who was completely oblivious to anything we ever said, and therefore could produce a pure example of French high-tech with lesser means than his English colleague.

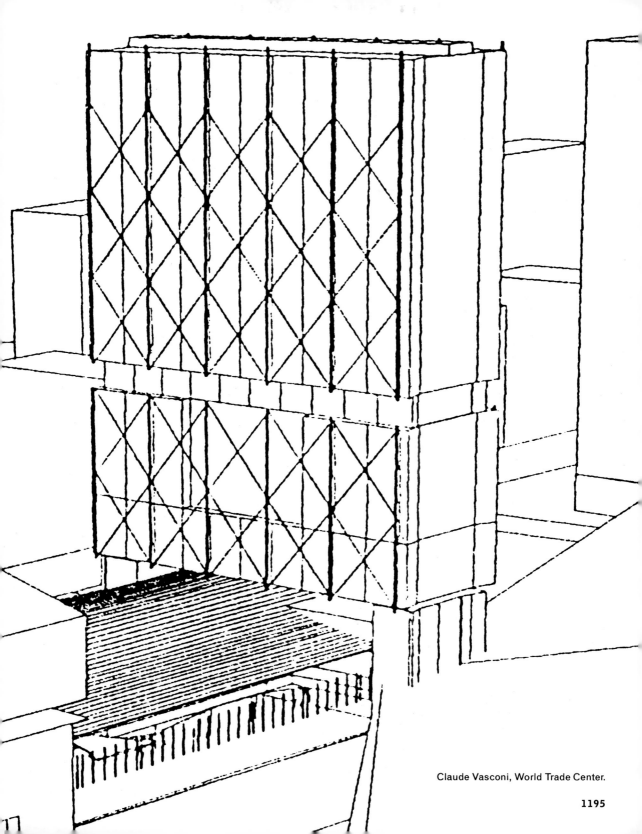

Claude Vasconi, World Trade Center.

has come in the form of 11 giant tunnel-boring machines (TBMs) costing up to $20 million each and weighing as much as 1,200 tons. Unlike the British, whose machines are mainly numbered, the French have given their TBMs women's names like Brigitte, Pascale and Catherine.

TECHNOLOGY

It may well be that what we have hitherto understood as architecture, and what we are beginning to understand of technology are incompatible disciplines. The architect who proposes to run with technology knows now that he will be in fast company, and that, in order to keep up, he may have to emulate the Futurists and discard his whole cultural load, including the professional garments by which he is recognized as an architect.

TELEVISION

Try to stop developmentwork broadcast-receivers and concentrate all efforts on television stop Television is our biggest chance stop Write on all doors and walls and blackboards TELEVISION stop Make everyone televisioncrazy stop We have enough people to do the job but most of them work on the wrong items stop There really is only one item: TELEVISION stop The only actual televisionfront we have at the moment is right here in U.S.A. stop WE are able to force it if we are ready to fight AND TO KEEP FIGHTING! stop Mobilise Eindhoven please stop No time to lose TELEVISION IS MARCHING ON HERE AND FROM HERE OVER THE WHOLE WORLD stop The only question is: WHO MARCHES ON THE TELEVISION, PHILIPS OR THE OTHERS? stop THE OTHERS ARE ALREADY MARCHING! PHILIPS EINDHOVEN, TAKE THE LEAD! fullstop

TEMPTATION

Imagine, dear boy, a young girl, beautiful and passionate, in the compartment of an express train. At one of the stations a young man gets in. From a good family. Night descends on the train. She falls asleep and in her sleep spreads her limbs. A glorious young creature. The young man — you know that

1197

type, bursting with sap but absolutely chaste — begins literally to lose his head.

TEST
Currently, the only technique that can reveal a toxic fish is bioassay, but it's a cumbersome procedure. It requires feeding suspect flesh to test animals. These assays nearly always depend on the death of the test animal to be useful. There can be little hope of determining if a test animal experiences a reversal of temperature sensation, or if its extremities tingle.

THEORETICALLY
Theoretically, Iridium could provide the world's first worldwide voice-communication system without any interference from governments. The world, however, is not quite ready for a "Global Village" concept, so the gateways in each country will be government-licensed, allowing the possibility of restricting access to the system.

THERE
It is hard to go on when you are nearly there but not near enough to hurry up to get there. That is where Rose was and she well she hardly could go on to get there. And where was there. She almost said it she almost whispered it to herself and to the chair. Where oh where is there.

THING
One shutter was shaking worse than the others. I grabbed it, to steady it, and it banged my thumb. When I pulled my hand away the boards began a fearful rattling and, before I could secure it, the whole shutter lifted, splintering one board and yanking screws out the hasp. Rain shot through the window. I reached for the flapping shutter and a cold wet thing closed over my hand. Before I could scream, another cold wet thing reached in and felt for my mouth.

THINKERS
The profoundest thinkers aren't those whose stars orbit cyclical pathways. To those who see inside themselves as if into the immense universe and who in themselves bear Milky Ways, the extreme irregularity of these constellations is well known; they lead directly to chaos and to a labyrinthine existence.

Jean Nouvel, Le Centre Euralille: tilted triangle emerging in historic city.

TRIANGLE DES GARES
The triangular plane that sloped to reveal the TGV became Jean Nouvel's commercial center.
Jean Nouvel is known for very expensive, very sophisticated buildings, but here he had a very brutal program: commercial center with offices, housing, hotels encrusted within. It became research by Nouvel into the issue of cheapness.
Cheapness is ideological in this situation because the virtual community can work only if the new Lille remains cheaper than the surrounding cities. Also, it was important that the first phase could already present a critical mass — we had to construct, with each franc, a maximum *quantity* of new urban substance. So cheapness had to be incorporated and recognized as a driving force, even in architecture.
To make the center truly urban, it had to offer more than the amorphous undifferentiated space — deliberate maze — of the typical shopping center. Nouvel organized it through public axes that cut through the commercial substance to connect the city to the station.
The project has become very beautiful and, for Nouvel, very Japanese. On the five towers, enormous blocks of neon will emit commercial, artistic, and ideological messages to the city. The entire building is clad in his favorite material — a kind of metallic grille, this time light gray.

there is an approach towards the final mutation, and that man only is in that he searches to be, plans to be, thumbing through words and modes of behavior and joy sprinkled with blood and other rhetorical pieces like this one.

THUMP
And then they started dancing, which was terrible because they were all so frustrated that they had to sort of stamp their feet — like architects. They're so stylized they can't let go, and when they do ... it's so awful, like a geometric Spanish Dance! It was a horrible party, everybody just hating each other. One had just won a competition and the others were all envious (and all their first wives were now the others' second wives — like the Dutch government — all the same people just changing places). You could feel the tension. Suddenly we heard a big smash and Richard Rogers had "thumped" somebody — he had thumped him on the face, and all the blood was running onto these white tiles. A real fight! And everybody pretended that nothing happened. They kept on dancing in the broken glass. And we were just watching, thinking, oh how awful! Why aren't there any other kinds of people like writers and painters? Why are there only architects, and all of them hating each other. Why is there only champagne and smoked salmon?

TIME[1]
The hands of all the four thousand electric clocks in all the Bloomsbury Centre's four thousand rooms marked twenty-seven minutes past two.

TIME[2]
Anyone who has used a VCR has likely had the experience of frustration and impatience when watching real-time broadcast TV that it can't be fast-forwarded. It is at such moments that time becomes a qualitatively new substance, commodity and effect.

TODAY
No! Today, today, today, today!

TOE
There is a toe sticking out from underneath a green blanket on my living-room sofa. A lovely toe; a pale and dainty toe. A toe that has never tested dirty bath water.

CONGREXPO
We built on the "wrong" side of the tracks, literally.

On a site separated from the station and commercial center by the railroad tracks, OMA did its own building. It is 300 meters long and has a very diagrammatic organization, with three major components: Zenith, a 5,000-seat concert hall; Congress, a conference center with three major auditoriums; and Expo, a 20,000 m² exposition hall. In the east-west direction, each of these components can be used independently, but openings between the components make it possible to use the building as a single entity on the north-south axis, to mix programs, to generate hybrids.

There are two huge metal doors between Zenith and Expo that can close or open, and if they open the separate parts become one, so you can also think of it as a theater with a 200-meter-deep backstage, or any other combination of these parts.

Architecturally, it is scandalously simple: an enormous plane of concrete, deformed into a scallop shape in the north, accommodates the concert hall; a concrete plate, folded according to the different auditorium slopes to become a bridge, forms the conference center. The bridge is simply placed on the field of the building, on enormous pilotis, in such a way that the connection — but also the separation — between the concert hall and the exhibition space can be made easily. The only gesture toward entity is a single roof under which all these elements are contained. It is not a building that defines a clear architectural identity but a building that creates and triggers potential, almost in an urbanistic sense.

This was when we began to realize that our architecture was changing through our experience in urbanism. It became interesting to do what we could do in urbanism — extend limits, generate possibilities — in architecture.

Congrexpo is a piece of equipment that with minimal dissociation from the generic urban plane, minimal means of intensification, accommodates the urban condition — but inside rather than outside.

There is an event planned for 1996: All the Mazda dealers of Europe are in Zenith; the doors are closed. The new model is driven through Expo; the doors open and it comes into the auditorium. The doors close; the dealers descend to the arena and throng around the car. In the meantime, the entire space of Expo is filled with 5,000 new Mazdas. The doors open; the dealers are guided to their own new Mazdas and drive out of the building. That event will take place in the space of 30 minutes.

Zenith: 5.500 seats

Congres: 3 halls, 1.500, 350 and 500 seats

Exposition: 18.000 m2

Parking: 1.230 places

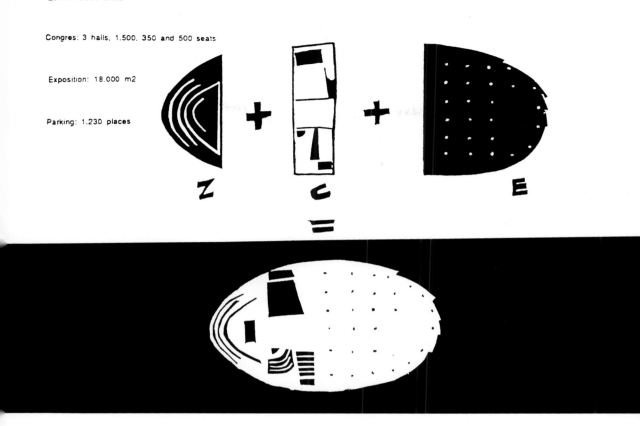

Z + C + E

=

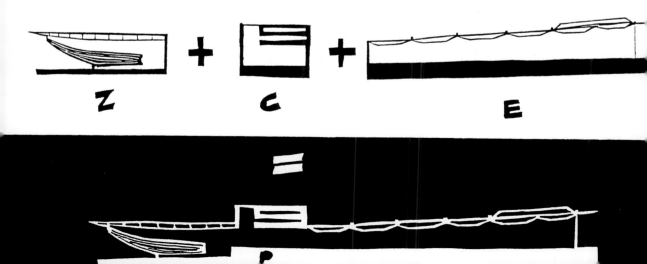

Z + C + E

=

P

TOGETHER

The funny thing is that architects are always incestuously together. They hate each other but they're always together.

TOILETS

Toilets in modern water closets rise up from the floor like white water lilies. The architect does all he can to make the body forget how paltry it is, and to make man ignore what happens to his intestinal wastes after the water from the tank flushed them down the drain. Even though the sewer pipelines reach far into our houses with their tentacles, they are carefully hidden from view, and we are happily ignorant of the invisible Venice of shit underlying our bathrooms, bedrooms, dance halls, and parliaments.

TOKYO[1]

35°40 N, 139°45 E

TOKYO[2]

[Tokyo] offers this precious paradox: it does possess a center, but this center is empty. The entire city turns around a site both forbidden and indifferent...Daily, in their rapid, energetic, bullet-like trajectories, the taxis avoid this circle, whose low crest, the visible form of invisibility, hides the sacred "nothing."
One of the two most powerful cities of modernity is thereby built around an opaque ring of walls, streams, roofs, and trees whose own center is no more than an evaporated notion, subsisting here, not in order to irradiate power, but to give to the entire urban movement the support of its central emptiness, forcing the traffic to make a perpetual detour. In this manner, we are told, the system of the imaginary is spread circularly, by detours and returns the length of an empty subject.

TOKYO[3]

Think of it like a rainforest made out of heavy metal.

TORMENTED

She always was, she always is, tormented by the problem of the external and the internal.

TORQUE

More importantly, that same V6 engine produces 160 foot-pounds of torque. Which means that even with all five seats filled, there is plenty of power to spare—even on steep grades.

EURALILLE

DYNAMIQUE D'ENFER

It was three years later, with the site already turned into a gargantuan infrastructural playground, that the "father" of the plan, Jean-Paul Baietto, revealed that our seemingly spontaneous action had been nothing but a figment of his imagination. As research for this book I asked him: "How come you never rejected the infernal complexity of our proposals? Why did you never say no to our most outrageous suggestions? Why have you allowed us to imagine, for instance, an operation on one particular site occupied by three owners layered on top of one another? Why didn't you simply send us back to the drawing board?"

"To create something worthwhile at the end of the 20th century," Baietto explained, "you need three conditions. First, you need limits. In the beginning of the century you could be a hero by offering generalizations; at its end only the hyper-specific is credible ... In Lille, we have a limited territory and make no claims beyond it."

Because the site had a border, it could be considered an enclave, a single entity, and therefore there was a hope in hell of realizing the project in a limited time.

"The second condition is external demand."

Since the entire hypothesis was based on the effect of the tunnel and the TGV, it was clear that there was an apparent need for the completion of the complex to coincide with the opening of the tunnel.

"With these two conditions, you create the third: you establish on your domain a *dynamique d'enfer*, a dynamic from hell ... So complex become all the interconnections, the mutual dependencies, the proliferation of interfaces, the superimposition of users and owners that together they form a group of prisoners, shackled by mutual obligation, exacerbated by the very complexity that you offered unwittingly."

It is only when they are all tied to the site by each other's demands, chained together by an overall vision never entirely revealed, when the dynamic from hell makes the entire situation irrevocable and the project is like quicksand from which no one can escape, that you can get away with such an enterprise in Europe.

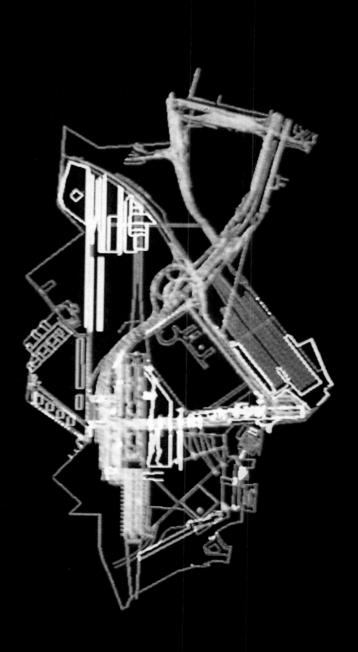

1209

WE WANTED TO INVESTIGATE AN ALTERNATIVE TO THE HEAVINESS OF REAL CONSTRUCTIONS OF CITIES.
WE WOULD CALL IT "LITE URBANISM," SPELLED THE AMERICAN WAY: L-I-T-E (LIKE THE BEER)—AN
URBANISM THAT WOULD NOT NECESSARILY HAVE PRETENSIONS TOWARD PERMANENCE OR STABILITY,

Programmatic Lava

Urban Design Forum
Yokohama, Japan
Project, 1992

東

京

湾

荒川

多摩川

1217

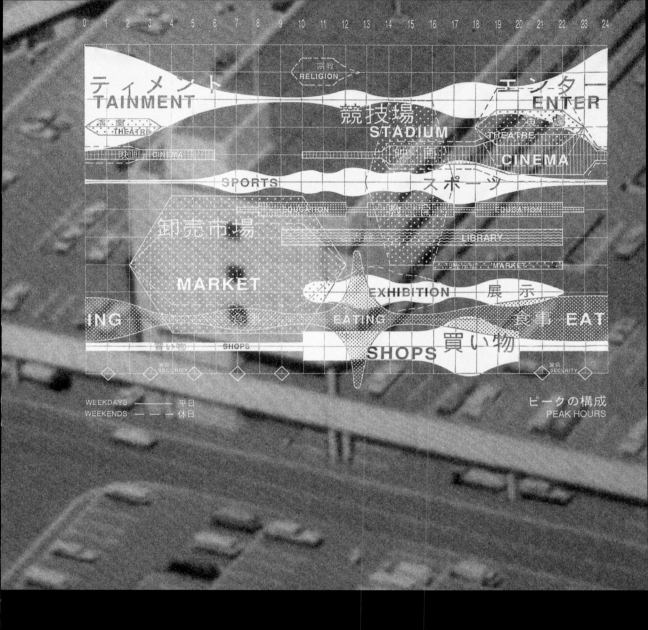

THE DIFFICULT THING ABOUT OUR SITE WAS THAT IT WAS ALREADY SPOKEN FOR: IT WAS ALMOST COM-
PLETELY OCCUPIED BY TWO ENORMOUS MARKET HALLS; ONE WAS ALSO A PARKING FACILITY. BECAUSE IN
20 YEARS THIS COULD BE ONE OF THE DENSEST AREAS OF JAPAN, THE PERMANENT PRESENCE OF THE
MARKET HALLS WAS GUARANTEED; IN OTHER WORDS, TO SERVE THE CITY, THEY HAD TO STAY.

BUT WE NOTICED THAT ALTHOUGH THEY PHYSICALLY DOMINATED THE ISLAND, THEY WERE USED INTENSELY
ONLY BETWEEN 4:00 AND 10:00 IN THE MORNING.
THE REST OF THE DAY NOTHING HAPPENED.

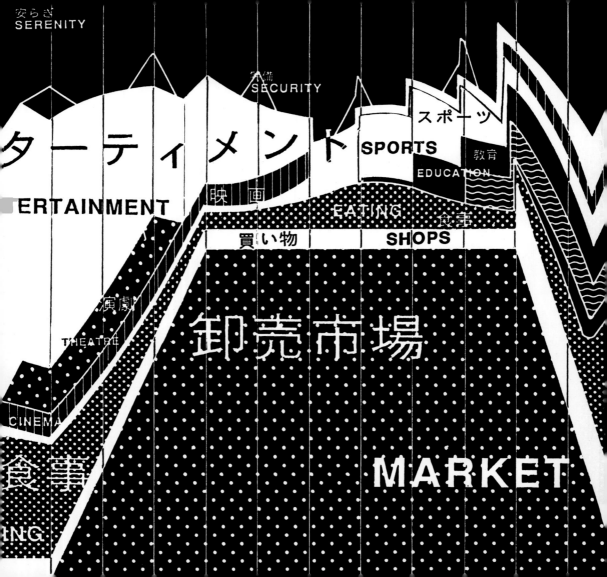

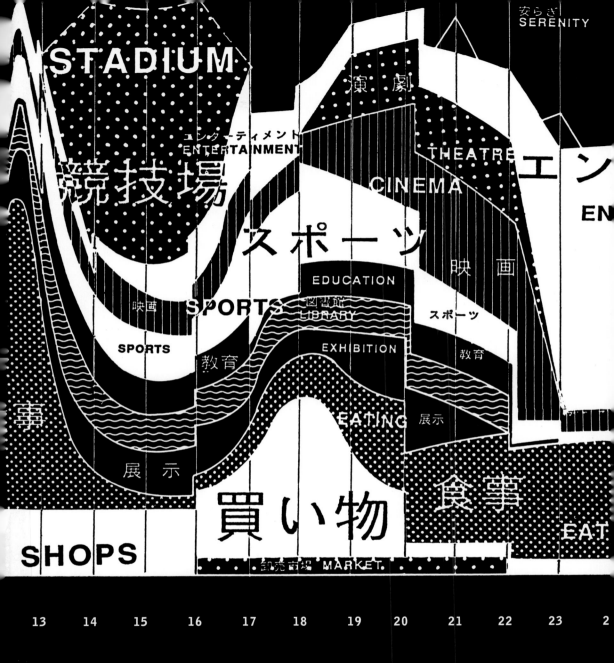

安らぎ
SERENITY

STADIUM

演　劇

THEATRE

エン

競技場

ユンターティメント
ENTERTAINMENT

CINEMA

EN

スポーツ

映　画

EDUCATION

映画

SPORTS

図書館
LIBRARY

スポーツ

SPORTS

EXHIBITION

教育

事

教育

展示

EATING

食事

展　示

買い物

SHOPS

EAT

卸売市場　MARKET

| 13 | 14 | 15 | 16 | 17 | 18 | 19 | 20 | 21 | 22 | 23 | 2 |

IT BECAME OBVIOUS THAT WE WOULD HAVE TO INVENT PROGRAMS TO FILL THE REST OF THE DAY, WHICH
WOULD ACHIEVE MAXIMUM USE OF THE EXISTING INFRASTRUCTURE.

WE THOUGHT WE COULD ADJUST THE PARKING LOT—CREATE A SINGLE WARPED PLANE THAT WOULD BE
SOMETIMES HIGHWAY, SOMETIMES RAMP, SOMETIMES PARKING, AND SOMETIMES ROOF AND THAT COULD
ACCOMMODATE THE ENDLESS PROGRAMS THAT WE WOULD INSERT IN AN AMORPHOUS AND INFORMAL
MANNER.

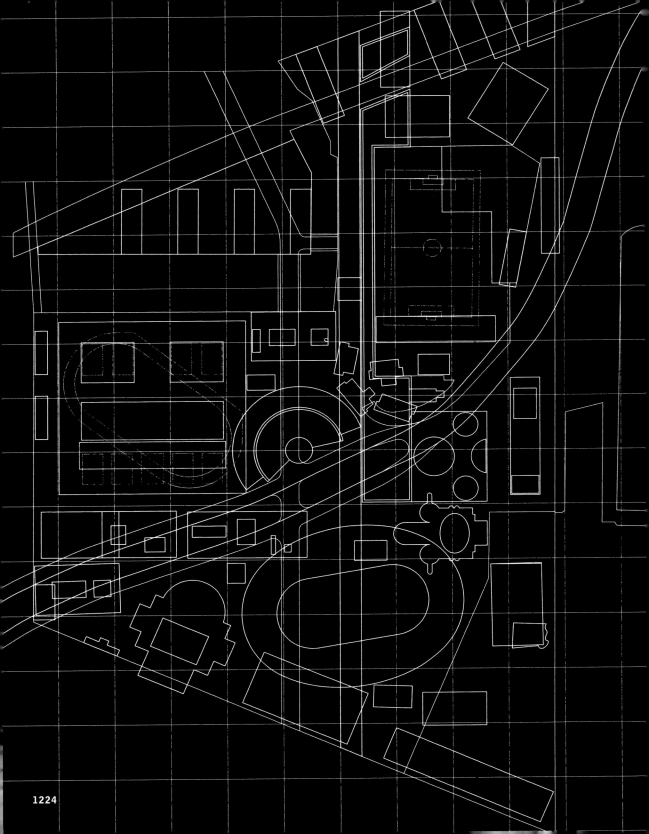

1224

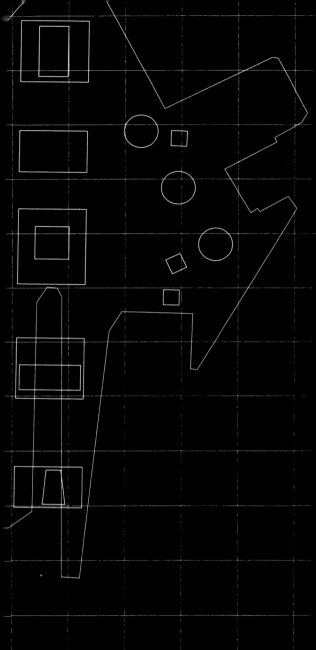

Our project is a hypothesis based on the unique conditions that we found on the site: two markets with a colossal number of parking places; the arrival on the site of railroads, cars (via the new highway), and ships; the proximity of Minato Mirai 21, a tremendous injection of density into an already congested urban condition. Together these elements define a situation with almost unlimited potential for triggering and supporting public life.

We have avoided designing buildings, with their inevitable limitations and separations; continuous and formless, the project engulfs the site like programmatic lava. Three layers of public activity are manipulated to support the largest possible number of events with the minimum amount of permanent definition. Noting that the peak hours of the market occur in the early morning, we propose a complementary spectrum of events that would fill the 24-hour cycle with a montage of successive and simultaneous peaks—a maximum exploitation of the location and its infrastructure—to create a 24-hour peak, a mosaic of heterogeneous 21st-century life.

Some parts are used as roads, some as parking places; minimal interventions provoke theaters, cinemas, nightclubs, restaurants, churches, sports fields, and other programs; the new givens of access, communication, artificiality, and technology are frozen in a momentary configuration. Covering the southeast section of the site, this programmatic tapestry leaves an area of the former docks intact, where conditions are ideal for housing: sea views, openness, density. Toward the city is a wedge of "center," which together with the housing will give a degree of three-dimensional anchoring to the site: this cluster of container "needles" connected to the superfast train station generates financial compensation for the "lite" urbanization of the island.

COMPOSITIONALLY IT WAS SIMPLY AN OPPORTUNISTIC INFILTRATION OF THE ISLAND'S RESIDUAL SPACE; INTO EVERY GAP AND EVERY SLIT AND EVERY AVAILABLE SPACE WE PUSHED PROGRAMS WITH MINIMAL CONTAINMENT, MINIMAL COVER, MINIMAL ARTICULATION OF MASS TO GENERATE THE GREATEST POSSIBLE DENSITY WITH THE LEAST POSSIBLE PERMANENCE.

0 | | | | | 100m

駐車場

◇ MARKET

生鮮卸売市場

SPORTS

SHISEIDO

Toyota

Noritake

Christian Dior
POLA
ROLEX
CHANEL
SHARP

MIKIMOTO

L'ORÉAL
PARIS

marie claire

Cardin

Christian Dior

FIAT

歌舞伎
KABUKI

GUCCI

OMEGA

NINA RICCI

CHANEL

HIGHWAY FROM 'MINATO-MIRAI 21'

TOYOTA

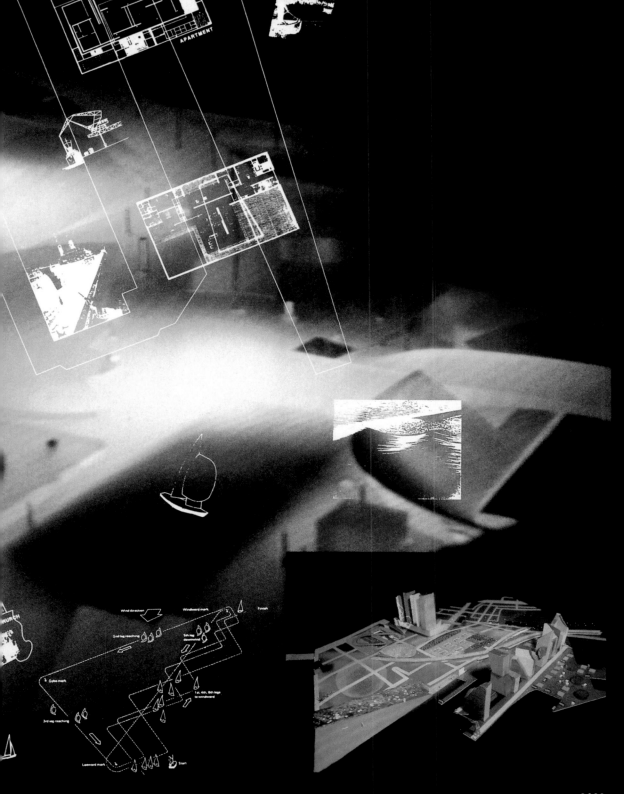

APARTMENT

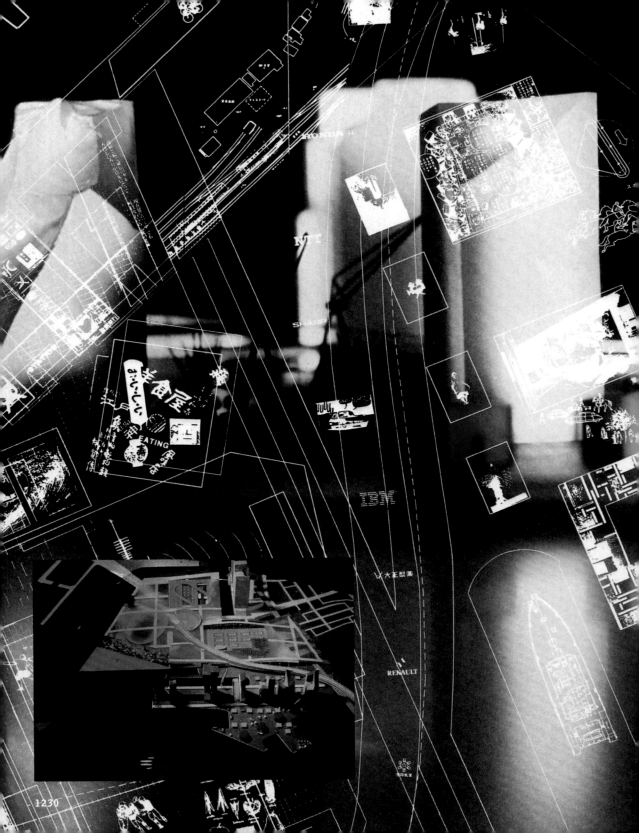

臨海公園

APARTMENT

1231

MARKET

青果卸売市場
'peak hours of the market'

OFFICE

PARKING
駐車場

SHISEIDO
Canon
CHANEL
CLINIQUE
L'OREAL

屋外劇場

EXHIBITION
OPEN

center 3-dimensional anchoring to the site

生鮮卸売市場

VOLVO

a modern FORUM

神奈

川区

千若町

HONDA (H)

NTT

SHARP

EATING

IBM

大正製薬

The Generic City

1240

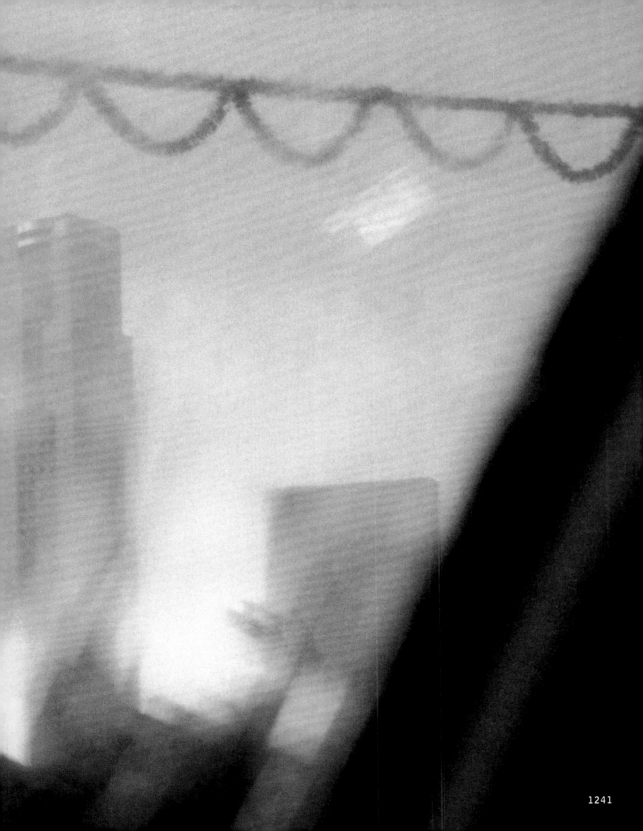

1241

1244

1245

1246

the *residual*. In the original model of the moderns, the residual was merely green, its controlled neatness a moralistic assertion of good intentions, discouraging association, use. In the Generic City, because the crust of its civilization is so thin, and through its immanent tropicality, the vegetal is transformed into *Edenic* Residue, the main carrier of its identity: a hybrid of politics and landscape. At the same time refuge of the illegal, the uncontrollable, and subject of endless manipulation, it represents a simultaneous triumph of the manicured and the primeval. Its immoral lushness compensates for the Generic City's other poverties. Supremely inorganic, the organic is the Generic City's strongest myth. **6.3** The street is dead. That discovery has coincided with frantic attempts at its resuscitation. Public art is everywhere — as if two deaths make a life. Pedestrianization — intended to preserve — merely channels the flow of those doomed to destroy the object of their intended reverence with their feet. **6.4** The Generic City is on its way from horizontality to verticality. The skyscraper looks as if it will be the final, definitive typology. It has swallowed everything else. It can exist anywhere: in a rice field, or downtown — it makes no difference anymore. The towers no longer stand together; they are spaced so that they don't interact. Density in isolation is the ideal. **6.5** Housing is not a problem. It has either been completely solved or totally left to chance; in the first case it is legal, in the second "illegal"; in the first case, towers or, usually, slabs (at the most, 15 meters deep), in the second (in perfect complementarity) a crust of improvised hovels. One solution consumes the sky, the other the ground. It is strange that those with the least money inhabit the most expensive commodity — earth; those who pay, what is free — air. In either case, housing proves to be surprisingly accommodating — not only does the population double every so many years, but also, with the loosening grip of the various religions, the average number of occupants per unit halves — through divorce and other family-dividing phenomena — with the same frequency that the city's population doubles; as its numbers swell, the Generic City's density is perpetually on the decrease. **6.6** All Generic Cities issue from the tabula rasa; if there was nothing, now they are there; if there was something, they have replaced it. They must, otherwise they would be historic. **6.7** The Generic Cityscape is usually an amalgam of overly ordered sections — dating from near the beginning of its development, when "the power" was still undiluted — and increasingly free arrangements everywhere else. **6.8** The Generic City is the apotheosis of the multiple-choice concept: all boxes crossed, an anthology of *all* the options. Usually the Generic City has been "planned," not in the usual sense of some bureaucratic organization controlling its development, but as if various echoes, spores, tropes, seeds fell on the ground randomly as in nature, took hold — exploiting the natural fertility of the terrain — and now form an ensemble: an arbitrary gene pool that sometimes produces amazing results. **6.9** The writing of the city may be indecipherable, flawed, but that does not mean that there *is* no writing; it may simply be that *we* developed a new illiteracy, a new blindness. Patient detection reveals the themes, particles, strands that can be isolated from the seeming murkiness of this Wagnerian *ur*-soup: notes left on a blackboard by a visiting genius 50 years ago, stenciled UN reports disintegrating in their Manhattan glass silo, discoveries by former colonial thinkers with a keen eye for the climate, unpredictable ricochets of design education gathering strength as a global laundering process. **6.10** The best definition of the aesthetic of the Generic City is "free style." How to describe it? Imagine an open space, a clearing in the forest, a leveled city. There are three elements: roads, buildings, and nature; they coexist in flexible relationships, seemingly without reason, in spectacular organizational diversity. Any one of the three may dominate: sometimes the "road" is lost — to be found meandering on an incomprehensible detour; sometimes *you see no building*, only nature; then, equally unpredictably, you are surrounded only by building. In certain frightening spots, all three are simultaneously absent. On these "sites" (actually, what is the opposite of a site? They are like holes bored through the concept of city) public art emerges like the Loch Ness Monster, equal parts figurative and abstract, usually self-cleaning. **6.11** Specific cities still seriously debate the mistakes of architects — for instance, their proposals to create raised pedestrian networks with tentacles leading from one block to the next as a solution to congestion — but the Generic City simply enjoys the benefits of their inventions: *decks*, *bridges*, *tunnels*, *motorways* — a huge proliferation of the paraphernalia of connection — frequently draped with ferns and flowers as if to ward off original sin, creating a vegetal congestion more severe than a fifties science-fiction movie. **6.12** The roads are only for cars. People (pedestrians) are led on rides (as in an amusement park), on "promenades" that lift them off the ground, then subject them to a catalog of exaggerated conditions — wind, heat, steepness, cold, interior, exterior, smells, fumes — in a sequence that is a grotesque caricature of life in the historic city. **6.13** There *is* horizontality in the Generic City, but it is on the way out. It consists either of history that is not yet erased or of Tudor-like enclaves that multiply around the center as newly minted emblems of preservation. **6.14** Ironically, though itself new, the Generic City is encircled by a constellation of New Towns: New

Towns are like year-rings. Somehow, New Towns age very quickly, the way a five-year-old child develops wrinkles and arthritis through the disease called progeria. **6.15** The Generic City presents the final death of planning. Why? Not because it is not planned—in fact, huge complementary universes of bureaucrats and developers funnel unimaginable flows of energy and money into its completion; for the same money, its plains can be fertilized by diamonds, its mud fields paved in gold bricks … But its most dangerous *and* most exhilarating discovery is that planning makes no difference whatsoever. Buildings may be placed well (a tower near a metro station) or badly (whole centers miles away from any road). They flourish/perish unpredictably. Networks become overstretched, age, rot, become obsolescent; populations double, triple, quadruple, suddenly disappear. The surface of the city explodes, the economy accelerates, slows down, bursts, collapses. Like ancient mothers that still nourish titanic embryos, whole cities are built on colonial infrastructures of which the oppressors took the blueprints back home. Nobody knows where, how, since when the sewers run, the exact location of the telephone lines, what the reason was for the position of the center, where monumental axes end. All it proves is that there are infinite hidden margins, colossal reservoirs of slack, a perpetual, organic process of adjustment, standards, behavior; expectations change with the biological intelligence of the most alert animal. In this apotheosis of multiple choice it will never be possible again to reconstruct cause and effect. They work—that is all. **6.16** The Generic City's aspiration toward tropicality automatically implies the rejection of any lingering reference to the city as fortress, as citadel; it is open and accommodating like a mangrove forest. **7. Politics** **7.1** The Generic City has a (sometimes distant) relationship with a more or less authoritarian regime—local or national. Usually the cronies of the "leader"—whoever that was—decided to develop a piece of "downtown" or the periphery, or even to start a new city in the middle of nowhere, and so triggered the boom that put the city on the map. **7.2** Very often, the regime has evolved to a surprising degree of invisibility, as if, through its very permissiveness, the Generic City resists the dictatorial. **8. Sociology** **8.1** It is very surprising that the triumph of the Generic City has not coincided with the triumph of sociology—a discipline whose "field" has been extended by the Generic City beyond its wildest imagination. The Generic City *is* sociology, happening. Each Generic City is a petri dish—or an infinitely patient blackboard on which almost any hypothesis can be "proven" and then erased, never again to reverberate in the minds of its authors or its audience. **8.2** Clearly, there is a proliferation of communities—a sociological zapping—that resists a single overriding interpretation. The Generic City is loosening every structure that made anything coalesce in the past. **8.3** While infinitely patient, the Generic City is also persistently resistant to speculation: it proves that sociology may be the worst system to capture sociology in the making. It outwits each established critique. It contributes huge amounts of evidence for and—in even more impressive quantities—against each hypothesis. In A tower blocks lead to suicide, in B to happiness ever after. In C they are seen as a first stepping stone toward emancipation (presumably under some kind of invisible "duress," however), in D simply as passé. Constructed in unimaginable numbers in K, they are being exploded in L. Creativity is inexplicably high in E, nonexistent in F. G is a seamless ethnic mosaic, H perpetually at the mercy of separatism, if not on the verge of civil war. Model Y will never last because of its tampering with family structure, but Z flourishes—a word no academic would ever apply to any activity in the Generic City—because of it. Religion is eroded in V, surviving in W, transmuted in X. **8.4** Strangely, nobody has thought that cumulatively the endless contradictions of these interpretations prove the richness of the Generic City; that is the one hypothesis that has been eliminated in advance. **9. Quarters**

9.1 There is always a quarter called Lipservice, where a minimum of the past is preserved: usually it has an old train/tramway or double-decker bus driving through it, ringing ominous bells—domesticated versions of the Flying Dutchman's phantom vessel. Its phone booths are either red and transplanted from London, or equipped with small Chinese roofs. Lipservice—also called Afterthought, Waterfront, Too Late, 42nd Street, simply the Village, or even Underground—is an elaborate mythic operation: it celebrates the past as only the recently conceived can. It is a machine. **9.2** The Generic City had a past, once. In its drive for prominence, large sections of it somehow disappeared, first unlamented—the past apparently was surprisingly unsanitary, even dangerous—then, without warning, relief turned into regret. Certain prophets—long white hair, gray socks, sandals—had always been warning that the past was necessary—a resource. Slowly, the destruction machine grinds to a halt; some random hovels on the laundered Euclidean plane are saved, restored to a splendor they never had... **9.3** In spite of its absence, history is the major preoccupation, even industry, of the Generic City. On the liberated grounds, around the restored hovels, still more hotels are constructed to receive additional tourists in direct proportion to the erasure of the past. Its disappearance has no influence on their numbers, or maybe it is just a last-minute rush. Tourism is now independent of destination … **9.4** Instead of specific memories, the associations the Generic City mobilizes are general memories, memories of memories: if not all memories at the same time, then at least an abstract, token memory, a déjà vu that never ends, generic memory. **9.5** In spite of its modest physical presence (Lipservice is never more than three stories high: homage to/revenge of Jane Jacobs?) it condenses the entire past in a single complex. History returns not as farce here, but as *service*: costumed merchants (funny hats, bare midriffs, veils) voluntarily enact the conditions (slavery, tyranny, disease, poverty, colony) — that their nation once went to war to abolish. Like a replicating virus, worldwide, the colonial seems the only inexhaustible source of the authentic. **9.6** 42nd Street: ostensibly the places where the past is preserved, they are actually the places where the past has changed the most, is the most distant — as if seen through the wrong end of a telescope — or even completely eliminated. **9.7** Only the memory of former excess is strong enough to charge the bland. As if they try to warm themselves at the heat of an extinguished volcano, the most popular sites (with tourists, and in the Generic City that includes everyone) are the ones once most intensely associated with sex and misconduct. Innocents invade the former haunts of pimps, prostitutes, hustlers, transvestites, and to a lesser degree, artists. Paradoxically, at the same moment that the information highway is about to deliver pornography by the truckload to their living rooms, it is as if the experience of walking on these warmed-over embers of transgression and sin makes them feel special, alive. In an age that does not generate new aura, the value of established aura skyrockets. Is walking on these ashes the nearest they will get to guilt? Existentialism diluted to the intensity of a Perrier? **9.8** Each Generic City has a waterfront, not necessarily with water — it can also be with desert, for instance — but at least an edge where it meets another condition, as if a position of near escape is the best guarantee for its enjoyment. Here tourists congregate in droves around a cluster of stalls. Hordes of "hawkers" try to sell them the "unique" aspects of the city. The unique parts of all Generic Cities together have created a universal souvenir, scientific cross between Eiffel Tower, Sacre Coeur, and Statue of Liberty: a tall building (usually between 200 and 300 meters) drowned in a small ball of water with snow or, if close to the equator, gold flakes; diaries with pockmarked leather covers; hippie sandals — even if real hippies are quickly repatriated. Tourists fondle these — nobody has ever witnessed a sale — and then sit down in exotic eateries that line the waterfront: they run the full gamut of food today: *spicy*: first and ultimately maybe most reliable indication of being elsewhere; *patty*: beef or

TORTURE

An American historian has pointed out that the English word "travel" was originally the same word as "travail" (meaning "work" or "torment"). And travail, in turn, was derived from the Latin word "tripalium," which was a three-staked instrument for torture.

TOTALITY

The whole point of thinking in terms of totality is the realization that we are part of it.

TOUCHED

He dreamt it as active, warm, secret, the size of a closed fist, of garnet colour in the penumbra of a human body as yet without face or sex; with minute love he dreamt it, for fourteen lucid nights. Each night he perceived it with greater clarity. He did not touch it, but limited himself to witnessing it, observing it, perhaps correcting it with his eyes. He perceived it, lived it, from many distances and many angles. On the fourteenth night he touched the pulmonary artery with his finger, and then the whole heart, inside and out. The examination satisfied him.

TOURIST

A person who travels from place to place for nonwork reasons. By UN definition, a tourist is someone who stays for more than one night and less than a year. Business and convention travel is included. This thinking is dominated by balance-of-trade concepts. Military personnel, diplomats, immigrants, and resident students are not tourists.

TRAGEDY

I don't believe anyone will ever be able to make any city council understand that from an urbanistic point of view, the most attractive parts of the city are precisely those areas where nobody has ever done anything. I believe a city, by definition, *wants* to have something done in those areas. That is the tragedy.

TRANSLATION

Where does this urge for translation come from? I do not want a translation to be possible. That would be the end of any event, any signature, and so on and so forth. Nevertheless, there is translation. We can't repress this desire for translation. So why, at the same time, translate and not translate?

synthetic; *raw*: atavistic practice that will be very popular in the third millennium. **9.9** Shrimp is the ultimate appetizer. Through the simplification of the food chain—and the vicissitudes of preparation—they taste like english muffins, i.e., nothingness. **10. Program** **10.1** Offices are still there, in ever greater numbers, in fact. People say they are no longer necessary. In five to ten years we will all work at home. But then we will need bigger homes, big enough to use for meetings. Offices will have to be converted to homes. **10.2** The only activity is shopping. But why not consider shopping as temporary, provisional? It awaits better times. It is our own fault—we didn't think of anything better to do. The same spaces inundated with other programs—libraries, baths, universities—would be terrific; we would be awed by their grandeur. **10.3** Hotels are becoming the generic accommodation of the Generic City, its most common building block. That used to be the office—which at least implied a coming and a going, assumed the presence of other important accommodations *elsewhere*. Hotels are now containers that, in the expansion and completeness of their facilities, make almost all other buildings redundant. Even doubling as shopping malls, they are the closest we have to urban *existence*, 21st-century style. **10.4** The hotel now implies imprisonment, voluntary house arrest; there is no competing place left to go; you come and stay. Cumulatively, it describes a city of ten million all locked in their rooms, a kind of reverse animation—density imploded.

11. Architecture **11.1** Close your eyes and imagine an explosion of beige. At its epicenter splashes the color of vaginal folds (unaroused), metallic-matte aubergine, khaki-tobacco, dusty pumpkin; all cars on their way to bridal whiteness … **11.2** There are interesting and boring buildings in the Generic City, as in all cities. Both trace their ancestry back to Mies van der Rohe: the first category to his irregular Friedrichstadt tower (1921), the second to the boxes he conceived not long afterward. This sequence is important: obviously, after initial experimentation, Mies made up his mind once and for all against interest, for boredom. At best, his later buildings capture the spirit of the earlier work— sublimated, repressed?—as a more or less noticeable absence, but he never proposed "interesting" projects as possible buildings again. The Generic City proves him wrong: its more daring architects have taken up the challenge Mies abandoned, to the point where it is now hard to find a box. Ironically, this exuberant homage to the interesting Mies shows that "the" Mies was wrong. **11.3** The architecture of the Generic City is by definition beautiful. Built at incredible speed, and conceived at even more incredible pace, there is an average of 27 aborted versions for every realized—but that is not quite the term—structure. They are prepared in the 10,000 architectural offices nobody has ever heard of, each vibrant with fresh inspiration. Presumably more modest than their well-known colleagues, these offices are bonded by a collective awareness that something is wrong with architecture that can only be rectified through *their* efforts. The power of numbers gives them a splendid, shining arrogance. They are the ones who design without any hesitation. They assemble, from 1,001 sources, with savage precision, more riches than any genius ever could. On average, their education has cost 30,000 dollars, excluding travel and housing. 23% have been laundered at American Ivy League universities, where they have been exposed—admittedly for very short periods—to the well-paid elite of the other, "official" profession. It follows that a combined total investment of 300 billion dollars ($300,000,000,000) worth of architectural education ($30,000 [average cost] x 100 [average number of workers per office] x 100,000 [number of worldwide offices]) is working in and producing Generic Cities at any moment. **11.4** Buildings that are complex in form depend on the curtain-wall industry, on ever more effective adhesives and sealants that turn each building into a mixture of straitjacket and oxygen tent. The use of silicone—"we are stretching the facade as far as it will go"—has flattened all facades, glued glass to stone to steel to concrete in a space-age impurity. These connections give the appearance of intellectual rigor through the liberal application of a transparent spermy compound that keeps everything together by intention rather than design—a triumph of glue over the integrity of materials. Like everything else in the Generic City, its architecture is the resistant made malleable, an epidemic of yielding no longer through the application of principle but through the *systematic* application of the unprincipled. **11.5** Because the Generic City is largely Asian, its architecture is generally air-conditioned; this is where the paradox of the recent paradigm shift—the city no longer represents maximum development but borderline underdevelopment—becomes acute: the brutal means by which universal conditioning is achieved mimic inside the building the climatic conditions that once "happened" outside—sudden storms, mini-tornadoes, freezing spells in the cafeteria, heat waves, even mist; a provincialism of the mechanical, deserted by gray matter in pursuit of the electronic. Incompetence or imagination? **11.6** The irony is that in this way the Generic City is at its most subversive, its most ideological; it elevates mediocrity to a higher level; it is like Kurt Schwitter's *Merzbau* at the scale of the city: the Generic City is a *Merzcity*. **11.7** The angle of the facades is the only reliable index of architectural genius: 3 points for sloping backward, 12 points for sloping forward,

2-point penalty for setbacks (too nostalgic). **11.8** The apparently solid substance of the Generic City is misleading. 51% of its volume consists of atrium. The atrium is a diabolical device in its ability to substantiate the insubstantial. Its Roman name is an eternal guarantor of architectural class — its historic origins make the theme inexhaustible. It accommodates the cave-dweller in its relentless provision of metropolitan comfort. **11.9** The atrium is void space: voids are the essential building block of the Generic City. Paradoxically, its hollowness insures its very physicality, the pumping up of the volume the only pretext for its physical manifestation. The more complete and repetitive its interiors, the less their essential repetition is noticed. **11.10** The style of choice is postmodern, *and will always remain so*. Postmodernism is the only movement that has succeeded in connecting the practice of architecture with the practice of panic. Postmodernism is not a doctrine based on a highly civilized reading of architectural history but a method, a mutation in professional architecture that produces results fast enough to keep pace with the Generic City's development. Instead of consciousness, as its original inventors may have hoped, it creates a new unconscious. It is modernization's little helper. Anyone can do it — a skyscraper based on the Chinese pagoda *and/or* a Tuscan hill town. **11.11** All resistance to postmodernism is anti-democratic. It creates a "stealth" wrapping around architecture that makes it irresistible, like a Christmas present from a charity. **11.12** Is there a connection between the predominance of mirror in the Generic City — is it to celebrate nothingness through its multiplication or a desperate effort to capture essences on their way to evaporation? — and the "gifts" that, for centuries, were supposed to be the most popular, efficient present for savages? **11.13** Maxim Gorky speaks in relation to Coney Island of "varied boredom." He clearly intends the term as an oxymoron. Variety cannot be boring. Boredom cannot be varied. But the infinite variety of the Generic City comes close, at least, to making variety normal: banalized, in a reversal of expectation, it is repetition that has become unusual, therefore, potentially, daring, exhilarating. But that is for the 21st century. **12. Geography** **12.1** The Generic City is in a warmer than usual climate; it is on its way to the south — toward the equator — away from the mess that the north made of the second millennium. It is a concept in a state of migration. Its ultimate destiny is to be tropical — better climate, more beautiful people. It is inhabited by those who do not like it elsewhere. **12.2** In the Generic City, people are not only more beautiful than their peers, they are also reputed to be more even-tempered, less anxious about work, less hostile, more pleasant — proof, in other words, that there *is* a connection between architecture and behavior, that the city can make better people through as yet unidentified methods. **12.3** One of the most potent characteristics of the Generic City is the stability of its weather — no seasons, outlook sunny — yet all forecasts are presented in terms of imminent change and future deterioration: clouds in Karachi. From the ethical and the religious, the issue of doom has shifted to the inescapable domain of the meteorological. Bad weather is about the only anxiety that hovers over the Generic City. **13. Identity** **13.1** There is a calculated (?) redundancy in the iconography that the Generic City adopts. If it is water-facing, then water-based symbols are distributed over its entire territory. If it is a port, then ships and cranes will appear far inland. (However, showing the containers themselves would make no sense: you can't particularize the generic through the Generic.) If it is Asian, then "delicate" (sensual, inscrutable) women appear in elastic poses, suggesting (religious, sexual) submission everywhere. If it has a mountain, each brochure, menu, ticket, billboard will insist on the hill, as if nothing less than a seamless tautology will convince. Its identity is like a mantra. **14. History** **14.1** Regret about history's absence is a tiresome reflex. It exposes an unspoken consensus that history's presence is desirable. But who says that is the case? A city is a plane inhabited in the most efficient way by people and processes, and in most cases, the presence of history only drags down its performance … **14.2** History present obstructs the pure exploitation of its theoretical value as absence. **14.3** Throughout the history of humankind — to start a paragraph the American way — cities have grown through a process of consolidation. Changes are made on the spot. Things are improved. Cultures flourish, decay, revive, disappear, are sacked, invaded, humiliated, raped, triumph, are reborn, have golden ages, fall suddenly silent — all on the same site. That is why archaeology is a profession of *digging*: it exposes layer after layer of civilization (i.e., city). The Generic City, like a sketch which is never elaborated, is not improved but abandoned. The idea of layering, intensification, completion are alien to it: it *has* no layers. Its next layer takes place somewhere else, either next door — that can be the size of a country — or even elsewhere altogether. The archaeologue (= archaeology with more interpretation) of the 20th century needs unlimited plane tickets, not a shovel. **14.4** In exporting/ejecting its improvements, the Generic City perpetuates its own amnesia (its only link with eternity?). Its archaeology will therefore be the evidence of its progressive forgetting, the documentation of its evaporation. Its genius will be empty-handed — not an emperor without clothes but an archaeologist without finds, or a site even.

15. Infrastructure **15.1** Infrastructures, which were mutually reinforcing and totalizing, are becoming more and more competitive and local; they no longer pretend to create functioning wholes but now spin off functional entities. Instead of network and organism, the new infrastructure creates enclave and impasse: no longer the *grand récit* but the parasitic swerve. (The city of Bangkok has approved plans for three competing airborne metro systems to get from A to B — may the strongest one win.) **15.2** Infrastructure is no longer a more or less delayed response to a more or less urgent need but a strategic weapon, a prediction: Harbor X is not enlarged to serve a hinterland of frantic consumers but to kill/reduce the chances that harbor Y will survive the 21st century. On a single island, southern metropolis Z, still in its infancy, is "given" a new subway system to make established metropolis W in the north look clumsy, congested, and ancient. Life in V is smoothed to make life in U eventually unbearable. **16. Culture**
16.1 Only the redundant counts. **16.2** In each time zone, there are at least three performances of *Cats*. The world is surrounded by a Saturn's ring of meowing. **16.3** The city used to be the great sexual hunting ground. The Generic City is like a dating agency: it efficiently matches supply and demand. Orgasm instead of agony: there *is* progress. The most obscene possibilities are announced in the cleanest typography; Helvetica has become pornographic. **17. End** **17.1** Imagine a Hollywood movie about the Bible. A city somewhere in the Holy Land. Market scene: from left and right extras cloaked in colorful rags, furs, silken robes walk into the frame yelling, gesticulating, rolling their eyes, starting fights, laughing, scratching their beards, hairpieces dripping with glue, thronging toward the center of the image waving sticks, fists, overturning stalls, trampling animals... People shout. Selling wares? Proclaiming futures? Invoking Gods? Purses are snatched, criminals pursued (or is it helped?) by the crowds. Priests pray for calm. Children run amok in an undergrowth of legs and robes. Animals bark. Statues topple. Women shriek — threatened? Ecstatic? The churning mass becomes oceanic. Waves break. Now switch off the sound — silence, a welcome relief — and reverse the film. The now mute but still visibly agitated men and women stumble backward; the viewer no longer registers only humans but begins to note spaces between them. The center empties; the last shadows evacuate the rectangle of the picture frame, probably complaining, but fortunately we don't hear them. Silence is now reinforced by emptiness: the image shows empty stalls, some debris that was trampled underfoot. Relief... it's over. That is the story of the city. The city is no longer. We can leave the theater now... **1994**

TRANSPLANT

Sometime in the early '90s, the first human-gene transplant will take place that is part of a medical treatment, likely a last ditch effort to save a child born with a fatal genetic illness … As science learns to alter those genes, some profound questions will arise: What constitutes a disorder, as opposed to mere differences in personal characteristics? Should genetic engineers fix nearsightedness, say, or a propensity to put on weight or lose hair? And if so, why stop there? Do you want your baby to have blue eyes or brown, blond hair or dark? The '90s won't introduce technology capable of making such choices, but we may have to decide whether we want to work toward that goal.

TREE-HOUSE

Over the years a wandering path had been hacked through the dense jungle beneath the tree, leading to the twenty broad stairs rising steeply to the wraparound porch. It seemed the tree was the house, of primary permanence, all else was simple landscape, feckless man-made ornament.

TREES

These trees are magnificent, but even more magnificent is the sublime and moving space between them, as though with their growth it too increased.

TREE TRUNKS

For we are like tree trunks in the snow. In appearance they lie sleekly and a little push should be enough to set them rolling. No, it can't be done, for they are firmly wedded to the ground. But see, even that is only appearance.

TRICK

These are traditional roles that women play, and here I am doing them, but that's not really what I'm doing.

TRICKS

"I know some good games we could play," / Said the cat. / "I know some new tricks," / Said the Cat in the Hat. / "A lot of good tricks. I will show them to you. / Your mother / Will not mind at all if I do." Then Sally and I / Did not know what to say. Our mother was out of the house / For the day.

TRIUMPH

Fukuoka housing is triumph.

TROPICAL

Fred was afraid of the night, afraid his body would slip away from him, dissolved in that purple velvet with diamond eyes, the tropical night. The tropical night did not lie inert, like a painted film-set, but was filled with whisperings, and seemed to have arms like the foliage.

TRUE

And this was the first time that he was positively certain of being a true and no imaginary knight errant, since he found himself treated just as he had read these knights were treated in past ages.

TRUTH[1]

Delusion possesses, as long as it lasts, an insurmountable truth.

TRUTH[2]

What is truth?

TRUTH[3]

Beauty is truth, truth beauty.

TRUTH[4]

I always speak the truth. Not the whole truth because there's no way to say it all. Saying the whole truth is materially impossible: words miss it. Yet it's through this very impossibility that the truth holds onto the real.

TRUTH[5]

Truth — the truth undiluted would crush them. The truth has to be parcelled out slowly, and even then not straight.

TRUTH[6]

Truth is out of style.

TRUTH[7]

No, truth is something desperate, an' she's got it. Believe me, it's somethin' desperate, an' she's got it.

TUNNEL[1]

The train entered a tunnel, turning their small traveling room into a sleeping compartment. She felt him stretch across and touch her hand.

TUNNEL[2]

See AIR[1].

TUNNEL VISION

Tunnel vision is a disease in which perception is restricted by ignorance and distorted by vested interest. Tunnel vision is caused by an optic fungus that multiplies when the brain is less energetic than the ego. It is complicated by exposure to politics. When a good idea is run through the filters and compressors of ordinary tunnel vision, it not only comes out reduced in scale and value but in its new dogmatic configuration produces effects the opposite of those for which it originally was intended.

TURBULENCE[1]

What is turbulence then? It is a mess of disorder at all scales, small eddies within large ones. It is unstable. It is highly dissipative, meaning that turbulence drains energy and creates drag. It is motion turned random. But how does flow change from smooth to turbulent?

TURBULENCE[2]

See POOL[1].

TURN-AROUND

Today there are many forces at work that would repudiate all distinction between the commercial and the creative. The greater the denial of this distinction, the more the denier thinks he is droll, intelligent, and informed. In effect, the denier is simply conveying a requirement of capitalism: the quick turn-around.

TUTTI

I call *full tutti* the combination of all melodic groups, strings, wind, and brass. By *partial tutti* I mean passages in which the brass group only takes part, whether two horns or two trumpets participate alone, or whether two horns are combined with one or three trombones, without tuba, trumpets, or the two remaining horns, etc.

TV

He watched a very great deal of TV, always had done, years and years of it, aeons of TV. Boy, did Keith burn that tube. And that tube burnt him, nuked him, its cathodes crackling like cancer. "TV," he thought, or "Modern reality" or "The world." It was the world of TV that told him what the world was. How does all the TV time work on a modern person, a person like Keith? The fact that he would have passed up a visit to the Louvre or the Prado in favour of ten minutes alone with a knicker catalogue — this, perhaps, was a personal quirk. But TV came at Keith like it came at everybody else; and he had nothing whatever to keep it out. He couldn't grade or filter it. So he thought TV was real … Of course, some of it *was* real.

TWILIGHT

But in the suburbs, Toni went on … you are in a strange intermediate area of sexual twilight. You might think of the suburbs — Metroland, for instance — as being erotically soporific; yet the grand itch animated the most unlikely people … It was here, he maintained, that the really interesting bits of sex took place.

TYRANNY
Under which tyranny would you like to live? Under none, but if I had to choose I should detest less the tyranny of one than the tyranny of several. A despot always has some good moments, an assembly of despots never has any.

U

UGLY
You must know how to make the best of ugliness itself.

ULTIMATE
Traveltopia also offers what it calls "the ultimate tour for human beings," a seven-year, 100 million-yen custom-designed trip to wherever in the world a particular traveler's interests can most effectively be pursued.

ULTRA
Get out of my way! I feel ultra-crabby today! "Ultra" means "going beyond the usual limit … excessive … to an extreme degree."

ULTRA-WIDE
Our new sophisticates collection of full fashioned ultra-wide neckwear in all silk, hand blocked Maharajah prints from India that fairly radiate the hot sun colors of the sub-continent. Available in great 4¼″ ties and 36″ squares. At only the finest stores.

UNCERTAINTY[1]
I believe in uncertainty.

UNCERTAINTY[2]
In the subatomic world, the act of measurement changes the system being measured, giving rise to what is known as the Heisenberg Uncertainty Principle. The principle tells us that if we choose to measure one quantity (e.g., the position of an electron), we inevitably alter the system itself and therefore can't be certain about other quantities (e.g., how fast the electron is moving). Since an interaction is involved in every measurement, and since measurements are involved in observations, physicists sometimes say that

the act of observation changes the system.

UNCOMFORTABLE
You tackle a stairway face on, for if you try it backwards or sideways, it ends up being particularly uncomfortable.

UNCOOPERATIVE
Gropius may be wrong in believing that architecture is a cooperative art. Architects were not meant to design together; it's either all his work or mine.

UNDER
Under his elegant tailored coat and linen his muscles were hard, visibly swelling when he moved. He was everything a man should be.

UNDERSTANDING
A sentence given me in unfamiliar code together with the key for deciphering it. Then in a certain sense, everything required for the understanding of the sentence has been given me. And yet if I were asked whether I understood the sentence I should reply "I must first decode it" and only when I had it in front of me as an English sentence, would I say "now I understand it." If we raise the question "At what moment of translating into English does understanding begin?" we get a glimpse into the nature of what is called "understanding."

UNFASHIONABLE
No, thank you. Sugar is not fashionable anymore.

UNFINISHED

UNIFORM
One of the most English institutions is the English policeman, with his odd helmet reminiscent of the topees that sahibs used to wear in India. To an Englishman a motorised policeman with a flat-topped cap looks somehow less assuring, more likely to be an enemy, than one with a helmet.

UNITY
All the arts, all the sciences can be ordered in a continuous array or spectrum ranging from pure discovery to pure invention. That they are all at some point on this continuum gives them a common but fragile

thread, justifying our thinking and talking of the unity of the arts and sciences.

UNLESS
A long silence. Then Giulio was overcome with irrepressible, convulsive shivering.
"I will not, I must not betray death. I'll kill myself tonight."
"Unless?" cried Prampolini.
"Unless?" repeated Fillìa.
"Unless?" concluded Marinetti, "unless you take us instantly to your splendid, well-stocked kitchens."

UNRELIABLE
They change shape at their own will, he said. I would have no quarrel, I wouldn't grumble, you see, if these rooms would remain the same, would keep some consistency. But they didn't. And I can't see the boundaries, the limits, which I've been led to believe are natural. That's the trouble. I'm all for the natural behaviour of rooms, doors, staircases, the lot. But I can't rely on them.

UP
Consequently, these city bodies extended in general not in breadth, but more and more upwards.

URBANISM
Urbanism doesn't exist; it is only an ideology in Marx's sense of the word. Architecture does really exist, like Coca-Cola: Though coated with ideology, it is a real production, falsely satisfying a falsified need. Urbanism is comparable to the advertising propagated around Coca-Cola — pure spectacular ideology. Modern capitalism, which organized the reduction of all social life to a spectacle, is incapable of presenting any spectacle other than that of our own alienation. Its urbanistic dream is its masterpiece.

USELESS
For many who before my time had achieved the highest degree of culture available to them could find nothing year after year to do with their knowledge, and drifted uselessly about with the most splendid architectural plans in their heads, and sank by thousands into hopelessness.

UTOPIA
Place has two meanings: *topic* — rhetorical and poetic thoughts and formulae — and *topographic* — a

CHRONOLOGY

1972

Exodus, or the Voluntary Prisoners of Architecture

Final project at the Architectural Association School of Architecture, London; entry for *Casabella*'s competition "The City as Meaningful Environment," first prize *ex eaquo*. Rem Koolhaas, Elia Zenghelis with Madelon Vriesendorp, Zoe Zenghelis.

City of the Captive Globe

Project for Manhattan. Rem Koolhaas. Paintings: Madelon Vriesendorp, Zoe Zenghelis.

1974

House in Miami

Miami, Florida. *Progressive Architecture* Award, 1974. Site: double lot facing ocean in dense suburb. Program: house for a family of five and frequent guests. In 1976, Arquitectonica built their project on the same site. Rem Koolhaas, Laurinda Spear.

1975

Roosevelt Island Housing

New York, NY. Competition. Rem Koolhaas, Elia Zenghelis with Livio Dimitriu, Richard Perlmutter, Ron Steiner.

Hotel Sphinx

New York, NY. Elia Zenghelis, Zoe Zenghelis.

1976

The Story of the Pool

Rem Koolhaas, Madelon Vriesendorp.

Welfare Palace Hotel

New York, NY. Rem Koolhaas with Derrick Snare, Madelon Vriesendorp.

New Welfare Island

New York, NY. Rem Koolhaas with German Martinez, Richard Perlmutter, Zoe Zenghelis.

1978

Extension of the Dutch Parliament

The Hague, Netherlands. Competition, first prize *ex eaquo*. Site: 13th-century fortress/government complex in The Hague city center. Program (distributed over new and existing facilities): assembly for 225 members with public gallery for 100; accommo-

dation for over 13 political parties to meet in committee; conference center; 340 rooms for representatives and assistants; accommodation for services (stenographers, printing works, police, etc.); complex of three restaurants. Rem Koolhaas, Zaha Hadid, Elia Zenghelis with Richard Perlmutter, Ron Steiner, Elias Veneris.

1979

Residence for the Irish Prime Minister

Phoenix Park, Dublin, Ireland. Competition. Program: official and private residence for prime minister and family with reception rooms, offices, private garden; guest house with private bedroom suites, communal living-dining areas. Rem Koolhaas, Elia Zenghelis with Alan Forster, Stefano de Martino, Ron Steiner.

Study for the Renovation of a Panopticon Prison

Arnhem, Netherlands. Client: Netherlands Government Buildings Agency. Situation: panopticon prison on the Rhine built in 1880 for solitary confinement: 180-foot diameter, 150-foot dome, four floors of 50 cells; grounds cluttered with sheds to house additional activities. Program: renovation of prison; addition of new facilities for work, education, sports, leisure; administrative offices. Project I (1979–81): Rem Koolhaas, Stefano de Martino. Project II (1982–85): Rem Koolhaas, Mike Guyer with Thijs de Haan, Vahe Kalousdian, Brigitte Kochta, Victor Mani, Luc Reuse, Georg Ritschl, Karin Rühle.

Boompjes TowerSlab

Rotterdam, Netherlands. Study for Rotterdam waterfront development. Client: city of Rotterdam. Site: 120-meter wedge, 20–40 meters wide, between canal and riverfront highway. Program: apartments, parking, shops, hotel, offices; reuse of 110-meter Willemsbrug segment. Rem Koolhaas, Stefano de Martino with Kees Christiaanse, Gerard Comello, Jeroen Thomas.

1980

Housing Kochstrasse/ Friedrichstrasse

Berlin, Germany. Internationale Bauausstellung (IBA) competi-

tion. Site: four-block area along Berlin Wall. Program: general scheme for four-block area with detailed proposal for Block 4 for housing (one area of 56 units, one area of 18 units), manual trade center, checkpoint facilities. Rem Koolhaas, Stefano de Martino with Herman de Kovel, Richard Perlmutter, Ricardo Simonini, Ron Steiner, Alex Wall. Model: Batsheva Ronen.

Housing Lützowstrasse

Berlin, Germany. Internationale Bauausstellung (IBA) competition, third prize. Site: narrow triangular site in South Tiergarten quarter; bordered on the south by Lützowstrasse, a war-damaged street; with five rows of 3½-story private dwellings. Program: social housing. Elia Zenghelis with Norman Chang, Omri Eytan, Katerina Galani, Andreas Kourkoulas, Batsheva Ronen, Ricardo Simonini, Ron Steiner, Alex Wall, Zoe Zenghelis.

1981

Netherlands Dance Theater, Project I

Scheveningen, The Hague, Netherlands. Client: Stichting Nederlands Dans Theater. Site: between Circus Theater and tramway at The Hague seaside, within partially realized Bakema renewal project. New site designated (see Netherlands Dance Theater, Project II). Program: performance and rehearsal facilities (26,000 m³) for Dutch modern dance company. Budget: $6.5 million (fl. 13 million). Rem Koolhaas, Jan Voorberg with Arjan Karssenberg, Stefano de Mar-

tino, Willem-Jan Neutelings, Jeroen Thomas. Engineer: Stefan Polonyi, Polonyi & Finck.

Y-Plein Urban Planning

Amsterdam North, Netherlands. Completed 1988. Client: city of Amsterdam. Site: 16-hectare former shipyard north of Y River, facing Amsterdam's historic center. Program: master plan for neighborhood quarter: 1,375 dwellings, public space, recreational facilities, school, shops, community center. Rem Koolhaas, Jan Voorberg with Kees Christiaanse, Herman de Kovel. Precedent studies: Dolf Dobbelaar, Paul de Vroom.

Oost III Housing and Shops

Y-Plein, Amsterdam North, Netherlands. Completed 1988. Client: city of Amsterdam. Program: two apartment buildings (11,860 m², 4,560 m²); 202 housing units (two, three, four, five rooms); shops. Cost: $9 million (fl. 18 million). Rem Koolhaas, Kees Christiaanse with Tony Adam, Xaveer de Geyter, Thijs de Haan, Leo van Immerzeel, Arjan Karssenberg, Jeroen Thomas, Paul de Vroom. Contractor: Heijmans Bouw.

School and Gymnasium

Y-Plein, Amsterdam North, Netherlands. Completed 1986. Client: city of Amsterdam. Program: school (700 m²), gymnasium (455 m²), outdoor play area. Cost: $450,000 (fl. 900,000). Jan Voorberg with Tony Adam, Leo van Immerzeel, Frank Roodbeen, Ruurd Roorda, Jeroen Thomas. Extension: completed 1992 by Kingma and Roorda Architects.

Villas Antiparos

Antiparos, Greece. Site: slope toward beach on small island in Aegean archipelago. Program: summer villas (some equipped for winter use) for sale and rentals; to use traditional local construction methods and materials. Elia Zenghelis with Ron

Steiner, Katerina Tsigaridas.

Hotel Therma

Lesbos, Greece. Site: shore of Bay of Gera, surrounded by mountains. Program: 300-bed hotel, marina with independent commercial and leisure facilities, villas, beachside bungalows. Elia Zenghelis with Katerina Galani, Ron Steiner, Elias Veneris, Alex Wall.

1982

Police Station

Almere-Haven, Netherlands. Completed 1985. Site: 1970s New Town on last Dutch polder. Program: district police station (2,600 m²), prison cells, two squad "penthouses." Cost: $700,000 (fl. 1.4 million). Arjan Karssenberg, Jeroen Thomas.

Parc de la Villette

Paris, France. Two-part competition, first prize. Built by Bernard Tschumi. Site: 55-hectare former slaughterhouse area in northwestern Paris, bordered to the north by the Périphérique, with Science Museum in converted slaughterhouses and Grande Halle (survivor of market buildings). Program: "Park for the 21st Century" to include entertainment facilities (7,500 m²); cultural information center (300 m²);

Retrospective Exhibition, Architecture Museum, Basel, 1988.

fragment of space possessing its own unity and (often) its own name. The name is a "no place," i.e., the very place of the text: *Utopia is not a topography but a topic*. It is often said that it is an imaginary place. Rather it is an indetermined place. Better yet, it is the very indetermination of place.

VACUUM[1]
Demand a vacuum cleaner.

VACUUM[2]
Well, they say nature hates a vacuum, Big Daddy.

VADDING
The word is vadding. It's a verb and it means the physical invasion of building space, usually the space above the ceiling tiles. You can remove these tiles and crawl around through the wiring on the floor — vadding. Hackers occasionally invade buildings and engage in vadding. They get a ladder, go up there, and crawl around all night. They're mapping the telephone lines and the computer lines in the building. I find it quite heartening that vadding even exists and that there are people willing to do it.

VAMPIRE
He lives outside of time and, as such, has no history, no memory, nor is he bound by the conventions of daily life. He must live at that time when all else is dead, at night. He lives in a dreaded state of anticipation and anxiety which carries with it a profound emptiness and loneliness not remedial even by death for he cannot easily die. He must spend his time watching the lives of others who are unconscious of his very existence. He cannot stand his reflection because it reminds him of his situation. He cannot constitute himself as an "other" through the mirror phase. He is doomed to be what he is, he cannot change the fact that he does not exist. The mirror does not lie here, does not allow him that feeling of mastery and control essential even to adult survival. It insists on showing him precisely the state he is in.

kiosks for small shows, games, temporary exhibits (1,200 m²); discovery workshops (7,100 m²); discovery gardens (20,500 m²); greenhouses (10,000 m²); children's discovery spaces (11,200 m²); space for permanent exhibits (3,200 m²); theme gardens (30,500 m²); outdoor ice-skating rink (1,200 m²); playgrounds (60,000 m²); outdoor hard-surface sports facilities (10,000 m²); children's play areas (16,000 m²); bathing/water elements (10,250 m²); restaurants (5,000 m²); catering (3,300 m²); snack bars (2,000 m²); picnic areas (2,750 m²); reception zones (2,200 m²); day-care facilities (2,500 m²); urban services (500 m²); shops (300 m²); accessory rental (300 m²); market (6,000 m²); offices (500 m²); circulation (35,000 m²); maintenance (4,200 m²); fire, police, and technical services (1,000 m²); first aid (200 m²); lavatories (200 m²); parking (17,800 m²). Rem Koolhaas, Elia Zenghelis with Kees Christiaanse, Stefano de Martino, Ruurd Roorda, Ron Steiner, Jan Voorberg, Alex Wall. Landscape consultants: Claire and Michel

OMA: The First Decade, Boymans–van Beuningen Museum, Rotterdam, 1989.

Corajoud. Model: Chiel van der Stelt, Hans Werlemann.

1983

Exposition Universelle 1989
Paris, France. Client: French government. Sites: Citroën Cevennes in west, Bercy in east, on both sides of the Seine. Program: concept/master plan for the 1989 World's Fair; in west, sites for participating countries; in east, area for exhibition/demonstration of information

technologies. Expo canceled. Rem Koolhaas, Elia Zenghelis with Kees Christiaanse, Stefano de Martino, Willem-Jan Neutelings, Ron Steiner, Alex Wall.

1984

Netherlands Dance Theater, Project II
Spui, The Hague, Netherlands. Completed 1987. Client: Stichting Nederlands Dans Theater. Site: cultural complex (master plan: Carel Weeber) in city center; building to share single volume with concert hall (van Mourik Architects); behind 12-story hotel (Carel Weeber); on 7.5-meter grid of new parking garage. Program: 1,001-seat auditorium; 32 x 20 x 24–meter stage with 18 x 9–meter proscenium; 18 x 14 x 9–meter backstage; 22.5-meter stage tower; orchestra pit; three rehearsal studios; offices; restaurant; staff/dancers' lounge; cafeteria; sauna; pool; dressing rooms; costume workshops; set workshops. Volume: 54,000 m³. Cost: $7 million (fl. 14 million). Structure/materials: steel, aluminum, sheet rock, stucco, marble, gold leaf. Rem Koolhaas with Jaap van Heest, Dirk Hendriks, Wim Kloosterboer, Willem-Jan Neutelings, Frank Roodbeen, Ron Steiner, Jeroen Thomas, Frans Vogelaar. Interior consultant: Petra Blaisse. Lighting: Hans Werlemann. Bars, restaurant furniture: Victor Mani, Chiel van der Stelt, Boa Contractors. Mural: Madelon Vriesendorp. Curtain: Petra Blaisse, execution in collaboration with Theatex, Holland. Structural engineers:

Polonyi & Finck, Aronsohn Structural Engineers. Acoustics: de Lange, Booy, TNO. Mechanical engineer: van Toorenburg. Stage installations: Stakebrand. Contractors: Bouwcombinatie Spui, Wilma, HBG. Extension, completed 1990 (rehearsal facilities and dressing rooms in parking garage): Wim Kloosterboer, Jeroen Thomas, Leo van Immerzeel. Studio 3 Café, completed 1992 (conversion of studio into café): Wim Kloosterboer.

Checkpoint Charlie Housing

Berlin, Germany. Completed January 1990. Client: Berliner Eigenheimbau GmbH. Site: Friedrichstrasse, next to Checkpoint Charlie. Program: housing, US Army facilities, customs, small indoctrination center, bus concourse, parking, dressing rooms, lecture room. Area: apartments (600 m²), ground floor (900 m²), basement including garage (900 m²). Structure: reinforced concrete. Finishes: plaster, ceramic tiles, corrugated metal. Cladding: special paint finishes, exposed concrete. Cost: $4.2 million (DM 7.5 million). Elia Zenghelis, Matthias Sauerbruch with Dirk Alten, Barbara Burren, Reni Keller, Alex Wall. Structural engineers: Polonyi & Finck. Support in Berlin: Hans Kollhoff.

De Brink Apartments

Groningen, Netherlands. Completed 1988. Client: Geerlings Vastgoed. Site: intersection of two canals near historic center. Program: two apartment blocks. Floor area: 2 x 8,600 m². Budget: $2 million (fl. 4 million). Rem Koolhaas, Stefano de Martino with Georg Ritschl, Jeroen Thomas, Paul de Vroom, Alex Wall.

Villa Dall'Ava

St. Cloud, Paris, France. Completed 1991. Prix d'architecture du Moniteur, 1991. Client: M and Mme Boudet. Site: 650 m² in Paris *banlieue* sloping toward Seine and Bois de Boulogne. Program: "glass house" for a family of three, rooftop pool with view of Eiffel Tower, two "apartments" (parents, daughter). Floor area: 250 m². Budget: $500,000 (FF 3 million). Structure: concrete, steel columns under front apartment. Cladding: sell pilarguli slate; exposed concrete; corrugated aluminum; clear, green, and sandblasted glass. Sunscreens: perforated aluminum, bamboo. Roof: plastic perforated tiles, moss, wood deck along swimming pool. Floors: terrazzo, black marble, black epoxy, linoleum, parquet. Kitchen: flat and corrugated polyester, cabinets of underlayment with Formica niches. Stairs: sandblasted steel, aluminum. Walls: waxed plaster. Ceilings: exposed concrete, perforated sheetrock. Rem Koolhaas, Xaveer de Geyter, Jeroen Thomas. Model: Ron Steiner. Site supervisor: Loïc Richalet. Interior consultant, curtains: Petra Blaisse. Garden: Yves Brunier. Finishing: Hans Werlemann. Engineer: Marc Mimram. General contractor: Entreprise Mare, Paris.

Churchillplein Office Tower

Rotterdam, Netherlands. Competition, first prize. Site: block at busy intersection in Rotterdam city center, next to renovated 17th-century mansion and bank by Dudok. Program: 24,000 m² flexible office space, public facilities, parking. Rem Koolhaas with Kees Christiaanse, Jaap van Heest, Götz Keller, Jeroen Thomas. Consultants: Aronsohn Structural Engineers, Hiensch Company.

1985

Byzantium

Amsterdam, Netherlands. Completed 1991. Client: Parkstede (MBO, Bouwfonds, Ballast Nedam). Site: previously occupied by power plant, facing historical/entertainment center and Vondelpark. Program: offices (2,800 m²), housing (10,000 m² with 74 units of 100–180 m², 5 penthouses), shops (2,300 m²), parking (580 spaces). Budget: $36 million (fl. 72 million). Materials: glazed brick, aluminum, concrete. Rem Koolhaas, Kees Christiaanse, Ron Steiner with Jaap van Heest, Georges Heintz, Dirk Hendriks, Götz Keller, Marty Kohn, Georg Ritschl, Jeroen Thomas. Structural engineers: Grabowsky & Poort. Mechanical engineers: Deerns, De Boer & Post. Contractor: Ballast Nedam.

Bus Station

Rotterdam, Netherlands. Competition. Completed 1987. Client: Public Transport Authority. Site: square in front of Rotterdam Central Station where subway, bus, tram, taxi, automobile, and bicycle traffic meet. Program: shelter for waiting passengers, ticket and information offices, access to subway, personnel facilities, tram and bus stop. Floor area: 300 m². Budget: $1.3 million (fl. 2.6 million). Materials: colored concrete (roof), green glazed brick, glass planks. Rem Koolhaas, Karin Rühle with Jaap van Heest, Götz Keller, Jeroen Thomas. Structural engineers: Partners and Van Putten, Gemeentewerken. Contractor: Vereniging Dura Bedrijven.

House for Two Friends

Rotterdam, Netherlands. Completed 1988. Client: Joop Linthorst. Site: 500 m² on dike. Floor area: 250m². Cost: $175,000 (fl. 350,000). Structure: rein-

VAN GOGH

Take as an example the performance in the role of Vincent van Gogh given by Takizawa Osamu, the last of the famous actors who helped create the traditions of the modern theatre movement in Japan. In preparing the part he went all the way to France; he even walked on the roads along which van Gogh had trudged. And when Takizawa heard that an old chair belonging to the artist had been found, he had a copy of it made and put on the stage. Yet the van Gogh that the actor was to play was actually the one created by the playwright Miyoshi Juro in his *Man of Flame*. As Miyoshi himself is Japanese, and the van Gogh he created was a part of his own thought, then his van Gogh would not sit on such a chair. In fact, he might well sit on the floor, on a Japanese cushion. Yet, to the actors in our modern theatre, so anxious to recreate the illusion of reality, this kind of natural, unassuming approach would be seen as impossible. For them, if van Gogh were to sit on a frayed and dirty cotton cushion, he would revert to being Takizawa same and not the character he was playing. But, to me at least, a play such as *Man of Flame* can evoke only a van Gogh who is nothing if not very theatrically Japanese.

VANITY

Vanity! That's what it is … The vanity of appearing as an author!

VEDALAND

Another developer has picked Orlando for a project on an even higher plane: a 195-hectare theme park called Vedaland, scheduled to open in 1993. The Maharishi Mahesh Yogi, the saffron-robed Indian guru who brought transcendental meditation to the world (and to the Beatles), has teamed up with magician Doug Henning to produce a spiritual equivalent of gourmet TV dinners, a high-tech, fakery-filled playground, ostensibly to help put man in harmony with nature.

VENEERED

Vilitzer did not turn his head to observe his enemy the governor. He looked straight ahead. As for the governor, he ran the interrogations with relish and exhibited his finest

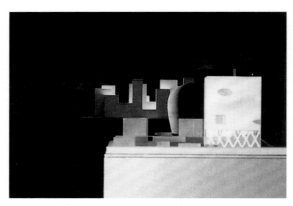

OMA: Fin de Siècle, Institut Français d'Architecture, Paris, 1990.

forced concrete, steel, wood. Materials: aluminum, glass, stucco, chipwood (interior wall), corrugated metal. Rem Koolhaas with Thijs de Haan, Georges Heintz, Götz Keller, Frank Roodbeen, Jeroen Thomas. Finishing: Jeroen Thomas, Hans Werlemann. Interior consultant, garden: Petra Blaisse.

Installation for the 1986 Milan Triennale
Rem Koolhaas, Frans Vogelaar, Alex Wall with Mike Guyer, Georges Heintz, Dirk Hendriks, Arjan Karssenberg.

Morgan Bank
Amsterdam, Netherlands. Competition. Client: Morgan Bank. Site: Apollolaan, boulevard in Berlage's extension plan, facing a small park. Program: bank/office building (10,000 m²), parking (46 cars), nine apartments (1,000 m²). Materials: dark gray granite "frame," marble "cut-out" entrance plaza, translucent glass-plank walls along garden. Rem Koolhaas, Götz Keller, Ron Steiner, Alex Wall, Elia Zenghelis with Kees Christiaanse, Xaveer de Geyter, Jaap van Heest, Georges Heintz, Karin Rühle. Interior consultant, entrance water garden: Petra Blaisse. Engineers: Cecil Balmond (structural) with Tudor Salisbury (mechanical), Ove Arup & Partners.

Parc Citroën Cevennes
Paris, France. Competition. Site: potential "arcadia" in urban area, bordered on one side by the Seine. Perimeter of site defined by existing and projected buildings. Previously site of Expo '89

project. Program: urban park. Elia Zenghelis with Eleni Gigantes, Georges Heintz, Matthias Sauerbruch, Alex Wall, Zoe Zenghelis. In collaboration with Claire and Michel Corajoud.

Bay of Koutavous Reconstruction
Argostoli, Greece. Client: Greek Ministry of Housing and Environment. Site: bay area of the Aegean island Cephalonia. Program: rejuvenation of bay area with parks and recreational facilities; bus station/boat rental facility, sports park, visitor information center, aquarium, marina. Elia Zenghelis with Stavros Aliferis, Jaap van Heest, Klaas Kingma, Ruurd Roorda, Matthias Sauerbruch, George Tombros, Elias Veneris, Alex Wall. Engineer: Dimitri Mantas.

1986

Uithof 2000
Utrecht, Netherlands. Master plan for University of Utrecht campus. Client: Universiteit Utrecht. Site: 240-hectare university campus in rural surroundings outside ring road east of city center. Program: phase I: three high schools (50,000 m² each), housing for 1,000 students, extension to academic hospital, new children's hospital, sports center, Educatorium (lecture/study facility); phase II: university library, relocation of law school from city center, various extensions to existing facilities. Preliminary design: Rem Koolhaas, Xaveer de Geyter, Willem-Jan Neutelings, Art Zaaijer. Realization: Art Zaaijer in collaboration with OMA.

Bijlmermeer Redevelopment

Amsterdam, Netherlands. Client: city of Amsterdam. Site: 1970s social-housing district in southeast Amsterdam with honeycomb layout of 11-story slabs based on 1930s CIAM principles; parking silos along highway, "interior" streets, shopping center beneath elevated roads, elevated metro line, parks; neglected and vandalized. Program: general renewal as alternative to proposed demolition. Rem Koolhaas with Yves Brunier, Xaveer de Geyter, Mike Guyer, Marty Kohn, Karin Rühle, Art Zaaijer.

The Hague City Hall

The Hague, Netherlands. Competition (OMA replaced Stirling Wilford halfway through 16-week design period), first prize. Commission later given to Richard Meier & Partners. Site: triangular wedge in city center of The Hague between historic city and new center, dominated by large seventies slabs; between OMA's Netherlands Dance Theater and the Binnenhof, site of the 1978 Parliament competition. Program: new city hall and central library (150,000 m²). Projected building cost: $175 million (fl. 350 million). Rem Koolhaas, Götz Keller, Willem-Jan Neutelings with Brigitte Kochta, Marty Kohn, Luc Reuse, Ron Steiner, Jeroen Thomas, Garciella Torre. Models: Herman Helle, Ron Steiner. Engineers: ABT; Cecil Balmond (structural) with John Berry (services), Ove Arup & Partners; Ketel Installateurs; Staalcentrum Nederland.

1987

Kunsthal I and II

Rotterdam, Netherlands. Project II completed October 1992. Site: 60 x 60–meter square along dike between major boulevard and southern edge of Museum Park (Boymans–van Beuningen Museum and Architecture Institute on northern side); next to Nature Museum; crossed by a secondary road. Program: hall for temporary exhibitions with three major exhibition spaces (1250 m², 1,000 m², and 640 m²), gallery (300 m²), auditorium (600 m²), independent restaurant (600 m²), offices (800 m²), seminar rooms. Total floor area: 7,000 m². Cost: $15 million (fl. 30 million). Structure: concrete, steel. Materials: black concrete, white concrete, travertine, glass, glass planks, corrugated polyester, wood, tree trunks, corrugated plastic. Project I: Rem Koolhaas, Ron Steiner, Gregor Mescherowsky. Project II: Rem Koolhaas, Fuminori Hoshino with Tony Adam, Isaac Batenburg, Leo van Immerzeel, Herman Jacobs, Eduardo Arroyo Munoz, Jim Njoo, Marc Peeters, Ron Steiner, Jeroen Thomas. Interior consultant: Petra Blaisse. Auditorium curtain: Petra Blaisse, James Rubery (sound), execution in collaboration with Theatex, Holland. Auditorium lighting: Hans Werlemann. Roof garden: Petra Blaisse. Restaurant ceiling, murals: Gunter Förg. Engineers: Cecil Balmond (structural) with Mirvat Bulbul (structural), Mohsen Zikri (mechanical), Mike Booth (electrical), Ove Arup & Partners; Gemeentewerken. Acoustics: TNO.

Ville Nouvelle Melun-Sénart

France. Competition; first prize: Coop Himmelblau. Site: 5,000-hectare, predominantly rural area south of Paris, to be developed as last New Town around Paris. Program: residential neighborhoods; industrial parks; infrastructure for educational, recreational, and cultural development; preservation of existing farmland and roads. Rem Koolhaas, Yves Brunier, Xaveer de Geyter, Mike Guyer. In collaboration with DBW: Yves Bories, Françoise Debuyst, Patrick Chavanne. Model: Herman Helle.

1988

Biocenter

University of Frankfurt, Germany. Competition. Client: University of Frankfurt. Site: 35,000 m² rural area to be developed as university campus. Program: laboratories, three lecture halls, library, restaurant, open-air theater, greenhouse, bicycle storage. Rem Koolhaas, Dirk Alten, Xaveer de Geyter, Alex Wall with Christian Delius, Christian Rapp, Luc Reuse, Edith Winkler. Engineers: Cecil Balmond (structural) with Mohsen Zikri (mechanical), Ove Arup & Partners.

Scientopia

Rotterdam, Netherlands. Client: city of Rotterdam. Site: Mueller Pier (5,000 m² obsolete harbor facility near city center). Program: science park for permanent and temporary exhibitions. Rem Koolhaas, Xaveer de Geyter, Yves Brunier.

skills, perfected in the courtroom. Before grand juries he must have been a formidable examiner—he was so big, sleek, thick in the throat, so smoothly groomed, fine as silk before the cameras but rough as hell in the interior.

VERTIGO

Not to be a man, to be the projection of another man's dream, what a feeling of humiliation, of vertigo! All fathers are interested in the children they have procreated (they have permitted to exist) in mere confusion or pleasure; it was natural that the magician should fear for the future of that son, created in thought, limb by limb and feature by feature in a thousand and one secret nights.

VERY

It's quite beautiful; it's either very great or very, very bad.

VIEW[1]

I like a view but I like to sit with my back turned to it.

VIEW[2]

The time for reflection is also the chance for turning back on the very conditions of reflection, in all senses of that word, as if with the help of a new optical device one could finally see sight, one could not only view the natural landscape, the city, the bridge and the abyss, but could view viewing.

VIEW[3]

The spectacular view always made Laing aware of his ambivalent feelings for this concrete landscape. Part of its appeal lay all too clearly in the fact that this was an environment built, not for man, but for man's absence.

VIOLENCE

With intellectuals, an astounding dullness in the eyes is often evident that comes not least of all from the continual violence done to the eyes by having to read things the eyes would not accept if they had their own way.

VIOLENT HUNGER

It is indecent to express any strong degree of those passions which arise from a certain situation or disposition of the body; because the company, not being in the same disposition, cannot be expected to sympathise with them. Violent hunger, for example, though upon many occa-

Architecture Museum

Rotterdam, Netherlands. Competition; first prize: Jo Coenen. Client: Nederlands Architectuur Institut. Site: triangle diagonally across from Boymans–van Beuningen Museum, facing Museum Park. Program: institute/museum to house Dutch architectural archives (drawings, models, etc.), facilities for permanent and temporary exhibitions (750 m², 300 m², 200 m², 130 m²), library, restaurant, auditorium. Materials: clear glass, green glass, corrugated polyester, chain-link sunblock curtain, concrete, travertine, silk. Rem Koolhaas, Xaveer de Geyter, Luc Reuse, Ron Steiner with Gregor Mescherowsky, Alexander Nowotny, Jeroen Thomas. Engineers: Cecil Balmond (structural) with Mirvat Bulbul (structural), Ove Arup & Partners. Model: Parthesius & de Rijk and Ron Steiner.

mann. Coordination, finance: Donald van Dansik. Models: Parthesius & de Rijk, Cor van der Hout, Ron Steiner, Kappers Trimensi, Chiel van der Stelt and Hans Werlemann. Sponsored by the Netherlands Ministry of Health, Welfare, and Cultural Affairs.

Renovation of Hotel Furka Blick

Furka Pass, Switzerland. Completed 1991. Client: Marc Hostetler. Situation: hotel built 1892 at summit of Furka Pass (altitude: 2,348 meters; accessible only in summer) as ten-room travelers' cottage; extension 1902 (27 rooms, kitchen, dining); reopened 1980 as artists' retreat/ tourist hotel; original conditions preserved. Program: new restaurant/bar with terrace, modernization of basement kitchen with "robot" connection to restaurant,

OMA: Fin de Siècle, Institut Français d'Architecture, Paris, 1990.

The Highway Projects

Studies for "150 kilometer-per-hour" buildings. Clients: Geerlings Vastgoed, Wilma Bouw, Multi Vastgoed. Site: four sites along or near highways in Scheveningen (The Hague), Arnhem, Oosterflank (near Rotterdam), and Rijnsweert (near Utrecht). Program: offices, housing. Rem Koolhaas, Jaap van Heest, Wim Kloosterboer, Luc Reuse, Ron Steiner, Jeroen Thomas.

Retrospective Exhibition

Architecture Museum, Basel, Switzerland. Design, installation: Petra Blaisse and Hans Werle-

new entrance. Budget: $500,000 (CHF 740,000). Rem Koolhaas, Jeroen Thomas with Maartje Lammers, Luc Reuse. Finishing: Hans Werlemann.

Euro Disney Hotels

Marne-la-Vallée, France. Competition. Client: Walt Disney Corp. Site: lakeside, 10–11 hectare area at Euro Disney. Programs: 500-room "motel"; 1,100-room hotel with two restaurants, snack bar, lounge, two meeting rooms, shops, pool, recreation facilities and health club, parking. Rem Koolhaas, Xaveer de Geyter, Luc Reuse, Ron Steiner, Alex Wall.

Netherlands Sports Museum

Flevohof, Netherlands. Client: Nederlands Sport Museum. Site: 5,000 m² along highway. Program: exhibition space for sports memorabilia, temporary exhibition space, library, video archives, sports and demonstration hall, auditorium, cafeteria, facilities for various indoor and outdoor sports activities (baseball, golf, mountaineering, cross-country skiing, swimming). Budget: $5 million (fl. 10 million). Rem Koolhaas, Luc Reuse.

Euralille: Centre International d'Affaires

Lille, France. Master plan, public spaces, general architectural supervision. Phase I completed 1994; phase II projected completion: 2005. Antonio Gaudí Prize, Olympic Awards, 1992. Client: Euralille public-private partnership. Site: 70 hectares in 1994, 120 hectares in 2005; east of the historic city formerly dominated by Vauban's 19th-century fortifications (now a highway), railroads, elevated motorways, and new TGV station; to become (with channel tunnel and TGV) the new center of the London-Paris-Brussels triangle. Program (phase I): investment: FF 5.2 billion ($865 million). 1. Le Centre Euralille (Triangle des Gares). By Jean Nouvel–Emmanuel Cattani and Associates. Clients: SNCF, Lille 93 (SOFAP, Groupe George V, Marignan Immobilier), Euralille. 236,600 m² with commercial center (92,000 m² leasable space with 31,000 m² sales space) including 130 shops, hypermarket (12,000 m²), 11 department stores; restaurants (5,250 m2); sports and recreation (5,900 m²); education (18,570 m²); Aeronef music theater (2,455 m²); public-private services (4,000 m²); professional services (17,538 m²); housing (13,566 m²); parking (81,600 m²: 3,400 places on two levels). Investment: FF 1.4 billion. 2. La Gare Lille-Europe. By Jean-Marie Duthilleul, SNCF. Client. SNCF. TGV station for 15,000 passengers per day in 1995; six tracks, two platforms, three pedestrian levels for 24 daily TGV connections to London, Brussels, Lyon, south of France. Investment: FF 270 million. 3. World Trade Center. By Claude Vasconi. Client: SCI, Cofracib Nord, SECL. Office tower (25,124

m²); atrium (15,449 m²): offices, exposition space, club, restaurant, etc. Investment: FF 530 million. 4. Tour Crédit Lyonnais. By Christian de Portzamparc. Client: Group George V, Crédit Lyonnais. 14,600 m² offices. Investment: FF 270 million. 5. FEVA. 8,500 m² center for architectural exhibition and research. 6. Four-Star Hotel. By François and Marie Delhay. Client: Cofracib Nord. 11,000 m², 204 rooms. Investment: FF 200 million. 7. Congrexpo (Lille Grand Palais). By OMA and François Delhay. Client: city of Lille, SAEM Euralille, Lille Grand Palais. 45,500 m² with Congress (meeting space, 18,000 m²), Zenith (rock theater, 7,500 m²), and Expo (exposition space, 20,000 m²). Investment: FF 350 million. 8. Le Parc Urbaine. By Empreinte in association with Gilles Clément, Claude Courtecuisse. 10 hectares. 9. Complementary infrastructure: (1) Parking between TGV station and *boulevard périphérique* (32,880 m², 1,370 places) by Antoine Béal and Ludovic Blanckaert; client: Euralille. (2) Metro station at Gare Lille-Europe by Martine and Jean Pattou; client: CUDL. (3) Tram station at Gare Lille-Europe by Thierry Grislain, Martine Proy; client: CUDL. (4) Viaduct Le Corbusier (172 meters long) by François Deslaugiers in association with Antoine Béal and Ludovic Blanckaert. Design sem-

inar, 1988: Rem Koolhaas, Donald van Dansik, Xaveer de Geyter, Georges Heintz, Willem-Jan Neutelings, Luc Reuse, Alex Wall, Art Zaaijer. Engineers: Cecil Balmond, Ove Arup & Partners. Collaborators, 1988–94: Rem Koolhaas, Donald van Dansik, Floris Alkemade with Age Alberts, Edzo Bindels, Eric van Daele, Richard Eelman, Douglas Grieco, Hassan Karamine, Jan-Willem van Kuilenburg, Alexander Lamboly, Mei-Ling Leung, Christine Machynia, Isabelle Menu, Eduardo Arroyo Munoz, Jim Njoo, Loes Oudenaarde, Karin Penning, Luc Reuse, Mark Schendel, Karolien de Schepper, Marleen Vink, Sarah Whiting, William Wilson, Stefan Witteman, Art Zaaijer. Engineers: Cecil Balmond (structure), Alain Marcetteau (geotechnics), Ahmed Bouariche (traffic), David Johnston (infrastructure), Ove Arup & Partners.

1989

Sea Terminal

Zeebrugge, Belgium. Competition, first prize. Site: pier at Zeebrugge harbor (on Belgian coast) extending three kilometers out to sea; departure/arrival point for channel ferries; landscape of mostly industrial forms. Program: terminal; customs; automobile, truck, and bus access; parking; hotel; conference center; entertainment facilities; casino. Rem Koolhaas, Xaveer de Geyter,

Jaap van Heest, Eric van Daele with Ramon Klein, Wim Kloosterboer, Maartje Lammers, Luc Reuse, Ron Steiner, Yushi Uehara. Engineers: Cecil Balmond (structural), Harry Saradjian (planning), Bob Cather (R & D), Ove Arup & Partners. Facade consultant: Frans de la Haye. Model: Parthesius & de Rijk with OMA. Plaster model: Parthesius & de Rijk.

Museum Park

Rotterdam, Netherlands. Completed 1994. Client: city of Rotterdam. Site: 12-hectare passageway linking city center to Rotterdam's Central Park; between Boymans–van Beuningen Museum, Kunsthal, and Architecture Museum. Program: urban park that can also accommodate passing shows/events. Budget: $2 million (fl. 4 million). Yves Brunier, Petra Blaisse, Rem Koolhaas with Tony Adam, Maartje Lammers, Gregor Mescherowsky.

Nexus World Housing

Kashii District, Fukuoka, Japan. Completed 1991. The Architectural Institute of Japan Prize for Best Building in Japan, 1991. Client: Fukuoka Jisho Co., Ltd. Site: part of Arata Isozaki's master plan for housing development at edge of Fukuoka City; plots of 1,791 m² and 1,706 m² in front of two future apartment towers by Isozaki. Program: 24 apartments, four shops, parking. Built area:

sions not only natural, but unavoidable, is always indecent; and to eat voraciously is universally regarded as a piece of ill manners.

VIRTUAL REALITY

A sound, smell and tactility-enhanced total video environment constructed of elaborate, flexible, interactive architectures that one may not only inhabit but actually move through, alter and invent. One inhabits virtual reality in real time, along with any number of others, by means of an electronic analog or deputy self through which all interactions are mediated. VR is not a simulated environment, but a new space altogether, made possible by telephones, data banks, computer graphics, and television.

VISIBILITY[1]

Maupassant often lunched at the restaurant in the Tower, though he didn't care much for the food: *It's the only place in Paris*, he used to say, *where I don't have to see it.* And it's true that you must take endless precautions, in Paris, not to see the Eiffel Tower; whatever the season, through mist and cloud, on overcast days or in sunshine, in rain — wherever you are, whatever the landscape of roofs, domes, or

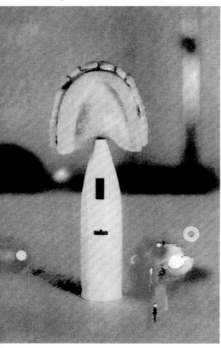

3,315 m² and 3,144 m². Cost: $15 million (¥1.4 billion). Structure: reinforced concrete. Major materials: black concrete wall, zinc roof, aluminum, various kinds of glass. Rem Koolhaas, Fuminori Hoshino with Jaap van Heest, Leo van Immerzeel, Shin-ichi Kanefuji, Ramon Klein, Maartje Lammers, Marc Peeters, Ron Steiner. Interior (model apartment): Kyoko Hoshino, Petra Blaisse. Local architect: Yoshikazu Kawamura. General contractor, structural consultants: Maeda Corp.

OMA: The First Decade

Exhibition, Boymans–van Beuningen Museum, Rotterdam, Netherlands. Design, direction, installation: Petra Blaisse and Hans Werlemann. Coordination, finance: Donald van Dansik. Video technique, sound: Claudi Cornaz, Hans Werlemann. Photography: Hectic Pictures. Models: OMA, Parthesius & de Rijk, Herman Helle, Cor van der Hout, Kappers Trimensi. With additional help from Eric van Daele, Ramon Klein, Luc Reuse, Jennifer Sigler, Art Zaaijer. Sponsors: Boymans–van Beuningen Museum; Cultuurfonds Bouwfonds Nederlands Gemeenten; Netherlands Architecture Institute; Geerlings Building Development; Netherlands Ministry of Welfare, Health, and Cultural Affairs; Multi-Vastgoed; Capi-Lux photographic services.

Zentrum für Kunst und Medientechnologie (Center for Art and Media Technology)

Karlsruhe, Germany. Competition, first prize. Construction canceled 1992. Client: Center for Art and Media Technology. Site: long narrow plot between railway lines and ring road, at edge of baroque city center. Program: 20,000 m² art and media center to include laboratories for sound, computer, and video (2 x 1,600 m²); media theater (1,500 m²); media museum and museum for contemporary art (4 x 1,000 m²); library (400 m²); lecture hall (500 m²); offices (7 x 200m²). Budget: $60 million (DM 108 million). Competition design: Rem Koolhaas, Heike Lohmann, Georges Heintz, Alex Wall with Christophe Cornubert, Rients Dijkstra, Xaveer de Geyter, Mark

Schendel, Ron Steiner. Engineers: Cecil Balmond, Ove Arup & Partners. Preliminary design: Rem Koolhaas, Wim Kloosterboer, Jacob van Rijs, Jeroen Thomas with Christian Basset, Ruud Cobussen, Marion Goerdt, Maartje Lammers, Heike Lohmann, Laura Weeber. Definitive design: Rem Koolhaas, Sven Ollmann, Jacob van Rijs, Christophe Cornubert with Frans Blok, Gro Bonesmo, Eric Carlson, Christine Enzmann, Kyoko Hoshino, Farshid Moussavi, Karin Penning, Markus Röthlisberger, Ron Steiner, Alejandro Zaera. Engineers: Cecil Balmond (structural), David Lewis (structural), Ove Arup & Partners. Local architect: Obermeyer.

Project for an Office City

Frankfurt Airport, Germany. Competition, first prize. Site: next to future (1994) airport terminal; bound by 16-lane *Autobahn*, secondary roads, future airport monorail; 28-meter height limit; occupied by office building (to be preserved). Program: offices. Rem Koolhaas, Eric van Daele, Luc Reuse, Ron Steiner. Models: Parthesius & de Rijk with Ron Steiner.

Très Grande Bibliothèque (Very Big Library)

Paris, France. Competition, honorable mention; commission to Dominique Perrault. Site: 250 x 300–meter rectangle in eastern part of Paris on left bank of Seine; faces (on right bank) sports arena, future Park de Bercy (to be linked to library site with pedestrian bridge), Ministry of Finance; 35-meter height limit. Program: Bibliothèque de France, Mitterrand's last *grand projet*; sound and moving image library/cinemathèque, recent acquisitions library (books, films, videos), reference library, catalog library, scientific research library. Area: 250,000 m². Rem Koolhaas, Art Zaaijer, Xaveer de Geyter, Georges Heintz, Heike Lohmann, Ron Steiner, Alex Wall with Christophe Cornubert, Ramon Klein, Yushi Uehara. Engineers: Cecil Balmond (structural), Mohsen Zikri (mechanical), Ove Arup & Partners. Competition model: Parthesius & de Rijk with OMA. Plaster models: Parthesius & de Rijk.

Sports Complex

Groningen, Netherlands. Client: city of Groningen. Site: future park between two suburbs near highway. Program: sports center with ice rink, indoor/outdoor swimming pool, indoor/outdoor tennis courts, sauna, locker rooms. Budget: $12.5 million (fl. 25 million). Rem Koolhaas, Eric van Daele, Winy Maas, Mark Schendel, Yushi Uehara.

Stad aan de Stroom

Antwerp, Belgium. Planning competition. Client: city of Antwerp. Site: ring road around city. Program: design for "inhabitation" of major infrastructural zone. Rem Koolhaas, Winy Maas, Ron Steiner, Yushi Uehara with Elizabeth Alford, Xaveer de Geyter, Kyoko Hoshino, Vince Scirano.

Video Bus Stop

Groningen, Netherlands. Project for exhibition "What a Wonderful World! Music Videos in Architecture." Completed 1991. Client: city of Groningen. Budget: $30,000 (fl. 60,000). Rem Koolhaas, Christian Basset.

1990

OMA: Fin de Siècle

Exhibition, Institut Français d'Architecture, Paris, France. Design, direction, installation: Petra Blaisse and Hans Werlemann. Coordination, finance: Donald van Dansik. Introduction collage: Petra Blaisse and Jennifer Sigler. Models: OMA, Herman Helle, Parthesius & de Rijk, Chiel van der Stelt and Hans Werlemann. Sound: Het Paleis van Boem. Technical installation: Claudi Cornaz and Hans Werlemann. Photography: Hectic Pictures. Graphic design (room 4): Hard Werken. Sponsors: First Europe (Group Pierre Premier); Netherlands Foundation for Fine Arts, Design, and Architecture, Amsterdam; Philips; Apple Computer. With special help from IFA, Theatex, Holland Ridderkerk.

OMA: Recent Work

Exhibition, Musée des Beaux-Arts, Lille, France. Design, direction, installation: Petra Blaisse and Hans Werlemann. Coordination, finance: Donald van Dansik.

Models: Herman Helle, Parthesius & de Rijk, OMA, Chiel van der Stelt and Hans Werlemann. Graphic design: Jos Stoopman. Slide show: Jennifer Sigler. Photography: Hectic Pictures. Sound: Het Paleis van Boem. Sound system, technical installations: Claudi Cornaz. Sponsors: First Europe (Groupe Pierre Premier); Netherlands Foundation for Fine Arts, Design, and Architecture, Amsterdam; Philips; Apple Computer; les Services Techniques de la Ville de Lille; Le Service de la Communication et de l'Information Municipale; Rabot-Dutilleul, Lille; Reprocolor, Lille; CRRAV secteur vidéo, Lille.

Energieen (Energies)

Group exhibition, Stedelijk Museum, Amsterdam. Organized by Wim Beeren, director. Artists included: Luciano Fabro, Gary Hill, Jenny Holzer, Anselm Kiefer, Rem Koolhaas, Jeff Koons, Walter de Maria, Issey Miyake, Bruce Nauman, Sigmar Polke, Rob Scholte, Cindy Sherman, Ettore

Sottsass, Frank Stella, Peter Struycken, Robert Wilson. OMA installation: Très Grande Bibliothèque. Design, installation: Petra Blaisse and Hans Werlemann. Text and image preparation: Jennifer Sigler. Models: Parthesius & de Rijk.

Palm Bay Seafront Hotel and Convention Center

Agadir, Morocco. Competition. Client: Palm Bay Company. Site: earthquake-prone dunes; end of axis from city center to seaside. Program: conference center, auditorium, exhibition space, 100-suite hotel, royal suites, parking. Rem Koolhaas, Winy Maas with Elizabeth Alford, Xaveer de Geyter, Ray Maggiore, Vince Scirano, Ron Steiner, Yushi Uehara. Engineers: Cecil Balmond (structural), Reiner Barthel (structural), Ove Arup & Partners. Models: Parthesius & de Rijk with Ron Steiner.

Hilton Hotel

The Hague, Netherlands. Study. Client: Van Cogg Group. Site:

Energieen, Stedelijk Museum, Amsterdam, 1990.

branches separating you from it, *the Tower is there*; incorporated into daily life until you can no longer grant it any specific attribute, determined merely to persist, like a rock or the river, it is as literal as a phenomenon of Nature whose meaning can be questioned to infinity but whose existence is incontestable.

VISIBILITY[2]
Visibility is a trap.

VISION
Transparency is achieved not by means of a single, privileged position but by the interpenetration of diverse points, that is, solely through the transformation of vision.

VOICE[1]
Well when you are all alone alone in the woods even if the woods are lovely and warm and there is a blue chair which can never be any harm, even so if you hear your own voice singing or even just talking well hearing anything even if it is all your own like your own voice is and you are all alone and you hear your own voice then it is frightening.

VOICE[2]
I've tried to drown myself in work, but I always come back to the surface in spite of myself, with a strange voice telling me I've forgotten something important.

VOID
See **AVOID**.

VOIDS
Voids in building sand amount to a third of the whole volume and must be filled to make the mix workable. To fill the voids with a binder, producing a mix of 1:3, would result in too strong a material in many cases. The quantity of binder is therefore reduced and made up by the addition of lime, e.g., 1 part cement: 2 parts lime: 9 parts sand.

VOLUME
Put PowerVox IV in your shirt pocket and realize to your amazement that you can hear whispered conversations up to 50 feet away, a pin drop 10 feet away, and even hear what people are talking about in the next room. A walk through the woods will reveal birds, deer, squirrels and even little crawly things that you never would have known about otherwise.

VOMIT
1. To disgorge the stomach contents.

Grote Marktstraat, busiest shopping street in The Hague. Program: 150-room hotel, convention hall, two restaurants, parking, shops. Budget: $21 million (fl. 42 million). Rem Koolhaas, Shin-ichi Kanefuji, Hassan Karamine, Winy Maas, Sarah Whiting.

Souterrain
The Hague, Netherlands. Projected completion: 1999. Client: city of The Hague. Site: 1,200-meter-long underground strip beneath Grote Marktstraat, The Hague's busiest shopping street. Program: parking garage for ±500 cars, two subway stations, tunnel for tram and subway, service street, lateral connections to existing and future parking facilities and department stores. Floor area: 16,500 m². Budget: $150 million (fl. 300 million). Materials: concrete, resins, wood, glass. Rem Koolhaas, Rients Dijkstra, René Heijne with Hernando Arrazola, Juliette Bekkering, Frans Blok, Udo Garritzmann, Jeanne Gang, Douglas Grieco, Fuminori Hoshino, Winy Maas, Ray Maggiore, Farshid Moussavi, Miguel Rodriguez, Karolien de Schepper, Hiroki Sugiyama, Willem Timmer, Tom Tulloch, Yushi Uehara, Jacques Vink. Engineers: SAT Engineering. Models: Parthesius & de Rijk, OMA.

Congrexpo (Lille Grand Palais)
Lille, France. Completed June 1994. Client: city of Lille (Pierre Mauroy, mayor); SAEM Euralille (Jean-Paul Baietto, general director); Lille Grand Palais (Jean Delannoy, vice president). Site: between railway lines and highways, historic city and periphery, facing future boulevard. Program: **1**. Zenith. Rock concert hall; theatrical, Greek, proscenium, and in-the-round auditorium. Floor area: 7,850 m², 1,000 m² stage area. 6,000 seats (3,200 fixed, 1,000 retractable mobile, 1,800 mobile). **2**. Congress. 1,500-seat conference auditorium for congress, European and international delegations (nine languages), interactive and/or formal meetings, theater, dance, cinema, product presentation; 500-seat auditorium for congress (nine languages), product presentation, recital, drama, cinema, classroom; 350-seat theater for dele-

gation-type congress, concert, recital, cinema, press conferences; 3,500 m² congress exposition space; 1,500-seat banquet space with full kitchen; two 200-place conference/classrooms; 12 80-place conference rooms; 2,500 m² administrative offices. **3**. Expo. 22,000 m² exposition space divisible into three equal spaces; 6,000 m² lobby and multipurpose spaces including meeting rooms, workshops, commercial space, office space, four bars, two restaurants. **4**. Parking. 1,500 enclosed spaces. Budget: $67 million (FF 400 million). Materials: concrete, metal, plastic, wood. Conception, realization: Rem Koolhaas/OMA, François Delhay, architects; Cecil Balmond, Ove Arup & Partners, engineer. Preliminary design workshop: Rem Koolhaas, Floris Alkemade, Douglas Grieco, Jan-Willem van Kuilenburg, Ray Maggiore, Eduardo Arroyo Munoz, Jim Njoo, Mark Schendel, Yushi Uehara, Sarah Whiting, William Wilson. Design development: OMA: Rem Koolhaas with Rients Dijkstra, Jan-Willem van Kuilenburg, Ray Maggiore, Mark Schendel, Yushi Uehara, Ron Witte, Dirk Zuiderveld; FM Delhay: François Delhay, François Brevart, Christophe d'Hulst. Definitive design: OMA: Rem Koolhaas with Ruud Cobussen, Jan-Willem van Kuilenburg, Ray Maggiore, Mark Schendel, Diana Stiles, Luc Veeger, Ron Witte; FM Delhay: François Delhay, François Brevart, Christophe d'Hulst, Shoreh Davar Panah, Isabelle Lemetay, James Lenglin, Olivier Tourraine. Construction: OMA: Rem Koolhaas, Mark Schendel with Ruud Cobussen, Jeanne Gang, Diana Stiles; FM Delhay: François Delhay, François Brevart with Xavier d'Alençon, Christophe d'Hulst, Bertrand Fages. Interior finishings, furniture: Petra Blaisse in collaboration with Julie Sfez. Textiles (auditorium curtains, Expo linen screen): Petra Blaisse. Structural engineers: Cecil Balmond, Rory McGowan, Robert Pugh, Mohsen Zikri (mechanical), Ove Arup & Partners. Services engineers: Joel Taquet, Pascal Beckaert, Gérard Cattuti, Bruno Fontana, Bruno Loiseleux, Sodeg. Facade consultant: Robert-Jan van Santen, Agence van Stanten. Scenography: Agence Ducks, Michel Cova. Acoustics: Rens van Luxemburg, TNO. Quantity surveyor: Bernard Gaillet, Jean-Marie Nuclain, Cabinet Gaillet. Bureau de contrôle: Christiaan Theys, Socotec. Planning: Mr. Talpin, Jean Foerderer, GEMO. Synthèse: SETIB, Yves de Ponthrud. General contractor: Dumez-Quillery SNEP.

OMA: Recent Work

Exhibition, Collegi d'Arquitectos de Catalunya, Barcelona, Spain. Design, direction, installation: Petra Blaisse and Hans Werlemann. Coordination, finance: Donald van Dansik. Introduction collage: Petra Blaisse and Jennifer Sigler. Models: OMA, Herman Helle, Parthesius & de Rijk, Ron Steiner, Hans Werlemann and Chiel van der Stelt. Sound: Het Paleis van Boem. Sound machine, technical installations: Claudi Cornaz with Hans Werlemann. Photography: Hectic Pictures. Graphic design ("newspaper"): Jos Stoopman. With additional help from Floris Alkemade, Gro Bonesmo, Douglas Grieco, Winy Maas, Ron Steiner,

William Wilson. Sponsors: First Europe (Groupe Pierre Premier); Netherlands Foundation for Fine Arts, Design, and Architecture, Amsterdam; Philips; Apple Computer; KLM; OCE; AKZO.

1991

Mission Grand Axe

La Défense, Paris, France. Competition. Client: EPAD, Paris. Site: 750-hectare EPAD territory, including La Défense; 120-meter-wide "path of the axis" extending three kilometers west from La Grande Arche, La Défense, to meet loop of Seine; sixties, seventies, eighties housing, offices, etc.; two cemeteries, university, park, future TGV and subway stations. Program: urban plan for EPAD territory. Rem Koolhaas, Winy Maas with Udo Garritzmann, Xaveer de Geyter, Douglas Grieco, Shin-ichi Kanefuji, Farshid Moussavi, Chidi Onwuka, Sarah Whiting, Alejandro Zaera. In collaboration with Yves Bories, Dominique Wurtz, DBW, Paris. Critics: Hans Kollhoff, Jacques Lucan, Fritz Neumeyer.

Duisburg Urban Planning

Duisburg, Germany. Competition. Client: city of Duisburg. Site: Duisburg's historic harbor area. Program: rehabilitation of waterfront; offices, housing, recreation, parking. Rem Koolhaas, Ron Steiner with Douglas Grieco, Alexander Lamboly, Winy Maas, Farshid Moussavi, Yushi Uehara, Sarah Whiting. In collaboration with Ag. Plan, Mühleim. Model: Parthesius & de Rijk with Ron Steiner.

Transferia

Competition for transportation exchange centers. Client: NBM Amstelland, CROW-Ede. Program: three Transferia for private-public transport exchange; part of Dutch program to reduce traffic congestion around major cities. Site 1: Moordrecht: the Green Heart of Randstad (Rotterdam, The Hague, Amsterdam, Utrecht). Site 2: Kralingen: edge of historic residential neighborhood on outskirts of central Rotterdam, neighboring eighties Brainpark office development.

Site 3: Lage Zwaluwe. Rem Koolhaas, Winy Maas with Udo Garritzmann, Shin-ichi Kanefuji, Chidi Onwuka, Ron Steiner, Arno de Vries, Sarah Whiting. Models: Parthesius & de Rijk.

Zac Danton Office Tower

La Défense, Paris, France. Competition, first prize. Client: Capri Entreprises. Site: triangular area in high-rise business complex north of Paris defined by elevated motorway, future square, and university project; neighbors Jean Nouvel's future 400-meter-

OMA: Recent Work, Collegi d'Arquitectos de Catalunya, Barcelona, 1990.

2. To spew forth: BELCH, GUSH.

VULNERABILITY

More and more, architecture is the imposition on the world of structures it never asked for. From this follows its vulnerability: it is forever in the humiliating position of a lover enumerating his positive qualities to someone who has lost interest.

W

WALL[1]

Berlin.

All of a sudden, I'm right there in front of it, without having realized. A long line of graffiti runs right across it, like the graffiti in the New York subway, like the West's mania for stickers. Suddenly, I have no historical imagination to cope with this wall, with this city cut in two like a brain severed by an artificial scalpel. The buildings which border upon it bear the charred traces of a hot history — cold history, for its part, feeds on cold signs; which reduce the imagination to despair (even graffiti are cold signs; the only funny signs are the rabbits hopping about in the barbed-wire friezes of *no-man's land*).

WALL[2]

In Japan a wall enters the consciousness in a quite different way. It is thin, often temporary, and more or less symbolic as a separation of inside and outside.

WALLS

And this palace was surrounded by ten walls, one inside the other, and all ten walls were made of water. And because the palace and walls consisted of water, it was impossible to enter there, for whoever tried to do so would surely drown.

WAR

War is the affair that decides the future of the country. Thus, if you wish to win the war, do not start war until you are confident of winning.

WAR-IN-BED

The two lovers devour half the ham. Large oysters follow, each with eleven drops of Muscat wine from Syracuse mixed into its sea water. Then a glass of Asti Spumante. Then the *War-in-Bed*. The bed, vast and already full of moonlight, fascinated,

OMA: Recent Work, Collegi d'Arquitectos de Catalunya, Barcelona, 1990.

high Tour Sans Fin. Program: offices (42,000 m²), restaurant (1,000 m²), club (350 m²), conference halls (350 m²), covered parking (600 spaces). Budget: $75 million (FF 447 million). Structure: 150-meter outriggered-prestressed in situ concrete columns around eight-meter core. Facade: clear glass with interior curtains and exterior concrete, colored glass louvers, iron screen with electronic "newspaper" billboard. Competition design: Rem Koolhaas, Winy Maas with Alexander Lamboly, Ray Maggiore, Farshid Moussavi, Sarah Whiting. Model: Parthesius & de Rijk. Preliminary design: Rem Koolhaas, Floris Alkemade, Christophe Cornubert, Anne Mie Depuydt, Christine Enzmann, Winy Maas, Farshid Moussavi with Floor Arons, George van Beers, Frans Blok, Arjen de Groot, Kyoko Hoshino, Willem Timmer, Paul van der Voort. Local architects: Michel Macary, Michael Halter, Patrick Ledigarcher, Jean Louis Vu Dinh Ba, Cabinet Macary, Paris. Engineers: Cecil Balmond (structural), Rory McGowan (structural), Crispin Matson (mechanical), Ove Arup & Partners; Coyne & Bellier; Trouvin Ingenierie.

Leipziger Messe

Leipzig, Germany. Competition. Client: Leipziger Messe GmbH. Site: highway between Leipzig and Dresden. Program: new exposition halls (100,000 m²), parking (150,000 m²), offices (40,000 m²). Rem Koolhaas, Winy Maas with Floris Alkemade, Hernando Arrazola, Rients Dijkstra,

Udo Garritzmann, Karin Penning, Marco Snijders, Ron Steiner, Tom Tulloch, Andy Woodcock.

1992

Urban Design Forum

Yokohama, Japan. Client: city of Yokohama. Site: one of five sites for development surrounding Yokohama's harbor, to be connected by a ring road/bridge; contains two market halls, large parking surface; future heavy traffic, railroads, ships; neighbors Minato Mirai 21, congested area undergoing further densification/development. Rem Koolhaas, Winy Maas, Yushi Uehara with Gro Bonesmo, Fuminori Hoshino, Kyoko Hoshino, Ron Steiner. Model: Parthesius & de Rijk with Ron Steiner, Claudi Cornaz (electrical).

Educatorium

University of Utrecht, Netherlands. Construction: June 1995. Client: Universiteit Utrecht. Site: flanked to north by botanical gardens; to south by 17-story office tower; to east by 185-meter-long, two-story classroom building; to west by pedestrian promenade, bicycle circuit, canal, green zone. Program: 10,000 m² multi-use academic facilities; entry hall, canteen for 1,000 people, two auditoriums for 400 and 500 people, three examination halls for 150, 200, and 300 people. Budget: $14.5 million (fl. 29 million). Proposed materials: exposed in situ prefabricated and sprayed concrete, travertine, clear and colored glazing, zinc, wood, slate, terrazzo, grass. Project I: Rem Koolhaas, Gary Bates, Jacob van Rijs, Ron

Steiner, Jeroen Thomas, Yushi Uehara with Gro Bonesmo, Xaveer de Geyter, Kyoko Hoshino, Markus Lüscher, Luc Veeger. Project II: Rem Koolhaas, Christophe Cornubert, Gary Bates with Richard Eelman. Engineering consultants: ABT Adviesburo voor Bouwtechniek and Ingenieursburo Linssen.

Holten House

Holten, Netherlands. Completed 1993. Site: 5,000 m² heavily wooded area on Dutch "mountain" (50 meters above sea level), with limited buildable area and four-meter height restriction. Program: house for two permanent residents (parents), three occasional residents (daughters). Floor area: 517 m². Cost: $500,000 (fl. 1 million). Rem Koolhaas, Gro Bonesmo, Jeroen Thomas. Model: Ron Steiner. Structural engineers: Cecil Balmond, Nick McMahon, Ove Arup & Partners; Bartels. Mechanical engineers: Van Losser; Linssen. Bathrooms, polyester roofs: Joep van Lieshout. General contractor: BCE Bouw.

Y-Oevers

Amsterdam, Netherlands. Master plan. Client: Amsterdam Waterfront, city of Amsterdam. Site: 515,000 m² along Y River behind Amsterdam Central Station, divided into six "islands." Program: housing (400,200 m²), commercial (692,200 m²), public space (161,300 m²). Collaborating offices: OMA, Neutelings and Roodbeen Architects, van Berkel & Bos Architects, Kees Christiaanse Architects, West 8 Landscape Architects, Judith Gor (light artist). OMA team: Rem Koolhaas, Rients Dijkstra with

Hernando Arrazola, René Heijne, Winy Maas, Miguel Rodriguez, Marco Snijders, Hiroki Sugiyama, Tom Tulloch, Andy Woodcock, Alejandro Zaera. Structural engineers: De Weger. Mechanical engineers: Peutz. Financial consultant: BBN. Traffic consultant: PTC Consultants.

Extension to the Stedelijk Museum

Amsterdam, Netherlands. Competition; first prize: Venturi, Scott Brown & Associates. Site: Amsterdam's museum of modern art sharing triangular Museumplein with Vincent van Gogh Museum and its future extension; defined by orthogonal intersection of Paulus Potterstraat (north) and van Baerlestraat (west), and diagonal Museumstraat axis (south) leading to Rijksmuseum; Concertgebouw to the west. Program: extension to museum with large exhibition space (750 m²), medium exhibition rooms (720 m²), small exhibition rooms (1,530 m²), auditorium (400 m²), conference rooms (100 m²), workshop/services/storage, restoration department, archives, canteen, information center, offices; extensions of lobby, museum shop, library, restaurant. Budget: $20 million (fl. 40 million). Rem Koolhaas, Farshid Moussavi, Ron Steiner, Francis Hsu, Xaveer de Geyter with Hernando Arrazola, Frans Blok, Nick Dragna, Christine Enzmann, Arjen de Groot, Glenn de Groot, Kyoko Hoshino, Markus Lüscher, Heidrun Reusch, Tom Tulloch, Wieland Vajen. Structural engineers: Cecil Balmond, Nick McMahon, Ove Arup & Partners. Garden: Petra Blaisse, Rosemarijn Nitzsche. Model: Vincent de Rijk.

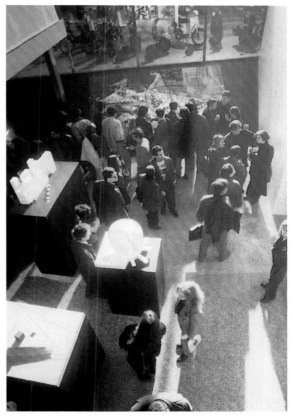

1993

Point City/South City

Project for redesigning Holland. Study for "Air Alexander." Program: one million new dwellings by 2015. Rem Koolhaas, Gary Bates with Winy Maas, Jacob van Rijs, Ron Steiner, Luc Veeger, Jeroen Veltman.

2 Bibliothèques Jussieu

Paris, France. Competition, first prize. Site: campus for 45,000 students; built by Albert in the 1960s (350,000 m² on 126,000 m²); unfinished due to May '68 riots; along Seine near Boulevard St. Germain and Nouvel's Institute du Monde Arab; crossed by subway lines. Program: library of humanities (8,000 m²), library of science and research (10,000 m²), reception and public space (1,000 m²), relogements (3,000 m²), parking (3,700 m²). Budget: $62 million (FF 372 million). Competition design: Rem Koolhaas, Christophe Cornubert, Xaveer de Geyter, René Heijne, Markus

Röthlisberger, Yushi Uehara with Hernando Arrazola, Siebe Bakker, Gary Bates, Gro Bonesmo, Arjen de Groot, Jerry Kopare, Markus Lüscher, Peter Oudshoorn, Jacob van Rijs, Roland Stuy. Preliminary design: Rem Koolhaas, Christophe Cornubert, Anne Mie Depuydt, René Heijne, Winy Maas, Jacob van Rijs with Matthias Bauer, Frans Blok, Patrick Cosmao, Michael Hsu, Ray Maggiore. Engineers: Cecil Balmond (structural), Rory McGowan (structural), Crispin Matson (mechanical), Sean Billings (facade), Ove Arup & Partners; Coyne Bellier. Program consultants: DA&DU. Adviser: Jean Attali. Model: Daan Bakker, René Heijne, Ad Kliphuis, Markus Lüscher, Gijs Niemeyer, Stein Vossen, Ronald Wall.

DICTIONARY REFEENCES

ABOLISH Susan Sontag, *The Benefactor* (London: Writers and Readers Publishing Cooperative, 1983).

ABSENCE Mangelos.

ACCEPTED Tama Janowitz, "In and Out of the Cat Bag," *Slaves of New York* (New York: Crown Publishers, 1986).

ACCIDENT James Gleick, *Chaos* (New York: Penguin Books, 1987).

ACCUMULATE Big Daddy, in Tennessee Williams, *Cat on a Hot Tin Roof*, 1955.

ACCURACY Henry Miller, *The Colossus of Maroussi*, 1941.

AD INFINITUM Ludwig Wittgenstein, *Philosophical Grammar*, ed. Rush Rhees, trans. Anthony Kenny (Oxford: Basil Blackwell, 1974).

ADJUST Lorus J. Milne and Margery Milne, *Insect Worlds* (New York: Charles Scribner's Sons, 1980).

ADVANTAGE John Fante, *Wait Until Spring, Bandini* (London: Paladin, 1990).

ADVICE *The Chinese Book of Odes*.

AESTHETIC John Gardner, *The Art of Fiction* (New York: Vintage, 1985).

AIR¹ Christopher Redman, "Breakthrough," *Time*, Nov. 12, 1990.

AIR² Joseph Gwilt, *The Encyclopedia of Architecture*, The Classic 1867 Edition (New York: Crown Publishers, 1982).

ALPHABETIZED Anne Tyler, *The Accidental Tourist* (New York: Alfred A. Knopf, 1985).

ALREADY Neal Ascherson, "The Borderlands," *Granta* 30 (Winter 1990).

ALTERNATE Charles Baudelaire, *Intimate Journals*, trans. Christopher Isherwood (San Francisco: City Lights Books, 1983).

ALWAYS¹ Arnold Schwarzenegger, as quoted by Bill Zehme, *Rolling Stone*, Aug. 22, 1991.

ALWAYS² Herman Hertzberger, lecture at Delft University, Sept. 1991.

ALWAYS³ Rem Koolhaas to Michael Graves, in *The Chicago Tapes* (New York: Rizzoli International Publications, 1987).

AMSTERDAMS *Times Atlas of the World* (London: The Times Publishing Co., 1955).

ANAGRAM Umberto Eco, *Foucault's Pendulum*, trans. William Weaver (New York: Harcourt Brace Jovanovich, 1989).

ANALOGY Umberto Eco, *Foucault's Pendulum*, trans. William Weaver (New York: Harcourt Brace Jovanovich, 1989).

ANDROID Philip K. Dick, *Do Androids Dream of Electric Sheep?* (London: Grafton Books, 1972). Filmed as *Blade Runner*.

ANGELIC Max Erlich, *The Edict* (New York: Bantam Books, 1972).

ANIMALS Demetri Porphyrios, "Heterotopia: A Study in the Ordering Sensibility in the Work of Alvar Aalto," in *Alvar Aalto* (London: Academy Editions Architectural Monographs, no. 4, 1978).

ANONYMOUS Ellsworth Kelly, as quoted in *Interview*, June 1991.

ANOTHER Kenneth Frampton, introduction to Pierre von Meiss, "Elements of Architecture."

APARTMENT Edouard Herriot, 1946.

ARBITRARY David Salle, "The Style, the Image, and the Arbitrary," in *Anyone*, ed. Cynthia C. Davidson (New York: Rizzoli International Publications, 1991).

ARCHITECTURE Peter Eisenman.

ARITHMETIC John Cage in conversation with Daniel Charles, *For the Birds*, trans. Richard Gardner (London: Marion Boyars Publishers, 1981).

ARRIVAL J. D. Salinger, *The Catcher in the Rye*, 1945.

ARROGANT Frank Lloyd Wright, as quoted in *Frank Lloyd Wright: His Living Voice*, ed. Bruce Brooks Pfeiffer (Fresno: The Press at California State University, 1987). Book and sound recording.

ARTIFICIAL Advertisement, soft drink, India.

ASSAULT Diane Ackerman, *A Natural History of the Senses* (New York: Vintage, 1991).

ASSOCIATION C. G. Jung, *The Psychogenesis of Mental Disease* (Princeton: Princeton University Press, 1960).

ATRIUM Piera Scuri, *Late Twentieth Century Skyscrapers* (New York: Van Nostrand Reinhold, 1990).

ATTRACTION Sam Seibert et al., "A Yen to Travel," *Newsweek*, Aug. 14, 1989.

ATTRACTORS Manuel DeLanda, "Nonorganic Life," in *Zone 6: Incorporations*, eds. Jonathan Crary and Sanford Kwinter (New York: Urzone, 1992).

AU Jorinde Seydel, "Rembrandt's Paniek," *Mediamatic* 6, no. 1 (Summer 1991).

AUDIENCE Lewis Coser.

AUTHENTIC Rem Koolhaas on The Hague City Hall, lecture at Delft University, 1987.

AUTHENTICITY Jurgen Habermas, "Modernity's Consciousness of Time," *The Philosophical Discourse of Modernity*, trans. Frederick Lawrence (Cambridge: MIT Press, 1990).

AUTOMONUMENT Rem Koolhaas, *Delirious New York* (New York: Oxford University Press, 1978; New York: The Monacelli Press, 1994).

AUTONOMOUS *Bertolucci by Bertolucci*, trans. David Ranvaud (London: Plexus, 1987).

AVOID Rem Koolhaas, 1991.

AWKWARDNESS Diane Arbus, introduction to *Diane Arbus* (New York: Aperture, 1972).

BABEL¹ Fritz Lang, *Metropolis* (Transit-Film Gesellschaft, 1926). Film. Published as *Metropolis* (London: Faber & Faber, 1989).

BABEL² Fyodor Dostoyevsky, *The Demons*.

BABEL³ Roland Barthes, "The Eiffel Tower," *The Eiffel Tower and Other Mythologies* (New York: Farrar, Straus & Giroux, 1979).

BABEL⁴ "The Great Wall of China," trans. Willa and Edwin Muir, *Franz Kafka, 1883–1924: The Complete Stories*, ed. Nahum N. Glazter (New York: Schocken Books, 1971).

BABOON Charles Moore in "The Yin, the Yang, and the Three Bears," *Charles Moore: Buildings and Projects, 1949–1986*, ed. Eugene J. Johnson (New York: Rizzoli International Publications, 1986).

BABY Eugène Ionesco, *Amédée, or How to Get Rid of It* (John Calder Publishers, 1958).

BADLY Maxim Gorky, *Boredom*.

BAD MUSIC Umberto Eco, *Foucault's Pendulum*, trans. William Weaver (New York: Harcourt Brace Jovanovich, 1989).

BALDNESS Advertisement, Beverly Hills Institute of Aesthetic & Reconstructive Surgery, *USAir Magazine*, Aug. 1991.

BALLS Madelon Vriesendorp, interview by Jennifer Sigler, June 1, 1991.

BANG[1] Fraser Cooke, "Rebel Rap," *The Face*, July 1991.

BANG[2] Japanese proverb.

BATH Mervyn Peake, *Titus Groan* (Harmondsworth: Penguin Books, 1968).

BAZAAR Fredric Jameson, lecture at Princeton University, April 1991.

BEACH Collective wisdom, May '68.

BEAT Chidi Onwuka.

BEAUTIFUL Paul Valéry, "The Conquest of Ubiquity," *Aesthetics*, trans. Ralph Manheim (New York: Pantheon Books, Bollingen Series, 1964).

BEAUTY[1] Charles Baudelaire, *Intimate Journals*, trans. Christopher Isherwood (San Francisco: City Lights Books, 1983).

BEAUTY[2] Thomas Mann, *Death in Venice*, 1912, trans. H. T. Lowe-Porter (New York: Alfred A. Knopf, 1930).

BED Joan Collins, as quoted in George Christy, "Joan's Bedroom," *Interview*, Oct. 1991.

BEDS Charles Baudelaire, *Any Where Out of This World!*

BEING THERE Francisco J. Varela, "The Reenchantment of the Concrete," in *Zone 6: Incorporations*, eds. Jonathan Crary and Sanford Kwinter (New York: Urzone, 1992).

BELLY James Joyce, *Ulysses*, 1922.

BERLIN Wim Wenders, interview by Hans Kollhoff, *Quaderns* 177 (April–June 1988).

BEST Advertisement, Kneading Fingers Massager,™ Kinsei Shiatsu, © 1991 Wellspring Products, *USAir Magazine*, Aug. 1991.

BETWEEN William Wharton, *Birdy* (New York: Avon, 1978).

BEYOND Fritz Neumeyer, "OMA's Berlin: The Polemic Island in the City," *Assemblage* 11.

BIFURCATIONS Manuel DeLanda, "Nonorganic Life," in *Zone 6: Incorporations*, eds. Jonathan Crary and Sanford Kwinter (New York: Urzone, 1992).

BIG[1] Nadine Gordimer, "The Ultimate Safari," *Jump and Other Stories* (London: Bloomsbury Publishing, 1991).

BIG[2] Donald Trump with Tony Schwartz, *Trump: The Art of the Deal* (New York: Warner Books, 1987).

BIGGER Superman, in Dan Jurgens, "The Mark of the Krypton Man," *Superman* 57 (July 1991).

BIKINI Chidi Onwuka.

BILLBOARD Bobbie Ann Mason, "Nancy Culpepper," *Shiloh and Other Stories* (New York: Perennial Library, 1985).

BINDING Fritz Neumeyer, "Reality as Discipline: Metropolitan Architecture and Urban Identity," *Quaderns* 183 (Oct.–Dec. 1989).

BLANCMANGE Dr. Gareth Roberts, neuroanatomist, on boxing, *The Independent*, Sept. 1991.

BLIMP Roger N. Dent, *Principles of Pneumatic Architecture* (London: Architectural Press, 1971).

BLINKED Rem Koolhaas, 1992.

BLONDE Philip Johnson, "Full Scale False Scale," *Writings* (New York: Oxford University Press, 1979).

BLUE John Hiatt, *Stolen Memories*.

BLUES John Lee Hooker.

BODY[1] Mario Vargas Llosa, *In Praise of the Stepmother*, trans. Helen Lane (New York: Penguin Books, 1991).

BODY[2] Alejandro Zaera, "Notes for a Topographic Survey," *El Croquis*, March 1992.

BODY[3] Voltaire, *Philosophical Dictionary*, ed., trans. Theodore Besterman (Harmondsworth.: Penguin Books, 1971).

BODY[4] Fredric Jameson, *The Ideologies of Theories: Essays* (Minneapolis: University of Minnesota Press, 1984).

BODY SNATCHER *Longman Dictionary of Contemporary English* (London: Longman Group Ltd., 1978).

BOREDOM[1] Max Beckman, "On My Painting," 1938, in *Modern Artists on Art*, ed. Robert L. Herbert (New York: Prentice Hall, 1964).

BOREDOM[2] Rem Koolhaas, interview by Bruno Fortier, *L'Architecture d'Aujourd'hui*, April 1989.

BORING[1] Jodie Foster, interview by Ingrid Sischy, *Interview*, Oct. 1991.

BORING[2] Andy Warhol.

BORROWER Norman Carrell, introduction to *Bach the Borrower* (Connecticut: Greenwood Press, 1967).

BOTH Sculpture title, "The General Jungle," *Gilbert & George: The Charcoal on Paper Sculptures, 1970–1974* (Bordeaux: Musée d'art contemporain, 1986).

BOUCLIERS *Paris Match*, May 1968.

BOUDOIR Heinz Tesar, "Future of the Boudoir: Privacy and Intimacy," in *Lotus Documents: Interior Landscapes*, ed. Georges Teyssot, 1987.

BOUQUET "Les Quatre petites filles," 1947–48, *Picasso: Collected Writings* (London: Aurum Press, 1989).

BOXES Reese Williams, "Common Origin," in *Blasted Allegories*, ed. Brian Wallis (New York: New Museum of Contemporary Art and MIT Press, 1987).

BRAIN[1] Piera Scuri, *Late Twentieth Century Skyscrapers* (New York: Van Nostrand Reinhold, 1990).

BRAIN[2] Henri Bergson, *Matter and Memory*, trans. N. M. Paul and W. S. Palmer (New York: Urzone, 1992).

BREATHING O. M. Ungers, *Morphologie City Metaphors* (Cologne: Verlag der Buchhandlung Walther König, 1982).

BRIDGE[1] "The Bridge," trans. Willa and Edwin Muir, *Franz Kafka, 1883–1924: The Complete Stories*, ed. Nahum N. Glazter (New York: Schocken Books, 1971).

BRIDGE[2] Indian proverb.

BROKEN[1] Nursery rhyme.

BROKEN[2] D. M. Thomas, *The White Hotel* (New York: Viking Press, 1981).

BUSY[1] OMA receptionist, to prospective employee.

BUSY[2] Lead singer of Floodland, interview by MTV, Nov. 10, 1991.

BUSY[3] Rem Koolhaas.

BUTTER[1] Melinda Wittstock, *The Times* (London), Oct. 25, 1991.

BUTTER[2] Label, Aunt Jemima® Butter Lite pancake syrup.

BUTTERFLIES Lorus J. Milne and Margery Milne, *Insect Worlds* (New York: Charles Scribner's Sons, 1980).

BUTTERFLY La Monte Young, "Composition 1960 #5," in *Happenings & Fluxus* (Koelnischer Kunstverein, 1970).

BUTTERFLY EFFECT James Gleick, *Chaos* (New York: Penguin Books, 1987).

CANNIBALIZE *Webster's Ninth New Collegiate Dictionary* (Springfield, Mass.: Merriam-Webster, 1990).

CANNIBALIZED Rem Koolhaas, *Delirious New York* (New York: Oxford University Press, 1978; New York: The Monacelli Press, 1994).

CAPITALISM Gilles Deleuze and Félix Guattari, *A Thousand Plateaus: Capitalism and Schizophrenia* (Minneapolis: University of Minnesota Press, 1987).

CAREFREE Piers Paul Read, *Polonaise* (London: Alison Press, 1976).

CATHEDRAL[1] Juliet Pomés Leiz and Ricardo Feriche, eds., *Barcelona Design Guide* (Barcelona: Gustavo Gili, 1990).

CATHEDRAL[2] David Byrne, *True Stories* (New York: Penguin Books, 1986).

CATHEDRAL[3] William Gibson, "Anyletter," in *Anyone*, ed. Cynthia C. Davidson (New York: Rizzoli International Publications, 1991).

CAUGHT Harry Mulisch, *Last Call* (London: Collins Hawill, 1987).

CAUTION Manual, Braun MR 300 Handblender.

CHANCE[1] Julio Cortazar, "The Instruction Manual: INSTRUCTIONS ON or rather EXAMPLES OF HOW TO BE AFRAID," *Cromopios and Famas*, trans. Paul Blackburn (New York: Pantheon Books, 1969).

CHANCE[2] Stephen W. Hawking, *A Brief History of Time* (London: Bantam Books, 1988).

CHANCE[3] Colette, *The Vagabond*, 1910, trans. Enid McLeod (New York: Farrar, Straus & Giroux, 1980).

CHANNEL Jerzy Kosinski, *Being There* (New York: Bantam Books, 1972).

CHAOS[1] Arthur C. Clarke, *2001: A Space Odyssey* (London: Arrow Books, 1968).

CHAOS[2] Rem Koolhaas, interview by Alejandro Zaera, "Finding Freedoms," *El Croquis*, March 1992.

CHARACTERS James Joyce, *Ulysses*, 1922.

CHARMING Marilyn Monroe on Brigitte Bardot, "Marilyn as a Comedienne," *Life*, May 25, 1959.

CHAUVINISM Parc de la Villette competition announcement, June 1982.

CHEERFULNESS Friedrich Nietzsche, *Twilight of the Idols*, 1889.

CHILD Milan Kundera, *Immortality*, trans. Peter Kussi (New York: HarperCollins Publishers, 1992).

CIRCLES Joseph Conrad, *The Secret Agent*, 1907.

CITED Jacques Derrida, "Signature, Event, Context," *Glyph* 1 (1977), as cited in Gregory L. Ulmer, "The Object of Post-Criticism," in *The Anti-Aesthetic: Essays of Postmodern* comes to meet them from the back of the open room. They get into it, toasting each other and sipping from the War-in-Bed. It is composed of pineapple juice, egg, cocoa, caviare, almond paste, a pinch of red pepper, a pinch of nutmeg and whole clove, all liquidized in Strega liqueur.

WARNING
Uncontrolled or uncoordinated emotion may be most harmful to a production.

WASTE
So on the one hand I really believe in empty spaces, but on the other hand, because I'm still making some art, I'm still making junk for people to put in their spaces that I believe should be empty: i.e., I'm helping people *waste* their space when what I really want to do is help them *empty* their space.

WAVE
When the crest of the wave was six feet from the step, Rubén plunged in: with his arms out like spears and his hair on end from the momentum of his leap, his body cut straight through the air and he fell without bending, without lowering his head or tucking his legs in; he bounced in the foam, scarcely went under, and immediately taking advantage of the tide, he glided out into the water, his arms surfacing and sinking in the midst of a frantic bubbling and his feet tracing a precise rapid wake.

WAVES
Our projects are not born out of reflexes that are known in advance … We are a little like a surfer — he does not control the waves, but he recognises them and knows how to go with them, even against them.

WEAK
God hath chosen the weak things of the world to confound the things which are mighty.

WEATHER[1]
Weather interests everyone, especially if the coverage area is likely to have violent weather from time to time.

WEATHER[2]
The global climate is explicable in terms of the movement of air masses and associated wind belts, resulting from temperature and pressure changes which in turn follow the variation in radiation input. This is

Culture, ed. Hal Foster (Seattle: Bay Press, 1989).

CITIES Phil Patton, *Open Road* (New York: Simon & Schuster, 1986).

CLASS Stella Adler, *The Technique of Acting* (Toronto: Bantam Books, 1988).

CLASSIC Jurgen Habermas, "Modernity's Consciousness of Time," *The Philosophical Discourse of Modernity*, trans. Frederick Lawrence (Cambridge: MIT Press, 1990).

CLEFT Susan Sontag, *The Benefactor* (London: Writers and Readers Publishing Cooperative, 1983).

CLICHES[1] Gregory Bateson, "Metalogue: About Games and Being Serious," *Steps to an Ecology of the Mind* (New York, 1972).

CLICHES[2] J. M. Richards, as quoted in Charles Jencks, *Modern Movements in Architecture* (London: Penguin Books, 1973).

CLIMATES Victoria Tokereva, "Centre of Gravity," trans. Michael Glenny, *Granta* 30 (Winter 1990).

CLIMAX Paul Starrett, *Changing the Skyline*.

CLOTHES[1] Diane Arbus on nudists, introduction to *Diane Arbus* (New York: Aperture, 1972).

CLOTHES[2] Jacques Lacan, *Le Seminaire, livre VII: L'Ethique de la psychanalyse* (Paris: Seuil, 1986).

142 Johannes Vermeer, *A Young Woman Seated at a Virginal*, 1673–75; National Gallery, London.

160–61 Paris Stock Exchange, August 2, 1993; photo: Lionel Cironneau, Associated Press.

CLOTHING Gertrude Jobes, *Dictionary of Mythology, Folklore, and Symbols* (New York: Scarecrow Press, 1962).

CLOUDS[1] John Ruskin, *Modern Painters*, ed. David Barrie (London: Deutsch, 1987).

CLOUDS[2] James Gleick, *Chaos* (New York: Penguin Books, 1987).

CLUB Comment on the profession of architecture, as quoted by Jeffrey Kipnis, lecture at Columbia University.

COACH Philip Roth, *The Great American Novel* (London: Cape, 1973).

COATING Charles Baudelaire, "The Painter of Modern Life," in *Selected Writings on Art and Artists* (New York: Harmondsworth, 1972).

CODE Carol Beckwith on a dance performed by the Wodaabe nomads of Niger, "Geerewol: The Art of Seduction," in *Fragments for a History of the Human Body*, part 2, ed. Michel Feher (New York: Urzone, 1989).

COINCIDENCE Jean-Paul Fargier, "Slave to the Rhythm," in *What a Wonderful World! Music Videos in Architecture*, eds. Jola Meijer and Ernie Tee (Groningen, Holland: Groninger Museum, 1990).

COLLAPSE Rem Koolhaas, *New York Architecture*, vol. 1 (New York: New York Chapter/American Institute of Architects, 1988).

COLLAPSED Daniel Defoe, *Robinson Crusoe*, 1719.

COLOUR[1] Advertisement, Harmony Hair Colour, *Cosmopolitan*, Sept. 1991.

COLOUR[2] Emile Zola, *L'Assommoir*, 1877, trans. Leonard Tancock (Harmondsworth: Penguin Books, 1970).

COLOURS Julian Barnes, *Metroland* (London: Pan Books, 1990).

COMMAND Nancy Friday, *Women on Top* (London: Arrow Books, 1991).

COMMAS Alice B. Toklas, in Gertrude Stein, *The Autobiography of Alice B. Toklas*, 1933.

COMMODITY Henri Lefebvre, *Everyday Life in the Modern World* (New York: Harper & Row, 1971).

COMPETITIVITE Riccardo Petrella, "L'Evangile de la compétitivité," *Le Monde Diplomatique*, Sept. 1991.

COMPLEXITY Ilya Prygogine and Isabelle Stengers, *Order Out of Chaos* (New York: Bantam New Age Books, 1984).

COMPLIMENT Madelon Vriesendorp, interview by Jennifer Sigler, June 1, 1991.

COMPULSION Sumerian text.

CONDENSER Rem Koolhaas, *Delirious New York* (New York: Oxford University Press, 1978; New York: The Monacelli Press, 1994).

CONDUCTOR Sidney Harrison, *How to Appreciate Music* (London: Elm Tree Books in association with EMI Music Publishing, 1981).

CONFIDENCE[1] Theo van Doesburg, Jan. 7, 1921, as quoted in Charles Jencks, *Modern Movements in Architecture* (London: Penguin Books, 1973).

CONFIDENCE[2] Dan McCosh on the 1992 Cadillac Seville, *Popular Science*, May 1991.

CONFINED Anthony Trollope, *Barchester Towers*, 1857.

CONFUSED Frank O. Gehry, as quoted in Janet Nairn, "Frank Gehry: The Search for a 'No Rules' Architecture," *Architectural Record*, June 1976.

CONNECTED Gilles Deleuze and Félix Guattari, *A Thousand Plateaus: Capitalism and Schizophrenia* (Minneapolis: University of Minnesota Press, 1987).

CONNECTIONS Jean Claude Garcias, "Tragic and Exhilarating: The Koolhaas Effect in France," *Casabella*, July–Aug. 1990.

CONSTRUCTION[1] Richard Hamilton, as quoted in Charles Jencks, *Modern Movements in Architecture* (London: Penguin Books, 1973).

CONSTRUCTION[2] Iakov Chernikhov, *The Construction of Architectural and Machine Forms*.

CONSUMER Vladimir Nabokov, *Lolita*, 1955.

CONTAINER Fredric Jameson, lecture at Princeton University, April 1991.

240 Egyptian statues.

CONTRADICT Estragon, in *Waiting for Godot*, 1955, in *Samuel Beckett: The Complete Dramatic Works* (London: Faber & Faber, 1986).

CONTRIBUTIONS Neil Coope, "The Art of Philosophy," *Philosophy* 66, no. 256.

CONTROL Kenzo Tange, "The Late Show," BBC.

CONVERSATION Tadao Sato, *Currents in Japanese Cinema*, trans. Gregory Barrett (Tokyo: Kodansha International, 1982).

COPIED Manolo Blahnik, shoe designer, interview by Michael Roberts, *Interview*, Sept. 1991.

COPYRIGHT Gregory L. Ulmer on the work of Sherrie Levine, "The Object of Post-Criticism," in *The Anti-Aesthetic: Essays of Postmodern Culture*, ed. Hal Foster (Seattle: Bay Press, 1989).

CORE Wim Wenders on Berlin, interview by

Hans Kollhoff, *Quaderns* 177 (April–June 1988).

CORPORATE Dorian Sagan, "Metametazoa: Biology and Multiplicity," in *Zone 6: Incorporations*, eds. Jonathan Crary and Sanford Kwinter (New York: Urzone, 1992).

COSTUME Richard Rayner, "Los Angeles Without a Map," *Granta* 19 (Summer 1986).

COUPLING Iakov Chernikhov, *Chernikhov, Fantasy and Construction*, ed. Catherine Cook (London: Academy Editions, 1984).

COURSE Clov, in *Endgame*, 1958, in *Samuel Beckett: The Complete Dramatic Works* (London: Faber & Faber, 1986).

COVER-UP "The Demon Princess," *Elijah's Violin and Other Jewish Folk Tales, as told by Harold Schwartz* (Harmondsworth: Penguin Books, 1983).

COWS Anthony Bailey, "Letter From the Netherlands," *The New Yorker*, Aug. 12, 1991.

CRANES[1] Jacques Derrida, *Glas*, trans. John Leavey and Richard Rand (Lincoln: University of Nebraska Press, 1986).

CRANES[2] David Leavit, *The Lost Language of Cranes* (London: Penguin Books, 1987).

270–71 "Russian doctors start treating V. I. Lenin for a stroke 70 years after his death"; photo: courtesy *Spy* Magazine.

CREAM-PUFF Charles Jencks, *Modern Movements in Architecture* (London: Penguin Books, 1973).

CRISIS[1] Martin Amis, *London Fields* (London: Penguin Books, 1990).

CRISIS[2] Julio Cortazar, *Hopscotch*, trans. Gregory Rabassa (New York: Random House, 1966).

276 P. Mondriaan, "Composition in Black and White"; Kröller-Müller Museum, Otterlo, Netherlands.

CUSHICLE Michael Webb, in *Archigram*, ed. Peter Cook (Great Britain: Studio Vista Publishers, 1972).

CYBER-SOMETHING Steve Jackson, interview by Gareth Branwyn, "The World's Oldest Secret Conspiracy," *Mondo 2000* 3 (Winter 1991).

CYBERSPACE[1] William Gibson, *Neuromancer* (London: Grafton Books, 1986).

CYBERSPACE[2] Sanford Kwinter, "Cyber Agonistes," *Newsline*, May/Summer 1991.

DANCE[1] Aurora S. Villacorta, *Step by Step to Ballroom Dancing* (Urbana-Champaign: University of Illinois Board of Trustees, Interstate Printers and Publishers, 1974).

DANCE[2] Anthony Vidler, "The Ironies of Metropolis: Notes on the Work of OMA," *Skyline*, May 1982.

DANCING Toni Morrison, *Beloved* (New York: Plume Books, 1988).

DANGER Letter to the editor, *De Volkskrant*, as quoted in "The Dike Holds," *Newsweek*, Jan. 22, 1990.

DATE[1] Advertisement, Dateline, *Cosmopolitan*, Sept. 1991.

DATE[2] Mogen Jul, *The Quality of Frozen Foods* (London: Academic Press, 1984).

DAY Juliet Pomés Leiz and Ricardo Feriche, eds., *Barcelona Design Guide* (Barcelona: Gustavo Gili, 1990).

DECIDE[1] Donald E. Westlake, *Drowned Hopes* (New York: Mysterious Press, 1990).

DECIDE[2] Shin-ichi Kanefuji, OMA, attempt to convince Udo Garritzmann to buy his Renault 4.

DECORATIVE Rem Koolhaas, interview by Alejandro Zaera, "Finding Freedoms," *El Croquis*, March 1992.

DEGLOVED Ian T. Jackson, "Osteotomies in the Craniofacial Area and Orthognathic Procedures," in *Rob & Smith's Operative Surgery*, 4th ed., eds. T. L. Barclay and Desmond A. Kernahan (London: Butterworths, 1986).

DEGRADATION Charles Darwin, *The Origin of Species*, 1859.

DELAY "Traffic Jams," *The Economist*, Feb. 18, 1989.

DEMENTED Spalding Gray, *Swimming to Cambodia* (New York: Theater Communications Group, 1985). Performance transcript.

DEMOLITION Description of Valsella VS-MT-DC general-purpose demolition charge, in *Jane's Military Vehicles and Ground Support Equipment 1986*, 7th ed., ed. Christopher F. Foss and Terry J. Gander (New York: Jane's Publishing Co., 1986).

DENSITY[1] Edgar M. Hoover and Raymond Vernon, *Anatomy of a Metropolis* (New York: Doubleday/Anchor).

DENSITY[2] Anthony Bailey, "Letter From the Netherlands," *The New Yorker*, Aug. 12, 1991.

DERIVE Guy Debord, in *Situationist International Anthology*, ed. Ken Knabb (Berkeley: Bureau of Public Secrets, 1981).

DESERT[1] Don DeLillo, *The Names* (London: Picador, 1987).

DESERT[2] Kazimir Malevich, "Suprematism," in *Modern Artists on Art*, ed. Robert L. Herbert (New York: Prentice Hall, 1964).

DESIRE[1] Salvador Dalí, "New York Salutes Me!" *Spain*, May 23, 1941.

DESIRE[2] Bruce Chatwin, *On the Black Hill* (London: Jonathan Cape, 1982).

DESTRATIFICATION Alejandro Zaera on the structural strategy of ZKM Karlsruhe, "Notes for a Topographic Survey," *El Croquis*, March 1992.

DETOURNEMENT "Definitions," in *Situationist International Anthology*, ed. Ken Knabb (Berkeley: Bureau of Public Secrets, 1981).

DIARY Anaïs Nin, as quoted in Elisabeth Barillé, *Anaïs Nin: Naked Under the Mask*, trans. Elfreda Powell (London: Minerva, 1993).

DICHOTOMY Peter Eisenman, *Misreading*.

DIMENSIONS AutoCAD Reference Manual (London: Autodesk, 1989).

DIRECTIONS Lewis Carroll, *Alice's Adventures in Wonderland*, 1865.

DIRTY REALISM Bill Buford, introduction to *Dirty Realism: New Writing from America* (Cambridge: Granta, 1983).

DISCIPLINE Glenn Wilson, *The Psychology of Performing Arts* (London: Croom Helm, 1985).

DISCOVER Hans Kollhoff, "Architecture versus Urban Design," *Quaderns* 183 (Oct.–Dec. 1989).

DISLOCATION Peter Eisenman, *Misreading*.

DISORDER Aldo Rossi.

DISORGANIZATION Jenny Holzer, *Truisms and Essays* (Halifax: Press of the Nova Scotia College of Art and Design, 1983).

DISRUPTED Paul Auster, *In the Country of Last Things* (New York: Viking Penguin, 1987).

DISTANCE[1] Alvin Toffler, *Future Shock* (New York: Bantam Books, 1970).

DISTANCE[2] Jerry, in Edward Albee, *The Zoo Story* (Jonathan Cape, 1962).

DISTRACTED Lorus J. Milne and Margery Milne, *Insect Worlds* (New York: Charles Scribner's Sons, 1980).

DIVORCE Rem Koolhaas, "Elegy for the Vacant Lot; *Delirious New York* Redux," *L'Architecture d' Aujourd' hui*, April 1985.

DOGMA[1] Tom Robbins, *Still Life with Woodpecker* (New York: Bantam Books, 1984).

DOGMA[2] Rem Koolhaas, *New York Architecture*, vol. 1 (New York: New York Chapter/American Institute of Architects, 1988).

DOLDRUMS *Webster's Ninth New Collegiate Dictionary* (Springfield, Mass.: Merriam-Webster, 1990).

DOOMED Rem Koolhaas, open letter to the Berlin Potsdamer/Leipziger Platz competition jury, Oct. 7, 1991.

DOOR Vikram Seth, *All You Who Sleep Tonight* (London: Faber & Faber, 1990).

DOUBLE Wilbur Shramm and William Porter, *Men, Women, Messages, and Media: Understanding Human Communication*, quoted in Richard Saul Wurman, *Information Anxiety* (New York: Doubleday, 1989).

DOUGHNUT[1] Rem Koolhaas, lecture at Columbia University, Nov. 1989.

DOUGHNUT[2] FBI Special Agent Dale Cooper of the television series "Twin Peaks," in *The Autobiography of FBI Special Agent Dale Cooper: My Life, My Tapes* (London: Penguin Books, 1991).

DRAG Angela Carter, *The Sadeian Woman* (New York: Pantheon Books, 1978).

DRAMA Oscar Wilde, *The Picture of Dorian Gray*, 1891.

DREAM Thomas Mann, *Death in Venice*, 1912, trans. H. T. Lowe-Porter (New York: Alfred A. Knopf, 1930).

DRESS Elsa Schiaparelli, *Shocking Life*, as quoted in Richard Martin, *Fashion and Surrealism* (New York: Rizzoli International Publications, 1987).

DRESSING ROOM Aldous Huxley, *Brave New World*, 1932.

DRIFTER Robert W. McIntosh and Charles R. Goeldner, *Tourism: Principles, Practices, Philosophies*, 5th ed. (New York: John Wiley and Sons, 1986).

DRIVE Robert Venturi, Denise Scott Brown, and Steven Izenour, *Learning from Las Vegas*, rev. ed. (Cambridge: MIT Press, 1988).

DRIVE-THRU Alejandro Zaera on the early concept for Congrexpo, "Notes for a Topographic Survey," *El Croquis*, March 1992.

DRUNK Charles Baudelaire, *Les Fleurs du mal*, 1857, 1861, 1868.

DUTCH[1] Bernard Stonehouse, *Philips Pocket Guide to the World* (London: George Philip, 1985).

DUTCH[2] Rem Koolhaas, interview by Hajime Yatsuka, *Telescope*, Winter 1989.

DUTCH[3] Hassan Karamine, OMA, on cycling in Holland, Nov. 1991.

DUTCH GREY John Hejduk, *Mask of Medusa*, ed. Kim Shkapich (New York: Rizzoli International Publications, 1986).

the result of the tilt of the earth's axis in relation to the ecliptic (the plane drawn through the sun and the earth's centre around which the earth rotates annually), the earth's rotation itself, the differential radiation absorption and reflection of large land and sea masses and major evaporative processes which utilise much of the sun's incident energy.

WEIGHTLESSNESS
Remember that astronauts who had to learn to manoeuvre weightlessly in the world had also to learn to urinate and defecate within their clothes, into systems designed to accommodate their body wastes to be sure, but nonetheless on their own bodies. From the sublime to the ridiculous, you might say.

WELFARE
My objective has been humanity's comprehensive welfare in the universe. I could have ended up with a pair of flying slippers.

WHAT
What should be the real intercommunion between all the architects of the world, and what should we tell the public?

WHITE
Every time we play this game, my response is the same: "White."

WHITE THREAD
Moreover, his stitching was reminiscent of today's jeans, for he used a white thread. There is a saying in Russian that a thing is "sewn with white thread" when we mean some trickery is obvious. It means that everything is visible.

WHORE
I am a whore.

WIND[1]
The river was swollen with snowmelt from the Andes, fast-running and rustling the reeds. Purple swallows were chasing bugs. When they flew above the cliff, the wind caught them and keeled them over in a fluttering reversal and they dropped again low over the river.

WIND[2]
The maximum speed of the wind in a tornado is not known for certain because whenever one of the storms has passed close to an anemometer, the instrument has either been wrecked or blown away.

WINDMILLS
As he spoke, he dug his spurs into

DUTCHNESS Simon Schama, *The Embarrassment of Riches: An Interpretation of Dutch Culture in the Golden Age* (William Collins Sons, 1987).

DUTY James Roderick, chairman, US Steel, 1979.

EDIBLE F. T. Marinetti, *La Cucina futurista* (The Futurist Cookbook), trans. Suzanne Brill (London: Trefoil Publications, 1989).

EDIT Zaha Hadid on the fourth-year unit at AA with Rem Koolhaas and Elia Zenghelis, in *AA Prospectus*, 1989–90.

EGG[1] Aldous Huxley, *Brave New World*, 1932.

EGG[2] Gertrude Jobes, *Dictionary of Mythology, Folklore, and Symbols* (New York: Scarecrow Press, 1962).

ELEVATED Charles Dickens, *Great Expectations*, 1860–61.

ELEVATOR Rem Koolhaas, *Delirious New York* (New York: Oxford University Press, 1978; New York: The Monacelli Press, 1994).

ELITISM Hans Hollein, *Arts and Architecture*, 1963.

EMEUTE Victor Hugo, *Les Misérables*, 1862, trans. Charles E. Wilbour (New York: Simon & Schuster, 1964).

EMPTY Martin Heidegger, "Art and Space," trans. Charles H. Seibert, *Man and World: An International Philosophical Review* 6, no. 1 (Feb. 1973).

ENERGY Vladimir Voinovich, *Moscow 2042* (London: Picador, 1986).

ENGINEER Rem Koolhaas, interview by Alejandro Zaera, "Finding Freedoms," *El Croquis*, March 1992.

ENLIGHTENING James Agee and Walker Evans, *Let Us Now Praise Famous Men*, 1939.

ENORMITIES Sir Thomas Browne, *Hydriotaphia: Urne Buriall*, 1658.

ENORMITY *Webster's Ninth New Collegiate Dictionary* (Springfield, Mass.: Merriam-Webster, 1990).

ENORMOUS Henry Miller, *Tropic of Cancer* (London: Grafton, 1965).

ENTROPY Robert Smithson, "A Tour of the Monuments of Passaic, New Jersey," published as "The Monuments of Passaic," *Artforum* 6, no. 4 (Dec. 1967).

ENVELOPE Rem Koolhaas, lecture at Delft University, April 1987.

ENVELOPED Roald Dahl, *Switch Bitch* (Penguin Books, 1965).

EPHEMERON Wim Wenders, interview by Hans Kollhoff, *Quaderns* 177 (April–June 1988).

EPIGRAM Oscar Wilde, *De Profundis*, 1905.

EPOCHE Roland Barthes, "The Image," 1978, in *The Rustle of Language*, trans. Richard Howard (Oxford: Basil Blackwell, 1986).

EQUAL[1] Jenny Holzer, *Truisms and Essays* (Halifax: Press of the Nova Scotia College of Art and Design, 1983).

EQUAL[2] Louis Kahn.

EROTICS Mario Perniola, "Between Clothing and Nudity," in *Fragments for a History of the Human Body*, part 2, ed. Michel Feher (New York: Urzone, 1989).

ESCAPED Peter Cowey, *Dutch Cinema: An Illustrated History* (South Brunswick: The Tantivy Press, 1979).

ESCAPE VELOCITY *Webster's Ninth New Collegiate Dictionary* (Springfield, Mass.: Merriam-Webster, 1990).

ETERNITY Frances A. Yates, *Theater of the World* (London: Routledge & Kegan Paul, 1969).

EUGENIC "People," *Time*, Dec. 22, 1947.

EVERY Advertisement, Steinway, 1948.

EVERYONE Richard Meier.

EX Eleanor James, "What Does Your Ex Expect?" *Cosmopolitan*, Sept. 1991.

EXAGGERATION "Rumpel-stilts-kin," *Grimms' Fairy Tales*, trans. Edgar Taylor (London: Scholar Press, 1979).

EXCEPTIONS Italo Calvino, *Invisible Cities*, trans. William Weaver (London: Pan Books, 1979).

EXCHANGE Imamura Shohei, "The Sun Legend of a Country Boy," in *Japanese Kings of the Bs* (Rotterdam: Stichting Film Festival, 1991).

EXCLUSION Michel Foucault.

EXPERIMENTAL *Situationist International Anthology*, ed. Ken Knabb (Berkeley: Bureau of Public Secrets, 1981).

EXPERIMENTS *Collins Wonder Book* (New York: Collins, 1920).

EXPLANATIONS "The Benefactor," *A Susan Sontag Reader* (New York: Vintage, 1983).

EXPLOITATION Maurice Nio, "The Ultra-Sexist Image," in *What a Wonderful World! Music Videos in Architecture*, eds. Jola Meijer and Ernie Tee (Groningen, Holland: Groninger Museum, 1990).

EXPLOSION Mario Vargas Llosa, "The Leaders," *The Cubs and Other Stories*, trans. Gregory Kolovakos and Ronald Christ (New York: Harper & Row, 1975).

EXPOSED Zhang Xian Liang, *Half of Man Is Woman* (London: Penguin Books, 1989).

EXPRESSION[1] Hermann Hesse, *Narziss and Goldmund*, 1930.

EXPRESSION[2] Walt Whitman.

EXTERIOR Roland Barthes, "The Eiffel Tower," *The Eiffel Tower and Other Mythologies* (New York: Farrar, Straus & Giroux, 1979).

EYES[1] Le Corbusier, *Towards a New Architecture*, 13th French ed., trans. Frederick Etchells (New York: Dover Publications, 1986).

EYES[2] Marcel Proust.

EYES[3] Jerzy Kosinski, *The Painted Bird*, 1965.

FACADE Rem Koolhaas.

FAC-DIFFERENT Umberto Eco, *Travels in Hyperreality*, trans. William Weaver (London: Pan Books with Secker & Warburg, 1987).

FACELIFT John Q. Owsley Jr., "Superficial Musculoaponeurotic System Platysma Facelift," in *Rob & Smith's Operative Surgery*, 4th ed., eds. T. L. Barclay and Desmond A. Kernahan (London: Butterworths, 1986).

FACELIFTS Robert Venturi, Denise Scott Brown, and Steven Izenour, *Learning from Las Vegas*, rev. ed. (Cambridge: MIT Press, 1988).

FACT Iris Murdoch, *The Sacred and Profane Love Machine* (London: Chatto & Windus, 1987).

FAITH Raymond Hood, as quoted in Rem Koolhaas, *Delirious New York* (New York: Oxford University Press, 1978; New York: The Monacelli Press, 1994).

FAKERS Cookie Mueller, "My Bio: Notes on an American Childhood, 1949–1959," *Bomb* 11 (Winter 1985).

FAKES[1] *Fake: The Art of Deception*, ed. Mark Jones (London: British Museum Publications, 1990).

FAKES[2] J. K. Huysman, *Against Nature*, 1882.

FALSE-DAY "The Third Window: An Interview with Paul Virilio," in *Global Television*, eds. Cynthia Schneider and Brian Wallis (Cambridge: MIT Press; New York: Wedge Press, 1988).

FAMOUS Advertisement, "The Six Most-Wanted Earrings" by Kenneth Jay Lane, "worn by the World's Most Admired Women."™

FANATIC Voltaire, *Philosophical Dictionary*, ed., trans. Theodore Besterman (Harmondsworth: Penguin Books, 1971).

FANTASTIC Rem Koolhaas, interview by Alejandro Zaera, "Finding Freedoms," *El Croquis*, March 1992.

FASHION Jean Baudrillard, *Cool Memories*, trans. Chris Turner (London: Verso, 1990).

FATE Martin Heidegger, *The Question Concerning Technology* (New York: Harper & Row, 1977).

FATHER Sigmund Freud, *A Phylogenetic Fantasy* (Cambridge: Harvard University Press, Belknap Press, 1987).

FATHERS *Bertolucci by Bertolucci*, trans. David Ranvaud (London: Plexus, 1987).

FAX Jules Older, "A Matter of FAX," *USAir Magazine*, Aug. 1991.

FEATURED Lucille Ball, as told to Cameron Shipp, *Women's Home Companion*, May 1953.

FEET Tadashi Suzuki, "The Grammar of Feet," *The Way of Acting*, trans. J. Thomas Rimer (New York: Theater Communications Group, 1986).

FICTIONS J. G. Ballard, introduction to *Crash* (New York: Vintage, 1989).

FIDGETY Mary Gaitskill, "Secretary," *Bad Behavior* (New York: Vintage, 1988).

FIGURE Rem Koolhaas, interview by Hajime Yatsuka, *Telescope*, Winter 1989.

FILING CABINET Henri Bosco, *Monsieur Carre-Benoit à la campagne*, as quoted in Gaston Bachelard, *The Poetics of Space*, trans. Maria Jolas (Boston: Beacon Press, 1969).

FILTERING Colin Rowe, as quoted in Piera Scuri, *Late Twentieth Century Skyscrapers* (New York: Van Nostrand Reinhold, 1990).

FINGERED George Orwell, *Down and Out in Paris and London*, 1933.

FIRE-FIGHTING Patricia Tutt and David Adler, eds., *New Metric Handbook: Planning and Design Data* (London: Butterworth Architecture, 1979).

FIRES Yves Klein.

FISHERMAN Ron Steiner, OMA, on competition for The Hague City Hall, interview by Jennifer Sigler, May 1990.

FIZZ Foster, in Harold Pinter, *No Man's Land* (London: Eyre Methuen, 1975).

FLANEURS[1] Walter Benjamin, *Charles Baudelaire: A Lyric Poet in the Era of High Capitalism*.

FLANEURS[2] Julian Barnes, *Metroland* (London: Pan Books, 1990).

FLAT[1] Peter Cowey, *Dutch Cinema: An Illustrated History* (South Brunswick: The Tativy Press, 1979).

FLAT[2] David Byrne, *True Stories* (New York: Penguin Books, 1986).

FLEETING Manolo Blahnik, shoe designer, interview by Michael Roberts, *Interview*, Sept. 1991.

FLUX[1] Michael Page, *The Power of Ch'i* (Northamptonshire: Aquarian Press, 1988).

FLUX[2] Jenny Holzer, *Truisms and Essays* (Halifax: Press of the Nova Scotia College of Art and Design, 1983).

FLUX[3] Gilles Deleuze and Félix Guattari, *A Thousand Plateaus: Capitalism and Schizophrenia* (Minneapolis: University of Minnesota Press, 1987).

FOOD Stanley Kahan, *Introduction to Acting*, 2nd ed. (Newton, Mass.: Allyn & Bacon, 1985).

FOREIGN[1] John David Morley, *Pictures From the Water Trade* (London: Fontana Paperbacks, 1986).

FOREIGN[2] Joseph Brodsky, "Democracy," *Granta* 30 (Winter 1990).

FORGET Karl Marx, *Surveys In Exile*, trans. Ben Fowkes (Pelican Books, 1973).

FORMULA[1] Rem Koolhaas, interview by Hajime Yatsuka, *Telescope*, Winter 1989.

FORMULA[2] Robert McGarvey, "The ABCs of Interviewing," *USAir Magazine*, Aug. 1991.

FRAGMENTS[1] Hans Kollhoff, "Architecture versus Urban Design," *Quaderns* 183 (Oct.–Dec. 1989).

FRAGMENTS[2] Paul Klee, "On Modern Art," 1924, in *Modern Artists on Art*, ed. Robert L. Herbert (New York: Prentice Hall, 1964).

FRICTION Carel Birnie, director, Netherlands Dance Theater, interview by Jennifer Sigler, Jan. 1990.

FRIENDLY Recipe for Oysters Rockefeller, *The Alice B. Toklas Cookbook*, 1954.

FROZEN Mercea Sinescu, "The State of Europe," trans. Fiona Tupper-Carey, *Granta* 30 (Winter 1990).

FRUGAL Jeff Smith (the Frugal Gourmet), as quoted in Adam Woog, "What's Cooking with Jeff Smith?" *USAir Magazine*, Aug. 1991.

FUKUOKA[1] *Webster's New Geographical Dictionary* (Springfield, Mass.: G & C Merriam Co., 1977).

FUKUOKA[2] Noriko Takiguchi and Makoto Murata, eds., *Fukuoka International Architects' Conference '89* (Fukuoka: Coordinating Office for FIAC '89, 1989).

FUMES "Traffic Jams," *The Economist*, Feb. 18, 1989.

FURNITURE Graham Greene, *The Ministry of Fear* (London: Heinemann, 1943).

FUTURE[1] Andy Warhol, *America* (New York: Harper & Row, 1985).

FUTURE[2] Brian Boigon, "A Cyberspatial Commentary," *Newsline*, Sept.–Oct. 1991.

FUTURE[3] Mies van der Rohe.

FUTURE[4] Douglas Coupland, *Shampoo Planet* (London: Simon & Schuster, 1992).

FUZZY Richard Ernsberger Jr. with Yuriko Hoshiai, "Computers With Human Logic," *Newsweek*, April 2, 1990.

GENEALOGY Jeffrey Kipnis, *In the Manor of Nietzsche* (New York: Calluna Farms Press, 1990).

GENESIS Henry Miller, *Plexus* (London: Panther, 1965).

GEOMETRY Tom Robbins, *Still Life with Woodpecker* (New York: Bantam Books, 1984).

GLANCE Janet Frame, *Living in the Manitoto*, 1981.

GLIDE F. Scott Fitzgerald, *The Great Gatsby*, 1925.

GLITTER Ron Steiner, OMA, interview by Jennifer Sigler, Jan. 1990.

GLOBAL[1] Jonathan Alter, "CNN's Global Village," *Newsweek*, June 18, 1990.

GLOBAL[2] Douglas Coupland, *Shampoo Planet* (London: Simon & Schuster, 1992).

GLOBALIZATION Rem Koolhaas, in *Progressive Architecture*, Jan. 1991.

GLOCAL Michael Johnson, "Decoding Business Buzzwords," *Newsweek*, June 10, 1991.

GO Rem Koolhaas, interview by Bruno Fortier, *L'Architecture d'Aujourd'hui*, April 1989.

GOODNESS Mike Kelley, *Plato's Cave, Rothko's Chapel, Lincoln's Profile* (Venice, Calif.: New City Editions, 1986).

GOPLACIA "Lines on the Island of Utopia by the Poet Laureate, Mr. Windbag, Nonsenso's sister's son," in Thomas More, *Utopia*, 1516, trans. Paul Turner (London: Penguin Books, 1965).

GORDIAN KNOT Gertrude Jobes, *Dictionary of Mythology, Folklore, and Symbols* (New York: Scarecrow Press, 1962).

GRACE[1] Riccardo Petrella, "L'Evangile de la compétitivité," *Le Monde Diplomatique*, Sept. 1991.

GRACE[2] B. Castiglione, *The Book of the Courtier*, trans. George Bull (New York: Penguin Books, 1967).

his steed Rocinante, paying no attention to his squire's shouted warning that beyond all doubt they were windmills and no giants he was advancing to attack. But he went on, so positive that they were giants that he neither listened to Sancho's cries nor noticed what they were, even when he got near them. Instead he went on shouting in a loud voice: "Do not fly, cowards, vile creature, for it is one knight alone who assails you."

WINDOW¹
(And does a window form part of the inside of a building or not?)

WINDOW²
In front of a window seen from inside a room, I placed a painting representing exactly that portion of the landscape covered by the painting. Thus, the tree in the pic-

GRAFT Jacques Derrida, *Dissemination*, trans. Barbara Johnson (Chicago: University of Chicago Press, 1981).

GRASP O. M. Ungers, *Morphologie City Metaphors* (Cologne: Verlag der Buchhandlung Walther König, 1982).

GREAT Mohammed Ali, 1963, as quoted in Batiaan Bommelje, review of *Mohammed Ali: His Life and Times* by Thomas Hauser, *NRC Handelsblad*, Sept. 21, 1991.

GREED Ivan Boesky, address to University of California Business School, 1985.

GREEN Magazine offer, salad bowls.

GREW Hermann Hesse, *Narziss and Goldmund*, 1930.

GRID Rem Koolhaas, *Delirious New York* (New York: Oxford University Press, 1978; New York: The Monacelli Press, 1994).

GROOVE Mrs. Edith Creed Bunker (Best Teacher of 1946).

GROTESQUE Ursula LeGuin, *The Left Hand of Darkness* (London: Futura, 1991).

GROVEL Ayn Rand, *The Fountainhead*, 1943.

GUARANTEE Advertisement, Crescourt Loft Conversions.

GUIDANCE Frank Lloyd Wright on the Beth Shalom Synagogue, letter to Rabbi Mortimer J. Cohen, April 22, 1958, in *Frank Lloyd Wright: Letters to Clients*, ed. Bruce Brooks Pfeiffer (London: Architectural Press, 1987).

GUZZLERS Catherine Queloz, "Hyperbation," *Forum*, July 1991.

HABITAT Tama Janowitz, "On and Off the African Veldt," *Slaves of New York* (New York: Crown Publishers, 1986).

HALLUCINATION Jean Baudrillard, *Cool Memories*, trans. Chris Turner (London: Verso, 1990).

HANDWRITING Susan Fromberg Schaeffer, *The Injured Party* (London: Hamilton, 1986).

HAPPEN John Cage in conversation with Daniel Charles, *For the Birds*, trans. Richard Gardner (London: Marion Boyars Publishers, 1981).

670 Robert Mapplethorpe, *Apollo 1988*; Estate of Robert Mapplethorpe.

HAPPIEST¹ Henry Miller, *Tropic of Cancer* (London: Grafton, 1965).

HAPPIEST² Bruce Mau, Toronto, 1992.

HARD Charlie Brown, in Charles M. Schultz, *Peanuts*. Cartoon.

HARDKAAS "La Cuisine Theoretique: Fine Obscure Architectural Discourse," *Telescope*.

HARMONY Georg Lukács, *The Process of Democratization*, trans. Susanne Bernhardt (Albany: State of New York Press, 1991).

HAZY Isaac Asimov, "No Connection," 1948, in *The Asimov Chronicles*, vol. 2, ed. Martin H. Greenberg (New York: Ace Books, 1990).

716 Andy Warhol, *Suicide*, 1962; silkscreen on paper; The Menil Collection, Houston; Gift of Adelaide de Menil Carpenter.

740–41 Giovanni Battista Tiepolo, *Apollo and the Continents* (detail), 1753; Prince-Bishop's Residenz, Würzburg; photo: Würzburg Congress & Tourismus Zentrale.

HEAVEN Tammy Faye Baker, as quoted in Priscilla Painton, "Fantasy's Reality," *Time*, May 27, 1991.

HEDGES Chidi Onwuka.

HEDONISM¹ OMA.

HEDONISM² Andrea Branzi, "The Remote-Controlled Home: Living in an Armchair," as cited in Daniel Libeskind, "Thresholds and Passages," in *Lotus Documents: Interior Landscapes*, ed. Georges Teyssot, 1987.

HERTZ *Durability of Concrete Road Bridges* (Paris: OECD Publications, 1990).

HEUREUSE "Le Désir attrape par la queue," 1941, *Picasso: Collected Writings* (London: Aurum Press, 1989).

HIDDEN Guy Debord, commentary on *Society of the Spectacle*, 1988.

HIERARCHY J. G. Ballard, *High-Rise* (London: Triad/Panther, 1985).

HIGHFALUTIN *Webster's Ninth New Collegiate Dictionary* (Springfield, Mass.: Merriam-Webster, 1990).

HISTORICAL François Sorlin, *Europe: The Comprehensive Effort*.

HISTORY Rem Koolhaas, lecture at Delft University, 1987.

HOLE¹ Henry Moore.

HOLE² *Happenings & Fluxus* (Koelnischer Kunstverein, 1970).

HOME Aldo Rossi, *A Scientific Autobiography* (Cambridge: Oppositions Books, 1981).

HONK Wim Wenders, interview by Hans Kollhoff, *Quaderns* 177 (April–June 1988).

HORRORSHOW Anthony Burgess, *A Clockwork Orange*, 1962.

HOTELS Douglas Coupland, *Shampoo Planet* (London: Simon & Schuster, 1992).

HUMAN Alejandro Zaera, "Notes for a Topographic Survey," *El Croquis*, March 1992.

HUMANITY Friedrich Nietzsche, *The Will to Power*.

HUNGRY Frank Lloyd Wright, "As 'Architect': The First Time," May 22, 1955, in *Frank Lloyd Wright: His Living Voice*, ed. Bruce Brooks Pfeiffer (Fresno: The Press at California State University, 1987). Book and sound recording.

HURRY Chidi Onwuka.

HYPERREAL Jean Baudrillard, *Simulacra and Simulations*.

IDEA Harold Brodkey, "The Animal Life of Ideas," *XX!st Century* 1 (Winter 1991–92).

IDENTITY Jane Gallop, *The Daughter's Seduction: Feminism and Psychoanalysis* (Ithaca: Cornell University Press).

IDIOT James Joyce, *Ulysses*, 1922.

IFFY *Webster's Ninth New Collegiate Dictionary* (Springfield, Mass.: Merriam-Webster, 1990).

ILLUSION Bruce Chatwin, *Patagonia* (London: Jonathan Cape, 1977).

IMAGE *Longman Dictionary of Contemporary English* (London: Longman Group Ltd., 1978).

IMAGES[1] Henri Bergson, *Matter and Memory*, trans. N. M. Paul and W. S. Palmer (New York: Urzone, 1991).

IMAGES[2] Jean Baudrillard, *The Ecstasy of Communication*, trans. Bernard and Caroline Schutze (New York: Semiotext(e)/Autonomedia, 1988).

IMAGINE Adilkno, "Topical Media," *Mediamatic* 6, no. 1 (Summer 1991).

IMPORT Noriko Takiguchi and Makoto Murata, eds., *Fukuoka International Architects' Conference '89* (Fukuoka: Coordinating Office for FIAC '89, 1989).

787 Yves Klein, *Anthropometry, ANT 61 (Héléna)*; photo: Christian Larrieu, from Pierre Restany, *Yves Klein* (Paris: Editions du Chêne, 1982).

IMPORTANT Kees Christiaanse on OMA's project for Parc de la Villette, interview by Jennifer Sigler, 1991.

IMPOSSIBILITIES Gilles Deleuze, "Mediators," in *Zone 6: Incorporations*, eds. Jonathan Crary and Sanford Kwinter (New York: Urzone, 1992).

IMPOSTER Frank Lloyd Wright, "As 'Architect': The First Time," May 22, 1955, in *Frank Lloyd Wright: His Living Voice*, ed. Bruce Brooks Pfeiffer (Fresno: The Press at California State University, 1987). Book and sound recording.

IMPUTETH "Of Innovation," *The Essays of Francis Bacon* (Mt. Vernon, NY: Peter Pauper Press).

796-97 *National Enquirer*, February 22, 1994.

INCOHERENCE Roland Barthes, "On Gide and His Journal," trans. Richard Howard, in *A Barthes Reader*, ed. Susan Sontag (New York: Hill and Wang, 1982).

INDECISION Michel de Montaigne, "How Our Mind Tangles Itself Up," *The Complete Essays* (Penguin, 1987).

INDUSTRY Gilles Deleuze and Félix Guattari, "The Anti-Oedipus," *A Thousand Plateaus: Capitalism and Schizophrenia* (Minneapolis: University of Minnesota Press, 1981).

INFERNO Italo Calvino, *Invisible Cities*, trans. William Weaver (London: Pan Books, 1979).

INFORMATION[1] Michael Synergy, in R. U. Sirius, "Synergy Speaks," *Mondo 2000* 3 (Winter 1991).

INFORMATION[2] John Cage in conversation with Daniel Charles, *For the Birds*, trans. Richard Gardner (London: Marion Boyars Publishers, 1981).

INFORMATION[3] David Byrne, *True Stories* (New York: Penguin Books, 1986).

INFORMATION[4] Jenny Holzer, *Truisms and Essays* (Halifax: Press of the Nova Scotia College of Art and Design, 1983).

INNOCENCE Jean Claude Garcias, "Tragic and Exhilarating: The Koolhaas Effect in France," *Casabella*, July–Aug. 1990.

INTEGRITY Charles Jencks, *Modern Movements in Architecture* (London: Penguin Books, 1973).

INTERESTING J. D. Salinger, *The Catcher in the Rye*, 1945.

INTERFACE Paul Virilio, "The Interface," *Lotus* 75, 1993.

INTERMEDIATE Fay Weldon, *The Life and Loves of a She-Devil* (Hodder and Stoughton, 1983).

INTERNATIONALIZATION Rem Koolhaas, interview by Alejandro Zaera, "Finding Freedoms," *El Croquis*, March 1992.

804-5 Airport plans, *Inflight Magazine*, American Airlines.

INTERRUPT[1] Martin Pawley, *Buckminster Fuller* (London: Trefoil Publications, 1990).

INTERRUPT[2] Julia, in T. S. Eliot, *The Cocktail Party* (London: Faber & Faber, 1950).

INTIMACY Georges Teyssot, "The Domestic Revolution," in *Lotus Documents: Interior Landscapes*, ed. Georges Teyssot, 1987.

INTO William Forsythe and David Levine, text from "The Loss of Small Detail," Ballett Frankfurt, 1991. Ballet.

INTUITION Enrico Fermi, physicist, as quoted in Trevor Leggett, *Zen and the Ways* (London: Routledge & Kegan Paul, 1978).

INVALID Frank Lloyd Wright, "Building Codes and the Guggenheim Museum," Aug. 2, 1953, in *Frank Lloyd Wright: His Living Voice*, ed. Bruce Brooks Pfeiffer (Fresno: The Press at California State University, 1987). Book and sound recording.

IRONING Eric de Kuyper on MTV, "Ironing Amid a Wealth of Images," in *What a Wonderful World! Music Videos in Architecture*, eds. Jola Meijer and Ernie Tee (Groningen, Holland: Groninger Museum, 1990).

IRONY Anthony Vidler, "The Ironies of Metropolis: Notes on the Work of OMA," *Skyline*, May 1982.

IRRATIONAL Alan Ryan, "When It's Irrational to be Rational," *New York Review of Books*, Oct. 10, 1991.

ISLANDS Milan Kundera, *Immortality*, trans. Peter Kussi (New York: HarperCollins Publishers, 1992).

ISORHYTHM Siegmund Levarie and Ernst Levy, *Musical Morphology* (Kent, Ohio: Kent State University Press, 1983).

JAM SESSION Umberto Eco, *Travels in Hyperreality*, trans. William Weaver (London: Pan Books with Secker & Warburg, 1987).

JARGON William Wegman, "Pathetic Readings," *Avalanche*, May–June 1974.

JERKED Jayne Anne Phillips, "Fast Lanes," *Granta* 19 (Summer 1986).

JOLLY Ayn Rand, *The Fountainhead*, 1943.

JUDGEMENTS Rem Koolhaas, interview by Alejandro Zaera, "Finding Freedoms," *El Croquis*, March 1992.

840 Michelangelo, *The Expulsion*, 1509-10, Sistine Chapel ceiling, Vatican; photo: Takashi Okamura; copyright Nippon Television Network Co., Tokyo.

JUNCTION J. G. Ballard, introduction to *Crash* (New York: Vintage, 1989).

JUSTE Jean-Luc Godard.

KILL *The New York Times*, Aug. 25, 1991.

KIPPLE Philip K. Dick, *Do Androids Dream of Electric Sheep?* (London: Grafton Books, 1972). Filmed as *Blade Runner*.

KNOCKING Stanlake Samkange, *The Mourned One* (Ibadan: Heinemann, 1975).

KNOW Madonna, interview by Carrie Fisher, *Elle*, Oct. 1991.

KNOWS Friedrich Nietzsche, *Twilight of the Idols*, 1889.

LABYRINTH Anaïs Nin, *Winter of Artifice*, in Julio Cortazar, *Hopscotch*, trans. Gregory Rabassa (New York: Random House, 1966).

LANDMARK David Naylor on the marquee of the Midland Theater, Kansas City, *Great American Movie Theaters* (Washington, DC: Preservation Press, 1987).

LANGUAGE Roland Barthes.

LAST Advertisement, Sitecraft planters and site furnishings, *Progressive Architecture*, Mid-Oct. 1988.

LEAK Michael Synergy, in R. U. Sirius, "Synergy Speaks," *Mondo 2000* 3 (Winter 1991).

LEASE *The Independent*, June 29, 1990.

LEFT FOOT Andrew MacNair, "Not Not Architecture," description of Koolhaas/MacNair studio at Harvard.

LEVEL[1] D. K. Chang, *Building Construction Illustrated* (New York: Van Nostrand Reinhold, 1975).

LEVEL[2] Brick, in Tennessee Williams, *Cat on a Hot Tin Roof*, 1955.

LEVERAGE Donald Trump with Tony Schwartz, *Trump: The Art of the Deal* (New York: Warner Books, 1987).

LIBERATING Glenn Wilson, *The Psychology of Performing Arts* (London: Croom Helm, 1985).

LIBERATOR Rem Koolhaas, lecture at Columbia University, Nov. 1989.

LIFE SENTENCE Wim Wenders, interview by Hans Kollhoff, *Quaderns* 177 (April–June 1988).

LIGHT-SCULPTURE Isamu Noguchi.

LILLE[1] *Frommer's Dollarwise Guide to France* (New York: Prentice Hall, 1987).

LILLE[2] Adapted from *Webster's New Geographical Dictionary* (Springfield, Mass.: G & C Merriam Co., 1977).

876 Lucio Fontana, *Concept spatial/Attentes*, 1966; private collection; from *Lucio Fontana* (Paris: Editions du Centre Pompidou, 1987).

900 Bandinelli, *Adam and Eve*; Firenze, Museo Nazionale, Giusti di S. Becocci.

904-5 Voters in South Africa; *de Volkskrant*, April 28, 1994; Associated Press.

LILLE[3] "Lille-Congrepo: Expositions-Congres-Spectacles," *Promotional News* (Lille: Congrexpo, 1992).

LILLE[4] Peter Wislocki, "Euralille," *Architect's Journal*, Sept. 1991.

LIMINAL Victor Turner, after van Gennep, *From Ritual to Theater* (New York: Performing Arts Journal Publications, 1982).

LIQUEFACTION Alejandro Zaera, "Notes for a Topographic Survey," *El Croquis*, March 1992.

LITE Label, Swiss Miss® Lite Hot Cocoa Mix.

LITE CITY Rem Koolhaas, notes for lecture at Rice University, 1992.

LITERATURE Gilles Deleuze, "Mediators," in *Zone 6: Incorporations*, eds. Jonathan Crary and Sanford Kwinter (New York: Urzone, 1992).

ture hid the tree behind it, outside the room. For the spectator, it was both inside the room within the painting and outside in the real landscape. This is how we see the world. We see it outside ourselves, and at the same time we only have a representation of it in ourselves. In the same way, we sometimes situate in the past that which is happening in the present. Time and space thus lose the vulgar meaning that only daily experience takes into account.

WINDOW[3]
This month Stanford became the first U.S. medical facility to install a computerized "window" that simulated the progress of daily light changes — and the passage of time — from sunrise to sunset ... The Stanford window is actually a computer-controlled light box behind a blowup of a 35mm slide. The scene depicts a peaceful pasture with billowing clouds in the background. An electronic digital timer produces 650 separate light changes every 24 hours, starting with the pale pink hues of sunrise and ending — on the opposite side of the window — with deeper shades of coral fading into dusk. An updated version will include a moon and twinkling stars.

WIPEOUT
All over the world, Moran decided, the past was being wiped out by condominiums.

WISHING
The alchemist is a dreamer who wishes, who enjoys wishing, who magnifies himself in his wishing big.

WIT
Wit: based on intuition, intelligence, knowledge, commitment and sense. The power of perceiving analogies and other relations between apparently incongruous ideas or of forming unexpected, striking or ludicrous combinations of them.

WORDS[1]
Many businesspeople in U.S. automobile and high-technology firms, for example, with Japanese competition much on their minds these days, like to use such Japanese words as *nemawa-shi* (consensus-building) and *kanban* (tight inventory management).

WORDS[2]
So papa teaches Josette the real meaning of words. A chair is a

1292

LITTLE STONES Heinz Kurth, *Concrete* (Tadworth: Windmill Press, 1972).

LIVERS "Preliminary Problems in Constructing a Situation," in *Situationist International Anthology*, ed. Ken Knabb (Berkeley: Bureau of Public Secrets, 1981).
LOBOTOMY Rem Koolhaas, *Delirious New York* (New York: Oxford University Press, 1978; New York: The Monacelli Press, 1994).
LOGIC *Longman Dictionary of Contemporary English* (London: Longman Group Ltd., 1978).
LONGER Advertisement, Antron carpet by Dupont, *Progressive Architecture*, Mid-Oct. 1988.
LOOK-ALIKE E. Ann Kaplan, "The Sacred Image of the Same," in *What a Wonderful World! Music Videos in Architecture*, eds. Jola Meijer and Ernie Tee (Groningen, Holland: Groninger Museum, 1990).
LOVE Hugo of St. Victor, *Didascalion*, trans. Jerome Taylor (New York: Columbia University Press, 1961).
LULLABY H. G. Wells, *The Dream* (London: Hogarth Press, 1987).
LUMBER John Irving, *The World According to Garp* (London: Transworld Publishers, 1979).
LURID Gore Vidal, *Washington, DC* (Boston: Little Brown and Co., 1967).
MA Arata Isozaki, "A Fragmentary Portrait of Anyone," in *Anyone*, ed. Cynthia C. Davidson (New York: Rizzoli International Publications, 1991).
MAD Norman Bates, in Alfred Hitchcock, *Psycho*, 1960. Film.
MADNESS Judith Barry, "Choros," in *Public Fantasy*, ed. Iwona Blazwick (London: Institute of Contemporary Arts, 1991).
MAINTENANCE Jagman Singh, *The Art of Earthmoving* (Rotterdam: A. A. Balkema, 1986).
MAKE Rem Koolhaas, interview by Alejandro Zaera, "Finding Freedoms," *El Croquis*, March 1992.
MAKE-UP The Diagram Group, *Man's Body: An Owner's Manual* (New York: Bantam Books, 1983).
MAMMALS J. G. Ballard, "Project for a Glossary of the 20th Century," in *Zone 6: Incorporations*, eds. Jonathan Crary and Sanford Kwinter (New York: Urzone, 1992).
MANEUVER Bertolt Brecht, *Tagebucher 1920–1922*.
MANUSCRIPTS Janny Scott, "The Great Paper Chase: Famous Scribbles in Demand," *The International Herald Tribune*, July 2, 1993.
MAP[1] Laurie Anderson, "Big Science" (Difficult Music [BMI], 1982). Sound recording.
MAP[2] Gilles Deleuze and Félix Guattari, *A Thousand Plateaus: Capitalism and Schizophrenia* (Minneapolis: University of Minnesota Press, 1987).
MAQUILLAGE André Corboz, "Looking for a City in America: Down These Mean Streets a Man Must Go–," in *Angel's Flight*, Occasional Papers from Los Angeles (Los

Angeles: The Getty Center for the History of Art and the Humanities, 1992).
MARBLE Gertrude Stein, *Lectures in America* (London: Virago Press, 1988).
MASKS[1] Olivia Vlahos, *Body: The Ultimate Symbol* (New York: J. P. Lippincott, 1979).
MASKS[2] Anaïs Nin, *Delta of Venus* (New York: Bantam Books, 1983).
MASTERPIECE Nancy and Malcolm Willey, letter to Frank Lloyd Wright, Nov. 21, 1934, in *Frank Lloyd Wright: Letters to Clients*, ed. Bruce Brooks Pfeiffer (London: Architectural Press, 1987).
MATADOR Primitivo, in Ernest Hemingway, *For Whom the Bell Tolls*, 1940.
MAY Paul Rudolph on Miami House by Rem Koolhaas and Laurinda Spear, *Progressive Architecture*, Jan. 1975.
ME Milan Kundera, *Immortality*, trans. Peter Kussi (New York: HarperCollins Publishers, 1992).
MEDIA[1] Jean Baudrillard, *Simulacra and Simulations*.
MEDIA[2] *Facts About Germany* (Gütersloh: Lexicothek Verlag, 1982).
MEDIATORS Gilles Deleuze, "Mediators," in *Zone 6: Incorporations*, eds. Jonathan Crary and Sanford Kwinter (New York: Urzone, 1992).
MEGALOMANIA Rem Koolhaas, lecture at Columbia University, Nov. 1989.
MELT Marshall Berman, *All That Is Solid Melts Into Air* (New York: Simon and Schuster, 1982).
MEMO Rem Koolhaas, memo to OMA office, July 10, 1991.
MEMORY Computer of Frans Blok, OMA.
MEN Jane Austen, *Emma*, 1815.
MESS Jack Kerouac, *Doctor Sax: Faust Part III*, 1959 (London: Deutsch, 1977).
MESSAGES J. G. Ballard, *Crash* (New York: Vintage, 1989).
MESSY Andrew MacNair, Rotterdam, 1993.
METAPHOR Peter Salter, in *AA Prospectus*, 1989–90.
METAPHORS O. M. Ungers, *Morphologie City Metaphors* (Cologne: Verlag der Buchhandlung Walther König, 1982).
METROPOLIS Alejandro Zaera, "Notes for a Topographic Survey," *El Croquis*, March 1992.
METROPOLITAN[1] OMA.
METROPOLITAN[2] Dan Jurgens, "The Mark of the Krypton Man," *Superman* 57 (July 1991).
MIDAS Rem Koolhaas, interview by Alejandro Zaera, "Finding Freedoms," *El Croquis*, March 1992.
MILESTONE Ron Steiner, OMA, interview by Jennifer Sigler, May 1990.
MIMESIS Rem Koolhaas, interview by Alejandro Zaera, "Finding Freedoms," *El Croquis*, March 1992.
MINUTE Alistair MacLean, *When Eight Bells Toll* (Fawcett Publications, 1966).
MISUNDERSTANDING Lucy, in Charles M. Schultz, *Peanuts*. Cartoon.
MOBIUS STRIP[1] Judy Jones and William Wilson, *An Incomplete Education* (New York: Ballantine Books, 1987).
MOBIUS STRIP[2] Paul Groot, "L'Eclipse: Narcisse, c'est moi ... " in *What a Wonderful World! Music Videos in Architecture*, eds. Jola Meijer and Ernie Tee (Groningen, Holland: Groninger Museum, 1990).

MODERN Advertisement, Armstrong's Linoleum, *Women's Home Companion*, Sept. 1954.

MODERNISM Rem Koolhaas, "Conversations with Students," *Architecture at Rice* (Houston: Rice University, 1991).

MODERNITY Charles Baudelaire, "The Painter of Modern Life," in *Selected Writings on Art and Artists* (New York: Harmondsworth, 1972).

MONEY Jonathan Crary, *Eclipse of the Spectacle* (London: Collins, 1979).

MONSTER George Langelaan, "The Fly," 1958, in *No, But I Saw the Movie*, ed. David Wheeler (New York: Penguin Books, 1989).

MONSTERS Jean Baudrillard, *Cool Memories*, trans. Chris Turner (London: Verso, 1990).

MONUMENTAL Arthur Drexler, *Transformations in Modern Architecture* (New York: Museum of Modern Art, 1979).

MORAL Friedrich Nietzsche, *Beyond Good and Evil*, 1886.

MORALITY Yukio Mishima, *Forbidden Colours*, trans. Alfred H. Marks (Penguin Books/Martin, Secker & Warburg, 1971).

MORE[1] Charles Dickens, *Oliver Twist*, 1837–39.

MORE[2] Daniel Libeskind, "Thresholds and Passages," in *Lotus Documents: Interior Landscapes*, ed. Georges Teyssot, 1987.

MORNING U. G. Brown, *Our Street* (London: Illusion Press, 1988).

MORPHOGENETIC Alejandro Zaera, "Notes for a Topographic Survey," *El Croquis*, March 1992.

MOUNTAIN Rem Koolhaas, *Delirious New York* (New York: Oxford University Press, 1978; New York: The Monacelli Press, 1994).

MOUSTIQUE Vice President, Toyota Motors research laboratory, as quoted in Paul Virilio, *La Loi de la proximité*.

MOUTH[1] Anaïs Nin, *Delta of Venus* (New York: Bantam Books, 1983).

MOUTH[2] Jenny Holzer, cast bronze plaque from "The Living Series" (1981–82), in Diane Waldman, *Jenny Holzer* (New York: Solomon R. Guggenheim Museum/Harry N. Abrams, 1989).

MOUTHS Charles Darwin, *The Origin of Species*, 1859.

MOVEMENT[1] Iakov Chernikhov, *The Construction of Architectural and Machine Forms*.

MOVEMENT[2] Marcel Duchamp in Pierre Cabanne, *Dialogues with Marcel Duchamp*, trans. Rojn Padgett (New York: Viking Press, 1971).

MULTIPLY Mario Buatta, as quoted in "Great Ideas," *HG*, Sept. 1991.

MUSEUM[1] Marcel Breuer at presentation of the Whitney Museum project, 1963.

MUSEUM[2] Tama Janowitz, "On and Off the African Veldt," *Slaves of New York* (New York: Crown Publishers, 1986).

MUSEUM[3] J. D. Salinger, *The Catcher in the Rye*, 1945.

MUST-HAVE *The Architect's Journal*, 1960, as quoted in Charles Jencks, *Modern Movements in Architecture* (London: Penguin Books, 1973).

MYSTERY[1] Robert Musil, *The Man Without Qualities*, trans. Eithne Wilkins and Ernst Kaiser (London: Secker & Warburg, 1954).

MYSTERY[2] John Nichols, *The Milagro Beanfield War* (New York: Ballantine Books, 1974).

MYTHICAL Rem Koolhaas, lecture at Columbia University, Nov. 1989.

NACH DRUBEN Fritz Neumeyer on "Exodus," Rem Koolhaas's AA thesis project, in "OMA's Berlin: The Polemic Island in the City," *Assemblage* 11.

NAME[1] Elvis Presley, Virginia housewife, on co-workers' reaction to her 1981 name change from Lilly May Painter, "Overheard," *Newsweek*, June 10, 1991.

NAME[2] Gertrude Stein, *The World is Round*, 1939.

NAME[3] Rem Koolhaas, office memo, Oct. 1992.

NAME[4] Ralph Hardy, *The Weather Book* (Boston: Little, Brown and Co., 1982).

NAME-DROP Joan Collins, *Past Imperfect*, 1978 (Coronet Books, 1985).

NAMELESS[1] Joseph Conrad, *Lord Jim*, 1900.

NAMELESS[2] Siri Hustvedt, "Mr. Morning," in *Best American Short Stories of 1991*, ed. Richard Ford (Boston: Houghton Mifflin, 1990).

NARCISSISM Sigmund Freud, *On Narcissism: An Introduction*, 1914 Standard Edition, vol. 14, trans. James Strackey (London: Hogarth Press, 1953).

NATURAL Leonardo da Vinci, "How to Make an Imaginary Animal Appear Natural," extract from the notebooks of Leonardo da Vinci, *Das Buch der Malerei*, ed. H. Ludwig (Vienna, 1882).

NEEDLES James Casebere, "Three Stories," in *Blasted Allegories*, ed. Brian Wallis (New York: New Museum of Contemporary Art and MIT Press, 1987).

NERVE Fyodor Dostoyevsky.

NERVED Sculpture title, "The General Jungle," *Gilbert & George: The Charcoal on Paper Sculptures, 1970–1974* (Bordeaux: Musée d'art contemporain, 1986).

NEUTRAL "The Aesthetics of Silence," *A Susan Sontag Reader* (New York: Vintage, 1983).

NEUTRALITY Marguerite Duras, *Blue Eyes Black Hair*, trans. Barbara Bray (New York: Pantheon Books, 1987).

NEW[1] Ivan Leonidov.

NEW[2] Advertisement, Pountney Clinic, London, *Cosmopolitan*, Sept. 1991.

NEW YORK[1] Rem Koolhaas, "The Contemporary City," lecture at Santander, Aug. 1988.

NEW YORK[2] Andrew Beresky, ed., *Fodor's New York City 1989* (New York: Fodor's Travel Publications, 1989).

NICE Ayrton Senna, Formula One driver, on an opponent after Portuguese Grand Prix, 1991.

NICER Frank O. Gehry.

NIGHTCAP John Le Carré, *Tinker Tailor Soldier Spy* (London: Pan Books, 1974).

NIGHTMARES Harry Mulisch, *Last Call*.

NOMAD Rem Koolhaas on Nexus housing, fax to Toyo Ito, July 17, 1991.

NON-CAPTIVE G. K. Chesterton, *The Club of Queer Trades* (London: Penguin Books, 1946).

NONSTOP Robert W. McIntosh and Charles R. Goeldner, *Tourism: Principles, Practices, Philosophies*, 5th ed. (New York: John Wiley and Sons, 1986).

NOODLES "Noodles in a Self-Heating Can," *Newsweek*, Jan. 15, 1990.

NORMAL Ueno Koshi, "The Road of

Kawashima Yuzo," in *Japanese Kings of the Bs* (Rotterdam: Stichting Film Festival, 1991).

NOT Jean Nouvel, *Jean Nouvel: L' Oeuvre récent 1987–1990* (Barcelona: Collegi d'Arquitectos de Catalunya, 1990).

NOVELLA Ivan Leonidov.

NUMBER Charles Baudelaire, *Intimate Journals*, trans. Christopher Isherwood (San Francisco: City Lights Books, 1983).

OBJECTLESSNESS Martin Heidegger, *The Question Concerning Technology* (New York: Harper & Row, 1977).

OBJECTS[1] Laurie Anderson.

OBJECTS[2] Tama Janowitz, "Spells," *Slaves of New York* (New York: Crown Publishers, 1986).

OBLIGATION Andre Higgins, *Independent* correspondent, on being expelled from China.

OBLIGATIONS Don DeLillo, *The Names* (London: Picador, 1987).

968 Lygia Clark, Air and Stone, 1966; inflated plastic bag and pebble.

OBLIVIOUS Denis Hollier, interview by Mark Taylor, *Newsline*, Nov. 1989.

OBSOLETE Joseph Abboud, fashion designer.

OBSTACLES L. G. O'Brien, "Moving In Space," *Geographical*, Aug. 1991.

OCCUPATION[1] Chidi Onwuka.

OCCUPATION[2] Rem Koolhaas, fax to Sven Ollmann, OMA, Sept. 24, 1991.

ODOR Arthur Drexler, *Transformations in Modern Architecture* (New York: Museum of Modern Art, 1979).

OLDER Jean Baudrillard, *Cool Memories*, trans. Chris Turner (London: Verso, 1990).

OOH *Webster's Ninth New Collegiate Dictionary* (Springfield, Mass.: Merriam-Webster, 1990).

OPPORTUNITY Advertisement, Olympus camera.

OPPOSITE Walter Benjamin, "The Work of Art in the Age of Mechanical Reproduction," trans. Harry Zohn, *Illuminations* (New York: Schocken Books, 1969).

ORDER Louis Kahn.

OTHER[1] Fredric Jameson, lecture at Princeton University, April 1991.

OTHER[2] Roland Barthes.

OXYGEN Arthur C. Clarke, *2001: A Space Odyssey* (London: Arrow Books, 1968).

OXYMORON *Webster's Ninth New Collegiate Dictionary* (Springfield, Mass.: Merriam-Webster, 1990).

PAID Kathy Acker, *Empire of the Senseless* (New York: Grove Press, 1988).

PANIC Jules Marshall, "Panic Biology," *Mediamatic* 6, no. 1 (Summer 1991).

PARANOIA Rem Koolhaas, *Delirious New York* (New York: Oxford University Press, 1978; New York: The Monacelli Press, 1994).

PARASITE J. Hillis Miller, as quoted in Gregory L. Ulmer, "The Object of Post-Criticism," in *The Anti-Aesthetic: Essays of Postmodern Culture*, ed. Hal Foster (Seattle: Bay Press, 1989).

PARIS Alexandre Lazareff, *Paris Rendezvous* (Paris: Hachette, 1991).

PARLEZ Subversive corporal, in Joseph Heller, *Catch 22*, 1961.

PARODIES Julian Barnes, *Talking it Over* (New York: Vintage, 1991).

PARTICIPATION Sigfried Giedion, *Walter

window. The window is a penholder. A pillow is a piece of bread. Bread is a bedside rug. Feet are ears. Arms are feet. A head is a behind. A behind is a head. Eyes are fingers. Fingers are eyes.

WORK¹
There were omnibuses, and it was raining. It rained for four days, and a leprous gray stretched out over everything. For three weeks I waited for the weight of my heart to lighten. I had to work at it, and most of all I wanted to love this place.

WORK²
I like work. It fascinates me. I can sit and look at it for hours!

WORKING
This vierendeel is working very very hard. We have modelled it on the computer and the results are such that these are the members required. I wish you would not call our members monstrous when they have a lot of work to do!! And we are trying to maintain economy and some degree of aesthetics.

WORLD
Then begins the *gigantic megalopolis*, the *city-as-world*, which suffers nothing besides itself and sets about annihilating the country picture.

WRONG¹
Sometimes you have to say: "What is the wrong thing. What is the wrong thing to do." And then do the wrong thing …

WRONG²
The developers who started building big new office complexes outside American cities in the 1970s assumed that their users would be able to speed to work along big, open freeways. They were wrong. In 1980 the suburbanite on his way to work was driving barely faster than the city dweller: 24 mph against 21 mph. Since he was also driving farther, 12 miles rather than 9, he actually spent longer behind the wheel.

WRONG³
In 1960, some months before his seventy-fifth birthday, when Ludwig Mies van der Rohe was asked to describe his working day, he answered: "I get up. I sit on the bed. I think, 'what the hell went wrong? We showed them what to do.'"

1294

Gropius: Work and Teamwork (London: Architectural Press, 1954).
PARTY Jerry Adler, "Age of the Push-Button," *Newsweek*, July 1990.
PASS Chieko Shiomi, "Passing Music for a Tree," from "Water Music," July 1964, in *Happenings & Fluxus* (Koelnischer Kunstverein, 1970).
PASTED Francis Picabia, "Le Premier Mai," *Literature* 14 (June 1920).
PATCHWORK Francisco J. Varela, "The Reenchantment of the Concrete," *Zone 6: Incorporations*, eds. Jonathan Crary and Sanford Kwinter (New York: Urzone, 1992).
PATIENCE Paul Valéry.
PCM Salvador Dalí, "The Conquest of the Irrational," appendix to *Conversations with Dalí* (New York: Dutton, 1969).
PC/VME Allen Brown, "Building a Toolbox for DSP Engineering," *Electronics World & Wireless World*, Sept. 1991.
PERCEPTION Aristotle, *De Anima*, trans. Hugh Lawson-Tancred (Harmondsworth: Penguin Books, 1986).
PERFECT Fred Astaire in *Top Hat* (lyrics by Irving Berlin).
PERISHABLE Charles Jencks, *Modern Movements in Architecture* (London: Penguin Books, 1973).
PERMANENT Paul Virilio, "The Overexposed City," in *Zone 1/2: The City* (New York: Urzone, 1987).
PHILOSOPHERS Marvin Minsky, as quoted in Stewart Brand, *The Media Lab*.
PHOBIAS Rem Koolhaas, interview by Alejandro Zaera, "Finding Freedoms," *El Croquis*, March 1992.
PHOTOGRAPHY Italo Calvino, "The Adventure of a Photographer," *Difficult Loves* (London: Picador, 1985).
PICTURES Eugene Ionesco, *Story Number 2 (for children under three years of age)*, trans. Calvin K. Towle (Harlin Quist, 1970).
PLACE¹ Charles Jencks, *Modern Movements in Architecture* (London: Penguin Books, 1973).
PLACE² Anonymous.
PLAN¹ Le Corbusier, *Towards a New Architecture*, 13th French ed., trans. Frederick Etchells (New York: Dover Publications, 1986).
PLAN² Raymond Hood, as quoted in Arthur Tappan North, *Raymond Hood* (New York: Whittlesey House, McGraw-Hill, 1931).
PLAN³ Umberto Eco, *Foucault's Pendulum*, trans. William Weaver (New York: Harcourt Brace Jovanovich, 1989).
PLANES Anne Tyler, *The Accidental Tourist* (New York: Alfred A. Knopf, 1985).
PLANETARY Maxine Hong Kingston, *The Woman Warrior*, 1976 (London: Pan Books, 1981).
PLANKTON Rem Koolhaas, "Whether Europe," lecture at Delft University, April 1988.
PLANNING Rem Koolhaas, interview by Alejandro Zaera, "Finding Freedoms," *El Croquis*, March 1992.

PLASTIC Chidi Onwuka.
PLAY Erik H. Erikson, psychoanalyst, as quoted in Edmund N. Bacon, *Design of Cities* (New York: Penguin Books, 1976).

PLENUMS Cecil Balmond, Ove Arup & Partners, with Rem Koolhaas, interview by *Kenchiku Bunka* Magazine, June 23, 1991.
PLOT Rem Koolhaas, *Delirious New York* (New York: Oxford University Press, 1978; New York: The Monacelli Press, 1994).
POETIC Samuel Hopkins Adams, "Night Bus," 1933, in *No, But I Saw the Movie*, ed. David Wheeler (New York: Penguin Books, 1989).
POINT P. L. Travers, *Mary Poppins* (London: Davies, 1934).
POLES¹ Robert A. M. Stern with Raymond W. Gastil, *Modern Classicism* (New York: Rizzoli International Publications, 1988).
POLES² Advertisement, Union Metal lighting poles, *Progressive Architecture*, Mid-Oct. 1988.

PONTIFICATE "The Fisherman and His Wife," *Grimms' Fairy Tales*, trans. Edgar Taylor (London: Scholar Press, 1979).
POODLE Tom Clark, *Shattuckworld*.
POOL¹ Paul Virilio, "The Last Vehicle," *Looking Back on the End of the World* (New York: Semiotext(e)/Autonomedia).
POOL² Rem Koolhaas, "The Story of the Pool," *Delirious New York* (New York: Oxford University Press, 1978; New York: The Monacelli Press, 1994).
POOL³ Rem Koolhaas on the Villa Dall'Ava, in *The Chicago Tapes* (New York: Rizzoli International Publications, 1987).
POP Drag queen, New York, as quoted in *The Face*.
POPULAR Donald Trump with Tony Schwartz, *Trump: The Art of the Deal* (New York: Warner Books, 1987).
POSITIONS¹ Donald Judd, "Donald Judd's 'Real' Furniture," *XX!st Century* 1 (Winter 1991–92).
POSITIONS² Aimee Rankin, "Legacies of Critical Practice in the 1980s," in *Discussions in Contemporary Culture*, ed. Hal Foster (Seattle: Bay Press, 1987).
POSTCARD Walker Percy, "The Loss of the Creature," *The Message in the Bottle*, 1954.
POSTCARDS¹ Toyo Ito on OMA's Fukuoka housing, fax to Rem Koolhaas, April 29, 1991.
POSTCARDS² Jacques Derrida, *The Post Card: From Socrates to Freud and Beyond*, trans. Alan Bass (Chicago: University of Chicago Press, 1987).
POST-MODERNISM Richard Meier, Royal Gold Medal Address, Royal Institute of British Architects, 1988.
POWER Michel Foucault, *Discipline and Punish*, trans. Alan Sheridan (London: Penguin Books, 1977).
POWERCUT Max Erlich, *The Edict* (New York: Bantam Books, 1972).
POWERLESS Norman Schwarzkopf, retired US general, on life after the Gulf War, "Overheard," *Newsweek*, Nov. 11, 1991.
POWERLESSNESS Friedrich Nietzsche, *On The Advantage and Disadvantage of History for Life* (Indianapolis: Hackett Pub. & Co., 1980).
PREGNANCY Rem Koolhaas on his late-1980s discovery that the principles explored

in *Delirious New York* could apply to Europe, interview by Alejandro Zaera, "Finding Freedoms," *El Croquis*, March 1992.

PREGNANT Caroline Walker Bynum, "The Female Body and Religious Practice in the Later Middle Ages," in *Fragments for a History of the Human Body*, part 1, ed. Michel Feher (New York: Urzone, 1989).

PRESENCE James Joyce, *Ulysses*, 1922.

PROBABILITY Ludwig Wittgenstein, *Philosophical Grammar*, ed. Rush Rhees, trans. Anthony Kenny (Oxford: Basil Blackwell, 1974).

PROCRUSTES Rem Koolhaas, "Our New Sobriety," in catalog for OMA exhibition at the Architectural Association, London, 1980.

PRODUCTION Henri Lefebvre, "Space, Social Product, and Use Value," *Critical Sociology* (New York: Irvington Publishers, 1979).

PROGRAMME Peter Salter, in *AA Prospectus*, 1989–90.

PROGRESS Fritz Neumeyer, "OMA's Berlin: The Polemic Island in the City," *Assemblage* 11.

PROPOSITION Ludwig Wittgenstein, *Philosophical Grammar*, ed. Rush Rhees, trans. Anthony Kenny (Oxford: Basil Blackwell, 1974).

PROPRIETY Anna Raeburn, *Keeper of Dreams* (London: Bodley Head, 1989).

PROTECT D. K. Chang, *Building Construction Illustrated* (New York: Van Nostrand Reinhold, 1975).

PROVOCATEUR Charles Jencks, *Modern Movements in Architecture* (London: Penguin Books, 1973).

PROXIMITY[1] J. D. Salinger, *The Catcher in the Rye*, 1945.

PROXIMITY[2] Rem Koolhaas, lecture on OMA's project for The Hague City Hall at Delft University, 1987.

PSEUDONYM Stephen King, interview by Mark Marvel, *Interview*, Oct. 1991.

PSYCHOGEOGRAPHY "Definitions," in *Situationist International Anthology*, ed. Ken Knabb (Berkeley: Bureau of Public Secrets, 1981).

PURGE Ian McEwan, *The Cement Garden* (New York: Simon & Schuster, 1978).

QUANTITY John Cage, *A Year from Monday* (Middletown: Wesleyan University Press, 1963).

QUASI-HISTORICAL Robert Maxwell, introduction to catalog for OMA exhibition at the Architectural Association, London, 1980.

QUERY "The Mouse and the Mole," *Bulgarian Folk Tales*, ed., trans. Assen Nicoloff (Cleveland, 1979).

QUOTE[1] Ralph Waldo Emerson, *Journals*, May 1849.

QUOTE[2] Madeleine Gagnon, "Body I," in *New French Feminisms*, eds. Elaine Marks and Isabelle de Courtivron (New York: Schocken Books, 1981), as cited in Kate Linker, *Love for Sale: The Words and Pictures of Barbara Kruger* (New York: Harry N. Abrams, 1990).

RADIUS Patricia Tutt and David Adler, eds., *New Metric Handbook: Planning and Design Data* (London: Butterworth Architecture, 1979).

RAIN John David Morley, *Pictures from the Water Trade* (London: Fontana Paperbacks, 1986).

RAINED James M. Cain, "Serenade," 1937, in *Three By Cain* (New York: Vintage, 1989).

RANDOM Cynthia Ozick, *The Messiah of Stockholm* (New York: Knopf, 1987).

RAPSODES Raymond Schwab.

RATIONALITY Iakov Chernikhov, *The Construction of Architectural and Machine Forms*.

RC Chidi Onwuka.

REACHABLE "Why the Sky Is High," *Bulgarian Folk Tales*, ed., trans. Assen Nicoloff (Cleveland, 1979).

REASON Sculpture title, "The General Jungle," *Gilbert & George: The Charcoal on Paper Sculptures, 1970–1974* (Bordeaux: Musée d'art contemporain, 1986).

REBEL Daniel Libeskind, "Berlin Museum," *Newsline*, Nov. 1989.

RED G. K. Chesterton.

REDOUBT Richard Ernsberger Jr., "Your Own Tearoom," *Newsweek*, Nov. 4, 1991.

REFLECTION Jurichiro Tamizaki, *Diary of an Old Man* (Oxford: Oxford University Press, 1988).

REFRACTION William Golding, *The Spire* (London: Faber & Faber, 1965).

REFUGE Thomas Pynchon, *Vineland* (London: Secker & Warburg, 1990).

REFUSE Leon Krier.

REGENERATION Wim Wenders, interview by Hans Kollhoff, *Quaderns* 177 (April–June 1988).

REGULATED Rem Koolhaas on OMA's Nexus housing, fax to Toyo Ito, July 17, 1991.

REINCARNATION[1] Attributed to captured US Air Force bomber pilot, Hanoi.

REINCARNATION[2] Kees van Kooten and Wim de Bie, Dutch comedians, 1977.

RELOCATED Jonathan E. Benjamin, ed., *Let's Go Greece* (London: Pan Books, 1989).

REMINDER Joseph Heller, *Catch 22*, 1961.

1098 Man Ray, *Hier, Aujourd'hui, Demain*, 1930–32 (detail).

REMINDERS Stephen Tyler.

REMNANT J. G. Ballard, *The Terminal Beach* (London: Gollancz, 1964).

REMONTAGE Manfredo Tafuri, "The Historical Project," *The Sphere and the Labyrinth* (Cambridge: MIT Press, 1987).

REPLICAS Janet Frame, *Living in the Manitoto*, 1981.

RESCUED Leo Tolstoy, *Anna Karenina*, 1875–77.

REST[1] Peter Sloterdijk, *Critique of Cynical Reason* (Minneapolis: University of Minnesota Press, 1987).

REST[2] Siegmund Levarie and Ernst Levy, *Musical Morphology* (Kent, Ohio: Kent State University Press, 1983).

REVERSAL Rem Koolhaas on The Hague City Hall, lecture at Delft University, 1987.

REVIVES USAir gift folio, *USAir Magazine*, Aug. 1991.

REVOLT William Burroughs with Keith Haring, *Apocalypse* (New York: George Mulder Fine Arts, 1988).

REVOLUTION[1] Alvar Aalto, speech to Royal Institute of British Architects, 1957.

REVOLUTION[2] Félix Guattari, "Regimes, Pathways, Subject," in *Zone 6: Incorporations*, eds. Jonathan Crary and Sanford Kwinter (New York: Urzone, 1992).

RHIZOME Gilles Deleuze and Félix Guattari,

"Rhizome," *A Thousand Plateaus: Capitalism and Schizophrenia* (Minneapolis: University of Minnesota Press, 1987).

RHIZOMORPHS J. K. Huysman, *Against Nature*, 1882.

1104–5 Michelangelo, Sistine Chapel ceiling (detail), 1509–10, Vatican; photo: Takashi Okamura; copyright Nippon Television Network Co., Tokyo.

RIGHT Lead singer of Floodland, interview by MTV, Nov. 10, 1991.

RINGING US soldier on the day's events, Gulf War coverage, CNN, Spring 1991.

RIP-OFF Rem Koolhaas on Ellerbe Becket and Dunlop Farrow's CN/Royal Trust Office Complex, in *Progressive Architecture*, Jan. 1991.

RISK John David Morley, *Pictures from the Water Trade* (London: Fontana Paperbacks, 1986).

RIVER Jean Baudrillard, *Cool Memories*, trans. Chris Turner (London: Verso, 1990).

ROAR Ron Steiner, OMA, interview by Jennifer Sigler, May 1990.

ROOM SERVICE Vladimir Voinovich, *Moscow 2042* (London: Picador, 1989).

ROTTERDAM[1] A. Green, *Holland in Full Colour* (Rijswijk: Eumar, 1979).

ROTTERDAM[2] Erich Mendelsohn, 1920s.

ROTTERDAM[3] Rem Koolhaas, "The Terrifying Beauty of the Twentieth Century," *L'Architecture d'Aujourd'hui*, April 1985.

ROTTERDAM[4] *Fodor's Holland 1988* (New York: Fodor's Travel Publications, 1987).

RUG Mae West, in *I'm No Angel*, 1933.

RUINS Fahed Abu Shaaer, manager of the Kuwait City Sheraton Hotel, which was severely damaged by Iraqi troops during the Gulf War, "Overheard," *Newsweek*, July 22, 1991.

RULE Alexey Brodovitch.

RUNNING BARNS William Faulkner, *The Sound and the Fury*, 1929.

RUSH Spalding Gray, *Swimming to Cambodia* (New York: Theater Communications Group, 1985). Performance transcript.

RUSHED Paul Klee, "On Modern Art," 1924, in *Modern Artists on Art*, ed. Robert L. Herbert (New York: Prentice Hall, 1964).

SAME Mary Gaitskill, "Secretary," *Bad Behavior* (New York: Vintage, 1988).

SANK Salvador Dalí, *Dalí by Dalí*, trans. Eleanor R. Morse (New York: Harry N. Abrams, 1970).

SAPPHIC Advertisement, Adam and Eve Video, *Penthouse*, July 1991.

SATISFACTION Anonymous.

SAW Peter Greenaway, *The Cook, The Thief, His Wife, and Her Lover*. Film.

SCALE Ron Steiner, OMA, interview by Jennifer Sigler, May 1990.

SCATTERBRAIN *The Book of J*, trans. David Rosenberg, commentary by Harold Bloom (New York: Vintage, 1991).

SCENT Thomas Mann, "A Man and His Dog," *Death in Venice and Seven Other Stories*, trans. H. T. Lowe-Porter (New York: Vintage, 1989).

SCHISM Rem Koolhaas, *Delirious New York* (New York: Oxford University Press, 1978; New York: The Monacelli Press, 1994).

SCOPOPHILIAC Arthur and Marilouise

X

XOCHIQUETZAL
In some legends, this goddess was the only female survivor of the great flood that destroyed the world preceding this one. With a man, she escaped the torrent in a small boat. Faced with the prospect of repopulating the world, they set to work as soon as the flood receded. But all of their children were born without speech. Finally a pigeon magically endowed them with language, but every child received a different tongue, so that each was unable to communicate with the others.

XXXXL
The pants, which hipsters wear five or six sizes too big and backward, come with a "permanent crease" and an expandable seam that promises "two sizes in one!" Colors include Lincoln green and Air Force blue. The pants go well with a work shirt that is "cut for comfort" — not surprisingly with sizes up to XXXXL.

Y

Y
The tide of red taillights flowed on ahead of them, and now they bothered him. In the darkness, amid this red swarm, he couldn't get his bearings. His sense of direction was slipping away. He must be heading north still. The down side of the bridge hadn't curved a great deal. But now there were only signs to go by. His entire stock of landmarks was gone, left behind. At the end of the bridge the expressway split into a Y. MAJOR DEEGAN GEO. WASHINGTON BRIDGE... BRUCKNER NEW ENGLAND... Major Deegan went upstate ... No! ... Veer right ... Suddenly another Y ... EAST BRONX NEW ENGLAND ... EAST 138TH BRUCKNER BOULEVARD ... Choose one, you ninny! Aceydeucey ... one finger, two fingers ... He veered right again ... EAST 138TH ... a ramp ... All at once there was no more ramp, no more clean cordoned expressway. He was at ground level. It was as if

Kroker, "The Virtual World," *Mediamatic* 6, no. 1 (Summer 1991).

SCREEN Shuhei Hosokawa, "Land of a Thousand Commercials," in *What a Wonderful World! Music Videos in Architecture*, eds. Jola Meijer and Ernie Tee (Groningen, Holland: Groninger Museum, 1990).

SCULPTURE Mino Rosso, futurist aerosculptor, "Network in the Sky" formula, in F. T. Marinetti, *La Cucina futurista* (The Futurist Cookbook), trans. Suzanne Brill (London: Trefoil Publications, 1989).

SEALED A. B. Yehoshua, *Five Seasons*, trans. Hillel Halkin (New York: Doubleday, 1989).

SEARCH Walker Percy, *The Moviegoer* (New York: Avon Books, 1980).

SEARCHING Philippe Starck, as quoted in Olivier Boissière, "Starck: A Spirit of the Times," in *Starck* (Cologne: Benedikt Taschen Verlag, 1991).

SECRETS[1] Rem Koolhaas, interview by Marta Cervello, *Quaderns* 183 (Oct.–Dec. 1989).

SECRETS[2] Douglas Coupland, *Shampoo Planet* (London: Simon & Schuster, 1992).

SECURITY Yoshinobu Ashihara, *The Aesthetic Townscape*, trans. Lynn E. Ricos (Cambridge: MIT Press, 1983).

SEDUCTION[1] Advertisement, SexScent, *Penthouse*, Dec. 1990.

SEDUCTION[2] Jean Baudrillard, *The Ecstasy of Communication*, trans. Bernard and Caroline Schutze (New York: Semiotext(e)/Autonomedia, 1988).

SEEMED Kazimir Malevich, "Suprematism," in *Modern Artists on Art*, ed. Robert L. Herbert (New York: Prentice Hall, 1964).

SEEMS William Shakespeare, *Hamlet*, c. 1600.

SEEN Elvis Presley, as quoted in Priscilla Beaulieu Presley with Sandra Harmon, *Elvis and Me* (London: Century Publishing, 1985).

SEMI-MYTH Bumper sticker.

SENSIBILITY "Notes on Camp," *A Susan Sontag Reader* (New York: Vintage, 1983).

SENSITIVE Victoria Hinton, *Country Homes and Interiors*, May 1990.

SENTENCES Georges Bataille.

SERENDIPITY *Webster's Ninth New Collegiate Dictionary* (Springfield, Mass.: Merriam-Webster, 1990).

SERVICE R. K. Narayan, *The Man-Eater of Malgudi* (Harmondsworth: Penguin Books, 1983).

SEVEN THOUSAND Advertisement, "Spain ... The Dream Never Ends," Tourist Offices of Spain, *The New Yorker*, Dec. 24, 1990.

SEWER Victor Hugo, *Les Misérables*, 1862, trans. Charles E. Wilbour (New York: Simon & Schuster, 1964).

SHACKS Bruce Chatwin, *Patagonia* (London: Jonathan Cape, 1977).

SHOCKING Charles Jencks on Vincent Scully, *Modern Movements in Architecture* (London: Penguin Books, 1973).

SHODDINESS "The Great Wall of China," trans. Willa and Edwin Muir, *Franz Kafka, 1883–1924: The Complete Stories*, ed. Nahum N. Glatzer (New York: Schocken Books, 1971).

SHOPPER Edgar Allen Poe, *The Man in the Crowd*, as cited in Kate Linker, *Love for Sale: The Words and Pictures of Barbara Kruger* (New York: Harry N. Abrams, 1990).

SHOPPING Judith Barry, "Casual Imagination," in *Public Fantasy*, ed. Iwona Blazwick (London: Institute of Contemporary Arts, 1991).

SHORT "Traffic Jams," *The Economist*, Feb. 18, 1989.

SHOWROOM Advertisement, Meon International faucets and lavatory accessories, *Progressive Architecture*, Mid-Oct. 1988.

SIGNATURE[1] Francesco Dal Co, "In Consideration of Time," in *Anyone*, ed. Cynthia C. Davidson (New York: Rizzoli International Publications, 1991).

SIGNATURE[2] Wole Soyinka, *Isara* (London: Methuen, 1990).

SIGNATURE[3] Jacques Derrida, "Summary of Impromptu Remarks," in *Anyone*, ed. Cynthia C. Davidson (New York: Rizzoli International Publications, 1991).

SIMPLE Peter Sloterdijk, *Critique of Cynical Reason* (Minneapolis: University of Minnesota Press, 1987).

SIMULACRUM Jean Baudrillard, *Simulacra and Simulations*.

SIMULATION Priscilla Painton, "Fantasy's Reality," *Time*, May 27, 1991.

SINCERITY George Burns.

SING James M. Cain, "Serenade," 1937, in *Three By Cain* (New York: Vintage, 1989).

SKELETON Rem Koolhaas, "Conversations with Students," *Architecture at Rice* (Houston: Rice University, 1991).

SKELETONS Peggy Norman, "Continuum," *Omni*, May 1991.

SKIMPY Anthony Bailey, "Letter From the Netherlands," *The New Yorker*, Aug. 12, 1991.

SKINNY Julio Cortazar, *Hopscotch*, trans. Gregory Rabassa (New York: Random House, 1966).

SKI SLOPE M. S. Casper, *Synthetic Turf and Sporting Surfaces* (New Jersey: Noyes Data Corporation, 1972).

SLAVES Peter Greenaway, lecture at the Boymans–van Beuningen Museum, Rotterdam, Oct. 26, 1991.

SLEDGEHAMMER Victoria Hinton on Lady Sheila Webster's building technique.

SLOW "Traffic Jams," *The Economist*, Feb. 18, 1989.

SLOWLY Phil Patton, *Open Road* (New York: Simon & Schuster, 1986).

SMALL Le Corbusier.

SMOKER Joy Williams, "Escapes," *Granta* 19 (Summer 1986).

SOBER Ron Steiner, OMA, interview by Jennifer Sigler, May 1990.

SO FAR Letter to the editor, *Cosmopolitan*, Sept. 1991.

SOLUTION Rem Koolhaas on vierendeel beams for ZKM Karlsruhe project, fax to David Lewis, Ove Arup & Partners.

SOMETIMES Donald Trump with Tony Schwartz, *Trump: The Art of the Deal* (New York: Warner Books, 1987).

SOUL[1] Yukio Mishima, *Forbidden Colours*, trans. Alfred H. Marks (Penguin Books/Martin, Secker & Warburg, 1971).

SOUL[2] Walt Whitman.

SPACE Laurie Anderson, "Words in Reverse," *Top Stories* 2 (Buffalo, N.Y.: Hallwalls, 1979).

SPACE-TIME Paul Virilio, "The Overexposed City," in *Zone 1/2: The City* (New York: Urzone, 1987).

SPEAK J. G. Ballard, introduction to *Crash* (New York: Vintage, 1989).

SPECIES Maurice Nio, "The Ultra-Sexist Image," in *What a Wonderful World! Music Videos in Architecture*, eds. Jola Meijer and Ernie Tee (Groningen, Holland: Groninger Museum, 1990).

SPEECH Paul Ricoeur.

SPEED[1] Richard Bach, *Jonathan Livingston Seagull*, 1970.

SPEED[2] Walter Benjamin, 1937, as quoted in Jonathan Crary, preface to "The Third Window: An Interview with Paul Virilio," in *Global Television*, eds. Cynthia Schneider and Brian Wallis (Cambridge: MIT Press; New York: Wedge Press, 1988).

SPEED[3] Gilles Deleuze and Félix Guattari, *Treatise on Nomadology*.

SPEED[4] Naguib Mahfouz, *Miramar* (Washington, DC: Three Continents Press, 1984).

SPIRAL Cecil Balmond, Ove Arup & Partners, with Rem Koolhaas, interview by *Kenchiku Bunka* Magazine, June 23, 1991.

SPLODGY Fay Weldon, *The Fat Woman's Joke* (London: Hodder & Stoughton, 1982).

SPOONFED Yamane Sadao, "Mori Issei: Man of the Water Surface," in *Japanese Film Kings of the Bs* (Rotterdam: Stichting Film Festival, 1991).

SQUARE Denis Hollier, interview by Mark Taylor, *Newsline*, Nov. 1989.

SQUASHED Tom Wolfe, *Bonfire of the Vanities* (New York: Bantam Books, 1988).

SQUAT Michael Dibdin, *Ratking* (London: Faber & Faber, 1988).

SQUIRREL Philip K. Dick, *Do Androids Dream of Electric Sheep?* (London: Grafton Books, 1972). Filmed as *Blade Runner*.

STAB Helen Zahavi, *Dirty Weekend* (London: Flamingo, 1992).

STADIUM Ron Arad, description of AA Soho stadium project, 1979, in *AA Prospectus*, 1987–88.

STAFF J. G. Ballard, *High-Rise* (London: Triad/Panther, 1985).

STAND-IN Willem-Jan Neutelings, OMA, interview by Jennifer Sigler, May 1990.

STARS Walker Percy, *The Moviegoer* (New York: Avon Books, 1980).

STATISTIC Kurt Vonnegut, *Player Piano* (London: Granada, 1981).

STIFLIN' Big Mama, in Tennessee Williams, *Cat on a Hot Tin Roof*, 1955.

STOLEN Molly Nesbitt, "The Rat's Ass," *October* 56 (Spring 1991).

STORIES[1] Mark Taylor, "Nuclear Architecture . . .," *Assemblage* 12.

STORIES[2] Jean-Luc Godard.

STORM Walter Benjamin, *Illuminations* (New York: Schocken Books, 1969).

STRANGER Jack Kerouac, *On The Road*, 1957.

STRANGLED Gilles Deleuze, "Mediators," in *Zone 6: Incorporations*, eds. Jonathan Crary and Sanford Kwinter (New York: Urzone, 1992).

STRATEGY Jean Baudrillard, *The Ecstasy of Communication*, trans. Bernard and Caroline Schutze (New York: Semiotext(e)/ Autonomedia, 1988).

STRATUM Mies van der Rohe.

STRESS R. H. Golde, *Lightning Protection* (London: Edward Arnold, 1973).

STUDIO Constantin Brancusi.

STUPID Don DeLillo, *The Names* (London: Picador, 1987).

STYLES[1] Gunnar Birkerts, dedication ceremony, University of Michigan Law Library addition, 1981.

STYLES[2] Le Corbusier, *Towards a New Architecture*, 13th French ed., trans. Frederick Etchells (New York: Dover Publications, 1986).

SUICIDE Aragon, "Suicide[18]," *L'Oeuvre poétique d'Aragon* (Monaco: Editions Alphée, 1974).

SUITS Sculpture title, "The General Jungle," *Gilbert & George: The Charcoal on Paper Sculptures, 1970–1974* (Bordeaux: Musée d'art contemporain, 1986).

SUPPLANTATION Charles Darwin, *The Origin of Species*, 1859.

SURPASS Friedrich Nietzsche, *The Will to Power*.

SURPRISE Franz Kafka, "Metamorphosis," *Metamorphosis and Other Stories*, trans. Willa and Edwin Muir (Harmondsworth: Penguin Books, 1983).

SURPRISED Milan Kundera, *The Unbearable Lightness of Being*, trans. Michael Henry Heim (New York: Harper & Row, 1987).

SURREAL Peter Eisenman, in *The Chicago Tapes* (New York: Rizzoli International Publications, 1987).

SURREALISM Rem Koolhaas, interview by Alejandro Zaera, "Finding Freedoms," *El Croquis*, March 1992.

SUSPENSE Gwendolyn, in Oscar Wilde, *The Importance of Being Earnest*, 1895.

SWALLOWED Phil Patton, *Open Road* (New York: Simon & Schuster, 1986).

SWARM Bill Powell, "Japan's Big Spenders," *Newsweek*, Aug. 6, 1990.

SWEAT SUIT Anne Tyler, *The Accidental Tourist* (New York: Alfred A. Knopf, 1985).

SWING M. S. Casper, *Synthetic Turf and Sporting Surfaces* (New Jersey: Noyes Data Corporation, 1972).

SWISH Charles Michael Kitteridge Thompson IV of the Pixies, as quoted in Simon Hill, "Fairy Tales," *Sky Magazine*, Nov. 1991.

SYNTHETIC Ernie Tee, "Red Skies Over a 'Wonderful World,'" in *What a Wonderful World! Music Videos in Architecture*, eds. Jola Meijer and Ernie Tee (Groningen, Holland: Groninger Museum, 1990).

SYSTEMATIZE Salvador Dalí, *La Femme visible* (Paris: Editions Surrealistes, 1930).

SYSTEMATIZERS Friedrich Nietzsche, *Twilight of the Idols*, 1889.

TACTICS J. R. R. Tolkien, *The Hobbit*, 1937.

TALENT[1] G. A. Dudley, *Dreams* (London: Aquarian Press, 1979).

TALENT[2] Paul Hindemith, *A Concentrated Course in Traditional Harmony — with emphasis on exercises and a minimum of rules* (London: Schott and Co., 1944).

TALL Frank Lloyd Wright, "The Mile High Skyscraper," Aug. 19, 1956, in *Frank Lloyd Wright: His Living Voice*, ed. Bruce Brooks

Pfeiffer (Fresno: The Press at California State University, 1987). Book and sound recording.

TAXI Chidi Onwuka, 1991.

TBMS Christopher Redman, "Breakthrough," *Time*, Nov. 12, 1990.

TECHNOLOGY Reyner Banham, 1960.

TELEVISION J. A. J. Bouman, Philips Corporation, telegram, March 5, 1948.

TEMPTATION Vladimir Nabokov, *The Defense*, 1930.

TEST Daniel G. Baden, "Toxic Fish," *Sea Frontiers*, May–June 1991.

THEORETICALLY Tim Furness, "Calling the World," *Flight International*, Aug. 1991.

THERE Gertrude Stein, *The World Is Round*, 1939.

THING Paul Theroux, *The Mosquito Coast* (London: Penguin Books, 1982).

THINKERS Friedrich Nietzsche, *The Gay Science*, 1882.

THIRD HAND Margaret Atwood, *Good Bones* (Toronto: Coach House Press, 1992).

THIRSTY Andy Warhol, *America* (New York: Harper & Row, 1985).

THOUGHTFUL Caption, *USAir Magazine*, Aug. 1991.

THROUGH Frank Lloyd Wright, letter to John Nesbitt, Dec. 31, 1941, in *Frank Lloyd Wright: Letters to Clients*, ed. Bruce Brooks Pfeiffer (London: Architectural Press, 1987).

THRUST "The Hundred Verses of the Spear," as cited in Trevor Leggett, *Zen and the Ways* (London: Routledge & Kegan Paul, 1978).

THUMBING Julio Cortazar, *Hopscotch*, trans. Gregory Rabassa (New York: Random House, 1966).

THUMP Madelon Vriesendorp, interview by Jennifer Sigler, June 1, 1991.

TIME[1] Aldous Huxley, *Brave New World*, 1932.

TIME[2] Jonathan Crary, preface to "The Third Window: An Interview with Paul Virilio," in *Global Television*, eds. Cynthia Schneider and Brian Wallis (Cambridge: MIT Press; New York: Wedge Press, 1988).

TODAY Madeline, in Eugene Ionesco, *Amédée, or How to Get Rid of It*, trans. Donald Watson (John Calder Publishers, 1958).

TOE Paul Quarrington, *Whale Music* (New York: Doubleday, 1990).

TOGETHER Madelon Vriesendorp, interview by Jennifer Sigler, June 1, 1991.

TOILETS Milan Kundera, *The Unbearable Lightness of Being*, trans. Michael Henry Heim (New York: Harper & Row, 1987).

TOKYO[1] *Times Atlas of the World* (London: The Times Publishing Co., 1955).

TOKYO[2] Roland Barthes, *Empire of Signs*, trans. Richard Howard (New York: Farrar, Straus & Giroux, Noonday Press, 1989).

TOKYO[3] Benjamin Wooley, "The Late Show," BBC, Nov. 2, 1991.

TORMENTED Alice B. Toklas on Gertrude Stein, in Gertrude Stein, *The Autobiography of Alice B. Toklas*, 1933.

TORTURE Michael Elliott, "Travel and Tourism," *The Economist*, March 23, 1991.

he had fallen into a junkyard.

YAK
But don't tie yourself down to these instructions. They will show you how to create an elephant mask, but maybe you'd rather be a tiger, a kangaroo or a yak.

YEARN
This yearning for innocence is undoubtedly the driving force behind his strong desire to make films without caring for a main theme or message.

YIELD
The only way to get rid of a temptation is to yield to it.

YOURSELF
The only way to be pure is to stay by yourself.

YOUTH
He was the youngest person I ever knew.

Z

ZEROS
What? You are seeking? You want to multiply yourself by ten, by a hundred? You are seeking followers? Seek zeros.

ZILLION
An indeterminately large number (~ of mosquitoes).

ZONE[1]
The zone where natives live is not complementary to the zone inhabited by the settlers. The two zones are opposed, but not in the service of higher unity. Obedient to the rules of pure Aristotelian logic, they both follow the principle of reciprocal exclusivity.

ZONE[2]
James Laver went to great lengths to relate the erotic charge of dress to changes in fashion. He did this by inventing the theory of the "shifting erogenous zone," arguing that at any period one position of the female body must be emphasised, but that this emphasis must continuously shift since otherwise men will become satiated.

ZONE CROSSING
Suppose the eight-fifteen breaks down between Mount Vernon and New Rochelle, breaks down beside a yellow cottage with a certain lobular stain on the wall which the

TOTALITY Raymond Williams.

TOUCHED Jorge Luis Borges, *Labyrinths* (New York: Penguin Books, 1970).

TOURIST Robert W. McIntosh and Charles R. Goeldner, "Glossary," *Tourism: Principles, Practices, Philosophies*, 5th ed. (New York: John Wiley and Sons, 1986).

TRAGEDY Wim Wenders, interview by Hans Kollhoff, *Quaderns 177* (April–June 1988).

TRANSLATION Jacques Derrida, conversation with Arata Isozaki, in *Anyone*, ed. Cynthia C. Davidson (New York: Rizzoli International Publications, 1991).

TRANSPLANT Michael Rogers, "The Tasty Tomato and Other Future Marvels," *Newsweek*, Jan. 1, 1990.

TREE-HOUSE Thomas Sanchez, *Mile Zero* (New York: Alfred A. Knopf, 1989).

TREES Rainer Maria Rilke.

TREE TRUNKS "The Trees," trans. Willa and Edwin Muir, in *Franz Kafka, 1883–1924: The Complete Stories*, ed. Nahum N. Glatzer (New York: Schocken Books, 1971).

TRICK Madonna, interview by Carrie Fisher, *Elle*, Oct. 1991.

TRICKS Dr. Seuss, *The Cat in the Hat*, 1957.

TRIUMPH Rem Koolhaas, fax to OMA office, Feb. 27, 1991.

TROPICAL Anaïs Nin, *Seduction of the Minotaur* (London: Peter Owen, 1961).

TRUE Miguel de Cervantes Saavedra, *The Adventures of Don Quixote* (1604, 1614), trans. J. M. Cohen (Harmondsworth: Penguin Books, 1985).

TRUTH[1] Goethe, *Wilhelm Meisters Wanderjahre*, 1807–28.

TRUTH[2] Pontius Pilate.

TRUTH[3] John Keats.

TRUTH[4] Jacques Lacan, "Television," trans. Denis Hollier, *October 40* (Spring 1987).

TRUTH[5] Mike Kelley, *Plato's Cave, Rothko's Chapel, Lincoln's Profile* (Venice, Calif.: New City Editions, 1986).

TRUTH[6] M.C. 900 Foot Jesus, *Hell with the Lid Off*. Sound recording.

TRUTH[7] Brick, in Tennessee Williams, *Cat on a Hot Tin Roof*, 1955.

TUNNEL[1] D. M. Thomas, *The White Hotel* (New York: Viking Press, 1981).

TUNNEL VISION Tom Robbins, *Still Life with Woodpecker* (New York: Bantam Books, 1984).

TURBULENCE[1] James Gleick, *Chaos* (New York: Penguin Books, 1987).

TURN-AROUND Gilles Deleuze, "Le Cerveau, c'est l'ecran," *Cahiers du Cinema 380* (Feb. 1986).

TUTTI Nikolay Rimsky-Korsakov, *Principles of Orchestration*, ed. Maximilian Steinberg, trans. Edward Agate (New York: Dover Publications, 1964).

TV Martin Amis, *London Fields* (London: Penguin Books, 1990).

TWILIGHT Julian Barnes, *Metroland* (London: Pan Books, 1990).

TYRANNY Voltaire, *Philosophical Dictionary*, ed., trans. Theodore Besterman (Harmondsworth: Penguin Books, 1971).

UGLY Charles Baudelaire, *Intimate Journals*, trans. Christopher Isherwood (San Francisco: City Lights Books, 1983).

ULTIMATE Sam Seibert et al., "A Yen to Travel," *Newsweek*, Aug. 14, 1989.

ULTRA Lucy, in Charles M. Schultz, *Peanuts*. Cartoon.

ULTRA-WIDE Advertisement, Resilio Traditional Neckwear, 1969.

UNCERTAINTY[1] Rem Koolhaas, interview by Alejandro Zaera, "Finding Freedoms," *El Croquis*, March 1992.

UNCERTAINTY[2] Judy Jones and William Wilson, *An Incomplete Education* (New York: Ballantine Books, 1987).

UNCOMFORTABLE Julio Cortazar, "The Instruction Manual: Instructions on How to Climb a Staircase," *Cromopios and Famas*, trans. Paul Blackburn (New York: Pantheon Books, 1969).

UNCOOPERATIVE Victor Lundy, as quoted in Charles Jencks, *Modern Movements in Architecture* (London: Penguin Books, 1973).

UNDER Alexandra Ripley, *Scarlett* (New York: Warner Books, 1991). Sequel to *Gone With the Wind*.

UNDERSTANDING Ludwig Wittgenstein, *Philosophical Grammar*, ed. Rush Rhees, trans. Anthony Kenny (Oxford: Basil Blackwell, 1974).

UNFASHIONABLE Gwendolyn, in Oscar Wilde, *The Importance of Being Earnest*, 1895.

UNFINISHED

UNIFORM Peter Bromhead, *Life in Modern Britain* (London: Longman, 1962).

UNITY Neil Coope, "The Art of Philosophy," *Philosophy 66*, no. 256.

UNLESS F. T. Marinetti, *La Cucina futurista* (The Futurist Cookbook), trans. Suzanne Brill (London: Trefoil Publications, 1989).

UNRELIABLE Harold Pinter, *The Dwarfs* (London: Faber & Faber, 1990).

UP Oswald Spengler, as quoted by Fredric Jameson, lecture at Princeton University, April 1991.

URBANISM "Elementary Program of the Bureau of Unitary Urbanism," in *Situationist International Anthology*, ed. Ken Knabb (Berkeley: Bureau of Public Secrets, 1981).

USELESS "The Great Wall of China," trans. Willa and Edwin Muir, *Franz Kafka, 1883–1924: The Complete Stories*, ed. Nahum N. Glatzer (New York: Schocken Books, 1971).

UTOPIA Louis Marin, *Utopics: Spatial Play* (Atlantic Highlands, NJ: Humanities Press, 1984).

VACUUM[1] Le Corbusier, *Towards a New Architecture*, 13th French ed., trans. Frederick Etchells (New York: Dover Publications, 1986).

VACUUM[2] Brick, in Tennessee Williams, *Cat on a Hot Tin Roof*, 1955.

VADDING William Gibson, in *Anyone*, ed. Cynthia C. Davidson (New York: Rizzoli International Publications, 1991).

VAMPIRE Judith Barry, "Wilful Amnesia," in *Public Fantasy*, ed. Iwona Blazwick (London: Institute of Contemporary Arts, 1991).

VAN GOGH Tadashi Suzuki, *The Way of Acting*, trans. J. Thomas Rimer (New York: Theater Communications Group, 1986).

VANITY Luige Pirandello, *Six Characters in Search of an Author*, trans. Frederick May (London: Heinemann Plays, 1954).

VEDALAND Priscilla Painton, "Fantasy's Reality," *Time*, May 27, 1991.

VENEERED Saul Bellow, *More Die of Heartbreak* (London: Penguin Books, 1988).

VERTIGO Jorge Luis Borges, *Labyrinths* (London: Penguin Books, 1970).

VERY Eberhard H. Zeidler on Miami House by Rem Koolhaas and Laurinda Spear, *Progressive Architecture*, Jan. 1975.

VIEW[1] Alice B. Toklas, in Gertrude Stein, *The Autobiography of Alice B. Toklas*, 1933.

VIEW² Jacques Derrida, "The Principle of Reason: The University in the Eyes of its Pupils," trans. Catherine Porter and Edward Morris, *Diacritics* 13, no. 3 (Fall 1983).

VIEW³ J. G. Ballard, *High-Rise* (London: Triad/Panther, 1985).

VIOLENCE Peter Sloterdijk, *Critique of Cynical Reason* (Minneapolis: University of Minnesota Press, 1984).

VIOLENT HUNGER Adam Smith, *Theory of Moral Sentiments*, 1759.

VIRTUAL REALITY Sanford Kwinter, in *Newsline*, May 1991.

VISIBILITY¹ Roland Barthes, "The Eiffel Tower," *The Eiffel Tower and Other Mythologies* (New York: Farrar, Straus & Giroux, 1979).

1278 Richard Hamilton, *The Critic Laughs*, 1968; from *Exteriors, Interiors, Objects, People* (Stuttgart: Edition Hansjörg Mayer, 1990).

VISIBILITY² Michel Foucault, *Discipline and Punish*, trans. Alan Sheridan (London: Penguin Books, 1977).

VISION Hiromi Fuji, *Concatenated, Multilayered Space.*

VOICE¹ Gertrude Stein, *The World is Round*, 1939.

VOICE² Naguib Mahfouz, *Miramar* (Washington, DC: Three Continents Press, 1984).

VOIDS B. F. Pegg and W. D. Stagg, *Plastering* (London: Granada, 1976).

VOLUME Advertisement, PowerVox IV, Haverhills, *The New Yorker*, Dec. 24, 1990.

VOMIT *Webster's Ninth New Collegiate Dictionary* (Springfield, Mass.: Merriam-Webster, 1990).

VULNERABILITY Rem Koolhaas, 1985.

WALL¹ Jean Baudrillard, *Cool Memories*, trans. Chris Turner (London: Verso, 1990).

WALL² Yoshinobu, *The Aesthetic Townscape*, trans. Lynn E. Ricos (Cambridge: MIT Press, 1983).

WALLS "The Water Palace," *Elijah's Violin and Other Jewish Folk Tales, as told by Harold Schwartz* (Harmondsworth: Penguin Books, 1983).

WAR Sonchi, *Theory of War.*

WAR-IN-BED Futurist Aeropoet, formula, in F. T. Marinetti, *La Cucina futurista* (The Futurist Cookbook), trans. Suzanne Brill (London: Trefoil Publications, 1989).

WARNING Stanley Kahan, *Introduction to Acting*, 2nd ed. (Newton, Mass.: Allyn & Bacon, 1985).

WASTE Andy Warhol, *The Philosophy of Andy Warhol* (New York: Harcourt Brace Jovanovich, 1975).

WAVE Mario Vargas Llosa, "On Sunday," *The Cubs and Other Stories*, trans. Gregory Kolovakos and Ronald Christ (New York: Harper & Row, 1975).

WAVES Rem Koolhaas, interview, *Techniques et Architecture*, Oct. 1988.

WEAK 1 Corinthians 1:27.

WEATHER¹ William Hawes, *The Performer in Mass Media* (New York: Hastings House Publishers).

WEATHER² T. A. Markus and E. N. Morris, *Buildings, Climate, and Energy* (London: Pitman Publishing, 1980).

WEIGHTLESSNESS Lionel Tiger, *The Manufacture of Evil* (New York: Harper & Row, 1987).

WELFARE R. Buckminster Fuller, *I Seem To Be a Verb* (New York: Bantam Books, 1970).

WHAT Alvar Aalto.

WHITE Richard Meier, in preface to *Richard Meier, Architect* (New York: Rizzoli International Publications, 1984).

WHITE THREAD Andrei Leonidov, "Reminiscences of My Father," *Leonidov* (London: Academy Editions, 1988).

WHORE Philip Johnson.

WIND¹ Bruce Chatwin, *Patagonia* (London: Jonathan Cape, 1977).

WIND² Ralph Hardy, *The Weather Book* (Boston: Little, Brown and Co., 1982).

WINDMILLS Miguel de Cervantes Saavedra, *The Adventures of Don Quixote* (1604, 1614), trans. J. M. Cohen (Harmondsworth: Penguin Books, 1985).

WINDOW¹ Jacques Derrida.

WINDOW² René Magritte, *La Ligne de vie II*, Feb. 1940.

1290 Jeff Koons, *Poodle*, 1991 (detail); courtesy Anthony d'Offay Gallery, London, and Jeff Koons.

WINDOW³ Jean Seligmann and Linda Buckley, "A Sickroom with a View," *Newsweek*, March 26, 1990.

WIPEOUT Elmore Leonard, *Cat Chaser*, in Martha Gelhorn, *View from the Ground* (London: Granta, 1989).

WISHING Gaston Bachelard.

WIT Pascal Schoning, unit description, in *AA Prospectus*, 1989–90.

WORDS¹ Michael Johnson, "Decoding Business Buzzwords," *Newsweek*, June 10, 1991.

WORDS² Eugene Ionesco, *Story Number 2 (for children under three years of age)*, trans. Calvin K. Towle (Harlin Quist, 1970).

WORK¹ Le Corbusier on Istanbul, *Journey to the East*, trans. Ivan Zaknic (Cambridge: MIT Press, 1987).

WORK² Jerome K. Jerome (1859–1927).

WORKING David Lewis, Ove Arup & Partners, on vierendeel beams for ZKM Karlsruhe project, to Rem Koolhaas.

WORLD Oswald Spengler, *The Decline of the West*, 1918–22.

WRONG¹ Robert Wilson, *Portrait Still Life Landscape* (Rotterdam: Museum Boymans–van Beuningen, 1993).

WRONG² "Traffic Jams," *The Economist*, Feb. 18, 1989.

WRONG³ Arthur Drexler, *Transformations in Modern Architecture* (New York: Museum of Modern Art, 1979).

XOCHIQUETZAL Patricia Monaghan, *The Book of Goddesses and Heroines* (New York: Dutton, 1981).

XXXXL Robert Tomsho, "Why Are Your Kids Beginning to Look Like Your Plumber?" *The Wall Street Journal*, May 4, 1993.

Y Tom Wolfe, *The Bonfire of the Vanities* (New York: Bantam Books, 1988).

YAK Ole Bruun-Rasmussen and Grete Petersen, *Make-Up, Costumes & Masks for the Stage* (New York: Sterling Publishing, 1976).

YEARN Yamane Sadao, "Mori Issei: Man of the Water Surface," in *Japanese Kings of the Bs* (Rotterdam: Stichting Film Festival, 1991).

YIELD Oscar Wilde.

YOURSELF Jenny Holzer, *Truisms and Essays* (Halifax: Press of the Nova Scotia College of Art and Design, 1983).

YOUTH Richard Saul Wurman on Louis Kahn.

ZEROS Friedrich Nietzsche, *Twilight of the Idols*, 1889.

ZILLION *Webster's Ninth New Collegiate Dictionary* (Springfield, Mass.: Merriam-Webster, 1990).

ZONE¹ Franz Fanon, *The Wretched of the Earth*, trans. Constance Farrington (New York: Grove Press, 1964).

ZONE² Elizabeth Wilson, *Adorned in Dreams* (London: Virago Press, 1987).

ZONE CROSSING Walker Percy, "The Man on the Train," *The Message in the Bottle*, 1954.

ZOOM James Gleick, *Chaos* (New York: Penguin Books, 1987).

ZOOM RATIO AutoCAD Reference Manual (London: Autodesk, 1989).

endpaper "Beijing residents admire a painting depicting Deng Xiaoping's tour of southern China in 1992"; *Hong Kong Standard*, September 26, 1994; Associated Press.

IMAGE CREDITS

The authors and the publisher have made every effort to obtain proper credit information and permission to reproduce images that are not the work of the Office for Metropolitan Architecture. Since some of the images were not traceable, the publisher would be grateful to receive information from any copyright holder not credited herein. Omissions will be corrected in subsequent editions.

For works of visual artists affiliated with the CISAC organization, the copyrights have been settled with Beeldrecht, Amsterdam, Netherlands. The photographs of the Villa Dall'Ava by Hans Werlemann were made possible by the Netherlands Foundation for Fine Arts, Design, and Architecture, Amsterdam.

OFFICE CHARTS Photos: front endpaper, i–vii, x–xi Jennifer Sigler. viii–ix OMA. xii–xiii Nigel Smith. Charts: Jeroen de Rijk, OMA.

DELIRIOUS NEW YORK 22 (lower left) see Dictionary References. 23–42 (photos) Robert Ouellette. Reprinted by permission of Oxford University Press, Inc.

LESS IS MORE 52–53 (large) Eloi Bonjoch. 56–61 (large) Hans Werlemann.

THE HOUSE THAT MADE MIES 62–63 courtesy of the Mies van der Rohe Archive, Museum of Modern Art, New York.

DUTCH SECTION 64–65, 70–71, 76–79 Hans Werlemann. 68–69 Peter Aaron, ESTO Photographics. 72–73, 76 see Dictionary References. 74–75 Petra Blaisse.

±13,000 POINTS 80–81, 101, 103, 105, 107 Petra Blaisse. 82–83, 108 (second from top), 124–25 courtesy Fukuoka Jisho Company. 86–87, 89 K. Monma. 88 (third from top) Nobuyoshi Araki. 90–91 Shinkenchiku-Cha (*Japan Architect* Magazine). 93, 97 Tomio Ohashi, *Kenchiku Bunka* Magazine. 95, 112–13 Fuminori Hoshino, OMA. 99 John Schnier, Toronto. 109 Richard Barnes. 111 H. Kawano.

WORTH A DETOUR 126–27 (large) Hans Werlemann. 126 (insets) Hans Werlemann. 127 (inset left) Marina Abramovic/Ulay, performance; (inset right) Daniel Buren, installation; postcards published by Hotel Furka Blick. 128–29 (large, small) Hans Werlemann and Jeroen Thomas.

OBSTACLES 132, 136–37, 140–43, 146–59, 162–65, 168–74, 192–93 Hans Werlemann. 142 (lower left), 160–61 see Dictionary References. 138–39, 144–45, 166–67 Peter Aaron, ESTO Photographics.

ONLY 90°, PLEASE 194–95, 197 (bottom) Hans Werlemann. 197 (top) Ger van der Vlugt.

IMAGINING NOTHINGNESS 198 courtesy Guillaume Bijl. 203 Ludwig Hilberseimer, *The New Regional Pattern* (Chicago: Paul Theobald, 1949), p. 148.

THE TERRIFYING BEAUTY OF THE TWENTIETH CENTURY 204 courtesy EPAD. 209 C. Michel/Masson.

FIELD TRIP 212–13 postcard. 218 (top) SIPA Press, 1961; Sunshine Photographics, Netherlands. 218 (bottom), 224 (top), 229 (top, bottom), 230 Rem Koolhaas, 1972.

REVISION 232–33, 235 Museum of Modern Art, New York, Film Stills Archive. 236 (bottom) University College London, Manuscripts and Rare Books Department. 238, 239 Hans Werlemann. 240 see Dictionary References. 241 (right) Paul Mellart; (left, right) courtesy Ministerie van VROM, The Hague.

SHIPWRECKED 254–55 Rem Koolhaas. 256 (right) Art Institute of Chicago. 257 (inset) Mies van der Rohe Archive, Museum of Modern Art, New York. 270–71, 276 see Dictionary References.

FINAL PUSH 278–79 (background) KLM Aerial Photography, Schiphol. 282 courtesy Colin Rowe. 286 courtesy Aldo van Eyck. 302–3 Hans Werlemann.

CADAVRE EXQUIS 304–5 Laan van Meerdervoort/City of The Hague. 308–9, 311, 312–13, 314–15 Hans Werlemann. 316–29 Hans Werlemann, Daria Scagliola. 328 see Dictionary References.

TYPICAL PLAN 334 Berenice Abbott/Commerce Graphics Ltd. 335–46 New York office plans from Robert F. R. Ballard, *Directory of Manhattan Office Buildings* (New York: McGraw Hill Books, 1978). 347 Neil Libbert. 348 (left) Mies van der Rohe Archive, The Museum of Modern Art, New York; (right) from Andrei Gozak and Andrei Leonidov, *Ivan Leonidov* (London: Academy Editions, 1988). 349 courtesy Andrea Branzi.

BYZANTIUM 354–61 Tomas Koolhaas and Louis Price, 1994.

GLOBALIZATION 362 Don McCullin/Mark George Photographics.

VANISHING ACT 370–71 Rients Dijkstra. 372–73 (background) Digital Color Center GmbH, Frankfurt. 372–73 (inset) Hans Werlemann.

ISLAM AFTER EINSTEIN 374–75 copyright 1960, Time, Inc.; reprinted by permission. 375 AFP Foto-Gilloon; reprinted by permission. 376–77 MASC Communication, Paris. 378–79 courtesy Palm Bay Company. 380–81, 393 Ron Steiner. 381 (inset) World View/Duncan Wherrett. 384 see Dictionary References. 384–85, 390–91, 392, 398–99 Hans Werlemann.

NEW ROTTERDAM 400–401 KLM Aerial Photography, Schiphol. 402 see Dictionary References. 404, 410–11, 418–19 Hans Werlemann. 422–25 (collages) Yves Brunier. 426–27 (drawing) Petra Blaisse. 430 (drawing) Paul Backewich.

LIFE IN THE BOX 432–41, 444–67 Hans Werlemann. 442–43 see Dictionary References.

NEUE SACHLICHKEIT 480–83, 486–87 (background) Bruce Mau. 484–85 see Dictionary References. 490–91 Rients Dijkstra.

BIGNESS 494 courtesy Wessel O'Connor Gallery, New York. 517 courtesy Gerhard Richter.

SOFT SUBSTANCE, HARSH TOWN 518–19, 526–32, 534–37, 542–53 Hans Werlemann. 523 (top) KLM Aerial Photography, Schiphol. 524–25 from *Die Neue Stadt* (Münster: Westfälischen Kunstverein, 1993), pp. 135, 151.

INDETERMINATE SPECIFICITY 544–53, 556–61 Hans Werlemann. 548, 554 (lower left), 554–55 see Dictionary References.

DIRTY REALISM 570–73 (aerial photos) courtesy City of The Hague; (Nervi's scheme from *Het Veranderend Stadsbeeld van Den Haag: Plannen en Processen in de Haagse Stedebouw 1890–1990*, ed. Victor Freijser (Zwolle: Waanders Uitgevers, 1991). 572 (second from top), 574 (top, bottom), 575 Hans Werlemann.

WORKING BABEL 579 Boymans–van Beuningen Museum, Rotterdam. 580 see Dictionary References. 580–81 OMA. 584–85 Jennifer Sigler. 586–87, 593, 596–99 Hans Werlemann.

STRATEGY OF THE VOID 602 Japanese pornography. 605 Michelangelo, *The Left Hand of Christ, Pietà*, 1498–99, in Ludwig Goldscheider, *Michelangelo* (London: Phaidon Press, 1963). 613 Françoise Hugier/Agence VU. 614, 622, 626, 630, 642 (sketches) Rem Koolhaas. 619 courtesy Chase Manhattan Bank. 620 Parthesius and de Rijk. 623 (top) Etienne-Louis Boullée, "Projet pour la Bibliothèque Royale, Paris"; courtesy Bibliotheque Nationale. 624, 628, 632, 634, 636, 638, 640, 645, 646, 648, 652, 654 OMA and Hans Werlemann. 625 (postcard) Ern Thill. 629 from Bertrand Lemoine, *Le Tunnel Sous La Manche* (Paris: Editions du Moniteur/ Eurotunnel, 1991), p. 148. 633 Robert Smithson, *Spiral Jetty*, 1970; Estate of Robert Smithson. 637 Lucio Fontana, *Concetto spaziale*, 1949. 639 Milton Humason, Carnegie Institute of Washington, Mount Wilson and Las Campanas Observatories. 643 Cindy Sherman, *Untitled Film Still #13*, 1978. 644 (drawing) Georges Heintz. 647 from Richard Saul Wurman, *Information Anxiety* (New York: Doubleday, 1989), p. 68. 650 Jennifer Sigler. 655 "A Loop Prominence" from David Bergamini, *Life Nature Library: The Universe* (New York: Time, Inc., 1966). 656 Hisao Suzuki. 658, 660, 661 Hans Werlemann.

LAST APPLES/MATH 662 Ove Arup and Partners. 669, 671 (sketches) Rem Koolhaas. 670 see Dictionary References.

DARWINIAN ARENA 690–93, 694, 697, 698, 700–701, 703, 709, 728–31, 736–37, 742–43, 746–47, 749, 753–54, 756–57, 760–61 Hans Werlemann. 707, 710–11, 712–13, 717, 718–19, 722–23, 726–27, 733, 738–39, 751, 758–59 Christophe Cornubert. 716, 740–41 see Dictionary References. 762 ABC Press/Magnum Photos.

THE ORGANIZATION OF APPEARANCES 764–65, 770–71 (large) Mark Schendel, OMA. 766–67, 773 (top), 775 (top, bottom), 777 (top, bottom), 781, 782, 783, 790 (bottom), 791, 794, 795, 802 (top), 808–9, 820–21 Hans Werlemann. 772 (top, bottom), 774, 778–80, 785, 788–89 François Dhaussy, Photo Poteau. 773 (bottom), 776, 784, 790 (top), 793 (bottom), 803 (bottom), 806 (top, bottom), 807, 810 (bottom) Philippe Ruault. 777 (top), 783 (top) OMA. 786–77 Phot'R Photographies Aériennes, Aéroport de Lille-Lesquin. 787, 796–97, 804–5 see Dictionary References. 792, 793 (top), 798 (top), 803 (top), 809 (bottom), 810 (top), 811 (top) Jean-Marie Monthiers. 799 Michel Arnaud/EDGE NY. 800–801, 802 (bottom) Duplan/Light Motiv.

PALACE OF THE SOVIETS 822 from Catherine Cooke and Igor Kazus, *Soviet Architectural Competitions, 1924–1936* (V+K). 824–25 Carl de Keyser, USSR/1989/CCCP (Amsterdam/The Hague: Focus/SDU, 1989).

830–31 Cartoon by Kouzi Kuroiwa in *Jackpot #7*, 1989.

ATLANTA 833–59 Rem Koolhaas, Petra Blaisse, Donald van Dansik, brochures. 840 (bottom) see Dictionary References.

LAS VEGAS OF THE WELFARE STATE 864–66, 868–70, 872–73, 875–876 OMA. 876 (lower left) see Dictionary References. 878–79 KLM Aerial Photography, Schiphol. 880–81, 885 Hans Werlemann.

CONGESTION WITHOUT MATTER 894–95 Parc de la Villette. 896–903, 906–19 Hans Werlemann. 900 (lower left), 904–5, 920 see Dictionary References. 938–39 courtesy Bernard Tschumi.

THEIR NEW SOBRIETY 956–57 Hans Werlemann.

WHAT EVER HAPPENED TO URBANISM? 958–59 Piranesi's Rome, from Gijs Wallis de Vries, *Piranesi: en idee van de prachtige stad* (Amsterdam: Uitgeverij Duizend & Een, 1990). 968 see Dictionary References.

SURRENDER 972–73 OMA. 976–77 courtesy Institut Geographique National, Paris. 988–89 Hans Werlemann.

DOLPHINS 990–91, 996, 998, 1004–5, 1006–7 Hans Werlemann. 1001 Ron Steiner.

SINGAPORE SONGLINES 1008, 1010, 1014 (4, 5), 1038 (4), 1040 (2), 1052 (3), 1066 (1–3), 1070 (1), 1074 (2), 1078 (3–6), 1084 (1) Jennifer Sigler. 1012 (top), 1018 (1–3) Urban Redevelopment Authority, *Living the Next Lap: Towards a Tropical City of Excellence*, 1991. 1014 (1, 2, 3, 6, 7) courtesy Ivan Tan, Bugis Street Management. 1016 (1) Li Fu Chen, *The Confucian Way* (London: KPI, 1987). 1016 (2), 1086 Urban Redevelopment Authority, *Living the Next Lap: Towards a Tropical City of Excellence* (brochure). 1020 (1–5), 1022, 1060 (2), 1068 (1) *The First Decade in Public Housing* (Singapore: Housing and Development Board, 1969). 1024, 1028 (2) Charles Abrams, Susumu Kobe, and Otto Koenigsberger, "Growth and Urban Renewal in Singapore" (report to the UN, 1963). 1026 see Dictionary References. 1028 (1) OMA, "Point City." 1032 (1–4, 7–9) Rodolphe de Koninck, *Singapour/re: An Atlas of the Revolution of Territory* (Montpellier: Reclus, 1992), pp. 39, 45, 87, 89. 1036 (1–3), 1080 (1–3), 1082 (3, 4, 5) Rem Koolhaas. 1036 (4), 1068 (4), 1074 (1) Ian Lloyd/R. Ian Lloyd Productions. 1038 (1, 2) Sentosa Press Kit. 1038 (3), 1076 (2), 1080 (4, 5), 1082 (1, 2) courtesy Singapore Parks and Recreation Department. 1040 (1) Ines Vente. 1042 (1) Saul Steinberg, (2) Dr. Pales, Collection Musée de l'Homme, from Bernard Rudofsky, *Architecture without Architects* (London: Academy Editions, 1964). 1042 (3), 1048 (2, 3), 1050 (1–3) Fumihiko Maki, *Investigations in Collective Form* (St. Louis: Washington University School of Architecture, 1964). 1046–47 see Dictionary References. 1048 (1, 4), 1050 (4) *Japan Architect* Magazine. 1052 (1), 1054 (2, 3), 1056 SPUR 65–67. 1052 (2) 1062, 1065 Daniel Castor. 1058 (1) Sunshine Photographics, Netherlands. 1058 (2), 1076 (3), 1078 (1, 2) *Singapore: The Next Lap* (Singapore: Times Editions, 1991). 1060 (1, 3), 1066 (4), 1068 (2, 3) Urban Redevelopment Authority, *Chronicle of Sale Sites*. 1063 Aaron Tan. 1064–65, 1070 (2, 3) drawings courtesy DP Architects. 1072–73 courtesy William Lim Associates.

TABULA RASA REVISITED 1092–93 (large, small) from *Paris, La Défense Metropole Européen des Affaires* (Paris, Editions du Moniteur, 1987). 1094–95, 1098–99 OMA. 1098 (lower left), 1104–5 see Dictionary References. 1102–3 Le Corbusier, Plan Voisin, from *La Ville Radieuse*. 1108–11, 1116–17, 1126–27, 1129, 1130–31, 1133, 1135 Hans Werlemann.

SIDE SHOW 1152–55 Hans Werlemann. 1152 (drawings) Ove Arup and Partners.

QUANTUM LEAP 1156–57 Jean-Claude Coutausse/Editing. 1157 (sketch) Rem Koolhaas. 1158 Spiekermann and Wegener, Institut für Raumplanung, Universität Dortmund. 1163 (inset), 1167 (large and inset), 1169 (inset), 1171–73, 1177 (large and inset), 1179 (inset), 1181 (inset), 1183 (inset), 1186, 1187 (large), 1193, 1198, 1199, 1202–3 (large) Hans Werlemann. 1174, 1188 see Dictionary References. 1187 (inset), 1203 (inset) Edwin Walvisch. 1190, 1191 (inset) courtesy François and Marie Delhay, Architects. 1191 (large) courtesy Kazuo Shinohara Atelier. 1188–89, 1196–97, 1206–7 Phot'R Photographies Aériennes, Aéroport de Lille-Lesquin.

PROGRAMMATIC LAVA 1212–13 (top), 1216–17 (large) courtesy Yokohama Urban Design Forum, City of Yokohama. 1217 (inset) courtesy Michael Graves. 1222–23, 1226–35 (background photos and insets) Hans Werlemann.

THE GENERIC CITY 1238–47, 1265–67 Rem Koolhaas. 1243, 1258–59 see Dictionary References.

CHRONOLOGY 1271–77, 1279, 1281–83 Hans Werlemann. 1278 see Dictionary References.

UNRAVELING 1304–5, 1308–11, 1314–17, 1326–43 Hans Werlemann. 1306 (top right) Bruno Barbey, ABC Press/Magnum Photos.

ENDPAPER see Dictionary References.

commuter knows as well as he knows the face of his wife. Suppose he takes a stroll along the right-of-way while the crew is at work. To his astonishment he hears someone speak to him; it is a man standing on the porch of the yellow house. They talk and the man offers to take him the rest of the way in his car. The commuter steps into the man's back yard and enters the house. This trivial event, which is of no significance objectively-empirically, is of considerable significance aesthetically-existentially. A zone crossing has taken place. It is of extraordinary interest to the commuter that he may step *out* of the New York Central right-of-way and into the yellow house. It is of extraordinary interest to stand in the kitchen and hear from the owner of the house who he is, how he came to build the house, etc. For he, the commuter, has done the impossible: he has stepped through the mirror into the *en soi*.

ZOOM

Imagine looking at the Volkswagen from closer and closer, zooming in with magnifying glass and microscope. At first the surface seems to get smoother, as the roundness of bumpers and hood passes out of view. But then the microscopic surface of steel turns out to be bumpy itself, in an apparently random way. It seems chaotic.

ZOOM RATIO

AutoCAD's "zoom ratio" is about ten trillion to one, more than adequate for most applications.

P.S.

1304

Unraveling

2 Bibliothèques Jussieu
Paris, France
Competition, 1993

The construction of two bibliothèques at Jussieu University should undo the social deficit that has accumulated since the construction of the campus was aborted after

UCLA

JUSSIEU

the events of May '68. While the project represents the insertion of a new core, it should
also resuscitate the significance of Albert's
original project.

Certainly beautiful, Albert's *parvis* — the roof of the podium — is
windy, cold, empty; but there are more important reasons for
its disfunctionality: Jussieu is a three-dimensional network, not
a building. Its endless connections absorb all circulation

psychologically exhaust in advance any attempt to inhabit it. Intended as the stage for social appearance — the essence of the campus — the *parvis* is experienced as residue, a mere slice of void sandwiched between socle and building.

To reassert its credibility, we imagine its surface as pliable, a social magic car-

density still, the two libraries are superimposed: science is embedded in the ground; humanities rises upward. Between them, the *parvis* — connected in the south with the

metro station and in the north with the Seine — runs into the building to become the *accueil*. These surfaces — a vertical, intensified landscape — are then "urban-

ized": the specific elements of the libraries
are reimplanted in the new public realm

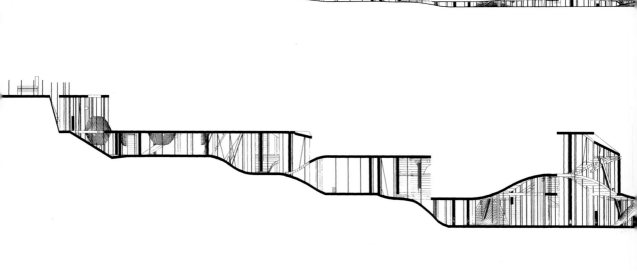

Instead of a s

of floors, sectio

are manipulated

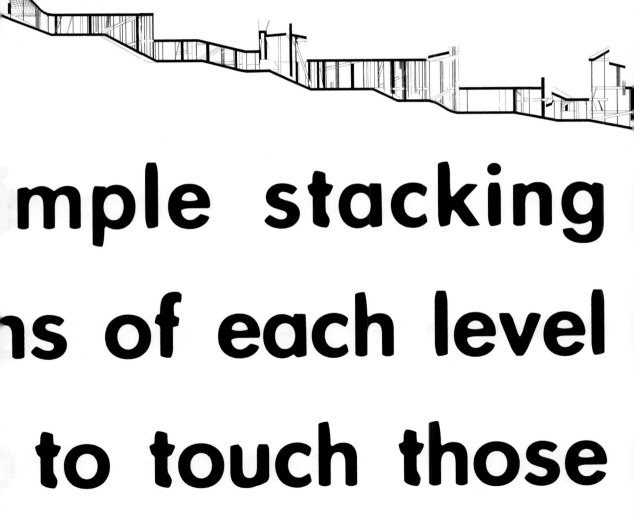

mple stacking

ns of each level

to touch those

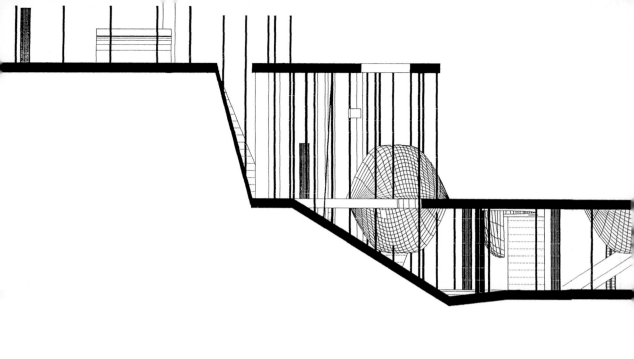

above and belo

are connected b

tory, a warped i

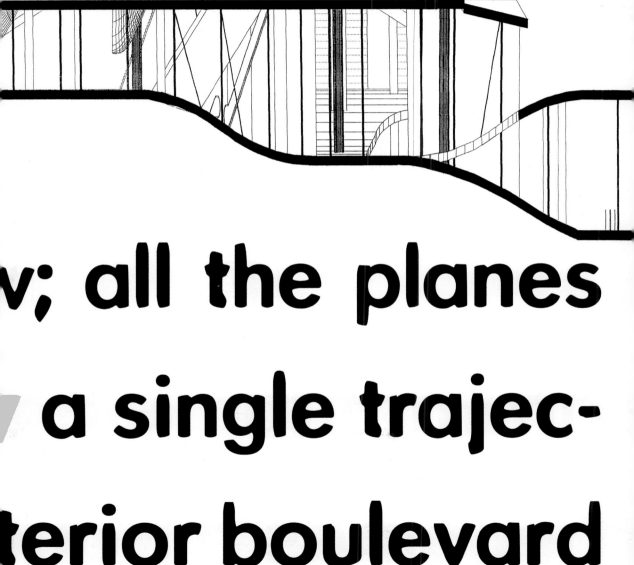

v; all the planes

a single trajec-

terior boulevard

that exposes an

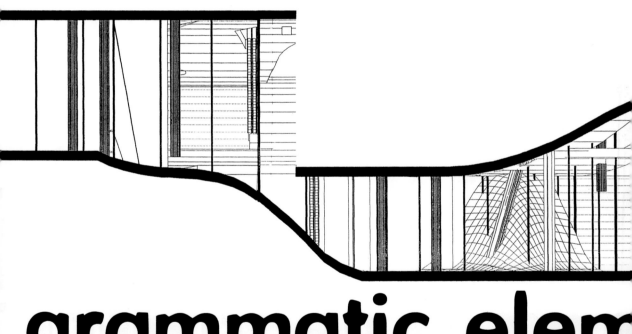

grammatic elem

becomes a Baud

relates all pro-

ents. The visitor

elairean *flâneur,*

inspecting and b

a world of book

— by the urban

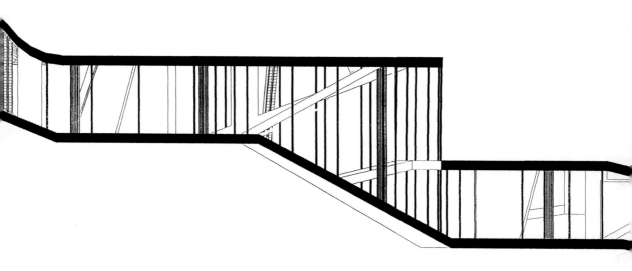

eing seduced by

and information

enario.

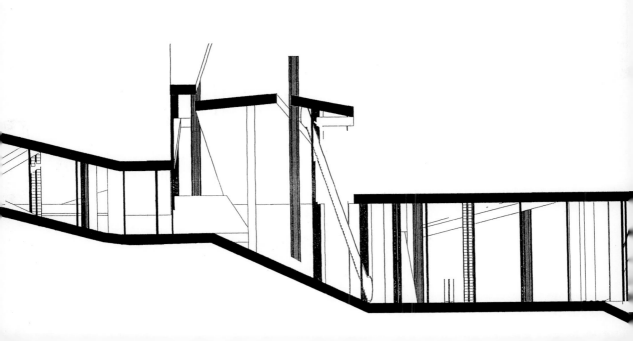

Through their scale and variety, the effect of the inhabited planes becomes almost that of a street; this boulevard generates a system of supra-programmatic "urban" elements in the interior: plazas, parks, monumental staircases, cafés, shops. To enrich the circulation experience, and to introduce more efficient and

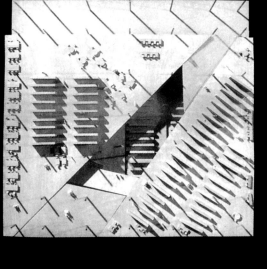
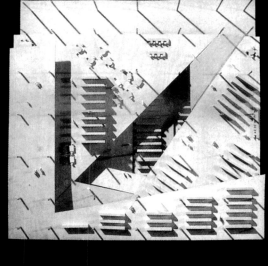
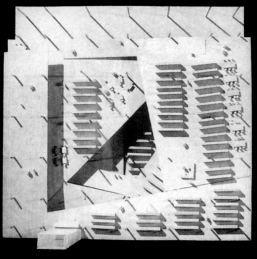
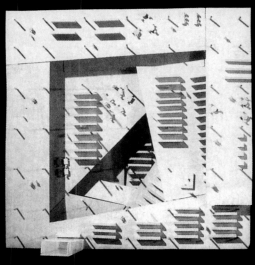

utilitarian paths, escalators and elevators create short circuits that complement pedestrian options with mechanical ones and establish the necessary programmatic connections. Vis-à-vis the monumental scale of the architecture — the average distance between floor and ceiling is seven meters — the 2.5-meter crust

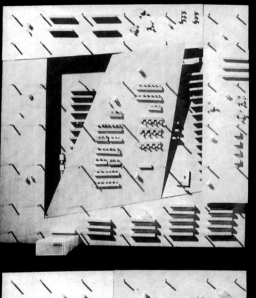

of human occupancy is insignificant. The architecture represents a serene background against which "life" unfolds in the foreground. In this urban concept the specific constructions of the libraries will have unlimited potential for individual expression and difference. Also, the life span of the structure and that of

the crust of the "settlements" are not necessarily the same; the
path and the public domain are analogous to the permanence of
the city, the infill of the libraries to that of individual architectures
In this structure, program can change continuously, without affect

1338

1339

1340

1341

1343

many tricks concerni· | An invitation by the Olym- | prevent the reunification
Taiwan issue" in re- | pic Council of Asia to Tai- | China through the
·rs. The official news- | wan's President Lee Teng-hui | Games," it claimed.

**ER BOARD: Beijing residents admire a painting depicting Deng Xiaoping's tour of southe·
·ngdong province, is on display at the Working People's Palace of Culture as part of celebr·**